SECURING YOUR ORGANIZATION'S FUTURE

A Complete Guide to Fundraising Strategies

Revised and Expanded Edition

Michael Seltzer

with the assistance of Kim Klein and David Barg

THE FOUNDATION CENTER

Library of Congress Cataloging-in-Publication Data
Seltzer, Michael, 1947-
 Securing your organization's future: a complete guide to fundraising strategies/
Michael Seltzer.--Rev. and expanded ed.
  p. cm.
 Includes bibliographical references and index.
 ISBN 0-87954-900-9
 1. Fund raising--United States. 2. Fund raising--Law and legislation--United States. 3.
Nonprofit organizations--United States--Finance. I. Title.

HV41.9.US S45 2001
658.15'224--dc21

00-054828

Dedicated to my collaborators,
Kim Klein and David Barg

"You say you want a revolution,
well you know,
we all want to change the world."

—John Lennon and Paul McCartney

Contents

Preface

The World of Nonprofits

The progress of the world will call for the best that all of us have to give.
—Mary McLeod Bethune

Learning must continue to be a lifelong experience that is informed by your direct involvement in the lives of your fellow citizens.
—John F. Kennedy, Jr.

In the simple title of this preface there are worlds of meaning. First, the obvious: nonprofits are a world in themselves, with their own language and culture that transcends other languages and cultures. Some nonprofits are recognized throughout the world, and many nonprofit leaders are considered the greatest humanitarians who have ever lived. A multi-billion dollar endeavor, the nonprofit world is one of the most important forces of the economy. In the United States, if nonprofits were a single industry, they would be the nation's largest. In Canada, ten percent of the workforce is employed in the nonprofit sector. In Holland, a country with one of the highest tax rates in the world, nine out of ten people regularly contribute to charity.

The "world of nonprofits" also encompasses the majority of efforts to make the world a more decent and humane place. Creative, innovative programs that feed the hungry, house the homeless, protect the environment, defend rights and civil liberties, end discrimination, teach, heal, or empower—all are brought to us by the world of nonprofits. Among the many nonprofit initiatives are theaters, schools, libraries, shelters, child-care centers, legal services, community organizing and advocacy groups, and the list goes on and on. The world would be a different place, a much more dismal one, without nonprofits, whether these groups are large, worldwide, and well-known, such as the Red Cross/Red Crescent Societies, OxFam, or Salvation Army, or local efforts that may not even be formally incorporated, such as neighborhood block clubs, sports teams for young people, or Sunday schools.

Ultimately, a nonprofit is a group expression of compassion, vision, and the belief that people acting together can effect change. Whenever a group of people decides to do something good for themselves and those around them, they embody the spirit, if not the form, of a nonprofit. Following are three examples that illustrate the power of nonprofits.

Idaho Rural Council, Boise, Idaho

The Idaho Rural Council (IRC) is a grassroots organization dedicated to the preservation of family farms, rural communities, and natural resources. Its members are citizens who are concerned about threats to Idaho's rural lifestyle and pristine environment. The IRC's issues include promoting sustainable agriculture and diversified food systems, developing a sound energy policy for Idaho, fighting for effective waste management and responsible mining practices, and ending corporate domination of the food system. With a budget of just under $200,000, IRC staff and board members have found it a challenge to work on all these issues; but the Council now receives money from sixteen foundations and so can hire more organizers and do more outreach for members. Membership is very affordable: $25 per individual and $30 per family. Members decide on the direction for IRC and elect its board, and are kept informed by an excellent newsletter, the *cIRCular*.

The IRC was formed in 1986 largely to address the financial crisis that devastated rural America and resulted in widespread farm foreclosures and bankruptcies. Since then, the Council has realized that the preservation of the family farm is threatened by many of the same factors that threaten the quality of life in urban environments—pollution, toxic waste dumping, and corporate control of the food chain. The IRC's capacity to raise money is directly correlated to its ability to communicate its concerns to both farmers and apartment dwellers. Its growth from a tiny handful of farmers to a solid organization with chapters all over Idaho indicates that it is doing that very well.

Habitat for Humanity International, Americus, Georgia

Habitat for Humanity International (HFHI) is an ecumenical Christian housing ministry that has built tens of thousands of simple, sturdy houses around the world to provide decent shelter for people who would otherwise have had to live in substandard housing. Habitat's vision is the eradication of inferior housing and homelessness from the earth, and making decent shelter for all a matter of conscience and action. A multi-million dollar worldwide service organization, HFHI is always high on the list of the fifty largest service organizations incorporated in the United States; its founder and director, Millard Fuller, a former businessman, remains the charismatic leader and visionary of this movement.

Like the IRC, Habitat believes in the power of volunteers and in involving the families who will be receiving homes; all the homes are built by volunteers. If any members of the family that will be living in the house can help with the construction, they are encouraged to do so. Habitat houses are sold to partner families at no profit, financed with affordable, no-interest mortgages, and built with "sweat equity"—families not only help build their own houses, but they are encouraged to volunteer their time to build houses for others as well.

Habitat's funding is raised entirely from individuals and congregations. Although Habitat describes itself as a Christian ministry, it has over the years worked with synagogues and with other religious groups. Its workbook for congregations describes Habitat's philosophy of fundraising very simply: "How do you get people to give? You ask. You ask again. And then you ask again. Timidity can only limit the possibilities."

Labor/Community Strategy Center, Los Angeles, California

The Labor/Community Strategy Center, founded in 1981, is a multiracial "think-tank, act-tank" committed to building democratic, internationalist social movements and challenging the ideological and political domination of multinational corporations. The Strategy Center's work addresses all aspects of urban life, including labor organizing, environmental justice, immigrants' rights, and adequate mass transportation. The Strategy Center works to confront poverty and call attention to the increasing preponderance of women and people of color among the world's poor.

The Center's $1 million budget comes from a combination of foundations, wealthy individuals, hundreds of small gifts from a large base of donors, fees, and the sale of products. Each of its campaigns must help raise money for itself as well as the organization as a whole. An example of a recent victory is the Center's successful Bus Riders Campaign. The Strategy Center, along with other organizations, formed a union of bus riders who insisted that Los Angeles radically improve its bus system, demanding better, safer buses and more frequent service. They called to the attention of the media, the city council, and finally the courts a highly discriminatory mass transit system: trains carrying primarily white professionals received the lion's share of funding, even though they carried one-tenth the ridership of L.A.'s much-neglected buses, which primarily transported people of color. The Metropolitan Transit Authority settled with the Bus Riders Union, freezing the cost of bus passes and adding 275 buses to its fleet.

These three groups have very different approaches. The Idaho Rural Council believes that small family farmers have a high quality of life that can be maintained. It enables people to decide for themselves what makes a quality life in the state of Idaho, and holds the government accountable to the will of the people rather than corporate interests. The Council's work focuses on one, primarily rural state.

The work of Habitat for Humanity International is firmly grounded in the Bible. The people they build houses for must only need a house—they need not be Christians, or even religious. By building thousands of houses all over the world, HFHI seeks to eliminate poverty one house at a time, with a partnership that includes churches, volunteers, and the families in need.

The staff and board of the Community Labor/Strategy Center must share a set of core beliefs. Very urban-based, the Center believes that urban life must be improved, that there is nothing pristine in the life of poor people in Los Angeles. They use a variety of tactics to win their campaigns.

All three groups envision a world without poverty, a world in which people have power over their own lives and destinies. All three organizations raise money from diverse sources and rely heavily on volunteers for money and for time. They hold onto their belief that the world can be a very different place despite the fact that their vision may be untenable to some. Belief in what on the surface would seem to be unachievable goals is the signature of the nonprofit community. Albert Einstein might have been speaking for all the nonprofits in the world when he said, "Imagination is more important than knowledge."

Introduction

It is one of the most beautiful compensations of life that no man can sincerely try to help another without helping himself.
—Ralph Waldo Emerson

From what we get, we can make a living; what we give, however, makes a life.
— Arthur Ashe

In the new millennium, we face much unfinished work from previous centuries—ending poverty, furthering democracy and preserving nations' unique cultural and environmental diversity, to name a few challenges. Much of this work is the mission of groups like the Daughters of Charity Orphanage in Kampala, Uganda; the Population and Community Development Association in Bangkok, Thailand; Red Road Productions in New York City, United States of America; and millions of other nonprofit, civil society, and nongovernmental organizations across the globe. For these organizations to succeed, they need to muster financial and human capital. This second edition of *Securing Your Organization's Future* is written for these social entrepreneurs to aid them in that task.

Throughout the world, fundraising for nonprofit organizations has evolved into a highly sophisticated and demanding endeavor. What was once a relatively straightforward activity has been dramatically affected by competition for available funds, by technological advances, and by legislation. To operate effectively, today's nonprofit organization needs a clear and far-reaching vision, a realistic plan to fulfill that vision, and the human and financial resources to carry out the plan, not just today but in the future. This book will help you get started, or, if you're a veteran, help maximize your efforts for the twenty-first century.

Whether your nonprofit organization operates in the United States or in any other country in the world (where such organizations are often called nongovernmental organizations, or NGOs), there have been fundamental changes in virtually every area of operations. Globalization has not only affected the world's free-market economies with unprecedented force, it also has an impact on the nonprofit sector. Today, instead of competition among organizations, for example, there's collaboration: a combining of interests, of shared visions, to produce newly effective results, even across sectors.

The most dramatic change, however, is probably in an organization's present and prospective constituency base. Today, people want to do more than just write a check; they want to become involved in the work of the organization they are supporting. Donors will volunteer and lobby, and they're prepared to take action, especially in the United States, where the baby-boomer generation is approaching retirement and has the skills, stamina, interest, and financial resources to make a measurable difference in a cherished cause. Because today's nonprofit must focus on a number of goals to operate effectively, these donors have become an invaluable new resource. Fundraising, in other words, has broader applications than just raising money: it's about meeting the organization's immediate and long-term goals, and building a popular and active base for its work.

Unquestionably, the constituents are there. The challenge is to attract and engage them by developing "signature" activities for your organization—an annual event, for instance, that is uniquely yours. Such yearly events can make a powerful contribution to an organization's ongoing financial health and provide a balance for the hit-or-miss perils of once-traditional fundraising. Today, sustainable fundraising and financing is critical to an organization's master plan.

This book deals with these and related issues in three main sections. Section 1, Getting Started, focuses on the founding and running of an organization, including chapters on defining vision and mission, setting up an organization legally, building a board of directors, planning programs, and developing budgets. Each chapter outlines a step-by-step process that any nonprofit can apply to its own situation. A checklist at the end of Section 1 provides the reader with a summary worksheet for personal use. Except for Chapter 2 (Making an Organization Legal), the tasks covered in Section 1 are ongoing during the life of an organization, and are intrinsic to successful fundraising.

Section 2, The World of Money, provides a comprehensive overview of the range of revenue sources available to nonprofits as well as step-by-step instructions on developing support from those sources. Chapters 7 through 14 focus on ways to secure support from individuals, including face-to-face solicitation, direct mail, special events, using the telephone, planned giving, earned and venture income, and utilizing the Internet. Chapters 15 through 21 provide a perspective on the array of institutional sources, including foundations, businesses and corporations, government, religious institutions, federated fundraising organizations, labor unions, and associations of individuals.

The purpose of each of these chapters is to enable readers to decide which of these sources are appropriate for their organization to pursue and to guide them in doing so effectively. Each chapter contains a worksheet on which to collect pertinent information useful to the needs of your organization. (Complete them, and you will be able to gauge which mix of sources will constitute your own funding mix in Section 3.)

Section 3, Developing Your Overall Fundraising Plan, aids readers in designing a fundraising strategy that focuses on developing support from a variety of funding sources by capitalizing on the uniqueness of their own nonprofit organization. Through a series of ten steps, nonprofit leaders will learn how to evaluate their organization's strengths and assets, choose their funding partners, set fundraising goals, design diversified strategies to secure both individual and institutional support, and plan and implement their fundraising efforts. Again, by completing the worksheets in this section, you will be able to apply what you have learned to your own situation.

As the numerous examples and case studies throughout this book illustrate, success in fundraising is within your grasp. Use this book as a workbook, a reference, and a guide as you go forward to raise the funds necessary to secure your organization's future.

Acknowledgements

I have been very fortunate to be able to tap the talents and generosity of many old and new friends to create this guide. First and foremost, I want to express my deep thanks to my collaborators Kim Klein and David Barg, whose contributions are inestimable. I am also indebted to Max-Karl Winkler for his whimsical illustrations; Rochelle Korman, Esquire of Patterson, Belknap, Webb & Tyler for her counsel; Dennis Payne for his help on a number of the chapters; Ellen Cassedy for the new chapter on labor; Holly Hall, Vince Stehle, Matthew A. Howe, and Kim Bobo for their inspiring profiles; Kate Rudin; Sam Gordon; and Blake West. A special thanks goes to Rick Schoff of the Foundation Center for all of his patience and good humor in facilitating the book's production.

On behalf of all of us, I bring you this book as a tool to help your organization build healthier communities and a healthier planet for all of us.

Michael Seltzer
September 17, 2000
New York, New York

Section 1

GETTING STARTED

Chapter 1

Defining Vision and Mission

Vision without action is a daydream. Action without vision is a nightmare.
—Japanese Proverb

It's kind of fun to do the impossible.   —Walt Disney

A clear vision and a well-defined mission are central to every nonprofit organization's success. Vision is the organization's optimal goal, the reason for its existence. Mission is what the organization plans to do in order to realize that vision. Vision is a view of the desired future, while mission describes the present and what is being done to close the gap between the two. An organization's history can thus be seen as a series of missions realized since its founding.

An organization's vision binds its membership, staff, and leaders together in their work; it communicates the organization's purpose and needs to its constituents, and sets the standard against which all plans, decisions, and actions must be measured. Defining both vision and mission is fundamental to an organization's creation and subsequent growth. Time must be devoted to articulating them clearly and powerfully. As the organization moves toward and perhaps even realizes its vision, these concepts may need to be redefined or expanded.

Vision and Mission Statements

> We hold these truths to be self-evident, that all men are created equal, that they are endowed by their Creator with certain unalienable Rights, that among these are Life, Liberty and the pursuit of Happiness. . . .

These words from the United States Declaration of Independence describe the founding fathers' *vision* for America. In the same way, vision statements for nonprofits and non-governmental organizations (NGOs) around the world provide the vital focus that gives their work meaning, scope, and direction. Vision statements put into words the essence of an organization's beliefs and values, and define its place in the world. They may be short and simple, but their message must be clear and powerful enough to attract people's attention and inspire their support. It is these words that will move members, donors, and volunteers to rally behind an organization's efforts—or to ignore them. Chosen wisely, a vision statement's words can echo far beyond the ears of the individuals or groups being targeted.

While vision statements express an organization's optimal goal and reason for existence, *mission* statements provide an overview of a group's plans to realize that vision by identifying an organization's service areas, target audience, values, and goals.

The following statements highlight the difference between vision and mission:

Biloxi AIDS Service Organization

Vision: Our ultimate goal is a world without HIV/AIDS.

Mission: The mission of the Biloxi AIDS Service Organization is to help people both infected and affected by HIV/AIDS to secure adequate nutritional and health support to enhance their lives.

The Latin American Guild for the Arts (LAGA)

Vision: LAGA's vision is enhanced by a desire to maintain a proud cultural institution where the arts are accessible to all who believe in the joy and the riches of culture from Latin America and Spain. This vision is carried on through resolution and determination to be counted among the best.

Mission: The Latin American Guild for the Arts is a Philadelphia-based, multi-disciplinary, nonprofit organization committed to the presentation, promotion, documentation, and preservation of the arts and cultures of Latin America and Spain.

The Importance of Vision and Mission Statements

With so many programs to develop and deliver, and so much money to raise, why should start-up nonprofits devote valuable time to stating what appears obvious? And why should mature organizations redefine what they've already been doing for years?

An organization's vision and mission are vital to its creation and subsequent growth. Far beyond merely projecting an organization's image or listing its programs, vision and mission statements differentiate one group from another. They establish the long-term direction that guides every aspect of an organization's daily operations, from informing decisions to providing highly effective tools for creating strategies and carrying them out—overriding any short-term considerations based on individual concerns or temporary circumstance. Vision and mission statements also promote shared values and expectations within an organization. Finally, they signal an organization's intent, and its commitment to worthy goals that deserve support.

Vision and mission statements are frequently drafted quickly for a new organization's bylaws, or for its application for federal tax exemption. Leaders of a fledgling effort should, however, make every effort—early on—to find the words that express their binding sentiments to the general public with the greatest resonance. In the case of a new effort, defining vision and mission enables the group to take its next step—establishing goals, the measurable achievements that move an organization forward.

Vital, up-to-date vision and mission statements are also indispensable for older, established organizations. Their statements should be reviewed periodically and, as appropriate, updated to reflect changes in society, and in the forces affecting them. A vision realized, for example, may suggest that it is time to create a new one and move on to other issues, constituencies, or locales. The March of Dimes, whose founding vision was the eradication of polio, is an excellent example. Discovery of the polio vaccine signaled that the organization's original vision would soon be realized. The March of Dimes then formulated a new one—a world without birth defects—and shifted its focus to an entirely different area of human suffering, and, in a sense, founded itself anew.

Older, established institutions may also, from time to time, experience the symptoms of fading vision, including declining membership, lack of public interest, or dwindling revenues, yet not recognize their vision is outdated and needs updating. Vision statements must be living documents that evolve in response to change and provide ongoing direction and inspiration for an organization's work

Creating Mission and Vision Statements

This chapter's opening quote was the work of the American colonies' Second Continental Congress, which assembled in Philadelphia in 1776. Most of the delegates were bound together by a shared vision—freedom and self-determination—which Thomas Jefferson then articulated in a vision statement for the future United States: the Declaration of Independence. He also described the Congress's mission: to declare independence from England.

The same process of drafting a nation's blueprint also applies to creating vision and mission statements for nonprofits. In both cases, a group with shared values meets to effect change and articulate its vision and mission, hoping that these statements will inspire their constituencies to action and that, over time, the group will be able to achieve its mission and realize its vision.

In an organization's founding stages, the task of drafting vision and mission statements should be shared by members of its core group. Each person will have a contribution to make, and spontaneous comments from those closely associated with the effort generally provide the best raw material for developing the final wording. Interested people outside the group can also play a part. Based on their experience or expertise, outsiders will frequently have insight into what is of critical importance and what is doable.

How can several individuals participate in the process at the same time? Invite a number of them to a special meeting with the stated intention of developing vision and mission statements. Ask the participants to consider the following question before the meeting so all can be prepared to make thoughtful contributions: "What would you like to see this organization accomplish and how do you think it can do so?" A less desirable but still serviceable approach is to ask one person to draft the statements and circulate them before the meeting. Regardless of which method you choose, the process of drawing from various sources will strengthen the final product.

Developing vision and mission statements with the organization's key internal and external players also serves to underline the importance of the statements and deepen the participants' commitment. This will, in turn, create a more powerful and visible identity for the organization and move its members to purposeful action. The following is a useful guide for achieving these results.

One Way To Draft Vision and Mission Statements

1. Announce a special meeting for a small number (five to fifteen) of those who share your vision and may be willing to become involved. To ensure maximum attendance, check in advance whether daytime or evenings, weekend or weekdays, are best. Offer to arrange a lift to the meeting if you sense that easy transportation might ensure the participants' attendance. Stress the importance of the gathering in writing and follow-up conversations. Tell your group that you are ready to set the direction of the fledgling organization by putting into words the ideas you've been discussing. Let them know that each has a unique contribution to make and that you value their input.

2. Select a meeting space that is accessible and comfortable; the walls should provide enough room for everyone to post a large sheet of paper. Make sure you have a sufficient supply of poster-size paper, marking pens, and masking tape.

3. Before the meeting, send a short letter to all the members of the group. Include the sample vision and mission statements of several nonprofits as guides. Ask your group to think about your organization and jot down some ideas before they come to the meeting. To help them understand the difference between the statements,

explain that a *vision* statement should answer the following questions: What do you hope to accomplish? What are the end results you would like to see? What are the changes you would like to effect in the society around you? To what end are your efforts focused? Simply stated, what would you like to see happen as a result of your efforts? Explain that a *mission* statement should answer these questions: What activities, programs, or services do you plan to undertake to accomplish your goals? How would you characterize these efforts? Are they service-related, advocacy-focused, or public education-oriented? Basically, the mission statement must outline how you plan to accomplish your stated aims.

4. The chair or facilitator opens the meeting by expressing thanks and reviewing the tasks that lie ahead. For example: "Our goal is to leave this meeting with clear statements of our vision and mission. We'll use the same process to create both statements. Let's start with the vision statement." The chair should then ask each person to write a statement expressing what he or she believes is the principal goal of the organization. Ask everyone to think about the concepts that strike them as crucial and to disregard for the moment any concerns for style or grammar. "Right now," you should explain, "we're searching for content. Let's concentrate on ideas; we'll get to the precise wording later." Take some time for questions and then ask everyone to write whatever comes to mind on his or her individual poster sheet. You can tell them, "Don't censor your thoughts. Write down as many words, phrases, and ideas as you can." Allow as much time as the group needs to finish, then invite everyone to read his or her own statements aloud, just as they were written.

5. Using a blackboard or paper, the chair should then record the most frequently mentioned thoughts and idea, as well as those that may have been mentioned by only one individual but that speak to everyone present. The chair's role here is crucial, for intelligence, intuition, and a keen sense of group dynamics must be used in deciding which phrases best convey the concepts the whole group perceives as central to the organization's vision.

6. After listing the words, expressions, phrases, and sentences the group agrees are most important, the chair should then ask for a collective effort to answer the question, "What would we ultimately like to change in the world?" Again, group members should not be concerned about grammar or style at this juncture, only concepts. The draft vision statement that develops can be refined later by answering the questions in the following section.

7. The group should then develop a mission statement using the same process. Working vision and mission statements will have been developed, and an increased sense of unity and commitment created among the participants.

Fine-Tuning Your Statements

Once working vision and mission statements have been agreed upon, check them by asking the following questions. For both vision and mission statements:

1. *Are they clear and concise?* People can be inspired to act by a minimum of rhetoric. Powerful messages often are best conveyed with very few words. The vision statements of the Isabella Geriatric Center and International Planned Parenthood provide examples that are both brief and meaningful: "To provide the finest care to older adults" for the former, and "We believe every child should be a wanted child" for the latter.

2. *Do they demonstrate a commitment to serving the public good?* To obtain and maintain tax-exempt status, which is akin to governmental approval for any charitable venture, an organization needs to show how its activities are charitable (see Chapter 2 for more on U.S. federal tax exemption). While the word "charitable" is usually defined in a broad sense by the Internal Revenue Service in the United States and its counterparts throughout the world, applicants must clearly demonstrate that their work is designed to serve the public good.

The following vision and mission statements of the Non-Profit Housing Association of Northern California (NPH) clearly focus on the public good:

Vision: A decent, safe, affordable home for every Northern California resident is the ultimate goal of NPH.

Mission: The Non-Profit Housing Association of Northern California (NPH) strives to preserve, develop, and manage quality housing, along with appropriate supportive services, to improve the lives of those in need, as well as revitalize and enhance communities and neighborhoods, through the support and promotion of nonprofit housing development corporations.

3. *Do they accurately reflect the values and beliefs that sustain your efforts?* The statements communicate an organization's beliefs and put them to work by mobilizing others into action. These beliefs constitute an organization's value system and might differentiate one group from others working in the same field, or reveal critical differences in approach or method.

The vision and mission statements of AVSC International illustrate this point:

Vision: We believe that individuals have the right to make informed decisions about their reproductive health and to receive care that meets their needs. We work in partnership with governments, institutions, and health care professionals to make this right a reality.

Mission: AVSC International works worldwide to improve the lives of individuals by making reproductive health services safe, available, and sustainable. We provide technical assistance, training, and information, with a focus on practical solutions that improve services where resources are scarce.

4. *Are they powerful?* One of the primary uses of vision and mission statements is to motivate and inspire others. The strength of these statements is their ability to touch the hearts of those whose support you hope to obtain. They should highlight the most compelling reason for people to rally behind your cause. Make sure yours communicate with impact. Do not confuse rhetoric with power.

The Reverend Martin Luther King, Jr.'s, "I have a dream" speech etched the vision of the American civil rights movement into the consciousness of the 1960's—and of the decades since.

Primarily for the mission statement:

1. *Is it realistic?* The mission statement should suggest clear parameters with regard to geographic scope, targeted constituency, and programmatic thrust. It should answer the question, "What can we realistically expect to accomplish if our work is successful?"

The mission statement of the International Rescue Committee, Inc., paints a clear picture of the intended results of its work and provides the basis for measuring the organization's performance, as does the mission statement of Caregivers:

> The International Rescue Committee, Inc., addresses the needs of refugees. In the United States, the Committee provides services to refugees through domestic resettlement. These services include job training, English-speaking classes, and programs to help refugees.

> Caregivers' mission is to make it possible for frail elders to maintain a reasonably independent lifestyle in the familiar and cherished surroundings of their own homes. Volunteers provide assistance such as transportation help, minor household chores and grocery shopping, assistance with reading and paperwork, and companionship. Our goal is to facilitate a long-term friendship between a homebound elder and a volunteer, so that the elder may have a stable, consistent, and reliable source of support.

2. *Does it indicate for whose specific benefit your organization exists?* An effective mission statement clearly identifies an organization's clients—the specific individuals it plans to serve. Begin by identifying which constituencies your organization plans to target, now or in the future. Be as specific as possible and avoid such phrases as, "serving the general public" (unless that is really true). Then define your prime constituents by age, sex, geographic locale, minority group status, income, or any other category, and specify the services to be provided. The mission statement of Hadassah—The Women's Zionist Organization of America—addresses all these points:

> Hadassah Medical Relief Association Inc. was founded in 1912 to assist Israel by providing medical services, medical research and teaching, services for immigrant Jewish children and youth, and education and vocational training.

The mission statement of the Idaho Black History Museum is similarly clear:

> The mission of the Idaho Black History Museum is to educate individuals of all races about the history and culture of African Americans with special emphasis on the Idaho African American experience.

In creating mission statements nonprofits should focus on communicating "WHAT services they will provide, WHO will receive those services, WHEN and WHERE services will be provided, and HOW the effectiveness of services will be measured. All of these considerations must be determined within the context of the ethical values of the organization."[1]

Putting the Statements to Work

After some careful polishing for style and grammar, your organization will be ready to unfurl its newly created banners and put them into action. You will be able to find many uses for your statements. They provide integral, consistent language for all of your printed materials, including brochures, programs, and newsletters. They are also important elements of proposals to corporations and foundations, and direct-mail fundraising appeals. You may even choose to include them on your letterhead. Depending on the particular audience you are approaching, you may elect to vary the exact wording, but your original statements will always provide good starting points and basic, useful scripts for supporters when describing your organization to others.

However an organization decides to communicate its vision and mission, it must put the words into action. How well an organization lives by its word will largely determine how well it is supported. Paying close attention to how you communicate your organization's vision and mission both internally and externally, combined with success in bringing the words to life, will ensure your own vitality and continued growth. This is equally true for organizations that are twenty-five years old and those that have just begun their work.

Tips

- Your organization's vision and mission statements should guide every aspect of your programs and operations; they provide a truly liberating component to your work, as they are, together, the steady compass that helps keep you on track.

- Revisit your founding statements periodically to make sure they continue to resonate with the times and inspire others to take action.

- Create personal vision and mission statements for yourself.

---

1. E. Jane Rutter, *The Self-Sustaining Nonprofit: Planning for Success* (Columbia, MO: Grants Link, Inc., 1997).

Developing Effective Vision and Mission Statements

1. Use the answers to the following questions as a guide to drafting appropriate statements for your organization. If your group is already in existence and has operative vision and mission statements, write them down below and then review them in light of these questions:

Vision

- What are the values or beliefs that inform your work?

- What would you ultimately hope to accomplish as a result of your efforts?

Mission

- How do you plan to work toward this broad vision?

- For whose specific benefit does the organization exist?

2. Weave together your responses to the above questions into two statements that communicate your organization's vision and mission:

3. Evaluate your statements in light of the following considerations:

- Are the statements clear and concise?

- Do the statements reflect your values and beliefs?

- Do the statements demonstrate a commitment to serving the public good?

- Are the statements powerful?

4. Jot down possible changes that you can make in light of the above responses.

5. Now modify your statements in ways that would strengthen them.

6. Share this draft with three people outside your organization for their comments. Be sure to include at least one person who is not familiar with your issues.

Additional Resources

Publications

Barthel, Diane. "The Role of 'Fictions' in the Redefinition of Mission." *Nonprofit and Voluntary Sector Quarterly* 26 (December 1997): 399–420.

Brinckerhoff, Peter C. *Mission-Based Management: Leading Your Not-for-Profit into the Twenty-First Century*. Dillon, CO: Alpine Guild, 1994. 258 pp.
   Guidebook for leadership in nonprofit organizations. Sections cover trends in the nonprofit sector, characteristics of successful nonprofits, board responsibilities and recruitment, management, marketing, planning, financial empowerment, flexibility, and handling change. Lists resources. Indexed.

Campbell, Bruce. "Do Your Donors Understand Your Mission?" *Fund Raising Management* 30 (August 1999): 47–48.
   Discusses research based on donor feedback, which implies that a nonprofit organization's mission is often misunderstood by its donors. Gives suggestions for a research plan that organizations can use to ascertain how informed their donors are, and the changes they need to make in order to communicate their mission most effectively.

Espy, Siri N. "Marketing Your Mission: Do You Use These Three Key Strategies? If Not, You'll Have Trouble Fulfilling Your Organization's Mission." *Nonprofit World* 14 (September–October 1996): 22–23.
   Explains how to develop a marketing orientation with three necessary elements.

Gehrke, John. "Organizational Alignment and Focus." *Advancing Philanthropy* 6 (Spring 1998): 39, 42–43.
   Analyzes four essential elements of nonprofit organizations: mission/vision, staff, strategies, and people the organization serves; stresses the need for these elements to be aligned independently as well as with each other.

Leet, Rebecca. *Marketing for Mission*. Washington, DC: National Center for Nonprofit Boards, 1998. 24 pp.

Levine, Judy. "Why People Give: The Importance of Mission-Driven Fundraising." *Grassroots Fundraising Journal* 13 (June 1994): 6–8.

Radtke, Janel M. "How To Write a Mission Statement." *Grantsmanship Center Magazine* 36 (Fall 1998): 30.

Sheehan, Robert M., Jr. "Mission Accomplishment as Philanthropic Organization Effectiveness: Key Findings from the Excellence in Philanthropy Project." *Nonprofit and Voluntary Sector* Quarterly 25 (March 1996): 110–123.

Vogt, Jean. "Demystifying the Mission Statement." *Nonprofit World* 12 (January–February 1994): 29–32.
   Provides concrete steps for constructing a nonprofit mission statement.

Chapter 2

Making an Organization Legal

One who is benevolent by nature adheres to the law. — Socrates

Now that you and your core group have agreed on and articulated the shared vision and mission that brought you together and inspired you to act, you are ready to establish your organization legally. This chapter examines the various United States legal structures available to your organization, and discusses the steps involved in choosing, and becoming, the one that best suits your group's needs.

Although the highest priorities for organizations at every stage of their development are usually fundraising, program delivery, and board development, the legal area must also be given thoughtful, ongoing attention for several reasons. First, an organization on the threshold of

incorporating must carefully choose the category in the Internal Revenue Service Code (the "Code") under which it seeks tax-exempt status, as each category contains important provisions about what can and cannot be done. Second, an organization's ability to secure funding depends largely on its reputation, which is based as much on its legal and fiscal credibility as it is on the quality of its programs. Third, the set of rules that determine how an organization operates—its bylaws—will increasingly be referred to over time to resolve important, even crucial, issues. Bylaws should therefore be drafted with great care, reviewed regularly, and updated as needed. Finally, it is essential that an organization address the legal issue of board members' personal liability if it hopes to attract and retain top volunteer leadership.

Nonprofit law is a vast, complex, and constantly evolving body of rules, regulations, and rulings. It is beyond the scope of this book to cover the subject in detail; the author's intention is to provide an overview of the topic and a list of resources that provide more in-depth information. Readers are urged to consult these references, as well as the counsel of experienced nonprofit practitioners, attorneys, and accountants with regard to the legal area of nonprofit operations.

Bylaws

Every nonprofit organization should establish the rules that will govern its internal operations and reflect its uniqueness and particular needs; these rules are its bylaws. Bylaws provide the board of directors with a set of rules to guide its transactions on behalf of the organization, and may contain provisions relating to its governance (within the constraints of the law). Although not always explicitly required by state governments, bylaws must accompany any organization's application to the Internal Revenue Service (IRS) for tax-exempt status.

Those who are most closely involved in launching a new organization should take great care in drafting bylaws and review them regularly for two reasons. First, they have important legal ramifications, including how conflicts are resolved between staff and board, as well as those arising within the board itself. Second, the rules they set forth govern your organization both now and in the future—when you and your colleagues may no longer be involved. It is easy to underestimate the importance of bylaws, as you feel an inherent trust for those friends and acquaintances you have recruited to work with you and to serve on the founding board of directors.

The most common bylaw provisions address:

- Members (if applicable)

- Meetings of members

- Voting members and quorums

- Board of directors (number of members, length of terms, vacancies, etc.)

- Committees of the board

- Officers of the board

- Provisions for adopting and amending the bylaws

Discuss the issue of bylaws with a lawyer, with other members of your organizing committee, and particularly with people who have extensive organizational experience. The bylaws of existing organizations are valuable references; you can request copies from other groups and check the Additional Resources section at the end of this chapter to learn more. Experienced legal counsel can also help your group develop its bylaws and assist you in deciding if yours should be a membership organization and, if so, which powers should rest with the members. (Note that in some states, nonprofit corporations must be membership organizations.)

You should also weigh the role of such officers as president and vice president(s), chairs and co-chairs, to determine the structure that would best serve your long-term interests. Again, seek the advice of other nonprofits (and refer to the Additional Resources section of Chapter 3 for more information on officers). Finally, don't let newly adopted bylaws gather dust on the proverbial shelf. Use them and update them when revision appears necessary. Bylaws can be detailed and specific, or somewhat general at an organization's founding to allow for flexibility as it grows and defines its operating procedures. In either case, bylaws will take on increasing importance as the organization develops and new people become active. Bylaws traditionally include the following information in a numbered article format:

1. Purposes stated in the charter elaborated in greater detail.

2. Qualifications for membership, methods of admission of members, rights and privileges.

3. Membership initiation or admission fees, dues, termination of membership for non-payment otherwise.

4. Rules for withdrawal, censure, suspension, and expulsion of members (including appeals).

5. Officers' titles, terms of office, times and manner of election or appointment, qualifications, powers, duties and compensation, if any (for each office, respectively).

6. Vacancies in offices or on the board of directors: when they shall be deemed to require action, and the method of filling such vacancies.

7. Voting by the members, including what number shall constitute a quorum. This may include cumulative voting, voting by bondholders on the basis of the number of bonds held, and other such special provisions, in many states, but not in all. Voting procedures should be carefully detailed.

8. Meetings for elections and for other than election purposes, including notice, quorums and agendas (general and special meetings).

9. Voting qualifications, individually or by groups, proxies, etc.

10. Directors' qualifications.

11. Classification of directors into two, three, four, or five classes, each to hold office so that the terms of one class shall expire every year.

12. Executive committees of the board of directors to exercise all (or certain) powers of the board between board meetings.

13. Directors' titles, terms of office, times and manner of election, meetings, powers, and duties.

14. Convention and assembly rules.

15. Property holding transfer.

16. The seal: its adoption, custody and method of use.

17. Bank depository, and which officers may act for the organization.

18. Bonding of the treasurer and other officers and agents.

19. Fiscal details: fiscal year, regular (at least annual) audits of books.

20. Principal office and other offices.

21. Books, records and reports.

22. Amendment methods and rules for the charter as well as for the bylaws.

23. Principal committees.

24. Dissolution procedures.

25. Disposition of surplus assets on dissolution.[1]

Forms of Nonprofit Legal Organization in the United States

In the United States, nonprofits can operate as unincorporated associations or corporations. There are fewer government reporting requirements for unincorporated associations, but they are not tax-exempt, they cannot receive grants from most foundations and corporations, and their supporters cannot deduct contributions for income tax purposes. While becoming and operating a nonprofit corporation both require considerable time and effort, the provisions of this form of legal organization make it the one most groups choose if they require substantial public support and if they expect their operations to be ongoing. New efforts can also choose to affiliate with an existing nonprofit corporation in lieu of creating their own. Obtain more information from the sources listed at the end of this chapter and seek the advice of experienced counsel in deciding which option makes the most sense for your group.

Because most organizations choose to operate as nonprofit corporations, we will discuss them first. We'll then consider unincorporated associations and also affiliation with an existing nonprofit.

---

1. Harold L. Oleck and Martha E. Stewart, *Nonprofit Corporations, Organizations, and Associations,* 1998/1999 cumulative supplement, (New Jersey: Prentice-Hall, Inc., 1998).

U.S. Nonprofit Corporations

The *American Heritage Desk Dictionary* defines a corporation as "a body of persons acting under a legal charter as a separate entity with its own rights, privileges and liabilities distinct from those of its individual members." People working together for charitable and other nonprofit pursuits usually choose the nonprofit corporation form of legal organization for the following reasons:

1. *Limited liability.* Incorporation ensures that the corporation, not its individual members, is liable for any legal actions brought against it. Individual members of the governing body (usually called the "board of directors," the "board of trustees," or sometimes the "steering committee") are unlikely to be held personally liable for the corporation's actions so long as they have acted prudently and responsibly.[2] Without incorporation, individual members of an association may be held personally liable in a court of law.

2. *Exemption from federal and state income taxes.* Nonprofit organizations that are granted tax-exempt status by the IRS do not have to pay federal or state income tax on their revenues. The central reason most organizations seek tax-exempt status is to enable contributors to take tax deductions for their gifts. Exemption from federal income tax is usually not the key factor, as most nonprofits do not realize significant net gains at the end of their fiscal year.

3. *Exemption from state, county, and city taxes.* IRS approval of an organization's application for exempt status usually ensures full or partial exemption from certain state, county, and city taxes, including sales, property, and other forms of local taxation. Laws vary; make sure to check the ones that apply to you.

4. *Charitable tax deductions for contributors.* Individual contributors may take a tax deduction with respect to their charitable contributions to organizations that are exempt under Section 501(c)(3) of the Code (that is, charitable, educational, scientific, literary, and similar organizations). In addition, lifetime gifts and bequests made by will to charitable organizations are not subject to transfer (gift, estate, or inheritance) taxes.[3] This crucial advantage of being able to attract deductible contributions is, however, offset by certain restrictions on organizations' activities; heavy penalties can be applied and enforced if those restrictions are not observed. There are such restrictions on private inurement (financial benefit to an individual)[4] and political activities (attempting to influence legislation or work on behalf of a candidate for public office).

---

2. The Volunteer Protection Act of 1997 provides certain protections to volunteers, nonprofit organizations, and government entities against lawsuits based on the activities of volunteers. It seeks to limit the erosion of volunteer resources that has resulted from members of boards and others withdrawing their volunteer participation from nonprofit organizations because of the potential for liability actions against them. The Act also offers protection from liability abuses.

3. The Better Business Bureau has published a useful pamphlet called "Tips on Tax Deductions for Charitable Contributions," which outlines in greater detail the deduction of contributions to nonprofit organizations. The pamphlet is available for free from the Council of Better Business Bureaus, Inc., 1515 Wilson Boulevard, Arlington, VA 22209.

4. Legislation passed in 1996 enables the IRS to impose fines on any 501(c)(3) organization (except a private foundation) or any 501(c)(4) organization engaged in private inurement. Private inurement occurs when the private interests of persons with a financial stake in the activities of the organization are furthered, and includes excessive compensation for executives and excessive economic benefit resulting from transactions.

5. *Eligibility for foundation and corporate grants.* Foundations and corporations generally restrict their grants to organizations that have obtained federal tax-exempt status under Section 501(c)(3) of the Code. While securing tax-exempt status does not ensure that an organization will be able to compete successfully with other nonprofits for foundation and corporate grants, lack of tax exemption does preclude, in the majority of cases, the possibility of receiving them.

6. *Annuity program for employees.* Employees of organizations exempt under Section 501(c)(3) may take advantage of certain special tax-sheltered annuities, commonly known as 403(b) plans. A nonprofit organization can choose to establish one of these plans, which make it possible for employees to deposit a portion of their salaries into interest-bearing accounts. These funds become subject to income taxes only when they are withdrawn by the employee. Such plans differ from standard IRA and Keogh plans in that employees can withdraw funds without a tax penalty in the event of retirement, death, disability, hardship, separation from the job, or attaining the age of 59½. To set up the plan, the nonprofit organization must qualify it with the IRS through an initial filing and continuing report and disclosure obligations.

7. *Reduced mailing rates.* Preferred second- and third-class mailing rates are available through the U.S. Postal Service to charitable, educational, literary, scientific, and similar nonprofit corporations.

8. *Credibility.* Many organizations think they will attract support because contributions they receive are deductible by donors. In fact, the "short form" tax return filed by some 80 percent of Americans currently permits no such deductions. Similarly, no tax benefits derive from charitable contributions in many other countries. The overarching value of an organization's tax-exempt status lies not in its ability to reduce donors' taxes but in the message it sends: this organization has passed the scrutiny of the IRS in the areas of purpose, structure, planning, governance, and accountability. People tend to trust and support organizations that have achieved nonprofit status, and donors who can deduct their gifts do receive an attractive tax benefit.

Categories of U.S. Nonprofit Corporations

Groups that have incorporated and are seeking tax-exempt status apply under one of the following categories listed in Section 501(c) of the Code:

- Corporations organized by act of Congress

- Title-holding companies

- Religious, charitable, scientific, literary, educational, public safety, etc., organizations

- Social welfare organizations

- Labor and agricultural organizations

- Business leagues

- Social and recreational clubs

- Fraternal beneficiary societies

- Voluntary employees' beneficiary societies

- Domestic fraternal beneficiary societies

- Teachers' retirement funds

- Benevolent life insurance associations

- Cemetery companies

- Credit unions

- Mutual insurance companies

- Corporations to finance crop operations

- Supplemental unemployment benefit trusts

- Employee-funded pension trusts

- War veterans' organizations

- Legal services organizations

- Black lung trusts

Most of the primarily public-serving nonprofit organizations in the United States apply for exemption under Section 501(c)(3) of the Code. To qualify under this section, IRS Publication #557 states that the "organization must show that it is organized and operated for purposes that are beneficial to the public interest." The same publication enumerates these purposes, which include educational, literary, scientific, religious, prevention of cruelty to animals, national and international sports, and "other purposes beneficial to the community." Not specified, but implied, are other purposes, such as the advancement of religion and education, and the relief of poverty. Organizations that achieve 501(c)(3) status are exempt from federal taxes, and contributions given to them are deductible by the donors for income tax purposes.

Although an organization's choice of category is primarily based on the fit with its mission, the organization should thoroughly explore the provisions of the category it is considering from several important perspectives.

Extent of Exposure to Unrelated Business Tax
Although an organization's choice of category rarely permits it to avoid paying taxes on earnings derived from the operation of a business that is unrelated to the organization's mission,[5] certain categories can limit the amount of tax it must pay, if any.

---

5. For example, income an opera company derived from sale of tickets to its performances would not be taxed, but revenues from the sale of automobiles, for example, would be.

Tax Deductibility of Contributions

Organizations that plan to solicit contributions from individuals should make sure that the category they select offers deductibility to contributors. Although all categories confer tax-exempt status, this status does not guarantee that contributors will be able to deduct donations for tax purposes. In fact, far more organizations are eligible for exemption from federal income tax than are eligible to receive tax-deductible contributions. Only organizations in these five categories can offer tax-deductibility to donors:

1. Charitable organizations, including educational, religious, and scientific groups.

2. States, possessions of the federal government, political subdivisions of either, the federal government itself, and the District of Columbia, as long as the gift is made for a public purpose.

3. Organizations of war veterans, and auxiliary units of foundations for veterans' organizations.

4. Many fraternal societies that operate under the lodge system, as long as the gift is to be used for charitable purposes.

5. Membership cemetery companies and corporations chartered for burial purposes as cemetery corporations.

Contributions to exempt organizations in other categories generally cannot be deducted by donors. Those organizations can, however, bypass this limitation by creating a new legal entity under Section 509(a)(2) of the Code: Service Provider Status—Charitable Support Organizations. This category confers "charitable support organization" status on the new entity, enabling it to raise money for the parent organization and offer donors tax deductibility for their contributions. This arrangement is frequently used by exempt organizations such as trade, business, and professional associations; social welfare organizations; labor unions and similar organizations; and social clubs.

Another consideration in an organization's choice of category concerns the extent to which individuals can deduct their gifts. In most cases, individuals making cash gifts to public charities cannot donate more than 50 percent of their adjusted gross income in any one year. The limit on other cash contributions (to private foundations and fraternal organizations, for example) is generally 30 percent. In both cases, however, any amount given over the allowed percentage can be carried forward and deducted over a period of up to five years. In the case of cash contributions to nonprofits by for-profit corporations, the limit is 10 percent of the corporation's taxable income; there are rules that permit carryover here, too. When gifts of property are involved, the rules are more complex. Such gifts are usually deductible, but there are limitations on the extent of the deductibility in any one tax year.

Lobbying

Lobbying is defined as an attempt to influence legislation, and includes activities that urge individuals to contact their legislators regarding specific legislation. While lobbying is, to varying degrees, a permissible activity for all charitable service organizations, organizations ruled as tax-exempt under Section 501(c)(3) of the Code are prohibited from devoting a "substantial" share (more than 20 percent of expenditures) of their energies to that area.

501(c)(4) Status

Organizations engaged primarily in lobbying activities are obliged to organize under a different section of the tax code—501(c)(4)—which sets no limitations on lobbying activities on behalf of an organization's exempt purpose. Organizations receiving tax-exempt status under Section 501(c)(4) of the Code have purposes similar to those of other nonprofits but pursue them by working primarily to influence legislation. A (c)(4) organization may participate in political campaign activities related to the nomination or election of public officials, but (c)(3)s are expressly forbidden from engaging in any political campaigning activities, at risk of forfeiting their tax-exempt status. However, 501(c)(4)s are not eligible to receive federal awards, grants, or loans and, as mentioned previously, their donors' contributions are not deductible.

Thanks to a 1983 U.S. Supreme Court decision, *Regan v. Taxation with Representation of Washington*, 501(c)(3) nonprofits wishing to expand and strengthen their lobbying abilities by establishing 501(c)(4) organizations are able to do so. Basing its decision on the First Amendment to the U.S. Constitution, the Court ruled that 501(c)(3) organizations are permitted to lobby through 501(c)(4) affiliates.

Before the *Regan v. Taxation with Representation of Washington* decision, the extent to which a nonprofit could act through a lobbying affiliate had never been entirely clear. As a result, few (c)(3)s had set up (c)(4)s to broaden their lobbying capabilities. The Supreme Court changed that by ruling that the only requirements for a (c)(4) engaged in lobbying on behalf of its (c)(3) parent were "that the affiliate be separately incorporated" and that it "keep records adequate to show that tax-deductible contributions are not used to pay for lobbying."[6]

501(h) Status

A 501(c)(3) organization may elect to become a 501(h) to gain additional temporary lobbying flexibility, and then revert back to (c)(3) status when the expanded lobbying options are no longer needed. The Nonprofit Coordinating Committee of New York provides information to help nonprofit organizations determine the implications of electing 501(h) status. The information is available on their Web site; see the Additional Resources section at the end of this chapter.

Section 527 Organizations: Political Action Committees (PACs)

If your group is organizing for the sole purpose of undertaking electoral activities, you must apply for exemption under Section 527 of the Code. Section 527-2(c)(1) of the Code defines electoral activities as "all activities that are directly related to and support the process of

---

6. *Regan v. Taxation with Representation of Washington*, 461 U.S. 540 (1983).

influencing or attempting to influence the selection, nomination, election, or appointment of any individual to public office."

PACs may exist as separate, segregated funds within a 501(c)(4) organization or as independent entities. In the first instance, they may only receive contributions from members of the parent organization; in the second, they are permitted to accept donations from the general public. The income PACs receive and spend on lobbying is subject to income tax, and the federal Regulation of Lobbying Act requires the filing of reports by anyone "who solicits, receives, or collects contributions" for lobbying through direct communication with members of Congress.

Unincorporated Association

Instead of incorporating, a group of people can form an association and function as a nonprofit organization in the United States without governmental approval. Associations are usually formed for limited, or clearly prescribed, volunteer efforts, such as sports and social groups, parent-teacher associations, volunteer firefighters, block clubs, tenants groups, and so on. As such, they can establish a bank account, accept contributions, and provide services. They can even claim exemption from federal, state, and local taxes as long as they:

- Do not exist to distribute profits to their officers and directors

- Adopt a set of basic rules spelling out the governance of their organization

- Establish procedures for disposing of assets upon dissolution

For much of the nation's history, nonprofit organizations functioned in precisely this way—as unincorporated associations operating as tax-exempt entities, but without official certification to that effect from the tax authorities.

A group's organizers might choose to form an unincorporated association rather than an exempt nonprofit corporation if they do not intend to raise substantial sums, hire staff, or provide tax deductions for members' dues or contributions. Such associations must still be governed by a set of bylaws and possibly even a set of articles of organization, or a constitution. They are not required to file federal tax returns as long as their annual gross receipts do not exceed $25,000. In addition, they do not have to pay tax on income or receipts as long as their deductible expenses equal, or exceed, their revenues.

A major disadvantage of unincorporated associations is that they are not separate legal entities from the individuals involved. As a result, members may be held personally liable for the actions of the association.

Unincorporated entities can file for federal tax exemption under Section 501(c)(3) of the Code as long as they have some form of articles of organization. Without tax-exempt status, however, they are not eligible for grants from most private foundations and corporations. Additionally, their donors cannot deduct contributions for income tax purposes. Because of these disadvantages—the potential for personal liability, and non-deductibility of contributions—relatively few nonprofits choose to operate as unincorporated associations.

Nonprofits and the Government

During the days of the Great Society, nonprofits went to Washington to solicit government support for their programs. But as more responsibilities for the public good are devolved, the federal government is channeling financial resources targeted for social needs to state and local government to use as they see fit and the focus has shifted from Washington to state and county capitals.

Nonprofit leaders are increasingly concerned about congressional legislative efforts to limit the ability to lobby as well as advocate, organize, or provide testimony and research in the public interest. Although the latest initiative to limit their lobbying ability—the Istook Amendment—was defeated, nonprofits must be aware of continuing efforts to curtail their advocacy activities, to restrict their fundraising ability, and to administer harsh, almost draconian punishment for activities judged to be noncompliant.

Included in the Istook Amendment were the following legislative proposals:

- Restricting and reducing the amount of money federally funded nonprofits could spend on lobbying

- Increasing the range of nonprofits these restrictions would apply to

- Expanding the definition of lobbying to include a wider range of activities

- Intensifying enforcement and penalties

Unfortunately, this example is only one of many recent legislative efforts to limit nonprofits' ability to effect social change. It was the concerted lobbying efforts of more than eight hundred nonprofits that led to the bill's defeat. Interestingly, several of those groups—and others—were deprived of federal funding as a result of their active opposition. Keeping in mind that the United States relies more on private nonprofits than any other industrialized country, and that workers in the nonprofit sector constitute roughly 7 percent of paid employment (just under half the size of the government workforce), nonprofit organizations have the leverage to vigorously oppose any restrictive legislation the government proposes.[7]

7. Jane Katz, "The Kindness of Neighbors," Federal Reserve Bank of Boston Regional Review (summer 1996): 613.

Securing Tax-Exempt Status

Success in securing state incorporation and federal tax-exempt status usually requires the assistance of an attorney with prior experience in the area of not-for-profit corporate law. Competent legal counsel helps the process move along smoothly and increases the likelihood that the various governmental bodies will act favorably. Because governmental approval is required to set up your organization, be sure to seek competent help. In other words, resist the temptation to jump in and complete the forms yourself, or to use the services of a lawyer who will work pro bono (free of charge) but is unfamiliar with nonprofit law.

The best solution is, of course, for your group to find a lawyer among its circle of friends, acquaintances, and colleagues who has experience in nonprofit law and is willing to work on a pro bono basis and in a timely manner. Failing that, there are several resources to turn to before spending money on legal counsel:

1. Contact other nonprofit organizations in your community and ask them who completed their original applications, and if it was done on a pro bono basis. At the same time, you can also request copies of their state incorporation and completed application for federal tax exemption to help you and your prospective lawyer.

2. Contact your local Community Legal Services office. This federally funded program provides pro bono legal assistance to U.S. organizations if at least one-half of their board of directors can meet their income guidelines and qualify as low income.

3. Ask local technical assistance or management support organizations that specialize in providing guidance to nonprofit organizations for the names of attorneys to contact.

4. Write to law firms to request pro bono assistance. The American Bar Association requests that its members undertake some pro bono work each year. Decisions on such requests from nonprofits are usually made by one of the partners of the firm, or by a special committee.

5. Finally, contact the local, county, or city bar association for recommendations; they generally maintain lawyer referral services specifically for this purpose.

While you should be prepared to pay for legal assistance, don't hesitate to begin by seeking pro bono help. But be sure you start off with qualified help. If the IRS rejects your application, you may reapply, but your chances for success the second time around may be slimmer. To gauge a prospective lawyer's capabilities, politely inquire about his or her past experience in the nonprofit field: Has he or she incorporated other organizations? How recently? You might even solicit the names of some of these organizations and contact them to ask what their experience was.

A pro bono arrangement may occasionally be a source of frustration, as lawyers, like other professionals, may give priority to their paying clients. After an attorney has agreed to work with you, clarify in advance when the work will begin and when it will be completed. Remember that you, too, are a client and are entitled to express your needs and expectations—and have them met.

State Incorporation

Before submitting an application to the IRS for federal tax exemption, an organization must incorporate. A corporation is a legal entity—with rights, privileges and liabilities—that is separate and distinct from its members and officers; most for-profit and nonprofit organizations in the United States operate as corporations. Corporate status affords nonprofits the standing and legal status donors are most comfortable with.

The first step in becoming a corporation is drafting the legal incorporation document—the articles of incorporation—and filing the document with the appropriate office within your state government, usually the office of the secretary of state or attorney general. It is not required that you incorporate in the state in which you plan to conduct your affairs, but most nonprofits do. The articles of incorporation form is available from the state government or from a large commercial stationery store. Whereas an organization's application for federal tax-exempt status normally takes at least four months, state incorporation is usually accomplished in a few weeks.

The following information is generally required for the articles of incorporation:

1. The name of the corporation.

2. The purpose of the corporation.

3. A statement that the corporation does not afford "pecuniary gain," or profit, to its members.

4. The period of duration of corporate existence, which may be perpetual.

5. The location, by city or community, of its registered office.

6. The name and address of each incorporator.

7. The number of directors constituting the first board of directors, the name and address of each director, and the tenure in office of the first directors.

8. The extent of personal liability, if any, of members for corporate obligations and the methods of enforcement and collection (there will be none, except in unusual circumstances).

9. Whether the corporation has capital stock (most nonprofit corporations do not have capital stock).

10. Provision for the distribution of corporate assets and for dissolution.

11. A statement whether or not there will be a membership separate from the board of directors. Without such a statement, it could be assumed that the corporation has a separate membership that elects the board of directors.

When the articles have been drafted, they should be sent to the appropriate state office; the same office will tell you the fee that should be sent along with the application. When the application is approved, a certification of incorporation will be sent to the organization.

Federal Tax Exemption

Both unincorporated associations and nonprofit corporations can file for federal tax exemption. Our discussion here describes the process of applying for tax-exempt status under Section

501(c)(3), but it also applies to other organizations applying in other categories in Section 501(c) of the Code.

Obtaining the necessary application forms is easy, and there is no filing fee. The IRS makes available four different publications to assist you in applying for recognition of exemption under Section 501 of the Code:

- Package 1023, which includes the actual application form (Form 1023) for Section 501(c)(3) organizations and instructions on how to complete it

- Package 1024, which includes the actual application form for other 501(c) categories

- Publication 557, *Tax-Exempt Status for Your Organization*, which details the application procedure and pertinent related matters

- *The Internal Revenue Service Exempt Organizations Handbook*, which discusses in even more specific detail requirements for receiving tax exemption

The first three publications are free. Simply call the tax information number in the phone book listed under "United States Government, Internal Revenue Service," or contact your local IRS tax forms office. The fourth item is available in any IRS Reading Room or may be purchased for by writing to the IRS, Attention: TX:D:P:RR, 1111 Constitution Avenue NW, Washington, DC. 20224. (Much of this information is also available on the IRS Web site.)

If, as is frequently the case, your organization began operating before applying for tax exemption, you must attach to your Form 1023 application a statement of receipts and expenditures, as well as a balance sheet for the current year and immediate prior year(s) (or however long the organization has been in existence, if less than three years). Make sure to enlist the help of an accountant or businessperson when preparing these—and any other—financial statements. Finally, the IRS requires a copy of your articles of incorporation and bylaws, signed by a principal officer of your organization and approved by your state's secretary of state.

Although you can complete Form 1023 without outside assistance, it is not advisable to do so. The form consists of eight parts containing more than one hundred questions, as well as seven additional schedules (related forms) that need to be filled out pertaining to different kinds of nonprofit organizations. Some of the information Form 1023 requires is:

- Full name of organization

- Employer identification number (see following section for explanation)

- A list of the organization's current or projected sources of financial support and fundraising plans

- A projected organizational budget for three years

- A brief narrative description of the present and future program activities of the organization (It is critical that the description of your organization's activities be consistent with the IRS' definition of what constitutes charitable activity.)

- Pertinent data on your governing body

While some of the questions in the application are fairly straightforward, others will prove challenging to the lay applicant. To complete the form successfully and minimize the chances the IRS will reject your application, approach the application process as a partnership between your organizing committee and your lawyer. Don't distance yourself from the process. Finally, ask your attorney to attend a meeting of your group to review the completed forms before submission and to answer any questions.

One last word of caution: your work is not over until the actual letter granting tax exemption arrives from the IRS. Before that, however, the IRS agent reviewing your application may request additional information. Again, you will want to consult with your lawyer before providing any additional data.

Last Legal Steps

When your incorporation is complete and the IRS has approved your request for tax-exempt status, the work to establish your organization's legal status is almost finished. Only a few steps remain. Most states and many localities require nonprofits to register with the Charities Registration Bureau of the state or locality where they'll be fundraising if they anticipate raising more than a certain amount every year from the general public. If your organization plans to fundraise actively in several states, you may have to register in each state. For specific requirements of each state, check Appendix A.

Nonprofit organizations that are exempt under Section 501(c)(3) may qualify for exemption from state sales tax as well as from property taxes if they own property. Check with your State Department of Finance or Taxation to secure the necessary forms. For property tax exemption, apply to your local (county, town, or city) tax assessor's office. Your organization may also qualify for a nonprofit bulk-mailing permit, which would dramatically reduce your cost for third-class bulk mailings (of no fewer than two hundred pieces). You can obtain a permit by applying to the main office of your local post office. An annual fee of less than $100 is required at the time of application.

If you plan to hire staff, you must learn about your legal and fiscal responsibilities as an employer. Obtain the Application for Employer Identification Number (Form SS-4) from the local IRS tax forms office. Filing this form with a regional IRS office will register your organization with both the state and federal governments for the purpose of withholding employee income tax. You will subsequently receive an employer identification number (EIN) and other relevant forms by mail. One of these forms has to accompany the quarterly deposits of withheld employee taxes that you must make at an authorized commercial bank or a Federal Reserve bank. Finally, you must register with the State Unemployment Insurance Program and the State Workers' Compensation Program.

An organization's responsibility to deposit taxes withheld from staff paychecks in a timely manner cannot be overemphasized. It is essential that an organization perform flawlessly in this area. Through the years, many have not and so have gone out of business. For organizations hard-pressed for cash, money withheld from paychecks that sits in a group's bank account waiting to be deposited and forwarded to the IRS can be a great temptation. These funds must be totally off-limits for any other purpose, no matter how pressing the need, as the law requires that withheld taxes be paid on time and imposes stiff penalties for late payment. Remember that staff members have, in effect, entrusted you with a portion of their salaries and you must follow through on your responsibility. Additionally, withheld taxes that are not paid represent the only liability for which board members are personally responsible.

To ensure that funds are available to make timely payment of withheld taxes, some organizations elect to use a payroll service. Payroll services calculate the proper deductions, write the paychecks, keep track of all taxes withheld, withdraw electronically the necessary amount from an organization's bank account, and forward those funds to the appropriate federal, state, and local tax agencies.

The help of a certified public accountant (CPA) with these procedures is as crucial as that of legal counsel in preparing Form 1023. Your registrations and filings with the IRS, timely deposit of withheld taxes, and financial record-keeping must be immaculate—always. Countless organizations have gone under—despite noble aims and good works—because their financial house was not in order. Don't let that happen to you.

Federal and State Reporting Requirements

Tax-exempt organizations are required to submit Form 990 (Return of Organization Exempt from Income Tax) or 990-EZ to the IRS annually. The completed Form 990 is the nonprofit organization's only mandated vehicle for public disclosure of information about its operations. As specified information must be tracked and reported according to prescribed standards, all tax-exempt organizations must become familiar with the information required by Form 990 and track this information in a timely and appropriate way throughout the year.

Effective June 1999, regulations contained in IRS Section 6104(d) require broader disclosure of a tax-exempt organization's completed Form 990 returns, including mailing a copy upon written request. A tax-exempt organization can make its completed 990 return available to consumers by posting it on the Internet—either on its own Web page or on a site maintained by another organization—as a way of complying with the new disclosure requirements. All of the regulations and forms, as well as tips and examples, are available on the Internet. Refer to the Additional Resources section at the end of this chapter.

As many states have additional reporting requirements, nonprofit organizations should confer with an accountant to be sure they are in compliance with all relevant state laws and regulations.

Recent changes in charity reporting and disclosure law have caused nonprofits to think more seriously about the quality of their reporting documents. These changes require nonprofits to disclose information about their programming, lobbying, and fundraising expenditures, as well as their levels of executive compensation. At this time, nonprofits are being encouraged to post this information on the World Wide Web as an efficient way of complying with the new disclosure laws. (It is hoped that publishing 990 forms on the Web will eliminate the need for multiple filings; currently, some of the larger nonprofits must file with the IRS and with thirty-eight states as well.)

The new public disclosure law will intensify the need for accurate and understandable returns. These changes are likely to elicit many previously unasked questions that require knowledgeable answers. "Board members should be aware that this [Form 990] is going to be *the* document."[8] Both board and the staff will be required to understand and interpret the form as the disclosure requirements place increased value and focus on its content.

Affiliation with an Existing Nonprofit Corporation

If an unincorporated association plans to approach individuals, foundations, and/or corporations in the United States for support but is not incorporated and federally tax-exempt, it may become affiliated with an exempt nonprofit corporation and raise money as if it were. Such an affiliation can last for a short period of time or can be permanent. Unincorporated associations usually affiliate with existing organizations in one of two ways:

- **Fiscal Sponsorship.** A group seeking tax-deductible contributions or institutional grants before receiving its own tax-exempt status may enter into a relationship with an existing exempt organization. The existing organization would receive funds to support the group's work and independently grant such funds to the sponsored group. The funds raised are contributed to the exempt organization with the understanding that they will, in turn, be used as a grant to the nonexempt group. The exempt organization must at all times retain discretion and control over the appropriate use of the funds by the ultimate beneficiary.

- **Adoption.** Adoption involves a somewhat more extensive relationship than fiscal sponsorship. Typically, a group is adopted by an exempt organization as a project; the exempt organization assumes full financial responsibility for, and legal control of, its adopted group. The adopted project is "housed" within the organizational structure of the adopting entity, which consequently has the power to influence program-related decisions that face their newly adopted project.

The reasons for a new, or even existing, nonexempt group to seek affiliation with a charitable organization are varied. For example:

1. The group may wish to undertake a short-term project and does not need a permanent organizational structure. Several filmmakers, for example, might be seeking grants to produce a film, or a group of artists might come together to produce a single exhibition.

2. During its start-up period, a group may wish to avoid the time and expense involved in securing federal tax exemption and instead become affiliated with an already exempt organization.

3. Similarly, the group plans to file for state incorporation and federal tax exemption but wants to start fundraising immediately. Affiliation with an existing nonprofit charitable organization enables it to do so.

---

8. Jennifer Moore and Grant Williams, "Return of the Future," *The Chronicle of Philanthropy* 11 (17 December 1998).

4. The group may wish to focus its initial energies on program activities rather than on administration. As a result, they turn to another organization to assume responsibility for such tasks as bookkeeping, payroll, financial reporting, and the like.

5. A group may be uncertain whether there is sufficient support for its work. Affiliation can provide an organizational haven while the group tests its ideas and programs. If the group finds that its work is received positively, it can then move out and become an independent organization.

6. A fledgling project may lack visibility and credibility as an organization. Associating with an existing, well-respected entity immediately provides it with some of these attributes.

7. Finally, the organizing committee of a new project may want to postpone the creation of a formal board of directors until it develops a track record. Affiliation provides the time the group needs to build the board, since the parent organization's board can serve as its legal interim governing body.

In considering an affiliation with an existing entity, you should also be aware of its potential disadvantages for your group:

1. Because in the case of adoption the parent organization assumes all legal and fiscal responsibilities for your group, it may seek to have some voice in matters that relate to those responsibilities. The parent organization may limit your autonomy by exercising this prerogative.

2. You may believe that a totally independent identity is essential to your group's success for a number of reasons, and that so close a relationship with another organization will detract from that image.

3. You will almost certainly have to pay a fee—usually a percentage of the grants and contributions you receive—to the parent organization or fiscal sponsor to cover the costs of the administrative services they provide. Such fees generally range from 5 to 15 percent of the revenues your organization generates.

4. You may be prevented by the parent organization or fiscal sponsor from approaching funding sources that have already been targeted for its own support.

Why might another nonprofit agree to become your parent or sponsoring organization? It might be interested solely on the basis of the importance and value it attributes to your vision and mission. It might also anticipate such benefits as enhanced reputation, increased visibility, and outreach to new constituencies as a result of the affiliation.

At the same time, there are reasons that might discourage organizations from serving as fiscal sponsors, or parents, of your work:

- They may be wary of assuming responsibility for a new undertaking whose capacity to attract funding is unknown.

- They may decide that the administrative fees they would receive will not offset the additional costs they would incur.

- They may be concerned that the association with your group could blur their own image in the eyes of the public.

In light of the above, the relationship between your group and the parent organization should be clearly understood and detailed in a written agreement before you enter into the affiliation. Be sure to include in the agreement a provision that allows for the two parties to dissolve their understanding at some specified future time.

Be aware that fiscal sponsorship requires accountability on your part to the parent organization only for the funds that you receive under its auspices, such as a grant from a foundation for a particular program you will implement. In this case, a grant agreement serves as the document that defines the relationship between the fiscal sponsor and the project, as well as between the fiscal sponsor and the funding source. The grant agreement becomes the document that describes in detail what the grantee may or may not do with the funds it receives. Typically, the agreement will provide that the grant be used only for charitable purposes, as broadly defined in Section 501(c)(3) of the Code, and not for political activities. In addition, the grant agreement will provide for periodic reporting on the use of the funds by the legal grantee to the donor.

Finding an Appropriate Sponsor or Parent Organization
The best candidates for sponsorship and adoption are organizations whose purposes and activities are compatible with your own. The first step in seeking out a possible sponsor or parent organization is to draw up a list of prospects. You can identify candidates for this list in several ways:

- Check available local directories of nonprofit organizations. Your local library will usually have such directories, perhaps in a community services section.

- Contact local consortium-style associations that correspond to your area of interest, such as the United Way, arts councils, health and welfare planning bodies, federations, and so on. Speak to their directors or public information officers and elicit their suggestions.

- Check national organizational reference books, such as the *Encyclopedia of Associations*, for other potential candidates.

- Finally, draw on the knowledge of the members of your organizing committee or board of directors; they probably already know some nonprofits that might be good sponsors. Arrange a meeting of your group to discuss candidates. Beforehand, ask several members of the group to research and investigate organizations using the avenues already mentioned, and to bring the results of their research to the meeting.

SAMPLE SPONSORSHIP AGREEMENT

SPONSORSHIP AGREEMENT

AGREEMENT made this ___ day of _____, 199_, by and between [insert name and address of exempt organization] (the "Sponsor"), and [insert name and address of non-exempt organization] (the "Project");

WITNESSETH:

WHEREAS, the sponsor, a not-for-profit corporation exempt from federal tax under section 501(c)(3) of the Internal Revenue Code of 1986, as amended (the "Code"), and exempt from New York State sales tax, is formed for the purpose(s) of [list charitable/educational purposes relevant to the project];

WHEREAS, the Project is a [type of entity] formed for the purpose(s) of [list charitable/educational purposes relevant to Project];

WHEREAS, the sponsor is willing to receive tax deductible charitable contributions (the "Funds") to be awarded by donors (the "Donors") to the sponsor for the benefit and use of implementing the Project; and

WHEREAS, the Project, with the administrative assistance of the Sponsor, desires to use the Funds in order to implement the Project;

NOW, THEREFORE, in consideration of the mutual promises, conditions and covenants contained herein, the parties hereto agree as follows:

1. The sponsor agrees to receive the Funds to be used for the Project, and to make the Funds available to the Project within three (3) business days from the date of receipt. The sponsor hereby authorizes the Project to make purchases, that, subject to paragraphs 2 and 4 below, the projects deems necessary and appropriate, on behalf of, and for the use of the project.

2. The project agrees to use any and all Funds received from the Sponsor solely for legitimate expenses on the Project, and to account fully to the Sponsor for the disbursement of all Funds received from it on a quarterly basis.

3. The Sponsor agrees that all Funds which it receives for the Project will be reported as contributions to it as required by law, and further agrees to acknowledge receipt of such Funds in writing and to furnish evidence of its status as an exempt organization under section 501 (c) (3) of the Code to any Donor upon request. The Sponsor agrees to notify the Project of any change in its tax-exempt status.

4. The Project agrees not to use Funds received from the Sponsor in any way which would jeopardize the tax-exempt status of the Sponsor. The project agrees to comply with any written request by the Sponsor that it cease activities which might jeopardize its tax-exempt status, and further agrees that the Sponsor's obligation to make Funds available to it is suspended and this Agreement shall be terminated in the event that it fails to comply with any such written request.

5. The Sponsor agrees to (a) send acknowledgement of the receipt of the Funds to the relevant Donors, (b) provide a copy of each such acknowledgement to the Project, (c) deposit such Funds in an interest-bearing account (the "Project Account") in the name of the Sponsor, established by the Sponsor and maintained at [name and address of bank], (d) provide mailing and postage services, including, but not limited to, metered mailing, (e) to the extent available under the Sponsor's general liability insurance policy, provide and maintain insurance for no less than three (3) and no more than eight (8) members of the Project and (f) provide incidental services in connection with the aforementioned.

6. The Sponsor shall be entitled to deduct from each separate cash award of Funds received from Donors an administrative fee of [five] percent ([5]%) of the amount such award, but in no event shall the aggregate of all such fees from all Donors deducted by the Sponsor during any fiscal year of the Sponsor exceed $[insert dollar amount].

7. The Sponsor shall maintain all books and financial records for Funds in accordance with generally accepted accounting principles. The Project account shall be segregated on the books of the Sponsor. Reports reflecting receipts, expenditures and balances will be delivered by the Sponsor to the Project on a monthly basis, within two (2) weeks after the end of each month, and on an annual basis, within three (3) months after the end of each fiscal year of the Sponsor.

8. The Sponsor shall prepare all requisite New York State and federal governmental reports and informational returns require in connection with the Project, including those required by the Internal Revenue Service. In the event the Project shall be audited by auditors selected by any Donor, the Sponsor shall cooperate in good faith with such auditors. The Sponsor shall retain all records relating to the Project for such period as shall be required by law.

9. The Sponsor shall permit the Project to operate freely within the guidelines of the Project's purposes and shall not interfer with such purposes, and subject to paragraphs 2 and 4 above, all right, title and other ownership interests in and to the Project including, without limitation, tangible and intangible property arising out of the Project and all income arising therefrom, shall be for the sole benefit of the Project.

10. This agreement may be terminated by (a) mutual agreement of the parties hereto which shall be in writing and signed by each of the parties hereto, or (b) one party, in event the other party breaches this Agreement, if such other party does not cure such breach within five (5) days after receiving written notice from the non-breaching party of such breach and the non-breaching party's intent to terminate this Agreement.

11. In the event this Agreement is terminated pursuant to paragraphs 4 or 10 above, the Funds shall not be transferred to individual or entity for any purpose without the consent of the Sponsor.

12. This agreement shall be governed by, constructed and interpreted in accordance with, the laws of the State of New York.

IN WITNESS WHEREOF, the parties have executed this Agreement the day and year first above written.

[NAME OF SPONSOR]

By: _____

[NAME OF SIGNATORY AND TITLE]

[NAME OF PROJECT]

By: _____

[NAME OF SIGNATORY AND TITLE]

Start off your meeting by listing the groups you and your researchers have identified on a blackboard or flip chart paper. Then ask everyone to brainstorm a list of other possible candidates with whom you might share an affinity by virtue of a common mission, issue, constituency, or location. Don't hesitate to include institutions you may consider too large, too removed, or too formidable. Continue this exercise until no new suggestions are forthcoming. Then stop and take stock of your list. The following criteria can help you rate the candidate organizations:

- Strong congruence with your vision, mission, and values

- Excellent administrative capabilities, especially in fiscal matters and grants management

- A record of accomplishment among funders

- A history of innovation and risk-taking, at least in terms of programs

You will probably want to add some criteria of your own. As you do, you will eliminate some of the smaller, less established organizations from your list. You may also find that you need more information about some of the candidates before your list of prospects is complete.

Once your list has been refined, make plans to meet with the leaders of organizations that remain to determine which may be most appropriate, supportive, and interested in adopting or sponsoring your project. The best approach is usually a letter that carefully outlines what you would like to accomplish. In the letter, request a meeting and then follow up with a phone call to schedule an appointment. If you know people personally at the organization, you may want to contact them to ask their advice on how best to approach the person in charge. Bring along another person from your core group to the meeting to show that others are seriously involved in your undertaking.

During the meeting, probe gently until you find out how an affiliated arrangement might work on a daily basis. Ask what administrative fees would be charged, and what they would cover. Find out whether the institution has entered into similar relationships in the past.

After a series of such meetings, your core group should be able to reach a decision. If you've found the "perfect match," work with your attorney to draw up a letter of understanding (if a parent) or a grant agreement (if a sponsor) that accurately sets forth your mutual understanding.

If you do not find an organization that gets high marks on the basis of your criteria, you might still want to consider one of them as a fiscal sponsor for a year or so. Such an arrangement would still enable you to concentrate on program development and fundraising rather than the considerable administrative work required to obtain tax exemption and run an organization.

Tips

- Legal and fiscal matters take time, but they should be given the highest priority.

- Draft bylaws with extreme care; they determine the rules by which your organization operates and provide the final word in the organizational challenges that inevitably arise over time. Using boilerplate bylaws may be faster, but working deliberately and seeking advice from managers of seasoned nonprofits is wiser.

Additional Resources

Publications

Blazek, Jody. *Tax Planning and Compliance for Tax-Exempt Organizations: Forms, Checklists, Procedures.* 3rd ed. New York: John Wiley & Sons, 1999. xxi, 818 p.

This compendium of compliance tools and information provides practitioners and nonprofit managers with step-by-step guidance to establishing and safeguarding the tax-exempt status of an organization. Contains an introduction to requirements and characteristics of a nonprofit organization, along with a chart comparing the various Section 501(c) categories for tax-exemption. Includes specific instructions for answering questions on IRS Form 1023 and 1024 when seeking approval for exempt status. Also explores the steps involved in the approval process and advice for contesting IRS determinations. Contains checklists to help all types of nonprofit organizations maintain their exemption through the successful preparation of annual compliance forms. Also examines unrelated business income definitions and exceptions, the various constraints placed on political and legislative activity, the rules governing private inurement or benefit (along with checklists to evaluate compensation or salaries, sales, exchanges or renting of property, loans, joint ventures and services rendered for membership), and the methods behind an IRS examination. Describes the special rules and sanctions applied to private foundations, including a description of the types of income subject to excise tax, and sample forms for complying with grant "expenditure responsibility" rules. Considers several aspects of financial management and planning for nonprofits, including checklists encompassing questions about tax exemption, compliance, and financial management in regards to the role of board members and financial managers, inventory of financial reports, short and long-term budgeting, ratio analysis to evaluate performance, overall financial management, and internal control. Includes glossary and bibliography. Updated by annual supplements.

Blumenberg, Anne. *Starting a Nonprofit Organization: A Practical Guide to Organizing, Incorporating and Obtaining Tax-Exempt Status.* 3rd ed. Baltimore: Community Law Center, 1996. 61 p.

Bromberger, Allen R., Richard S. Hobish, and Barbara A. Schatz, eds. *Getting Organized.* 5th ed. New York: Lawyers Alliance for New York, 1999. xx, 371 p.

Introductory manual for attorneys representing organizations that wish to incorporate and to secure recognition of federal and state tax-exempt status. Forms and instructions for state tax-exemption are therefore geared toward organizations in New York. Appendices provide important addresses and telephone numbers; and sample forms and exhibits.

Colvin, Gregory L. *Fiscal Sponsorship: Six Ways To Do it Right.* San Francisco: Study Center Press, 1993. viii, 82 p.

Describes the six forms of fiscal sponsorship recognized by the Internal Revenue Service (IRS), with examples, charts and diagrams. Includes hypothetical scenarios, a sample sponsorship agreement, IRS Revenue Rulings, criticism and commentary.

Davis, Pamela. "The Politics of Risk: Are Nonprofits More Vulnerable Than You Think?" *Nonprofit World* 17 (July–August 1999): 33–37.

The Nonprofits' Insurance Alliance of California was formed in 1989 and is operated by the nonprofits it insures. A brief history of NIAC and how it works is offered here. The extent to which the model of NIAC can be replicated in other states is examined.

DeBoe, Margaret A. *Classifying 501 (c) Nonprofits.* Washington, DC: Accountants for the Public Interest (What a Difference Understanding Makes: Guide to Nonprofit Management Series), 1994. 17 p.

Covers characteristics of 501(c)(3) organizations, obtaining exemption, group exemptions, public and private charities, mergers, and other activities. Includes references and resources.

Gianfagna, Jean M. "Understanding UBIT." *Currents* 23 (June 1997): 36–40.

Goddeeris, John H., and Burton A. Weisbrod. *Conversion from Nonprofit to For-Profit Legal Status: Why Does It Happen and Should We Care?* Evanston, IL: Northwestern University. Institute for Policy Research, 1997. 38 p.

Examines recent activity in health care conversions, options for the transfer of assets from a nonprofit to a for-profit, possible motives for such a conversion, and resulting public policy implications. With bibliographic references.

Greig, Louise J.A., and M. Elena Hoffstein. "Issues Arising from Mergers and Fusions of Charitable Organizations." *Philanthropist/Le Philanthrope* 15 (August 1999): 40–56.

Provides an overview of the legal issues related to the mergers and amalgamations of charitable organizations in Canada. Discusses the liability of trustees and directors as well as regulatory issues.

Grobman, Gary M. *The Non-Profit Handbook.* Harrisburg, PA: White Hat Communications, 1997. viii, 302 p.

Hobish, Richard S. *Good Work in Hard Times: Reorganization, Dissolution and Bankruptcy: A Legal Primer for Nonprofit Organizations Coping with Financial Distress.* New York: Lawyers Alliance for New York, 1997. 28 p.

Provides practical, specific, and concise guidelines for board members and executives who are considering restructuring or dissolution of a nonprofit organization. Appendices cite the pertinent New York State laws.

Hopkins, Bruce R. *An Overview of Basic and Current Tax Law Affecting Association-Related Foundations.* Washington, DC: Association Foundation Group, 1999. 36 p.

Hopkins, Bruce R. *The Law of Fund-Raising,* 2nd ed. New York: John Wiley & Sons (Nonprofit Law, Finance, and Management Series), 1996. xxi, 762 p.
> Covers all aspects of state and federal nonprofit fundraising law, including the evolution of government regulation, comprehensive summaries of each state's charitable solicitation acts, a comparative analysis of these acts, legal issues in state regulation of fundraising, federal regulations, proposals and issues in prospective federal regulations, and overviews and commentaries. Appendices include copies of relevant IRS forms for exempt organizations, the eighty-two-item IRS checklist for monitoring charitable fundraising, a table of cases, and a table of IRS rulings and other pronouncements. Updated by supplements.

Hopkins, Bruce R. *The Law of Fund-Raising: 1998 Cumulative Supplement.* New York: John Wiley & Sons (Nonprofit Law, Finance, and Management Series), 1997. xii, 102 p.

Hopkins, Bruce R. *The Law of Fund-Raising: 1999 Cumulative Supplement.* New York: John Wiley & Sons (Nonprofit Law, Finance, and Management Series), 1998. xiii, 130 p.

Hopkins, Bruce R. *The Law of Tax-Exempt Organizations.* 7th ed. New York: John Wiley & Sons, 1998. xxii, 930 p.
> Contents are divided into six parts, beginning with an introduction to tax-exempt organizations. Other sections include charitable organizations; other tax-exempt organizations; general exempt organization laws; the commerciality doctrine and unrelated business income taxation; and inter-organizational structures and operational forms. The appendix contains Internal Revenue Code Sections; a table of cases; a table of IRS Revenue Rulings and Revenue Procedures; a table of IRS Private Letter Rulings and Other Items; and a table of IRS Private Determinations Cited in Text. Also contains an index. Updated with annual supplements.

Hopkins, Bruce R. *A Legal Guide to Starting and Managing a Nonprofit Organization.* 2nd ed. New York: John Wiley & Sons (Nonprofit Law, Finance, and Management Series), 1993. xvi, 304 p.
> Readable exploration of the fundamental laws affecting the operation of nonprofit organizations. Examines virtually all aspects of starting and operating a nonprofit group, including reporting revenue, tax exemption, the rules pertaining to charitable giving, compensating the nonprofit employee, lobbying, and successful techniques for using for-profit subsidiaries, partnerships, and planned giving. Throughout the book, the fictional "Campaign to Clean Up America" serves to illustrate salient points. The final section examines challenges which nonprofits will face over the coming decades. Includes a glossary of important legal terms, and an index.

Hopkins, Bruce R. *The Second Legal Answer Book for Nonprofit Organizations.* New York: John Wiley & Sons, 1998. xxxii, 303 p.

Designed for nonprofit executives, board members, fundraising professionals, lawyers, and accountants who need quick and authoritative answers concerning the law governing nonprofit organizations. The question and answer format offers a guide to understanding complex legal issues. Topics discussed include intermediate sanctions, competition and commerciality, partnerships and joint ventures, tax-exempt status, associations, social welfare organizations, social clubs and political organizations, private foundation rules, interests in business enterprises, preparation of annual returns, and disclosure and distribution requirements. Provides citations as research aids for those who need to pursue particular items in greater detail. Indexed.

Hopkins, Bruce R., and D. Benson Tesdahl. *Intermediate Sanctions: Curbing Nonprofit Abuse.* New York: John Wiley & Sons, 1997. xiii, 194 p.

Reviews the history and background of the intermediate sanctions law, which places an emphasis on the taxation of those who engaged in impermissible private transactions with tax-exempt public charities and social welfare organizations, rather than revocation of the tax exemption of these entities. With this approach, tax sanctions, structured as penalty excise taxes, may be imposed on disqualified persons who improperly benefited from the transactions and on organization managers who participated in any transation while knowing that it was improper. Sections cover specific applications of the sanctions and planning for compliance. Includes glossary, bibliography, and index.

Hummel, Joan. *Starting and Running a Nonprofit Organization.* 2nd ed. Minneapolis: University of Minnesota Press, 1996. ix, 152 p.

Handbook explains the steps involved in setting up a nonprofit organization: how to define goals and plan programs, put together a board of directors, incorporate, become tax exempt, develop a budget, raise funds, set up a bookkeeping system, hire staff, and plan a program of community relations. Includes bibliography.

Johnston, Janis, ed. *Turning Vision into Reality: What the Founding Board Should Know about Starting a Nonprofit Organization.* Washington, DC: National Center for Nonprofit Boards, 1999. 38 p.

Kirschten, Barbara L. *Nonprofit Corporation Forms Handbook.* 2000 ed. Eagan, MN: West Group, 2000. xxiv, ca. 1200 p.

Covers registration and reporting requirements for Internal Revenue Service (IRS) designated tax-exempt organizations. Provides sample document forms to illustrate incorporation and operation of nonprofits under the jurisdictions of California, Delaware, District of Columbia, Illinois, Maryland, Massachusetts, New York, Texas, and Virginia. Offers guidelines for applying for IRS 501(c)(3) or 501(c)(6) exempt status.

Leavins, John A., and Darshan Wadhwa. "Are Your Activities Safe from UBIT?" *Nonprofit World* 16 (September–October 1998): 49–51.
  Explains the background of the original unrelated business income tax law and the current law and its application.

Leifer, Jacqueline Covey, and Michael B. Glomb. *The Legal Obligations of Nonprofit Boards: A Guidebook for Board Members.* Washington, DC: National Center for Nonprofit Boards, 1997. 38 p.

Mahoney, John W. "Volunteer Protection Act: What Does It Mean for You." *Nonprofit World* 16 (March–April 1998): 36–37.
  Highlights major points of this new legislation, which is intended to protect volunteers and nonprofit organizations from excessive and frivolous lawsuits.

Mancuso, Anthony. *How To Form a Nonprofit Corporation.* 4th ed. Berkeley, CA: Nolo Press, 1997.
  Written by an attorney, this is a practical step-by-step guide to forming a nonprofit organization that meets the requirements for a federal corporate income tax exemption under Section 501(c)(3) of the Internal Revenue Code. In order to qualify for this status, nonprofits must be organized for religious, charitable, educational, scientific or literary purposes. Contains eleven chapters: Overview of Nonprofit Corporations; Nonprofit Corporation Law; The Federal 501(c)(3) Nonprofit Income Tax Exemption; 501(c)(3) Public Charities and Private Foundations; Other Nonprofit Tax Issues and Reporting Requirements; Steps to Organize a Nonprofit Corporation; Prepare Your Bylaws; Apply for Your Federal 501(c)(3) Tax Exemption; Final Steps in Organizing Your Nonprofit Corporation; After Your Corporation is Organized; Lawyers and Accountants. Appendix consists of forms and state sheets which provide the following for each state: secretary of state information, corporate name requirements, articles of incorporation, bylaws, state corporate tax exemption. Includes index.

Nober, Jane C. "Keep, File, Toss." *Foundation News & Commentary* 39 (March–April 1998): 47–49.
  Explains how to choose what to toss, and what to save in order to stay in compliance with the Internal Revenue Service.

Oleck, Howard L., and Martha E. Stewart. *Nonprofit Corporations, Organizations, and Associations.* 6th ed. Englewood Cliffs, NJ: Prentice-Hall, 1994. xxiv, 1632 p.
  Offers practical information concerning every aspect of organization, administration, regulation, taxation, mergers and dissolutions. Includes details on qualifying for nonprofit status, protecting tax-exempt status, utilizing powers and purposes clauses, conducting directors' meetings, forming committees, removing or suspending nonprofit directors, drafting bylaws, recognizing unauthorized and improper acts, dealing with lawsuits or bankruptcy, when and how donations can be solicited, new limits on charitable deductions,

standards for nonprofit accounting, federal and state lobbying laws, management techniques, mixing profit and nonprofit activities, and parliamentary law. Provides model business and tax forms, such as the annual report, resolution on salaries, appointment of an agent, ballot for election, articles to amend charter, bylaws of large and small nonprofits, and applicable Internal Revenue Service documentation.

Oleck, Howard L., and Martha E. Stewart. *Nonprofit Corporations, Organizations, and Associations: 1998/1999 Cumulative Supplement.* Englewood Cliffs, NJ: Prentice-Hall, 1998. xxii, 478 p.
> Provides updated information on new court rulings and changes in tax policy of current relevance to the operation of various types of nonprofit organizations. The cumulative index includes entries for the sixth edition and the supplement.

Olenick, Arnold J., and Philip R. Olenick. *A Nonprofit Organization Operating Manual: Planning for Survival and Growth.* New York: The Foundation Center, 1991. xxiii, 484 p.
> Manual addresses the essential financial and legal aspects of managing a nonprofit organization. Divided into four parts, Part 1 ("Long-Range Considerations") includes chapters which cover each step of the nonprofit incorporation procedure, the limits on political and legislative activity, methods for devising the proper organizational structure, information to include when drafting articles and bylaws, the elements of strategic planning, and the responsibilities of the board and staff. Part 2 ("The Vital Role of Financial Management") contains chapters on the operating budget (including a step-by-step guide to preparing a budget worksheet), program budgeting, cash and capital budgeting, fundraising, income-producing ventures, the "Generally Accepted Accounting Principles" (written for non-accountants), establishing a management information system, and a practical approach to accounting. Part 3 ("Operational Management") covers financial reports and cash management, and Part 4 ("Outside Accountability") discusses required financial reports, grant management, the "IRS Form 990: Return of organization exempt from income tax," and other tax-reporting obligations. Includes figures and tables, illustrations and step-by-step guides, sample forms, and annotated bibliography.

Salamon, Lester M. *The International Guide to Nonprofit Law.* New York: John Wiley & Sons, 1997. xxxii, 400 p.
> Serves as a layman's guide to the basic law of nonprofit organizations in the following countries: Australia, Brazil, Canada, Egypt, France, Germany, Hungary, India, Republic of Ireland, Israel, Italy, Japan, Mexico, the Netherlands, Poland, the Russian Federation, South Africa, Spain, Sweden, Thailand, United Kingdom, and the United States. Noting that in a global arena the concept of the nonprofit sector is an ambiguous one, the scope of the comparison of laws covers a wide array of types of organizations. Yet, according to Salamon, there are some common elements that seem to be in place in each country analyzed, so that 'nonprofit' entities are 1) private, that is, separate from government; 2) organized, that is, institutionalized to some extent; 3) voluntary, that is, noncompulsory, and involving some meaningful degree of voluntary participation; 4) self-governing, that

is, controlled according to their own internal procedures; and 5) non-profit-distributing, that is, not returning any profits they may generate to their owners or directors. Appendices include extracts from "Handbook on Good Practices for Laws Relating to NGOs," a 1997 discussion draft by the World Bank. Includes bibliographic references and an index.

Schadler, B. Holly. *The Connection: Strategies for Creating and Operating 501(c)(3)s, 501(c)(4)s, and PACs.* Washington, DC: Alliance for Justice, 1998. viii, 62 p.
Explains the differences between 501(c)(3) organizations and 501(c)(4) organizations. The latter may conduct educational, lobbying and political activities, but donations to it are not tax deductible. 501(c)(3)s may engage in only a limited amount of lobbying. Defines two types of political action committees (PACs) and outlines the activities they may pursue. Provides detailed information about establishing 501(c)(4)s and PACs and how to structure and manage the relationships between the three types of organizations in order to engage in public policy activities.

Sherman, Karen, ed. *New York Not-for-Profit Organization: Charitable Compliance Requirements & Tax Exemptions with Registration, Reporting & Tax Forms.* New York: Lawyers Alliance for New York, 1997. vi, 24 p. and appendices.
Contains concise details about charitable registration, annual reporting requirements, and federal and state tax exemption for New York State nonprofits. Appendices duplicate numerous government forms and related instruction sheets.

Simon, Karla W., and Leon E. Irish. "Legal Mechanisms To Encourage Development Partnerships." *International Journal of Not-for-Profit Law* 1 (September 1998): 40–46.
In the introduction, the authors explain the establishment and growth of the International Center for Not-for-Profit Law (ICNL) and the initiatives on which the organization is currently focused. The majority of the article outlines and describes the primary legislative issues that need to be addressed in order for nongovernmental organizations (NGOs) to form partnerships with business or government in their region or country. Some of the foundations needed are 1) general framework legislation; 2) procurement legislation; 3) fiscal legislation; 4) privatization mechanisms; and 5) specialized local government grantmaking authority. An appendix provides a list of other legislation, national and local, in brief. With bibliographic references.

Sobczak, Carol A. "Acts of Self-Dealing: Are You a Disqualified Person?" *Trusts & Estates* 137 (October 1998): 27, 30, 32, 34.
Examines the term "disqualified person" in relation to the self-dealing rules of the Tax Reform Act of 1969.

Suhrke, Henry C. "Earmarked Contributions and the Risk of Private Benefit: A New Chapter?" *Philanthropy Monthly* 30 (March 1997): 5–11.
The Internal Revenue Service has partially blessed a new form of fundraising, "deputized fundraising," enabling donors to designate the use of funds for specific individuals or their

expenses or projects. The blessing is partial because the IRS insists the awarding of 501(c)(3)status to the practitioner is non-precedential.

Teitell, Conrad, and Richard A. Siegal. *Avoiding Intermediate Sanctions.* Boston: Warren, Gorham & Lamont, 1998. xii, various pagings.

Tesdahl, D. Benson, and Jodi Finder. "Don't Wait for Intermediate Sanctions Guidance." *Nonprofit World* 16 (January–February 1998): 22–24.
> Provides guidelines to follow to avoid penalties associated with section 4958 of the IRS Code. Intermediate sanctions are excise taxes that can be imposed on certain individuals receiving an excessive benefit from their dealings with a charity or social welfare organization.

United States, Internal Revenue Service. Application for Recognition of Exemption Under Section 501(a) or for Determination Under Section 120 (Package 1024), Washington, DC: Internal Revenue Service. Free. (Order from: local IRS Tax Forms Office)
> Includes the actual application forms for exemption from federal income tax for organizations covered under other parts of Section 501(c) besides Section 501(c)(3).

United States, Internal Revenue Service. Application for Recognition of-Exemption Under Section 501(c)(3) of the Internal Revenue Code (Package 1023), Washington, DC: Internal Revenue Service. 8 pp. plus forms. Free. (Order from: local IRS Tax Forms Office)
> Application forms for tax-exempt status (Forms 1023 and 872-C) along with instructions for completing them.

United States, Internal Revenue Service. *Internal Revenue Service Exempt Organizations Handbook.* Washington, DC: Internal Revenue Service. $54.00. (Available in any Internal Revenue Service Reading Room, or order from: IRS, Attention: TX:D:P:RR, 1111 Constitution Avenue, N.W., Washington, DC 20224)
> Detailed discussion of the specific requirements for receiving tax-exempt status.

United States, Internal Revenue Service. *Tax-Exempt Status for Your Organization* (Publication 557). Washington, DC: Internal Revenue Service, February 1984. 44 pp. Free. (Order from: local IRS Tax Forms Office)
> Discusses the rules and procedures for organizations seeking to obtain exemption from federal income tax under Section 501(c) of the Internal Revenue Code.

Volunteer Lawyers for the Arts. *To Be or Not To Be: An Artist's Guide to Not-for-Profit Incorporation.* New York: Volunteer Lawyers for the Arts. 1982. 12 pp.
> Discusses pros and cons of corporate status, legal responsibilities, and information needed to file for incorporation and to apply for tax-exempt status. Alternatives to incorporation are also covered.

Williams, Grant. "Intermediate Opinions." *Chronicle of Philanthropy* 11 (28 January 1999): 23–25.
> Provides preliminary comments from nonprofits about the IRS's draft of legislation about intermediate sanctions.

Williams, Grant. "IRS Is Urged To Make Some Revisions in Plan To Enforce Disclosure Law." *Chronicle of Philanthropy* 10 (12 February 1998): 41–42.
> Nonprofit advocates recommend that the IRS not create too great a burden for organizations that try to comply with the new information-disclosure law. A law passed by Congress in 1996 required charities to make their Form 990 readily available to the public. The IRS's proposed regulations describe in detail how nonprofits can comply with the law. Article states the government's plan and responses from nonprofit representatives.

Zeitlin, Kim Arthur, and Susan E. Dorn. *The Nonprofit Board's Guide to Bylaws: Creating a Framework for Effective Governance.* Washington, DC: National Center for Nonprofit Boards, 1996. 24 p.
> Provides a basic definition of bylaws and an overview of the issues and areas bylaws should address. Gives examples to illustrate the relationship between state law and bylaws. Includes bibliography.

Internet

The Alliance for Justice (www.afj.org)
> Maintains a Web site with useful links and a summary of its publications for nonprofits; which include "The Connection: Strategies for Creating and Operating 501(c)(3)s, 501(c)(4)s, and PACs." The Alliance produces publications that guide nonprofit organizations in legal matters related to advocacy (lobbying, ballot campaigns, tax status). The site lists state offices regulating incorporation by nonprofits.

Council of Better Business Bureaus (www.bbb.org)
> Nonprofit organizations might find the site useful. It proposes standards for charitable solicitations and gives a good sense of what business donors' expectations can be from the charitable organizations they support.

ExemptLaw.com (www.exemptlaw.com/)
> This web site will help answer your questions about the many legal and tax issues that affect nonprofit organizations in the United States. Includes numerous FAQs and links to IRS forms.

Financial Accounting Standards Board (FASB); FASB Order Department; 401 Merritt 7, P.O. Box 5116; Norwalk, CT 06586-5116 (www.rutgers.edu/Accounting/raw/fasb)
> Standards and other documents can be obtained from this site.

Federal Election Commission (www.fec.gov)
 Reporting forms are found on their Web site. Nonprofits can also file forms electronically.

Internal Revenue Service Site for Tax-Exempt Organizations
(www.irs.ustreas.gov/prod/bus_info/eo)
 Information for American tax-exempt organizations provided directly by the Internal
 Revenue Service, including rules, pronouncements, guidelines, and contact information.

The Internet Nonprofit Center (www.nonprofits.org)
 Maintains a broad-ranging Web site that provides information for and about nonprofit
 organizations. The Center is a project of the Evergreen State Society, a nonprofit
 organization based in Seattle, WA. The site is a good source of information about IRS
 Form 990 and Financial Accounting Standards Board (FASB) Standards. The site includes
 a categorized bibliography of print literature related to nonprofits. The site is an excellent
 starting point for obtaining information about how to set-up and operate a nonprofit
 organization.

The National Center for Nonprofit Boards and Independent Sector (www.ncnb.org,
www.independentsector.org)
 Resources to help nonprofits determine how much lobbying they can engage in.

Nonprofitlaw.com (www.nonprofitlaw.com)
 Allows you to download tax status applications forms, as well as 990 and 990-EZ forms
 and instructions. A concise matrix comparing various aspects of the different tax statuses is
 also on the site, which is maintained by a private organization.

Nonprofit Coordinating Committee of New York (www.npccny.org)
 The Nonprofit Coordinating Committee of New York provides members with technical
 and managerial support, informs members of government activities that impact them,
 represents the nonprofit sector in legislative matters, and promotes a better understanding
 of the role of nonprofits in the economy and culture of New York.

990online.com (www.990online.com)
 A very comprehensive site regarding Form 990 and related regulations.

1800net.com (www.1800net.com/nprc)
 Industry-specific documents and pronouncements designed for nonprofit organizations, as
 well as practical information on how to start a nonprofit organization.

Chapter 3

Building a Board of Directors

Honest differences are often a healthy sign of progress.
—Mohatma Gandhi

The vast body of literature about nonprofit boards of directors speaks volumes, literally, about their importance. A nonprofit organization lacking dedicated individuals with diverse skills and expertise on its board of directors has little hope of realizing its vision. Committed board members bring planning, management, financial, and program expertise to the organization. They also provide contributions, fundraising contacts, and influential voices in the community to speak of the organization's importance and needs. Their stewardship and ability to involve

others will keep both new and mature organizations on track as they work to realize their mission and vision.

In the United States and other countries with established nonprofit sectors, boards of directors (or trustees) are charged with the governance of an organization. In countries without a formal nonprofit sector, a group of people still must assume a high level of responsibility for an organization's governance and well-being. While the original vision and impetus that launched an organization may have come from one or a few individuals, many others are needed to turn that vision into reality, including staff and committee members, volunteers, and donors.

But those who serve on the board play a special role, as it is largely the quality of their leadership that will determine an organization's success. Their profile in the community will directly influence how the organization will be regarded and supported, and it is no exaggeration to say that their personal integrity can either make or break a venture. The importance of choosing board members wisely—especially in an organization's founding stage when the effort is vulnerable yet the need for committed and proactive leadership is pressing—cannot be overemphasized.

If an organization is founded mainly through the efforts of one person, that individual will generally aspire to leadership, either as a staff member (i.e., executive director) or officer of the board of directors (i.e., president, or chair). He or she might choose to serve in both capacities or to step aside once other responsible and committed leadership emerges. In any event, wise founders will make it a top priority at the very outset to involve new people as members of a planning, steering, or organizing committee. This core group will provide initial leadership until a board of directors is formally established.

By inviting new people to serve on an interim or organizing committee, founders and core groups can identify candidates for board membership, benefit from their talents right away, and learn more about them—and their ability to support the founder's vision—by working together. Some of these individuals will continue their involvement as board members; others may continue to play a part in the life of the organization, but not necessarily on the board or staff.

Start-ups may find it difficult to resist the temptation of inviting people to join the board without first getting to know them. Actually, founders and young organizations are in stronger positions than they realize to solicit the participation of highly desirable individuals because board membership can bestow knowledge, power, visibility, status, contacts, and satisfaction. In fact, a study conducted by James E. Austin in 1996 at Harvard found that U.S. executives—individuals many organizations want on their boards—say that board membership helps them make valuable business contacts, affords opportunities to sharpen their business skills in a new setting, and provides personal satisfaction. The study found that some 81 percent of managers and executives surveyed were significantly involved in the nonprofit sector; that 82 percent of the 316 CEOs polled served on boards; and that most sat on more than one board, and 36 percent sat on six or more.

Organizations, then, would do well to solicit board membership from a position of strength—since they have so much to offer—and not involve a person formally until they have become totally comfortable with that prospective board member's character, motivation, commitment, and skills. No child should be entrusted to a stranger.

The following overview of board selection, structure, responsibilities, and dynamics is not meant to be exhaustive. The intent of this chapter is to offer a kind of expanded checklist that founders, staff members, board members, and others can apply to their own organization. The Additional Resources section at the end of this chapter enumerates excellent sources for in-depth study.

Key Elements of Board Operations

A nonprofit board comprises a number of elements, all of which must work together harmoniously for an organization to achieve its mission.

- *Members* establish and update the organization's vision and mission.

- The *chairperson* coordinates, motivates, mediates, trains, and encourages board members; leads board evaluation; makes sure the board focuses on governance, not management; acts as chief representative of the organization to its constituencies, and as the principal fundraiser; and works closely with the executive director.

- *Other officers* work with the executive director and chair to coordinate the board's work and help make things happen.

- *Standing committees*—development, executive, finance, fundraising, nominating, program—meet regularly.

- *Other committees*—audit, bylaws, personnel, strategic planning, vision/mission review, and special ad hoc committees such as special events—meet as necessary.

- *Meetings* address organizational priorities without micromanaging, and result in action on committee findings and recommendations.

- *Agendas* are developed by the chair and executive director to accomplish the board's business.

- *Board minutes* serve as a brief, readable report of actions taken, items discussed but held over, items postponed, and new business.

- The *executive director* brings information and new trends to the board's attention and carries out the board's instructions.

The Board of Directors: Its Responsibilities

Once more, an organization's vision and mission provide the starting point for our discussion. In Chapter 2 we saw that a group's vision and mission provide the basis for its choice of legal operating structure. We now turn to a nonprofit's governing structure—the board of directors—to explore how it can help the organization achieve its mission and realize its vision.

The board of directors is the governing body of an organization, the mechanism for channeling and directing the time and energy of other volunteer leaders. A basic understanding of board members' responsibilities is actually provided by law: "A board member must act as a prudent person." A board member is not required to know everything about running an organization. Neither is he or she expected to anticipate all outcomes, but rather to use common sense and to act accordingly. Board members act prudently, for example, by not committing an organization to new programs until sufficient funding is either pledged or in hand.

Meeting according to a schedule prescribed in the bylaws, nonprofit boards discuss and vote on an organization's highest priority issues. They set policy and perform such vital functions as hiring and evaluating key staff, approving operating budgets, establishing long-term plans, and carrying out fundraising activities. They also address vision and mission review; budget review and adoption; ongoing monitoring of expenses and income; and the board's own renewal process, including recruitment and orientation of new members, and assessing its own performance.

Although the literature abounds with lists of nonprofit boards' responsibilities, the following ten are frequently chosen by many nonprofit experts:

1. Ensure adequate resources

2. Determine the organization's mission and purposes

3. Select and support the executive director, review his or her performance, and establish personnel policies

4. Ensure effective management and planning

5. Ensure effective fiscal management and legally compliant operations

6. Organize the board so that it works efficiently

7. Approve budgets, and determine and monitor the organization's programs and services

8. Select and orient new board members

9. Enhance the organization's public image

10. Evaluate the board's own performance

1. Ensure Adequate Resources

Perhaps no board responsibility is more important than fundraising. This responsibility must be institutionalized so that when members of a board approve a project or organizational budget, they know that it is up to them to make sure adequate funds are available.

That board members have an obligation to donate money (as well as time and energy) to an organization should, with few exceptions, be a condition of board membership, and should be discussed early on with prospective board members. In addition to providing a guaranteed level of support each year, board giving sends a message of utmost importance to donors—that the board is active and committed.

Most board members are also expected to solicit contributions, and it would be difficult for a board member unwilling to contribute to the organization to solicit from others. To be sure, there are exceptions to this rule. A person who cannot make a significant donation but who can raise sums from others or provide essential expertise, representation, or reputation can still be a valuable board member. At the same time, "give or get" is the prevailing view on the matter, and an organization able to report 100 percent board giving gains a great deal of leverage.

It's best that either the board's chairperson or members of the development committee, not the executive director, solicit contributions from other board members, as people generally give more to their peers. This approach will raise more money and also avoids placing the director in an uncomfortable position, even if he or she is an excellent fundraiser and solicitor.

The goal for board giving should increase each year. Board members with substantial means and commitment to the organization can be asked to consider making a significant pledge, which could be paid over several years. Such gifts not only assure an organization of ongoing support and increase its ability to plan; they also stimulate giving at higher levels by setting an example.

With the government reducing its support of the nonprofit sector while at the same time restricting nonprofits' advocacy activities, the role of board members in fundraising has never been more important. Today more than ever, successful fundraising requires board members to open doors, solicit large donors, join staff in visiting prospective foundations and corporate contributors, and participate in planning fundraising and public education campaigns. In addition to donating cash, stock, and other property, board members can undertake many other fundraising tasks, including selling tickets to special events, soliciting memberships, participating in meetings with prospective funding sources, hosting benefits at home, and speaking to gatherings of potential supporters.

All board members should learn the art of raising money and should be willing to exercise that ability on behalf of their organization. Chapter 11 of this book, "Face-to-Face Solicitation," will prove helpful to board (and development committee) members who are willing to solicit but need some background. The majority of today's nonprofit leaders—both board and staff members—have learned these skills through their own direct experience; they have not had to depend solely on wisdom passed down by word of mouth through successive generations within an institution, as was once the case. The nonprofit sector's enormous growth has created the need for more formal education, and the various aspects of fundraising are being codified and taught at colleges and universities, workshops, and seminars.

2. Determine the Organization's Mission and Purposes

The discussion in Chapter 1 highlights the role board members, or members of a start-up's core group, can play in developing an organization's vision and mission statements. Once vision and mission have been framed, the board should review the statements from time to time to assess their currency, and revise or update them if necessary. Just as board members will refer to their group's vision and mission in speaking with others, they should keep the statements in mind when reviewing program and budget proposals, considering candidates for board membership, and, generally, in all their deliberations.

3. Select and Support the Executive Director, Review His or Her Performance, and Establish Personnel Policies

Selecting an organization's chief executive is perhaps the most important decision a board can make. Revisiting vision and mission statements should be the first step in the hiring process, as the director's job is to move the organization ahead on the path set forth. The board should then take stock of the organization's current needs and resources. Because different strengths are required of chief executives at different stages of an organization's development, this inventory will suggest the kind of individual to hire. Boards must also make sure that the organization's working environment will support the new director in meeting their expectations.

Based on this information, a job description should be drafted and decisions made about compensation, benefits, and so on. However the search is then conducted—by board members, by a committee of the board, or by a search firm—the final choice belongs to the board. Once the new director has been hired, it is the board's job to support that person in every way, a task frequently assigned to its executive committee. This support includes making sure expectations are clear; providing ongoing feedback; making introductions to community leaders, organizations, and significant donors; including the new director in social events; and being aware of the director's personal situation.

Clearly stated expectations also form the basis for assessing the new director's performance. Concrete goals, mutually agreed upon, facilitate the assessment, which should be undertaken in the spirit of helping the director perform most effectively. Of course, the board's own performance must also be considered. It's virtually impossible for a chief officer to do his job if board members are not doing theirs. To provide a measure of objectivity in the assessment process, boards sometimes hire an outside consultant.

Most nonprofit organizations are employers at one time or another. In fact, colleges and hospitals may be among a community's largest employers. However, some nonprofits, especially smaller ones, see traditional employer–employee issues as incompatible with their idealistic, altruistic aspirations. Many old-fashioned nonprofit bosses hold the attitude that working for a charitable purpose affords psychological benefits so great as to outweigh any mere material compensation such as salary increases and better benefits packages. Such an attitude fosters unnecessary conflict and tension—nonprofit employees obviously have the same needs as workers in the for-profit sector.

Because the nonprofit's products are usually the services of their employees and volunteers, tending to their concerns is of paramount importance. The effective hiring, training, evaluation, and compensation of employees is one of the best ways for an organization to accomplish its work. The board, therefore, should include individuals with expertise in human resources. Although few boards can match the personnel resources available to large corporations, most organizations can enlist human resource specialists or other professionals in the helping professions, such as training, social work, and psychology.

Board and staff work together to accomplish the same objectives, but the relationship is hierarchical out of necessity, since the board is ultimately responsible for fulfilling the organization's purposes. Board and staff roles can easily become clouded by such factors as proprietary feelings on the part of an executive director, particularly when he or she is the group's founder; a history as a passive or rubber-stamp board; a negative interaction of personalities; or a desire to avoid conflict. An effective organization is guided by a carefully crafted balance between staff and board authority. Simply put, staff members are responsible for day-to-day operations, whereas the board sets long-term policies.

4. Ensure Effective Management and Planning

Although these two terms have not always been associated with the nonprofit sector, they are indispensable to the effective implementation of programs. Management means guiding the available human and financial resources toward the smooth and efficient accomplishment of established goals. A board of directors hires an executive director to serve as the manager of an organization, but the board still needs to make sure that this function is adequately carried out.

Planning refers to the mapping out of an organization's programs, activities, and finances so that it can operate in a coherent and focused manner. Whether you are planning a short-term project such as a fundraising event, developing a new program area, or undertaking long-term strategic planning, it is the quality of your planning that will largely determine the success of your efforts. (See Chapter 4 for a more detailed discussion of planning.)

By paying careful attention to both management and planning functions, board and staff can help move an organization along the best possible course toward advancing its mission. Increasingly, college courses and degrees in management and planning, as well as workshops and seminars, are being offered to nonprofits. Board members and staff should seek out such opportunities, or recruit individuals with expertise in these fields from other nonprofits or businesses.

5. Ensure Effective Fiscal Management and Legally Compliant Operations

A board of directors is not an advisory body. A board has the actual power to establish the major policies that govern the affairs of an organization—in fact, in many countries it is accorded this responsibility by law. A board also has the ethical and, in some areas, legal responsibility to make sure the organization operates in accordance with the law. For example, in the United States, if an organization fails to pay its employees' withholding taxes to the Internal Revenue Service, the board, collectively and individually, is ultimately responsible for the full payment of those taxes. Directors' and officers' insurance cannot protect board members from this responsibility—many boards have been taught a painful and unexpected lesson in this regard. Faced with both important legal and ethical responsibilities, a board is urged to exert its authority.

Most people can learn to understand the fiscal matters that come before a nonprofit board, but it is crucial that at least one member have substantial experience in financial management to serve as the board's guide. Such a person would logically serve as treasurer. Prospective candidates for this office include accountants, comptrollers, and others with finance experience, either in the nonprofit, corporate, or public sectors.

Once this competency is added to its ranks, a board is in a better position to understand its regular financial statements and to make informed financial decisions entailed in reviewing and approving the annual operating budget, assessing anticipated revenues, and approving new expenditures. Although the treasurer is likely to be the board member with the greatest financial expertise, all board members should understand basic financial concepts and be familiar with the organization's numbers. An organization's credibility can sink if its finances are poorly understood or handled. For instance, in the United States, in addition to penalties for late payment of employees' federal withholding taxes, incorrect expenditures of foundation grant monies can result in serious repercussions.

How do you negotiate a lease for office space with a prospective landlord? What are permissible grassroots lobbying activities for U.S. nonprofit organizations under Section 501(c)(3) of the Code? What laws should a board of directors be aware of when firing an employee? What types of fundraising activity require special reporting procedures to the state in which your organization conducts its business?

The list of legal issues you will face during the life of your organization goes on and on. Some boards believe that occasional legal questions can be handled easily by calling a lawyer friend. That might work sometimes, but it won't always; having a qualified lawyer on a board will help ensure that all legal matters are dealt with properly. At the same time, all board members should familiarize themselves with the basics of nonprofit law. As in financial management, legal foresight is the best way to make sure that problems do not arise.

The need for professional legal help becomes clearest during periods of crisis, when documents such as bylaws must provide the means of resolving thorny issues. But legal oversight is no less important in other areas, such as filing annually with the charities registration bureau or government agencies, or informing the board what constitutes a quorum for decision-making purposes, when necessary.

6. Organize the Board So That It Works Efficiently

Board Structure: Officers

Who guides a board in its work? Who makes sure that a board does its job? These tasks fall to the officers of a board, who are appointed, selected, or elected by their peers. Officers are usually referred to as president and vice president(s), or chair and co-chair(s), as well as secretary and treasurer. Nonprofits are often required by law to list board officers in their articles of incorporation and enumerate their functions in a set of bylaws. Active, responsible officers are essential if a board is to function smoothly and efficiently, and ensure that its members derive satisfaction from their work. Officers play an important role in making sure that the board and its committee tackle their work efficiently and effectively.

Board Structure: Committees

Board committees help a board work effectively by investigating and developing policy options for the board's consideration, and by distributing the work equally. Committees are the vehicles for drawing on members' skills and expertise and for expanding their participation beyond meeting attendance. When committees function well, they enrich the experience of the group's

Learning the Hard Way

When I was 23, I learned the hard way about my fiscal responsibilities as a board member. I joined the board of an innovative, state-funded alcohol recovery program geared to the gay and lesbian community. It was one of the first programs to be geared to a specific community, and was innovative because all the people that worked within the program had to be recovering alcoholics with a year or less of sobriety. The idea was that the whole staff would be very close to the problems that their clients faced. Board members, on the other hand, did not have to meet these criteria. In fact, many of us had little experience with drug and alcohol problems, and could not have anticipated the problems we would face.

The executive director was a brilliant woman who had been through many recovery programs. She was tough, funny, and articulate, and I never questioned anything she said. I thought my job was simply to come to meetings and to help raise money. Before a year had passed, the director started coming late to board meetings, and eventually, stopped coming completely. The treasurer of the board reported getting phone calls from creditors, and then the director disappeared. She left a pile of unpaid bills with no paper trail of how money had been spent—financial chaos. She had not stolen the funds, but it was clear that neither she nor any of her staff had managed the money properly.

Payments on the grant from the state were suspended and the state revenue service's audit deemed that the money had been squandered and that the agency had to pay most of it back. The audit noted carelessness but no wrongdoing, and expressed that the board had not exercised appropriate supervision.

Since the organization disbanded, it was able to settle with the state for much less than was owed—about $2,000 per board member. Although this was a very generous deal on the part of the state, it was a third of my salary and took me three years to pay. I look back on it as one of the cheapest lessons I have ever learned. I will never underestimate the responsibilities of the board again.

—Kim Klein

members, create more productive and interesting meetings, and give the members a chance to develop closer relationships.

A committee can be composed of both board members and nonmembers. In fact, an important (though unstated) committee function is to serve as a vehicle for getting to know prospective board members. Candidates with the skills and expertise needed by committees can be asked to serve in a definite capacity rather than simply being invited to "join the board." By presenting the organization's expectations and requirements to a prospective board member before he or she is elected—and by giving that candidate the opportunity to accept the "job description" and show that they understood it—a board can avoid some of the problems of ineffectual "rubber-stamp" boards.

A board's standing committees should be enumerated in an organization's bylaws. They most frequently include the executive, development, finance, nominating, and program committees. Following is a brief description of the function each performs:

1. The *executive committee* is a smaller body empowered to act on behalf of the full board between regularly scheduled meetings. Central to an organization's operations, it usually comprises the board's officers and meets regularly to deal with pressing issues, to hold preliminary conversations about certain matters needing refinement and focus before being presented to the full board, and to make routine decisions that don't need the full board's approval. The executive committee works closely with the executive director and other senior staff members, as appropriate.

2. The *development committee* directs the board's fundraising activities. It educates board members about the organization's programs and funding needs, and helps them become better informed about, and comfortable with, the fundraising process. Working closely with the executive director and board chair, it focuses members' work in identifying, cultivating, and soliciting contributions from the outside community, and, together with the board chair, soliciting gifts from other board members.

3. The *finance committee* oversees the organization's financial operations. This committee performs the final review of the annual budget, recommends it to the full board, and then monitors its implementation. It works closely with the executive, development, and financial directors in the role of reviewer and advisor, but it does not become involved in daily operations unless there is no staff.

4. The *nominating committee* performs the vital role of identifying and recommending candidates for board membership, as well as cultivating and nominating officers. The importance of this committee is frequently overlooked, but the results of its work will largely determine an organization's success. This committee is also responsible for the orientation and training of new board members, and for the board evaluation process.

5. The *program committee* monitors an organization's programs for implementation and consistency with the strategic plan. Working with the executive and program directors, the program committee also presents program proposals developed by staff to the board, makes recommendations, and reports progress. As with all other board committees, the program committee limits its involvement to oversight and planning.

Other standing committees can include building and grounds, investment, personnel, public affairs, strategic planning, and others, as appropriate. Nonstanding committees are usually formed for short periods to perform specific functions. These would include audit, vision/mission review, special events, and strategic planning committees, to name a few.

One final word about committees. The board must value their work and take their recommendations seriously. On the other hand, committee members must understand that the board as a whole must make the final decision on their recommendations.

Board Structure: Meetings

Two keys to productive board meetings are focusing on governance, not administration, and using time efficiently. The board chair—with the help of the executive director—is responsible for maintaining the meeting's focus and efficiency, and making sure that the organization's top priorities are addressed. The chair and executive director should review the minutes of the last meeting for action items and, as appropriate, contact those responsible to make sure their work has been done and that they are ready to make their report. Of course, the chair should know the report's findings well before the board meeting.

To ensure that meetings are energizing and productive, a good presiding officer sets the agenda in consultation with other members of the executive committee and staff leadership well in advance of upcoming meetings. It is then essential that the agenda, along with background information, be sent to board members. A member of the executive committee might even phone board members to see if they have any questions. Not only will these procedures ensure that discussions and decisions are more substantial, but board members will take their responsibilities more seriously if they can come to the meeting well-informed.

During the meeting, the chair must be attuned to the sense that more information is needed. If pre-meeting preparation has been thorough, this should rarely occur. But if it does, the chair can delegate the matter to a board committee for further investigation. That committee can then present its findings and recommendations at the next board meeting.

If a board finds itself focusing on details rather than major policy issues, something is awry. Executive directors and board leadership must ensure that issues are framed properly to elicit the best thinking of board members, who are taking time from work, family, and friends to attend meetings. By eliciting opinions on the matters at hand, keeping the discussion on track, and moving matters along, the chair can help maximize members' participation. If board members become disinterested and inactive as a result of unproductive meetings, absences and resignations will shortly follow, and new candidates will hesitate to join a board known to have a lot of deadwood.

Carefully prepared meetings—where substantive issues are thoughtfully presented, discussed, and acted on—will, on the other hand, deepen board members' commitment, for they will see that their time and expertise are highly valued. The organization will have sent the message that their opinions matter, that they are important. Feeling appreciated is a basic human desire. Applying this principle to institutional development almost guarantees success.

7. Approve Budgets, and Determine and Monitor the Organization's Programs and Services

These tasks are the essence of a board's governance function. Boards will, correctly, devote substantial time to planning, but they must also make sure that the plans are being implemented properly, and must also address whether an organization has sufficient resources to carry out the plans they've developed. In its oversight capacity, a board must resist the temptation to micromanage the organization. Not only does this blur the division of responsibilities between board and staff, it also sends a harmful message to the staff: "We don't trust your work." Additionally, involvement in administration and program activity distracts a board's attention from its primary governance and development responsibilities.

8. Select and Orient New Board Members

Nonprofit leadership must always be on the lookout for new board candidates for several reasons:

- No matter how active and committed a board may be, it will welcome the stimulation provided by a new board member's ideas, expertise, contacts, and enthusiasm.

- Few organizations consistently have the necessary complement of skills on their boards.

- As an organization's funding mix changes—from predominantly government and foundation sources to individual and corporate donors, for example—the board will need to recruit people with expertise and experience in personal solicitations and corporate fundraising.

- A board's numbers must be replenished continually: members' terms regularly expire, some members rarely attend meetings, and others may resign.

In seeking out new board members, organizations must avoid choosing people whose only qualification is that they share the same vision and values. They must instead reach out to the wider community to identify people with the expertise they need; if the candidates are not already sympathetic to their goals and values, the organization must then share with them the importance of their vision. This is the more productive approach to building a board.

Prospective board candidates with desired skills can be identified through other nonprofit organizations, including larger agencies, institutions, hospitals, universities, professional trade associations of fundraisers and public relations professionals, and even public relations and fundraising firms themselves.

Professionals in these fields certainly can strengthen your board of directors, but you should not be discouraged if you are unable to engage them as board members. What is important is that the board members you do recruit are committed to learning about fundraising. Raising funds from individuals and other philanthropic sources is a skill that can be learned and that may well develop into a deeply satisfying experience. Remind them that in asking for support, they also are giving a gift to the prospective donor: the opportunity to feel good about himself or herself by making a difference in the world.

Identifying Skills and Expertise

Just as a contractor secures the services of electricians, carpenters, plumbers, and bricklayers to build a house, the organizers of a new nonprofit venture should identify the tasks before them. Once again: it is the group's vision and mission that determine what those tasks are. Once the tasks are defined, the organizers can then identify the skills and expertise needed by the board to get the work done. Candidates for board membership with these qualificaitons can be seen as belonging to one of three "clusters."

1. *Natural constituents.* Natural constituents are the people with whom you are working to bring about the changes that will directly improve their lives. This group
   clearly has the greatest practical investment in the work, and as a result, may well
   provide the passion and drive to inspire others to make similar commitments. This
   group often devotes the most time and energy to your efforts—again, because its
   stake in the group's success is high. Also, a board should reflect the people it represents in one way or another. In part, the passion that people bring to a board is fueled
   by their personal experience in dealing with the issue at hand. Bear in mind, too, that
   many foundations look for racial, ethnic, and gender diversity on the boards and
   staffs of organizations whose grant requests they are considering.

2. *People with program expertise.* People with program-related expertise in your field
   may or may not be immediately affected by your work. If, for example, you are
   establishing a public-interest law center or a women's health program, you would
   want experienced lawyers and medical practitioners on your board. For financial
   reasons, it's unlikely you'll be able to hire all the experts you need; including program experts on your board is a practical alternative. Assuredly, they must sympa-
   thize with your mission and be willing to support it. For example, the Long Island
   Mothers Against Drunk Driving (MADD) chapter has on its board a psychologist
   who also runs weekly victim support groups, as well as doctors, elected officials,
   and civic leaders who bring to the board specific and relevant areas of expertise. A
   good way to proceed in building your board is to identify the occupations that bear
   directly on your work. If your field is public-interest law, for example, your list
   should include lawyers, judges, law professors, and legal workers.

3. *People with nonprofit expertise.* The third cluster consists of people with skills pertinent to the general needs of nonprofit organizations. Such areas of expertise
   include:

   - Accounting (and other knowledge in fiscal matters)

   - Law, especially nonprofit corporation law

   - Fundraising and development

   - Marketing, communications, and public relations

   - Human resources and personnel

   - General management

   - Planning

   - New information technologies

Soliciting Board Membership:
Two Board Recruitment Stories (Successful and Otherwise)

Case 1

Several years ago, I was invited by letter to join the board of a well-respected organization in New York City, my hometown. Accompanying the invitation was an extensive packet of literature about the organization. They even enclosed an addressed and stamped reply envelope. After weighing their invitation for a week, I declined. Why?

I was naturally flattered, and initially receptive to the idea. Then I asked myself a practical question: "Why are they interested in me as a board member?" Sounds like common sense, doesn't it? I needed to know before I jumped in for "the good of the cause." While I was sure to derive some satisfaction from knowing that X organization was working on a matter close to my concerns, I considered the invitation further in the light of my own interests, which included

1. increasing my own knowledge of issues;

2. enjoying the company of like-minded people;

3. serving in a leadership capacity among my peers;

4. meeting new people;

5. broadening my experience to enhance my consulting skills.

I was unable to answer fully how participating on the board of this organization would match my interests. Also, no one from X organization took the trouble to contact me personally to ask if I had any questions. Working under the press of other matters, I chose not to contact them to suggest a meeting and merely declined their invitation.

- Accounting and fiscal expertise

- Advocacy and public policy

Unfortunately, too many nonprofit leaders do not recruit beyond their immediate circle of friends and acquaintances or do not go beyond the first cluster—natural constituents. They may suspect that professionals, and businesspeople in particular, will not be sympathetic to their pursuits. In response to these concerns, you should seek out likely prospective board candidates and discuss with them what your organization is about and what your needs are. You will then be in a better position to judge whether your initial concerns were well founded.

By keeping the three clusters before you, you will have a shopping list of the human resources you need for your organization to grow and prosper.

Case 2

Around the same time, I had the task of recruiting new fundraising committee members for an organization whose board I co-chaired. A fellow board member recommended someone who was skilled in areas our organization currently lacked. As a first step, I called up our prospect to suggest that we meet to discuss our organization's work and explore if she would serve on our fundraising committee. Before the meeting, I invited the executive director to join us and mailed our prospect a packet of our literature. At the meeting, we discussed our organization, its vision, and its values and explained in some detail why we thought our prospect could make a valuable contribution to our work. She thanked us for our invitation and promised us a decision shortly. Within ten days, she decided to join us and became an active and hard-working member of our committee.

Why did one organization fail while the other succeeded? Because in the second case, the approach was better prepared and more personal. It was clear that we had inventoried our own needs and given serious thought to the specific contributions she could make. Gratified by the worth we placed on her abilities, she also realized that she could derive good feelings and personal satisfaction from her involvement.

The obvious lesson of these two stories is that thoughtful approaches to potential board or committee candidates pay off. A second lesson is that the hardest workers in an organization are those who know that their talents are valued.

— Michael Seltzer

Finding Board Candidates

Once an organization has inventoried the skills and expertise needed by the board, it needs to identify candidates for board members. Here are a number of methods for finding qualified prospects:

1. Approach local corporations and businesses. Contact the department responsible for community relations, human resources, public affairs, or charitable contributions to see if there is an employee recruitment program to match employees with community service opportunities.

2. Approach your local Volunteer Action Council or its counterpart, or any other agencies that specialize in recruiting volunteers.

3. Seek out the advice of local funders, such as foundation staff, United Way officials, and government officials who have an interest in your field of endeavor.

4. Contact executive directors and board officers of large, established nonprofit institutions in your community, as well as of those whose efforts are similar to yours, for their suggestions.

5. Speak to religious leaders in your locale to see if they can recommend any candidates, particularly from their own congregations.

6. Include in any promotional and membership materials pleas for volunteers with the specific skills you are seeking.

7. Ask for volunteers at any canvassing efforts, open houses, special events, and benefits that your organization sponsors.

8. Check with local chapters of professional trade associations such as the Bar Association, Chamber of Commerce, and Public Relations Society.

9. Discuss your needs with representatives of civic groups, such as Kiwanis, Soroptomists, Hadassah, Junior League, Rotary, Lions, Jaycees, and the like.

10. Find out if any hospitality organizations, such as Welcome Wagon, exist in your community, and if so, inform them of your needs. They very often provide the first contacts for a community's newcomers, who are potential recruits for civic efforts.

The process of identifying, cultivating, and soliciting individuals for board membership is virtually the same as the fundraising process. It's also the same as the process for securing pro bono work, soliciting chairs and committees for special fundraising events, recruiting advisory committee members, and virtually any other activity that involves people. The factors common to all these activities are thoughtful planning, identifying how the person being approached will benefit, being clear about your expectations, and considerate, efficient communication.

Plato might not have been referring to nonprofit boards when he said, "The beginning of the work is the most important part." But his words give additional weight to the importance of telling prospective board members—during your first serious discussion—what will be expected. Providing a prospective candidate with a written description of what his specific responsibilities would be is essential. A written description not only helps a prospect decide whether to continue or end his or her candidacy, but it also should amount to an informal contract should the candidate eventually join the board.

After a candidate agrees to undertake the outlined responsibilities, he or she should be invited to work with the organization for a time to make sure the fit is right for both parties. If it is, the candidate can then be recommended by the nominating committee to the board, which will vote on the candidate.

9. Enhance the Organization's Public Image

Board members may be called on to appear in public on behalf of the organization at fundraising events, conferences, rallies, seminars, and the like. These are wonderful opportunities for members to demonstrate the group's talents and expertise, and to enhance the organization's public profile.

Directors' and Officers' Insurance

Directors and officers of nonprofit organizations, like their corporate counterparts, are occasionally the subjects of lawsuits. Commercial liability insurance does not normally protect the board members against such allegations as wrongful termination or discrimination in hiring practices. Nonprofits are, therefore, strongly advised to purchase Directors' and Officers' Insurance to provide protection against allegations of wrongdoing, especially in regard to employment practices. This form of insurance will cover all past, present, and future directors and officers, volunteers, trustees, committee members, and the nonprofit entity itself. Premiums in 1999 were roughly $1,000 per $1 million of coverage; policies can be purchased from insurance brokers or over the Internet from various providers (search words: directors officers insurance).

10. Evaluate the Board's Own Performance

The board of directors of a nonprofit organization evolves and changes over time, even as the organization itself progresses through its own life cycle. Often, a start-up nonprofit will rely on board members to engage directly in the operation of the organization until staff resources are developed. The nature of the board's work then typically shifts to policy, strategy, and infrastructure development, with an executive and staff handling the management and administrative functions of the organization. Because this delineation of responsibilities is not always clear, it is essential that board and staff functions be spelled out precisely. Only in this way will it be possible to evaluate the board's performance fairly.

Ensuring adequate orientation of new board members and maintaining communication between the board and the executive director are prerequisites to any serious board evaluation effort. Evaluating the effectiveness of one's board requires a clear understanding of what is generally expected of its members.

The objective of board evaluations should be to identify ways of best utilizing the time and resources that members bring to the organization, and to understand better how to make the experience of leading the organization as rewarding as possible for those who volunteer their time. However, evaluations do not substitute for the solid orientation of board members, and should not be viewed as opportunities to educate or steer boards; this should be accomplished through more direct means of communication.

Boards must not only monitor a nonprofit's programs and finances; they must also encourage and enforce a culture of nondiscrimination, personal dignity, and freedom from any form of harassment. They must make sure that procedures have been created to address complaints both within and outside the organization relating to discrimination and, specifically, sexual harassment. While staff leadership must make sure that a group's day-to-day work is free of any hint of discrimination or harassment, the board is the court of last resort for resolving issues arising from either. The board may designate a personnel committee to address these areas, or it may act

Conflict-of-Interest Policy

It is prudent for nonprofits to establish a conflict-of-interest policy to prevent situations from developing where board members appear to have derived personal profit or gain from their involvement. Such a policy may require that board members disclose their affiliations with other agencies or organizations, and may require members with such affiliations to refrain from participating in decisions involving the affiliated agency. An organization's conflict-of-interest policy can be applied to board members, staff, consultants, and volunteers.

Here is a sample conflict-of-interest policy:

This conflict of interest policy is designed to help directors, officers and employees of the [ORGANIZATION NAME] identify situations that present potential conflicts of interest and to provide [ORGANIZATION NAME] with a procedure which, if observed, will allow a transaction to be treated as valid and binding even though a director, officer or employee has or may have a conflict of interest with respect to the transaction. The policy is intended to comply with the procedure prescribed in Minnesota Statutes, Section 317A.255, governing conflicts of interest for directors of nonprofit corporations. In the event there is an inconsistency between the requirements and procedures prescribed herein and those in section 317A.255, the statute shall control. All capitalized terms are defined in Part 2 of this policy.

1. Conflict of Interest Defined. For purposes of this policy, the following circumstances shall be deemed to create Conflicts of Interest:

Outside Interests.

(i) A Contract or Transaction between [ORGANIZATION NAME] and a Responsible Person or Family Member.

(ii) A Contract or Transaction between [ORGANIZATION NAME] and an entity in which a Responsible Person or Family Member has a Material Financial Interest or of which such person is a director, officer, agent, partner, associate, trustee, personal representative, receiver, guardian, custodian, conservator or other legal representative.

Outside Activities.

(i) A Responsible Person competing with [ORGANIZATION NAME] in the rendering of services or in any other Contract or Transaction with a third party.

(ii) A Responsible Person's having a Material Financial Interest in; or serving as a director, officer, employee, agent, partner, associate, trustee, personal representative, receiver, guardian, custodian, conservator or other legal representative of, or consultant to; an entity or individual that competes with [ORGANIZATION NAME] in the provision of services or in any other Contract or Transaction with a third party.

Gifts, Gratuities and Entertainment. A Responsible Person accepting gifts, entertainment or other favors from any individual or entity that:

    (i) does or is seeking to do business with, or is a competitor of [ORGANIZATION NAME]; or

    (ii) has received, is receiving or is seeking to receive a loan or grant, or to secure other financial commitments from [ORGANIZATION NAME];

    (iii) is a charitable organization operating in Minnesota;

under circumstances where it might be inferred that such action was intended to influence or possibly would influence the Responsible Person in the performance of his or her duties. This does not preclude the acceptance of items of nominal or insignificant value or entertainment of nominal or insignificant value which are not related to any particular transaction or activity of [ORGANIZATION NAME].

2. Definitions.

    A. "Conflict of Interest" is any circumstance described in Part 1 of this Policy.

    B. " Responsible Person" is any person serving as an officer, employee or member of the Board of Directors of [ORGANIZATION NAME].

    C. "Family Member" is a spouse, parent, child or spouse of a child, brother, sister, or spouse of a brother or sister, of a Responsible Person.

    H. "Material Financial Interest" in an entity is a financial interest of any kind, which, in view of all the circumstances, is substantial enough that it would, or reasonably could, affect a Responsible Person's or Family Member's judgment with respect to transactions to which the entity is a party.

    E. "Contract or Transaction" is any agreement or relationship involving the sale or purchase of goods, services, or rights of any kind, the providing or receipt of a loan or grant, the establishment of any other type of pecuniary relationship, or review of a charitable organization by [ORGANIZATION NAME]. The making of a gift to [ORGANIZATION NAME] is not a Contract or Transaction.

3. Procedures.

    A. Prior to board or committee action on a Contract or Transaction involving a Conflict of Interest, a director or committee member having a Conflict of Interest and who is in attendance at the meeting shall disclose all facts material to the Conflict of Interest. Such disclosure shall be reflected in the minutes of the meeting.

    B. A director or committee member who plans not to attend a meeting at which he or she has reason to believe that the board or committee will act on a matter in which the person has a Conflict of Interest shall disclose to the chair of the meeting all facts material to the Conflict of Interest. The chair shall report the disclosure at the meeting and the disclosure shall be reflected in the minutes of the meeting.

    C. A person who has a Conflict of Interest shall not participate in or be permitted to hear the board's or committee's discussion of the matter except to disclose material facts and to respond to questions. Such person shall not attempt to exert his or her personal influence with respect to the matter, either at or outside the meeting.

D. A person who has a Conflict of Interest with respect to a Contract or Transaction that will be voted on at a meeting shall not be counted in determining the presence of a quorum for purposes of the vote. The person having a conflict of interest may not vote on the Contract or Transaction and shall not be present in the meeting room when the vote is taken, unless the vote is by secret ballot. Such person's ineligibility to vote shall be reflected in the minutes of the meeting. For purposes of this paragraph, a member of the Board of Directors of [ORGANIZATION NAME] has a Conflict of Interest when he or she stands for election as an officer or for re-election as a member of the Board of Directors.

E. Responsible Persons who are not members of the Board of Directors of [ORGANIZATION NAME], or who have a Conflict of Interest with respect to a Contract or Transaction that is not the subject of Board or committee action, shall disclose to the Chair or the Chair's designee any Conflict of Interest that such Responsible Person has with respect to a Contract or Transaction. Such disclosure shall be made as soon as the Conflict of Interest is known to the Responsible Person. The Responsible Person shall refrain from any action that may affect [ORGANIZATION NAME]'s participation in such Contract or Transaction.

In the event it is not entirely clear that a Conflict of Interest exists, the individual with the potential conflict shall disclose the circumstances to the Chair or the Chair's designee, who shall determine whether there exists a Conflict of Interest that is subject to this policy.

4. Confidentiality. Each Responsible Person shall exercise care not to disclose confidential information acquired in connection with such status or information the disclosure of which might be adverse to the interests of [ORGANIZATION NAME]. Furthermore, a Responsible Person shall not disclose or use information relating to the business of [ORGANIZATION NAME] for the personal profit or advantage of the Responsible Person or a Family Member.

5. Review of policy.

A. Each new Responsible Person shall be required to review a copy of this policy and to acknowledge in writing that he or she has done so.

B. Each Responsible Person shall annually complete a disclosure form identifying any relationships, positions or circumstances in which the Responsible Person is involved that he or she believes could contribute to a Conflict of Interest arising. Such relationships, positions or circumstances might include service as a director of or consultant to a nonprofit organization, or ownership of a business that might provide goods or services to [ORGANIZATION NAME]. Any such information regarding business interests of a Responsible Person or a Family Member shall be treated as confidential and shall generally be made available only to the Chair, the Executive Director, and any committee appointed to address Conflicts of Interest, except to the extent additional disclosure is necessary in connection with the implementation of this Policy.

C. This policy shall be reviewed annually by each member of the Board of Directors. Any changes to the policy shall be communicated immediately to all Responsible Persons.

as a whole. Many mature organizations do not have separate personnel committees, but new and developing nonprofits should consider creating such a committee to develop personnel policies and procedures, and to ensure that these are clearly stated in an up-to-date manual. In any event, board and personnel committee members must be careful not to undermine the authority of the chief executive in these areas.

Tips

- It is essential that prospective board members be told what is expected of them before they are proposed for election. Asking people to join the board without providing a "job description" is sure to create an ineffective board.

- Build a board slowly; doing so actually accelerates the work of an organization if supportive, active members are chosen as a result. Proceeding carefully can provide the necessary time for learning why an individual wants to become a board member, and deciding whether their agenda is compatible with your culture, vision, and mission.

- Cultivate board members continually. Do not assume that once members are elected to the board, they don't need nurturing; in most cases, their participation and giving depends on it. Make sure you know what benefits they expect to derive from membership, and if their work warrants it, make sure to deliver those benefits.

Additional Resources

Publications

Abbey, Leslie A. *Corporate Governance: A Guide for Not-for-Profit Corporations.* New York: Lawyers Alliance for New York, 1996. 50 p.
> Designed to assist managers and directors of New York nonprofits in complying with the New York Not-for-Profit Corporation Law. Sections cover the purpose and content of corporate documents including the certificate of incorporation, by-laws, resolutions, minute book, and the corporate seal; an overview of the structure of nonprofit corporations including the roles of members, directors, officers, and staff; and a discussion of the duties and potential liabilities of the board of directors.

Andringa, Robert C., and Ted W. Engstrom. *Nonprofit Board Answer Book: Practical Guidelines for Board Members and Chief Executives.* Washington, DC: National Center for Nonprofit Boards, 1997. viii, 197 pages.
> Written in question-and-answer format, provides basic information about the functions, structure, tasks, and selection of nonprofit boards. Indexed.

Axelrod, Nancy R.; Centro Mexicano para la Filantropia. El papel que juega un director ejecutivo en la conformacion y desarrollo del consejo directivo en las organizaciones sin fines de lucro = The chief executive's role in developing the nonprofit board [in Spanish]. Spanish edition. Washington, DC: National Center for Nonprofit Boards, 1997. 23 p.

Bernstein, Philip. *Best Practices of Effective Nonprofit Organizations: A Practitioner's Guide.* New York, NY: The Foundation Center, 1997. vii, 183 p.
    Identifies and explains the organizational processes adopted by successful nonprofits. Topics covered include defining purposes and goals, creating comprehensive financing plans, evaluating services, and effective communication.

Bonavoglia, Angela. *The Trustee Connection: Making a Difference.* New York: Women and Foundations/Corporate Philanthropy (Far From Done Reports; No. 6), 1994. 36 pages.
    Presents a detailed account of women and foundation trustees, based on in-depth personal interviews with seventeen women trustees of various foundations representing different regions, ages, backgrounds, races, classes, ethnicities, and types of foundations. Provides insight into the workings and thinkings of a seldom-studied but highly influential group. With bibliography and resource list.

Bowen, William G. *Inside the Boardroom: Governance By Directors and Trustees.* New York: John Wiley & Sons, 1994. xx, 184 p.
    The author, who has served on the boards of six prestigious nonprofit institutions as well as high-profile business organizations, explores the role of the board of directors in nonprofit and for-profit organizations, and offers recommendations on how boards can better serve the interests of their organizations and stakeholders. Appendices include presumptive norms and capsule profiles of selected organizations. With bibliographical references and index.

Brudney, Jeffrey L., and Vic Murray. "Do Intentional Efforts To Improve Boards Really Work? The Views of Nonprofit CEOs." *Nonprofit Management & Leadership* 8 (Summer 1998): 333–348.
    Based on a survey of more than 3,000 Canadian nonprofit organizations (851 returns were received), the authors identify some of the factors that lead nonprofits to implement changes in their boards. With bibliographic references.

Carver, John. *Boards that Make a Difference: A New Design for Leadership in Nonprofit and Public Organizations.* 2nd ed. San Francisco: Jossey-Bass Publishers (Nonprofit and Public Management Series), 1997. xxiv, 241 p.
    Orients board members to their role as strategic leaders, emphasizing the necessary aspects of governance: making policy, articulating the organization's mission, and sustaining its vision. Helps boards to concentrate their energies on the overall purpose of their organization and guides them in working with managers to accomplish that purpose. Presents procedures for evaluating the executive staff, delegating authority to management,

making decisions as a board, and establishing bylaws for the board's self-governance. Bibliographical references.

Carver, John, and Miriam Mayhew Carver. *Reinventing Your Board: A Step-By-Step Guide To Implementing Policy Governance.* San Francisco: Jossey-Bass Publishers (Nonprofit and Public Management Series), 1997. xxi, 232 p.

> Provides practical advice to implement the theoretical framework outlined in the author's work "Boards that Make a Difference." At the core of the program is the creation of a set of policies for governance of an organization, and achievement of board and staff commitment to those policies. Numerous sample policy documents are provided. Indexed.

Chait, Richard, Thomas Holland, and Barbara E. Taylor. *Improving the Performance of Governing Boards.* Phoenix, AZ: Oryx Press (American Council on Education/Oryx Press Series on Higher Education), 1996. xiv, 161 p.

Connors, Tracy Daniel, ed. *The Nonprofit Handbook: Management.* 2nd ed. New York: John Wiley & Sons (Nonprofit Law, Finance, and Management Series), 1997. xxi, 809 p.

> This handbook is a comprehensive reference guide to the policies and procedures shared by a great majority of small- and medium-sized nonprofit organizations. Contains drafts of policies and procedures as well as sample plans, forms, records, and reports. Divided into four parts: Interactive Strategic Planning, Quality Management, and Leadership; Human Resources; Communication, Fund Raising, and Information Management; and Accounting, Finance, and Legal Issues. Includes bibliographic references, a glossary, and an index.

Daley, John M., F. Ellen Netting, and Julio Angulo. "Languages, Ideologies, and Cultures in Nonprofit Boards." *Nonprofit Management & Leadership* 6 (Spring 1996): 227–240.

> Examines three types of languages that are dominant within the board of directors of nonprofit human services agencies: mission, operations, and manners. Suggests that these languages are connected to values and express ideology.

Dart, Ray, Pat Bradshaw, Victor Murray, and Jacob Wolpin. "Boards of Directors in Nonprofit Organizations: Do They Follow a Life-Cycle Model?" *Nonprofit Management & Leadership* 6 (Summer 1996): 367–379.

> Uses data from a survey of Canadian nonprofit organizations to empirically test the life-cycle model of a nonprofit's board of directors. Suggests that while formal structural elements of board behavior change in the manner suggested by life-cycle models, the more behavioral aspects of nonprofit boards do not.

Donovan, James A. *Fifty Ways to Motivate Your Board: A Guide for Nonprofit Executives.* Orlando, FL: Donovan Management, 1997. 108 p.

Dorsey, Eugene C.; Centro Mexicano para la Filantropia. El papel que desempena el presidente del consejo directivo en las organizaciones sin fines de lucro = The role of the board chairperson [in Spanish]. Spanish edition. Washington, DC: National Center for Nonprofit Boards, 1997. 27 p.

Spanish translation of "The Role of the Board Chairperson," originally published in 1992.)

Firstenberg, Paul B. *The Twenty-First Century Nonprofit: Remaking the Organization in the Post-Government Era.* New York: The Foundation Center, 1996. xxii, 247 p.

Provides a road map for organizations seeking to enhance their performance both in program design and execution and in achieving financial health. Encourages managers to: adopt the strategies developed by the for-profit sector in recent years; expand their revenue base by diversifying grant sources and exploiting the possibilities of for-profit enterprises; develop human resources by learning how to attract and retain talented people; and explore the nature of leadershipages. Provides profiles of three nonprofit CEOs: McGeorge Bundy, William G. Bowen, and Joan Ganz Cooney. Includes bibliographic references and index.

Fram, Eugene H., and Judy Withers. "Conflict of Interest in the Board Room?" *Nonprofit World* 17 (March–April 1999): 19–21.

Frank, Everett, and Karen Simmons. "Board Chair Succession: A Plan that Keeps Your Organization Running." *NonProfit Times* 12 (March 1998): 17, 24.

Frantzreb, Arthur C. *Not On This Board You Don't: Making Your Trustees More Effective.* Chicago: Bonus Books, 1997. x, 255 p.

Gives an overview of the board member's role. Chapters cover the mission of governance, ministry of philanthropy, motivation of giving, management process, and methods of accountability. Includes bibliography and index.

Fry, Robert P., Jr. *Creating and Using Investment Policies: A Guide for Nonprofit Boards.* Washington, DC: National Center for Nonprofit Boards, 1997. 24 p.

Guides nonprofit board members through the basics of investing and formulating investment policies for their organizations. Provides sample investment policies. Includes glossary and bibliography.

Gruber, David A. "Financial Reporting: Vital Tools for Board Members." *NonProfit Times* 13 (April 1999): 37, 58.

Lists several financial reports that board members might find useful for effective stewardship of an organization.

Harrison, Bill J. "When Board Members Don't Give." *Fund Raising Management* 29 (May 1998): 14–17.

Examines methods for dealing with board members who don't contribute as much as they might.

Harrison, Bill J. "Your Board Members Must Be Donors." *501(c)(3) Monthly Letter* 17 (September–October 1997): 1, 3.
  Many nonprofit organizations have board members who do not make financial contributions to their organizations, but the author posits that financial support is the principal goal of board members.

Harrow, Jenny, and Paul Palmer. "Reassessing Charity Trusteeship in Britain? Toward Conservatism, Not Change." *Voluntas* 9 (June 1998): 171–185.
  Assesses the changing nature of the governance role of trustees in Great Britain, presenting seven types of trustees and their predominant behavior or attitude regarding their relationship to the charity. With bibliographic references.

Herman, Melanie L., and Leslie T. White. *Leaving Nothing to Chance: Achieving Board Accountability Through Risk Management.* Washington, DC: National Center for Nonprofit Boards, 1998. 34 p.

Herman, Melanie L., and Leslie T. White. *D & O: What You Need To Know.* Washington, DC: Nonprofit Risk Management Center, 1998. 76 p.
  Answers the most frequently asked questions about liability protection for directors and officers of nonprofit organizations. Briefly discusses risk management, then outlines the legal duties of board members (though state laws differ) and suggests specific steps nonprofit administrators should take to monitor their exposure to risk. Technical descriptions of the elements of directors' and officers' (D & O) insurance are provided, with citations from actual policy forms. Includes glossary.

Herrington, J. Bryce. *The Nonprofit Board's Role in Establishing Financial Policies.* Washington, DC: National Center for Nonprofit Boards, 1996. 31 p.

Hirzy, Ellen Cochran. *The Chair's Role in Leading the Nonprofit Board.* Washington, DC: National Center for Nonprofit Boards, 1998. 16 p.
  A board chair must bring vision, objectivity, decisiveness, energy, and commitment to the position. Outlines ten essential tasks the chair should do in order to create and sustain an effective board. With bibliographic references.

Holland, Thomas P. "Strengthening Board Performance: Findings and Lessons from Demonstration Projects." *Nonprofit Management & Leadership* 9 (Winter 1998): 121–134.
  Reports findings from a multi-year study of the boards of twenty-four nonprofit organizations. The study used a control group design to assess the impact of interventions intended to improve the performance of the participant boards. Over a three-year period, ten boards received developmental interventions, and the other fourteen served as controls, receiving no interventions. It was found that the experimental group demonstrated marked improvements, while the comparison group did not. The study revealed that some of the obstacles to improving board performance are unfocused expectations, lack of clarity and

accountability, and resistance to trying new approaches. The research underscores the importance of engaging board members in creating their own development program, formulating their own goals for the board, and periodically evaluating their progress. Methods of reforming board governance structures and procedures are discussed. With bibliographic references.

Howe, Fisher. *The Board Member's Guide to Strategic Planning: A Practical Approach to Strengthening Nonprofit Organizations.* San Francisco: Jossey-Bass Publishers (Nonprofit Sector Series), 1997. xiii, 114 p.

Howe, Fisher. *Fund-Raising and the Nonprofit Board.* 2nd ed. Washington, DC: National Center for Nonprofit Boards, 1998. 16 p.
  Examines five key principles of fundraising as they pertain to nonprofit board members. These principles explain why board members must be involved in fundraising in order to be truly effective. The first principle states that the board alone is ultimately responsible for attracting funding resources to ensure the financial viability of the organization and its programs. The second principle clarifies the motivations of donors, explaining them as natural processes. The third principle involves the importance of the case statement to successful fundraising. Board members should be involved in preparing this statement, and should be able to explain the case persuasively to prospective donors. The fourth principle urges every board member to employ his or her own skills and interests in support of the fundraising effort. And the fifth principle examines ways to motivate board members to actively fulfill their fundraising responsibilities. Includes a board member's fundraising checklist, and a brief bibliography.

Hughes, Sandra R. *To Go Forward, Retreat!: The Board Retreat Handbook.* Washington, DC: National Center for Nonprofit Boards, 1999. 36 p.

Hughes, Sandra R., Berit M. Lakey, Marla J. Bobowick. *The Board Building Cycle: Nine Steps To Finding, Recruiting, and Engaging Nonprofit Board Members.* Washington, DC: National Center for Nonprofit Boards, 2000. 52 p.
  Includes a computer disk with sample worksheets, evaluation surveys, and other items for prospective and current board members.

Jackson, Douglas K., and Thomas P. Holland. "Measuring the Effectiveness of Nonprofit Boards." *Nonprofit and Voluntary Sector Quarterly* 27 (June 1998): 159–182.
  Authors offer evidence that the Board Self-Assessment Questionnaire (BSAQ), which they developed based on earlier research, provides "reliable, valid, and sensitive measures" of nonprofit board effectiveness and performance. The BSAQ, composed of sixty-five questions, was administered to 623 board members in thirty-four nonprofits. The questionnaire is reprinted. Includes bibliographic references.

Johnston, Janis, ed. *Turning Vision into Reality: What the Founding Board Should Know about Starting a Nonprofit Organization.* Washington, DC: National Center for Nonprofit Boards, 1999. 38 p.

Kile, Robert W., J. Michael Loscavio, and Jamie Whaley, ed. *Strategic Board Recruitment: The Not-for-Profit Model.* Frederick, MD: Aspen Publishers, 1996. xv, 141 p.
   Intended to explain the process, systems, and techniques used by executive search professionals in order to illuminate effective board recruiting strategies. Suggests an eight-step process: 1) assembling the board development team; 2) assessing the organization's needs; 3) developing board position profiles; 4) scripting the organization's story; 5) researching candidate sources; 6) developing third-party referral networks; 7) contacting and meeting candidates; and 8) evaluating and selecting new board members.

Lansdowne, David. *Fund Raising Realities Every Board Member Must Face: A One-Hour Crash Course On Raising Major Gifts for Nonprofit Organizations.* Medfield, MA: Emerson & Church, 1997. 109 p.

Leifer, Jacqueline Covey, and Michael B. Glomb. *The Legal Obligations of Nonprofit Boards: A Guidebook for Board Members.* Washington, DC: National Center for Nonprofit Boards, 1997. 38 p.

Maiers, Randy. "Selection Process: The Business Approach to Nominating." *NonProfit Times* 13 (April 1999): 41–42.
   Lists seven strategies used by for-profit entities, but rarely used by nonprofits, for selecting potential board candidates.

Maron, Rebecca M. "Self-Assessment: A Remedy for Dysfunctional Board Behaviors." *Association Management* 49 (January 1997): 51–53.
   Provides a questionnaire and suggestions for improving a board's internal processes.

Martinelli, Frank. "The Board of Directors: Foundation for Success." *New Directions for Philanthropic Fundraising* 20 (Summer 1998): 25–43.
   Wisdom about the responsibilities of nonprofit boards, specifically within the smaller organization, with suggestions for how to deal with common pitfalls. Explains the roles of board committees, such as the executive committee and the fundraising committee. Recommends assessment of board members' performance, as well as their self-evaluation, and provides a sample form. With bibliographic references.

Martinelli, Frank. "Encouraging Visionary Board Leadership." *Nonprofit World* 16 (July–August 1998): 11–14.
   Provides a list of eight characteristics possessed by visionary leaders, seven barriers to visionary leadership, and details five key strategies necessary for building effective visionary leadership.

Masaoka, Jan. *All Hands on Board: The Board of Directors in an All-Volunteer Organization.* Washington, DC: National Center for Nonprofit Boards, 1999. 22 p.
   Concise information specific to governance of an all-volunteer organization (AVO), with checklists, suggested readings, and resource list.

Mathiasen, Karl, and Teresa Santos, trans. Centro Mexicano para la Filantropia. El Consejo En Transicion: Tres Momentos Claves En El Ciclo De Vida Del Consejo Directivo = Board Passages: Three Key Stages in a Nonprofit Board's Life Cycle [in Spanish]. Washington, DC: National Center for Nonprofit Boards, 1997. 27 p.

Michalko, Michael. "Seven Creative Ways To Energize Your Board Meetings." *Nonprofit World* 16 (May–June 1998): 11–12.

Miller, Barbara. "Creative Brainstorming with Your Board." *Fund Raising Management* 27 (January 1997): 18–20.
   Advocates that fundraising professionals hold at least two brainstorming sessions a year with their board of directors to generate ideas and ease frustration.

Miller, Judith L., Kathleen Fletcher, and Rikki Abzug. *Perspectives on Nonprofit Board Diversity.* Washington, DC: National Center for Nonprofit Boards, 1999. 35 p.

Moyers, Richard L. "Making Plans for the Board of the Future." *NonProfit Times* 13 (July 1999): 21–22.
   The changes in trends of board leadership are outlined and discussed.

Moyers, Richard L., ed. "Building a Bold New Board: Matching Mission with Minds." *Board Member* 8 (January 1999): 10–13.

Murray, Vic. "Improving Board Performance." *Philanthropist/Le Philanthrope* 13 (January 1997): 33–37.
   Presents a review of what it takes to create effective boards for nonprofit organizations. Identifies the main factors affecting a board's operation. Gives typical problems that can arise and various approaches to handling them.

National Center for Family Philanthropy. *The Trustee Notebook: An Orientation for Family Foundation Board Members.* Washington, DC: National Center for Family Philanthropy, 1999. ix, 83 p.
   An introduction to managing a foundation for those new to the field. Explains what trustees must do and cannot do, how to be an effective grantmaker, how to develop the board, how to ensure public accountability, among other issues. Provides several resource lists, and sample forms and policies related to grantmaking and board membership.

National Center for Nonprofit Boards. *Self-Assessment for Nonprofit Governing Boards: User's Guide and Questionnaire.* rev. ed. Washington, DC: National Center for Nonprofit Boards, 1999. 59 p.

Discusses how self-assessment strengthens a board and the organization it governs, provides advice on administering the enclosed questionnaire, and describes how to interpret questionnaire responses. Also provides guidance on implementing a self-assessment retreat. Includes questionnaire/checklist, worksheets, and suggested resources. The set includes multiple copies of the questionnaire.

National Center for Nonprofit Boards; Suarez, Ray (narrator). *Meeting the Challenge: An Orientation to Nonprofit Board Service* [video]. Washington, DC: National Center for Nonprofit Boards, 1998. 35 minutes.

Covers four critical areas of board responsibility: mission, oversight, resources, and outreach. With accompanying user guide.

Newman, Raquel H. "Handling a Troublesome Trustee." *Fund Raising Management* 28 (April 1997): 22–23.

O'Connell, Brian. *The Board Member's Book: Making a Difference in Voluntary Organizations.* 2nd ed. New York: The Foundation Center, 1993. 198 p.

Written for board members, this practical guide to the essential functions of voluntary boards, covering such areas as: the role of nonprofit boards; finding, developing, and recognizing good board members; the role of the board president; working with committees; the board's role in fundraising; ethics; and evaluating the results. Bibliography and index.

O'Connell, Brian. *Board Overboard: Laughs and Lessons for All But the Perfect Nonprofit.* San Francisco: Jossey-Bass Publishers, 1996. xvii, 221 p.

Spoof of nonprofit organizations written by Brian O'Connell, founding president of Independent Sector. Presented in the form of minutes from a fictitious nonprofit's board meetings.

O'Connor, Judith. *The Planning Committee: Shaping Your Organization's Future.* Washington, DC: National Center for Nonprofit Boards, 1997. 20 p.

Oliver, Caroline, ed. *The Policy Governance Fieldbook: Practical Lessons, Tips, and Tools from the Experience of Real-World Boards.* San Francisco: Jossey-Bass Publishers, 1999. xxviii, 242 p.

Based on the policy governance model designed by John Carver, provides lessons derived from nonprofit boards that are dealing with various challenges. Each chapter is introduced with a challenge, then addresses it with real-life experiences and strategic recommendations. Includes numerous lists that outline the major points. Indexed.

Orlikoff, James E. "Seven Practices of Super Boards." *Association Management* 50 (January 1998): 52–58.

Panas, Jerold. *The Magic Partnership: What Good Board Members Do* [Video]. Chicago: Institute for Charitable Giving, 1998. 69 minutes. (SkilFilm Series).

Richards, Randall R. "Crafting a Dynamic Board Retreat." *Association Management* 50 (January 1998): 93–97.

Robertson, Brian. "Board Member or Bored Member?: How Do You Rate?" Nonprofit World 17 (May–June 1999): 20–21.
  Provides a self-assessment test for board members.

Robinson, Maureen K. *The Chief Executive's Role in Developing the Nonprofit Board.* Washington, DC: National Center for Nonprofit Boards, 1998. 16 p.
  Sets forth eight initiatives that chief executive officers can take to develop and work effectively with their governing boards. The strategies recommended by the author include: 1) exercise authority; 2) maintain a healthy and mutually supportive relationship with the board chairperson; 3) encourage leadership; 4) participate in board recruitment; 5) provide thorough orientation for new board members; 6) plan and hold effective board meetings; 7) practice good communication; and 8) advocate and help plan board retreats or special workshops, including periodic board self-study sessions of its responsibilities, membership, organization, and performance. With bibliographic references.

Roth, Stephanie. "How Does Your Board Measure Up?" *Grassroots Fundraising Journal* 17 (August 1998): 5–8.
  Provides a chart to evaluate board strengths and weaknesses in areas of selection and composition, orientation and training, structure and organization, and the board at work. Also provides a list of other resources to help strengthen boards.

Ruiz, Rosemarie. "Are You Fulfilling Your Financial Trust?" *Nonprofit World* 17 (January–February 1999): 22–23.
  Explains the role auditors, board members, and the executive director play in the financial future of an organization.

Scott, Katherine Tyler. *Creating Caring and Capable Boards: Reclaiming the Passion for Active Trusteeship.* San Francisco: Jossey-Bass Publishers, 2000. xix, 199 p.
  An examination of the achievement of excellence in governance leadership. Those charged with trusteeship of nonprofits can cultivate a deeper understanding of their responsibilities through "depth education," which includes studying the history, mission and publics of the nonprofit. Includes bibliographic references and index.

Simmons, Karen, and Ann Schmieg. "No Surrender: Designing a Great Board Retreat." *NonProfit Times* 11 (October 1997): 16, 18.

Simmons, Karen, and Gary J. Stern. *Creating Strong Board-Staff Partnerships.* Washington, DC: National Center for Nonprofit Boards, 1999. 20 p.
    Delineates and discusses organizational issues and practical considerations involved in the effort to create strong bonds between board and staff. With bibliographic references.

Suhrke, Henry C. "Why Do Nonprofits Have Boards, and What Do Boards Do?" *Philanthropy Monthly* 30 (September 1997): 21–23.
    Responds to frequently asked questions about nonprofit boards.

Supple, Chuck. "The Changing Face of the Board: A Younger Generation Finds a Place at the Board Table." *Board Member* 8 (April 1999): 6–7.
    Three young board members offer ideas to engage young people and encourage them to volunteer as board members.

Swanson, Andrew. "A Board Member Self-Assessment." *Nonprofit World* 15 (November–December 1997): 21.
    A short quiz for board members to assess their own performance.

Szanton, Peter. *Evaluation and the Nonprofit Board.* Washington, DC: National Center for Nonprofit Boards, 1998. 18 p.

Taylor, Barbara E., Richard P. Chait, and Thomas P. Holland. "The New Work of the Nonprofit Board." *Harvard Business Review* (September–October 1996): 4–11.

Tebbe, Donald. *For the Good of the Cause: Board-Building Lessons from Highly Effective Nonprofits.* San Jose, CA: Center for Excellence in Nonprofits, 1998. 134 p.
    Based on interviews conducted by the author, the book is directed to executive directors, board chairs, and board committee chairmen. Tebbe outlines five key roles, five success traits, and lessons for nonprofit boards. Case studies of twenty organizations are presented. Each case study focuses on a key challenge faced by the organization, and describes how the board was involved.

Tempel, Eugene R. "Blending Three Generations into Effective Volunteers and Nonprofit Boards." *NonProfit Times* 13 (July 1999): 23–24.

Vartorella, William F. "A Worksheet for Evaluating Your Board." *FRI Monthly Portfolio* 37 (June 1998): 1–2.

Volunteer Consulting Group. *The Board Marketplace Program: A Community Action Plan To Bridge the Gap Between Nonprofit Boards and Potential Board Members.* New York: Volunteer Consulting Group, 1998. x, looseleaf pages.
> A Board Marketplace Program (BMP) is a community-wide initiative that opens two-way communication between local boards and people who wish to serve on them. This manual outlines the steps for establishing a program, and supplies worksheets and samples to facilitate the process.

Wagner, Lilya, and Mark A. Hager. "Board Members Beware: Warning Signs of a Dysfunctional Organization," *Nonprofit World* 16 (March–April 1998): 18–21.

Weisman, Carol E., comp. and ed. *Secrets of Successful Boards: The Best from the Non-Profit Pros.* St. Louis, MO: F. E. Robbins & Sons Press, 1998. 192 p.
> Various writers contribute chapters on topics including board meetings, strategic planning, legal issues, relationship with the executive director, volunteers, and use of the Internet.

Wood, Miriam M., ed. *Nonprofit Boards and Leadership: Cases On Governance, Change, and Board-Staff Dynamics.* San Francisco: Jossey-Bass Publishers (Nonprofit Sector Series), 1996. xviii, 246 p.
> Contains thirteen cases based on real-life issues in governance and leadership encountered by nonprofit board members, executive directors, presidents, and consultants. Questions for discussion and an annotated interdisciplinary bibliography are included at the end of each case. The cases are divided into three sections covering the role of external stakeholders in governance, complexities in the board-staff relationship, and interpreting mission and accountability. Includes index.

Internet
To get to the following links, go to: www.clark.net/pub/pwalker/ General_Nonprofit_Resources/Oversight_Groups

Council of Better Business Bureaus, Inc.
> Now on-line; includes a Directory of Better Business Bureaus. It also includes on-line information about charities. This site is growing quickly and provides a wealth of information.

The Internet Nonprofit Center (www.nonprofits.org)
> Provides a sample conflict-of-interest policy and links to other samples, as well as sample position descriptions for board president, chairperson, chief voluntary officer, and vice president/vice chair.

Mississippi State University Extension Servic (www.xt.msstate.edu/pubs)
> Provides staff position descriptions and sample job descriptions for board officers provided by the Support Center of San Francisco.

The National Center for Nonprofit Boards (www.ncnb.org/main.htm)

The National Center for Nonprofit Boards (NCNB) is dedicated to increasing the effectiveness of nonprofit organizations by strengthening their boards of directors. Through its programs and services, NCNB provides solutions and tools to improve board performance, acts as convener and facilitator in the development of knowledge about boards, promotes change and innovation to strengthen governance, and serves as an advocate for the value of board service and the importance of effective governance.

Volunteer's Legal Handbook: (www.ptialaska.net/~jdewitt/vlh)

Details on the legal liabilities of nonprofit organizations, including tax regulations, reporting requirements, and screening of volunteers.

Chapter 4

Putting Your Purpose to Work: Planning Your Programs

If you have built castles in the air, your work need not be lost; that is where they should be. Now put the foundations under them.

—Henry David Thoreau

This chapter discusses a subject that can make or break a nonprofit organization: planning. Plans provide guidelines for making decisions in every area of an organization's operations, and serve as blueprints for achieving its objectives, its mission, and, hopefully, its vision. Nonprofits develop many different kinds of plans, but all good ones share these essential features: they

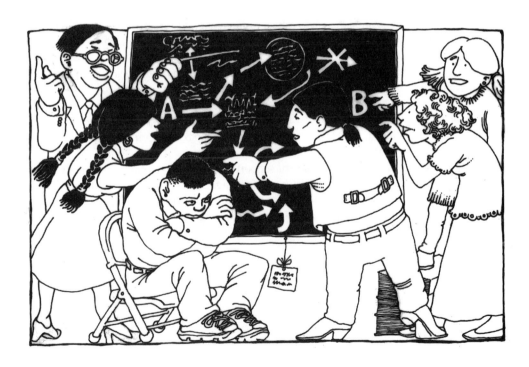

specify a time frame; they inventory the financial and human resources needed to achieve specific results in both the internal and external environments; and they detail how the plan will be implemented and the results assessed.

An organization's history can provide important information for the planning process, but plans can only be developed on the basis of information available and valid at the time they are drafted. Because internal and external factors constantly change, they become out of date almost immediately. It is essential, therefore, that both well-established nonprofits and fledgling efforts regard plans as living documents to be reviewed frequently and modified as circumstances change.

Planning is critical to a start-up's ability to present itself clearly and convincingly to its emerging constituencies, to initiate a track record of successful program delivery, to secure the resources it needs, and to establish its credibility. Mature organizations must also engage in planning because their ongoing success depends upon continued efficient utilization of resources and delivery of products and services. Further, planning ensures that an organization will be driven by its vision, and not the quest for funds. Below is an example of an organization that did not plan, became fund-driven, and while still doing good work, failed not only to accomplish its original mission, but may have endangered its future.

Despite the fact that the organization described below is no longer aligned with its founders' vision, it still provides valuable services. However, if organizations with similar histories do not formalize their mission by means of a long-range plan, they are unlikely to develop a stable base of support. Instead, the organization may be forced to change its focus constantly in order to secure funding from new sources for new programs, as present funders will be unlikely to renew their support of an organization that lacks a clear mission or plans for its achievement. In the case described below, continued lack of planning may ultimately cause it to lose its focus and identity, and jeopardize its future.

In an earlier chapter, we used the March of Dimes to illustrate how an organization can evolve when its vision is realized (the eradication of polio) and it develops a new one (a world without birth defects). Unlike the constantly changing mission of our example, the March of Dimes' new vision was arrived at consciously, and work toward its realization proceeded according to a long-range plan. As a result, the March of Dimes continues to be supported by the same funding sources that helped it achieve its initial vision.

In today's climate of reduced government support and increased competition among rapidly growing numbers of nonprofits and NGOs for funding, individual and institutional funding sources are becoming more rigorous in their funding decisions.[1] As a result, nonprofits are seeking to become more businesslike by applying practices more traditionally associated with for-profit corporations; careful, thorough planning is one of the most important of these practices.

---

1. See Lester M. Salamon's report for the Nathan Cummings Foundation, *Holding the Center: America's Nonprofit Sector at a Crossroads,* for a perceptive and provocative discussion of this and a wide variety of other challenges and trends. (*Holding the Center: America's Nonprofit Sector at a Crossroads.* New York: Nathan Cummings Foundation, 1997. Available from the Foundation Center, 79 Fifth Ave., New York, NY 10003 and www.fdncenter.org).

Case Study

Morphing the Mission

Operating out of space donated by a church, two students, two tenants and one long-time housing advocate started a tenants' rights group in a low-income urban neighborhood. After negotiations for improvements to the tenants' building fail, the group organizes a rent strike that attracts considerable publicity and, after only two months, the landlord makes the improvements. Heartened, the group focuses its attention on the next apartment building. The all-volunteer group's limited financial needs are met by the church and by passing the hat at tenant organizing meetings; their publicity occasionally attracts unsolicited donations.

One day, the organization receives a foundation grant for $10,000 and uses the funds to hire a part-time manager to solicit more grants. Although inexperienced in community organizing, the manager quickly generates $45,000 in additional grants, becomes full-time, and the founding group rents a storefront office to continue its successful organizing work.

The manager's first task should have been to create an organizational plan. Priorities established by the plan would have determined: 1) Whether the $45,000 should have been allocated to salary, or to organizing more buildings, thus fulfilling the group's original intention and building a stronger track record; 2) the need to incur rental and other office expenses. Presenting a plan to the foundation and asking for feedback would have built the relationship by evidencing the organization's foresight and fiscal responsibility.

Looking to the future, the group decides to create an income stream by writing and marketing a manual on tenant organizing based on its impressive track record. The foundation they approach to fund the manual asks that a unit on researching housing, family, and neighborhood demographics be included. Although not convinced of the value of such a unit, the manager and group agree on its inclusion since the foundation is willing to contribute $75,000 a year for two years to fund the manual.

Lacking a plan, the group launched an earned/venture income initiative rather than leveraging its two foundation grants to solicit additional support from individuals, businesses, and more foundations, and building a governance infrastructure. A plan outlining development activities and detailing staff and volunteer time allocation would have helped build a fundraising base without diverting human resources from the group's mission. The organization's agreement to undertake research in order to secure the $150,000 foundation grant now indicates that it has become fund-driven, rather than mission-driven. A plan would have determined whether research was part of the organization's mission and, if so, where it fit into the program priority list. The plan could have served as a point of reference in the group's conversations with the foundation that asked for the research component, resulting, possibly, in a grant more in line with their mission.

Grant money in hand, the organization hires a research firm and follows its suggestion that tenant groups be created in each building to do the advocacy work while the group itself dedicates itself to research. At this point, the founders have moved on to other things and the director creates an independent tax-exempt entity with its own board of directors. A foundation previously approached for the research grant then expresses interest in funding leadership development training and makes a grant. We leave this group as it moves out of the neighborhood where it had done its tenants' rights organizing to larger offices in a more upscale neighborhood and hires two more staff members.

At this point, the funding tail is wagging the organizational dog, so to speak. Its mission already altered by adding the research element, the organization takes another step away from the founders' vision by accepting funding for leadership training. Should they visit their creation at this point, the founders might well wonder how many disadvantaged tenants living in substandard housing were being directly served by the now fully staffed, well-supported, and well-housed organization.

Now financially stable, the organization continues to this day doing research, writing, publishing, and training on issues related to community organizing, tenants' rights, and urban, low-income neighborhoods.

—Kim Klein. Taken from the *Grassroots Fundraising Journal,* April 1999. Used by permission.

What Are the Advantages of Planning?

The advantages of planning include the following:

1. Planning forces an organization to establish program priorities so it can most effectively use its limited resources, challenging the notion that a group should do everything.

2. The planning process requires that an organization ask and answer specific long-term questions, such as:

   • Why do we exist?

   • Whom do we serve?

   • How will we make a difference?

3. Planning gives an organization a blueprint to chart its own future.

4. Planning improves communication at all levels within an organization, generating greater participation, trust, and results.

5. Planning saves time. Either time is invested in the planning process before a project is launched, or time must be spent later on labor-intensive remedial activities to solve the problems resulting from the initial lack of planning.

6. Planning maximizes an organization's human resources by defining the specific roles of staff, board, and volunteers.

7. Planning provides staff and board with criteria to measure their effectiveness.

What Are the Perceived Disadvantages of Planning?

The perceived disadvantages of planning include:

1. Planning creates long-range solutions but does not immediately solve impending crises. It is difficult for an organization to think about long-range planning when, for example, its payroll for the coming month is not in hand.

2. Planning creates change, and change can be threatening. Many people are comfortable with the status quo and resist change, even when it may be for the better.

3. Planning is time-consuming and requires considerable thought before action can be taken. Nonprofit leaders are usually doers and activists, impatient with the problems they see and anxious to take immediate corrective steps.

4. Some organizations perceive that planning is:

   • restrictive, discouraging creativity;

- inflexible, limiting an organization's ability to take advantage of new developments;

- misleading, and based on future conditions whose certainty is unknown.

On the contrary, planning supports creativity by turning creative ideas into reality. Plans also provide guidelines for determining whether new developments—funding, program, or other—are in line with an organization's mission. Rather than limiting a nonprofit's ability to respond to new opportunities, plans help identify the ones that will support its mandated work. Finally, plans ensure that an organization's programs will be expressions of its vision and mission, rather than expressions of leadership's fears about the availability of resources in the future.

Short-Term and Long-Term Planning

The two basic kinds of planning are short-term and long-term (also called long-range, or strategic) planning. Short-term planning takes two forms. Start-ups develop an organizational and program plan for one year and may sketch plans for a second. Short-term plans are also drafted to detail the step-by-step implementation of long-term plans developed by more mature nonprofits. Long-term planning looks forward three to five years or longer, states where the organization wants to be at that time, and outlines how to get there. Organizations engaged in long-term planning (many do so on a regular basis) will then work backward, so to speak, and develop shorter-term goals and plans for all areas of its operations.

The concepts and vocabulary of planning can be daunting, but the many short- and long-range plans that individuals routinely make in their own lives show that planning need be neither onerous nor off-putting. Planning a shopping excursion, for instance, includes virtually the same elements as a short-term organizational plan. After the goal of the excursion has been decided (what to buy); a strategy is developed (check which stores have the merchandise, get in the car, buy gas, pick up a friend, and go); a budget is created (how much can be spent); responsibility is assigned (who will do the shopping); and a timetable is established (when the shopping will be done).

Plans must be flexible. Decisions may have to be made during the excursion if one store is out of an item; if the price has gone up past what you were prepared to spend; if you remember something that had been left off the list; or if a family emergency arises and the shopping must be cancelled. Finally, you can evaluate how effective your plans were by asking how you might have done the shopping more quickly (by ordering some items from a catalog for home delivery, or shopping on-line); if you could have spent less money (by looking through ads in the paper or reading consumer publications); or if you could have saved time by calling ahead to be sure an item was available.

Longer-range plans made by individuals and families also resemble those made by nonprofits. Planning the purchase of a major appliance, car, or home; undertaking financial planning to make sure college tuition is available; planning for retirement; and preparing and updating a will—all are familiar examples of long-range planning, and all require a similar planning process.

Our discussion of short-range and long-range planning will include these considerations: purpose, preparation, process and timeline, parties involved, and implementation and monitoring. Finally, we will consider an essential element of the planning process: evaluation, or self-assessment. We have already pointed out that as the number of nonprofits seeking funding grows, and as government funding declines, it is increasingly important that organizations be able to demonstrate the effectiveness of their work. Evaluation is an important tool organizations can use to improve the quality of their work, and to prove their worthiness to present and potential funders.

Short-Term Planning for New Organizations

There are so many things for a start-up to do—seemingly all at the same time—that planning can seem more of an inhibitor of action than an enabler. Founders are frequently people of action, anxious to get going and to feel that they are making progress. But while spontaneous action creates immediately gratifying movement and momentum, only action directed by thoughtful planning can create lasting progress and structure that can be built on. Founders would do well to "make haste slowly."

An organization planning for its first year of operation should follow a sequence of logical steps similar to the following:

Step 1. Decide To Plan
Successful planning requires the support and participation of the start-up organization's core group, including its founder(s), board of directors, and other key individuals. A less-than-full commitment to the process means that any plans that are developed are unlikely to be implemented. Just as the process described in Chapter 1 for creating vision and mission statements can be a unifying experience, the planning process for an emerging organization's first year can bind the participants together.

Step 2. Assign Responsibility for Planning
If there are enough members of the core group, a committee can be created to undertake the planning process. Start-ups would be well advised to solicit the participation of outside people with nonprofit and planning experience. In addition to bringing their experience and expertise to your planning process, they may become interested in your work and eventually become volunteers and contributors. Make sure that all those who participate in the planning process are aligned with your vision and mission.

Step 3. Assess the Extent of the Problem and/or Opportunity
An essential part of program planning is the clear identification and assessment of what the organization aims to address. Either before or during the planning process, an organization must understand the problem or the opportunity thoroughly in order to design sound, relevant

programs. Information-gathering might involve researching the existing literature on the issues as well as holding in-depth discussions with both constituents and key informants. This stage of program planning is sometimes described as undertaking a needs assessment.

Remember that your assessment should flow from your stated mission and should set the stage for the subsequent objectives and programs that you will develop. Your analysis should also consider similar efforts undertaken by other organizations. If you do not include these groups in your appraisal, you cannot establish a unique course of action for your own programs, and you will therefore diminish your chances of receiving adequate funding and ultimate success. Make sure you ask questions such as:

- What would be the value added of our work?

- What would differentiate us from other organizations in the same field of endeavor?

- What unique niche might we fill?

Step 4. Set Program Objectives
Needs assessment provides data that helps an organization set objectives. An objective—the desired outcome of a program—should be stated in the form of the specific change or result an organization seeks, or a list of the services it plans to deliver. Objectives also provide benchmarks by which organizations and potential funders can gauge progress and effectiveness. Too often, objectives are confused either with broader goals that might be found in a mission statement or with methods of accomplishing objectives.

In order to qualify as an objective, a statement needs to be SMART—Specific, Measurable, Achievable, Realistic, and Time-limited. Accomplished objectives become your history, a track record that inspires donors to trust your organization to accomplish what it has set out to do. Here are some examples of clear objectives based on needs assessment data:

- To increase the reading skills of five hundred ten-year-old children in our three school districts so that all read at or above grade level within two years, and through this project to ensure that 90 percent of school-age children in our community will always read at or above grade level.

- To decrease the incidence of teen drug abuse in our neighborhood by 50 percent in one year by providing a basketball court that can be used day and night.

- To lessen the loneliness and isolation of homebound seniors in our town through a visitor program that will match one hundred volunteer visitors with one hundred homebound seniors for weekly visits and monthly outings.

- To perform three concerts between September and May so that at least one hundred children from each of the four local elementary schools can be introduced to the traditional music of India, the Andes, and Azerbaijan.

The results of programs with such clear objectives can be easily measured:

- How many school-age children have advanced their reading skills?

- How much has the rate of teen drug abuse declined?

- How many seniors have become involved in social activities?

- How many children from each school attended the concerts?

By setting clear objectives, organizations can more effectively prioritize and focus their activities, optimize their limited resources, and evaluate their success.

Step 5. Design Programs

At this juncture, you can proceed to plan programs—developing the sequence of activities that will advance your objectives. All too often, organizations make this Step 1, overlooking the vital previous steps that ensure that all programs are linked to the organization's objectives and will further its stated mission. Programs initiated without thorough research and preparation may accomplish some good yet not achieve the specific results the organization seeks.

In designing programs, be specific. Think of your programs as strategies or maneuvers that will best position your organization to accomplish its objectives. During the design process answer the following questions:

- What are you going to do? Enumerate all the tasks involved.

- How are you going to do it? Do you need any special expertise?

- Where is it going to take place? Locally? Nationally?

- Who has the responsibility for implementation? Staff? Which staff? Others?

- When will the program take place? When will it start, and when will it end?

- How much is the program going to cost in terms of both staff and nonpersonnel expenses?

Thorough, effective planning answers all these questions. The what, how, where, who, and when of any program may have been imagined at one time or another, consciously or otherwise, with or without formal planning. But deliberate program designing enables an organization to control the program planning process from start to finish and creates a powerful end product to guide its activities.

Step 6. Develop a Work Plan

By accomplishing the previous steps, you will have gathered the data needed to create a work plan, a checklist of tasks and deadlines that provides an organization with an invaluable tool for undertaking its work in a systematic fashion. Once established, the plan clarifies the responsibilities each party must fulfill to make the project happen, and can serve as an informal contract between staff, board of directors, and funders.

To develop a work plan, list all the tasks involved in carrying out a program, organized by function. For example, group all printing or promotion or organizing tasks together. Next to each task list the name of the party or parties responsible. Then, chart out the optimal timeline for the completion of the entire program, including all the tasks enumerated. The following charts provide examples of work plans for two particular programs.

Sample Work Plan A

Establishing a Program to Meet the Needs of New Immigrants to Our Community

Tasks	Who	When: Timeline

Tasks	Who	Sept.	O	N	D	J	F	M	A	M	J	J	A
1. Reviewing Mission Statement	Staff/Board/ Committee		⊢----->										
2. Undertaking Needs Assesment	Staff/ Volunteers			⊢--------->									
3. Setting Program Objectives	Staff/Board/ Committee					⊢----->							
4. Designing Program	Staff					⊢-------------->							
5. Seeking Financial Support for Program	Board/Staff							x-----------x--->					
6. Implementing Program	Staff/ Volunteers								x-----------x----------->				
7. Monitoring and Evaluation	Board/Staff									⊢-------------->			

Step 7. Monitor and Evaluate Progress

Common sense is the rule in this last step. If a certain set of tasks is not completed on schedule, find out why. Elicit thoughts and suggestions from the responsible parties and involve them in the monitoring and evaluation process. Ask questions such as: Did we underestimate the amount of time necessary to complete the task? What corrective action needs to be taken? Do we need to reset any deadlines for completion of the project? The thrust of monitoring a project's progress is to enable all involved to do their jobs most effectively. Take care to make the tone of these conversations positive and nonjudgmental.

It is best to establish in advance the criteria you will use to evaluate your work. State objectives clearly so that staff and volunteers know your expectations and the criteria by which their work will be measured. Also, schedule in advance those times when the program will be evaluated (three months, six months, twelve months, and so on).

Sample Work Plan B

Organizing a National Tour of "X" Theater Company

Tasks	Who	When: Timeline													
		Sept.	O	N	D	J	F	M	A	M	J	J	A	S	O	N	Dec.
1. Establish Purposes of the Tour	Board/ Staff	⊢--→													
2. Map Out Schedule of Appearances	Executive Directors/ Logistics Coordinator		⊢--------→												
3. Select Plays to be Performed	Artistic Director	⊢-------→													
4. Commence Fundraising	Board/ Executive Director	⊢------------→													
5. Organize Tour Publicity	Publicity Coordinator/ Local Publicists								⊢--------x---------------→						
6. Organize Local Publicity	Local Contacts									⊢----------------→					
7. Rehearse Performers	Actors and Cast								⊢----------------------→						

Long-Term (Strategic) Planning[2]

While an organization's vision and mission statements will guide its work at every stage of its development, few start-ups expect to fulfill their mission and realize their vision right away. Their focus must necessarily be on taking the first few steps in that direction by beginning the work, by developing support and structure, and, most important, by staying alive. These priorities, combined with uncertainty regarding people, program success, and funding sources, make planning for one year only—and perhaps outlining a second—the most appropriate approach for new initiatives.

---

2. For more help on this stage of planning, see *Strategic Planning Workbook for Nonprofit Organizations,* published by the Amherst Wilder Foundation, 1997. This resource has a number of helpful worksheets and sample plans, as well as suggestions on how to compile all the information needed for proper program planning.

Nonprofits and NGOs already delivering programs, developing new ones, and leveraging their human and financial resources can—and must—take the longer view. Achieving their mission and vision is a long-term undertaking that requires planning that looks three to five, and perhaps ten, years into the future. Some organizations, such as the YMCA of New York, engage in this process every year. Most nonprofits will use their current fiscal year as the base year, and the next fiscal year as year two of the plan. Long-term plans have elements in common with short-term ones, but a more mature organization's scope requires a more rigorous process.

There are different approaches to long-term planning; materials describing some of them are listed in the Additional Resources section of this chapter. By reviewing these resources, speaking with experienced planners in both the nonprofit and for-profit worlds, and studying the long-term plans of similar organizations, you can identify the most appropriate approach for your organization, modify it if necessary, and apply it to your work. The following overview of long-term planning can serve the leadership of start-ups by providing a glimpse of the planning work to be done once their organizations are up and running, and can suggest considerations and approaches that might be relevant even at the incorporation stage. For those embarking on their first long-term planning exercise, the outline provides an overview to help put each step of the process in perspective. Finally, for those who already have done long-term planning, the overview may serve as a useful checklist and review of the basics. The process is divided into three phases: preparation, drafting the plan, and review and approval of the plan.

Phase 1. Preparation

Step 1. Decide To Plan
The short-term planning process usually begins when a start-up's core group agrees that planning should take place. For long-term plans, a formal decision to plan is made by the board, either because the bylaws require periodic planning, because the latest long-term plan has expired, or because board or staff leadership has recommended it. The decision specifies the term of the plan, usually three, five, or ten years. One person should oversee the planning process to make sure that all necessary steps are taken according to an established schedule.

The board can create a committee of its members to work with staff, or the executive director can set up a staff-level committee to make recommendations to the board. In either case, the committee solicits input from others; ultimately, everyone in the organization plays some role in planning. The greater the board's involvement in the planning process, the greater will be its investment in implementing the plan. A retreat facilitated by a planning expert may help inspire and guide the planning process.

Step 2. Review Vision and Mission Statements
Before beginning the planning process, initiate an organization-wide review of your organization's vision and mission statements to make sure they still capture the essence of the group's prime purposes. These statements provide the litmus test for all planning decisions, and because the external conditions that affect a group's intentions are constantly in flux, reviewing an organization's founding statements is always in order.

Step 3. Survey the Environment

Long-range planning requires that an organization consider both the internal and external environments in which it operates from several perspectives.

- **Competition.** Which organizations have a mission similar to your own? Are you aware of any new developments or new organizations? Are any organizations planning to close, thereby creating an opportunity for your organization to expand, hire laid-off staff, and expand its donor base?

- **Overall economic trends.** How do this year's economic indices compare with last year's? With projections for next year? Will changes affect your fundraising and earned income efforts? Are there specialized indices you should consult in this regard? What effect do you think long-term economic projections will have on your organization?

- **Field trends.** Has your reading of periodicals highlighted any significant developments or trends in your sector that should be considered in your planning? If you belong to a professional association, do their statistics or reports indicate growth and increased funding in a particular program area? Are any areas clearly on the wane?

- **External opportunities and threats.** Does your survey reveal potential major opportunities or significant threats? If you operate a homeless shelter, you must know if a law may be enacted to sweep your city's homeless off the streets, and that funding is available for new residential care facilities. If you are an arts organization, you should be aware of a movement gaining momentum at the board of education to eliminate arts education in the schools; you might work to stop the movement, or prepare community education programs to replace any that are cancelled.

- **Public sector.** All organizations (especially those receiving substantial support from or having significant contracts with units of government) will want to stay informed about political developments at all levels—and not just at planning time.

- **Social, cultural, and demographic trends.** What are the local, regional, national, and international trends that you should take into consideration? If the population you're serving is shrinking, building a new facility may not be a high priority. But if a local ethnic population is reviving its culture, say, or if immigrants are an increasingly large part of your community, you need to be aware of those changes so that you can plan to diversify your board membership or hire new staff with native fluency in the immigrants' language.

- **Strengths and weaknesses.** Make an honest inventory of your organization's strengths and weaknesses. Examine such areas as program quality, staff professionalism and effectiveness, board composition and participation, committee effectiveness, advocacy efforts, community relations, prospect cultivation, marketing, and so on. Also consider such factors as adequacy of space, computer hardware and software, communications capability, staff morale, and the like. Solicit opinions from a variety of people who serve within your organization, as well as from a few who do not.

Phase 2. Drafting the Plan

Step 1. Solicit Recommendations
Board members should write a description of how they see the organization three (or five or ten) years from now. Staff members, including program directors and managers, should also write down what they would like to see happening in their area three (or five or ten) years down the road. For now, money should not be a consideration so that creative thinking is not inhibited. This is the time to dream. Each respondent should be given a report discussing the findings of the environment study (described in Step 3 of Phase 1) so that all are working under the same set of assumptions. Using the same forms for staff assessment and recommendations will also facilitate the process of writing the plan.

Step 2. Assemble the Recommendations for the Board
After the staff considers the recommendations from the standpoints of priority and timing, the recommendations then should be merged into a single document. The document should be sent to board members well before their meeting so that the ensuing discussion will be more informed, and any preliminary questions can be clarified by the appropriate staff or planning committee member. At its meeting, the board should focus on the worthiness of the recommendations solely in the context of the organization's vision and mission; financial considerations should still not enter the discussion. The key question is, "If funds were available to implement these recommendations, is this the very best we can do?"

Step 3. Elaborate the Plan and Create Budgets
The board then returns the document to the planning coordinator (or committee, or designated staff member) with its own recommendations so that the plan can be worked out in detail and budgets developed. It is essential to develop an operational component to the plan, whereby responsibility is assigned for tasks and objectives, deadlines are set for their achievement, and monthly, weekly, and perhaps even daily benchmarks are established. Without the "how" provided by the operational plan, the "what" of a long-range plan will never be achieved.

After the board's finance committee analyzes the soundness of the figures, the fundraising committee considers the proposed financial goals in light of the organization's present and potential sources of earned and contributed income. Those committees may choose to develop several budgets based on different income projections, and ask that the recommendations be adopted subject to revenues raised.

Phase 3. Final Review and Approval of the Plan

Step 1. Board Review and Final Modifications
Once the planning staff adapts the initial recommendations to the different budget models, the revised versions of the plan are sent to board members. The board discusses the plans at a meeting and then forwards them to management so that any board-suggested modifications can be made. It may prove helpful for the organization's director and the chairs of its finance and fundraising committees to review the plans at the board meeting and answer questions that arise.

Step 2. Final Redraft and Vote
After the latest modifications have been made, the several versions of the plan, now in their final form, are sent once more to the board. A formal vote is held on which version of the plan will be approved. Versions of the plan projecting less revenues than the approved version should be ready for implementation in the event that fundraising goals are not met.

Planning and Fundraising

Careful program planning increases the likelihood that a project will find support. Today, funders are reading proposals with heightened attention to the quality of the submitting organization's planning process. They are demanding that an organization's management be as solid as its vision is inspiring. With this is mind, note that the planning process parallels some of the major components of writing a proposal: stating the problem or assessing the needs; setting program objectives; describing program methods and the evaluation plan. (A resource with more information about integrating program planning with the proposal writing processes is *Program Planning and Proposal Writing*, by Norton J. Kiritz, published in reprint form by the Grantsmanship Center, Los Angeles, California, www.tgci.com/.).

You will find that your planning work also will aid you in writing copy for annual campaign and promotional materials (brochures, direct mail letters, case statements, etc.). Board members and staff also will be able to use some of the data gathered in presentations to inform prospective donors and others.

Finally, once reported, the results of your work will demonstrate to both your individual and institutional supporters the value of their assistance. They will then see the return on their charitable "investment" and be likely to renew their support and speak well of your work. Careful forethought when planning programs increases the likelihood of their success in advance of their execution, and aids the fundraising process as well.

Tips

- Proper planning takes time. Ultimately, not having a plan is more time-consuming.

- Program planning precedes any successful effort to raise funds. Donors want to know what specifically your group will do to address the need you have identified.

- The most important part of the plan details the objectives. From objectives you can create a work plan and evaluate work already done. Objectives are SMART—Specific, Measurable, Achievable, Realistic, and Time-limited.

Additional Resources

Publications

Allison, Michael. *Strategic Planning for Nonprofit Organizations: A Practical Guide and Workbook.* New York: John Wiley & Sons, 1997. 277 p.

Arsenault, Jane. *Forging Nonprofit Alliances: A Comprehensive Guide to Enhancing Your Mission through Joint Ventures and Partnerships, Management Service Organizations, Parent Corporations, Mergers.* San Francisco: Jossey-Bass Publishers (Nonprofit & Public Management Series), 1998. xvii, 198 p.

Barry, Bryan W. *Strategic Planning Workbook for Nonprofit Organizations.* rev. ed. St. Paul, MN: Amherst H. Wilder Foundation, 1997. x, 129 p.
  Clearly written workbook describes the step-by-step process for developing and effecting a strategic plan. Numerous worksheets and planning tips help both experienced nonprofit executives and volunteer leaders envision the future of their organization and construct the best path to reach that goal. Appendices include an example of a strategic plan and a bibliography.

Brinckerhoff, Peter C. *Social Entrepreneurship: The Art of Mission-Based Venture Development.* New York: John Wiley & Sons, 2000. xvi, 238 p.
  Brinckerhoff states that nonprofits are mission-based businesses, not charities. He defines social entrepreneurs as "people who take risks on behalf of the people their organization serves," and in this book he seeks to teach business development skills in order to facilitate successful risk-taking ability. Since planning is an essential first step in the process, details are provided for developing a business plan, including financial projections, for a nonprofit. Numerous worksheets, charts, and examples are given. Indexed.

Bryce, Herrington J. *Financial and Strategic Management for Nonprofit Organizations.* 3rd ed. San Francisco: Jossey-Bass Publishers (Nonprofit & Public Management Series), 2000. xxxviii, 776 p.
  A comprehensive desk reference organized into five parts. Part One focuses on the mission or purpose of a nonprofit; maintenance of tax-exempt status; forms of nonprofit corporations, foundations, and associations; and the role of trustees. Part Two deals with

increasing contributions; uses of trusts, annuities and endowments; consequences of business ventures; and marketing and advocacy. Part Three discusses budgets, including compensation and benefits; and managing claims against the organization. Part Four analyzes finances, including statements and goal-setting. Part Five deals with strategic planning, collaboration, alliances, and reorganization. Appendices include a sample of a conflict-of-interest policy; various IRS documents; the unified registration statement ("Standardized Registration for Nonprofit Organizations Under State Charitable Solicitation Laws"); and glossary. With suggested readings and an index.

Bryson, John M., and Farnun K. Alston. *Creating and Implementing Your Strategic Plan: A Workbook for Public and Nonprofit Organizations.* San Francisco: Jossey-Bass Publishers (Public Administration Series; Nonprofit Sector Series), 1996. xx, 117 p.

Bryson, John M. *Strategic Planning for Public and Nonprofit Organizations: A Guide to Strengthening and Sustaining Organizational Achievement.* rev. ed. San Francisco: Jossey-Bass Publishers, 1995. xxi, 325 p.
> Introduces the dynamics and benefits of strategic planning. Provides four case studies of organizations that underwent the strategic planning process, and outlines the Strategy Change Cycle, developed by the author. Eight chapters emphasize the planning aspects of the approach. The roles and responsibilities of management leaders, and guidance on starting the planning process, are provided. Includes bibliographic references and index.

Coolsen, Peter. "What Nonprofit Organizations Need Are More Left-Handed Planners." *Nonprofit World 18* (March–April 2000): 29–32.
> Gives suggestions for effective strategic planning in nonprofit organizations. With bibliographic references.

Howe, Fisher. *The Board Member's Guide to Strategic Planning: A Practical Approach to Strengthening Nonprofit Organizations.* San Francisco: Jossey-Bass Publishers (Nonprofit Sector Series), 1997. xiii, 114 p.

Joyaux, Simone P. *Strategic Fund Development: Building Profitable Relationships that Last.* Frederick, MD: Aspen Publishers (Fund Raising Series for the 21st Century), 1997. xiii, 213 p.
> Argues that four relationships are critical for a nonprofit organization's survival. The first relationship is within the organization and involves creating a healthy infrastructure. The second is with the community, which evolves through strategic planning. The third is with the organization's constituents so they will be ready to give. Finally, the fourth is with the organization's volunteers to enable them to take action on behalf of the organization. Includes bibliographic references and index.

Kearns, Kevin P. *Private Sector Strategies for Social Sector Success: The Guide to Strategy and Planning for Public and Nonprofit Organizations.* San Francisco: Jossey-Bass Publishers, 2000. xxvii, 344 p.

> Kearns delves into the realm of strategic thinking as practiced by the business sector, and how these methods can be best utilized by the public and nonprofit sectors. He claims that, essentially, the models can be growth, retrenchment, or stability, and he studies these options thoroughly. Some of the areas he explores are the increasingly competitive environments, entrepreneurial initiatives, strategic collaborations, and advancing the mission. With bibliographic references and an index.

Light, Paul C. *Sustaining Innovation: Creating Nonprofit and Government Organizations that Innovate Naturally.* San Francisco: Jossey-Bass Publishers (Nonprofit and Public Management Series), 1998. xxx, 299 p.

> Presents case studies and lessons from the Surviving Innovation Project, a five-year research effort funded by the Ford, McKnight, and General Mills foundations. Though the resulting data show that there is no one true path to innovating, the most successful organizations focused on assets and mission rather than liabilities.

O'Connor, Judith. *The Planning Committee: Shaping Your Organization's Future.* Washington, DC: National Center for Nonprofit Boards, 1997. 20 p.

Oster, Sharon M. *Strategic Management for Nonprofit Organizations: Theory and Cases.* New York: Oxford University Press, 1995. ix, 350 p.

> Applies the concepts of strategic management developed originally in the for-profit sector to the management of nonprofits. Describes the preparation of a strategic plan that is consistent with the resources available, analyzes the operational tasks in executing the plan, and outlines the ways in which nonprofits need to change in order to remain competitive. Topics examined include the role and mission of the nonprofit, fundraising, accounting, evaluation, volunteers, and the board of directors. Provides in-depth case studies of nine nonprofit organizations from diverse areas of the nonprofit sector. Includes numerous charts and graphs, bibliographic references, and index.

Rutter, E. Jane. T*he Self-Sustaining Nonprofit: Planning for Success.* Columbia, MO: Grants Link, Inc., 1997. ix, 117 p.

> Provides practical guidelines and advice to nonprofits that are making the transition from a volunteer organization to a formal structure. Covers topics of incorporation, developing internal structures, financial and service planning, and growth. Includes bibliographical references.

Wyzbinski, Patricia, Pam Moore, and Scott Gelzer. "Beyond a Hit List: Income Planning for Small Nonprofit Organizations." *New Directions for Philanthropic Fundraising* 20 (Summer 1998): 9–23.

> Recommends that nonprofits create an income plan to 1) state goals and objectives; 2) reflect long-term planning; 3) apportion responsibilities to various parties; and 4) use as an evaluation tool. Explains in detail the planning process and the roles of staff and board. Provides a sample of such a plan, with instructions about implementation.

Internet

About.com (www.nonprofit.tqn.com/library/weekly/aa030998.htm)

> Extensive resources, links, software relating to nonprofit planning.

Applied Research & Development
(www.ardi.org/cgi-bin/ardi?action=Resources2&cat=Planning)

> Information on nonprofit strategic planning

Business Planning Site (www.planware.org/index.html)

> Business plan software and freeware, white papers on business planning, financial planning, and strategy development.

Charity Village (www.charityvillage.com/charityvillage)

> Planning resources are only one area covered by this vast Canadian site, which contains information, links, and resources about virtually every area of a nonprofit's activities.

The Grantsmanship Center (http://www.tgci.com/)

> TGCI offers grantsmanship training and low-cost publications to nonprofit organizations and government agencies. TGCI conducts some 200 workshops annually in grantsmanship and proposal writing. More than 100 local agencies host these workshops.

InnoNet Non-Profit Toolbox (www.innonet.org/)

> Created by Innovation Network, a nonprofit consulting organization in Washington that helps charities plan and evaluate programs, this Web site offers interactive work sheets that help nonprofit staff members develop program, fundraising, and evaluation plans for their projects. The site plans to post sample evaluation tools, such as surveys and questions for focus groups, that can be downloaded, as well as links to other Internet resources for nonprofit organizations.

Nonprofit Links (www.uwex.edu/li/links_strategic.html)

> Provides many links to organizations specializing in nonprofit planning; includes on-line articles and worksheet.

Nonprofit Organizational Assessment Tool (www.uwex.edu/li/assess1.html)
   A 29-page on-line description of the nonprofit planning model, with charts, by LI faculty
   member Frank Martinelli. This section of the Nonprofit Organizational Assessment Tool
   can help guide a group discussion about an organization's strategic planning process. This
   group discussion ideally should include board members, staff, volunteers, and service
   recipients, but could be used as a self-assessment tool by anyone associated with a
   nonprofit organization.

Planware (www.planware.org/buslink-i.htm)
   A variety of software to support the process of institutional planning

Strategic Planning in Nonprofit and Public Sector Organizations Description of Planning
Model (on-line article) (www.mapnp.org/library/mgmnt/np_progs.htm#anchor4294895830)
   Information in this document explains a basic (and increasingly common) framework in
   which nonprofit programs can be developed. The framework suggested in this document
   will produce a program that is highly integrated with the organization's mission and other
   programs. The framework serves as a sound basis for writing program proposals to
   funders, as well, because the framework closely follows that of the standard proposal
   document. In addition, the program will be clearly structured for a straightforward program
   evaluation. This document includes the following sections: What's a Nonprofit Program? 6
   Cornerstones for Solid Program Planning; 8 Guidelines to Keep Program Planning on
   Track; Program Direction: Goals and Objectives; Program Process (Process, Resources
   and Budget); Program Evaluation. Extensive links and other resources.

Chapter 5

Developing Budgets

Mathematics is the language with which God has written the universe.
—Galileo Galilei

Imagine the following scenario. You knock on the door of a prospective donor to ask for a contribution. Your prospect listens to your request, then asks, "How much do you need to get this project off the ground?" You stammer and finally say, "Well, whatever we can raise." The prospect tries to help from another angle: "How much do you want from me?" You respond, "We can use whatever you can give us." Frustrated by your lack of knowledge and preparation, the prospect politely terminates the conversation. Crestfallen and certainly no richer than before, you leave.

Knowing the precise cost of your proposed program could have helped you avoid this scenario and might well have saved the day!

Prospective backers, both individual and institutional, respond most favorably to solicitations that are based on the concrete costs of an organization's work. Preparing a budget is the process of determining those costs, and identifying potential sources of revenue to meet them. Careful budgeting and budget administration will move your organization forward by assuring prospective and current supporters that any dollars they invest in your work will be used wisely, and will pay dividends. And doing your budget homework before meeting with a potential funder means that you'll have an answer ready when asked the inevitable question, "How much do you need?" It also sends several important messages to your prospect: that you value your prospect's time and interest enough to have prepared for the meeting; that you were able to prepare because your organization is thorough in its budgeting and, by implication, in all its financial operations; that your prospect can trust that any contribution he or she makes will be well used.

What Is Budgeting?

In its narrowest definition, budgeting means calculating the cost of what you need to spend as you work to accomplish your mission (expenses), and the amount needed to be raised to pay for them (income). Budget creation flows from the planning process; it details in financial terms how an organization's resources will be allocated to accomplish what has been planned. The process of developing and monitoring budgets also performs other important functions.

1. *Budgeting is a management tool.* An organization's hard-earned, limited resources are usually insufficient to fund all the programs an organization wishes to deliver; the budgeting process forces an organization's board and staff to engage in fruitful, relationship-building deliberations in order to establish its priorities and choose which programs to fund. Budgeting is thus a strong tool for management to cultivate the board's involvement.

2. *Budgeting is a program tool.* It helps determine how much funding is needed—and how much may be available—to launch a new program. This process will, in turn, determine the scope and shape of the program. If less than the total projected program expenses is raised, previously established strategies will determine how the program can be modified to accommodate the shortfall. If it is found that the project cannot continue, established budgeting priorities will direct the allocation of the funds that have been raised to other operational areas.

3. *Budgets that must be revised significantly send a strong message.* The practice of continually making sure there's enough money can alert you to important dynamics that may develop but remain hidden. Frequently modifying programs because of a lack of resources sends a message to the community that an organization may not be operating at maximum efficiency. Clients, audiences, or other targeted

constituencies who are negatively affected by program changes will not be an organization's best public relations agents in the community.

4. *Budgeting is a financial planning tool.* It forces an organization to anticipate its expenses and revenues on a regular basis. The issue of when expenses must be incurred and when revenues may be received is addressed by a document based on the budget: the cash flow chart. The chart's timing of expenses and revenues provides essential information to the nonprofit's managers and board members, who may need to arrange short-term loans or undertake additional fundraising to cover periodic shortfalls.

5. *Budgeting is a form of management control over expenditures.* The processes of preparing, administering, and revising a budget provides an organization with an ongoing monitoring system. By comparing on a monthly basis its actual expenditures and receipts against those projected in the budget, an organization can, if necessary, modify its operations. With increasing competition for limited resources, organizations that are able to document sound financial management will have a decided advantage in their fundraising.

6. *Budgeting is a development tool.* An organization's budget calculates the amount that must be raised through its fundraising activities. As will be discussed later, the budget can serve as a fundraising tool, as some items may offer attractive underwriting opportunities. Finally, a board of directors becomes more committed to raising money when its members decide together how it will be spent. The executive director plays a central role in this process by helping the board understand how the budget was developed. Conversations with board members in person and on the phone about the budget (or any other matter) give the executive director opportunities to answer questions and, at the same time, forge closer relationships. While an executive director may prefer to concentrate on operations and program delivery, it would be unwise to completely relegate money issues to a board treasurer, comptroller, accountant, or bookkeeper. Doing so would diminish the effectiveness of both the executive director and the budget-making process in rallying an organization's constituencies in support of its financial goals.

A final budget expresses the organization's program and activity priorities in financial terms; once approved it becomes the reference point for all spending decisions. Its thoughtful creation and implementation are absolutely central to the mission, programs, and management of the organization.

Budget Planning

Preparing an ongoing organization's annual budget involves its board of directors, executive committee, staff, program directors, and treasurer (or chief financial officer). For a start-up

The Budget as a Fundraising Tool

A grassroots environmental group asked an annual contributor of $500 to discuss the possibility of increasing her gift. She asked for their budget. At the meeting, she pulled it out and said to the director, "You know what I learn from this budget? I learn that you are responsible, you think clearly about what things will cost, and know how to balance income and expenses."

Pleased with her statement, the director asked her if she would consider doubling her annual gift. She replied, "You know what else I learn from this budget? You think too small. Your work is going to take a lot more money, and you need to be asking for a lot more. Send me a budget that justifies a request for $10,000 and I'll consider making such a gift." The director realized that the budget—and not the vision—was driving program. He changed the budget, received $10,000 from this donor, and doubled the organization's income in only six months. Remember that budgets are tools, not ends in themselves.

organization the core group creates its first-year budget. In both cases, the organization's vision and mission statements should guide the budgeting process.

The budgeting process should be initiated well in advance of the new fiscal year, and, in the case of ongoing organizations, is usually based on the previous year's budget. Staff members of ongoing organizations can make valuable contributions to calculating budgets, as they are closest to the daily operations. Their input helps the executive director compute the program and operating budgets and prepare the total organizational budget for the board's consideration. For start-ups, thorough research of projected expenses; conversations with other nonprofit managers, businesspeople, and an accountant; and careful, conservative estimates of potential income form the basis for their first-year budget. The following sample calendar of Budget Development Activity offers a thorough guide to budget planning.

Kinds of Budgets

Start-up organizations usually develop an overall budget for their first year of operations that projects staff, supplies, space, services, and program expenses, as well as anticipated revenues from contributions, grants, and fees. Because a new organization has no history on which to base its first-year budget, staff must thoroughly research expenses and talk with other nonprofit managers, businesspeople, and an accountant familiar with nonprofit practice. Projecting revenues for a new organization is likely to be more difficult. Revenues cannot be projected the same way expenses are estimated because it would be inappropriate, in most cases, to call potential supporters and ask if—or what—they plan to give. We will discuss this challenge below.

More mature organizations develop both an organizational budget that projects total expenses and revenues, as well as program budgets that attribute both direct and indirect

Budget Development Activity

Week	Activity
1	Gather all documents, historical reports, previous planning information, program status reports, etc. necessary to begin budget-planning process.
2	Analyze historical information. Begin development of budget assumptions. Review environmental factors affecting future year fundraising program. Prepare budget questionnaire. Develop budget narrative on program strategy.
3	Begin budget planning process; staff and leadership to complete budget questionnaire. Complete the budget assumptions affecting salaries, benefits, and other administrative objectives.
4	Begin development of program objectives. Begin to assemble financial information necessary to carry out program objectives. Meet with employees to review personnel performances and assign salary changes to personnel budget.
5	Finalize program and budget objectives for next year. Present program objectives to leadership for reaction and review.
6	Present draft budget to finance committee for review. Revise budget and program objectives based on further staff and volunteer concerns.
7	Review, compare, and contrast current budget information with historical data, local financial information, and national trends.
8	Finalize all budget information.
9	Prepare final documents for presentation and approval.
10	Present final budget documents to administration, finance committee, or board of directors for final approval.[1]

1. James M. Greenfield, ed. *The Nonprofit Handbook: Fund Raising,* 2nd edition (New York: John Wiley & Sons, Inc., 1997).

expenses and revenues on a program-by-program basis. Organizational and program expense budgets consist of two parts: personnel items and non-personnel items. Personnel items include salaried staff, contracted assistance (consultants, accountants, lawyers, etc.), short-term employees (interns, work/study students, temporary workers), and fringe benefits for salaried staff (workman's compensation, health insurance, pension plans, unemployment compensation, etc.). Non-personnel items include office rent and supplies, utilities, telephone, printing, office equipment and repair, postage, travel, liability insurance, and the like.

Nonprofits engaging in long-term (strategic) planning usually translate those plans into a strategic budget that lays out fiscal and fundraising goals for a three- to five-year period. The following section discusses organizational and program budgets.

Organizational Budgets

Organizational budgets project overall expenses and revenues for one year of operations. As each expense and revenue is entered on a separate line, these budgets are sometimes called *line-item budgets*. Organizational budgets facilitate comparisons with previous years' financial results, and are the budgets normally submitted with proposals for unrestricted grants and contributions. These budgets also quickly reveal whether an organization will have sufficient revenues to pay for its operations. To better understand the organizational budget, let's look below at the numbers a small orchestra has projected for its third season.

The orchestra's organizational budget reveals a deficit of close to $10,000 for its upcoming season. If its leadership does not want to open the new season with a projected deficit, it must take action to either increase revenues or decrease expenses. Let's assume that the revenue projections are on the optimistic side, and that it will be a significant accomplishment to achieve them, let alone raise an additional $10,000 to cover the projected deficit. The alternative, then, is to reduce expenses. However, it is difficult to look at an organizational budget and know what part of the orchestra's activities each expense item represents, or what impact cutting expenses would have. In order to determine where reductions can be made without compromising the organization's ability to operate, the orchestra's leadership identifies five program areas: concerts and education are its two primary programs, and administration, fundraising, and publicity/public relations are its support programs. In order to determine the cost of each of these programs and identify expenses that can be safely reduced, program budgets are developed for each area.

Program Budgets

Program budgets project the expenses and revenues associated with a discrete element of an organization's work. Because they reveal the true expenses for each area of an organization's operations, they are valuable management tools. In program budgets, expenses and revenues are calculated in two ways: *directly,* that is, 100 percent of the item is related to the program; or *indirectly,* when a percentage of an organization's resources (salary, office space, telephone, computer, etc.) or revenues (unrestricted gifts from foundations, corporations, or individuals) is attributed to the program.

Revenues

Earned

Ticket Sales	$ 47,860
Program Advertising	6,000
Concessions	2,000
Total Earned	**$ 55,860**

Unearned

Individuals	
Contributions	$ 71,500
Memberships	20,000
Major Gifts	50,000
In-Kind Donations	1,600
Special Events	30,000
Direct Mail Solicitation	7,500
Phonathon	6,100
Grants	
Foundations	19,500
Businesses	5,750
Corporations	26,000
Government	8,250
Total Unearned	**$246,200**
Total Earned	**$ 55,860**
Total Revenue	**$302,060**

Expenses

Personnel	
Artistic	$126,759
Administrative	95,000
Payroll@15%	14,250
Total Personnel	**$236,009**
Non-Personnel	
Concert Production	38,571
Office Rent	3,600
Utilities	720
Telephone	2,400
Printing	15,340
Office Equipment	2,650
Office Supplies	1,350
Postage	4,600
Travel	1,875
Insurance	4,200
Dues	250
Total Non-Personnel	**$ 75,556**
Total Personnel	**$236,009**
Total Expenses	**$311,565**
Total Revenue	**$302,069**
NET	**($ 9,496)**

Overhead Strikes Again

The Alcoholism Center for Teens (ACT) learned the hard way about overhead costs. They applied for funding for an innovative program to send young outreach workers into teenage hangouts to talk to teens about responsible alcohol consumption. Schools, fraternities, community centers, and ball games were some of the many venues they visited. The cost of the outreach workers was the main expense, with materials to hand out the only other tangible cost. They applied for, and received, funding for these costs.

However, overhead costs for the program soon became apparent. The outreach workers needed a desk when they came into the office to work. They needed a phone at that desk to make follow-up calls or to request permission to go to a school campus. They used stationery to write thank-you notes to people who were helpful to them, and they needed computer time to log in the results of their visits and to avoid having two workers visiting the same venue. They had out-of-pocket costs, such as parking and meals that had not been taken into account, and they had to be included in the staff meetings and retreats. Not only did this program not generate any extra money for the general operating needs of the group (including the staff time it took to keep finding funding for the program), but the program cost the organization a few thousand dollars a year. Fortunately, they realized the problem and were able to correct it in their next round of funding proposals.

Examples of *direct expenses* are the fees paid to the dancers by a dance company specifically for their outreach work in local schools, and the price of the land purchased by a conservation group. *Revenues directly attributable* to a program are any fees paid by the schools to the dance company for its outreach program, or a foundation grant to a rehabilitation center restricted to funding its peer counseling program.

Don't Overlook Indirect Expenses

In preparing program and project budgets, organizations sometimes overlook—or underestimate—indirect costs and present only a program's direct costs as the total expense. This faulty budgeting can prove dangerous, perhaps even precipitating a financial crisis if the real costs of a program significantly exceed revenues. The "simple" oversight of failing to include indirect costs in a program budget could result in a serious debt situation or cause a significant, unanticipated drain on general (unrestricted) revenues.

Examples of *indirect* expenses are that part of the annual cost of a bus owned by the dance company for transporting its dancers to the schools, and the portion of the salary of the rehabilitation center's executive director that can be allocated to the peer counseling program. *Revenues indirectly attributable* to a program would include a proportional share of the total unrestricted funds an organization receives. Projecting direct expenses and revenues is relatively straightforward; calculating all-important indirect expenses requires additional work.

Indirect costs can be substantial; in the accompanying orchestra example, indirect costs were 39.6 percent of the organizations total budget. Some federal agencies allow their grantees to add as much as 40 percent of a project's direct costs as indirect costs, or overhead; many universities project 50 percent in overhead costs. Smaller organizations should project 10 to 20 percent in overhead costs. For example, if the direct costs of a project total $40,000, another $4,000 to $8,000 (10 to 20 percent of $40,000) should be added to cover indirect costs, bringing the total project budget to $44,000 to $48,000.

In preparing a project budget, it may be preferable to itemize all indirect costs in your budget. However, some funders allow only a fixed percentage of the project's total budget (personnel plus non-personnel) to be designated as overhead cost. If a prospective funder's requirements are not made clear in their pre-grant application literature, ask them if they have any preference.

Direct Expenses

The first step in developing the orchestra's program budget is for its staff to calculate direct expenses for each program:

Budget Worksheet A

Direct Program Expense Projections

| | PRIMARY | | SUPPORT | | | |
| | | | | | Publicity/ | |
Item	Concerts	Education	Administration	Fundraising	PR	Total
Musicians	$61,160	$20,970		$13,065	$640	$95,835
Travel, per diem	8,430	2,640		1,454		12,524
Conductor, Soloist	10,000	4,000	$1,150	3,250		18,400
Music purchase	1,625	175		321		2,121
Rehearsal space	2,650	400		500		3,550
Concert production	11,980	2,780				14,760
Receptions	900			9,760		10,660
Advertising	5,800			1,680		7,480
Printing	5,100		1,350	5,690		12,140
Total	$107,645	$30,965	$2,500	$35,720	$640	$177,470

One hundred percent of these expenses will appear in the program budget since they will be incurred in their entirety in the delivery of the respective programs. For instance, the receptions will be held only after concerts ($900) and in connection with fundraising events ($9,760); advertising will be placed only for the concerts ($5,800) and for fundraising events ($1,680).

The printing expenses do not represent the orchestra's total printing budget—only the printing of concert programs ($5,100), office forms ($1,350), and special fundraising event invitations and programs ($5,690).

Indirect Expenses

To project the orchestra's indirect program expenses, its staff will first calculate personnel costs, then the cost of non-personnel items. The first step in determining the personnel costs is to create a time budget; that is, to estimate the amount of time each staff member spends on each activity.

Budget Worksheet B

Indirect Program Expenses: Personnel Time

| | PRIMARY | | SUPPORT | | | |
| | | | | | Publicity/ | |
Position	Concerts	Education	Administration	Fundraising	PR	Total
Executive Director	15%	10%	35%	35%	5%	100%
Artistic Director	40%	30%	10%	10%	10%	100%
Secretary	10%	10%	40%	35%	5%	100%

To calculate the amounts to include in each program budget, staff members' salaries are then multiplied by the percentage of time they devote to each program, and payroll is added.

Budget Worksheet C

Indirect Program Expenses: Personnel Salaries

| | PRIMARY | | SUPPORT | | | |
| | | | | | Publicity/ | |
Position	Concerts	Education	Administration	Fundraising	PR	Total
Executive Director	$6,750	$4,500	$15,750	$15,750	$2,250	$45,000
Artistic Director	12,000	9,000	3,000	3,000	3,000	30,000
Secretary	2,000	2,000	8,000	7,000	1,000	20,000
Payroll @15%	3,113	2,325	4,013	3,863	938	14,252
Total	$23,863	$17,825	$30,763	$29,613	$7,188	$109,252

The orchestra's indirect non-personnel expenses are then calculated by estimating the proportion of each expense item that is devoted to the different program areas.

Budget Worksheet D

Indirect Program Expenses: Non-Personnel

	PRIMARY		SUPPORT			
Item	Concerts	Education	Administration	Fundraising	Publicity/ PR	Total
Office Rent	$360	$180	$1,260	$1,440	$360	$3,600
Utilities	72	36	252	288	72	720
Telephone	240	120	840	960	240	2,400
Printing	320	160	1,120	1,280	320	3,200
Office equipment	265	132	928	1,060	265	2,650
Office supplies	135	68	473	540	134	1,350
Postage	460	230	1,610	1,840	460	4,600
Travel	188	94	655	750	188	1,875
Insurances	420	210	1,470	1,680	420	4,200
Dues	25	12	88	100	25	250
Total	**$2,485**	**$1,242**	**$8,696**	**$9,938**	**$2,484**	**$24,845**

We derived the figures in Budget Worksheet D by calculating the cost of the concerts at 10 percent of the annual total, education at 5 percent, administration at 35 percent, fundraising at 40 percent, and publicity/public relations at 10 percent. We are now able to calculate the orchestra's program expenses by adding its projected direct expenses (Budget Worksheet A) to its total projected indirect expenses (Budget Worksheets C and D).

Budget Worksheet E

Total Projected Program Expenses

	PRIMARY		SUPPORT			
Expense	**Concerts**	**Education**	**Administration**	**Fundraising**	**Publicity/ PR**	**Total**
Direct	$107,645	$30,965	$2,500	$35,720	$640	$177,470
Indirect						
Personnel	23,863	17,825	30,763	29,613	7,188	109,252
Non-personnel	2,485	1,242	8,696	9,938	2,484	24,845

Projecting Revenues

For start-ups, projecting first-year revenues is a challenging exercise because there is no history upon which to base the numbers. A good way to develop this projection is to hold a meeting of your core group to create a list of potential sources of revenue for both program (restricted) and general (unrestricted) support. Those sources will include contributions, memberships, and major gifts from individuals; revenue from special events, direct mail solicitations, and phonathons; grants from foundations; contributions and grants from businesses, corporations, religious institutions, labor unions, federations, and associations; grants and contracts from government agencies; revenue from earned income ventures; and any other relevant sources. While it is unlikely that a new organization will receive revenues from each of these sources, it's still worth considering all categories to stimulate your group's thinking. You might also ask group members to invite friends and acquaintances outside the group who know the community well and might be willing to participate in this process. Inviting these people to the meeting could be the first step in cultivating their interest in your work. (Make sure you don't miss opportunities to involve people you trust in your organization's planning processes, and remember that almost any activity can be used to involve and cultivate prospective volunteers, donors, and leaders.)

After finalizing your list and researching each source, hold another meeting of your core group to "rate" each potential source; that is, estimate the amount of revenue your organization might generate within the next twelve months.

Because not all the sources you've listed will respond at the level you initially project, subtract 33 percent from the overall total, then ask your group if the resulting number appears realistic. Although this process is highly subjective and a bit like flying blind, the revenues you've projected may not differ substantially from what actually comes in. Of course, the more research that can be done on each potential source, the more accurate your ratings will be (see Chapter 11 for more about researching prospects). When you compare your ratings with the revenue you've actually received by the end of your first fiscal year, you can almost count on being surprised. Sources you expected to be generous will have given much less than you expected—or nothing. The opposite will also be true: surprisingly generous gifts will have arrived from unexpected sources, providing not only welcome financial support but also additional motivation and momentum.

The revenue projections from all sources can then be totaled and compared to the organization's total projected expenses. If there is a modest shortfall, that amount might be raised from sources not yet identified. The deficit might also be covered by an additional gift from a contributor at the end of the season. One of fundraising's basic tenets is: "Those who are most likely to give are those who have already given." If the difference between projected expenses and revenues is significant, expenses will have to be reduced. Program budgets give an organization's leadership a clear picture of the true costs of its activities, and facilitate the creation of a prioritized list of potential expense reductions. You can use a spreadsheet program to create a number of "what if?" scenarios based on raising varying percentages of your projected revenues. By calculating the revenues that are available if 95 percent, 90 percent, 85 percent, etc., of your projections is realized, you can create a list of potential expense reductions to make in each case.

More mature organizations will have data for past years, making the job of projecting revenues somewhat easier (except in the case of new programs and initiatives for which the organization has never before solicited support). Staff and leadership will base revenue projections on a

Budget Worksheet F

Program Revenue Projections

| | CONCERTS (Restricted) | | | | |
| | 1997–98 | | 1998–99 | | 1999–00 |
SOURCE	Proj.	Actual	Proj.	Actual	Proj.
Earned					
Tickets	36,580	33,478	41,995	43,640	44,060
Program Advertising	4,480	4,173	5,100	5,345	5,200
Concessions	1,400	800	1,580	1,540	2,000
Unearned					
Individuals	25,000	16,750	22,500	20,000	22,500
Foundations	5,000	5,000	6,000	5,500	6,000
Businesses	2,500	1,250	2,000	1,860	2,250
Corporations	5,000	6,500	7,500	7,250	7,500
Government	0	0	0	0	2,500
Total	$79,960	$67,951	$86,675	$85,135	$92,010

Budget Worksheet F (continued)

Program Revenue Projections

	EDUCATION (Restricted)				
	1997–98		1998–99		1999–00
SOURCE	Proj.	Actual	Proj.	Actual	Proj.
Earned					
Tickets	3,240	1,845	3,720	3,695	3,800
Program Advertising	500	675	650	700	800
Concessions	0	0	0	0	0
Unearned					
Individuals	4,500	3,750	4,000	4,000	4,000
Foundations	2,000	1,500	2,000	3,500	2,500
Businesses	1,000	600	750	850	1,000
Corporations	2,000	2,500	2,500	3,000	3,500
Government	750	750	1,000	1,000	1,250
Total	$13,990	$11,620	$14,620	$16,745	$16,850

	FUNDRAISING (Unrestricted)				
	1997–98		1998–99		1999–00
SOURCE	Proj.	Actual	Proj.	Actual	Proj.
Individuals					
Contributions	$30,000	$24,500	$30,000	$37,650	$45,000
Memberships	15,000	13,050	15,000	14,255	20,000
Major Gifts	25,000	15,000	20,000	37,500	50,000
In-kind	1,000	585	1,000	1,266	1,600
Special Events	10,000	12,680	15,000	21,750	30,000
Direct Mail	6,500	3,560	5,000	4,760	7,500
Phonathon	3,250	3,000	3,500	4,150	6,100
Grants					
Foundations	5,000	5,000	5,000	6,500	11,000
Businesses	2,500	1,875	2,000	2,260	2,500
Corporations	10,000	6,700	7,500	12,500	15,000
Government	1,000	1,000	1,000	1,000	4,500
TOTAL	$109,250	$86,950	$105,000	$143,591	$193,200

careful analysis of recent revenue data, as well as on recent organizational developments, the general funding environment and, ultimately, on their own good judgment.

Returning to the orchestra we discussed earlier, we find that its staff and leadership have based their revenue projections on the revenue that was projected and the revenue that was actually received for each of the past two years.

There is a tremendous advantage to analyzing the results of previous years' revenue projections and actual income received: the comparisons indicate the accuracy of revenue projections. Realizing that their projections were too high in 1997–98, staff and leadership projected more conservative figures for 1998–99, and, helped by the orchestra's growth, met their projections.

Other important information can be derived from this kind of analysis. For instance, revenue received from major gifts from individuals and special events was substantially higher than projected, and grew quickly. This indicates that the orchestra should spend more time soliciting major gifts and arranging special fundraising events than, say, pursuing grants from government sources.

Projected revenue from government sources for 1999–2000, however, is significantly higher than before, since the organization, now that it is three years old, has become qualified to apply for grants from certain federal agencies to which it could not apply before. This is an example of the kind of new developments in an organization that will impact its program revenue projections. Another example of this is the higher projection for foundation grants; a woman who made a major gift told the orchestra's executive director that she will bring a proposal for funding to her family foundation, and that the orchestra can count on the money because she makes the decisions.

Program Budget Summary

Now that the orchestra has projected its program revenues and expenses for the coming year, it can create a program budget summary that compares the two.

Budget Worksheet G

Program Summary Budget

Program	Expenses	Revenues	Net
Concerts	$133,993	$92,010	($41,974)
Education	50,032	16,850	(33,182)
Administration	41,959	0	(41,959)
Fundraising	75,271	0	(75,271)
Publicity/PR	10,312	0	(10,312)
Unrestricted revenue	0	193,200	193,200
Total All Programs	**$311,567**	**$302,060**	**($9,507)**

As a result of developing program budgets, it becomes clear to the orchestra's leadership that no expenses should be reduced from the support programs since they generate a significant surplus. Instead, expenses associated with the concerts and educational programs will be scrutinized to determine where $10,000 can be saved to balance the budget. Perhaps pieces will be performed that require fewer musicians, or soloists can be hired for lower fees. It is possible that including season subscription brochures with annual fund mailings will increase the purchase of season tickets to the point where the advertising budget can be reduced. Printing concert programs on lighter paper, asking friends of the orchestra to bring pot luck suppers to the concert hall for the musicians so that their per diems can be reduced, and sending fewer musicians into the schools are examples of the kind of expense reduction that will combine to eliminate the projected deficit.

Had the orchestra not developed a program budget in addition to its organizational budget, its leaders might have looked at the organizational budget and decided to cut expenses from the support programs. Such action would be likely to increase the orchestra's projected deficit—not eliminate it—since the support programs generate a surplus and should not be weakened.

General Support vs. Project Support

In our development of the orchestra's program budgets, we categorized grants and donations as either "program" (restricted) or "general" (unrestricted). Contributions and grants earmarked for specific programs carry the legal obligation to be spent only for those programs. Contributions and grants made for general purposes—that is, where the donor has not specified the use of the funds—can be used by the recipient organization for any purpose, and so are highly prized by nonprofits. The orchestra would have no problem whatsoever in receiving additional contributions restricted to its concerts and education programs because contributions restricted to those areas are projected to be some $75,000 less than expenses.

A central issue for organizations soliciting funds from private sources is whether they should solicit funds for specific programs or for general operating support to be used as they see fit. In this matter, nonprofits and their prospective supporters are sometimes at odds. Institutional needs are often practical, requiring unrestricted dollars to cover such pedestrian expenses as rent and utilities. Generally speaking, though, there is more money available from institutional sources for programs than for general purposes.

The Need To Maintain Core Programs
Ongoing core programs are beset by such prosaic expenses as staff salaries, rent, and related administrative costs. More often than not, these expenses cannot be included in new project budgets. Yet core programs remain the source from which new initiatives eventually spring. Given the fragility of nonprofit funding today, exclusively project-specific support can actually undermine the financial condition of the recipient by contributing to its limbs without attending to its heart.

An organization unduly preoccupied with its own survival is not likely to develop much in the way of new and innovative projects. Unrestricted grant dollars enable recipients to develop new

Financial Accounting Standards Board

The Financial Accounting Standards Board (FASB) is a private sector organization in charge of establishing standards of financial accounting and reporting; FASB makes the rules that govern generally accepted accounting principles in the United States. FASB recently issued two guidelines concerning the way nonprofits report their financial performance and account for their fundraising support, because the wide variety of accounting and reporting formats in the nonprofit sector made it difficult for readers to compare organizations.

FASB 116 on Contributions Made and Received governs how and when to account for pledges receivable in addition to donated assets. This standard also addresses noncash contributions such as building and equipment, and contributed services, such as the time of volunteers.

FASB 117 on Financial Statement Display details how nonprofits should account for contributions and net assets (using three categories: unrestricted, temporarily restricted, and permanently restricted). This standard also requires that a statement of cash flows be added to the set of financial statements expected to be maintained by nonprofit organizations. (Other financial statements should include a balance sheet, a statement of activity, and, for voluntary health and welfare organizations, a statement of functional expenses.)

In addition, certain watchdog groups and workplace fundraising organizations have established their own standards for monitoring nonprofit organizations' operations. Organizations such as the Council of Better Business Bureaus and the United Way ask participating nonprofits to collect and submit information beyond what is required for Form 990 by the IRS.

All U.S. nonprofit organizations must be aware of these, and other FASB guidelines. In addition to the issue of legal compliance, preparing budgets in accordance with FASB guidelines will facilitate the filing of reports required by state and federal agencies.

programs and projects more easily. Many new ideas are never developed due to lack of discretionary money for investment at the early stages. In these instances, unrestricted revenues serve as a source of venture capital for new initiatives.

Budgeting in the nonprofit sector is a learned skill, and is not possessed by all in equal measure. Some smaller organizations doing highly valuable work may lack financial expertise. Unrestricted funding enables such an organization to pool its revenues rather than engage in more sophisticated bookkeeping, which may burden a small staff.

Gaps in Government Support
Most nonprofits that receive government support find that those grants and contracts do not sufficiently cover all the related costs of their work. Foundations and corporations have traditionally been relied upon to help "bridge the gap" with unrestricted support not offered by most

---

Determining When an Organization Might Seek General Support

A nonprofit might choose to apply to a foundation for a general support grant when

- Its mission is consistent with the central thrust of the funder's program strategies.

- It is receiving funds for multiple projects cutting across several different program areas within the foundation. In some cases, it may be in the best interests of both the funder and the grantee to consolidate several separate program grants into one general support grant.

- Its work is of ongoing, historic interest to the funder.

- A funder is interested in building and sustaining institutions within its particular field of endeavor.

---

government agencies. The recent decline in unrestricted grants from foundations and corporations, however, increases the challenge these nonprofits face.

Guidelines to Budgeting

A good starting point for creating your budget is to fill out the worksheets that follow this section. Here are some guidelines to help you apply sound business and budgeting principles when you do:

1. *Be concrete and specific in your projections.* Base expense projections on carefully itemized and researched resources, services, and personnel needed for program and operating activities. Base contribution projections on donors' giving histories, if any, as well as your ratings. Break down expense and income categories in as much detail as possible; the more specific you are, the more accurate your projections will be. The following worksheets can help you. For example, all personnel expenses can be calculated using the following formula:

(Title of Staff Position)
$ ___,___$ / month x ____ months x ____ % x ____ positions

"$" denotes the monthly salary allocated to this position; "months" indicates exactly how many months that position will be filled during a given year; and "%" tells whether the position is full-time (100%) half-time (50%), etc. If there is one such position within your organization, you would multiply these figures by 1; for two such staff positions, multiply these figures by 2, and so forth.

No category of expenses or revenue sources should be overlooked. In itemizing telephone costs, for example, make separate projections for local and long-distance calls, as well as for the purchase of phone equipment. If an expense (such as long-distance charges) is expected to vary from month to month, project a monthly unit cost on the basis of averaging out yearly costs over twelve months. Do not, however, take this principle to its extreme by projecting how many pencils you might need to buy each month. Look first at categories of expenses, and then at major subcategories, if they exist. If during the year, you need to conserve funds by decreasing expenses, such detailing will help you identify where you can spend less.

2. *Be conservative in your projections.* In making estimates, err on the high side for expenditures and on the low side for revenues; it's far better to be surprised with unanticipated revenues than with unpaid bills. Many organizations, however, tend to do just the opposite and are forced to learn—if they are able to remain in business—that building slowly and surely is actually the fastest way to succeed.

   For example, project the same net income from a special event as that event generated the previous year, even if you expect to raise more (revenues from the event might increase, but so might your costs, resulting in no greater profit). By erring on the safe side, your organization will develop a track record of realistic budgeting. This will prove to be an enormous asset when reviewing your organization's financial performance with potential funding sources.

3. *Ascribe a dollar value to key volunteer labor* (see the following example). If your organization comprises only volunteers and no one has yet been placed on salary, there are still people devoting long hours to the work normally performed by paid staff members. The value of their work must be estimated and included for two reasons. First, budgets must accurately represent an organization's personnel resources. Second, including the value of your key volunteers' time increases your budget, and prospective funders frequently judge the significance of an organization's efforts by the size of its budget.

   In addition, adding the value of your key volunteers' work to the budget in the "Donated" column acknowledges their importance to your staff, organization, prospective funders, and, most importantly, to them. These volunteers cannot, however, take a tax deduction for time they donate, no matter how valuable it is to an organization. Not all volunteers' work should be valuated and included in the budget, however. Include in your program and organizational operating budgets only those volunteers whose labor is vital to the operation of an individual project, or to the organization as a whole.

Sample Operating Budget for South Valley Community Organizing Project

January 1999 to December 1999

	Requested	Donated	Total
Personnel			
A. Coordinator (2)			
($2,500 x 12 months x 100% x 2)		$60,000*	$60,000
B. Block Captains (5)			
($1,000 x 12 months x 25% x5)		15,000*	15,000
Total Personal Expenses		$75,000	$75,000

*Unsalaried volunteers currently fill these positions. We have ascribed salaries to them on a par with employees at similar organizations with comparable responsibilities.

4. *Ascribe a dollar value to donated non-personnel items as well* (see the next example). The dollar value of donated items such as office space, telephones, furniture, printing, and other in-kind contributions should also be included in an organization's budget. Although donated items don't represent a direct cost to the organization, they do have value because you might have purchased them had they not been donated. Note that it is the organization, sometimes in consultation with experts, that must declare the value of a donated item, not the donor. These items, however, do have significance to those who contributed them: the value your organization has ascribed to the items can be deducted for tax purposes. Listing donated items in your budget conveys your appreciation to donors, and highlights the range of support—beyond cash contributions—your organization is able to attract.

   You can also list in the "Donated" column those expense items that have already been paid for, either by a funder or by your own organization. In either case, annotate the sources of these funds. Should you ever seek a matching or challenge grant, this method of budgeting will enable you to document how precise your record-keeping is, thus giving an indication that you can be depended upon to abide by the terms of your grant agreement.

Sample Operating Budget of Highland County

Teen Hotline, 1999–2000

	Requested	Donated	Total
Non-Personnel Operating Expenses			
A. Office Rent			
($200/month x 12 months)		$2,400*	$2,400
B. Telephone			
Answering Machine		175**	175
Basic Service			
(3 lines x 12 months x 70 = $2,520	2,520		2,520
C. Printing			
5,000 brochures		1,800***	1,800
10, palm cards		600***	600
Total Requested from "X" Corporation	2,520		
Total Donated		4,975	4,975
Total Budget for Non-Personnel Expenses			**$7,495**

* Office space donated by First United Methodist Church
** Answering machine donated by Barney's Hardware Store
*** Printing donated by Highland Savings Bank

5. *Distinguish carefully between organizational budgets and program budgets.* An organizational budget presents the group's entire financial picture—all its expenses and all its revenues. A program budget includes only those expenses and revenues that apply to a specific project. Most groups need both types of budgets. Bookkeeping, fundraising, and public relations are as much a part of delivering programs, services, and events as they are of operations.

   If an organization sends a proposal to a funder for general (unrestricted) support, it submits the overall organizational budget. If, on the other hand, it submits a proposal to fund a particular project (restricted support), it includes a project budget.

6. *Make your proposal budgets realistic.* Don't ask for the moon when preparing budgets for proposals, and don't approach the budgeting process as if you were spending the winnings from a lottery ticket. Remember that potential funders will look for evidence of realistic expense projections and will relate them to the results you hope to produce: Do a project's anticipated benefits justify the expense?

Base salaries for staff positions on those for comparable positions at similar organizations. Contact your local United Way, health and welfare planning organization, or relevant trade organization for information on salary scales. If you cannot pay your staff market salaries, you should know what they are and consider getting closer by giving raises as finances permit. For non-personnel expense items, secure quotes from several vendors and keep your consumer instincts operative as you shop for a fax machine, a computer, or long-distance telephone service. To be sure, your organization need not have an outmoded, inefficient office, but neither should it try to compete with the decor and equipment in the offices of large businesses. Funders deeply appreciate the attention you give to maximizing the impact of the dollars they entrust to you.

7. *Establish minimum internal budgets.* Too often budgets are determined by the amount of money that has been raised to complete a project, rather than by the minimum actually needed to carry out the project with some measurable success. Every organization should strive to establish a minimum budget for its programs, which, if achieved, would enable the organization to accomplish programmatic goals to the satisfaction of its supporters.

Your fundraising budget is your optimal operating budget. It should reflect all the expenses your work would require if you were to secure as much funding as you could reasonably expect to address the problem outlined in your proposal. If you do not secure all the funding outlined in your optimal budget, your funders will certainly understand a modified budget, as long as the program now associated with this budget still seems possible.

This modified budget should represent no less than the minimum budget required to make a difference in the problems your organization is addressing. If, however, you raise less than the minimal operating budget, you should consider abandoning the project and returning its specified funds to the donor. Another option in this situation is to negotiate with the donor to use the funds for another purpose, such as a less costly program. On the other hand, if you succeed in raising more, you might ask the funder for permission to expand the project, or to use the funds for another purpose.

By completing the following worksheets, you will identify the expenditures you need to make to carry out the work of your organization, or your special program.

WORKSHEET A

Organizational Expense Budget

First Year of Operations

Personnel Costs

A. Executive director

    $___ x 12 months x 100% = $_____

    (Note: 100% denotes full-time employment)

B. Program coordinator

    $___ x 12 months x 100% = $_____

C. Administrative assistant

    $___ x 12 months x 100% = $_____

D. Fringe benefits (employee benefits)

Note: Fringe Benefits can either be computed by itemizing all fringe benefits, or by computing a fixed percentage of the total payroll of an organization or of a project

    1. State unemployment insurance

        _____% x $____ (total payroll) = $_____

    2. Worker's compensation ( ) = $_____

    3. FICA/Social Security ( ) = $_____

    4. Health insurance ( ) = $_____

    5. Life insurance ( ) = $_____

    6. Pension ( ) = $_____

    7. Staff training ( ) = $_____

    8. Child care reimbursement ( ) = $_____

E. Outside Contracted Services

    1. Bookkeeper

    $____/ day x ____days/year = $_____

    2. Consultant

    $____/ day x ____ days/year = $_____

Total Personnel Costs for First Year of Operations $_____

Non-Personnel Costs

A. Office space rental

   $____ x 12 months = $_____

B. Utilities (gas, electricity, etc.)

   $ ____ x 12 months = $_____

C. Telephone (monthly service, including long-distance,
      internet access, and on-line charges)

   $ ____ x 12 months = $_____

D. Printing (including newsletters, brochures, annual reports,
      program publications, etc.)

   $ ____ x 12 months = $_____

E. Duplication

   $ ____ x 12 months = $_____

F. Equipment (including rental, leasing and purchasing of
      computers, photocopy machines, etc.)

   $ ____ x 12 months = $_____

G. Office supplies

   $ ____ x 12 months = $_____

H. Postage

   _____% x $____ (total payroll) = $_____

I. Travel (including - trips to attend conferences of _____ and _____, etc.)

J. Office and liability insurance $_____

K. Membership and professional dues $_____

Total Non-Personnel Costs for First Year of Operations $_____

Total Costs for First Year of Operation $_____

WORKSHEET B

Program or Project Expense Budget

First Year of Operations

Personnel Costs

A. Project director

$___ x 12 months x 100% = $_____

(Note: 100% denotes full-time employment)

B. Community organizers (2)

$___ x 12 months x 100% x 2 = $_____

C. Executive director

$___ x 12 months x 20% = $_____

D. Administrative assistant

$___ x 12 months x 30% = $_____

E. Fringe benefits (employee benefits)

1. State unemployment insurance

_____% x $____ (total payroll) = $_____

2. Worker's compensation ( ) = $_____

3. FICA/Social Security ( ) = $_____

4. Health insurance ( ) = $_____

5. Life insurance ( ) = $_____

6. Pension ( ) = $_____

7. Staff training ( ) = $_____

8. Child care reimbursement ( ) = $_____

F. Outside Contracted Services:

1. Bookkeeper

$____/day x ____days/year = $_____

2. Consultant

$____/day x ____ days/year = $_____

Total Personnel Costs for First Year of Operations $_____

Non-Personnel Costs

A. Office space rental

    $____ x 12 months x 25% = $_____

B. Utilities (gas, electricity, etc.)

    $ ____ x 12 months x 25% = $_____

C. Telephone (monthly servicei and internet access,
     including long-distance)

    $ ____ x 12 months x 25% = $_____

D. Printing (including brochures, program reports,
     promotional literature, etc.)

    $ ____ x 12 months x 25% = $_____

E. Photocopying

    $ ____ x 12 months x 25% = $_____

F. Equipment (including rental, leasing and purchasing of
     computers, photocopy machines, fax machines, etc.)

    $ ____ x 12 months x 25% = $_____

G. Office supplies

    $ ____ x 12 months x 25% = $_____

H. Postage

    $ ____ x 12 months x 25% = $_____

I. Travel (includin—trips to attend conferences of ____ and ____, etc.)

    $ ____ x 12 months x 25% = $_____

J. Office and liability insurance $_____

    $ ____ x 12 months x 25% = $_____

K. Membership and professional dues $_____

    $ ____ x 12 months x 25% = $_____

Total Non-Personnel Costs for First Year of Operations $_____

Total Costs for First Year of Operation $_____

    Note that program budget projections are based on a rough estimate that the activities involved in conducting a particular program constitute 25 percent of all the work of the organization during this twelve-month time period. Each group has to make a similar calculation for their own programs and projects.

The next worksheet will help you identify potential sources of the revenue needed for your work, and to project the amount each might give—the income side of budgeting.

WORKSHEET C

Organizational Revenue Budget

Projecting Income for First Year of Operation

Income Sources

A. Individuals

    1. Contributions/memberships $_____

    2. Monthly pledges $_____

    3. Large donor gifts $_____

    4. Special events $_____

    5. Payroll deductions $_____

    6. Direct mail $_____

B. Foundation Grants $_____

C. Businesses and Corporations

    1. Contributions $_____

    2. Grants $_____

D. Government (city, town, county, state, federal)

    1. Grants $_____

    2. Contracts $_____

E. Religious Institutions

    1. Special offerings $_____

    2. Contributions $_____

    3. Grants $_____

F. Earned Income Ventures

    1. Sales of "x" product or service $_____

    2. Miscellaneous program-related income $_____

G. Other Income:

    1. _____ $_____

    2. _____ $_____

Total Income $_____

WORKSHEET D

Budget and Cash Flow Planning Sheet

Income	Jan	Feb	Mar	Apr	May	Jun	Jul	Aug	Sept	Oct	Nov	Dec
(Cash on hand as of first of month)	$	$	$	$	$	$	$	$	$	$	$	$
Individuals												
Foundation Grants												
Businesses and Corporations												
Government												
Other												
Total revenue in hand	$	$	$	$	$	$	$	$	$	$	$	$

Expenses	Jan	Feb	Mar	Apr	May	Jun	Jul	Aug	Sept	Oct	Nov	Dec
Personnel:												
Non-Personnel												
Total Monthly Expenses	$	$	$	$	$	$	$	$	$	$	$	$
Cash on hand as of end of month	$	$	$	$	$	$	$	$	$	$	$	$

Budget Approval

By law, in all nonprofit organizations the board of directors has the ultimate financial responsibility and must determine whether expenditures and fundraising projections for the coming year are realistic before giving their approval. For responsible boards, approving a budget is far more than a routine administrative procedure; the board must agree to make sure that enough money is raised to cover the organization's expenses.

Working together, staff, program directors, and officers of the board will arrive at a final budget draft. This draft should then be sent to board members well before the meeting at which it will be considered, so comments and opinions can be informed. When the budget is sent out, all items must be explained so that board members can understand how the numbers were generated. Including numbers—both budgeted and actual—from previous years can provide a valuable point of reference. Here is a suggested format for such a comparison:

	1999–2000	1998–99		1997–98	
	(Projected)	*(Budgeted)*	*(Actual)*	*Budgeted)*	*(Actual)*
Office supplies					

After the review process, which may take more than one meeting, the board will be ready to vote on the general operating budget for the upcoming fiscal year.

Budget Administration

Approval by the board of an organization's proposed budget is just part of the budgeting process. Because the timing and the amount of actual revenues and expenditures will vary from those projected, constant monitoring is in order.

The board's treasurer plays a key role in monitoring revenues and expenditures (as well as in all aspects of the budgeting process) by working with the executive director or the chief staff financial officer and advising the board. The treasurer may also serve as a counselor to the executive director and a coach to board members who are less familiar with finances. To ensure the detection of any impropriety or error, and to keep total financial responsibility from resting with one person, most organizations divide these duties, including the monitoring function, among several people.

The executive director generally assumes a much more hands-on role, approving expenditures up to a specified amount, supervising payroll, and monitoring income. The director may also delegate an even more detailed role to a comptroller or finance manager. If the organization is large (or fortunate) enough to have an active treasurer, this person can play an important role in preparing financial reports for the board's review, and in monitoring overall financial performance.

Staff members must know how much is budgeted for their area of operations and plan accordingly. Should they find at some point that they cannot remain within budget ceilings, they must request permission from the board to raise the limits on the expenditure category in question, and, optimally, be able to suggest ways of generating the additional amount.

Those who monitor an organization's economics are vital not only to that organization's financial management but also to its overall integrity. According to Leon Haller, author of

Financial Resource Management for Nonprofit Organizations, the executive director or other manager who fills this role must everyday:

- See to it that all financial transactions are recorded

- Control use of the organization's assets

- Assure preparation of accurate financial reports

- Anticipate financial problems

- Comply with state and federal reporting requirements.[1]

In an all-volunteer organization, these daily responsibilities would fall to the treasurer, who would rely on a larger finance committee for help.

Leveraging Resources

Nonprofit corporations, like for-profit corporations, work hard to leverage resources, contain expenses and maximize income. Here are several strategies that may help your organization relieve pressure on its budget.

1. *Exploit opportunities to deliver public services.* Nonprofits that generate healthy earned income, thereby reducing the organization's dependence on contributions, send a positive signal to potential funders. Many local and state governments, especially in urban areas, now contract out to nonprofit organizations the provision of services that have traditionally been the responsibility of government. This phenomenon, often called "privatization," is not without controversy, but the signs are that it will continue to grow. The corporate sector is also beginning to follow this practice. Entrepreneurial nonprofits, especially human service agencies, can explore contract opportunities with local government officials as a means of increasing earned income. Additional benefits include heightened visibility and credibility, establishing a governmental track record, and creating support for general operations. In San Francisco, community boards resolve neighborhood problems with trained volunteer mediators. These local boards now handle and settle more cases than the San Francisco municipal court. Money is saved and community residents gain a sense of civic empowerment.

2. *Barter talents, goods and services with other organizations.* Nonprofit organizations are far from asset-poor. Their staff, board, and volunteers possess talents and experience desired by others. They may also have other goods and services that are in great demand, such as equipment or mailing lists. Nonprofit entrepreneurs can exchange or lend something or someone of value to other organizations.

---

1. Leon Haller, *Financial Resource Management for Nonprofit Organizations* (Englewood Cliffs, NJ: Prentice-Hall, Inc., 1982).

3. *Budget more aggressively, monitor expenses carefully, and bank more wisely.* Nonprofits should work continually to pinpoint all true costs—both direct and in-kind—of its operations to make sure that all true expenses are reflected. In preparing budgets, nonprofits often underestimate such items as staff time, program expenses, indirect costs, and overhead. Additionally, donated labor and services are often underreported or invisible in grant applications. Nonprofit budgeteers must make every effort to identify all real costs, include them in the budget sections of their proposal, and regularly review all cost items to assess where savings can be made. Finally, more nonprofits need to be familiar with bank policies and procedures involving loans and lines of credit.

4. *Collaborate with other institutions.* Although working with other organizations is rarely simple and problem-free, pooling resources can be well worth the effort. Both small and large agencies have much to gain in designing program initiatives that draw on complementary strengths of collaborating organizations. Also, funders increasingly look more favorably on grant requests that are submitted by partnerships and consortia. When AIDS Housing of Washington in Seattle set out to build and run the nation's first skilled-nursing residence designed specifically for people living with AIDS, their founders recruited Virginia Mason Medical Center, a large and prestigious hospital, to operate the facility. Countless examples of other successful collaborations exist.

   Nonprofits can also join forces on a smaller scale, such as co-producing a newsletter, journal or magazine. For example, more than thirty zoos, zoological parks, and societies co-publish *Wildlife Conservation*. Each society adds a members' bulletin insert with information on its own institution.

5. *Negotiate unrestricted and multi-year grants.* The old grantsmanship philosophy—that foundations provide seed funds for projects, which ultimately attract ongoing government support—is no longer realistic in many situations. Additionally, many new program initiatives need longer start-up periods, requiring multi-year support from their funders.

6. *Share services and space with other organizations.* To reduce operating costs and to raise new revenues, nonprofits are moving in with each other and developing creative ways to pool expenses. In Los Angeles, the Mexican American Legal Defense and Educational Fund (MALDEF) is seeking nonprofit subtenants for its renovated historic downtown headquarters. All tenants will be able to reduce expenses by sharing conference and meeting rooms, reception areas, and kitchen facilities. Similarly, in lower Manhattan in New York City, Battery Dance rents out its two dance studios to other dance companies. The resulting income helps underwrite the core budget of the company.

   Despite its best efforts, an organization must sometimes take sterner measures to ensure its survival or the continuity of its mission. The final two strategies address this possibility.

7. *Downscale or discard programs.* There is probably nothing more painful for an executive director and a board of directors to do than to turn away clients in need or to abandon a program. At the same time, pruning some branches of the organizational tree may well help it regain health.

After a year of careful deliberation, the Gay Men's Health Crisis in New York City, the world's largest AIDS service organization, set a cap on new client admissions for the first time in its history: no more than twenty-five new clients would be admitted each week. Their board acted most reluctantly, but in the face of increasing requests for assistance and insufficient financial resources, it was convinced that this type of managed growth would ensure the continuing quality of their services.

It is important for agencies to address the human and personal issues associated with any cutback in services. Unless properly managed, such changes can prove devastating not only to clients, but to the morale of staff, board, and volunteers as well. Every effort must be made to engage members of an organization's immediate and external communities in discussion about the problem, and the organization's steps to remedy it.

8. *Merge with another organization.* If a nonprofit is unable to attract sufficient resources to finance its work, it should consider affiliating with a stronger, kindred organization. Many nonprofits find that strategic planning provides their leadership the opportunity and appropriate context to consider such an option.

In 1987, the country's two leading national disarmament organizations, SANE and the Nuclear Freeze Campaign, merged to create SANE/FREEZE. The thirty-year-old SANE had a respected national presence in Washington, D.C., while the Nuclear Freeze Campaign had an extensive network of more than 1,300 local activist groups. Together they were able to create the most potent grassroots lobbying organization for peace and justice issues in the nation.

Budgeting Forever

Budgeting is not simply an activity to be carried out once a year, or whenever a proposal is being prepared. An organization's budget, like its bylaws, is a working document for the staff and the board's continued use throughout the year. Make sure that actual expenses and receipts are regularly measured against it on at least a monthly basis.

Budgets also provide the standard against which an organization's performance must be measured. If actual expenditures or revenues vary significantly from budget projections, look closely at every aspect of your operations to identify if the variance results from faulty budget projections, inaccurate prospect ratings, sub-par performance in development, or other organizational activities—or all of the above. Once weaknesses have been identified and addressed, an organization can actually become stronger as a result of unexpected financial problems. In this process, as in all others, frank, open discussion among staff and board members can actually turn a challenge into an opportunity to grow.

Tips

- Involve all staff and board members in creating or approving the budget and make the process as transparent as possible. This will create enthusiasm and ownership of the program and will make fundraising easier.

- A budget is as much a management and program planning tool as a financial tool. Vision should drive program creation, and program drives budget creation. A budget is not an end in itself.

- Take the time required to put together a good budget. If you shortchange the process, you will pay—literally and figuratively—later.

Additional Resources

Publications

Accountants for the Public Interest. *What a Difference Nonprofits Make: A Guide to Accounting Procedures.* 3rd ed., rev. Washington, DC: Accountants for the Public Interest, 1995. vi, 76 p.

Summarizes basic principles of nonprofit accounting and key management concerns designed to assist accounting and business professionals who volunteer their time and expertise to the nonprofit sector. Includes sample financial statements and covers special topics such as cash and accrual accounting, nonprofit revenues, capitalizing and depreciating fixed assets, accounting for restricted contributions, common fund types, and inter-fund receivables and payables. Appendices include the qualifications for IRS 501(c)(3) nonprofit status and restrictions on such organizations, other tax-exempt classifications, federal tax and reporting requirements, IRS forms and publications, a sample Form 990 and Schedule A, and a selected bibliography.

Blazek, Jody. *Financial Planning for Nonprofit Organizations.* New York: John Wiley & Sons (Nonprofit Law, Finance, and Management Series), 1996. xix, 275 p.

Provides a step-by-step process through the major areas of financial planning including general administration; the roles and responsibilities of staff, board members, and professional advisors; developing and implementing budgets; asset and resource management; and internal controls to prevent waste and fraud. Includes the National Charities Information Bureau's standards in philanthropy, a bibliography, glossary, and index.

Bremser, Wayne G. *Tracking Special Monies.* Washington, DC: Accountants for the Public
Interest (What a Difference Understanding Makes: Guides to Nonprofit Management Series),
1994. 14 p.

   Discusses the effects of two new accounting standards issued by the Financial Accounting
   Standards Board in June 1993. Covers restricted funds, capital campaigns, fund
   accounting, special events, member dues, and unrelated business income. Shows a
   simulated subsidiary ledger.

Brinckerhoff, Peter C. *Financial Empowerment: More Money for More Mission.* Dillon, CO:
Alpine Guild (The Mission-Based Management Series), 1996. 238 p.

   Written for the senior staff and board members of not-for-profit organizations. Based on
   Brinckerhoff's three core philosophies of not-for-profits: (1) a not-for-profit is a
   mission-based business; (2) no one gives a not-for-profit money—all money is earned; and
   (3) not-for-profit does not mean nonprofit. Chapters cover characteristics and outcomes of
   empowerment, how to estimate cash needs, working with traditional funders, how to
   develop a new business, financial reporting, a review of different financing options,
   budgeting from the bottom up, pricing for empowerment, corporate structures, roles of the
   CEO and the board, a sample empowerment plan, and a summary of key ideas. Includes
   bibliographic references and index.

Dabel, Gregory J. *Saving Money in Nonprofit Organizations: More than 100 Money-Saving
Ideas, Tips, and Strategies for Reducing Expenses without Cutting Your Budget.* San
Francisco: Jossey-Bass Publishers, 1998. xii, 115 p.

   Listing of cost-saving ideas with brief explanations. The methods cover numerous
   categories such as budgeting and tracking of expenses; investing and planning; wise
   purchasing practices; protecting the organization from lawsuits; personnel and benefits
   costs; occupancy and equipment costs.

Dropkin, Murray, and Bill La Touche, *The Budget-Building Book for Nonprofits: A
Step-by-Step Guide for Managers and Boards.* San Francisco: Jossey-Bass Publishers
(Nonprofit and Public Management Series), 1998. xxii, 157 p.

Financial Accounting Standards Board. *Statement of Financial Accounting Standards No.
116: Accounting for Contributions Received and Contributions Made.* Stamford, CT:
Financial Accounting Standards Board (Financial Accounting Series), 1993. 69 p.

Financial Accounting Standards Board. *Statement of Financial Accounting Standards No.
117: Financial Statements of Not-for-Profit Organizations.* Stamford, CT: Financial
Accounting Standards Board (Financial Accounting Series), 1993. 79 p.

Garner, C. William. *Accounting and Budgeting in Public and Nonprofit Organizations: A Manager's Guide.* San Francisco: Jossey-Bass Publishers, 1991. xvii, 252 p.

Provides practical knowledge of interactive accounting and budgeting systems for managers with no formal preparation in the subjects. Chapters cover history of accounting and budgeting; six types of funds typically used in public and nonprofit organizations; the approval, adoption, and allocation subsystems of budgeting; the language of accounting and the various types of accounts; the tracking of financial information; three basic financial statements; the six points of interaction between accounting and budgeting systems; the purpose of adjustments; and the auditing and analysis of financial information. Bibliography. Appendixes include a glossary of common budgeting terms, a list of income sources, definitions of object expense categories (from United Way of America's "UWASIS Chart of Accounts"), and a recommended reading list.

Hankin, Jo Ann, Alan G. Seidner, and John T. Zietlow, *Financial Management for Nonprofit Organizations.* New York: John Wiley & Sons (Nonprofit Law, Finance, and Management Series), 1998. xii, 610 p.

Handbook written for managers with responsibility for financial decision-making in nonprofit organizations. Coverage includes discussion of financial roles and responsibilities; development of a financial plan and financial reports; cash management and banking relations; risk management; investment principles and policies; safeguarding assets; and evaluation.

Herzlinger, Regina E., and Denise Nitterhouse. *Financial Accounting and Managerial Control for Non-Profit Organizations.* Cincinnati: College Division South-Western Publishing Co., 1994. 878 p.

Maddox, David C. *Budgeting for Not-for-Profit Organizations.* New York: John Wiley & Sons, 1999. xvi, 269 p.

A comprehensive treatment of the budgeting process, from basic principles to in-depth analysis and prediction of trends. Follows case studies of four nonprofits to illustrate the budget planning process and management of finances. Some of the issues discussed include the budget cycle, operating and capital budgets, evaluation and analysis, human resources, and cost cutting. The four hypothetical case studies are the University of Okoboji, a Victim Assistance Association, a Community Arts Council, and a Presbyterian church. With glossary, index, and bibliographic references.

Miller, Terry, and Partnership for Democracy Financial Management Program. *Managing for Change: A Common Sense Guide To Evaluating Financial Management Health for Grassroots Organizations.* Washington, DC: Partnership for Democracy, 1992. viii, 137 p.

Provides overview of basic financial management techniques for small organizations with budgets in the range of $50,000 to $200,000. Explains planning, budgeting, cash flow projections, accounting and financial statements, reporting requirements, governance, control and staffing. Discusses how to read and present a financial statement; allocation of costs; and questions concerning accountants and auditors, as well as independent contractors and employees. Provides worksheets for budgeting, board of directors, organization chart, and symptoms of major financial management problems.

Olenick, Arnold J., and Philip R. Olenick. *A Nonprofit Organization Operating Manual: Planning for Survival and Growth.* New York: Foundation Center, 1991. xxiii, 484 p.
    Manual addresses the essential financial and legal aspects of managing a nonprofit organization. Divided into four parts, Part 1 ("Long-Range Considerations") includes chapters which cover each step of the nonprofit incorporation procedure, the limits on political and legislative activity, methods for devising the proper organizational structure, information to include when drafting articles and bylaws, the elements of strategic planning, and the responsibilities of the board and staff. Part 2 ("The Vital Role of Financial Management") contains chapters on the operating budget (including a step-by-step guide to preparing a budget worksheet), program budgeting, cash and capital budgeting, fundraising, income-producing ventures, the "Generally Accepted Accounting Principles" (written for non-accountants), establishing a management information system, and a practical approach to accounting. Part 3 ("Operational Management") covers financial reports and cash management, and Part 4 ("Outside Accountability") discusses required financial reports, grant management, the "IRS Form 990: Return of organization exempt from income tax," and other tax-reporting obligations. Includes figures and tables, illustrations and step-by-step guides, sample forms and annotated bibliography.

Rotondi, Ann M. "Create a Budget that Works for You." *Nonprofit World* 15 (July–August 1997): 46–51.
    Details the making of a budget and provides illustrations.

Shim, Jae K., Joel G. Siegel, and Abrahan J. Simon. *Handbook of Budgeting for Nonprofit Organizations.* Englewood Cliffs, NJ: Prentice Hall, 1996. xvii, 510 p.

Solloway, Richard. "Don't Forget Your Indirect Costs." *Nonprofit World* 14 (September–October 1996): 46–51.
    Discusses the importance of including indirect costs in a nonprofit organization's budget.

Sumariwalla, Russy D., and Wilson C. Levis. *Unified Financial Reporting System for Not-for-Profit Organizations: A Comprehensive Guide To Unifying GAAP, IRS Form 990, and Other Financial Reports Using a Unified Chart of Accounts.* San Francisco: Jossey-Bass Publishers (Nonprofit and Public Management Series), 2000. xxvii, 355 p.
    Utilization of the unified chart of accounts (UCOA) can enhance and streamline the preparation by nonprofits of various required financial reports, which include the 990, GAAP financial statements, reports to United Ways and to grantmakers, and internal reports. Provides the complete UCOA, examples of various forms, a summary of state registation requirements, as well as a history of financial reporting requirements. With bibliographic references and an index.

Section 1 Summary Worksheet

SECTION 1 CHECKLIST:

Getting Your House in Order (See Chapter 1 if you need assistance)
Name of Your Organization:

_____

1. Vision/Mission Statement

   The vision/ mission of this organization is:

   _____

   _____

   _____

   _____

   _____

   _____

   _____

   _____

   _____

2. Structure (See Chapter 2 if you need assistance)

   Our organization has: (check the appropriate boxes)

   a. INCORPORATION
   ❑ filed for incorporation as a not-for-profit corporation with the State
   of _____, and expects to have a response by _____.
   (date)

   ❑ received notice from the State of _____, that its application for
   incorporation has been accepted as of_____.
   (date)

   b. FEDERAL TAX-EXEMPTION
   ❑ filed for exemption from Federal Income Tax with the Internal Revenue
   Service, and expects to have a response by _____.
   (date)

   ❑ received notice from the Internal Revenue Service that it has been
   awarded an exemption from Federal income tax under section 501 (c) (3)
   of the IRS Code as of _____.
   (date)

   c. ADOPTION
   ❑ been adopted as a project of (name) _____ which is incorporated within

The State of _____ and is federally tax-exempt under section 501(c)(3) of the Internal Revenue Code.

d. FISCAL SPONSORSHIP
❑ secured (name of non-profit organization) _____ as a fiscal sponsor of our activities.

e. UNINCORPORATED ASSOCIATION
❑ decided to operate as a unincorporated association.

3. Governance (See Chapter 3 if you need assistance)
   a. We have written a set of bylaws that designates the

   _____

   (board of directors, steering committee, etc.)

   as the prime decision-making body within our organization.

4. Programs (See Chapter 4 if you need assistance)

   a. We are currently conducting the following programs:

      1)

      2)

      3)

      4)

   b. We would like to establish the additional following programs:

      1)

      2)

      3)

      4)

5. Budgets

   a. The total operating budget for our organization for the upcoming year is: $_____.

   b. The estimated budgets for our projected programs for that year are:

Programs	12-Month Budget
1)	$
2)	$
3)	$
4)	$
5)	$

Section 2

THE WORLD OF MONEY

Chapter 6

The Many Sources of Funding and Support

Don't say you don't have enough time. You have exactly the same number of hours per day that were given to Helen Keller, Pasteur, Michelangelo, Mother Teresa, Leonardo da Vinci, Thomas Jefferson, and Albert Einstein.
—H. Jackson Brown

Section 1 of this book provided guidance for start-up nonprofits in establishing themselves, and for established organizations in revisiting nonprofit basics for review and updating. Developing Budgets, the last chapter of Section 1, discusses how an organization projects revenue, and lists potential sources for that revenue. In today's highly competitive world of nonprofit fundraising,

organizations must seek to develop funding from a mix of individual and institutional sources in order to remain viable. Section 2 of this book discusses the multiplicity of traditional—and new—sources available to nonprofits and suggests how they may be approached. All organizations are urged to solicit as many of these sources as is practical and appropriate in order to develop the highly diversified support base that is so vital to an institution's health.

Fortunately, the vast number of individuals and institutions that support nonprofit initiatives around the world attests to the universality of the philanthropic instinct. Individuals extend their support in myriad ways: they make contributions and pledges in response to direct mail requests, phonathons, appeals on the Internet, door-to-door canvassing, and face-to-face solicitations. They give at their offices through workplace solicitation and payroll deductions, and consult their financial advisors to choose planned giving vehicles. Individuals also contribute in their communities by attending special events and purchasing goods and services from nonprofits, ranging from gifts, cards, and theater tickets to school tuition and hospital care.

Institutions that provide both financial and in-kind support to nonprofits include foundations; businesses and corporations; local, state, and federal governments; religious institutions; and labor unions. Additionally, thousands of local and national civic associations, usually nonprofit themselves, extend some kind of aid to charitable and philanthropic undertakings, as do federated fundraising organizations, such as the United Way. The existence around the world of millions of nonprofit organizations—more than one million are registered with the government in the United States alone—attests to the depth and breadth of individual and institutional resources that are committed to supporting their work.

Tapping these resources is the ongoing work of those who raise money for nonprofit organizations. Their work, popularly referred to as "development" by fundraising professionals, encompasses a wide range of activities, only one of which is the actual solicitation of individuals and institutions for contributions. Development work ranges from organizing a street fair to raise several thousand dollars, to meeting with business and social leaders to develop an invitation list for a special event with a $350,000 goal, to undertaking a yearlong planning process for a $10 million capital campaign.

Development also includes such activities as visiting the Foundation Center in New York City, one of its field offices, or its Web site to research foundations whose guidelines and giving history make them candidates for support, as well as designing and writing proposals, solicitation letters, direct mail pieces, and newsletters. Development activities also include meeting with staff members of other nonprofit organizations to seek advice, create joint programs, or review fundraising schedules to avoid conflicts, as well as meeting with board and committee officers and members to develop relationships, discuss work in progress, identify and discuss problems, or review candidates for volunteer leadership positions.

All these activities—and so many more—are undertaken to raise money in the vast, complex, constantly changing, and highly competitive world of nonprofit finance. Enormous though this range is, two fundamental principles of fundraising lie at the center of this enterprise.

The first principle is that successful fundraising requires careful forethought and planning. The second is that no organization should depend so much on a single funding source that the group would be unable to function without it. All planning needs to be guided by this second principle, because an organization that is totally dependent on government grants and contracts, for example, is extremely vulnerable. The group that receives support from foundations, a federated fundraising body, and a pool of individuals *in addition* to government agencies is clearly stronger and more secure. In 1869 the Metropolitan Museum of Art turned solely to New York City's wealthy citizens for support. More than a century later, it still welcomes contributions from a large number of individuals, but it also receives support from the local, state, and federal government, from corporations, and from foundations as well.

Today, diversification of support is vital, and no organization can hope to finance its work successfully from any one source. Even if it does succeed in obtaining that one large, elusive grant, there's no guarantee the grant will be renewed each year, and the organization's future will not be secure. Moreover, funding sources like to see that an organization's funding is diversified, for this shows broad-based agreement that its mission is important and worthy of support.

Where Do Novice and Veteran Fundraisers Begin?

By becoming acquainted with the entire array of available funding sources, fundraisers can select those most appropriate to their own organization. The chapters in this section and the worksheets at the conclusion of each chapter will help you identify which sources may consider supporting your organization. Remember that it is highly unlikely that every source will be interested in your work, and so, with limited fundraising resources, you will need to choose your "best bets." The chapter and worksheets in Section 3 will help you refine your list to include only those sources that might become part of your particular funding "mix." You will then be able to map out your fundraising action plan.

Individuals

All philanthropy can, almost without exception, trace its origins to individuals rather than to governments, businesses, or foundations. The "founding" philanthropists of the United States were individuals such as Benjamin Franklin, whose generosity and vision led to the creation of several of Philadelphia's earliest nonprofit institutions, including the University of Pennsylvania and Pennsylvania Hospital.

During the Middle Ages, Europe's cathedrals were built not only through the largesse of kings, queens, and other nobility, but also through the generosity of tradespeople and artisans. Many members of merchant and guild associations, including bakers, carpenters, weavers, shoemakers, butchers, masons, fishmongers, furriers, and others contributed to the building of the famed cathedral in Chartres, France; their funding underwrote the creation of many of its breathtaking stained glass windows.

Today, individuals are actually the largest source of unrestricted dollars for most nonprofit organizations after the federal government (whose funding is actually provided in large part by individuals through taxes). In the United States, for example, individuals gave nearly $160 billion in 1999 to nonprofit organizations (including bequests), and regularly provide almost 90 percent of all charitable contributions in a given year. Each and every one of us is today's philanthropist. Whether we respond to a direct mail solicitation, attend a special event, or donate construction supplies to build a homeless shelter, it is our combined efforts that make nonprofit endeavors possible.

What distinguishes individual philanthropy today from that of previous eras is its depth and unmatched variety. This is the direct result of nonprofit leaders' creativity in developing their approaches to individuals. The most popular and effective methods of soliciting contributions from individuals today are discussed in Chapters 8 through 14.

Foundations

The purpose of a foundation is to make grants and contributions to other nonprofit organizations. Whereas some foundations are created through the gifts of a single wealthy individual or family, others, such as community foundations and certain public charities, receive their income from a number of different individuals and families. Some corporations also create foundations to distribute a portion of their profits to charitable causes.

Although foundations date back more than a thousand years in Turkey, modern foundations, relatively recent arrivals on the philanthropic scene, can trace their origins to the late nineteenth and early twentieth centuries, when industrialists such as John D. Rockefeller and Andrew Carnegie in the United States, and J.R. Tata in India, established foundations to distribute portions of their huge fortunes for charitable purposes.

There are currently more than fifty thousand foundations in the United States, ranging from small, unstaffed, local foundations to endowed international ones with professional staffs. Although American foundations have impressive assets, their collective annual grantmaking may reach approximately 10 percent of all United States charitable giving in any given year. Consequently, nonprofits cannot look to foundations to supply the majority of their contributed income on an ongoing basis.

During the 1980s and 1990s, there was an enormous proliferation of nonendowed grantmaking institutions—legally defined as "public charities"—which derive their income from a large number of individuals. Examples include community foundations; dozens of women's funds around the country that support grassroots women's groups; the Paul Robeson Fund, which funds social issue media; and the Funding Exchange Network, which makes grants to social change initiatives.

Other countries have also seen a rapid increase in the number of these funds. InterPares, in Ottawa, Canada, funds economic development projects in developing countries with the money it raises in Canada. MamaCash, with headquarters in the Netherlands, funds an impressive array of community-organizing women's projects around the world. Community foundations in Antigua, Mexico City, Mumbai (India), Warsaw, and other places are adapting this first world tradition with some exciting results.

As a result of government cutbacks in their support of social programs in many countries made during the 1980s and 1990s, foundations are now receiving a greater volume of requests than ever before. Since their grantmaking budgets do not usually increase significantly from year to year, their ability to respond to new inquiries is limited. The result is that more and more foundations are looking for ways to increase the impact of their dollars. Some make challenge, or matching, grants that have to be matched by other sources. Not only do such grants leverage foundations' ability to make their dollars go further, but they also stimulate grantees' fundraising efforts. Other foundations endeavor to increase a group's fundraising capability by making grants to support direct mail efforts, create income-producing Web sites, or hire consultants. Chapter 15 offers more information on how foundations operate and the best ways to approach them for support.

Businesses and Corporations

From the neighborhood mom-and-pop store to the giant multinational corporation, the business sector provides support for nonprofit organizations around the world. Local merchants have probably always played a role in enhancing the quality of life in their communities, but corporations are relative newcomers to the philanthropic scene.

Corporate giving in the United States started in the late 1800s, when the railroads began their long association with the Young Men's Christian Association (YMCA). As the railroads expanded westward, the need arose for inexpensive, temporary housing for their employees. To meet that need, the railroad companies helped build "railroad YMCAs." Hence, from its very beginning, commerce found that it could serve its own interests through charitable activities.

What distinguishes corporate philanthropy is the diversity of ways that businesses assist nonprofits, apart from cash grants and contributions. Companies, especially large ones, have vast human and material resources that they can make available to groups. A neighborhood store can place a canister next to its cash register for contributions, put flyers and posters in its window, and sponsor a special event. One day of every month, Wild Oats Natural Food Stores (and other chains) donate 5 percent of their receipts to a different community group. This is rarely less than $2,000 in the urban settings where Wild Oats operates. Corporations can donate materials, office equipment, and products; provide free quality printing of newsletters, ad books, annual reports, raffle tickets, and other promotional materials; and serve as a source of volunteers. They can directly promote nonprofit activities through joint promotions. As long as there is mutual interest, businesses and nonprofits can work together in boundless ways.

Corporate giving in the United States totaled $11.02 billion in 1999.[1] Although U.S. corporate giving has more than kept pace with the rate of inflation every year during the 1990s, corporate giving as a percentage of pre-tax profits has declined slightly since its high point in 1986 to 1.3 percent in 1999. Much corporate and business giving is hard to track, however, as it often takes the form of in-kind donations such as computers and software, office furniture, paper, and printing.

Like foundations, corporations are experiencing an increased volume of requests. As a result, nonprofits are well advised to solicit noncash support from business, and to develop creative partnerships that benefit both parties. Chapter 16 provides further insights into corporate philanthropy, and suggests how nonprofits should approach business for support.

---

1. Ann E. Kaplan, ed., *Giving USA: The Annual Report on Philanthropy for the Year 1999* (New York: American Association of Fund-Raising Counsel, 2000).

Government

Although government has assumed greater responsibility for promoting social welfare since the nineteenth century, many would argue that it has regressed in the last twenty years. The discussion regarding the government's role is the same now as it was in the late 1800s: who should care for the disadvantaged? Should it be part of a government's mandate, or is this function best accomplished by turning it over to private charity? Many of today's civic institutions, such as fire departments and libraries, were previously operated by nonprofit associations rather than by a governmental body; some continue to be. In many cases, nonprofits have been the trailblazers for later government involvement. Even a program as well known as the U.S. Peace Corps took its philosophy from such nonprofit precursors as Operation Crossroads Africa, which continues to send American and Canadian college students to African countries each summer to work on development projects.

In the late 1970s and 1980s, local, state and federal governments were well-entrenched partners with nonprofit organizations in protecting and promoting the well-being of the citizenry. That alliance has undergone deep challenges and changes ever since the Reagan and Thatcher administrations attempted to shift some of this responsibility away from the federal government. In the United States, beginning with the passage of the Gramm-Rudman-Hollings Act in 1986 and continuing with the dismantling of welfare and other entitlements under the Clinton administration, the role of government continues to be questioned and debated. In the meantime, nonprofits are increasingly called upon to provide more services to greater numbers of individuals, services that had previously been supplied, or underwritten, by the government.

However, despite these reductions in federal, state, and local support, all levels of government are expected to continue providing funds to the nonprofit sector in the areas of social services, health, housing, education, employment, and the arts and humanities, to name a few. (It is common for governmental units actually to "contract" for services with nonprofit entities. A contract involves a much more clearly defined relationship between two parties than does a grant.) It is hard to calculate the total of annual financial support that government provides to nonprofits through grants and contracts. Experts estimate that the various government bodies in the United States provide more than $170 billion in grants and contracts.

As governments shift their funding priorities, no other segment of nonprofit financing is expected to undergo as much change in the near future. Pressure from conservatives to reduce social spending will continue to wreak havoc on the established framework for governmental financing of human services, which reached its peak in the 1970s. However, whatever realignment occurs between federal, state, and local units of government in the future, it appears that government's preeminent role in financing nonprofit providers of human services will remain intact. Chapter 17 offers information on government support and outlines how nonprofits can identify and approach government agencies at the local, state, and national levels.

Religious Institutions

Organized religion has been the vehicle for transmitting charitable traditions from one generation to the next, and for reminding believers that charity and philanthropy are moral imperatives.

Close to 50 percent of the charitable dollars donated each year by individuals in the United States is given to religious bodies and their related institutions and agencies.

It is difficult to measure how much financial support religious institutions provide to other nonprofits, but the amount is significant. For example, the Campaign for Human Development of the United States Catholic Conference grants more than $12 million every year to social change and economic development projects. Religious bodies, from the local parish to the national governing body, provide a range of resources extending beyond the financial, including office and meeting space, volunteers, and advocacy support, among others.

Of course, giving is not the province of any one particular religion; its spirit is common to all and is expressed in many different ways. Some religious groups prefer to establish their own nonprofit organizations, while others choose to make grants to other nonprofit entities. Others may actually undertake both roles and become direct service providers as well as grantmakers.

At a time when the federal government is drastically cutting back and devolving its social welfare expenditures, funding from religious sources is becoming more visible and appreciated for its depth and consistency. Chapter 18 explores the world of religious philanthropy and provides suggestions on how to seek your share.

Labor Unions

Labor unions are rarely sources of significant cash contributions, but their support of nonprofits—by providing volunteers, advice, political contacts, facilities, and services—is on the rise. Unions have become keener to establish relationships with local nonprofit organizations to help break down their isolation and strengthen their community ties in order to reach more potential members. This is good news for nonprofits, and the time is now ripe for them to develop mutually beneficial partnerships with labor unions.

Developing ties with nonprofits is only one aspect of U.S. labor unions' intense efforts to reverse the sharp decline in membership that began in the mid-1950s. At that time, some 35 percent of all workers in the United States were union members, but by the mid-1990s, union membership had fallen to 14 percent of the U.S. workforce. With the election of John J. Sweeney to the presidency of the AFL-CIO in 1995, however, a campaign was launched to increase union membership; working with nonprofits was one of the strategies developed toward this end.

Labor's support of nonprofit organizations has a clear agenda: allocate resources to support its own goal of increasing union membership. If your organization can raise and enhance the visibility of a union, or improve its workers' quality of life through the services you provide in your community, it may well be a candidate for developing a mutually beneficial relationship with a union. Chapter 19 discusses how unions support the work of nonprofits, what they expect in return, and how your organization might develop a relationship that advances your common goals.

Federated Fundraising Organizations

Federated fundraising organizations, such the United Way of America, are nonprofits organized along geographic, constituency, or issue lines for the purpose of raising funds from the general public and distributing them to a variety of designated nonprofits. Federated organizations generally organize annual fundraising campaigns in the workplace to solicit contributions from employees in the form of payroll deductions at regular intervals. Paying out their contributions over 52 weeks enables individuals to make larger gifts than they could if they wrote a single check; this is the reason behind much of federated fundraising's success.

In communities across the United States, nonprofits have discovered that they can maximize their fundraising potential by forming a fundraising coalition. Close to two hundred such coalitions now raise money to support many areas of nonprofit concern, among them issues of gender and racial discrimination, housing, health care, the arts, neighborhood development, and the environment. Examples include Earth Share, which raises money for national and international environmental organizations; Children's Charities of America, which funds teaching, feeding, and protection programs for children in the United States and abroad; and the National Black United Fund, which promotes organizations working for the advancement of the African-American community.

The amount of money raised by federated fundraising organizations shows that theirs is a very successful method. The United Way, for example, reports that its 1,400 autonomous locals across the United States received pledges of more than $3.77 billion in 1999. According to the National Committee for Responsive Philanthropy, "alternative" funds raised more than $700 million in 1996, and are expected to raise more than $1 billion per year. (In this context, "alternative" is used primarily to distinguish these funds from the United Way as well as to indicate these funds attempt to address the root causes of social needs.) In coming years, more nonprofits are expected to knock on the doors of their local United Ways to get access to those funds, while others will unite to create new fundraising federations in their communities. Chapter 20 discusses federated fundraising organizations and outlines procedures for seeking their support.

Associations of Individuals

People with like-minded interests often work together for a common goal by creating associations; today, more than forty thousand such groups operate in the United States alone. Additionally, there are countless numbers of grassroots self-help groups.

While the prime motivating force behind such efforts may not necessarily be philanthropic, it is quite common for associations to embrace some charitable or civic activity as part of their mandate. They may choose to administer such activities themselves, or work in partnership with other nonprofit organizations. The Junior League is an example of an association that does both. Service clubs such as the Lions, Rotary, or Soroptomists often organize special events to benefit local charities.

Associations can be a prime source of volunteers for nonprofits and can also serve as partners in advocacy programs. Some groups, such as the League of Women Voters, have been active in issues like voter registration and international affairs for many years. The key for a nonprofit hoping to tap this resource is to identify which associations have similar concerns and might be willing to work together. As competition for financial support increases, nonprofit organizations can improve their success rate by demonstrating the support of associations in their communities. Chapter 21 presents the world of associations in greater detail and describes how nonprofits can seek their support.

Summary

Sound fundraising involves reviewing all potential revenue sources and targeting those whose interests and giving histories indicate a possible match with a particular nonprofit. While your search for funding sources will begin by compiling a lengthy list, your time and energy are limited; refine the list through research to determine which sources are the best to tap. Once you have selected the mix of revenue sources that best suits your work, you will be able to develop a fundraising strategy and plan to guide you.

The chapters in this section detail the range of financial resources available to nonprofits, help you select the most appropriate ones to approach, and outline the actual solicitation process. Complete the worksheets at the end of each chapter. Then proceed confidently to Section 3, which will advise you how to develop a fundraising plan suited to the mix of funding partners you have chosen.

Tips

- If you want to create a stable, healthy organization—regardless of size or location—you must secure funds from a diverse array of sources. A wide and varied base of support decreases a nonprofit's vulnerability and communicates to other potential funders that your organization's work is widely valued and deserving of their support.

- To help determine your organization's ideal funding mix, research the mix of organizations that have similar purposes and are comparable to yours in size, location, and longevity. While individuals account for the bulk of charitable giving in some countries, your research may reveal that organizations similar to yours do not receive the bulk of their revenues from them. The equation will differ for each type of nonprofit, and even among nonprofits with similar missions.

- Remember that the many sources of funding are not discrete entities; working with one will often lead to another, and still another. An individual donor who becomes interested in your organization's success may have ties to a foundation or be involved in the charitable activities of the corporation where he or she works. In the same way, volunteers provided by an association or labor union may become personally interested in your work and expand their involvement.

PART A

APPROACHING INDIVIDUALS FOR SUPPORT

Chapter 7

Giving from Individuals: An Overview

Years ago, my mother taught me that there are three kinds of people in this world. One kind of person goes through life and leaves nothing behind. Not even their name. Another kind of person does bad things to people. And another kind of person leaves life just a little bit better than they found it. How could I let my mother down?
                                                        —Nelson Mandela

Rooted in the religious and cultural traditions of societies the world over, the inclination of individuals to give cash and material goods has made them the largest source of contributions to nonprofits. It is the support of individuals that enables organizations to be born, and provides the

substance and credibility they will often need to secure funding from foundations, corporations, and other institutions.

The following chapters in this part of the book—Approaching Individuals for Support—discuss the seven most important ways of soliciting gifts from individuals: special events, direct mail, telephoning, face-to-face solicitation, planned giving programs, using the Internet, and earned and venture initiatives.

The Magnitude of Individual Giving

Giving USA's 2000 annual report concludes that individuals give the most charitable dollars year in and year out: $159.32 billion to U.S. nonprofit organizations in 1999—84 percent of all charitable gifts made that year. In Canada, the figure was approximately 80 percent. In 1995, Independent Sector ("a national leadership forum working to encourage giving, volunteering, not-for-profit initiative, and citizen action") reported that approximately 70 percent of all Americans made a charitable contribution during the previous year; in the same year, eight out of ten Canadians gave almost Can$15 billion. In the Netherlands, a country where one of the world's highest tax rates sharply reduces disposable income, nine out of every ten people still made charitable contributions.

Equally impressive—and surprising—is the data on individual donors' income. While "Lords and Ladies Bountiful" still exist, the wealthy do not give the most. In fact, 1994 estimates suggest that individuals with household incomes below $60,000 made 82.6 percent of all individual gifts that year. Households with incomes of less than $10,000 gave away an average of 4 percent of their income, whereas families whose income exceeded $100,000 gave an average of 3.4 percent.[1]

Canadian statistics tell a similar story. Households with average incomes exceeding Can$110,000 donated 2.9 percent of their income; households with an average income of $13,000 donated 4.6 percent. Jim Stanford, an economist with the Canadian Autoworkers, notes, "A similar trend is visible across provinces. No province gives more generously than hard-hit Saskatchewan, where donations from the average household were 40 percent higher than in Ontario, where personal incomes are the highest in Canada."

The actual amount of money individuals give away is in fact much greater than these figures indicate. Millions of dollars are given away in cash every year to door-to-door solicitors; to church, mosque, and synagogue collections; to volunteer firefighters collecting money at busy intersections; and to veteran's groups selling paper flowers to workers on their lunch breaks. And if charitable intent could be measured, the numbers would rise even higher; significant amounts are given away in quarters and dollar bills to homeless people in the street, and by family members to their less well-off relatives.

In the last ten years, however, there has been a precipitous decline in the number of people making contributions in the United States and Canada. In 1987, when the first edition of this

---

1. Virginia A. Hodgkinson and Murray S. Weitzman, eds., *Giving and Volunteering in the United States* (Washington, D.C.: Independent Sector, 1994).

book was published, a Gallup poll commissioned by Independent Sector, the National Society of Fund Raising Executives, and the 501(c)(3) Group showed that 86 percent of all Americans made charitable contributions. Eight years later, Virginia Hodgkinson, then vice president for research at the Independent Sector, reported that four million fewer households had made donations in 1994 than in 1993. And according to journalist Andre Picard, writing for *The Star*, "Canadians give less to charity today than they did in 1984, and the number of people making donations has fallen steadily since 1990." It is not yet clear if this is a worldwide trend, but it is certainly one that U.S. and Canadian nonprofits must monitor.

Hodgkinson attributed much of this decrease to organizations' overemphasis on soliciting "mega gifts," and to the publicity such gifts create. She reasoned that mega gifts have made smaller donors feel insignificant and have catalyzed the decline in the number of people being asked. Her survey further reported that only 60 percent of Americans were asked for money in 1995—17 percent fewer than were asked in 1994. The silver lining in this news, however, is that 78 percent of the (mostly younger) people who had never been solicited responded positively, as compared to 70 percent of the population as a whole.

What emerges from these statistics is the fact that individuals are still the driving force in philanthropy, whatever the size or frequency of their gifts. They are the source, year in and year out, of 80 to 90 percent of the charitable dollars given. Individuals make contributions to nonprofit organizations in a number of ways.

- They give cash to door-to-door canvassers soliciting on behalf of the local volunteer fire department, a public interest campaign, health charity, or the like.

- They attend movie premieres, theater parties, dances, dinners, and other special fundraising events.

- They respond to letters (direct mail appeals) and telephone calls (phonathons) that reach them at their homes.

- They give large gifts when asked personally by someone from an organization that has earned their trust.

- They write their favorite organizations into their wills, designate them as recipients of their property after their death, and participate in other forms of planned giving.

- They purchase second-hand or homemade clothing and household items at thrift shops, bazaars, tag sales, garage sales, or auctions, and they purchase greeting cards, calendars, cookies, and other products sold by nonprofits. (These methods are discussed further in Chapter 8, Special Events, and in Chapter 14, Earned and Venture Income.)

- They give via the Internet by responding to appeals sent by e-mail and by joining organizations whose Web sites they've visited.

- They give their time by volunteering. While not strictly a cash gift, volunteering benefits an organization in many ways.

This list of the ways individuals contribute suggests an overall fundraising strategy that applies to almost all nonprofits, and raises the question, "How should I approach the many and diverse individuals who may support my organization?"

The base of most organizations' support is their membership—the large number of donors who make relatively modest contributions each year, usually to an annual fund appeal. Almost every individual whose first gift to an organization is less than $250 becomes a prospect for the annual fund campaign. The annual fund campaign is an essential element, perhaps *the* essential element, in an organization's development plan because of its ability to expand the donor base and identify prospects for larger and planned gifts—this, in addition to generating contributions. The campaign can be accomplished by direct mail, personal contact, a phonathon, or a combination of all these methods. Fundraisers would do well to concentrate on building this base of support instead of hoping for an immense gift from one individual that would solve an organization's financial problems forever, or theorizing that one dollar from every member of a community would do the same.

The Ladder of Effective Communication

Face-to-face conversation

small group discussion

telephone conversation

handwritten letter

word processed letter

e-mail

fax

large group discussion

video

mass-produced letter

"list serve" e-mail

brochure/pamphlet

news item

advertisement

Message 1: Always use the highest rung you can when asking for money.

Message 2: Don't count on publicity to raise money.

Message 3: Don't expect a big response when a board member simply writes to his corporate friends.

Source: Harvard Business Review. An exhibit from "What You Need to Know about Fund Raising," by Fisher Howe (March/April 1985). Amended by Fisher Howe and Michael Seltzer (March 1999).

Organizations often set up gift clubs to induce individuals to "graduate" from making modest yearly contributions to giving more, thereby becoming members of a President's Circle or, in the case of a symphony orchestra, a Conductor's Club. In return for making larger annual gifts ($1,000, $2,500, or $5,000, for example), club members are invited to exclusive events, acknowledged in an organization's printed materials, and generally made to feel "special."

Some club members, and others, may become so committed to your organization that they become prospects for a major gift. After they have been carefully cultivated and researched, they can be asked in person for a substantial contribution or pledge to support a specific program, to memorialize someone by making a "naming gift," or to provide the general, unrestricted operating support that is the financial lifeblood of an organization.

The essence of this strategy is to build a broad base of support and then identify individuals to build relationships with so that they become increasingly active in the affairs of the organization, make larger gifts, and, hopefully, involve their friends and institutional contacts in giving money.

What Induces People To Contribute?

There is no one simple answer; people's charitable giving patterns are as varied as their shopping habits. What is clear, however, is that people derive both emotional and material benefits from supporting the work of nonprofit organizations. While pure altruism may well be a good part of what motivates individuals' charitable actions, common sense suggests there is more. Individuals can, and do, receive many benefits as a result of making a contribution, including recognition, a sense of belonging and of being appreciated, personal satisfaction, increased self-esteem, and any material benefits a recipient organization might offer, such as gifts, subscriptions, newsletters, and opportunities to attend special events.

Let's examine why individuals are moved to become philanthropists. As we do, remember that the struggling low-income family that manages to give a can of food in a food drive is moved by the same philanthropic impulse as a George Soros, or other well-known, generous people of means.

Values and Benefits

Individuals are primarily motivated by their own value systems, which are, in turn, shaped by their life experiences. If a person has encountered discrimination as a result of race, gender, sexual orientation, ethnicity, or class, he or she knows too well the personal costs of bigotry, and may be moved to help make life easier for others who face similar situations. If someone has grown up in a poor neighborhood that offered few opportunities for exposure to knowledge, yet became enriched because a library was close by, that person will probably never forget its value. Such an experience is precisely what moved Andrew Carnegie to contribute millions to the founding of libraries throughout the English-speaking world in the 1800s. Similarly, if someone experiences the loss or disability of a loved one resulting from a specific disease, he or she may become motivated to support organizations that work to reduce the incidence of that particular affliction.

Not surprisingly, these same experiences, values, and beliefs are frequently what move the founders of organizations to create them. Many organizations devoted to discovering cures for debilitating and fatal diseases were founded by individuals who suffered from the disease. The creation of the March of Dimes in 1938 by a polio survivor, President Franklin D. Roosevelt, epitomizes this point. To launch the National Foundation for Infantile Paralysis (as the March of Dimes was originally called), Roosevelt assembled a group of wealthy men nicknamed the Silver Spoon Club to raise money. Their efforts met with only limited success, so Roosevelt's wife, Eleanor, tried a different approach. She issued a nationwide call for women of all backgrounds to march through the streets of America collecting dimes for the Foundation. This effort was extremely successful financially and gave enormous visibility to the work. The organization became known by its fundraising strategy—the March of Dimes—and eventually changed its name to just that.

Sense of Community

In times past, residents of smaller communities derived a strong sense of identity and belonging from their daily interaction with family and neighbors. Although this is still the case in many towns and villages throughout the world, experiencing a sense of belonging in crowded urban centers or sprawling suburbs now comes less easily, and frequently must be manufactured. In these settings, the natural yearning to belong may be satisfied by voluntary association with any one of countless organizations ranging from block clubs, tenant coalitions, co-ops, and social groups to adult education programs and self-help efforts. Participating in activities that speak out on such issues as the equality of women, protection of civil liberties, and saving the whales is another way for like-minded people to find each other. Similarly, working on behalf of the local symphony or ballet can bring together people who share a passion for the arts.

Sense of Personal Worth

Self-esteem may well be the foundation of happiness, yet contemporary life tends to deprive people of that precious commodity. Most societies value wealth, youth, beauty, and power but few members can acquire and/or hold onto these things. The vast majority won't attain or retain them and usually cannot resist feeling somehow inferior. In addition, the typical workplace does not necessarily reinforce individuals' sense of worth but, rather, may erode it through tedium and the pervasive message that everyone is dispensable. Participation in the activities of nonprofit organizations can nurture people's sense of self-worth by providing the recognition, satisfaction, and sense of making a difference often not found in the workplace.

There are also those who enjoy material success as a result of their work but still feel somewhat inadequate, unappreciated, or alone. Such individuals might well offer their services and resources as a volunteer, board member, or donor, in the hope that recognition and validation may be more forthcoming in the nonprofit environment.

Posterity

Few of us can afford to have a building named for us in recognition of our contribution. Nonetheless, the same desire to make a personal and lasting stamp on the future that inspires a millionaire to endow a wing of a hospital resides within us all. Just as parents often see their children as extensions of themselves, so too can individuals claim a stake in the future by contributing time, money, or both to the causes and organizations that have touched their lives most deeply. This desire to leave a mark has undoubtedly inspired many of the individuals who, together, bequeathed a total of over $15 billion to nonprofit organizations in 1999 in the United States alone.

Sheer Fun and Pleasure

For many people, donating, volunteering, and attending fundraising events such as gala movie premieres, theater parties, and walkathons is out-and-out fun. If they weren't fun, these events would long ago have ceased to attract the large numbers of people they do each year.

Feeling Good

How many times have you seen someone smile—or have you smiled—with satisfaction after giving some coins to the Santa Claus outside a department store at Christmas? No doubt moved by religious and cultural traditions to behavior that is almost reflexive, millions make this small gesture every year—and feel better as a result.

Affirming values and beliefs, developing feelings of belonging and personal worth, contributing to posterity, having fun, and feeling good—with so many possible benefits, it is no mystery that so many people participate in philanthropic activities each year. Fundraisers would do well to remember that nonprofits have, in a sense, as much to give as the potential donor. Armed with this knowledge, fundraisers can raise significantly more money by considering donors' needs to be as important as the organization's. In this regard, as in all others, preparation is the key. By researching a prospect's aspirations, interests, personality, giving patterns, and so on, a fundraiser can increase the chances of success by making a solicitation designed to benefit both parties. The importance of this perspective was recently underlined for me when a fundraiser shared the reaction of a wealthy prospect she had solicited. The donor-to-be said that it was an honor and great personal compliment to be asked.

Can Your Organization Raise Money from Individuals?

In Chapter 6 we suggested that nonprofits be guided in determining their funding mix by researching the mix developed by comparable organizations. If your own research indicates that groups similar to yours have successfully solicited contributions from individuals, it is likely that you too will develop a revenue stream from that source.

Profile of Three Donors

Sarah Silber: Growing Up Giving

From the time she was born, Sarah Silber received small gifts of money on her birthday and Hanukkah. When she was nine, her parents deposited this money in a special "gift" account and explained to her the meaning of the account's interest and balance figures. When Sarah was 16, her grandmother encouraged her to begin contributing some of her savings (then $3,200) and her time to projects that interested her and the two struck a deal: for every hour Sarah volunteered and for every dollar she gave of her own money, her grandmother would contribute a dollar to Sarah's "Giving Fund" for future use.

Sarah began keeping articles, brochures, and fliers about issues and groups that interested her, eventually noticing that most of the information she had collected was about dolphins and abused children. She realized that one way she could do something to help in these areas was to give money to projects that excited her.

To help her decide which groups to support, Sarah went to the library and researched the organizations mentioned in her collection of materials. There, she found that three organizations on her list that rehabilitated injured dolphins were mentioned in a book on environmental nonprofits. She also learned about the Environmental Support Center in Washington, D.C. and wrote for more ideas. Based on her research, Sarah began making donations and now, at age 23, continues researching organizations and making contributions.[2]

John Gage: Living and Giving Simply

A former monk, 50-year-old John Gage left the Jesuit order ten years ago but still keeps his vow of simplicity. He feels strongly that America is caught up in over-consumption and is troubled that most people do not see or feel the effects of what he considers to be global greed. Although he lives on less than $8,000 a year, John gives away $480 annually (6 percent of his income). He still focuses his giving on the goal of "restoring right relationship between peoples and the planet" that informed the giving practices of his Jesuit order.[3]

This process is made much easier, of course, if the organization can enlist the support of a well-known person. Fundraising for HIV and AIDS groups was immeasurably helped, for instance, when people such as Elizabeth Taylor, Elton John, and Arthur Ashe became involved as spokespersons and supporters of people living with HIV/AIDS. Efforts to ban land mines took a quantum leap forward with the support of Princess Diana, and raised even more money after her tragic and untimely death. Although many, if not most, organizations cannot attract such high-profile people, especially in their founding stages, they can adapt and apply this principle by identifying local opinion leaders and soliciting their help.

Often a fundraising effort takes time to gather momentum, but once under way raises money very quickly. The Cathedral of Christ the Savior in Moscow has been raising money since the

---

Gilbert Rivera: "I'm a big believer in giving back."

Gilbert Rivera did not think twice before making his $10,000 gift to the American Red Cross's relief efforts for victims of Hurricane Georges. Mr. Rivera, who was born in Puerto Rico and is a co-owner of a multimillion dollar roofing and waterproofing business in the Bedford-Stuyvesant section of Brooklyn, says, "Almost all my community and my customers are Hispanic, and I've got a little money now, so I said, 'Whatever you need, I'll give it.'"

For Mr. Rivera, 41, charitable giving is a habit. Since setting up his business 18 years ago, he has sponsored Little League teams, raised money for Hispanic scholarships and sent neighborhood children to summer camps. This is not the first disaster relief or hurricane relief fund to receive a donation from Mr. Rivera. And the amounts he donates have been substantial: from $5,000 to the Williamsburg Little League to more than $100,000 to refurbish the Roman Catholic Church he attends.[4]

---

2. Tracy Gary and Melissa Kohner, *Inspired Philanthropy: Creating a Giving Plan* (Berkeley, CA: Chardon Press, 1998).

3. Ibid.

4. Fernandez, Sandy M. "Hispanics Erase Myths with Money." *New York Times* (18 November 1998): sec. G, p.16.

1980s using a number of grassroots strategies and working primarily with its Orthodox believers. In the late 1990s, the fundraising effort suddenly took off when the mayor of Moscow realized the importance of the cathedral to the morale of all Muscovites—and the impact on tourism another beautifully restored site could create. Three years after the mayor became involved, enough money had been raised to virtually finish the restoration.

Again, few organizations can attract the support of a country's leading political figure, but all can work with dedication and purpose, thereby creating the momentum that somehow attracts people, resources, and opportunities to its work.

That momentum will largely be created by the people who make the actual solicitations. Who are they? The CEO, executive director, or founder of an organization is in an excellent position to solicit contributions from selected individuals of means if he or she has developed a personal relationship with those individuals. Members and officers of advisory boards and the board of directors who have agreed to fundraise on behalf of an organization should be counted on to raise significant funds from friends and contacts. Strive to involve current donors as solicitors; they already have a demonstrated stake in the organization that empowers them to ask others, and more and more contributors want to expand their support beyond writing a check to an organization once a year. Their involvement in the fundraising process—or other activities—will deepen their commitment, satisfaction, and level of support. Remember that the work of identifying individuals who may become involved is ongoing and should be a top priority.

Identifying Your Own Individual Support Base

Tom Boyd, a trainer and consultant to nonprofits based in New York City, offers a very useful tool for identifying an organization's potential support base: the "concentric circles" model. Assemble the members of your organization's core group and ask them to come up with a list of constituencies that might be willing to support the organization if approached. One way to identify them is by asking group members the following question: Which constituencies are—or could be—the most committed to our organization's vision? Participants should list categories of individuals, and then specific individuals. Let everyone in your group contribute suggestions before you stop, then organize their responses. Take a compass, and on a piece of poster-size paper or a blackboard draw one large circle and then two circles within that circle, all emanating from the same point (see the worksheet at the end of this chapter).

The First Circle

The first circle, the bull's-eye, contains the individuals with the greatest stake or interest in the success of your undertaking. Who are they? First, those whom your activities most directly benefit; they will best understand its value. If you are running a day-care center, you know that all the parents using your facility are likely to make contributions. What about the children's grandparents? Don't they also appreciate that their grandchildren are receiving quality care when their own son or daughter is at work? Individuals in these groups are good candidates for the first circle of contributors to your day-care center. Not everyone will be able to make large donations, but we are not talking about the size of gifts yet. Simply start by listing your own constituents, whoever they may be.

Are there other candidates for the first circle? Well, yes—we forgot ourselves. How can we ask our friends to contribute to something that we don't already give to? Add the members of your board of directors, your volunteers, and even your staff. Again, the amount of expected contributions is not important yet, but the principle is.

Those who are selected for the first circle can be defined as your *internal constituency*: they are really the insiders of your organization, each with a direct stake in the success of your effort.

The Second Circle

In making choices for the second circle, select constituencies already known to these insiders. A new theater group, for example, realized that the personal friends of all the actors, directors, and others involved in the venture were likely supporters. They collected the holiday mailing lists of the members of their organizing committee and each member then wrote a personal note on each appeal letter. This approach was so successful that they raised $15,000! Begin to place in the second circle individuals and constituencies who are kindred souls. Ask yourselves, "Do we know anyone who may develop an interest in our work?"

The Third Circle

Once your group has finished choosing candidates for your second circle, turn to groups of individuals with whom you have no existing or prior personal contact but who you presume would be responsive. Let's call these people your prospective supporters; place them in the third circle. For example, when Mothers Against Drunk Driving (MADD) first formed in Fair Oaks, California, the founders knew that they could appeal not only to mothers who had lost a child in an alcohol-related accident in their own community, but to mothers throughout the country who had experienced or could experience a similar loss.

If you are establishing a center to help new mothers raise their infants, you might add to your third circle local pediatricians, nurses, social workers, family counselors, and others whose professional lives bear on your work. The third circle will help you make generalizations about the types of individuals who might be receptive to your cause. If you find a significant number of pediatricians on your list, you may want to target all the pediatricians in your community as prospects. Continue to ask, "What other categories of people might respond to a request for contributions?" This is a good opportunity to brainstorm; consider all possibilities, even if at first they seem remote.

Finally, ask yourselves which individuals or categories of individuals that have not yet surfaced through this exercise might respond to a request. Again, using the day-care center as a model, how about senior citizens, or even single people who enjoy children? Clearly, these two groups are not the likeliest prospects, nor are they particularly easy to identify, but still they are prospects.

Developing a Fundraising Strategy

Once you have completed the concentric circles exercise, your next task is to develop strategies for cultivating the interest, involvement, and financial support of the individuals you've identified. The strategies will be different for each constituency, and will be based on a number of factors, including an individual's interest, inclination to give, and financial means; the degree of personal contact the organization has, or can establish, with that individual; and the organization's own visibility, track record, and resources.

The next seven chapters discuss seven vehicles for approaching individuals for support: special events, direct mail solicitation, telephoning, face-to-face solicitation, planned giving programs, using the Internet, and earned and venture income initiatives. As you read about these fundraising vehicles in detail, be aware of the myriad ways individuals can become involved with an organization; soliciting an individual for a contribution should be seen as only one step in the larger process of involving that person in the life of an organization. Following is an outline of the strategy many organizations use for developing individuals' involvement and support. As you follow each step, keep in mind the individual's personal interests and reasons for involvement. The more personal contact an organization has with an individual, the further each step will take both.

Circles 1 and 2

1. Individual is identified by member of core group, board, or by friend of the organization.

2. Potential for involvement and financial support is discussed and a solicitation strategy created, including designating a person to carry out the strategy.

3. Individual is cultivated by personal contact, by mail, or by invitation to attend a meeting, special event, or program.

4. According to degree of interest shown, person is then invited to volunteer, to attend another gathering, to receive more information, or is solicited.

5. Solicitation is made, as appropriate, in person or by mail; or person volunteers or has other contact with organization and is then solicited.

6. If gift is received, donor becomes prospect for annual fund, and, as indicated by size of gift and interest demonstrated, a candidate for additional volunteer opportunities, including committee membership.

7. Donors of moderate interest and gifts are cultivated through invitations to events, informational mailings, etc., and solicited for annual fund contributions as well as for support of special projects.

8. Donors of larger gifts who do not wish further involvement are also cultivated through invitations and mailings and become candidates for annual fund requests and face-to-face solicitations for contributions, pledges, and planned giving.

9. Larger donors wishing to become more involved may become prospects for face-to-face solicitations for substantial gifts and pledges, planned giving, and membership on the board or board and advisory committees.

Circle 3

1. Individuals are identified through their inclusion in relevant constituencies or on purchased or exchanged mailing lists.

2. They are asked to support the organization by a direct mail solicitation.

3. For those who respond, cultivation begins by starting with step 3, above.

Case Study

Seniors with Power United for Rights (SPUR), New Orleans, Louisiana

SPUR is a community organizing effort of and for low-income seniors. Its constituency has little money and limited access to people who do. They discovered, however, that these facts do not necessarily prevent a group from raising money. They educated themselves on the principles of fundraising by watching a series of videotapes obtained by the Headwaters Fund of Minneapolis, Minnesota, in which Kim Klein conducts fundraising training sessions. John Graham, then the development director, said, "I think I have seen those tapes so much I could do your hand motions with that magic marker in my sleep."

By identifying diverse sources of funding and using as many ways as possible to ask people for money, they were able to increase individual giving from $11,500 to $20,000 in less than a year. They did this using three fundraising strategies: a special event, a membership campaign, and the sale of publications. They also decided to use their annual convention as a fundraising event as well as a time to educate themselves and plan for the next year. As a result, attendance increased 30 percent over the previous year, and profit increased from $432 to $5, 512! Methods for raising this money included: selling tables of ten to an organization in exchange for reserved seating and group recognition; securing corporate sponsorship of tables for seniors unable to pay the $7 ticket price; engaging Secretary Bobby Jindal of the Louisiana Department of Health and Hospitals to speak about the expansion of home and community based care for seniors. This strategy created much free publicity and strong ticket sales.

Their second fundraising source was membership dues. For years, the organization paid no attention to the number of new members needed to grow and to replace those who had dropped out. They were losing ground until 1997, when a strong membership drive brought in 81 new individual members, and 8 new organizational memberships at $100 each. Finally, they published their first ever "Silver Services Directory," which was distributed to 25,000 seniors in the greater New Orleans area. Although conceptualized primarily as a service to seniors, SPUR decided to try to make the directory at least break even by offering advertising space to small businesses. Board members solicited ads from friends, colleagues, places where they shopped, and vendors that they used. The $5,224 they generated in advertising revenue allowed them to publish the directory, and created a $800 surplus to be used for programs.

—Kim Klein (Special thanks to John Graham and SPUR.)

Tips

- When listing prospective contributors, don't omit people because you think they won't make a gift. Never say no for someone else; you may lose a contribution and deprive the person of an opportunity to make a difference.

- Remember that you never know where your next board member or major donor may come from. Again, make sure your lists are inclusive, and that you speak with as many people as possible to identify the greatest possible number of prospective donors.

- Whatever the prevailing trends in giving or the current direction of the economy, people will make contributions. These factors will affect overall giving to some extent, but people who say, "It's impossible to raise money today," or, "People won't give for that kind of thing, especially with business so bad,"—or anything similar—can pretty much be ignored. People give, and will continue to give, no matter what.

Worksheet

Approaching Individuals for Support

Getting Your House in Order (See Chapter 1 if you need assistance)
Name of Your Organization:

_____

1. Building on Individual Support to Date

    a. Have any individuals ever supported your work in the past?
       ❑ yes   ❑ no

    b. If yes, how many? _____

    c. What characteristics and interests do these individuals share?
    Comments:

    _____
    _____
    _____

    d. What is your sense of what they valued in your organization's work?
    Comments:

    _____
    _____
    _____

    e. How did you approach them for financial support in the past?

    ❑ Face-to-face solicitation
    ❑ Planned giving
    ❑ Direct mail
    ❑ Earned or venture income projects
    ❑ Special events
    ❑ Other

2. Targeting Your Prospective Individual Supporters

    Complete the accompanying "concentric circles" chart to target your own individual prospects. Remember that you should fill in the circles in the following manner:

    First Circle—your most likely contributors (your internal constituency: members of the board of directors, clients, current donors and members, staff, volunteers, etc.).

    Second Circle—other individuals you know who have a direct stake in the success of your efforts (friends, colleagues, acquaintances).

Third Circle—prospective supporters who are new to you; other individuals and categories of individuals who conceivably would respond positively to a request from your organization. Pay particular attention here to unusual possibilities that may not have occurred to you initially.

3. Making the Match (For the previously identified constituencies, complete the following exercises (use your own blank paper):

   a. Write whatever thoughts immediately come to mind about why individual X or X constituency would be interested in supporting your work.

   b. Come up with one or two sentences relating your work to the interests of the individuals you are approaching.

4. Assessing Potential Individual Support

   On the basis of what you have determined, how would you rank your chances of securing support from individuals?

   ❏ Very Good
   ❏ Possible
   ❏ Unlikely

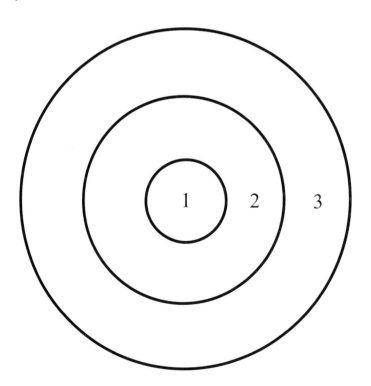

Additional Resources

Publications

Albo, Amy. "The Benefactor 100: The Most Generous Among Us: An Exclusive Ranking Based on Total Donations." *Worth* 8 (April 1999): 110–122.
  Ranks America's most generous individuals based on lifetime donations.

Alexander, Lamar. "The Civic Entrepreneur: Fixing American Giving." *National Civic Review* 86 (Winter 1997): 287–90.
  Presents the major conclusions of the National Commission on Philanthropy and Civic Renewal, chaired by Mr. Alexander.

Avery, Laura J., and John L. Gliha. "Computer-Assisted Prospect Management and Research." *New Directions for Philanthropic Fundraising* 11 (Spring 1996): 85–103.
  Discusses the use of computers to access data on prospects and how managers can take advantage of this technology to efficiently support a research operation.

Barth, Steve. "Finding the Needle in the Haystack." *Currents* 24 (June 1998): 32–38.
  Explains how to use computer screening and database analysis to find hidden major gift prospects.

Blanton, Carol. "Building the Upgrade Ladder." *Grassroots Fundraising Journal* 13 (June 1994): 9–11.
  Describes how to use the donor pyramid, the graphic depiction of an organization's overall donor base, in an annual campaign, to create a strategy for moving donors up to higher levels of giving.

Burlingame, Dwight F., ed. *Critical Issues in Fund Raising.* New York: John Wiley & Sons (NSFRE/Wiley Fund Development series), 1997. xxii, 266 p.
  Researchers and practitioners address the major issues in the current state of fundraising, including demographics and donor motivation, strategies, marketing, ethics, regulation and law, cost-effectiveness and financial management. Also provides perspective on fundraising in Western Europe. Indexed.

Carson, Emmett D. *A Hand Up: Black Philanthropy and Self-Help in America.* Washington, DC: Joint Center for Political and Economic Studies, 1993. 66 p.
  Provides an historical overview of black philanthropy, providing key developments, events and institutions, in order to both challenge the perception of black dependency in the past, and to enhance the effectiveness of black philanthropic initiatives in the future. Chronicles religious, benevolent and fraternal institutions, and self-help, from the Colonial era to the present. Concludes that black philanthropy is a rich tapestry that is still being woven today. With bibliography.

Costa, Nick G. "Reading the Minds of Major Donors." *Advancing Philanthropy* 5 (Summer 1997): 39–41.
    Examines seven donor profiles that were identified in a recent study, with an eye at helping fundraising professionals better understand their donors' needs.

Council on Foundations. *Cultures of Caring: Philanthropy in Diverse American Communities.* Washington, DC: Council on Foundations, 1999. 305 p.
    Four separate studies of philanthropy in diverse communities: African Americans, Asian Americans, Latinos, and Native Americans. Researchers interviewed 15-25 donors from each group who gave at least $10,000 each year, other individuals with knowledge about the giving of each group, and studied the literature on motivations for giving, among other techniques. Contents include: "Native-American Philanthropy: Expanding Social Participation and Self-Determination" by Mindy L. Berry; "Reflections on Endowment Building in the African-American Community" by Mary-Frances Winters; "Latino Philanthropy: Expanding U.S. Models of Giving and Civic Participation" by Henry A. J. Ramos; "Asian-American Philanthropy: Expanding Circles of Participation" by Jessica Chao. Also included is a study by Diana S. Newman, "The Role of Community Foundations in Establishing and Growing Endowment Funds by and for Diverse Ethnic Communities," and an introduction by Joanne Scanlan.

Cox, Michael W., and Richard Alm. "The Accidental Philanthropist." *Philanthropy* 12 (November–December 1998): 10–12.
    Discusses the ways the wealthy contribute to society.

Dundjerski, Marina, and Holly Hall (contributor). "Tapping the Wealth of Hispanics: Charities May Be Overlooking a Golden Opportunity To Reach a Rapidly Growing Group of Donors." *Chronicle of Philanthropy* 9 (31 October 1996): 33–36.

Evenson, Robert A. "Asking and Giving: A Relationship of Trust and Promise." *501(c)(3) Monthly Letter* 17 (August 1997): 9–10.
    Emphasizes the importance of a trusting relationship between organization and donor.

Fernandez, Sandy M. "Hispanics Erase Myths with Money." *New York Times,* (18 November 1998): sec. G, p. 16.
    Hispanics are becoming more prominent as philanthropists and nonprofit board members. Much of the recent charitable giving for disaster relief in Latin America has come from Hispanic donors. Though there is little data about Hispanics as philanthropists, Independent Sector has determined that per-household giving increased 55 percent between 1987 and 1995.

Ferree, G. Donald, Jr., John W. Barry, and Bruno V. Manno. *The National Survey on Philanthropy & Civic Renewal 1997-1998: Americans on Giving, Volunteering, and Strengthening Community Institutions.* Washington, DC: National Commission on Philanthropy and Civic Renewal, 1998. 96 p.

> Presents the findings of the National Survey on Philanthropy and Civic Renewal conducted by researchers at the University of Connecticut, who interviewed more than one thousand people by telephone. Additional surveys were conducted with representatives from racial/ethnic and other minority groups, and with wealthy persons. The survey questions are reprinted in Appendix 1.

Gary, Tracy, and Melissa Kohner. *Inspired Philanthropy: Creating a Giving Plan: A Workbook.* Berkeley, CA: Chardon Press, 1998. xvii, 103 p.

> Authors offer to individual givers their insights and suggestions for creating a program of focused, effective, and meaningful philanthropy. Presented in a step-by-step workbook format with numerous exercises. Appendices include a Donor Bill of Rights, sample letters, site visit questions, and resource lists. Indexed.

Glynn, Jeannette E. *Who Knows Who: Networking Through Corporate Boards.* 10th ed. Berkeley, CA: Who Knows Who Publishers, 1998. iii, 837 p.

> Traces the networks among the most influential people in America, the boards of directors of 1,066 companies and 112 foundations.

Gower, April. "The Donor Profile." *Fund Raising Management* 29 (December 1998): 22–23.

> Briefly discusses the importance of accurately matching the attributes of current and potential individual donors through the use of donor profiles.

Greene, Stephen G. "Ranks of Volunteers Swell to a Record but Donations Dip, Survey Finds." *Chronicle of Philanthropy* 11 (21 October 1999): 16, 18.

> Describes the findings of a recent survey conducted by Independent Sector, which indicates that Americans are volunteering in record numbers, although their charitable giving has slightly decreased. Sidebars provide statistics on household giving to charity, 1987-1998; giving and volunteering in America, by sex, race, age, income, marital status, employment status, and education level; comparisons of people who itemize tax deductions and those who do not; and public views on charitable organizations.

Halfpenny, Peter. "Economic and Sociological Theories of Individual Charitable Giving: Complementary or Contradictory?" *Voluntas* 10 (September 1999): 197–215.

> Compares microeconomic and sociological analytical frameworks for examining individual giving to charitable organizations. Considers rational-action theories and the qualitative tradition in the discussion of sociological analysis of charitable giving. With bibliographic references.

Hall, Holly. "Forging Ties to the Money Pros." *Chronicle of Philanthropy* 9 (7 August 1997): 1, 12, 14.

To offset government cuts and to tap into the $10 trillion that baby boomers are expected to inherit, charities are experimenting with various means of enabling financial professionals to actively encourage their clients to consider philanthropy. Whereas some charities have already achieved impressive results using such techniques, among the many barriers to their widespread use are: the reluctance of most financial professionals to bring up the issue for fear of losing business, their lack of proficiency in the complexities of planned giving, and their discomfort in discussing value-laden matters with their clients.

Hartsook, Robert F. "15 Fund-Raising Opportunities with the Millionaire Next Door." *Fund Raising Management* 29 (November 1998): 16–17, 27.

Hartsook, Robert F. "77 Reasons Why People Give." *Fund Raising Management* 29 (December 1998): 18–19.

Hartsook, Robert F. "Practice Your ABC's: Cultivating Donors Equals Receiving Gifts." *Fund Raising Management* 27 (November 1996): 14–16.

Kaplan, Ann E. *Giving USA: The Annual Report on Philanthropy for the Year 1999.* 45th ed. New York: American Association of Fund-Raising Counsel, 2000.

Statistical analysis of charitable giving contributions, distribution, donors, recipients, sources of philanthropy, and areas of philanthropic opportunity in 1999. Sources analyzed include individuals, bequests, foundations, and corporations. Areas of philanthropic opportunity reviewed are religion; education; health; human services; arts, culture, and humanities; public/society benefit; environment/wildlife; and international affairs. A separate section reviews giving worldwide. Contains numerous charts, lists, and statistical tables. Among the statistical tables are total giving, uses of contributions, the growth of contributions, and inflation-adjusted giving. Includes a resource guide and a table of the National Taxonomy of Exempt Entities.

Keirouz, Kathryn S., Robert T. Grimm, Jr., and Richard Steinberg. "The Philanthropic Giving Index: A New Indicator of the Climate for Raising Funds." *Nonprofit and Voluntary Sector Quarterly* 28 (December 1999): 491–99.

The Philanthropic Giving Index, developed by the Indiana University Center on Philanthropy, measures the "climate for philanthropic gifts and fund-raising in the United States." Through semi-annual surveys of development professionals, the resulting index measures anticipated donor behavior, and unlike other studies, looks forward rather than to the past. The PGI also assesses the future success of different types of fundraising techniques, and cross-references those with broad nonprofit fields of activity. The initial survey was distributed in February 1998; potential uses of the PGI are given. With bibliographic references.

Klein, Kim. "Donors Are Not Water Faucets." *Grassroots Fundraising Journal* 15 (June 1996): 6–8.
>   Recommends that fundraisers think of donors as individuals rather than part of a homogeneous group. Analyzes three typical incidents where donors were mistreated.

Klein, Kim. "Profile of a Major Donor: From Family Business to Family Gift." *Grassroots Fundraising Journal* 15 (August 1996): 13–14.

Lane, Carole A. Edited by Helen Burwell and Owen B. Davies. *Naked in Cyberspace: How To Find Personal Information Online.* Somerville, MA: Pemberton Press Books, 1997. xxvii, 513 p.

Lipman, Harvy. "Rise in Giving Tracks Growth in Americans' Income, IRS Data Shows." *Chronicle of Philanthropy* 12 (10 August 2000): 12.

Maclean, Charles B., and Jana B. Greenberger. *Philanthropy Now: Seeding the New Generation of Entrepreneurial Givers.* Executive briefing. Portland, OR: Charles B. Maclean, 1998.

McAllister, Pamela. *The Charity's Guide to Charitable Contributions.* Seattle: Conlee-Gibbs Publishing, 1998. vii, 138 p.
>   Focuses on common situations that most fundraisers encounter, and answers questions that may be asked by potential donors. Several chapters explain IRS rules; additional chapters deal with particular types of contributions and fundraising methods; one chapter is devoted to planned giving; the final chapter discusses state laws. Appendices include reprints of IRS Publication 526 (Charitable Contributions); Publication 561 (Determining the Value of Donated Property); Form 8283 (Noncash Charitable Contributions); and Form 8282 (Donee Information Return). Indexed.

McDonald, Kathleen. "Uncommon Knowledge: Peer Screening Can Fill the Holes in Your Prospect Records." *Currents* 23 (July–August 1997): 30–36.
>   The peer-screening process involves identifying potential donors among friends, classmates, neighbors, etc., as a first step toward prospect identification. Various stages and aspects of the screening process are discussed, such as preliminary planning, selection of participants, compiling of lists, running of sessions, and recording of data.

Miller, Judith. "A Hands-On Generation Transforms the Landscape of Philanthropy." *New York Times* (9 December 1997), sec. G, p. 8.
>   Discusses the interest of many "baby boom generation" philanthropists to become directly involved in the charities they support.

Newman, Raquel H. "Transforming Donors into Strategic Funders." *Fund Raising Management* 29 (March 1998): 31, 42.

> Examines differences between donors and strategic funders. Donors are defined as a person who writes checks to organizations of their choice, whereas strategic funders seek a relationship with an organization and are willing to take risks with their philanthropy.

Ostrower, Francie. *Why the Wealthy Give: The Culture of Elite Philanthropy.* Princeton, N.J.: Princeton University Press, 1995. xii, 190 p.

> An in-depth analysis of philanthropy by the elite based on a series of personal interviews with ninety-nine wealthy donors from the New York City area. Shows that the wealthy take philanthropy and adapt it into an entire way of life that serves as a vehicle for the social and cultural life of their class. Discovers divergent patterns of giving that reflect alternative sources of donor identity, such as religion, ethnicity, and gender. Includes index, notes on methodology, and bibliographic references.

Prince, Russ Alan, and Karen Maru File. *The Seven Faces of Philanthopy: A New Approach to Cultivating Major Donors.* San Francisco: Jossey-Bass Publishers (Nonprofit Sector Series), 1994. xvi, 219 p.

> Identifies and profiles seven types of major donors and offers detailed strategies on how fundraisers can approach them. The seven types—the communitarian, the devout, the investor, the socialite, the altruist, the repayer, and the dynast—emerged from a comprehensive study of wealthy donors. Explains why each type requires a different approach, and how fundraisers can identify and understand the motivations of each type of donor. Includes research methodology, references, and index.

Robinson, Andy. "Finding Major Donors by Mail." *Grassroots Fundraising Journal* 16 (June 1997): 6–8.

Waltman Associates. *National Connections: Directory of Corporate & Nonprofit Boards.* Minneapolis, MN: Waltman Associates, 1999. CD-ROM.

> Database listing individuals and their board affiliations with corporations, major nonprofits, foundations, and civic organizations. Searchable fields include name, board affiliation, type of board, city and state, and occupation.

Williams, Karla A. *Donor Focused Strategies for Annual Giving.* Frederick, MD: Aspen Publishers (Aspen's Fund Raising Series for the 21st Century), 1997. xi, 287 p.

> A step-by-step approach to establishing an annual giving program is presented, including guidance on how to create a hospitable environment, build a constituent base, set giving objectives, and design an infrastructure.

Williams, Roger M. "Where the Money Comes From." *Foundation News & Commentary* 40 (March-April 1999): 54–59.

> Examines trends in giving from individuals such as Oseola McCarty, a washer woman who gave $100,000 to the University of Southern Mississippi for scholarships.

Zimmerman, Robert, and Ann W. Lehman. "Researching Funding Sources on the Web." *Grassroots Fundraising Journal* 17 (August 1998): 12–13.

Internet

Association of Professional Researchers for Advancement (http://www.aprahome.org)

> Maintained by the professional organization for fundraisers who conduct research on potential donors, this Web site provides answers to questions frequently asked about fundraising research and links to Web sites that contain information about private and corporate grantmakers, as well as individual donors.

Annual Giving

> An on-line forum to discuss annual giving, maintained by T. Greg Prince, Associate Director for Annual Giving at the University of North Carolina at Chapel Hill. To subscribe, send an e-mail message to listserv@unc.edu that states in the body of the message "subscribe annfund Your Name". Leave the subject blank, and do not include e-mail addresses in the body of the message.

Online Directories

Anywho (http://www.anywho.com)

> 90-million-plus consumer listings in the United States. Includes reverse directory, direct phone connections, partial name searching, Web addresses, fax and toll-free numbers.

Infospace (http://www.infospace.com)

> Database of 100 million listings in the U.S., 200 million in Europe; 16 million American yellow-page listings. Includes reverse directory, fax numbers, e-mail, partial name searches.

Lycos (http://www.lycos.com)

> More than 90 million phone listings in the United States. Uses Whowhere. Includes e-mail addresses; allows searches by partial spelling.

Switchboard (www.switchboard.com)

> 120 million listings. Uses Info USA. Includes e-mail addresses and a knock-knock button, which is used to find out whether listed people want to receive mail from searchers.

Chapter 8

Special Events

If social capital serves as the basis of trust in democracy, special events
provide the instrument. —Michael Seltzer

After face-to-face solicitation, special event fundraising—people coming together for a common purpose and generating revenue—is the oldest form of fundraising under the sun. In the frontier days of the United States, there was barn raising—people donating their time to help neighbors build barns without spending money. During the Great Depression, people held special fundraising events called rent parties.

Some of the most successful fundraising events blend local culture and traditions of mutual responsibility into an event that benefits an organization. Among the most striking examples are

the events that have been held by immigrant groups in the United States since the beginning of the twentieth century to raise funds for newly arrived fellow countrymen. Without doubt, the American model of fundraising is a useful example, and provides a wealth of information on every aspect of nonprofit and NGO operations to groups around the world. However, fundraisers should look to their own communities and develop events that tap into local cultural, civic, and religious traditions.

Whatever its inspiration or cause may be, a successful special event will create publicity, attract new members, educate the public, reinforce and strengthen an organization's relationships with its donors, volunteers, and members, and make money. These events are indeed special, for they bring people together to have fun, to celebrate, to be moved by others, and to mingle with their peers in an inviting and hospitable setting. The warm, even treasured, memories that special events can create for participants can turn "friendraising" into fundraising, and prompt favorable responses when attendees are later asked for help.

Of all the forms of fundraising, special events are the most frequently used by organizations ranging from local volunteer fire departments to metropolitan arts centers. The array of these events is staggering: garage sales, craft fairs, bowlathons, house tours, auctions, running races, bake sales, awards banquets, concerts, dinners, cocktail parties, wine and cheese receptions, street bazaars, and so on, ad infinitum.

Proceeds from special event fundraising can range from a few hundred dollars from events like raffles to hundreds of thousands of dollars from auctions, when items to bid on may include dresses that belonged to the late Princess Diana, or an evening with Barbra Streisand. A major charity ball in a large city might net $250,000 to $1,000,000, while a garage sale in a suburban community might raise $2,000. Some events may aim to generate good publicity and cultivate donors who might make substantial gifts in the future. As in other forms of fundraising, the timing, advance planning, and inherent appeal of an event will determine the extent of its success.

What Are the Advantages of Raising Money through Special Events?

Successful special events can produce a wide range of immediate and long-term benefits.

1. *Raise money.* Well-planned efforts are almost guaranteed to generate immediate revenue. Successful annual events generate income that can be estimated with some certainty, thus helping an organization project revenues more accurately. Lessons learned from past events will also help contain costs and identify ticket pricing that works, thus increasing net income.

2. *Cultivate current and prospective donors.* Special events can be effective tools for organizations with well-developed cultivation strategies to increase giving from contributors, and win support from new sources—now and later.

3. *Expand your donor base.* Individuals who are not familiar with an organization's work might attend an event because of their desire to meet people, as a way of

fulfilling a social or business obligation, or out of an interest in the event itself. Successful special events almost invariably result in new donors of both gifts and time.

4. *Increase your visibility.* Your organization's visibility can be increased, and its mission and programs become more widely known, as a result of the media coverage that a special event can generate—from a large invitation mailing, and from the general buzz an upcoming event often creates.

5. *Align and energize your staff, leadership, and volunteers.* A well-planned event can bring together all of an organization's constituencies through their work toward an immediate, shared goal: creating a successful occasion.

6. *Update your mailing list.* Sending invitations for a special event by first class mail is a good way to confirm addresses, as the U.S. Post Office will return any such mail that cannot be delivered.

7. *Meet an immediate need.* A smaller organization might fill an unexpected need with funds generated by a quickly organized event. A larger nonprofit might place a telephone call or two and solve the problem. Other groups, however, might not yet have special friends of means to call—but they could generate both cash and good feelings by holding a garage or bake sale with minimal or no investment.

What Are the Disadvantages of Raising Money through Special Events?

Most potential disadvantages of special events concern an organization's human and financial resources.

1. *Extensive work is required.* Planning, implementing, and following up a successful event require substantial human resources; just how much depends on the event's size and scope. Large-scale events such as walkathons, testimonial dinners, and benefit concerts require that many people, staff and volunteers, work for months if not longer. Organizations may desire the many benefits afforded by a successful event, but lack the people power to organize one.

2. *Initial outlay of funds.* Like direct mail campaigns, most special events need an outlay of funds before any income is realized; hotels almost always require a deposit to reserve a ballroom for a dinner, and theaters also require deposits for a benefit. Other expenses, such as designing, printing, and mailing invitations; holding kickoff parties; generating publicity; and hiring additional staff, may increase the up-front investment to a level that strains an organization's financial resources. Working under the pressure of cash flow problems is stressful and distracting.

3. *Possibility of failure.* Young organizations, especially those staging an untried event, must consider the possibility of failure. Before undertaking a special event, a

Case Study

A Birthday Present for AIWA

The Asian Immigrant Women Advocates (AIWA), a group based in Oakland, California, that organizes garment and computer assembly workers, needed to raise $1,500 quickly. A long-time donor offered to use her forty-fourth birthday party as the occasion to raise this money. She told the people she invited to bring a check made out to AIWA instead of a present. More than forty people came to the birthday party, and AIWA walked away with checks totaling $1,770 at no cost to them since the hostess paid for everything. Everyone had a good time and afterwards two people confessed to their hostess that this was the kind of party they liked best. Why? Because it saved them from having to agonize over what to buy!

nonprofit should consider its ability to weather the expense, the loss of momentum, the adverse impact on staff and volunteer morale, and the potential harm to its reputation caused by a less-than-successful event.

Deciding Whether To Launch a Special Event

The decision to schedule a special event is best made during the planning process, either as part of a one-year plan, or a three- to five-year long-range plan. At that time, the organization will allocate its projected human and financial resources among its programs according to priorities established by leadership. (It may be useful at this point to review the program planning section of Chapter 5, Developing Budgets.) If the resources are available to undertake a fundraising event; if the organization's constituency can be counted on to support it; and if the projected return in terms of both fundraising and "friendraising" justify committing those resources, the planners may be inclined to schedule the event. Two other important factors, however, should be considered before the decision is made.

- The event must fit into the flow of the organization's other development activities. For instance, is there enough time before and after to prepare, deliver, and follow up the event? This question should be considered from both the staff's point of view (can they devote enough time to it?) as well as from that of the organization's constituency (will they feel they're being asked too often?).

- An event requires sustained effort by an organization's board, staff, and volunteers; all must be totally committed to the event in order to maintain the necessary enthusiasm and attention. If there are problems within an organization, or too many demands on everyone's time, it may be difficult to elicit this commitment. At the same time, organizing an event offers an excellent opportunity to involve new potential leaders.

If, for instance, staff members and volunteers are ready and willing but board members are overcommitted, an event leadership committee might be recruited to undertake such responsibilities as making a financial contribution to the event; committing to bring a specified number of friends and associates to the event; helping create publicity for the event; soliciting donations of goods and services; and so on. In the process, members of this ad hoc committee might deepen their commitment to the organization, expand its donor base, and demonstrate leadership qualities that the organization might tap in the future.

Piggyback If You Can't Go It Alone

If your organization decides it can't create an event from the ground up, all is not lost! No doubt you already engage in certain activities or events that are perfect vehicles for special event fundraising. Fundraising can frequently be "piggybacked" onto, or incorporated into, a programmatic activity without much additional work. If, for example, your organization holds an annual meeting to brief members and constituents on its work, you could easily add an auction, raffle, or program ad book (a publication in which individuals and businesses are advertised for a fee). Because you'll already be doing the publicity for the annual membership meeting, you're sure to have an audience; the fundraising element can easily be added.

Faith communities, clubs, and service organizations often rely on this piggyback method. A church's annual bazaar with booths, food, and rides offers an ideal opportunity to set up a table and raffle something of value, such as a car, at no additional expense.

Another way to piggyback fundraising is organize an activity as part of a larger public event (such as a street fair or carnival) sponsored by another organization that assumes responsibility for promotion and advertising. If you decide to do this, decide which products (baked goods,

---

Piggybacking and Lifestyle Fundraising

In planning special events, organizations need to anticipate and assess the types of social, cultural, and civic activities that current and prospective constituents already engage in. This concept of "lifestyle fundraising" is well illustrated by the work of Lambda Legal Defense and Education Fund. Jack Schlegel, a dedicated volunteer, loved going to the theater and the ballet. To help fund the organization, he started buying group rate discount tickets to dance and theater performances, recruited friends to give wine and cheese receptions at their homes before or after performances, and sold tickets to the organization's supporters at a higher price. By adding a fundraising component to activities that the group's constituents already engaged in, the organization has been raising money and involving new people for more than twelve years.

sandwiches, beverages, bumper stickers, buttons, posters) or activities (carnival games) would most appeal to the event's market. Did you attend the last street fair in your community? What were most of the booths selling? Food? Antiques? Thrift sale items? Just as a small business can hawk its wares at an annual town celebration, so can your organization. Familiarize yourself with the consumer instincts of your potential customers, and when the day arrives, you'll be ready for business.

The principles behind our two piggyback examples are straightforward: choose a winning idea or product, and an occasion that already attracts a crowd. If you feel this may be appropriate for your organization, make a list of the events and programs that you normally organize in a given year, as well as a list of major public events in your community. Then review each list for piggyback fundraising opportunities.

There is another important element in this fundraising technique. Not only does it publicize your work, but it also shows donors and prospects that you are reaching out to the community at large, that your support is broad-based, and that you are not relying only on their support. Make sure these contributors and prospects know about the events, and make a special effort to have them attend. They'll like to see your volunteers at work, and will feel good about being introduced as valued benefactors, or potential supporters.

Why Do People Attend Special Events?

Understanding what motivates people to spend hundreds, sometimes thousands, of dollars, pounds, francs, and so on to support organizations they frequently don't know much about bears further examination. What do they want? What do they hope their contributions will bring them? Fundraisers who study human nature and understand what compels people to give are headed in the right direction.

People's desire to perform good works and to help others transcends culture, religion, and time. One way people act on this desire is by supporting charitable institutions; attending a non-profit's special event shows that a person cares about its cause. If nonprofits and NGOs, however, depended solely on the support of people who genuinely cared, the charitable sector would almost entirely disappear. Unfortunately, by itself, caring is not sufficient. It is the need for appreciation, a sense of achievement, and an increased feeling of self-worth that motivates most charitable giving. Special events planned with an awareness of these motivations are usually well-attended and profitable, as they can deliver satisfaction on all counts.

Planning Special Events

You've weighed the advantages and disadvantages of staging a special event, you've considered its timing, and you've decided to go ahead with an event. Now, where to start? With thorough planning, of course! Planning is essential to the success of any event. Nothing is as depressing as opening a theater on the benefit night to find fifty people—rather than four hundred—in the

> ## Do We Have To Go?
>
> ### Definitely—We Do So Much Business with Her Company!
>
> Nothing fills a room faster than honoring individuals—or or even organizations—for their civic leadership. Banquets, parties, luncheons, dinners, and even picnics can be vehicles for recognizing those who have made extraordinary contributions to your own organization or to the community at large.
>
> What makes these events work is that, for a variety of reasons, the individuals being honored will draw a crowd. That person may be such a shining light that people will attend simply to express their appreciation. If the honoree is a top officer of a significant business or corporation, almost every supplier, vendor, consultant—in short, anyone doing business with the honoree's corporation—will attend. Honorees will know that one of the main reasons they're being honored is because they will attract attendees, and will, therefore, expect to be asked for their mailing list.

theater. Planning is the means to ensure a full house. Following are the most important aspects of event planning.

Choosing the Right Event for Your Organization

Your choice of event should be compatible with your organization's mission, needs, and image. A black tie dinner-dance in a hotel ballroom seems just right as a benefit for an arts organization, but somehow all wrong as a fundraiser for a homeless shelter. Producing a horse show or hunt to underwrite construction of a private school's new gym is a good fit, but how well would such an event be attended by supporters of an animal rights organization?

After making sure that the nature of the event is appropriate to your mission, think about your current and targeted constituencies' demographics, interests, and financial resources. If you are targeting a younger group, a sporting event or discotheque evening might be successful. Are there many tennis players among your constituency? If so, why not put on a round-robin tennis tournament? If you do, include some local pros; they'll attract their students and club members, and amateurs love to play on the same court as the pros. Consider, too, the kinds of events that have already succeeded in your community. What have groups similar to yours organized? Which went well and which did not?

Here is a basic list of some of the more traditional special events.

- Art gallery openings
- Art shows
- Auctions
- Award presentations
- Bake sales
- Benefit performances
- Block parties
- Book sales
- Designer showcases
- Fairs
- Fashion shows

- Festivals
- Garage sales
- Kick-off events
- Movie screenings
- Picnics
- Private parties
- Sporting events
- Theater parties
- Tours
- Tribute dinners

You hardly need limit your thinking to these or other traditional events. Don't be afraid to develop a unique event that might intrigue your constituents, or a group of people that has not previously been involved. With a little ingenuity and a lot of planning, your special event can be something out of the ordinary that people will talk about for months—as well as a financial success. All the better for next year's event, too! Here are some examples of successful creative special events.

- In 1994, an initiative was put on the California ballot to create a single payer health-care system. Although ultimately unsuccessful, the fundraising for this initiative is instructive. Activist and political consultant Dave Fleischer created the plan: one thousand house parties in six months all over the state of California. The campaign organizers created house-party packets that included generic invitations, a timeline, a sample pitch, and even signs and posters to put up on the walls of the house where the party took place. The invitations were simple fliers that were easily photocopied. The fliers made it clear (as all such invitations should) that the parties were to be fundraising events by stating at the bottom, "Bring your questions and your checkbooks." Ultimately, 1,300 house parties took place, raising a total of $1,400,000.

- Many communities hold fundraisers called The Pasta Bowls. Upscale restaurants or well-known chefs compete in categories such as "best pasta sauce," or "most unusual," "most innovative," or "most authentic." The judges might be city council members, clergy, food critics for the local paper, and volunteers from the food bank. People pay $15 to attend these all-you-can-eat extravaganzas, and the food banks receive from $5,000 to $15,000 from these popular, well-attended events. The food is donated by the restaurant or by a grocery store, so costs are minimal.

It is important to mention why restaurants and grocery stores contribute food to such events. A desire to support good works may well be a factor in their decision. Another might be that someone who gives them a lot of business asks them. Perhaps the most important factor, though, might be their desire for a targeted group of people to know that they are good neighbors and so should be patronized. Seen in this light, their donations are actually marketing tools. The organization's side of the deal, so to speak, is the publicity they provide to restaurants by making sure their names are prominently displayed at the venue.

- The Center for Third World Organizing (CTWO), which spearheaded the National Welfare Rights Organization in the United States, has held an annual dinner for seventeen years. Each year they give an award named after activist George Wiley to a person of color who has contributed in a special way to end racism; the event always draws three to four hundred people and nets anywhere from $10,000 to $30,000. The invitations to the event are very clever: each year's invitation is a take-off on what that year would be in an individual's life. For example, the sixteenth annual dinner invitation said, "Sweet Sixteen and Learning To Drive." It featured a picture of a driver's license with the words "licensed to organize" in the space for what you are allowed to do. The seventeenth annual dinner was a take-off on *Seventeen Magazine* and the eighteenth was "Finally Legal." The success of these dinners is found in the fact they are both fun and serious, and known for excellent and bountiful food.

Setting the Date

Select your date carefully. Avoid holidays, tax season, election days, major sports events, religious observances, dates of competing events, and so forth. On a blank calendar for the year, cross out all the dates that would be inappropriate due to these and other kinds of conflicts. Then decide which dates might be most attractive to your constituency, and make sure your key people are available and will hold the date. Once you've set a date, notify other groups in your community so they can avoid scheduling their own events too closely. Extend them the same courtesy. Negotiation, if necessary, is worth the effort; it's much better to negotiate than to fail.

Creating a Budget

Your overall event budget should have been established during the planning process, but now is the time to elaborate the details.

Assigning Responsibility

All special events, regardless of their size, have similar components, and responsibility must be assigned for each. For smaller organizations, one person may have to oversee several operational areas.

- **Manager of the event.** The event manager is responsible for supervising and coordinating all components of the event.

- **Volunteers.** Volunteers are virtually indispensable to producing special events. The volunteer chair recruits, assigns, trains, and schedules the volunteers.

- **Marketing.** The person who leads the marketing effort assumes responsibility for a variety of tasks, including advertising and publicizing the event, creating all printed materials, and seeking sponsors for the event.

- **Legal.** An attorney should be recruited to review any contracts the organization must sign, and to arrange insurance coverage.

- **Finance.** Establishing a system to record expenses and income, tracking an event's financial progress, and discussing the implications with other members of the event leadership are jobs of the financial director. If, for instance, corporations are expected to buy a certain number of tables but the checks are not arriving, the finance chair will alert board and event committee members who can call their corporate contacts to boost the numbers. If checks are slow to come in from people on a particular committee member's list, the finance chair should call that person so that he or she can follow up.[1]

- **Development.** Responsibility must be assigned for both aspects of an event's development activities: generating income, and establishing strategies for cultivating selected attendees. This vital area will be covered in detail below in the section Maximizing Income.

- **Event Management.** A person must be designated to supervise logistics at the event.

Controlling Expenses

Securing donated items is one way to keep costs down. Try to get *everything* donated—the costs of renting space; printing tickets, posters, brochures, and ad books; and purchasing refreshments and other items all add up and consume potential profits. Try to obtain these things for free before deciding to spend money on them.

---

1. Committee members should write personal notes on the invitations your organization sends to people on their list. Make sure that you secure a copy of their list and assure them that you will not contact those people for any reason without first asking; this is very important. When responses are received, check them against committee members' lists and let the member know when "her [or his] people" respond.

Case Study

The Fortune Society's No-Benefit Benefit

For some, it is intriguing NOT to attend a benefit. For years, the Fortune Society, one of New York's leading criminal justice organizations, capitalized on the feeling of many that the hustle and bustle of benefit events in any given season can become overwhelming. Their solution? They sent out a compelling invitation to potential supporters, asking them to stay home. The solicitation letter describes parties that might have been—a dinner at an upscale hotel or a party at a discotheque—as well as the reactions that might have been—groans and moans at the thought of attending a party that would end at 1:00 AM on a weeknight. In the end, the Fortune staff tells the reader that they thought better of it all and invited people to stay at home, curl up with a book, and "help Fortune with all the money you will save by not going out."

The approach is clever, and it clearly works. The No-Benefit Benefit has netted the organization tens of thousands of dollars. Fortune estimates they've spent approximately $1,200 each year for postage and mimeograph paper for invitations. Close to a thousand people respond each year.

Why do Fortune's constituents give so generously for a cause that is surely not one of the most popular around—providing services to ex-offenders? The staff believes it has something to do with the fact that Fortune takes a light-hearted approach. People get a chuckle out of the idea, and the message gets around that Fortune would rather spend its money on services than on parties, an attitude that obviously touches a chord in donors. The thought that their money will be used wisely may, in fact, encourage people to give more.

Other organizations have made variations on this theme: a No-Baby Baby Shower to raise money for low-income families, and a No-Banquet Banquet held by the Little League in Hoboken, New Jersey. Whatever nonevent you decide to hold, make your concept and invitation clever, but be sure to include serious information about your programs. Fortune includes a list of its programs, and describes the populations aided by the money raised.

—Kate Chieco

Be sure to get volunteers to organize your event. Traditionally, volunteers organize most special events of limited scope. Organizing a special event, particularly a large-scale one, can be laborious and time-consuming, but it can also be immensely rewarding. Using volunteers to provide the people power is not only cost effective for the organization, but also gratifying for volunteers. They find pleasure in the work and provide the assistance without which no special event can succeed. Moreover, people of any age can join in, from teenagers who organize walkathons in their communities to grandmothers who sell their own homemade pies and cakes at a street fair. Volunteers are the planners and the administrators, as well as the envelope stuffers, the chauffeurs, the cooks, leafleteers, and so on. As the scope of the event increases, salaried staff will become involved. Outside fundraising firms or consultants are often hired to plan and implement a very large fundraising special event, but this increases the cost significantly.

Maximizing Income

Sponsorship

There are two basic kinds of sponsorship, both of which can be solicited for the same event: event sponsorship by a business, corporation, or individual; and event sponsorship at lesser levels, such as patron, sponsor, and benefactor; or bronze, silver, and gold.

The chief consideration for a business or corporation regarding sponsorship of a charity's special event (or in considering a contribution) is the potential payoff in terms of publicity or more business. Since sponsorship dollars frequently come from a business's marketing budget, nonprofits that solicit such sponsorship must be ready to state clearly the benefits that the business might derive from their contribution. The organization can become, in effect, a public relations agent for the potential sponsor. In many cases, the same holds true for individuals: what will motivate their sponsorship? Social recognition? Enhanced visibility with potential clients attending the function? Organizations should think in very business-like terms when soliciting both institutional and individual event sponsorship.

Event sponsorship at lower levels should also be solicited from institutions and individuals. While a single event sponsor naturally receives the greatest exposure, sponsors at lower levels can have their participation highlighted by one, several, or all of the following: a listing on invitations, advertising, and publicity; special program listing; seating priority; access to exclusive pre-event receptions, and so on.

The work of soliciting both kinds of sponsorship is undertaken by the organization's board, development committee, and event committee. The event committee—a group of individuals who have committed to bring a certain number of friends and associates to the event—deserves some attention. Increasing the number of event attendees is only one function this committee can serve. It also can engage the participation of someone the organization has targeted for increased involvement, but who has declined to date; serving on the event committee requires only a specific and limited obligation. Once someone is on the event committee, he or she can learn the benefits to be derived from ongoing involvement with the organization. Committee membership is thus a valuable cultivation tool. And from the member's perspective, serving on an event committee provides a person entrée to business or social circles that might otherwise not be accessible.

It's important for an organization to plan the development component of its event with foresight and insight. Too often, the logistics take precedence over marketing.

Pricing

Both for-profits and nonprofits need to establish pricing schedules that generate sufficient revenues while also remaining acceptable to customers. The for-profit world depends heavily on test marketing and focus groups to provide the solution. Whether a nonprofit is presenting an event for the thirty-second consecutive year or for the first time, it must be sensitive to the capacity of

Case Study

Walkathons: Planning for Success

Walkathons were launched in Europe and Canada in the 1960s by the International Freedom from Hunger campaign of the United Nations' Food and Agriculture Organization. The first walk in the United States took place in Fargo, North Dakota, in 1969, when one thousand high school and college students walked twenty-five miles to raise funds for self-help development projects at home and abroad, and to raise consciousness about the root causes of poverty and malnutrition.

Each volunteer secured sponsors who paid from twenty-five cents to five dollars for every mile the volunteer walked. The walks were called Hunger Hikes, or Walks for Development. So great was their success that, within four years, committees in more than a thousand communities had followed Fargo's example under the auspices of the American Freedom from Hunger Foundation. They raised more than $10 million to alleviate human suffering, foster development, and increase the number of trained, socially committed young leaders.

These walks were the predecessors of the walkathons, bikeathons, and swimathons that so many organizations now use to raise both visibility and funds. Even in their early years, Walks for Development mobilized literally hundreds of thousands of participants, who raised $100,000 to $250,000 per walk in large urban centers from these one-day-long activities. These walks were organized by students from local colleges, high schools, and junior high schools. A successor to these early walkathons are the AIDS Walks held in many major U.S. cities each year that generate millions of dollars for AIDS research, advocacy, and care.

What was involved in organizing these walks? What made them successful? How can today's organizations replicate these earlier successes? To illustrate how to plan a special event effectively, let's examine a sample timetable in organizing a walk.

its constituents and, like for-profits, undertake some test marketing. By initiating discussions with managers of other local nonprofits and with its constituents, a nonprofit can come up with an event pricing schedule that works.

Ad Journal

An ad journal is a publication that may contain a variety of "advertisements": messages congratulating the organization or the individual the organization is honoring; simple ads that say, "compliments of"; or perhaps just the name of the person, couple, family, or company that wishes to advertise. For some, buying an ad is a way to support an organization; for others, ads provide visibility. Either way, an organization can increase its income from an event by selling ads in a journal. Organizations that are short of volunteers can hire professional advertising salespeople to sell ads for them on a commission basis. The ads can be full-page, half-page, quarter-page, or less.

Walkathon Sample Timeline

3 months before walk date	2 months before walk date	1 month before walk date
Publicity	**Publicity**	**Publicity**
1. Meetings with key media people for programming and articles 2. Endorsements of local and state officials 3. Brochure planned	1. Schedule of press releases and news conferences covering walk logistics, office address, route maps, walk beneficiary, etc.	1. Radio and TV publicity and promo blitz begins. 2. Begin button and sticker sales
Recruitment of Walkers	**Recruitment of Walkers**	**Recruitment of Walkers**
1. Invitations to walk 2. Get on agendas and into meetings, school assemblies 3. Get on agenda of city councils, school boards	1. School assemblies, meetings with civic leaders and groups, and other speaking engagements	1. Dispersal of walk cards and project information
Logistics	**Logistics**	**Logistics**
1. Recipients of funds designated 2. Checkpoint and starting points approved 3. Planning of walk-daylogistics, including transportation and communication, VIPs, and ceromonies	1. Office secured 2. Accountant secured 3. Overhead account secured 4. Meeting with police for approval of checkpoints, route, and starting point 5. Walk card layout to printer	1. Walk bank account secured 2. Final approval of route and checkpoints
		After Walk
		1. Process walk cards

Silent Auction and Raffle

The theory behind adding silent auctions and raffles to special events is that money has already been spent to attract people and to create a lively, expansive atmosphere. Why not, then, offer guests additional opportunities to support the organization, enjoy the announcements of winning bids and numbers throughout the event, and possibly win something exciting in return? This is another example of piggyback fundraising discussed earlier in this chapter.

Group Sales

If you are organizing a large-scale event, such as a concert, consider selling blocks of tickets to other groups at a discount (group rates). These groups, in turn, will add a few dollars to the ticket price and sell them to their own constituents. By doing this, you are more likely to cover all your costs and maximize your profits. If you feel your organization may not have the resources to undertake a special event by itself, go a step further and co-host a special event with another organization.

Holding the Event

Careful planning should ensure that an event runs smoothly. The people in charge of each component should review task lists with their volunteers to make sure that instructions and goals are clear, and that alternative plans have been developed in case problems arise. For example, extra tables, chairs, and seating cards should be ready in case more people attend the event than expected. Staff and volunteer leadership should be prepared to step in for a board or committee member who must cancel at the last moment, so that cultivation assignments are still carried out.

Follow-Up

It's essential that follow-up to a special event be as carefully planned as the event itself, and that all involved understand that a very important part of the event takes place after everyone has gone home. The following four categories of follow-up steps—logistics, development, organization, and assessment—will help you organize your work to leverage the success of your event.

Logistics

1. Return all rented and borrowed equipment in good condition.

2. Deliver any remaining fresh flowers to people who worked behind the scenes, or to another local nonprofit, such as a nursing home, shelter, or club as a way of saying, "Thank you."

3. Send unserved food to the local equivalents of Meals on Wheels organizations, such as God's Love We Deliver or City Harvest, which will deliver it to those in need.

Development

1. Send hand-signed, personalized thank-you notes to all attendees, to those who did not attend but sent contributions, and to all those who worked on the event. For those who attended, make sure to fulfill the IRS's requirement that you state the amount of their ticket price, which is tax-deductible.

Case Study

The Balm in Gilead

The Balm in Gilead (The Balm) is a national nonprofit organization founded in New York City by Pernessa C. Seele in 1989. Working through Black churches, The Balm aims to stop the spread of HIV/AIDS in the African-American community, and to support those infected with, and affected by, HIV/AIDS. The Balm, recognized as one of the most effective and inspiring AIDS initiatives aimed at faith communities, successfully engages denominational leaders, clergy, congregations, and individual parishioners in the AIDS struggle. It is the only AIDS service organization that has been endorsed by more than ten Black church denominations. These endorsements provide the organization with the potential to bring AIDS prevention and treatment information to more than 20 million Black Americans through their religious affiliations.

The vision of creating an organization that would bring such significant benefits to so many was Ms. Seele's, as was the vision of creating a special event of enormous scope to raise funds for, and increase the visibility of the organization and HIV/AIDS. As happens with so many projects, nonprofits, and institutions, everything began with one inspired, determined individual.

Ms. Seele conceived a special event whose proportions reflected those of the HIV/AIDS pandemic: a benefit concert at Riverside Church, in New York, featuring the world-famous mezzo-soprano Jessye Norman. Writing in the concert program, Ms. Seele said, " Five years ago, God placed a vision in my heart and mind of a performance by Ms. Norman that would highlight the legacy of strength, courage and refuge that African Americans have found in the bosom of their churches throughout our history."

How she turned that vision into a reality that was supported by corporations, foundations, religious institutions, individuals, and some of the world's most prominent artists, writers, poets, and humanitarians is a testament to the strength of the human spirit, and an inspiration to nonprofits the world over. As Ms. Seele explains it, "When God is within you, you can accomplish just about anything."

The first step in developing her concept was to interest Ms. Norman in the project. After writing for more than a year to Ms. Norman's manager, Ms. Seele arranged a meeting with the singer's representatives. Once they were convinced that the project was viable, a meeting ("high tea") was finally set up between Ms. Norman and Ms. Seele, at which their common roots—as two black girls from the South who had drawn great strength from their local churches—established a bond that still exists today. Before Ms. Seele could even begin to explain her plans, however, Ms. Norman led off with a full-blown vision she had of the event—and proceeded to articulate what The Balm's founder had been dreaming of for the previous two years!

Ms. Norman's commitment to the project was only the beginning of the long journey to Riverside Church, and to the Emmy the concert video would eventually win. As she developed her approach to secure underwriting for the concert, Ms. Seele realized that she had absolutely no knowledge of the largely white world of classical music and its sponsorship. Nevertheless, her networking brought her into contact with Evelyn Cunningham and

Dean Sayles, whose mentorship enabled Ms. Seele to learn—and to keep learning—what she had to, and led her to the funding sources that eventually underwrote the event. Her observation about finding the considerable human and financial resources that were needed to create the miracle of the concert should be well-noted by everyone involved with the activities of a nonprofit organization: "Everything we need already exists; the only challenge is accessing it."

This perspective of abundance rather than scarcity was a major factor in enabling Ms. Seele to persevere through continuing challenges, disappointments, and frustrations, including, to her enormous surprise, the fact that nobody initially believed that Ms. Norman had agreed to appear! The event gained momentum nevertheless, as increasing numbers of sponsors came forward and artists offered their services. Staff was hired, volunteers found, television broadcast secured; the event took on a life of its own, beyond even what Ms. Seele and Ms. Norman had envisioned. The key to the benefit for The Balm in Gilead—" Jessye Norman Sings for the Healing of AIDS"—was that the people who created the evening developed a sense of ownership and derived personal satisfaction and inspiration from their work. In Ms. Seele's words, "Everything comes out of relationships."

The effort and dedication of the performers, producers, sponsors, staff, and volunteers combined to create an evening that gave hope, inspired faith, and raised enough money to secure the future of The Balm's work on behalf of HIV/AIDS in the Black community. Additionally, the event gave The Balm's board and donors an increased sense of the impact of their work and support, and brought the organization's message of healing to millions though the television broadcast and concert videotapes.

Ms. Seele's outlook regarding the availability of resources, the power of conviction, and the importance of relationships is a primer for special events fundraising, for fundraising in general, and for lives that make a difference. And her tenacity in recruiting Jessye Norman for the concert is a blueprint for securing the services of spokespeople and celebrities—be they internationally known divas, or local talent. The "campaign to recruit Jessye Norman" was based on a few principles: finding an individual with visibility, integrity, and appeal to an organization's target audience; intensive networking so that an initial approach can be supported by credible people who are known to the individual, or to the individual's representatives; working with representatives, agents, and other people who screen charity requests; preparing the proposal; finding common ground with the individual whose services an organization is seeking to secure; and understanding that the cultivation process must continue, and even intensify, after the individual accepts.

Volunteers and committee members working on special events—of this or any other magnitude—must have clear job descriptions and deadlines. Additionally, their interest and active participation should be cultivated on an ongoing basis from the moment they commit to the event. Make sure that the larger purpose of the event is brought to their attention continuously. Provide regular progress updates to renew their enthusiasm. Know why your key volunteers and committee members are involved, understand their expectations, and, as appropriate, make sure your organization fulfills them.

—David Barg

2. Publicize the results of the event.

3. Call key organization people who attended—event chair or co-chairs, benefit committee members, major donors, and the like—to thank them and solicit their feedback.

4. If staff members or volunteer leaders were assigned to speak to targeted individuals and cultivate their interest, speak with them, note their comments on the individuals' cultivation records, and update your strategies.

5. Research new prospects who attended, develop appropriate cultivation strategies, and assign responsibility for their implementation.

6. Invite benefactors and patrons of the occasion to visit facilities and program sites, to attend performances, to visit with scholarship recipients, and so on, so they can see how the funds raised at the event are being used.

7. If there was a photographer at the event, mail pictures to current and prospective donors. Of course, send out only the most flattering photos!

8. To provide a sense of closure for the volunteers who helped, and to cultivate them for the next event, plan a party in their honor. At the gathering, thank the key volunteers, report the results of the event and, if possible, provide a small gift or memento to express your appreciation for their time and effort. Be sure to have a photographer there, and publish a group picture in your next newsletter as a way of reinforcing your gratitude.

9. Send a reminder to people who attended but did not pay.

Organization

1. Make an accounting of the evening's finances and send the financial report to the appropriate individuals.

2. Enter data for each attendee in your records (e.g., amount paid, amount owed, change of address, etc.).

3. Check vendors' invoices against goods and services actually provided, and pay outstanding invoices.

Assessment

As soon as possible after the event, meet with board and staff members, event leadership, and key volunteers to discuss such questions as:

1. What brought most people to the event? Invitations? Publicity? Calls from board and committee members?

2. Who attended? Did we succeed in reaching our targeted constituents?

3. What motivated them to come?

4. What made the event enjoyable?

5. What would have made it more enjoyable?

6. Were financial, public relations, and cultivation goals achieved?

7. Should the event be repeated next year?

8. If so, which elements should be kept? Which should be changed?

After the meeting, summarize and distribute the results, and plan to apply what you've learned to upcoming events.

The maxim "Nothing breeds success like success" applies as much to special event fundraising as to any other activity. If you organize an event that attracts new constituents, reaches its fundraising goal, and enhances your organization's public profile, you should build on that success right away to keep the momentum going. Remember that a successful special event can be the beginning. Look ahead to the next year as you close the pages on this year's event, and start working right away to make your special event a new annual tradition for your organization and its community.

Tips

- Make your events annual traditions. If a special event has been successful, there is no reason why it will not succeed in subsequent years. Build on your past success by billing your events Second Annual, Fifth Annual, Tenth Annual, and so on. As long as people enjoy themselves, you will enable them to have the same pleasure again and again. Successful events held annually, "signature events," help promote an organization and attract new people and businesses.

- Remember that people attend special events mainly for social reasons. While many will be pleased to support the sponsoring organization, they mainly come to socialize, network, and meet new people. Ticket prices for large special events can be high, so make sure to give attendees what they want—a terrific social evening. At the same time, be sure to get what *you* want by carrying out your carefully planned cultivation strategies.

- To maximize turnout for a special event, involve as many people as possible in planning and staging the event. People can be asked to serve on the sponsoring committee for the program, on any of the volunteer working committees (decorating, tickets, food, etc.), or as hosts and greeters at the event itself. In these ways, you're increasing the investment of more people in the success of the event. A secondary advantage is that you will have identified a core group of volunteers for the event next year.

Summary Worksheet

for _____

(name of your organization)

Approaching Individuals for Support: Special Events

Building on Special Events to Date

1. Are you already organizing special events to raise funds?

   _____ yes　　_____ no

   If so, what are they?　　　　　　　　　What are their net proceeds?
   　　　　　　　　　　　　　　　　　　　(gross income minus expenses)

   a. _____　　　　　$ _____
   b. _____　　　　　$ _____
   c. _____　　　　　$ _____
   d. _____　　　　　$ _____

2. Which of these events rely more on volunteer energies than on staff energies?

   a. _____
   b. _____
   c. _____

3. Which of those special events are "proven" traditions (i.e., continue to attract more people each year, raise more funds each year, etc.)?

   a. _____
   b. _____
   c. _____

4. Which events should be discarded (due to declining numbers of participants and sagging receipts) or vastly overhauled?

   a. _____
   b. _____
   c. _____

5. How can you enhance the income potential for any of these events (e.g., maximize use of volunteers, get more costs donated, etc.)?

   Additional Actions Needed
   Planning New Special Events

   a. _____
   b. _____
   c. _____
   d. _____
   e. _____

6. What new ideas for special events would you like to explore further? (Note: Convene a brainstorming meeting of your fundraising committee or board to come up with ideas.)

    a. _____

    b. _____

    c. _____

    d. _____

7. Have others tried any of these events in your community? What has been their experience? Have you approached them for advice?

    Names of Other Organization

    a. _____

    b. _____

    c. _____

8. What realistic fundraising goals can you set for each of your special events programs, individually and collectively?

    Total:
    Each event
    Current: New:

    $ _____ $ _____

    $ _____ $ _____

    $ _____ $ _____

9. How much people power is needed to organize each event? How much time should be allocated up front to plan each event successfully?

    Event   Planning Time Needed   People Power

    _____   _____   _____

    _____   _____   _____

    _____   _____   _____

10. Finding Assistance and Counsel
    Name three or more individuals who might be able to advise you on how to more effectively organize special events.

    a. _____

    b. _____

    c. _____

    d. _____

11. Rating Your Special Event's Potential

    On the basis of what you have learned, how would you rank your chances of raising funds through special events?

    ___ Very Good   ___ Possible   ___ Unlikely   ___ Still Unknown

Special Event Planning Form

1. Where will the event be held?

   _____

2. Can the location be seen as a drawing element?

   _____ yes _____ no

3. What up-front monetary resources will be needed?

   $ _____

4. Is there an interest in this type of event in the community?

   _____ yes _____ no

5. Will the event draw an audience?

   _____ yes _____ no

   If yes, what is the reason for them to attend?

   _____

   _____

6. What will you be giving to those who attend (e.g., exposure, social time, etc.)?

   _____

7. When will the event be held?

   _____

8. Will the event conflict with other events that would interest the same audience?

   _____ yes _____ no

9. How much planning time does the group need to put the event together?

   _____

10. How will organizational information be introduced?

    _____

11. How will you market the event? For example, are there related groups with newsletters that would advertise for you?

    _____

12. Whom do you know? Whom do your friends know? How can you effectively network to attract people to the event?

    _____

13. Does the event lend itself to honoring anyone?

    _____ yes _____ no

14. Is the event attractive enough to be an annual tradition for your organization?

    _____ yes _____ no

15. Are there two people whom you could approach to be co-chairs of the event?

_____ yes   _____ no

If yes, who are they?

a. _____

b. _____

Who should approach them?

_____

16. Finally, what plans are you making to ensure that attendees have a good time?

_____

_____

_____

_____

_____

Source: Adapted from a form used by Amnesty International U.S.A.

Additional Resources

Publications

Allen, Judy. *Event Planning: The Ultimate Guide to Successful Meetings, Corporate Events, Fundraising Galas, Conferences, Conventions, Incentives and Other Special Events.* New York: John Wiley & Sons, 2000. xiv, 306 p.

> A textbook about special events from planning, budgeting, timing, location selection and requirements, menu planning, and considerations for guests, such as transportation. The appendix contains sample worksheets for different types of events. Indexed.

Brody, Ralph, and Marcie Goodman. *Fund Raising Events: Strategies and Programs for Success.* New York: Human Sciences Press, 1988. 291 p.

> Focuses on fundraising activities designed to provide contributors with something in return for their financial support. Part 1 describes generic principles and concepts to guide strategic thinking involving all of a nonprofit's events; Part 2 describes actual fundraising events in detail. Includes bibliography.

Devney, Darcy Campion. *Organizing Special Events and Conferences: A Practical Guide for Busy Volunteers and Staff.* Sarasota, FL: Pineapple Press, 1990. 129 p.

> Hands-on guide to organizing and managing special events and conferences. The step-by-step structure of the book includes checklists, schedules, models, and sample forms and worksheets. Part 1 provides a broad overview of the event manager's responsibilities. Part 2 focuses on planning and logistics, including financial management, site selection, and facilities. Part 3 examines publicity, media relations, and registration, including tips on writing press releases and designing posters. Part 4 helps the event manager select and schedule programming, activities, and entertainments. Part 5 covers food and includes chapters on menu planning, quantity shopping and cooking, and quality presentation and serving. The appendix lists publications and organizations for further information.

Dickey, Marilyn. "Adventures in Joint Fund Raising." *Chronicle of Philanthropy* 11 (11 March 1999): 25–27.

> Many nonprofit organizations have begun to collaborate their fundraising activities with other nonprofits in an effort to increase exposure to potential volunteers and donors and to reduce the number of grant proposals to grantmakers.

Espinosa, Rick. *The Carnival Handbook: And Other Fundraising Ideas.* Los Angeles: Century West Enterprises, 1995. v, 218 p.

Franks, Aaron M., and Norman E. Franks. *Cash Now: A Manual of Twenty-Nine Successful Fundraising Events.* Vancouver, British Columbia: Creative Fundraising, 1993. xvii, 260 p.

Freedman, Harry A., and Karen Feldman. *The Business of Special Events: Fundraising Strategies for Changing Times*. Sarasota, FL: Pineapple Press, 1998. x, 149 p.
  Directed at both experienced and novice event planners, provides practical advice and detailed checklists.

Freedman, Harry A., and Karen Feldman Smith. *Black Tie Optional: The Ultimate Guide to Planning and Producing Successful Special Events*. Rockville, MD: Fund Raising Institute, 1991. x, 247 p.
  Complete guide to planning and managing special events, from sidewalk sales to tennis tournaments, celebrity concerts, or cruises. Filled with checklists, flow charts, worksheets and sample forms to develop budgets, set prices, organize committees, design invitations and more. Includes chapters on working with celebrities, and food issues. A " tools of the trade" section lists helpful organizations and publications, with an extensive listing of ways to contact celebrities. Indexed.

Geier, Ted. *Make Your Events Special: How To Plan and Organize Successful Special Events Programs for Nonprofit Organizations*. 2nd ed. New York: Cause Effective, Inc., 1992. ii, 123 p.
  Detailed workbook includes sections on how to establish goals for special events; prepare and manage the program, fundraising, promotion and marketing; coordinate technical and logistical operations; enlist and coordinate personnel; and evaluate a special events programs. Each section includes worksheets.

Gordon, Micki. *The Fundraising Manual: A Step by Step Guide To Creating the Perfect Event*. Gaithersburg, MD: FIG Press, 1997. x, 184 p.

Hall, Holly. "How To Avoid Pitfalls in Raising Money with Special Events." *Chronicle of Philanthropy* 5 (4 May 1993): 35–36.

Hall, Holly. "Recruiting Celebrities: Charities Often Bungle Requests, Negotiation." *Chronicle of Philanthropy* 5 (1 December 1992): 24, 26.
  Discusses the advantages and disadvantages of involving celebrities in fundraising special events. The Celebrity Outreach Foundation in Los Angeles specializes in matching celebrities with charities. Several other similar agencies are profiled. The article states common mistakes nonprofits should avoid when working with celebrity representatives.

Hall, Holly. "A Walkathon, Step by Step." *Chronicle of Philanthropy* 1 (30 May 1989): 7–11.
  The twentieth annual Walk for Hunger, organized by the Boston nonprofit Project Bread, had 35,000 participants, 2,000 volunteers, and 700,000 sponsors. The walkers raised $3.5 million for 250 emergency food facilities serving forty-nine Massachusetts communities. This article examines the history of the Walk for Hunger, and details how the grassroots event is organized—including awareness promotion, participant recruitment, volunteer training, and the handling of the day's events. Shoshana Pakciarz, the executive director of

Project Bread, believes the walkathon strengthens Boston's sense of community while at the same time doing good for others.

Harris, April L. "New Tools for the Trade." *Currents* 24 (February 1998): 39–43.
High-tech strategies to use in planning special events.

Harris, April L. *Special Events: Planning for Success.* 2nd ed. Washington, DC: Council for Advancement and Support of Education, 1998. vii, 153 p.
Step-by-step guide to a successful special event, from initial planning to invitations and publicity to paying the bills when the party's over. Harris states that special events offer a unique opportunity to showcase an institution in interesting, time-effective, and creative ways that at the same time allow for personal contact. They help to educate, make a point, build friendships, enable constituents to feel like insiders, and foster a sense of community. But special events do not exist in isolation, Harris cautions; instead, they should be integrated into an institution's total advancement program.

Harris, April L. *Raising Money and Cultivating Donors through Special Events.* Washington, DC: Council for Advancement and Support of Education, 1991. 57 p.
A companion volume to the author's *Special Events: Planning for Success,* this work leads the reader step-by-step through the planning and completion of special events fundraising.

Hauser, Cindy. *Aspen's Guide to Sixty Successful Special Events: How To Plan, Organize, and Conduct Outstanding Fund Raisers.* Frederick, MD: Aspen Publishers, 1996. viii, 318 p.

Kaitcer, Cindy R. *Raising Big Bucks: The Complete Guide to Producing Pledge-Based Special Events.* Chicago: Bonus Books, 1996. xiv, 240 p.

Klein, Kim. "The Correct Use of Special Events." *Grassroots Fundraising Journal* 18 (February 1999): 9–10.
Reviews reasons for conducting a special event and recommends completion of three preliminary tasks to ensure success.

Klein, Kim. "Putting On a House party." *Grassroots Fundraising Journal* 18 (August 1999): 11–13.
Step-by-step guidance for creating a fundraising event in your home.

Levy, Barbara R., and Barbara H. Marion. *Successful Special Events: Planning, Hosting, and Evaluating.* Frederick, MD: Aspen Publishers, 1997. xiii, 233 p.
Presents an overview of planning, hosting, and evaluating successful special events, from the definition of a special event, through goal setting, choice of theme and site, determinations of cost, time frame, and human resources needed, to decor, public relations, and legal considerations.

Liddell, Jamise. "Are You Covered?" *Currents* 25 (March 1999): 19–23.
   Insurance basics for event planners.

Nelson, Dave. "Pricing Correctness vs. Political Incorrectness." *Fund Raising Management* 28 (February 1998): 34–35.
   Author comments on the pricing of special events.

Nonprofits' Insurance Alliance of California, Nonprofit Risk Management Center. *Managing Special Events Risks: Ten Steps to Safety.* Washington, DC: Nonprofit Risk Management Center, 1997. 54 p.

Stallings, Betty, and Donna McMillion. *How To Produce Fabulous Fundraising Events: Reap Remarkable Returns with Minimal Effort.* Pleasanton, CA: Building Better Skills, 1999. 168p.
   Divided into two sections, the first provides advice about choosing the right special event, selecting volunteers, planning, publicizing, and evaluating the event. The second section is a how-to guide for planning and managing a dinner event, and includes worksheets, checklists, and insider's tips. An accompanying computer disk is included.

Swarden, Carlotta G. "Outsourcing Events: Reduce Stress While Generating Revenue." *NonProfit Times* 10 (May 1996): 26, 37.

Ukman, Lesa, ed. *IEG Sponsorship Sourcebook: The Comprehensive Guide to Sponsors, Properties, Agencies, and Suppliers.* 1999 ed. Chicago: IEG, Inc., 1998. 478 p.
   Compiled for the benefit of corporations looking for sponsorship opportunities, the *IEG Sponsorship Sourcebook* can also be helpful for nonprofits seeking sponsors for their events. The directory is arranged in nine sections. Section one includes contact name, address, and telephone and fax numbers of the 300 most often-mentioned sponsors, arranged alphabetically. Section two is an alphabetical list of sponsors. Sections three through six list sponsorship opportunities by location, by U.S. Region and foreign country, and by category. Section seven contains a directory of sponsored events by month. Sections eight and nine indicate numbers attending sponsored events and budget categories. Section ten lists sponsorship agencies. Industry yellow pages and a master index complete the final two sections of the volume.

Wendroff, Alan L. *Special Events: Proven Strategies for Nonprofit Fund Raising.* New York: John Wiley & Sons (Nonprofit Law, Finance, and Management Series), 1999. xx, 214 p.
   Provides a strategy for conducting special events, using the Master Event Timetable (METT) as a guide. Provides worksheets and illustrations of real-life examples from launch through evaluation. Accompanied by computer disk.

Williams, Warren. *User Friendly Fundraising: A Step by Step Guide to Profitable Special Events*. Nashville, TN: Associated Publishers Group, 1994. 144 p.

> Written as a how-to manual for novice fundraisers. Describes various kinds of special events: auctions, tournaments, carnivals and fairs, theme parties, sporting events, house and garden tours, seminars, and casino fundraisers. Includes examples of a planning calendar, an outline of auction procedures, and various forms and checklists. Also includes a bibliography.

Internet Resources

The following websites contain information about special events management software, as well as a wide range of other fundraising-related software and sites.

www.fundraiser-software.com/donormgt.html

www.nonprofit-info.org/npofaq/05/

www.npo.net/nponet/computer/fundacct.htm

www.coyotecm.com/tips.html

Chapter 9

Direct Mail

Short words are best and old words when short are best of all.
—Sir Winston Churchill

Often described as the least personal way to raise funds, direct mail is the most personal way to raise funds after face-to-face solicitation and telephone contact. Direct mail fundraising—the mailing of appeal letters to individuals for financial support—differs from other forms of fund-raising from individuals in that you are soliciting large numbers of people for reasonably small donations—usually less than $100. Mailings can range from a few handwritten pleas sent out to friends, to a word-processed or personalized form letter sent to a few dozen or hundred

supporters, to a highly designed, multifaceted printed packet mailed to thousands or hundreds of thousands of people.

Although its success is largely based on getting out a high enough volume of letters to the right people that even a small response rate still generates donors and cash, direct mail is also one of the few fundraising strategies that allows you to get your message into the hands—literally—of anyone for whom you have an address. Unlike interviews or news reports, you control the message; and at a fraction of the cost of advertising, direct mail remains a staple in the fundraiser's toolkit.

Large international and national nonprofit organizations such as Amnesty International, Oxfam, Greenpeace, Save the Children, CARE, Smithsonian Institution, National Audubon Society, National Organization for Women, and Planned Parenthood have utilized direct mail for a long time. Since the early 1980s, local nonprofits of all sizes have been systematically using direct mail to seek out contributors as well.

Depending on the initial investment of funds to cover your start-up direct mail costs (such as printing, postage, and purchase of lists of potential donors), you may realize anywhere from several hundred to tens of thousands of dollars from a direct mail effort.

A cautionary note: direct mail is really an investment in your financial future. The first-year costs of establishing a direct mail program may exceed the actual dollars that you will raise. However, carefully planned direct mail efforts in subsequent years will produce greater profits and thus justify the initial investment.

What Are the Advantages of Raising Money by Direct Mail?

1. *It's effective.* Direct mail is the most effective way to get your message across to new people with something they can hold in their hands and read at their leisure. E-mail is the only other means of sending prospects a "letter" that arrives at their home, where it can be read in private. Although many people claim to hate direct mail, most do respond to mailings some of the time, and in many surveys, 71 percent of people polled say their favorite part of their day is opening their mail.

2. *It's efficient.* Direct mail is an efficient use of your organization's time and money because successful mail appeals bring in new supporters as well as identify prospective larger donors. People who contribute $100 or more might well respond to other forms of solicitation. If someone responds to your organization's first mail solicitation by sending a check, that person is likely to contribute again.

3. *It produces measurable results.* You can count the number of letters mailed out and the exact costs of a particular appeal, and also determine the number of responses, the total dollars received, and the names and addresses of the contributors. As a result, you can measure whether your direct mail efforts have been profitable.

4. *It generates a donor profile.* For organizations that purchase mailing lists, direct mail solicitations can build the profile of a "typical" donor. By measuring and

analyzing responses from lists with different characteristics, an organization can identify the traits shared by those who contribute.

5. *It educates others.* Direct mail can educate new and old constituents. New-comers—your prospects—might read just the message on the outside of your envelope, or they may scan the contents within. Even if people don't respond immediately with a contribution, they may become more sensitive to your issue. In the same sense, your existing constituents can become better informed about issues of mutual concern and be moved to give again and/or to give more, and can be enlisted for other types of activities, such as advocacy work and volunteering.

What Are the Disadvantages of Raising Money by Direct Mail?

1. *It requires an investment.* With direct mail you have to spend money to make money. Approaching individuals for contributions via mail for the first time is a potentially costly process. Choosing unlikely lists of contributors initially will cost you money that you may not recoup until a second or third mailing. A response of between 0.5 and 1 percent (fifty to one hundred people from a mailing of ten thousand) is considered good for first-time mailings to people who haven't given before.

2. *It's expensive.* Although cheap on a per-unit basis, significant direct mail campaigns can be expensive because of the volume required to make them worthwhile. Finding those vital names and addresses requires time and, more important, money. Direct costs are incurred through printing, postage, and, perhaps, the rental of prospective donor lists. Indirect costs include the time it takes your salaried staff to prepare and coordinate the mailings and, possibly, to organize volunteers to stuff your appeal envelopes.

3. *It's risky.* You can estimate only roughly how much money you might net, based on your previous experiences. If you're approaching individuals for the first time, you are even more in the dark about their potential.

More than any other fundraising strategy, direct mail demonstrates the importance of thinking in terms of an overall plan. For example, once you attract donors by mail, if you want to relate to them only by mail, you will raise far less money than if you are willing to meet some of them in person, invite them to events, and begin to build a relationship. A basic premise of direct mail is that if you are not willing to get into fundraising all the way, don't get into it at all. Direct mail in and of itself is too expensive and risky, but when combined with other strategies and seen as a means to build relationships, it is a wonderful strategy.

Understanding Key Direct Mail Concepts

Response Rate and Donor Profile

The number of letters mailed relative to the number of contributions received is called the response rate. For example, if you mail an appeal to a purchased list of one thousand names and receive ten contributions, you have achieved a response rate of 1 percent—the typical rate for a quality mailing to a purchased list. The response rate is the most important variable in direct mail fundraising; it tells you how well a list of prospective givers is working. By comparing the response rates of lists of people with different traits, an organization can, over time, build a profile of the type of people most likely to respond to mail appeals from your group.

Response Cost

In determining the effectiveness of a mailing, it is important to know how much it cost to generate each response. This cost is determined by dividing the total cost of the mailing by the number of positive responses received. If mailing one thousand letters costs $500 and generates 10 responses, the cost per response is $50 ($500/10). If each donor contributed $50, the total received is $500 (10 x $50); the organization will have created 10 new donors at zero cost and zero profit. If each donor contributes $35, which is more likely, then the organization has created 10 new donors at a cost of $150 ($50 cost per donor minus $35 income = $15 net cost per donor x 10 donors = $150).

Direct Mail as an Investment

While spending $500 on a mailing that nets $0 (or even loses $150, as in the case where each of the 10 donors gave $35) may seem to be a failure, it is in reality a successful investment in an organization's future. Why? Because the organization now has 10 new people to ask for extra gifts, to invite to special events, and to become renewable donors. In addition, some of those new donors may eventually give large gifts and become more involved in the organization.

Let's contrast this with another example: suppose that the mailing produced not 10 responses, but only 3—a response rate of 0.3 percent instead of 1 percent—but one of those gifts was $1,000. If you look at the total raised, the second appeal would appear to be the more successful one. But while it is wonderful to have found a $1,000 donor using a mail appeal, the second appeal must be termed a failure because the organization's donor base was increased by only 3 and not 10; and because the lower response rate failed to help build the donor profile that is so critical to the success of direct mail fundraising.

Worksheet

Estimating the Potential Income of First-Time Prospect Mail Appeals

1. Set a range of gifts for the solicitations. Estimate roughly the average dollar response that mailings to these individuals have netted for other organizations. You can sometimes obtain this data by asking the organization whose list you are utilizing. Look at past direct mail appeals of that organization and see what the range of gifts requested is. The lowest category often represents the gift the group expects to receive most often. For example, if an organization is asking for contributions in the range of:

   _____ $25   _____ $50   _____ $100 $_____ (other)

   then $25 represents the gift received most often.
   Your Anticipated Average Gift = $ _____ .

2. Now, set the top possible gift, which is frequently $100. The "Other" category is for those who wish to give less than $25, more than $100, or some unlisted amount in between.

   Your Top Average Anticipated Gift = $100.

3. Fill in the rest of your range of gift sizes. Usually you give your potential supporters four to five possible options, including "Other" as the last option listed.
   a. $ _____
   b. $ _____
   c. $ _____
   d. $ _____
   e. $ _____
   f. Other: _____

4. Using the accepted reference of 0.5 to 1 percent return on initial mailings, calculate the potential range of income. For example, if you mail out 10,000 pieces asking for $25 as the lowest gift,

   0.5 percent x 10,000 = 50 people
   50 people x $25 = $1,250
   1 percent x 10,000 = 100 people
   100 people x $25 = $2,500

   Your gross potential range of income for this mailing is $1,250 to $2,500.

Comparing Projected Income Against Projected Expenses

Total Expenses -	$ _____	
Minus Potential Range of Income:	$ _____	to $ _____
Net:	$ _____	to $ _____

If your income exceeds your expenses, your direct mail effort is likely to be profitable.

If your income equals your expenses, you have not wasted your time, for you have acquired up to one hundred potential new donors who can be approached a second and a third time for support.

If your income is substantially or alarmingly less than your expenses, you need to find a less expensive way to reach those ten thousand prospects. You might cut your production costs by seeking out donated printing or artwork, use volunteer labor, or swap prospect lists rather than buy them. You might also start your gift table at a higher level to raise your anticipated income

Deciding Whether To Use Direct Mail Solicitation for Your Organization

Practically every kind and size of nonprofit organization can use direct mail. Almost all nonprofits use the mail to communicate with stakeholders, including donors, anyway. However, the potential to net contributions varies considerably depending upon a number of factors, such as start-up funds to cover initial costs, the appeal of your issues to individuals, and the persuasiveness of your case.

It is not easy to determine whether direct mail solicitations will prove worth your effort in time and money, but let's examine some of the considerations involved.

1. *Cost.* Every group can afford a low-cost direct mail effort, as described below. Of course, if you have an existing list of supporters to whom you are already mailing newsletters or literature, the cost of adding an appeal for funds to any of these mailings would be minimal. You certainly can and should be asking your existing contacts or readers for money. If, on the other hand, that list is relatively small and does not really encompass your universe of potentially interested individuals, it is really not your best source of income. It is obviously more expensive to approach "untested" groups of individuals for contributions, since you have no prior first-hand experience with these prospects. If you are approaching totally new prospects and/or will have to cover all the costs of a pilot mailing, you will need to gauge in advance your relative costs versus your potential income. The worksheet below can serve as a guide for this computation.

2. *Availability of prospects.* Does your organization already have mailing lists of supporters that might be used for direct mail purposes? Do you collect names and addresses of people who attend your special events or who call or write your group for information or request your newsletter? Have you a list, too, of individuals to whom you may have provided services?

   Any of these lists can be used for direct mail purposes. In fact, these lists contribute to what is known in direct mail circles as an organization's "house list." A house list is made up of individuals who have some previously established relationship with your organization; the strongest element of a house list is people who have given money before. Generally speaking, two-thirds of donors who have given before will, if asked, renew their support over the course of a year. People on your house list who are not donors but have some other kind of relationship to your group—vendors, volunteers, alumni, and so on—should be asked to give at least once a year. An organization can generally convert at least 25 percent of its house list into donors. Of course, there is no guarantee that you will receive X number of positive responses from such a mailing; a list of that sort, however, does say you've got some names of people who have already expressed an interest in your work, and they are your most likely supporters.

If you have no lists of your own, do you have access to the mailing lists of similar organizations? People who are attracted to such organizations might also respond affirmatively to yours. Simply contact these organizations directly and ask if you can do a mailing on their list.

You may find that some organizations are unwilling to give you their list for a mailing. Others may make their lists available only for a fee or in exchange for your own list. If you are approaching a national organization but your work has only local appeal, you will want to request only the names of people who live nearby. You can also rent mailing lists of potential sympathizers from direct mail list brokers (check for listings in your local telephone directory). And don't forget how to be a smart shopper; call other nonprofits that have used a specific list broker and find out what their experiences were.

3. *Precedents.* Are there other organizations similar to your own that have been successful in raising money through direct mail appeals? If so, they have already determined for you that direct mail can be effective in eliciting contributions from potential supporters.

If you have responded affirmatively to any of the above items, you certainly should consider direct mail as part of your overall fundraising effort. Check the summary worksheet at the end of the chapter.

How To Organize a Direct Mail Effort?

Direct mail should not be a single event but rather a sustained effort throughout the year to present your organization to potential supporters on a regular basis. In many cases, the more times you mail out to a list of supporters (particularly your house list), the more money you will ultimately raise. Some well-established organizations successfully mail once a month to their regular contributors, and others may mail two or three times each year with equal success. There is no fixed number of times an organization "should" mail, but don't be afraid to mail more than once a year.

Direct mail can fit very nicely into your overall fundraising program, your advocacy work, and your public education efforts. For example, the donors you acquire through direct mail ("prospecting") become possible candidates for major contributions, or participants in special events, or volunteers, or lobbyists, or consumers of any products that you might market (such as calendars, gift cards, or posters). The following steps outline the procedures for organizing a direct mail campaign.

Step 1. Create Your List, Identify Prospective Supporters

Refer back to the concentric circles exercise in Chapter 7. Select the people with whom you have already established some contact through the mail as candidates for your first mail appeal. Of course, include anyone who has already given you unsolicited contributions of any size. If the list of those individuals is modest in size (fewer than five hundred names), you might consider augmenting it with other names. Even if your initial list is a good size, you may still consider getting additional names and undertaking an expanded mailing.

Step 2. Augment Your Initial Mailing List

You can expand your initial list in a number of ways.

1. Swap your current list with groups that have similar constituencies. Exchanging names and addresses with another organization expands your potential list without incurring any costs. Of course, some groups may be protective of their mailing lists and refuse to exchange or even sell their lists.

2. Compile a list of the friends, relatives, colleagues, co-workers, business associates, vendors and neighbors. If each of your principal supporters gives you ten new names and addresses, you have increased the size of your list tenfold.

3. Beg or borrow lists from organizations. Convince them of the value of your work and ask for a one-time loan of their list.

4. Rent existing lists of donors from groups with similar constituencies. The average contributors list available for rental ranges in price from $45 to $150 per thousand names, with a usual minimum rental of two thousand names. Sometimes you can rent directly from the organization, but more likely you will have to rent from a professional list broker. Once you know to whom you are mailing, you can then determine what you are mailing.

5. Make use of free publicity outlets in your community, such as notices in local newsletters, public service announcements on radio, Web sites, and other ways to spread the word about your work and to encourage inquiries. Once you get the name and address of an interested individual, you have a candidate for your direct mail efforts. Your initial investment in labor may consist of only a press release mailing to local media.

Step 3. Develop the Mailing Piece or Package

Direct mail packages traditionally include the following:

• Outside envelope which can include a "teaser" (a slogan or quotation to compel people to open the envelope)

- Letter, which can range from one to six pages (most frequently one or two 8½-by-11-inch sheet printed on both sides)

- Reply device (a card restating the request for money), which fits into the reply envelope

- Return envelope, with or without a postage imprint

Mailings, however, can also consist of a self-mailer—a flyer with a coupon or even a post-card, depending on the circumstances and funds available. You can also include other items in a mailing, such as a photograph, a newsletter, a cover note from your president or a local celebrity, or a calendar of events.

Within certain postal guidelines, you can mail anything you want. However, it's best to limit your enclosures to items pertaining to the request for a contribution. Concentrate on your written copy for the letter, envelope, reply device, and, possibly, the return envelope. Also, be sure to pay attention to the artwork, color, typeface, and overall design. The presentation of your message does influence your chances of success.

Step 4. Write Copy for the Mailing

Through your copy you need to establish in the most definitive terms the reason(s) recipients should support your work. You might present only one reason. Stress why your cause or program is unique. Describe your mission and how the money will be used without being too wordy. Highlight key points. Make your letter easy to read. If possible, build a story around your central idea, or recount the history of your issue or cause. Set a tone for your writing. It can be whimsical, dramatic, serious, emotional, or otherwise, but whatever tone you choose has to be conveyed consistently throughout the mailing package.

Pay close attention to the concept of segmentation. For instance, the letter mailed to cold prospects from a purchased list should not be the same as the one sent to current donors. Like-wise, different letters should be sent to donors making smaller donations and those making larger ones. Be careful not to include top donors in your direct mail solicitation; they may be offended that you are treating them like everyone else. Send them the solicitation package, and handwrite across the top, "I thought you'd like to see what our mail solicitation looks like." Do the same with members of the board and advisory committee, and other individuals who play an important part in the life of your organization.

Computer technology has made it easier than ever to keep good records and make mailings as personal as possible. It's wonderful to be able to thank a donor for his past gift(s) and state the amount of the gift, when the gift was made, and, if appropriate, the purpose. Describing in the letter what that person's contribution, together with the gifts of others, has made possible can make the donor feel that he or she has made a difference regardless of the size of the gift.

Here are some openings for good direct mail appeals, followed by brief comments on why they work:

From the Christian Appalachian Project, Lancaster, Kentucky, a 50-year-old organization that provides a wide variety of self-help programs in central Appalachia, is this opening to a letter to someone who has not given before:

Dear Friend,

Did you ever feel that life had placed a mountain in front of you that was too steep to climb?

Comment: A one-sentence opening paragraph is easy to read. Furthermore, the question posed is one that almost any person would answer, and piques the reader's curiosity to find out what mountain is being referred to. This kind of opening is designed to draw people into the letter.

From the Gay and Lesbian Alliance Against Defamation (GLAAD), Los Angeles, California, which challenges homophobic images in the media and applauds positive representations of gay and lesbian life:

Dear Friend,

Last fall, our Executive Director, Joan Garry, wrote to ask you to renew your GLAAD membership and to update you about our activities. Since then, we haven't heard from you, but as Co-Chairs of the Board of Directors, we hope that you will take this opportunity to renew your financial commitment to GLAAD by returning the coupon at the bottom of this page along with your contribution.

Comment: Addressed to an insider, the letter simply states what GLAAD thinks has recently happened. It gives the impression that the lapsed member is so important that now the board chairs are taking the time to write. Informing people of their importance to your organization and the importance of their gift is a key element in successful direct mail fundraising.

From the Siskiyou Project in Cave Junction, Oregon, which seeks to protect wilderness from exploitation and to educate people on the critical importance of the region they work in, is this letter to a current member:

Dear Friend,

It's official. A proposed gold mine on the banks of the Chetco River in the heart of the rugged Kalmiopsis Wilderness will never happen, and 2,000 acres of additional mining claims in the Wilderness will be terminated!

Comment: This is a short, easy-to-read paragraph celebrating a victory. The member can feel good that his or her donation helped save this wilderness, and can be confident that future donations will be as effective.

The copy should always offer something to the reader, even if that something is intangible, such as an offer to protect his or her constitutional rights with the money that's contributed. The donor might also derive some sense of protection or well-being from the gift, as well as a feeling of satisfaction in participating in a cause. Membership in an arts organization, for example, might provide both social cachet and new contacts. Material rewards might include a newsletter, a schedule of events, a magazine, or even "membership" with or without specific benefits. In any case, the reader should be aware that there is something to be gained in exchange for a contribution.

All the components of the mailing piece should mention one of the offers. For example, the reply card can start off with a statement like, "Dear Ira, You can count on me to help the American Civil Liberties Union resist this historic swing against individual liberties." (Note the fact that the reply is personalized—"Dear Ira"—and uses the pronoun "you.")

It is usually recommended that the minimum gift amount be mentioned somewhere in the letter to encourage at least that level of gift. In addition, your reply card should list four or five categories of giving levels, including "other." You can set an overall financial goal in the letter itself; for example, "We need to raise an additional $2,500 to open the doors of our second shelter. If 100 readers of this appeal each give us $25, we will meet our goal."

You want to at least cover the costs of the mailing itself so that you don't lose money. You hope to net more. Generally, people who give will contribute the amount you have requested. Also, identifying levels of giving with appropriate names, such as patron or benefactor for your highest category, helps stimulate higher giving. Listing categories also encourages donors to aspire to higher levels of giving in the future.

It can be very effective to tell the reader exactly what a certain amount makes possible; for instance, $25 feeds a hungry infant for a month. The more a donor can visualize the connection between writing a check and helping someone, the more likely that that person will write a check; or, if the recipient is already a supporter, that he or she will increase the size of their gift. Regarding this last scenario: there is nothing wrong with asking for more, but be sure to justify your request.

Finally, your copy must inform the reader how to mail in a contribution; for example, "Use the enclosed reply card and envelope to let me hear from you today."

No matter how good the letter is, the recipient must first be enticed to open the envelope. A "teaser" on the envelope will encourage a prospective donor to read on. The Southern Poverty Law Center in Montgomery, Alabama, for example, included a photograph in its package. On the envelope was a bright yellow sticker that said "Photo Enclosed, Please Do Not Bend." In a direct mail solicitation for members, the California State Parks Foundation used this teaser: "Your FREE Hiking Guide to California." Both of these methods are very effective.

Step 5. Design the Mailing

Once you have a rough copy of your appeal, you can proceed to the design stage. Some kind of artwork is always desirable, no matter how limited your budget. One approach is to use the same type style in each piece of the mailing; all the pieces in the package should support the letter, which is heavily weighted with copy. You might simply use your organization's letterhead and a uniform type style to produce a standard 8½-by-11-inch two-sided letter. Using parts of your letterhead as artwork for other pieces of the mailing helps give the package a uniform graphic look. High-quality photographs that support the copy can be a boost to a mailing. Photos of anonymous people standing in a line and smiling are not useful. On the other hand, photos of actions, of demonstrations, of children performing or reading, of wilderness that has been saved can be quite effective. Photographs are often used on the reply card or even on the outside envelope to encourage people to open the mailing. Use parts of your letterhead for the artwork of other pieces of the mailing, since you do want the mailing to present a uniform graphic image.

A Note about Brochures. The evidence is now very clear that brochures do not help appeals and may in fact lower the rate of response. Brochures are for distributing at forums, for giving to potential major donors before soliciting them, for sending to friends with a personal note, and so on.

Step 6. Arrange Printing and Mailing

Before deciding how many pieces to include in your mailing—letter, return envelope, reply card, photos and other possible enclosures, and the outside envelope (the "carrier")—and their respective sizes, check postal regulations about maximum and minimum size and weight for bulk and first-class mailings. This will help you decide the size and total number of your own enclosures. The most common approach is to use a No. 10-sized envelope. Next, investigate local offset printing concerns. Obtain at least three bids before you select a company. Make sure that your three contacts are bidding on the basis of the same specifications and that they give you a detailed bid, including a paper sample. If a printer is a member of your board or your family, your printing might be donated. (Unless you have a really strong personal relationship with a printer, this is unlikely.) Ascertain whether the price of the printing includes delivery. Be sure that the bid includes such factors as perforations, if any. With more and more people expressing concern for the state of the environment, you can increase your response by printing on recycled papers; organizations working on environmental issues will wish to explore the cost of "tree-free" paper such as hemp, cotton, or kenaf. (For more information on tree-free or recycled options, contact Coop America in Washington, D.C. and ask for their publication *Woodwise*. Their phone number is 202-872-5307; their Web site is www.coopamerica.org.)

Typically, you will want your printer to fold your letters. You can plan a volunteer night to stuff your mailing and to bundle it appropriately for the post office. If you have more than five thousand outgoing pieces, you should consider engaging a letter shop to affix labels, to stuff envelopes, and to bundle for mailing. If you have a large volunteer force, you might want to do these jobs yourself.

After affixing labels on a bulk-rate mailing, you need to organize the mailing by zip code. Check the bulk-rate office of your main post office, or check with your local postmaster for details on bulk-rate mailing. There are nonprofit mailing houses and sheltered workshops that also do business by stuffing nonprofit mailings.

Step 7. Monitor Daily Returns to Your Mailing

Plan on the necessary people power to open your mail, starting two to three weeks after a third-class bulk mailing and about one week after a first-class mailing.

All contributions should be acknowledged with a personalized thank-you note within seventy-two hours, or as soon as possible. The acknowledgment builds goodwill and provides a receipt for a donation. Some organizations include a small envelope for an additional contribution. Your thank-you note can be very brief, and should specify the amount of the donation. (IRS regulations require you to acknowledge any contribution over $250, and to specify if any goods or services were received for the gift.)

For example,

Dear Ms. Jones,

Thank you so much for your gift of $50 to Wetlands Protection League. Your gift will go a long way to educating the public about the importance of wetlands and in protecting the habitat of the many birds that live in them. No goods or services were provided for your gift.

Sincerely, Joe Director

Tabulate the number of responses and the dollar amounts so that the response rate and the average gift can be calculated. And to help you predict cash flow in response to future mailings, note the number of responses received each day and gauge the trend of the responses.

Step 8. Assess the Results

In evaluating your results, you will be looking perhaps at weekly report summaries. You will be appraising the success or failure of the campaign in terms of total responses, total dollars earned, average gift, and dollars earned versus dollars spent.

Remember, if this was your first mailing to a list of names and your income roughly equals your expenses, you can think of yourself as fairly successful, since you have gained a number of donors who will respond again to your requests for support. If your expenses exceeded your income by a wide margin (more than 30 percent), then you may want to reassess the suitability of direct mail for you altogether, unless you can isolate the exact reasons that the mailing failed and correct them in your next attempt. A mailing might fail because of bad timing, high costs, or wrongly targeted lists.

Step 9. Schedule Future Mailings

Nearing breakeven or profitability in your first mailing should inspire you to repeat the campaign. Although you should definitely schedule another mailing on the anniversary of your initial effort, you will not want to wait a year until your next mailing. Deciding when to mail again is your next task. Many organizations mail successfully at the following times:

- September 1 to October 15: Post-Labor Day Season

- November 7 to November 21: Year-End Holiday Period (Appeals at this time of the year reach people during a season of generosity and also, for Americans itemizing their taxes, afford them a tax write-off just before the end of the year. Appeals sent after November 21 run into too much competition for attention. Unless you are a soup kitchen, a homeless shelter, or some kind of agency serving a lot of people in December, your appeal will not do as well that month.)

- January 1 to February 1: Post-Holiday Appeal (People are looking for opportunities to make themselves feel better.)

- March: Spring Appeal

There are almost as many potential times for mailings as there are weeks in the year. A significant factor is your own seasonality, that is, when your own programs occur or when you experience a particular emergency. You usually plan a fixed mailing schedule of three to four mailings a year, with the opportunity for additional emergency appeals as the situation warrants. After engaging in direct mail for one year, you will be able to gauge what times of the year engender the best responses to your requests. Calculations based on average gift, response rate, and profitability (as measured by costs versus revenues) provide you with the data necessary to decide when to schedule your mailings. For example, you may reserve your mailings to new lists for the time of the year when you received the most responses previously. You can continue to mail out to your regular list at the other scheduled times.

Summary Worksheet

for _____

(name of your organization)

Approaching Individuals for Support: Direct Mail

Building on Direct Mail Efforts to Date

1. Are you already using direct mail to raise funds?

   ____ yes   ____ no

   If yes, during which months have you been sending out appeals? Or, how many times each year, if your timing varies?

   a. _____

   b. _____

   c. _____

   d. _____

   e. _____

2. What is the net income and number of donors responding for each of these appeals?

   a. $ _____; ____ # of donors: new ____ renewing ____

   b. $ _____; ____ # of donors: new ____ renewing ____

   c. $ _____; ____ # of donors: new ____ renewing ____

   d. $ _____; ____ # of donors: new ____ renewing ____

   e. $ _____; ____ # of donors: new ____ renewing ____

3. How can you enhance the income potential for any of these appeals?
   Additional Actions Needed:

   a. (e.g., Fall Appeal)_____

   _____

   _____

   _____

   b. (e.g. Holiday Appeal) _____

   _____

   _____

   _____

   c. (e.g. Spring Appeal) _____

   _____

   _____

   _____

d. _____

_____

e. _____

_____

4. Which of those special appeals are "proven" traditions (i.e., more people respond, more funds are raised each time, etc.)?

a. _____

b. _____

c. _____

5. Which appeals should be discarded (due to declining numbers of responses or lower receipts) or vastly overhauled?

a. _____

b. _____

c. _____

Assessing Your Organization's Direct Mail Readiness

6. Have you identified the particular constituencies that you can approach for support by direct mail?

_____ yes   _____ no

They are:
a. "house list"

a. _____

b. _____

c. _____

d. _____

7. Does your organization already have mailing lists of these constituencies?

_____ yes   _____ no

8. If not, do you have access to such mailing lists (through friends and colleagues, other organizations, etc.)?

_____ yes   _____ no   _____ untested

9. Have you determined the fixed costs versus potential revenues of a direct mail effort to gauge your potential net income?

_____ yes   _____ no

Projected Costs $ _____
Projected Income $ _____

10. Does the anticipated return in dollars and new donors justify the time expended?

_____ yes _____ no

Finding Assistance and Counsel

11. Name three or more individuals who can advise you on starting or enhancing your direct mail effort.

a. _____

b. _____

c. _____

d. _____

e. _____

Rating Your Direct Mail Potential

12. On the basis of what you have determined, how would you rank your chances of securing individuals' support through direct mail?

___ Very Good ___ Possible ___ Unlikely ___ Still Unknown

Additional Resources

Publications

Barnes, Roscoe. "What Daytime Soaps Can Teach Us about Writing Good Copy." *Fund Raising Management* 30 (April 2000): 36–37.
    Suggests how to "hook" readers by using effective last sentences or paragraphs on each page of fundraising letters or brochures.

Bazerman, Charles. "Green Giving: Engagement, Values, Activism, and Community Life." *New Directions for Philanthropic Fundraising* 22 (Winter 1998): 7–21.
    Analysis of fundraising appeals, with emphasis on the efforts of the Community Environmental Council in Santa Barbara, California. Their fundraising documents stressed maintaining the community's way of life, and were very successful. With bibliographic references.

Christ, Rick. "Put Your Direct Mail to the Test." *Currents* 24 (May 1998): 20–26.
    Explains the need for testing of direct mail campaigns and suggests strategies on what to test, how to test, and what to expect from testing.

Clark, Connie. "Designing Your Outer Envelope: To Tease or Not To Tease?" *FRI Monthly Portfolio* 35 (August 1996): 3–4.
    Lists several proven techniques for getting a potential donor to open a fundraising letter.

De Vries, Dan. "Building a Donor Base with Personal Letters." *Grassroots Fundraising Journal* 18 (August 1999): 3–6.
    Offers ideas for personalizing direct mail solicitations.

Dickey, Marilyn. "Give a Little, Get a Lot?" *Chronicle of Philanthropy* 10 (11 December 1997): 32–36.
    Nonprofit groups are becoming creative when it comes to using small gifts, also know as premiums, to attract direct mail donors.

Hall, Holly. "Fund Raisers Put Their Direct-Mail Solicitations to the Test." *Chronicle of Philanthropy* 10 (8 October 1998): 34–37.
    Highlights changes that several nonprofit groups made to their direct mail campaigns that improved their fundraising results.

Huntsinger, Jerry. "Beating Your Control: What Are You Going To Test This Time?" *NonProfit Times* 13 (January 1999): 26–27.
    Provides a list of direct mail techniques, their advantage or disadvantage, unseen traps, and any possible percent increases or decreases in their use.

Jardine, Fred, and Don Schoenleber. "And the Winner Is." *Fund Raising Management* 29 (April 1998): 20–22.
Examines what works and fails when using premiums and incentives in fundraising.

Kauper, Laura. "Reaching Out Regionally with FSIs." *Fund Raising Management* 27 (January 1997): 14–17.
Describes how United Cerebral Palsy Associations of New Jersey successfully used freestanding inserts, which are coupon-type ads in Sunday newspapers, to foster greater awareness of their cause and build a more extensive database of prospective donors.

Klein, Kim, and Stephanie Roth. "Choosing the Right Fundraising Strategy." *Grassroots Fundraising Journal* 18 (June 1999): 3–6.
Describes several common fundraising strategies, what each one is best used for, and the expected response from each.

Lewis, Herschell Gordon. "Direct Mail Fund Raising Tactics." *Fund Raising Management* 28 (July 1997): 17–19.
Direct mail campaigning is a classical means to raise funds. The author posits that in order to use this technique effectively into the next century, fundraisers ought to abandon tired cliches and adapt their pitches to a changing world.

Lewis, Herschell Gordon. "Open Me: Does Your Envelope Plead, Scream or Demand?" *Fund Raising Management* 25 (January 1995): 17–19.
Recommends fundraisers test their envelope treatments to be sure they are not inadvertently alienating prospects instead of attracting them.

Munoz, Pat, and Amy O'Connor. "Testing and Tracking Your Results." *Grassroots Fundraising Journal* 17 (June 1998): 5–8.
Discusses direct mail testing of lists and elements of a direct mail package. Also provides a discussion on how to track and analyze test results.

NonProfit Times Direct Marketing Edition (ISSN 0896-5048) is published six times a year by NPT Information Services, Inc. 240 Cedar Knolls Road, Suite 318, Cedar Knolls, NJ 07927. To subscribe call 973-734-1700 or e mail: circmngr@nptimes.com

Rieck, Dean. "Powerful Fund-Raising Letters from A to Z: Part One of Three." *Fund Raising Management* 29 (April 1998): 25–28.

Rieck, Dean. "Powerful Fund-Raising Letters from A to Z: Part Two of Three." *Fund Raising Management* 29 (May 1998): 30–33.

Rieck, Dean. "Powerful Fund-Raising Letters from A to Z: Part Three of Three." *Fund Raising Management* 29 (June 1998): 28–31.

Rieck, Dean. "Using an Emotional Appeal To Boost Your Direct Mail Response." *Fund Raising Management* 30 (May 2000): 24–25.

Ritzenhein, Donald N. "Content Analysis of Fundraising Letters." *New Directions for Philanthropic Fundraising* 22 (Winter 1998): 23–36.
    The author analyzed 21 examples of direct mail letters from the book *Direct Mail Fundraising: Letters that Work* (Plenum, 1988) by Torre and Bendixen. Letters were coded according to four categories: reason for the appeal, proof offered of the need, basis of proof (emotional or logical), and suggested reward to the donor. Within each category, percentages of variations were tabulated and are presented here—wth conclusions about what fundraisers think persuades donors. With bibliographic references.

Robinson, Andy, and Amy O'Connor. "The Direct Mail Debate." *Grassroots Fundraising Journal* 17 (December 1998): 8–13.
    Presents two viewpoints on the use of direct mail as a mechanism for acquiring new members by small grassroots organizations. The first author, Andy Robinson, presents "The case against direct mail for small grassroots groups"; while author Amy O'Connor weighs in with "There's still life in direct mail." Includes suggestions by Mr. Robinson on alternatives to direct mail.

Sinclair, Townes & Company. *Writing for Dollars.* Atlanta, GA: Sinclair, Townes & Company, 1999. 77 looseleaf pages.
    Advice about writing for direct solicitation and for foundation grants. Includes numerous samples.

Squires, Conrad. "Snatching Victory from the Jaws of Defeat." *Fund Raising Management* 27 (January 1997): 32–33.
    Gives suggestions for improving the success rate of a direct mail campaign.

Torre, Robert L., and Mary Anne Bendixen. *Direct Mail Fund Raising: Letters that Work.* New York: Plenum, 1988. xi, 314 p.
    Comprehensive but concise text to aid fundraisers create a direct mail program or improve an existing one. Briefly discusses effective direct mail strategies, writing principles that increase contributions, and criteria needed to develop the best fundraising letter possible. Examines 100 successful direct mail appeals from across the United States, chosen because they provide a good match between effective copy and the intended audience, make it easy for prospects to do whatever it is the mailing asks them to do, clearly define a specific reason and objective for the mailing, and avoid incorrect assumptions and condescension. The appeals are divided into sections for hospitals, health care, and education/social services. Appendixes include selected packages and a calendar of events listing all holidays as well as designated periods of special recognition.

Warwick, Mal, Deborah Block, Stephen Hitchcock, Ivan Levinson, and Joseph H. White, Jr. *999 Tips, Trends and Guidelines for Successful Direct Mail and Telephone Fundraising.* Berkeley, CA: Strathmoor Press, 1993. 316 p.

Watt, Charles V. "Acknowledging the Gift: The Most Important Aspect of Fund Raising." *Fund Raising Management,* 30 (February 2000): 36, 40–42.
> Detailed discussion of the process of sending acknowledgments for contributions received by nonprofit organizations.

Weinstein, Stanley. *The Complete Guide to Fund-Raising Management.* New York: John Wiley & Sons, 1999. xii, 307 p.
> A comprehensive treatment of fundraising principles and practices, including information about creating case statements, record-keeping, prospect research, cultivating donors, major gifts, grants, direct mail, telemarketing, special events, planned giving, and capital campaigns. Covers management and human resources issues, planning, budgeting, ethics, and evaluation of a fundraising program. Includes disk. Indexed.

Internet Resources

Alliance of Nonprofit Mailers (www.nonprofitmailers.org)
> Maintained by the Alliance of Nonprofit Mailers in Washington, D.C., a coalition of nonprofit organizations, this Web site provides information on nonprofit postal rates and regulations as well as updates on postal issues that are pending before Congress and the Postal Rate Commission.

Direct Mail Response Rate Calculator
(www.moore.com/solutions/integratedsvcs/dirmailcalc.html)
> Developed by Moore Corporation Limited, a communications company in Lincolnshire, Illinois, this Web site includes forms that helps fundraisers determine how large a test mailing is necessary to test a new direct mail fundraising appeal, calculate how many recipients must make a gift for a mailing to cover its costs, and test whether the results are statistically significant. The site also allows fundraisers to calculate how large the full-scale mailing should be to match the response rate to the test mailing, and to figure out how large a variance to expect between the results of the test mailing and the full-scale mailing.

Internet Prospector (www.internet-prospector.org/index.html)
> This Web site provides the current and back issues of the *Internet Prospector,* an on-line newsletter that offers news, advice, and links to Web sites that help fundraisers use the Internet to gather information about foundations, corporations, and individuals in the United States and abroad. To recieve the monthly newsletter via e-mail, send a blank e-mail message to chlowe@uci.edu. In the subject field, type "Subscribe Internet Prospector."

Mal Warwick & Associates, Inc. (www.malwarwick.com)
>   Maintained by Mal Warwick & Associates, Inc., a fundraising consulting company in
>   Berkeley, California, this site provides articles on direct mail and Internet fundraising.
>   Topics include how to start a direct mail program, choose the right mailing lists, write
>   effective fundraising letters, build monthly donor programs, attract visitors to a charity's
>   Web site, and use e-mail to raise money.

The following Web sites contain information about direct mail fundraising software, as well
as a wide range of other fundraising-related software and sites:

www.fundraiser-software.com/donormgt.html

www.nonprofit-info.org/npofaq/05/

www.npo.net/nponet/computer/fundacct.htm

www.coyotecom.com/tips.html

Chapter 10

Using the Telephone

There are no such things as strangers, only friends that we have not yet met.
— Unknown

Two fundraising maxims—"People give to people," and "The greater the degree of personal contact, the greater the chance for a gift,"—are borne out by the success of phonathons. People give because they are asked, particularly when they are asked personally, and phoning is the most personal approach a solicitor can make without actually paying a visit. Phonathons are fundraising events held by a wide variety of nonprofits to follow up direct mail appeals, to solicit or upgrade annual fund contributors, or to conclude capital campaigns, special needs campaigns, and a variety of other endeavors.

While there is much talk that people hate to be called at home and asked for money, the telephone is an increasingly effective fundraising tool that frequently generates better results than direct mail. This is especially true when large numbers of people who are unfamiliar with an organization (such as those on a rented list) are solicited, as a phone conversation provides the personal touch that direct mail cannot deliver.

What Are the Advantages of Raising Support by Telephone?

Following are some of the reasons for the effectiveness of telephone solicitations:

1. The telephone is an internationally accepted medium for holding serious conversations; people are familiar with being asked for money over the phone.

2. Unlike door-to-door soliciting, phoning is safe for both caller and prospect.

3 Volunteers are generally more comfortable phoning strangers than meeting with them personally.

4. Phoning is the highest volume fundraising strategy after direct mail; many hundreds of calls can be made in one evening.

5. People's questions can be answered on the spot; questions prompted by direct mail or televised appeals remain unanswered. This is very important because a simple question or slight doubt can prevent a person from making a donation.

6. Prospects for larger donations, as well as for board and committee membership, can be identified during phone conversations.

7. Phonathons bring all of an organization's constituencies together, building camaraderie among board, staff, and volunteers and creating organizational momentum.

8. In addition to raising funds, phonathons also have public relations value; calls can bring an organization to the attention of people who are not aware of its work.

9. Speaking with lapsed donors can generate renewed support.

10. Phonathons are relatively straightforward fundraising events and don't normally require significant expenditures, extensive preparation, or involved logistics.

What Are the Disadvantages of Raising Support by Telephone?

Fundraising by telephone also has its disadvantages, which include the following:

1. Some prospective donors feel that unsolicited calls are intrusions, and few people would honestly say that they like being solicited over the phone. An organization

runs the risk, therefore, of alienating some prospects who might contribute if approached differently.

2. As a result of the unethical and sometimes illegal practices of some telemarketers and fundraisers, people who were once responsive to phone solicitations may have become fearful and stopped responding.

3. Calls from unfamiliar sources can be identified and avoided through caller-ID technology.

4. Many people must be called, and many people must give, in order to justify the expenditure of money and staff and volunteer time.

5. Callers who are not familiar with a person's giving history may alienate current or lapsed donors.

6. Solicitors cannot see or respond to the facial expression or body language of the person they're calling.

7. It's easier to turn down a request on the phone than it is in person.

Some of these disadvantages can be avoided through careful planning, including reviewing the contribution histories of current and lapsed donors before the calls are made, and making sure the callers are personable, sensitive, enthusiastic, and knowledgeable. Others, such as the inability to sense a person's nonverbal reactions, must be considered in light of the phonathon's purpose: calling large numbers of people because visiting everyone on the call list is both impractical, and, in most cases, inappropriate.

While the advantages would appear to outweigh the disadvantages, organizations must go beyond theory before deciding to hold a phonathon. The principal consideration is, of course, financial. It is difficult to predict the results of any fundraising approach with absolute certainty, but there have been enough phonathons and studies of phonathons to provide reliable data. Perhaps the most important information these studies report is their findings about who responds to telephone solicitations, and what the overall response rates are.

Calculating the Cost Effectiveness of a Phone Campaign

The groups most likely to make contributions when solicited by phone are:

- People who have never given to an organization but have contributed to similar groups; studies show that about 5 percent will respond positively.

- An organization's current donors; about 15 percent will make an extra gift for a special project when asked by phone.

- An organization's lapsed donors; between 10 and 30 percent will contribute when called.[1]

---

1. Kim Klein, "Revisiting the Phon-a-thon," *Grassroots Fundraising Journal* 18 (April 1999): 7–11.

Knowing which groups are most likely to respond to telephone solicitations, as well as their average response rates, enables an organization to project how much might be raised by a phonathon. Measuring these revenues against expenses will indicate whether or not you should hold a phonathon. Use the above formulas to calculate your organization's potential income from a phonathon.

The set of figures in the following example is based on calling people who have not given to your organization but have supported similar ones. Community-based organizations should adapt to their situation the numbers of individuals called to calculate potential income from the phonathon.

According to our formula, if you call 1,000 people in the first group described above, 50 (5 percent of 1,000) will contribute. Let's say you've targeted $35 as the average gift you hope the calls will generate. Your donations will then theoretically total $1,750 (50 gifts at $35) and you will be making $1,750 for every 1,000 attempted calls, or $1.75 per call. Volunteers or paid solicitors normally reach fifteen prospects per hour (not including reaching answering machines, disconnects, etc.), so each caller is raising $26.25 per hour (15 calls per hour at $1.75 per call). With good preparation and training, as well as a bit of luck (a few gifts of $50 or $100), it is possible to raise more per hour. Using paid callers is expensive, so most organizations should use volunteers as much as possible.

After calculating the total projected gifts from this group of prospective donors, perform the same calculation for members of the second group—current donors being asked for extra gifts—but apply an average response rate of 15 percent. Finally, go through this exercise a third time and project the total gifts from members of the last group—lapsed donors—using an average response rate of 20 percent. When the projected gift totals from the three groups are added and compared with the projected expenses, an organization should be able to project the results of its phonathon.

Preparing for a Phonathon

Once an organization has decided that the projected revenues will justify the effort, the phonathon must be carefully planned to increase the chances of success. Planners should do their utmost to create a festive, high-energy event; festive because those involved should enjoy their volunteer work, and high-energy because the callers' level of enthusiasm is a key factor in making successful calls. Here are some basic steps an organization should take in preparing for a phonathon.

1. *Set a date.* In setting a date for the phonathon, pay close attention to what's going on in your community, and on the television. Avoid calling during the last episode of a popular television show, for example, or when several charity or sporting events are scheduled. (It's never possible to avoid conflicts completely, of course.) Most organizations have found that calling on a Tuesday, Wednesday, or Thursday between six and nine in the evening (don't call later than nine o'clock) at the beginning of the month generally works best. You may want to conduct your phonathon over two

nights; the second night provides another chance to reach some of the people who couldn't be reached on the first night.

2. *Find a location.* The venue for the phonathon should have enough room and phones; it's best if everyone is in the same room. If the phones are close together, it's easier for callers to support each other and share the good news that builds momentum. Real estate and law offices, mail order houses, and any companies that do a lot of business on the phone are good prospects for allowing you to use their phones at night, especially if they receive some publicity for their contribution. Members of an organization's core group may be helpful in finding the location and negotiating the terms of its use. Be prepared to pay for toll calls.

3. *Publicize the phonathon.* In order to increase the number of people who will respond when called, it's a good idea to publicize the phonathon in as many ways as possible. While a phonathon may not in itself be hot news in the eyes of local journalists and broadcasters, you might be able to attract their interest by issuing press releases about the phonathon's cause.

4. *Make a list of people to call.* Organize your list into groups of current donors, lapsed donors, and people who donate to similar organizations but not to yours; assign the easiest group—your current donors—to volunteers who have never participated in a phonathon before. They might also call lapsed donors, who are also usually friendly and whose contributions probably ended as a result of an oversight. Only rarely will donors stop giving because they have developed a dislike for your organization.

   Your list should include the person's name, address, phone number, and a place to summarize the call. For current and lapsed donors, add a column with the dates and amounts of the person's last few gifts and, if possible, the purpose of those gifts. Including a prospect's giving history provides the caller with a natural opening line: thanking the donor for what he or she has already done.

5. *Prepare materials for volunteer callers.* Draft an instruction sheet discussing the most common situations that arise during telephone solicitations and how to handle them. Also, list the questions that prospects are most likely to ask, and provide the best answers.

6. *Write a script for volunteers to read.* Volunteers will generally be able to "ad lib" after the first few conversations, but a script will provide a feeling of security for the initial calls.

7. *Prepare follow-up letters.* You'll need to send three different letters after the calls are made and callers' reports are turned in. One letter thanks the donor for his gift of $____; the second expresses the organization's thanks for speaking with the caller and includes more information about the group; the third letter is sent to people who could not be reached, along with the organization's information. Send these letters with return envelopes and return cards specifying how much the donors pledged on the phone.

Sample Phoning Form A

XYZ Organization Phonathon Form

Volunteer Name: _____

Donor Name: _____   Spouse: _____

Address: _____   Giving History:

City: _____   Grand Total: _____

State, Zip: _____   Largest Amount: _____

Phone (H): _____   Last Amount: _____

Phone (W): _____   Last Date: _____

Amount Pledged: _____   Most recent in-kind donation:

Date Pledged: _____   Description: _____

_____

Payment Date: _____   Date: _____ Value: _____

__ Now __ Other Please specify: _____

__ Would like listing as donor to appear in annual report and other material

__ Anonymous

Comments

_____

_____

_____

_____

_____

_____

_____

_____

Adapted by permission from DonorPerfect-Starkland Systems.

Sample Phoning Form B

Name: _____   Pledge: $ _____ Matching gift: $ _____

Address: _____   __ New donor/Increased

City: _____   __ Will give (unspecified)

State: _____ Zip code: _____   __ Undecided

Telephone   __ Refused/Reason: _____

Home: _____   __ Do not call

Work: _____   __ Sent gift earlier

                                     __ Send information

Credit card information

__ Mastercard __ Visa __ Amex   New address __ Home __ Business

Exp. Date: _____   _____

                                    _____

                                    _____

                                    Telephone: _____

Call Record

Caller: Date/Time   Comments:

_____

_____

_____

_____

_____

_____

_____

_____

_____

_____

_____

_____

Sample Tips for Phoners

The following tips can be useful in a group setting or can be used by the solo caller.

- **Invest in your organization.** Your personal contribution is a tangible sign that you believe in your organization and its mission. If you have not done so already, please make your contribution or fill in your pledge on the appropriate call report form. Your calls to others will be more successful when you have made your early contribution.

- **Plan each call. Review the giving or membership history.** Decide on an appropriate request amount (always more than last year). Take a second to review any sample scripts or think through what you are going to say.

- **Smile and dial.** People can hear the smile in your voice. Smile before you dial. Smile when speaking.

- **Know your organization's case for support.** Your reasons for supporting the organization are most persuasive. Your sincere and convincing understanding will translate into financial support from the prospective donors you call. Let the prospect know why you support the organization. And tell the prospect why it needs financial support.

- **Always ask for or suggest a specific giving amount.** Again, please remember to suggest more than the donor gave last year.

    EXAMPLE (if the donor gave $75 last year): "With your support, X Organization has been able to accomplish so very much . . .and I hope you're in a position to consider a donation of $100 or more to help us carry on this work."

- **Don't accept the first "no." Negotiate.** Suggest alternatives. Maybe the no is only "no" to the request amount you suggested. Ask: "With what amount would you be comfortable?"

---

8. *Select volunteer callers.* In selecting callers for a phonathon, use the same criteria and sensitivity you'd use to select people to make face-to-face solicitations (see the following chapter). To determine how many callers are needed, estimate that one person can make thirty to thirty-five calls per hour (not all of these will reach the intended party, of course). Since the phoning session will last about four hours (three hours of calling, thirty minutes of warm-up and thirty minutes of debriefing and wrap-up), each volunteer should be given about one hundred names to call.

Some groups, hoping for better results, choose not to use volunteers for telemarketing and employ paid solicitors. If you choose to hire a firm for this purpose, you still need to prepare callers thoroughly to answer questions on topics concerning your organization's vision and mission, funding mix, and programs. Paid solicitors are generally given an hourly wage plus a bonus for

- **Strive to reach agreement on a specific donation amount.** *If the donor doesn't pledge a specific contribution amount, it's the same as a refusal.* Prospects who say, "I'll send something in" rarely do. Try a "let me" phrase.

  EXAMPLE: "Let me enter that as a pledge of $25. You can send that in when we send the reminder—or if you want to, you can always add to that amount."

- **Always repeat the amount pledged.**

- **Always repeat any special payment schedules or information.**

- **Be warm and polite to everyone.** If the prospect made a pledge, say "Thank you." If the prospect gives you a firm refusal, say "Thank you for your time. I hope you'll consider supporting X Organization in the future."

- **Record the results of the call.**
  1. Specific dollar amount of the pledge
  2. Instructions for reminder statements (any special information about when the pledge will be paid)
  3. Check the spelling of the donor's name—how does the donor wish to be acknowledged?
  4. Your name as the volunteer caller
  5. If refusal, clearly write "refusal"

- **Turn in all appropriate paperwork.**

Adapted by permission of DonorPerfect-Starkland Systems.

each successful call. While paid solicitors can be very effective, some donors are put off by them. Your group will have to weigh the pros and cons of professional solicitors and make your decision.

9. *Recruit volunteer coordinators.* Recruit volunteers to handle the evening's logistics and support the callers during the phonathon. By bringing refreshments, spreading news of a successful call, and so on, these volunteers can energize callers and increase their effectiveness.

The Phonathon Itself

1. *Train the callers.* Ask callers to arrive at the phonathon location about a half hour before the phoning is to begin. Make sure you have copies of the instructions, the question and answer sheet you mailed to them, and the prospect forms. Review the sheets with them. Do not skip this step. Then walk the callers through the solicitation script, which might begin in this way:

Sample Telephone Script A: Public Interest Communications, Inc.

Common Cause Virginia Presentation

Hello, may I speak with Mr./Ms._____, please? . . . Hi, Mr./Ms. _____. This is _____ calling from PIC on behalf of Common Cause of Virginia. Are you able to hear me clearly?

Fine, Mr./Ms._____. Thanks for your support of Common Cause of Virginia. It helped make the past session of the General Assembly our most successful one *ever*. Using funds provided by friends like you, we were able to mail *thousands* of action alert postcards to Common Cause members throughout Virginia about the need to pass three major reforms. Many legislators said that the calls and letters they received from Common Cause members made the critical difference in the passage of all three reform measures.

But as significant as those victories were, we have a lot more work to do. You see, most states limit the amount of money an individual, corporation, or political action committee can contribute to candidates. But not Virginia!

What chance does the ordinary citizen have when wealthy special interests can spend hundreds of thousands of dollars to get their way in Richmond? We need to win political fundraising limits and soft money restrictions. But we need your help. Our operating budget for the year is $53,000. That's pocket change to those who oppose reform. But until we limit the money special interests contribute to our lawmakers, Virginia will continue to be for sale to the highest bidder.

This Spring appeal is one of our most important sources of funding. All the money we generate from this telephone appeal will stay home in Virginia to help clean up our Commonwealth. Will you invest in good government and renew your support of Common Cause of Virginia with a gift of $ _____?

(If no) I understand, Mr./Ms._____. But here's the effect of unlimited campaign spending: You telephone your legislator because of a matter that's important to you. At the

"Hello, is John Smith available?" If it is John, continue. "My name is Vivian Volunteer, and I am on the board of Friends of Birds. May I speak with you for a minute?" (PAUSE) Be respectful of the answer. If Mr. Smith does not want to continue the conversation, ask if you can call back later. If the response is "no," thank him politely, hang up, and record this result. If he says, "I never make contributions over the phone," ask if you can mail some information so they can decide when the time is right.

If Mr. Smith is willing to listen, you might continue as follows: "Friends of Birds has a simple mission — to preserve the birds' habitat. We started ten years ago because of a dramatic decline in the songbird population in our community. Because of our work, the songbird population has stabilized, and is beginning to grow. Have you heard of our work?"

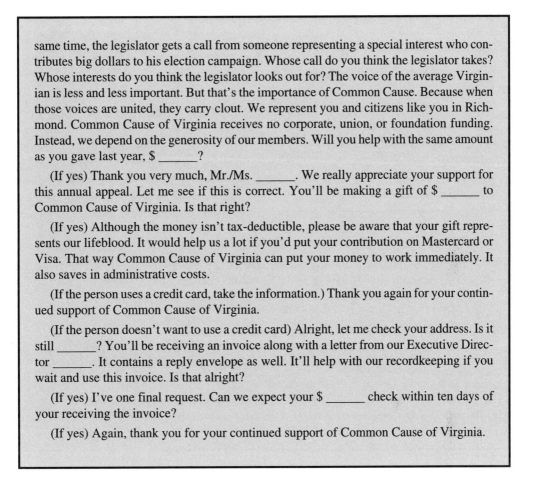

same time, the legislator gets a call from someone representing a special interest who contributes big dollars to his election campaign. Whose call do you think the legislator takes? Whose interests do you think the legislator looks out for? The voice of the average Virginian is less and less important. But that's the importance of Common Cause. Because when those voices are united, they carry clout. We represent you and citizens like you in Richmond. Common Cause of Virginia receives no corporate, union, or foundation funding. Instead, we depend on the generosity of our members. Will you help with the same amount as you gave last year, $ _____ ?

(If yes) Thank you very much, Mr./Ms. _____. We really appreciate your support for this annual appeal. Let me see if this is correct. You'll be making a gift of $ _____ to Common Cause of Virginia. Is that right?

(If yes) Although the money isn't tax-deductible, please be aware that your gift represents our lifeblood. It would help us a lot if you'd put your contribution on Mastercard or Visa. That way Common Cause of Virginia can put your money to work immediately. It also saves in administrative costs.

(If the person uses a credit card, take the information.) Thank you again for your continued support of Common Cause of Virginia.

(If the person doesn't want to use a credit card) Alright, let me check your address. Is it still _____? You'll be receiving an invoice along with a letter from our Executive Director _____. It contains a reply envelope as well. It'll help with our recordkeeping if you wait and use this invoice. Is that alright?

(If yes) I've one final request. Can we expect your $ _____ check within ten days of your receiving the invoice?

(If yes) Again, thank you for your continued support of Common Cause of Virginia.

(PAUSE) If yes, ask what Mr. Smith knows, adding, "I don't want to take your time repeating what you already know." If he is not familiar with your work, you might say, "Let me just share two recent accomplishments that best demonstrate our work. After I do, I want to ask you to help support what we do." The two examples should be brief — one or two short sentences each. For example, "Friends of Birds convinced the local tanning plant to install scrubbers on their chimneys. This reduced smog in our community significantly, helping not only songbirds but also people with asthma and other respiratory illnesses. Do those accomplishments seem worthwhile to you, Mr. Smith?"

Sample Telephone Script B: Public Interest Communications, Inc.

Chesapeake Bay Foundation Special Appeal Script

Hello, may I speak with Mr./Ms. _____, please? . . .Hi, Mr./Ms. _____. This is _____ calling from PIC for the Chesapeake Bay Foundation. We appreciate your support for our efforts to save the Bay.

As you know, the Chesapeake Bay Foundation has worked very hard to stop the decline of the Bay's health. I'm calling because the Bay's so far out of balance that it's no longer enough to just prevent further decline. *We need to restore what's been lost.* And that's a very tall order.

For example, oysters are now less than 1 percent of their original population! The Bay has also lost the majority of its wetlands, underwater grasses, and forested buffers. Meanwhile, toxic chemicals and polluting nutrients are choking the Bay's waters.

The Chesapeake Bay Foundation is dedicated to restoring the natural balance of the Bay. This includes taking steps like adding 400,000 oysters to Bay waters . . .restoring wetlands . . .replanting forested buffers . . .growing new underwater grasses . . .and working to cut the toxic pollution *in half!*

All of this takes money. That's why I'm calling! We need your help. Will you make a special tax-deductible gift to the Chesapeake Bay Foundation of $ _____?

(If no) I understand, Mr./Ms. _____. But the loss of the Bay's natural balance has left the door open for Pfiesteria. This lethal microbe killed more than a *billion* fish in North Carolina! Last summer, it killed tens of thousands of fish in several Maryland rivers. Pfiesteria has also been implicated in a wide range of human health problems, as well.

(PAUSE) If Mr. Smith agrees that your examples are good things, then say, "Tonight we are looking for one hundred new members, and I hope you might join Friends of Birds with a gift of $35." (PAUSE) If he agrees, arrange for the donation to be paid by credit card or check. If he says, "Thirty-five dollars is a lot," suggest that he pay it in two installments. If that is not possible, tell him that a gift of any amount is helpful and deeply appreciated; then ask what he would like to give. Thank him for whatever he decides to do.

After reviewing the script with the callers and having them practice with each other, remind them that only five of one hundred people they call are likely to make a gift. Most will not be home, some will not give on the phone, some will be curt, and some will engage in pleasant conversation but not make a gift. Remind your callers that practically every conversation brings the organization and its work to people's attention.

The only way we can truly address the Pfiesteria problem is to replenish the Bay's natural systems. Mr./Ms. _____, this is a job that's never been so critical as it is today. Will you help? Will you make a special tax-deductible gift of $ _____ to the Chesapeake Bay Foundation?

(If no) Alright, Mr./Ms. _____. But, thank you again for your support of the Chesapeake Bay Foundation.

(If yes at any amount) Thank you very much, Mr./Ms. _____. We really appreciate your special pledge of support for the Chesapeake Bay Foundation. Let me see if this is correct. You'll be making a special gift of $ _____, is that right? (If yes) Wonderful. It would save us a lot in administrative and processing expenses if you'd put your contribution on Mastercard or Visa. By charging your gift, the Chesapeake Bay Foundation will also be able to put your money to work immediately. Would you like to charge your gift to your Visa or Mastercard, Mr./Ms. _____? (If the person uses a credit card, take the information.) Great, Mr./Ms. _____. Thank you again for your special support of the Chesapeake Bay Foundation's efforts to restore the Bay's natural balance.

(If the person doesn't want to use a credit card) Alright, Mr./Ms. _____. Is your address still _____? You'll be receiving a special invoice along with a letter from the Chesapeake Bay Foundation's president, _____. It contains a postage-paid reply envelope as well. It'll help us with our recordkeeping if you wait and use this invoice. Is that alright?

(If yes) I've one final request. Can we expect your $ _____ check within ten days of your receiving the invoice? (If yes) Thank you again for your very generous support, Mr./Ms. _____. It will really help the Chesapeake Bay Foundation's efforts to restore the Bay's natural balance.

2. *Place the calls!* Make sure the volunteers keep the atmosphere lively. Ask your coordinators to circulate among the callers to express their thanks, ask questions, spread the word about successful calls, and generally create a positive atmosphere.

After the Event

1. *Send donor follow-up letters.* Fill out the follow-up letters that you wrote ahead of time and send them out no more than twenty-four hours after the calls were made. See page 243 for a sample thank-you note for a pledge made during the course of a phonathon.

2. *Thank participants.* Send thank-you notes immediately to all those who participated in the phonathon and tell them the results.

Sample Letter of Confirmation to Phonathon Volunteers

May 1, 2000
Jennifer Goodheart
1234 Volunteer Lane
Anycity, TX 78000

Dear Jennifer,

Thanks so much for agreeing to serve as a volunteer caller for the XYZ Nonprofit Organization June Phonathon. The calling will take place at _____ (location).

To confirm, I see that you signed up for the evening of Monday, June 12, 2000. There will be a brief orientation that evening beginning at 6:30. Calling will begin immediately after the orientation and will continue until 9:00 PM.

Volunteers who have participated in our phonathons frequently have remarked that they enjoyed the experience and were surprised at how much could be raised using this simple approach.

I believe you will enjoy the experience also. Besides, we will have pizza and light refreshments for the volunteer callers.

Again, let me express my appreciation for all you do for the XYZ Nonprofit Organization.

With best regards,

Jan Enright
Director of Volunteers

3. *Publicize the outcome.* Spread the good news about the success of your phonathon. Communicate with your internal constituents through your newsletter or a special mailing. Let your community know the extent to which it supports your mission through press releases to the print and electronic media. Your release is more likely to make the news if it comes from a prominent member of the community who is involved with your organization, or if you describe the actual benefits to the community made possible by the phonathon. Make sure to follow up the releases by phone (of course!) and persevere until you are able to speak to the person to whom you sent the release.

Sample Thank-You Note and Phonathon Reminder

May 1, 2000
Mr. and Mrs. Samuel Betts
7521 Phone Responsive Rd.
Anytown, TX 78302

Dear Sam and Mildred,

Thank you so much for your pledge of $125 to the XYZ Nonprofit Organization's 2000 fund drive. When our volunteer called last night, you were kind enough to respond generously to our June phonathon. Please know that your contribution will help us feed the hungry, cure the sick, enrich lives through arts and cultural events, and promote spiritual growth for the thousands of people who use our services each year.

I have enclosed a postage-free envelope for your convenience in making your pledge contribution. I have also enclosed a receipt for your records.

You can feel confident that you have made an important investment in the economic, cultural, health care, educational, and spiritual life of our city and state. When you use our services, please enjoy them with the knowledge that you have done so much to make the work of the XYZ Nonprofit Organization possible.

Again, thanks and best wishes to you and yours.

Arthur G. Whizz
Executive Director

Phoning After a Mail Appeal

Following up a direct mail appeal with a phonathon invariably increases the appeal's success. The process is very straightforward. Two weeks after the appeal is mailed, everyone who has responded is taken off the list, and those who haven't responded are called. The script varies slightly from the phonathon just described in that a sentence is added such as, "I am Jean Vasquez from the Women's Shelter. We recently sent you a letter about our work. Did you have a chance to read it?" If the person has read it, you can move right to the close, "Will you be able to help us with a gift of $35 tonight?"

On the other hand, if the person cannot remember the letter or claims not to have received it, callers should follow a script and move into a fuller conversation, "If you will give me a few minutes right now, I'll tell you what it said."

Common Mistakes

- If a person says he or she doesn't give by phone but would like to see some information, don't assume that you are being put off. Many people will not give to a caller right away, but that doesn't mean that they will not give at all. Send them your literature.

- Don't ask emotionally charged and leading questions that have only one answer, such as, "Do you care about retarded children?" or "Don't you wish we had fewer children killed by guns in our community?" Such manipulative questions will undermine any atmosphere of trust that a caller may have created. If you want to establish lasting relationships that will encourage donors to pledge support on a continuing basis, you must first win their trust by treating them with respect. While some people will give money once because of guilt, shame, fear, or greed, they will not give a second time. Nobody likes to be made to feel bad.

- Your script should be a few short sentences, and should get to the point quickly. Make sure that you pause for breath while talking. If you are describing something complicated, punctuate your script with questions: "Did you see the article about that in the paper last week?" or "Do you know about our group—I don't want to tell you things you already know."

Tips

- There are four "P"s to phoning: be Prepared, Polite, and Precise (don't go on and on), and do Proper follow-up (especially thank-you notes).

- Remember that most people will say "no" to a phone solicitation. Don't take this personally—it has nothing to do with you. And remember: every no brings you closer to the next yes and, in addition, brings your organization to the attention of a new person who may ultimately become a donor.

- The way people relate to their telephone is constantly changing with new technologies, and depends to some extent on the age of the person, how long he or she has had a phone, how common phones are in his or her part of the world, and so on. Therefore, there are no hard and fast rules about raising money by phone, except those posed in the preceding tip.

Case Study

Phonathon Relay: DES Action, Oakland, California

DES Action finds people exposed to the drug diethylstibestrol (DES), which pregnant women were given in the 1950s, 1960s, and 1970s to prevent miscarriage. The drug caused a rare form of vaginal cancer in some DES daughters and a variety of reproductive problems in the children of women who took the drug. DES daughters in the Action has worked to find everyone exposed to the drug, help them monitor side effects of the drug, and insure that such drugs cannot ever go on the market again.

DES Action's quarterly newsletter, *DES Action Voice*, is read by more than 3,000 people. Local DES chapters receive two-thirds of the $30 annual subscription fee, which provides the bulk of their income. The phonathon described here was an attempt to improve upon the membership renewal rate of 33 percent. DES' national office organized the phonathon and provided materials to local chapters. The national office felt that local volunteers were competent to answer questions and would make cheaper and better callers than paid solicitors. To avoid long distance charges, they organized a relay. The following description is what they sent their local chapters:

The relay starts on the East Coast. Groups in the Eastern time zone will begin calling their lapsed subscribers at 6 p.m. Eastern Standard Time (EST). At 7 p.m. EST, a designated chapter will call a local chapter in the Midwest, where it will then be 6 p.m., and they will report how much money the East Coast groups have raised so far. Midwest groups will then begin calling. At 9 p.m. EST, East Coast groups will end their phonathon, tally up their results and call the local Midwest chapter, who will report to the other chapters. In turn, the designated Midwest chapter will call the San Francisco office at 8 p.m. Central Time, and report on their success and the success of the East Coast groups. All groups on Pacific Standard Time will be informed of success so far and begin calling. The West Coast phoning will end at 9 p.m. The phonathon will have lasted for nine hours; three in each time zone. With each successive tally of how much has been raised, callers can tell the people they call how much has been brought in, thus increasing excitement.

Results

Using an average of three volunteers each, the seven local chapters called a total of 800 people and contacted 300. Renewal rates varied from 15 to 35 percent per chapter. 100 people agreed to renew their subscription and eighty ultimately did so. Those people who were not reached received a "Sorry we missed you" letter that generated another 35 renewals. The $3,000 gross income was divided among the chapters according to their results. Twenty-one volunteers worked three hours each for a total of 63 volunteer hours. The income for this event was $47.60 per hour. There were no long distance charges, and costs were minimal as each chapter provided volunteers with dinner and soft drinks.

—Pat Cody and Nancy Adess

Summary Worksheet

for _____

Approaching Individuals for Support: Using the Telephone

Using the Telephone To Get Lapsed Donors To Renew

1. How many previous donors have not given within the last 18 months? _____

2. How many mail appeals have you sent seeking their renewal? _____

3. Note percent of response to each appeal:
   Direct Mail Appeal 1: __% Direct Mail Appeal 2: __% Mail Appeal 3: __%

4. Does it seem that you have gotten as many people to renew by mail as possible?
   _____ yes _____ no

5. For how many of your lapsed donors do you have phone numbers? _____

6. How many volunteers would it take to call them? (Assume each volunteer can make 100 calls per evening) _____

7. Assuming a 20-percent response rate and an average gift of $35, how much money could you raise using this strategy? _____

   (Sometimes it is helpful to figure out how much money is being raised per person per hour. You can then decide if this is the best strategy by looking at the number and then thinking of other ways these same volunteers could be raising money with the same amount of effort.)

8. Shall you use telephone calls to try to renew lapsed donors?
   _____ yes _____ no Why?_____

Using the Telephone To Raise Money from Current Donors

1. How many donors have given at least once in the last 18 months? _____

2. Do you have an exciting project or challenge that can be explained quickly and easily over the phone? Write a short sample script here:

   _____
   _____
   _____
   _____
   _____

3. How many volunteers would it take to call them? _____ (Assume each caller can make 90 calls per evening. Current donors and members may want to talk about the issue, so callers won't be able to get through their lists quite as fast.)

4. Assuming a 10- to 15-percent response rate and an average gift of $35, how much money could you raise using this strategy? $ _____

5. Shall you call current donors?

    _____ yes   _____ no

Using the Telephone To Raise Money from People Who Have Not Given Before

1. List three kindred organizations that might give you their list, or exchange lists, of people with correct phone numbers:

    a. _____

    b. _____

    c. _____

2. Create two sample scripts that describe your organization in two or three sentences in a compelling way:

    a. _____

    _____

    _____

    _____

    b. _____

    _____

    _____

    _____

3. How many volunteers would it take to call these lists? _____

4. Assuming a 5-percent return and an average $25 gift, how much money would you raise and how many new donors would you get? $ _____ ; _____ new donors

5. Compare the numbers of donors—the money you would raise, the cost in time and money—of a telephone solicitation to a direct mail appeal sent to these same people. What do you conclude?

6. Shall you call people who have not contributed before?

    _____ yes   _____ no Why?_____

    In each of the above cases, you may want to compare the costs of using paid solicitors as well.

Rating Your Telephone Solicitation Potential

On the basis of what you have learned, how would you rank your capability to elicit support from individuals through telephone solicitations?

___ Very Good   ___ Possible   ___ Unlikely   ___ Still Unknown

Additional Resources

Publications

Alford, Jimmie R. "Asking for Money." *Nonprofit World* 17 (May–June 1999): 13–15.
Shares insights for successful solicitation calls.

Brody, Leslie. *Effective Fund Raising: Tools and Techniques for Success.* Acton, MA: Copley Publishing Group, 1994. x, 157 p.
Basic primer for executive directors, board members, and volunteers wishing to raise funds to maintain needed services or develop new programs. Covers mobilization, annual appeals, phonathons, corporate approaches, soliciting foundations, special events, and consultants. Includes an appendix of master forms for reproduction, and an acrostic.

Dickey, Marilyn. "Dialing for Big Dollars." *Chronicle of Philanthropy* 11 (8 April 1999): 24–26.
Nonprofit organizations have begun to use paid telemarketers to solicit major gifts from donors.

Flanagan, Joan. "Memberships." *Grantsmanship Center Magazine* 41 (Summer 2000): 6–8.
Explains the importance of a membership base and techniques for expanding it, including membership drives and phonathons.

Gafke, Roger. "On Telemarketing's 20th Anniversary: Disturbing Trends, Great Possibilities." *Fund Raising Management* 29 (April 1998): 32–33.

Heuermann, Robert. "Phonathon Training: A Guide for Callers." *Currents* 23 (April 1997): 16–33.

Klein, Kim. "Revisiting the Phone-a-thon." *Grassroots Fundraising Journal* 18 (April 1999): 7–11.
Details the effective use and management of a phonathon.

Klein, Kim, and Stephanie Roth. "Choosing the Right Fundraising Strategy." *Grassroots Fundraising Journal* 18 (June 1999): 3–6.
Describes several common fundraising strategies, what each one is best used for, and the expected response from each.

Korol, Iris S. "Thank You—You Can Never Say It Too Many Times." *Fund Raising Management* 30 (March 1999): 20–21.
Provides tips on a new development technique called the "thank-a-thon."

LeBlanc, Jeffrey. "Why Making the Best Call is the Right Call for You." *Fund Raising Management* 29 (October 1998): 34–35.

Metz, Amy Talbert. "Phonathon Training: A Guide for Development Staff." *Currents* 23 (April 1997): 10–14.

Pollack, Rachel H. "Hold the Phone." *Currents* 24 (May 1998): 28-32.
    Examines the use of higher asks, better fulfillment, and motivated callers to increase telemarketing funds.

Ryan, Ellen. "Annual Fund Answers: Experts in Direct Mail, Phonathons, and In-Person Asks Tackle Some of the Annual Fund's Perennial Problems." *Currents* 22 (May 1996): 30–37.

Ryan, Ellen. "On the Phone Again." Currents 17 (March 1991): 28–32.
    Provides sixty ways to train callers, motivate donors, and come through the phonathon experience with success and sanity.

Suhrke, Henry C. "Fund Raising and the Telemarketing Sales Rule." *Philanthropy Monthly* 28 (October 1995): 19–25.
    Reprints the telemarketing sales rule as declared by the Federal Trade Commission and the American Telemarketing Fundraisers Association.

Suhrke, Henry C. "Telemarketing: The Real Success Story and the Attorney General Reports." *Philanthropy Monthly* 32 (September–October 1999): 20–26.
    Analyzes recent reports issued by the Attorney General regarding the results of telemarketing campaigns.

Twardowski, Timothy. "The Sounds of Success." *Fund Raising Management* 28 (August 1997): 19–21.
    Offers criteria any nonprofit organization should consider when evaluating a telemarketing firm for their fundraising event.

Wallace, Jodi Meryl. "Universities Graduate to Call Center Automation." *Fund Raising Management* 27 (November 1996): 26–29.
    Discusses call automation systems that can dial numbers automatically and switch only answered calls to telemarketers. These systems can also provide information about a prospect's interests and giving history and display an appropriate script. Lists ten questions to ask a vendor about call automation technology.

Warwick, Mal. "Telephone Tactics: Seven Steps to Make Your Phonathon Script a Winner from Hello to Thank You and Good Night." *Currents* 22 (May 1996): 24–28.

Warwick, Mal, Deborah Block, Stephen Hitchcock, Ivan Levinson, and Joseph H.White, Jr. *999 Tips, Trends and Guidelines for Successful Direct Mail and Telephone Fundraising.* Berkeley, CA: Strathmoor Press, 1993. 316 p.

Weinstein, Stanley. *The Complete Guide to Fund-Raising Management.* New York: John Wiley & Sons, 1999. xii, 307 p.

> A comprehensive treatment of fundraising principles and practices, including information about creating case statements, recordkeeping, prospect research, cultivating donors, major gifts, grants, direct mail, telemarketing, special events, planned giving, and capital campaigns. Covers management and human resources issues, planning, budgeting, ethics, and evaluation of a fundraising program. Includes disk. Indexed.

Internet Resources

The following Web sites contain information about phonathon fundraising software, as well as a wide range of other fundraising-related software and sites:

www.fundraiser-software.com/donormgt.html

www.nonprofit-info.org/npofaq/05/

www.npo.net/nponet/computer/fundacct.htm

www.coyotecom.com/tips.htm

Chapter 11

Face-to-Face Solicitation

I like to listen. I have learned a great deal from listening carefully. Most
people never listen.
— Ernest Hemingway

Face-to-face solicitation is the best way for many nonprofit organizations to solicit support from people with the means to give it. When solicitors meet with people they know, the response rate is about 50 percent. When solicitors personally ask people they don't know, as in a canvass, the response is about 15 percent. Face-to-face solicitations of either kind yield dramatically higher response rates than when there is no personal contact. For instance, a direct mail appeal is considered successful when it generates a response rate of 1 to 3 percent.

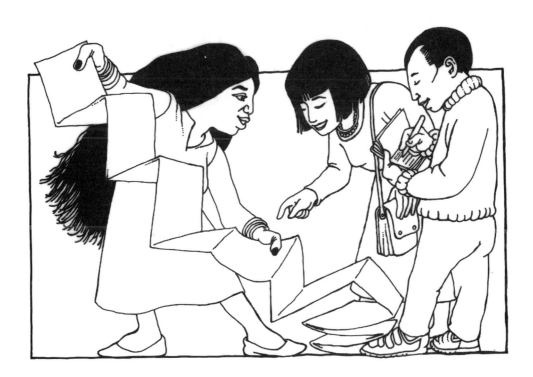

These response rates illustrate yet again one of the cardinal rules of fundraising: people give to people. In fact, study after study has shown that some 80 percent of those surveyed said they made their most recent contribution simply because someone asked them. Only 50 percent of this group could name the organization they gave to, but 90 percent remembered the person who asked them! Even if the person was a stranger, the donor will be able to describe the person in great detail: "It was a nice young man, dressed in a suit—and so polite." The principle that people give to people—is as true for the trustee of the local museum who pays a visit to a wealthy philanthropist as it is for the public interest canvasser who knocks on all the doors in a neighborhood.

Learning how to engage others in a lively discussion of your work and endeavoring to win them over as supporters paves the way for your organization to become a potential recipient of both small and large donations. More often than not, the return for your efforts will more than compensate for the time and energy expended.

If you need to enlist the support of a large number of people (such as contributors, petition signers, volunteers, and so on), personalized approaches—setting up tables at a busy shopping center or well-traveled street intersection, perhaps, or meeting at someone's home—can be very effective. Moreover, these experiences can be very rewarding for many people, for they involve contact with others. In fact, personal solicitation is the only form of fundraising in which you get immediate feedback on your ideas and visions, and, often, excellent new ideas from the person you're soliciting.

Most nonprofit organizations, from the smallest to the largest, can learn how to successfully solicit funds from individuals by face-to-face solicitation, regardless of the type of constituents the organization serves, and whether the solicitations are carried out by canvassing a neighborhood or at scheduled appointments with long-time donors.

What Are the Advantages of Raising Money by Face-to-Face Solicitation?

1. A personal visit or meeting is generally the most effective form of solicitation an organization can undertake.

2. Pledges secured through face-to-face solicitations are usually paid quickly.

3. Face-to-face solicitations offer opportunities to build relationships that may lead to increased support from a donor in the future.

4. A gracious, well-prepared personal solicitation can enhance your organization's reputation and increase its donor base, as the person you've solicited may well share a positive experience with peers. A properly cultivated donor may even be willing to approach friends or associates—or contacts at foundations and corporations—on your organization's behalf.

5. Solicitors who find the work gratifying and feel as if they're making a difference are likely to help with soliciting again.

What Are the Disadvantages of Raising Money by Face-to-Face Solicitation?

1. Identifying and researching prospects; recruiting, training, and servicing volunteer askers; carrying out and following up on the solicitations; and keeping accurate records are all tasks that require time, effort, and money. An organization's resources must be allocated carefully, and so the rate of return in relation to effort expended must be high; this cannot be guaranteed for groups that are creating a donor base from scratch.

2. Additional resources and benefits—such as producing special events for generous contributors or arranging to have a space named for someone—will be needed to cultivate relationships with donors who have responded to personal solicitations.

3. Constancy of effort is mandatory; supporters must be kept abreast of your work with some regularity, not only when you need money.

4. Solicitors who become discouraged might decline further involvement in your organization's fundraising activities.

Deciding Whether To Try Face-to-Face Solicitation

To determine whether personal soliciting will prove worthwhile, consider the effort it will take in time and money and the results of any past experiences. Your own experience will be your best guide. Beyond that, look at some other considerations in the following list and in the summary worksheet at the end of this chapter.

1. *Can you demonstrate a real need for individual charitable dollars?* If you currently receive the bulk of your income from public sources—city, county, state, federal—you may have to overcome your constituents' impression that the government will provide ongoing support for all your needs. This should not be difficult, as most people know that government is continually cutting back its role, and many statistics are available to support this decline.

    However, some prospective donors may feel that your programs should be completely funded by the government, even if they are not presently. You will need to make clear that it is highly unlikely that government support can be generated, and that (if it is the case) part of your organization's mission is to get government funding restored to previous levels. In any event, before meeting with your potential donors you should have prepared a list of reasons why it is appropriate for the public to provide a significant portion of your funding. A clear presentation of your programs and sources of revenue will help a prospective donor understand which programs, if any, receive public underwriting and which do not.

Similarly, if you do not receive, or anticipate receiving, any significant grants or contracts from foundations, corporations, or the government, you will be able to make a stronger case for the need for individual support.

2. *Do you have a potential constituency to approach?* Check your concentric circles exercise (see Chapter 7) again to determine whether your prospective supporters are close enough to be solicited personally. If, for example, your mission is to save a species of butterfly in a remote region in Brazil from extinction, but your potential large donors live in different corners of the world, your chances of meeting them all personally are decidedly limited (see the case study later in this chapter for ways of personally soliciting a scattered donor base). If, however, your potential donors are more accessible, as for most nonprofits, you will probably have identified in your circles exercise different prospective constituents to approach, one-to-one, for support.

3. *Will the return in dollars justify the time expended?* Your own experience, as well as that of other organizations, will serve as your best guide. Keep in mind that requesting money in person is the most effective way to elicit support from individuals. As a result, most organizations should include personal solicitation in their fundraising mix.

4. *Have the prospects you've identified for personal solicitations been sufficiently cultivated?* Can you recruit solicitors to whom these prospects are likely to respond? Asking too soon, or having the wrong person make the request, can not only result in a smaller gift (or none at all), but it might alienate the prospect and ruin your chances for receiving the significant support that might have been forthcoming if you had waited for the right time and the right solicitor.

If you have planned thoughtfully, you already will have considered these questions and the preceding discussion can serve as a guide to review your plan in light of any internal and external developments since the plan was created and adopted.

How Does Face-to-Face Solicitation Work?

Remember the kids who knocked on doors at Halloween saying, "Trick or treat for UNICEF"? Or the mothers who scoured neighborhoods on a door-to-door basis on behalf of the original March of Dimes? While those kids and mothers hardly fit the stereotype of face-to-face fundraisers—the arts patron who is visited by a peer on behalf of the local museum, say—the fact is that people of all ages and walks of life will ask someone for a contribution at some point in their lives. Similarly, nonprofit organizations of all shapes and sizes engage in some form of personal solicitation at some point. An organization that has decided to undertake a face-to-face solicitation campaign should take the following steps:

Step 1. Review Your Goal for the Campaign

Project a goal for total individual contributions by setting targets for gifts at specified levels on a gift range chart. The gift range chart is based on the simple premise that a few people will give big gifts, some people will give medium-size gifts, and most people will give smaller gifts. The chart forms a triangle, and is generally calculated as follows:

1–2 gifts =
10% of the goal
2–4 gifts = 10% of the goal
5–10 gifts = 10% of the goal

Continue down the chart with more gifts at lower amounts.

SAMPLE GIFT RANGE CHART
Goal = $50,000

No. of Gifts	Gift Amount
2	$5,000
4	$2,500
10	$1,000
20	$500
40	$250

You can adapt this chart to your targeted constituencies. Suppose, for example, that many of your potential donors cannot afford a gift higher than $100; you might then look for 100 gifts at $100 and no gifts at $5,000. Perhaps you have a donor who will give you $10,000 on the condition that her gift is matched by gifts in the $250 to $500 range. Such a condition would help you determine the number of gifts to put in that part of your gift range chart. The chart is a tool to test the reality of your goal, and to help you figure out how many prospects you will need to meet your goal.

Because current and prospective donor profiles vary from nonprofit to nonprofit, each organization must establish for itself the minimum gift amount that justifies a personal solicitation. Large, established charities that as a matter of course receive contributions of $500 and $1,000 in response to mailings may schedule face-to-face meetings to ask for no less than $5,000. Smaller organizations, on the other hand, may solicit contributions of $250 in person. If the larger nonprofit has identified a potential major donor but feels that a request for $5,000 would be premature, it may attempt to schedule a personal solicitation for a smaller amount as part of a long-term cultivation strategy. Thorough advance work will have addressed these issues.

Step 2. Identify Your Prospects

Working with the fundraising committee, the director of development or the key staffer responsible for fundraising then designs and carries out cultivation strategies for each prospect.

Many novice fundraisers feel that they don't know anyone who "has money." They make the mistake of looking for people who are affluent rather than people who are givers; but many people who have a lot of money don't give any away. Many people who have very little money also do not contribute to charity. On the other hand, many wealthy people and many more middle class, working class, and low-income people contribute generously. In looking for people to ask, start with people you know, and note which of them believes in your cause or something similar. Then decide what to ask for.

Organizations should, therefore, begin planning their face-to-face campaign by counting the number of people listed in the first circle of the circles exercise (described in Chapter 7) while keeping in mind their human resources, i.e., how many "askers" actually can be counted on to knock on doors or make personal calls. If you identified fifty individuals in your first circle and have ten volunteers willing to ask, it's realistic to think that each of those fifty might be approached personally.

If you've rated lawyers as strong prospects in your third circle, say, you'll want to learn how many live or work in your community. If the local bar association directory lists thousands, you would need hundreds of askers to solicit all of them face-to-face; a direct mail appeal would clearly be the only way to ask for their support. Those who responded and, over time, continued giving might eventually become prospects for face-to-face solicitations.

If you have a few lawyers in your core group willing to involve some colleagues in raising money for your organization, you're likely to be able to arrange some personal solicitations without waiting for prospects to identify themselves by responding to a mail appeal. Your lawyers group would meet to review the list of attorneys and identify colleagues they'd be willing to solicit in person. This process of recruiting people to work together on fundraising projects forms the basis for many of an organization's development activities. Many steps are involved in this process, and each one is important.

1. Speak to the lawyers in your core group (personally, of course) to explain the project. Before the conversation, you might want to mail, fax, or e-mail a letter outlining the project. Include the list of lawyers and ask each recipient to choose the ones he or she would feel comfortable asking to join the group. Clearly state what you want him or her to do.

2. Be sure to let people know that you appreciate them and value their time. It's also good to avoid putting people in a position where they have to say no to you. By describing the project before you ask for a commitment, you give the other person an opportunity to decline more gracefully.

3. The easier you can make it for others to help, the more willing they will be. When you meet with one of the lawyers in your core group, bring along some background material on your organization that will help him make the calls. Offer to send any materials on his or her behalf and ask what else you can do to support his work. Identify exactly what you need the person to do, and make sure you do the rest. In this case, you want your lawyer friend to make a call to a colleague, not to check contact information, write and mail materials, and the like.

4. At the meeting, review the project and the benefits it will bring to the organization. Review the list and secure your lawyer friend's commitment to invite one or two colleagues to join the group. Come prepared with a project timeline and tell the lawyer exactly what you want and when it needs to be accomplished. Setting deadlines

is essential. Repeat these steps with all the lawyers who have agreed to recruit colleagues to join the group.

5. At the same time, poll your lawyer group for the best time and place to hold the first meeting; it's always good to get a few possibilities. It can be helpful if one of them hosts the meeting, as this tends to increase a person's commitment.

6. Follow up to see how the recruitment is going, and when the group is set write a note thanking the members in advance for their help. Enclose the same list, background materials, and time schedule.

Each one of the above steps is important to assembling the group and priming it for action. By following these steps you'll show both present and new supporters that you know how to work with volunteer leaders, which will increase their confidence in your organization and their willingness to work on its behalf.

Note that soliciting the participation of people outside the core group for special groups, as well as for board and special event committee membership, is done in the same way. What is the common factor? It's a slight variation on the first principle of fundraising: People give to people. This fundamental maxim must never be far from the consciousness of every multi-tasking nonprofit manager and board member. This is, of course, more easily said than done. The pace of nonprofit life is fast, and the pressure is considerable to focus on the logistics of program and service delivery, administration, and cash flow rather than people. But all concerned with the growth of an organization must keep this principle in mind at all times.

The lawyers that the solicitors are in contact with are solicited in person, and the rest are solicited by direct mail. An organization's lawyer also might seek opportunities to address local meetings of attorneys to lay the groundwork for a later appeal by mail (see Chapter 20 for more information on approaching associations for support).

Step 3. Research Your Prospects

Now for the next guiding principle in individual fundraising: Know your donor. Learn why each prospective donor may be interested in supporting your organization. Before anything else, make sure that you know that this person does, in fact, give away money. Many well meaning and good-hearted people do not give money to charities, and approaching people known to be "nongivers" is almost invariably a waste of time. Conducting research on each prospect for personal solicitation is, therefore, essential for the following reasons:

- Research provides the information an organization needs to design an effective cultivation strategy.

- Research reveals the interests, patterns, and, perhaps, the needs that can help an organization know how much to ask for, and for what purpose.

- Research helps identify the best person—or the best kind of person—to set up and make the solicitation.

- Research provides information that facilitates the conversation between solicitor and prospect, thus showing that the organization has done its homework.

Prospect research is so important that many large nonprofit institutions employ full-time researchers to support their development efforts. The Additional Resources section at the end of this chapter lists some of the many sources of information available in print and on the Internet about researching prospects. Conversations with friends of your organization can also yield valuable information. The basic areas your research should cover are listed on the Sample Prospect Identification Form later in this chapter.

Step 4. Recruit and Train Your Askers

Once again, it's vital to remember our first guiding principle of fundraising: The more personal the contact, the more successful a solicitation is likely to be. If, for example, you approach friends and acquaintances for contributions, it is highly likely that the responses will be favorable. This is one of the primary reasons for the success of walkathons and the like, events in which participants are sponsored by friends and family.

Our second guiding principle flows from the first: People are likelier to give to individuals they respect, or with whom they identify—or both. Social workers respond to other social workers, to counselors, and to others in the helping professions whom they admire. They also respond to individuals associated with organizations they respect. Even if most local lawyers, for example, do not know your name, your membership in the local chapter of the bar association might increase their willingness to contribute. This explains why so many organizations list on their letterheads a number of individuals together with their affiliations as sponsors, patrons, or advisors, even though a disclaimer may appear at the end of the list, saying "Organizations listed for identification purposes only." Look at yourself first and ask, "Whom do I respect and look up to in my community?" Is it a local religious leader, an elected official, an artist, a writer? Your own responses will not be considerably different from those of the people you will be approaching.

You might now recruit some of these local celebrities or influential people to join your efforts, either as askers, sponsors, or roving ambassadors. If someone does become a sponsor, inform other prospective supporters (donors) that "so-and-so" has signed on as a sponsor of your organization, and ask them to consider joining him or her as a member; even better, ask the new sponsor to make the "ask," if possible.

Undoubtedly, becoming an asker is not always easy. As with almost everything else in life, one learns best by doing. It is also imperative that the first person you ask is yourself—which means that the first time you ask you'll get the gift! If you won't give, it will be hard for you to ask others to give. When you have made a gift, you can ask people to join you in making a contribution. It might help to remember that you are not asking someone merely to give you money; you are asking for help in supporting something you believe in, and that you think they will believe in as well.

You can prepare yourself in several ways: by role playing different scenarios with your other askers; by inviting a veteran asker from another organization to hold a training session; and finally, by first asking a friend whom you can tell that you are practicing. If you choose to approach a friend, it's a good idea to use the buddy system; ask a fellow asker to come along, and work as a team. Afterward, you can discuss the solicitation. Your donor friend might even give you some valuable feedback on the meeting.

In recruiting solicitors, be precise in stating your expectations, setting deadlines, and specifying reporting and follow-up procedures. Make sure they are comfortable visiting the people assigned to them. A staff, committee, or board member involved in the personal solicitation campaign should visit each solicitor to review the research performed on their prospects, to discuss strategy, and to answer questions.

It's frequently a good idea to review your entire list of prospects with your cadre of askers, since they may identify people they already know and would like to solicit. Such a review might also reveal information about prospects known to your asker that had not previously surfaced as a result of your own research. Of course, you will want to make sure that all your askers are thoroughly familiar with your organization's vision, mission, programs, overall finances, and plans for the future.

Cultivating askers' involvement doesn't end with their agreement to undertake the solicitation; rather, it begins at that time. Tell your solicitors how the organization plans to support their efforts; arrange for them to be called regularly for encouragement and feedback; share good news with them; and, above all, be generous in expressing your appreciation for their time and efforts.

Step 5. Schedule the Appointment

For many volunteer and professional fundraisers, asking for an appointment can feel like a greater personal risk than asking for the gift itself. Perhaps they anticipate feeling more deeply rejected if prospects will not even meet with them than they would if they did meet but declined to make a gift. How to overcome this fear of personal rejection? Remembering that you are asking on behalf of the organization, not yourself, rings true intellectually but may not allay any fears. As in most matters, the only way to prevail is by forcing yourself to make the call purely by dint of will. And, as in most matters, you will find that your fears are groundless; that prospects who have been properly chosen and cultivated usually agree to meet; and that they are frequently pleased, enthusiastic—and even, on occasion, grateful—to learn how they might make a difference in the world through a contribution.

Therefore, don't hesitate to be direct when you are writing the letter or placing the phone call to set up an appointment. Explain clearly why you wish to meet with the prospect. You might say, for example, "I am involved with a new organization that is currently doing critically important work. Because I know that you share my interest in ___, I would like to get together to tell you what we are doing, and to ask for a contribution." Its also a good idea to mention how long the meeting will last, as this may be a factor in the prospect's decision to meet or not. It also communicates your respect for his or her time.

Consider carefully the best location for the meeting. If the prospect expresses interest, the solicitor should ask where he or she would prefer to meet, or perhaps gently suggest that the meeting be held at the organization's facility, or at (one of) the site(s) of its programs. In any event, the solicitor should defer to the prospect. It's generally advisable not to eat if an important solicitation is being made, unless it is the prospect who suggests a restaurant or club setting. The interruptions that occur during the course of a meal can be distracting, and tables are usually too small to accommodate any materials used for the solicitation.

Once the appointment has been made, send a hand-written note thanking the prospect for agreeing to meet, and confirming the date, time, location, and purpose of the meeting. Make sure to call the day of the meeting to re-confirm.

Step 6. Make the Solicitation

Just before the meeting, review the information your organization has provided, and the strategy and goal of the solicitation. Just as the quality of a runner's performance during a race depends on his or her training, so too will the results of your solicitation be largely determined by what has preceded the meeting. If the research and cultivation processes have been thorough and effective and have identified the prospect's capacity, inclination, and motivation for giving; if you have familiarized yourself with the organization and your prospect; and if you are committed to the campaign's success, it is highly likely that your solicitation will be effective.

Remember that you are not only asking for something; you are also offering something—the opportunity for the prospect to make a difference in the world. Your tone of voice, posture, and energy should communicate this gift that you are able to give to the prospect. Be a good listener, and pay close attention to what the prospect's body language communicates about his or her mood, quality of attention, and degree of interest.

Prospective donors will want to know how much you need to advance your organization's mission or to launch a new project or build an endowment. Tell them. You might begin by saying, "We need to raise $10,000 by December 1st so that we can rent an office and purchase the supplies we need to open our doors for work. I am giving $250. Would you consider giving a similar amount?" Remember that people are free to refuse or to ask for some time to make a decision. Be sure to wait for a response: after you ask for the gift do not say anything until the prospect has replied. If a prospective donor needs some help in arriving at a decision, you might indicate a number of options and a range of possible gifts. The prospective donor can then think within that range and come to a decision.

Step 7. Follow Up the Meeting

Immediately after the meeting, send a letter thanking the prospect for his or her pledge, if one was made, or reviewing the main points of your conversation if he or she has asked for time to consider your request. Make sure you then follow your organization's procedures for reporting on the results of the meeting.

The Door-to-Door Canvass

One of the most popular ways to raise money in person is through door-to-door canvassing. This strategy works best when the organization has something dramatic and brief to explain to the person answering the door, and when the issue directly affects the person being solicited. Canvasses work well on issues such as utility rate reform, local schools, environmental issues (especially toxic waste, smog, or landfills), domestic violence, and the like. People are often accustomed to young girls selling Girl Scout cookies, high school band members raising money to go on a trip, or a neighbor collecting money for various health-related concerns.

Case Study

The Wildlands Project

The goal of the Wildlands Project, a conservation group operating from Tucson, Arizona, is to establish a network of linked wilderness reserves across North America. The group's annual budget in 1996 was around $300,000, almost entirely from foundations. Understandably nervous about relying on such a narrow funding base, the project sought help to diversify foundation support and to build a major donor program. It contracted with noted fundraising consultant, Andy Robinson. Robinson had to work with two restricting factors:

- The Wildlands Project will never be a membership group. It works primarily with other conservation groups and does not wish to manage a large base of small donors, nor does it wish to appear to be in competition with membership-based conservation groups.

- The project could not solicit many gifts in personal meetings because it works all over North America and their donor base is very far flung.

The project decided to build a campaign around small, very personalized mailings, gifts from board members, and a handful of small benefit events. The goal was to find 200 people who would give at least $100, with a lead gift of $5,000, for a total of $50,000 in 1996.

The group found its prospects in its current donor list, which included 265 people who had given $50 or more during the previous two years, and in lists of names brought to the group by board members and others. In all, the Wildlands Project sent 700 major donor letters. Each letter was personalized to the donor, e.g., "Dear Fran." The letter was one and one-half pages long—printed on one page front and back on board letterhead—and each letter was signed by the chair and the board president, who are both well known in conservation circles. The letters were then taken to the next board meeting, where people were asked to put personal notes on the bottom of a letter of anyone they knew.

In the end, the Wildlands Project contacted 700 people, most of them through this very personal mail appeal. One hundred and seventy-seven people responded with gifts of $100 or more, for a total of $65,600. They received one big gift of $10,000 and two of $5,000; the $10,000 gift and one of the $5,000 gifts came through the mail. The gift they got most often was $100; they received 90 of these.

Thanks to Andy Robinson for this information.

Case Study

From Rags to Riches in Only Three Years

Money has always been one of the main topics at the Wisconsin Coordinating Committee on Nicaragua (WCCN). We have worked to recruit and train board members who take fundraising seriously. It's been a real learning experience and many of our best lessons have come from the school of hard knocks.

For our first major donor campaign, we set a goal of $5,000. The staff did everything they could to lighten the board's burden. They prepared personalized letters and gave each board member a list of potential donors and a phone script to use in calling them. The only thing board members had to do was sign and mail the letters and make an average of five calls apiece. The campaign raised a total of $445. As we look back, we can see that the staff made the campaign so painless that most of us didn't notice it was happening. Recently, I went through some records about that campaign and was surprised to find my name next to a list of seven donors that I had been assigned to contact. I didn't remember having seen the list previously. In fact, I only recognized two of the names on the list and I'm sure I never called those two. My non-participation was typical of the level of board involvement in that campaign. Despite the shortcomings of that campaign, it laid the groundwork for future success. The following year, we established a Development Committee, composed of active board members, and began planning a campaign that would rectify past mistakes.

This time, instead of presenting board members with lists of assigned names, members of the development committee met personally with each board member and went over our entire donor list, asking them to select the names they would be most willing to contact. We stressed the importance of contacting each donor personally, at least by telephone if not face to face.

We kicked off the campaign in October with a special weekend board training session. Subsequently members of the Development Committee periodically phoned other board members to check up on their progress. We also set a definite closing date for the campaign by scheduling a post-campaign party in November. Not all board members completed all of their calls by the closing date, but most did. The result of this campaign was a total of $33,409—a lot better than the previous year's $445! Nothing in our experience prior to that campaign would have suggested that we could expect that level of success.

The main lessons we learned were the following:

- Major donor campaigns do work.

- Participation of board members and volunteers is essential to the success of fundraising. It is much easier to persuade volunteers to participate in the work of fundraising if they've participated in the planning.[1]

---

1. Sheldon Rampton, "From Rags to Riches in Only Three Years!" *Grassroots Fundraising Journal* 10 (December 1991): 10–12.

The actual canvass idea seems simple enough. Trained, paid workers go door-to-door in predetermined sympathetic neighborhoods, enlisting people's support for an issue. But initial appearances belie the complexity of canvassing.

Mounting a successful canvassing operation requires proficiency in long-term planning, administration, budgeting and fiscal management, and personnel matters. For example, recruiting qualified canvassers is not simple. Candidates have to be willing to work in all kinds of weather, be adaptable, be able to deal with rejection, and believe in the goals of the organization they are representing. As many canvass directors have discovered, good candidates are hard to find.

Before canvassers go out in the field, they participate in training and strategy sessions covering such topics as how to get into apartment buildings and how "to educate not debate" someone who wants to give the canvasser a hard time. The trainees also learn about eye contact, body language, and preparing their "rap" so that the who, what, and where of the organization comes across in the first minute of conversation. To assure their personal safety, they are urged to leave any situation the minute they feel uneasy. They are also taught self-defense techniques. Before they go into any neighborhood, the canvass director gives the local police a list of their names and sends a press release to the local newspaper to let people know they're coming. Finally, they review last year's map and donor list, and discuss the targeted community's political and socioeconomic make-up.

Many groups have discovered that canvassing is a good way to introduce people to their organization, but because of the cost and planning involved, a canvass has to be done in the context of other strategies. It is not uncommon for very successful canvasses to gross $500,000 but net only $100,000 to $150,000 after all staff costs are deducted. Therefore, canvassing must be seen as an educational tool as well as a fundraising strategy.

Tips

- When preparing to make a face-to-face solicitation, think about what the prospective donor's interests are. Learn as much as you can about the person you'll be visiting with, especially what motivates and moves him or her.

- The more questions you ask, the better. In the course of answering, your prospect is likely to reveal a fair amount; and because you will be listening with full attention, it's likely that you'll find a direction to develop that will lead to the ask.

- Make sure you understand that you are asking neither for yourself nor for the organization per se. You are asking for a cause. More than asking, you are giving—giving someone the opportunity to make a difference today and tomorrow.

Summary Worksheet

for _____

(name of your organization)

Approaching Individuals for Support: Face-to-Face Solicitation

Efforts to Date

1. Are you already approaching individuals directly for support?
   _____ yes   _____ no

2. If yes, which of the following approaches have you used?
   _____ Personal visits
   _____ Canvassing
   _____ Other _____

3. Which approaches have proven successful (i.e., revenues exceed costs, people continue to respond affirmatively to requests, etc.)?

   a. _____
   _____
   _____

   b. _____
   _____
   _____

   c. _____
   _____
   _____

4. Which approaches should be discarded or overhauled?

   a. _____
   _____
   _____

   b. _____
   _____
   _____

   c. _____
   _____
   _____

Planning New Efforts

1. List ways you can enhance the income potential of the face-to-face solicitation approaches you will continue:

   a. _____

   _____

   _____

   b. _____

   _____

   _____

   c. _____

   _____

   _____

   d. _____

   _____

   _____

   e. _____

   _____

   _____

   f. _____

   _____

   _____

   g. _____

   _____

   _____

   h. _____

   _____

   _____

   i. _____

   _____

   _____

If your organization has not solicited individuals in person but plans to, which organizations in your community can share their experience and advice on face-to-face solicitations? Who can make the inquiry effectively on your behalf?

Organization	Contact Information	Person Assigned	Report Due

Rating Your Face-to-Face Solicitation Potential

On the basis of what you have learned, how would you rank your capability to elicit support from individuals through face-to-face solicitation?

__ Very Good   __ Possible   __ Unlikely   __ Still Unknown

Sample Prospect Identification Form

Name: _____

Address:_____

Phone (home):_____

      (work):_____

E-mail:_____

Where else does this prospect give money?

    a. _____

    b. _____

    c. _____

Who knows this prospect best, and what is that person's relationship to the prospect?

Contact: _____

Relationship to prospect: _____

_____

Personal information about prospect: _____

Occupation: _____

Age: ____

Length of time with current employer: _____

Other interests, e.g., civic groups, religious groups, trade associations:

_____

_____

What will this prospect most like about our work? About what area will he or she will have most questions?

_____

Can this prospect make a decision alone? If no, who else must be consulted?

_____

_____

Solicitor information:

_____ I can call this prospect.

_____ I cannot call this prospect but you may use my name.

_____ I cannot call this prospect; do not use my name

Name of solicitor:_____

Amount being requested _____

Result:_____

_____

_____

_____

Additional Resources

Publications

lbo, Amy. "The Benefactor 100: The Most Generous Among Us: An Exclusive Ranking Based on Total Donations. *Worth* 8 (April 1999): 110–122.

Alford, Jimmie R. "Asking for Money." *Nonprofit World* 17 (May–June 1999): 13–15.
  Shares insights for successful solicitation calls.

Baird, John A., Jr. "Trading Up." *Fund Raising Management* 29 (May 1998): 18–19, 25.
  Describes three procedures for improving a solicitation program.

Bloom, Judy. *Being Rich Is Not a Piece of Cake*. New York. National Film Archive of Philanthropy, 1998. Video recording. 37 minutes.

Brewer, Randy W. "Getting Past First Base with Your New Donor: Three Rules for Getting a Second Date." *Fund Raising Management* 30 (April 1999): 32–33.
  Discusses three strategies for sustaining a healthy donor relationship after the first gift.

Clemow, Susan B. "The Fun of Asking for Money in Twelve Easy Steps." *Fund Raising Management* 30 (April 2000): 30–33.
  Provides twelve suggestions for successful fundraising.

Dahnert, Sachs Jennifer. "12 Ways to Block the Ask." *Currents* 24 (November–December 1998): 16–20.
  Provides a list of common solicitations errors, and suggestions for preventing them.

Dee, Jay R., and Alan B. Henkin. "Communication and Donor Relations: A Social Skills Perspective." *Nonprofit Management & Leadership* 8 (Winter 1997): 107–119.
  Discusses the findings of a study entitled "Fairness and Reputation Effects in a Provision Point Contribution Process," conducted by Melanie Beth Marks and D. Eric Schansberg, which looks at how much information fundraisers should tell potential donors and the effects of disclosing certain information.

Edwards, Paul. *The Tapestry of the Uultimate Ask: The Strategy, Design and Motivation that Ensures Your Success* [video recording]. Chicago: Institute for Charitable Giving, 1999. 3 vols. 321:00 minutes.
  Three separate videotapes.

Goettler, Ralph H. "The Four Ws of Major Gift Solicitation." *Nonprofit World* 16 (May–June 1998): 16–18.

Graham, Christine. *Asking: A Hands-On Learner's Guide to Gift Solicitation.* Shaftsbury, VT: CPG Enterprises, 1998. 20 p.

Graham, Christine. *Practice Makes Perfect: Short Solicitation Exercises You Can Use with Your Board and Volunteers.* Shaftsury, VT: CPG Enterprises, 1998. 32 p.
    Offers exercises for the techniques outlined in the companion volume, *Asking.*

Hartsook, Robert F. *Closing that Gift: How To Be Successful 99% of the Time.* Wichita, KS: ASR Philanthropic Publishing, 1998. 160 p.
    How to make the ask and get the donation.

Hartsook, Robert F. "15 Fund-Raising Opportunities with the Millionaire Next Door." *Fund Raising Management* 29 (November 1998): 16–17, 27.

Jaye, Melinda. "Guide for the Successful Campaign Solicitor." *Fund Raising Management* 30 (May 2000): 26–27.

Kirsch, Rodney P., and Martin W. Shell. "Achieving Leadership Gifts: The Investment Returns of Lasting Relationships." *New Directions for Philanthropic Fundraising* 21 (Fall 1998): 35-60.
    Explains the various ways of defining what constitutes a leadership gift and how development staff can create an environment that encourages this type of giving. Stresses the importance of partnering with volunteers, building relationships over time with donors, and maximizing the CEO's commitment. Outlines the role played by development staff, and techniques they may successfully utilize in securing leadership gifts. Finally, discusses other considerations, such as relationship with the donor's spouse and family, recognition and publicity, and gifts of appreciated securities. Includes bibliographic references.

Klein, Kim. "Asking Current Donors for Money: Why, How and How Often." *Grassroots Fundraising Journal* 19 (February 2000): 3–6.

Lawson, David M. "Read the Writing on the Wall Street." *Currents* 25 (June 1999): 20–25.
    Activities in the business markets may influence the interest and ability of donors to make tax-favored major gifts. Initial public offerings, mergers, hostile takeovers, and stock options may create donor deadlines that the wise development officer needs to understand.

Makar, Arthur. "Gays and Lesbians: An Untapped Donor Resource." *Advancing Philanthropy* (Spring 1999): 28–30.
    Lists questions about inclusion, institutional policies, outreach, and institutional perception that gays and lesbians may ask before deciding whether to give to an organization.

Matheny, Richard E. *Major Gifts: Solicitation Strategies.* Washington, DC: Council for Advancement and Support of Education, 1994. v, 165 p.

Consists of three sections. Section one comprises fourteen chapters that lead a reader through the development of major gift solicitation, focusing on the face-to-face communication process with prospective donors. Section two contains eleven case studies designed to test your knowledge of solicitation strategies. Section three presents possible solutions to the questions posed by the case study situations.

Merrilees, Sue. "Donor Rating for Small Organizations." *Grassroots Fundraising Journal* 17 (June 1998): 3–4.

Explores the usefulness of donor rating systems, explains the inclination and ability component of a rating system, and concludes by detailing how to begin and maintain the system.

Nicklin, Julie L. "Turning Young Tycoons into Tomorrow's Carnegies." *Chronicle of Higher Education* 44 (17 July 1998): A47–50.

Development officers at many higher education institutions are altering their fundraising techniques in order to obtain donations from wealthy young people.

Panas, Jerold. *Shaking the Money Tree: What Motivates Donors.* Chicago: Institute for Charitable Giving (SkilFilm Series), 1995. Video recording. 53 minutes.

Phillips Communications. *Techniques of Personal Solicitation.* Los Angeles: Phillips Communications (Focus on Fundraising video series), 1994. Video recording. 21 minutes.

Roth, Stephanie. "Common Mistakes in Building Relationships with Donors (And How To Avoid Them)." *Grassroots Fundraising Journal,* 19 (June 2000): 6-8.

Seymour, Si. *Designs for Fundraising.* Detroit: The Taft Group, 1966.

A classic work on developing campaigns, understanding people and why they give, and solicitation techniques, as well as enduring insights and fundraising wisdom.

Staub, Scott C. "Is the Asian Community Different?" *Advancing Philanthropy* (Spring 1999): 10–11.

Considerations for fundraising strategies that are effective with Asian-Americans.

Sturtevant, William T. *The Successful Ask, Part I: Winning the Gift.* Chicago: Institute for Charitable Giving, 1995. Video recording. 54 minutes.

Sturtevant, William T. *The Successful Ask, Part II: Winning the Gift.* Chicago: Institute for Charitable Giving, 1995. Video recording. 86 minutes.

Wylie, Peter. "Look to Your Donor Database." *Advancing Philanthropy* 6 (Fall–Winter 1998): 36–38.

  Describes the cycle of information-gathering and the relationship necessary to cultivate major donors.

Internet

Internet Prospector (www.internet-prospector.org)

  Monthly newsletter focusing on information for prospect researchers.

www.leadershipdirectories.com

  The Leadership Library is a unique database of personnel information that helps subscribers reach leaders in United States government, business, professional, and nonprofit organizations. A wide range of book titles is included in the library.

www.APRAhome.org/

  Association addressing the changing needs and wide scope of skills required of advancement researchers and advancement service professionals working within the nonprofit community.

Chapter 12

Beyond the Simple Cash Contribution: Planned Giving

It is easier for a camel to go through the eye of a needle, than for a rich man to enter the kingdom of God.

— St. Matthew, Chapter 19, Verse 24

The growing number of nonprofits and NGOs around the world and the increasing need for their services have created unprecedented interest in innovative revenue generation strategies. In the United States alone, the growth of the nonprofit sector has been dramatic: in 1946, there were 100,000 nonprofits; in 1963, 500,000; and by 1996, there were more than 1,300,000.[1] As a

273

result, organizations are charting new fundraising directions to underwrite their work; raising money via the Internet and engaging in earned and venture income initiatives are just two examples.

Nonprofits are also turning to a traditional form of fundraising—planned giving—for its potential to generate substantial revenues, for the benefits it provides to both donors and the organization, and for its ability to create support for the present and the future. "Planned giving" is the broad term used to describe the integration of estate, tax, and overall financial planning with philanthropic planning so as to maximize a gift's benefits to the donor, the donor's family, and the recipient charity.

Nonprofits with the resources to launch, or intensify, planned giving programs can use this powerful tool to foster their solvency and cover increased costs while building long-term organizational viability, especially through establishing and increasing endowments, fulfilling long-range plans, and providing a cushion for emergencies. In increasing numbers, donors are now allocating their resources to benefit an organization during, or after, their lifetime through a planned gift.

Pooled income funds; charitable remainder, lead, and income trusts; gift annuities; and gifts of securities, real estate, works of art, and other property are some examples of planned gifts that benefit an organization, and the donor, during a donor's lifetime. Vehicles that take effect after a donor's death include naming an organization as the beneficiary of life insurance, and bequests—the most popular planned giving vehicle. In the most mature planned giving programs in Canada, bequests account for some 80 percent of all planned gifts.[2] The level of bequest giving in the United States in 1999 ($15.61 billion[3]) attests to the impact this one form of planned giving can have on the work of nonprofits.

The Growth of Planned Giving

Although it is not as well known as other fundraising strategies, the number of nonprofits undertaking planned giving programs has increased substantially over the last few decades. In the United States, this increase has been driven by several factors, including the ongoing development of planned giving financial instruments; an increase in the number of planned giving professionals, lawyers, accountants, development officers, and other nonprofit staffers familiar with these vehicles; and the increasing transfer of wealth from one generation to another as the baby boomers gray. At the turn of the century, some $6 to $8 trillion was expected to have passed from the baby boomers' parents to their children, doubling or tripling the number of millionaires in the United States from approximately 1.5 million to as many as 4.5 million.[4] From a strategic point of view, planned giving is a powerful means for nonprofit organizations to tap into a significant share of this transfer.

---

1. From an address by demographer Judith Nichols to the Ohio Prospect Research Group in 1997.

2. Malcolm Burrrows and Ann Rosenfiel, "Bequest-Based Programs: Basic, Boring, and Profitable," *Canadian Fundraiser* (30 October 1996).

3. Ann E. Kaplan, ed., Giving USA: *The Annual Report on Philanthropy for the Year 1999* (New York: American Association of Fund-Raising Counsel).

4. Council on Foundations, *Organized Philanthropy in the United States.* (Washington, D.C.: Council on Foundations).

Planned giving is, however, hardly a new idea. Plato made one of the earliest recorded planned gifts when he left money for his Academy's maintenance after his death. In his will Shakespeare earmarked ten pounds for the poor living in Stratford, England, and Giuseppe Verdi's will specified that royalties from the performance of his operas be used to benefit a home for retired singers and musicians in Milan, Italy. Alfred Nobel's estate endowed the Nobel Prizes, and the provisions of James Smithson's will established The Smithsonian Institution in Washington, D.C. The Kamehameha School for children of Hawaiian descent was established by Princess Bernice Pauahi Bishop, who established a trust to support it. And the David and Lucile Packard Foundation was established by the co-founder of the Hewlett-Packard Corporation, David Packard.

Today, the potential for nonprofits and NGOs the world over to help secure their future through planned giving programs is enormous—and largely untapped. In the United States (population: 285 million) alone, for example, about two million people die every year, and some 60,000 estate tax forms (required for estates in excess of $600,000) are filed with the U.S. federal government. Only 17 percent of these forms list a charitable gift, and 83 percent of the country's wealthiest individuals leave nothing at all to charity.

Further evidence for such optimism can be found in remarks made by Canadian fundraiser Dr. Edward H. Pearce as reported in 1995.

> Most of us now know that a growing proportion of the Canadian population is getting older and living longer, that the smaller nuclear family has resulted in fewer potential beneficiaries, that people 50 or older are in control of 75 percent of all assets, that they hold an estimated $250 billion in real estate, and that an increasing number of people have become cash poor but asset rich as the result of inflation.
>
> However, many may not be privy to the findings of the October 1994 Royal Trust Wealth Management Poll, a survey of the top 25% of Canadians by income. According to that research, 45% of respondents indicated that they expected to receive an inheritance. Fully 81% described themselves as middle class, and of those whose assets were over $500,000, 35% still described themselves as middle class.
>
> This perception will certainly impact the ways that planned gifts are approached and marketed in the future. The priorities of those surveyed were as follows: 90% would pass on their estate to their heirs; 88% wished to minimize taxes on their estate; and 95% wanted to preserve the value of their assets after retirement. One final finding of note: of the 45% who expected to receive an inheritance, a high percentage indicated that they would consider making a charitable gift.

For organizations with sufficient resources and prospects to launch a planned giving program, the time is right to take a closer look at planned giving for the potentially significant role it can play in their funding mix. Even for nonprofits that are too new to have built the constituencies, resources, and track record to launch such a program, the following discussion will help them prepare for the future.

What Are the Advantages of Raising Money by Planned Giving?

1. A planned giving program sends a strong message to its constituents: "We know that the issues that we are addressing will not totally disappear in our lifetime, so we are creating a planned giving program to make sure that our efforts can continue." Soliciting planned gifts is an important step organizations can take now to create revenues that will secure their future.

2. Provided that expenses are limited to the cost of printed materials, legal counsel, and mailings, an organization's planned giving campaign may be launched with only modest up-front capital. Of course, there are the indirect costs of staff and volunteer time, and the cost of any materials or seminars that you attend to further your own understanding of this area of charitable giving.

3. Undertaking a planned giving program extends the scope of an organization's planning process from years to decades, and sharpens its financial management by forcing it to consider the financial and human resources needed today to create revenues tomorrow.

4. Planned giving can increase an organization's revenues without asking its supporters to give more. At the same time, planned giving provides current donors with an option for giving more without decreasing their income.

5. Planned gifts enable donors to leverage use of their assets and enjoy recognition now for making a gift that, at the moment, need not reduce their assets or income.

6. Planned gifts frequently contribute to an organization's lifeline—funds for operating expenses. As institutional funders increasingly restrict their giving to specific programs, planned gifts—which frequently do not specify a purpose for the funds' use—can provide the vital unrestricted support organizations need for operating expenses.

7. Planned gifts can help an organization create an endowment. For nonprofits that normally cannot divert dollars from paying bills and salaries to build an endowment, planned gifts can provide revenue that can be used for building up an endowment.

8. Knowing that significant funds are committed to an organization in the future assures both individual and institutional funders of its long-term viability.

What Are the Disadvantages of Raising Money by Planned Giving?

1. An organization must commit time and money to raise funds that don't pay next month's bills, or even next year's. Because planned giving usually provides

deferred income to an organization, you are soliciting gifts that cannot be used for your organization's present programs and needs. With wills, life insurance policies, or most charitable remainder trusts, proceeds become available only when the donor dies. You will want to think carefully about allocating time and money to planned giving programs if your organization cannot meet its immediate cash needs.

2. Planned giving can involve large sums of money, substantial personal contributions, lifetime commitments, and serious fiduciary responsibilities. Any nonprofit considering entering this area should, therefore, approach it carefully and methodically, and consult with planned giving experts.

3. Executive directors without experience and training in this area can be justifiably wary of such an undertaking, especially since it may involve an organization's most significant donors. Some may also be uncomfortable in discussing bequests with a donor.

4. Members of your board must be among the first to participate; an organization will find it difficult to secure the participation of others unless its top leaders have chosen to participate.

The Different Kinds of Planned Giving

Laws governing planned giving vary greatly from country to country, and are frequently revised. The discussion that follows describes planned giving vehicles in their generic form for nonprofit organizations in the United States.[5] Further, in the United States the laws of the various states may affect planned giving. Readers are strongly advised to consult an attorney and an accountant who specialize in planned giving before making—or soliciting—a planned gift.

Immediate Funds for the Nonprofit: Outright Gifts of Property

Younger organizations undertaking planned giving programs usually need immediate support, and would do well to solicit gifts of property—such as securities and real estate—that can be easily converted into cash.

Individuals making gifts of appreciated securities to nonprofit organizations receive their full value as a deduction and avoid any capital gains tax resulting from the securities' appreciation.

---

5. U.S. law qualifies every nonprofit tax-exempt organization whose activities have been designated as charitable by the Internal Revenue Service under Section 501(c)(3) of the Internal Revenue Code (evidenced by receipt of a "determination" letter of federal tax exemption from the IRS) as potential recipients of any planned gifts. The IRS lists all such organizations in Publication 78, which is available for $35 by writing the Superintendent of Documents, U.S. Government Printing Office, Washington, DC 20402, or can be accessed on the World Wide Web (updated and corrected quarterly). Of course, a donor may make a contribution to an organization or designate it in a will, regardless of tax status. However, unless the group is designated as charitable, the donor (or his estate) may not receive all tax advantages.

Donors can transfer securities by sending stock certificates or by instructing their broker to transfer them electronically to the nonprofit's account.

Outright gifts of real estate generate benefits for both organization and donor: they are easily converted into cash by the organization; they entitle the donor to a tax deduction in the amount of the sale price; and they permit the donor to avoid paying capital gains tax on the amount the property has appreciated since purchase. This may be especially interesting to a donor who has, for example, lived in a house whose value has appreciated substantially over the long period the owner has resided there. It is also possible to donate a portion of a property, to make the gift in stages, or to make a gift of real estate known as the "part gift/part sale," or "bargain sale." In this case, a donor sells property to an organization for a "bargain price" that is substantially below market value and is credited with a gift in the amount of the difference between the property's market value and the price for which it was sold. The donor can take a deduction for—and avoid paying capital gains tax on—the amount of the transaction considered a gift. However, the portion of the capital gains allocable to the "sale" is taxable. The transfer of real estate is done through a simple deed containing text similar to the following:

> I/we hereby give the property at (insert address or description of property being donated) to (insert name of recipient organization).

Outright gifts can be made of other kinds of property, such as land, automobiles, clothing, furniture, art collections, gas and oil rights, partnership rights—anything an individual might own. The amount of income tax deduction is based on a number of variables, such as the current value of the property, the nature of the property, whether the giver owned it for more than one year ("long-term"), and whether the nonprofit can use the gift for its tax-exempt purposes. It is advisable to conduct (or ask the donor to secure) a Phase One environmental study of any proposed gift of real estate. Also, the charity should calculate the cost of holding real property in the event that it is not readily salable. Gifts of partnership interests should be analyzed for unrelated business income tax issues and potential "phantom income" problems.

Immediate Funds for the Nonprofit: Life Income Gifts

Individuals wishing to make a significant gift without losing income from assets that are donated can make a life income gift. Each type of life income gift has its own special features, but they all share one basic concept: the donor receives satisfaction and recognition for making the gift, yet still receives income from the donated assets. Other benefits to donors of life income gifts include avoiding capital gains tax on transfers of appreciated assets; receiving immediate tax deduction; and possibly enhancing retirement plans and reducing eventual estate taxes.

Annuities and Trusts

Life income gifts commonly take the form of specialized gift annuities and trusts. An *annuity* is a form of investment on which a person receives fixed payments for a lifetime or a certain number of years. A *trust* is a fiduciary arrangement in which property is held and managed by one party for the benefit of another. Gift annuities and trusts are often referred to as "deferred" gifts, since the recipient organization has to wait until the donor's death to use the gift.

In order for the donor to obtain a charitable tax deduction at the time of the gift, whether it is an annuity or a trust, that gift must be irrevocable; once the gift is made, the donor cannot cancel the arrangement at a later date. For this reason, among others, individuals considering such gifts should always be encouraged to consult their legal and financial advisors. Donors making gifts through living trusts or bequests can specify whether the funds are to be used for restricted or unrestricted purposes. Such gifts can be made in the donor's name, or in honor or memory of a family member, friend, or associate. The donor's desires regarding the use and ongoing acknowledgment of the gifts should be clearly spelled out in the establishing documents, and reviewed by legal counsel. Let's review each major type of gift annuity and trust arrangement.

Gift Annuity. Perhaps the most straightforward kind of planned gift is the gift annuity. A donor makes a gift to a nonprofit organization and periodically receives a fixed sum for life as well as a charitable deduction on his or her federal income taxes for a portion of the gift at the time it is made. The assets used to purchase a gift annuity may be in the form of cash, securities, or real or personal property. In exchange, the charity promises to make fixed payments (annuities) to the donor and/or another named person for the duration of his or her life. Usually a portion of the annuity is excluded from the recipient's gross income and is thus tax-free.

The recipient nonprofit is able to use the donated funds after the death of the donor or the last beneficiary. In the meanwhile, it can plan, build, or borrow on the basis of the value of the gift that will be available to it in the future. If the recipient nonprofit prefers not to assume the obligation of making the annuity payments, it can still establish the gift annuity by reinsuring the annuity through a commercial insurance carrier.

"Reinsuring" means that the nonprofit sells the annuity to a commercial insurance carrier, which then takes responsibility for the annuity. The legal obligation is thus transferred. When the nonprofit sells the annuity to an insurance company, the nonprofit then receives in cash a portion of the gift annuity it would have received when the owner died had it chosen not to sell. That portion will, of course, be less than the amount the nonprofit would have ultimately received, but it can be used immediately by the organization.

Charitable gift annuity programs typically are regulated by the state in which the charity is based.

Charitable Remainder Trust. In this arrangement the donor makes a gift in trust to the recipient organization in the form of cash, securities, or real estate. The gift entitles the donor and/or another named person to income for life (or for a stated period of years) and the donor receives a tax deduction for the present value of the remainder portion in the year the gift is made. At the end of the period, the nonprofit may use what is left in the trust—the remainder. Depending on how well the funds have been managed, the amount will be either larger or smaller than the original gift. Contributions of real property are possible, but typically require more complicated planning.

There are two types of charitable remainder trusts: the *unitrust* and the *annuity trust.* Unitrusts provide a fluctuating amount of annual income to the donor or someone else named. The amount is based on annual valuation of the trust and the stated percentage that the trust pays out (at least 5 percent). Annuity trusts provide a fixed amount of yearly income to the donor or

The Gift Annuity Serves Two Purposes: Giving and Receiving

Suppose you are age 75 and want to give $10,000 to the American Cancer Society and receive annual payments of 8.2 percent for as long as you live. Here is a summary of the results:

1. You transfer $10,000 for a gift annuity agreement.

2. You are permitted to deduct over $4,770 as a charitable gift in the year the gift is made. (Note: If this is more than you can deduct in the year of the gift, you can carry over any excess deduction into the five succeeding tax years.) The exact deductible amount may vary from month to month.

3. You will receive $820 each year for as long as you live. When you file your federal income tax each year, you report only $396 for approximately the next 12 years. During that time, $424 of each payment does not have to be reported as income. Afterward, the entire payment is taxable. (Note: The length of time that payments are partially tax-free depends upon your age when the gift annuity is created.)

4. At death, the American Cancer Society's obligation to make the payments ends, yet your gift continues to be used in the work you wished to further.[6]

---

6. From the American Cancer Society Web site: http://cancersociety.org

---

person named. The amount is determined at the time of the gift, and may be either a stated percentage or a fixed amount (in either case, at least 5 percent of the original gift amount).

Charitable Lead or Charitable Income Trust. The charitable lead trust can be an important tool in a donor's estate planning, as there are beneficial income, gift, and estate tax implications. There are different kinds of lead trusts that meet the varying tax needs of different individuals. Organizations may use income from charitable lead or charitable income trusts for a specified period of time. What remains after that time reverts to the donor or other person named by the donor; this is the reverse of the charitable remainder trust. In all cases, the remainder of the trust goes to whomever the donor designates. There are various ways to structure charitable lead trusts depending upon the grantor's tax needs and philanthropic and personal desires. It is very important to consult with qualified legal counsel.

Pooled Income Fund. Similar to a mutual fund, a pooled income fund enables individuals to invest their funds with others. However, through a pooled income fund the ultimate beneficiary is a designated nonprofit organization. It works as follows: a donor invests money or property in a pooled income fund established by a nonprofit. The donor designates those individuals who will receive regular interest payments; when all beneficiaries have died, the designated nonprofit receives a charitable tax deduction equal to the calculated present value of what eventually will pass to the nonprofit.

This type of gift creates additional benefits for the donor. Since a nonprofit will benefit from any permanent improvement to the property it receives (such as a new roof), the donor who makes the improvement can declare the portion of the cost allocable to the charity's remainder interest as a charitable deduction. The donor/resident is, however, still responsible for any mortgage on the property, as well as for paying real estate and other taxes on the property while living in it. If the donor chooses to move and relinquish the right to live in that home, the donor can claim an additional tax deduction based, as before, on the property's value and age. This gift also helps a donor avoid the trouble and expense of disposing of the property later.

The nonprofit organization receiving this type of gift benefits not only from eventual possession of the donated property; it is able to carry the present value of its remainder interest as an asset on its balance sheet. A gift of a donor's personal residence, or a portion thereof, is an ideal planned gift to an organization. It can be a simple deed, and there are minimal administrative responsibilities for the nonprofit.

Providing Support Beyond the Donor's Lifetime

Bequests

Individuals may increase their support for an organization during their lifetime by providing for gifts to be made after their death. This is usually done through a will, the legal document that tells how to dispose of what a person owns upon death. The gift itself is known as a *bequest*. A person may give all or part of what he or she owns to a nonprofit organization, a specific dollar amount, a percentage of the entire estate, a gift in trust, or specific items, such as paintings or antiques, a book or stamp collection, or one hundred shares of Company X. It is also possible to give part ownership in an item, such as 50 percent "partial interest" in real estate or in a painting (in which case the nonprofit would hold and use the property for six months of the year). In the United States, charitable gifts made through a will are 100 percent deductible for estate tax purposes, and, by reducing the taxable amount of the estate, reduce estate taxes.

Unlike gift annuities and trusts, which may be irrevocable, bequests are revocable: a donor may change his or her will at any time, removing one organization or adding another. For this reason, an organization must never count income from bequests until it is received. It also should develop a simple stewardship program to continue cultivating donors who have already named the organization in their will.

Gifts by will can be worded as follows: "I give, devise, and bequeath to (insert name of recipient organization) for its general purposes (or for a specific purpose) all (or a fraction or percentage) of the rest, residue, and remainder of my estate, both real or personal."

Life Insurance

A nonprofit may be named as beneficiary of a new or existing life insurance policy, subject to restrictions in some states. The nonprofit may be the first ("primary") beneficiary, or a second, third, or later contingent beneficiary for all or part of the policy's proceeds. Individuals may also

Profile:

Moderate Gifts—Life Estate

Even donors of moderate means can make a substantial and meaningful gift to non-profit organizations using a life estate arrangement. The following is a profile of a donor who came forward and expressed her interest in making a gift to a charitable organization in Northeast Ohio.

Mrs. Smith* attended a gift-motivating seminar which was hosted by the nonprofit organization. Although she did not consider herself a candidate for a planned gift, she approached the organization with her strong desire to make a gift that would perpetuate her concern for the organization and those it served.

Mrs. Smith's Concerns: She was living on a fixed income and was concerned about her investments keeping pace with inflation. She had limited options for her maturing Series E and EE bonds, and she wanted to avoid tax consequences and be able to increase her income. She was also concerned about the disposition of her home, both in life and after death.

Mrs. Smith's assets totaled $465,000. They included $250,000 in government bonds; a home valued at $110,000; an Individual Retirement Account valued at $45,000; $25,000 worth of personal property; and stocks and bonds worth $35,000.

The Solution: Mrs. Smith gifted her home to the charity while retaining the right to live in it for the remainder of her lifetime. Since disposition during life was a concern, the life estate offered various options while she was alive. She could gift her remainder interest to the charity and receive another charitable tax deduction. An alternative would be for the house to be sold and her remainder interest paid in cash or given through a gift annuity. As a result of the gift, she was entitled to a $50,000 charitable income tax deduction that helped offset the gain from the sale of her bonds.

Although Mrs. Smith never believed she had the capacity to make a charitable gift to this organization, she was able to make a gift that satisfied her charitable and philanthropic goals and was a significant and meaningful gift for the organization. In other words, a charitable planning strategy helped solve her personal financial goals.[7]

---

* Name has been changed to ensure confidentiality

7. Peggy Wallace Bender, "Profile: Moderate Gift – Life Estate," *TRENDS* (Cleveland: Strategies for Planned Giving, Fall 1995).

---

transfer ownership of life insurance policies to nonprofit organizations and gain income tax deductions. The donor deducts the cost basis in the policy or the policy's replacement value—whichever is less—as charitable contributions for income tax purposes.

Life insurance can be a convenient vehicle for charitable giving simply because an individual may find that the original reason for purchasing their life insurance policy is no longer as pressing. For example, they may have wanted to make financial provisions for children in the event of their premature death, but then decide to make a favorite charity the beneficiary of their life insurance policy when those children are grown and self-supporting.

Deciding Whether To Launch a Planned Giving Program

If you have decided that the advantages of establishing a planned giving program (as they apply specifically to your organization) significantly outweigh the disadvantages, you will still want to answer several questions before embarking on your planned giving campaign.

1. *Will your work be ongoing?* Does your organization plan to be around for the next generation? Do you anticipate that your vision and mission will be as vitally important at the end of the twenty-first century as it is at the beginning? A planned giving program makes sense only if your leadership agrees that the organization and the need for its work are ongoing. If you think that your mission will be accomplished and your vision a reality within ten years, and that you do not plan to develop new ones, then launching a planned giving program is clearly not a wise use of resources.

   For example, if you are a college or a hospital, your mission is unending, and planned giving has a clear place in your fundraising. If you're a public interest advocacy group seeking to stop construction of a nuclear power plant or improve your community's mass transit system, however, you may well fulfill your mission in a matter of years; if you do not plan to address new issues on an ongoing basis, you will probably choose not to undertake a planned giving campaign.

2. *Is your organization solid?* You must be able to demonstrate to prospective donors of planned gifts—and their advisors—that your organization has the following characteristics of a sound institution:

   - An organizational vision sufficiently powerful to attract and justify financial support in the future

   - An active, responsible, publicly acknowledged governing body that supports planned giving both in concept and in fact

   - Sound finances as evidenced by audited financial statements

   - Sufficient staff and access to experts to administer planned gifts

   In short, an organization interested in receiving planned gifts—or any other form of substantial contributions—must demonstrate that it is financially sound, well-managed, and fully capable of administering those gifts, now and in the future. Brand new and recently established groups are not the best candidates for planned giving programs since they have just begun to reach out to the public for support. Individuals are unlikely to respond to solicitations for planned gifts by these organizations. More mature organizations with a strong network of regular donors are likelier candidates.

3. *Do you have prospects for planned giving?* Review your concentric circles exercise (see the end of Chapter 7). Do you currently have donors with the financial ability and loyalty to your organization to make such a commitment? Note that the commitment need not be enormous. Everyone is going to die, and since no one can take very much to whatever awaits, gifts of one's personal possessions usually can be put to good use by a recipient organization.

   Discussing planned gifts with board members and other key supporters is a good way to learn if your organization has enough qualified prospects to launch a planned giving program. In your conversations, remember that you are only raising a trial balloon, and phrase your questions accordingly, e.g., "We are considering an outreach effort to inform people how they could designate our organization as beneficiary in their wills (or as a beneficiary of a life insurance policy). Since you are close to our work and know us, we were hoping that you could tell us what you think about the idea." You will not only obtain some pertinent data, but you will also be laying the groundwork for actual solicitations further down the road.

4. *What kind of experiences have comparable organizations had with planned giving?* Check with nonprofits whose standing and donor base are similar to your own to learn if their experiences with planned giving have netted positive results. Ask about the pitfalls as well.

Organizing a Planned Giving Effort

Despite the legal and financial complexities of planned giving vehicles and administration, the process of soliciting planned gifts is based on the same principles that underlie any other kind of solicitation. In fact, our frequently repeated maxims—"People give to people," and "The more personal, the more effective"—are nowhere more applicable than in the area of soliciting planned gifts. Making a planned gift is a highly personal matter, and personal contact is needed to establish the necessary level of trust.

More people than one would imagine make planned gifts. Older and larger nonprofit institutions such as hospitals and universities have traditionally solicited bequests from major donors; but now individuals from all walks of life are solicited for a variety of planned gifts by organizations both large and small. Nevertheless, for some nonprofit managers, creating a planned giving program represents a real challenge, as it requires an ongoing commitment in an area that demands extensive legal and financial expertise. Fortunately, organizations can be assured that prospective donors will consult their own legal and financial advisors, and planned giving experts can be retained.

Solicitors of planned gifts should not feel uncomfortable in discussing such gifts, as the focus is life—the life of the organization, and the improved lives of those who have been or will be helped by planned gifts. Moreover, the literature and planned giving software libraries are extensive, and the many professional associations of planned givers offer conferences and seminars at

The Royal Ontario Museum Foundation Planned Giving Advisors

It's virtually impossible for even the largest nonprofit organizations to have the specialized expertise they need in-house. But most organizations can enlist the help of attorneys and accountants who specialize in trusts and estates, as well as bank trust officers and financial planners, by convening a planned giving advisors committee. Here is the Description of Responsibilities and the Mandate for the Planned Giving Advisors created by the Royal Ontario Museum (ROM) Foundation:

> Planned Giving Advisors to the Major Gifts and Planned Giving Committee of the ROM Foundation will bring professional expertise to the planned givers, accountants, financial planners, insurance executives, investment counselors, trust and estate officers, and brokers. They will bring invaluable knowledge to the marketing and promotion of planned gifts in support of the Museum. It is anticipated that there will be about ten advisors who will serve the Foundation in this capacity.
>
> Specifically, Advisors will:
>
> • participate in presentations at seminars on estate and financial planning for Museum members;
>
> • suggest and/or contribute articles to Museum publications about the tax aspects of giving and about planned giving;
>
> • promote the Museum and may, at times, have opportunity to refer a potential donor to the professional staff of the Foundation;
>
> • from time to time be called upon to advise on marketing strategies, to vet articles, marketing materials and prototype planned gift agreements;
>
> • be called upon to brief Foundation staff on legal, technical or regulatory changes and developments;
>
> • meet from time to time as a group to discuss issues of common concern and to learn about the programs and activities of the Museum.
>
> Professional staff at the Foundation may refer a potential donor to an Advisor to obtain professional advice. Referrals will be provided at the request of the donor only. Unless at the request of the potential donor, Advisors will not be involved directly in the solicitation of planned gifts.

many levels for nonprofit managers (see the Additional Resources section at the end of this chapter).

Soliciting an organization's first few planned gifts can be simpler than it might seem. Since the vast majority of planned gifts involve bequests (as mentioned earlier, 80 percent of all planned gifts made in Canada are bequests), encouraging donors to include your organization in their will covers at least 80 percent of your market. Bequests can, in fact, be the beginning of a donor's involvement with an organization. If a donor includes an organization in his or her will, it is possible that, with proper stewardship and cultivation, the donor's confidence and commitment will grow and a planned giving plan may develop; the donor may even make cash contributions in addition to the bequest.

The growth of an organization's planned giving program can be compared to building a highway in an area where there is currently little traffic. Almost invariably, the highway attracts traffic; once the structure is in place, activity increases. The same can be true for a planned giving program; once it is announced and a basic structure has been created, activity will increase, and the structure will expand to handle all situations.

A Step-by-Step Guide To Launching a Planned Giving Program

Step 1. Prepare Materials
Many specialized planned giving consultants will readily provide samples of brochures and newsletters that can be personalized with your organization's name or logo. Publishers of these newsletters have access to resources that many nonprofits cannot readily afford. To find the right specialist for your institution, ask for recommendations from fundraisers at institutions similar to yours, or check professional magazines, books, or journals to identify planned giving experts. Respond to direct mail invitations to obtain further information about planned giving publications and seminars.

Additionally, hospitals, colleges, large social service agencies such as the Salvation Army, and religious societies often have planned giving materials available upon request that can guide you in preparing your own promotional material. Finally, the books listed in the Additional Resources section at the end of this chapter provide excellent, in-depth information.

A few words of caution: You are dealing in legal matters, intricate gifts, and large sums of money. If you choose to prepare your own materials, seek the counsel of a tax lawyer and a financial advisor, such as an accountant.

Step 2. Solicit Your Board Members
Just as the general financial support of your board sends an important message to your constituents, so too does the board's participation in your planned giving program. The board's own gifts demonstrate each member's commitment to the concept, thereby setting an example to others; such gifts also make board members' solicitations more effective.

Step 3. Market the Program
Marketing your planned giving program will be most effective if it encompasses two thrusts: a broad outreach to your general constituency, and a more focused effort directed toward a

Planned Parenthood Federation of America

Planned Parenthood distributes six-paneled, color informational brochures on "Giving Through Your Will," "Charitable Remainder Trusts," and the "Planned Parenthood Pooled Income Fund." Each is accompanied by a response form. The organization also periodically publishes an 8½-by-11-inch, four-sided newsletter highlighting individuals and families who have made planned gifts to them. The newsletter also includes a message from the organization's president, some factual information, and a response form. Finally, the newsletter introduces their donors and others to the Heritage Club, which honors individuals who made a commitment to support the Planned Parenthood Federation of America through a bequest or other planned gift.

smaller, more targeted group. Creating a "Legacy Society"—a variation on the gift club concept—gives structure and visibility to your planned giving program.

Nonprofits should include a notice about their planned giving programs in every piece of literature that reaches their members. You might, for example, begin your campaign by simply using your newsletter or annual report to outline the ways in which individuals can earmark planned or deferred gifts to your organization, and invite them to designate your organization in their wills.

For selected individuals, you might consider positioning your organization as a source of planned giving information. Creating and sending out "tax-update newsletters" and brochures addressing such topics as the importance of having a will and how to go about estate planning, for example, may well prompt some of your prospects to explore planned giving. Include a response card with these mailings so that readers can ask for more information and, in the process, change their status from suspect to prospect. You might also hold a series of seminars where planned giving experts discuss such general topics as planned giving, tax law changes, wills, and estate planning. If you do, make sure that the seminars are not thinly disguised group solicitations; people will sense this and attendance is likely to be minimal.

As in a face-to-face solicitation campaign, create a schedule for your planned giving campaign. Decide the specific time of the year to announce the program in your newsletter, annual report, and other promotional materials. Events such as a group's tenth or twenty-fifth anniversary can serve as ideal occasions to launch a planned giving effort. Also decide when you might actually make targeted approaches to prospective participants.

Finally, consider creating a planned giving committee at the board level. Properly constituted, such a committee can give immediate credibility to your program; additionally, committee members can identify, cultivate, and solicit prospective donors among their peers and associates. Members should be expected to make their own planned gifts as a condition of participation.

The Royal Ontario Museum Foundation Planned Giving and Major Gifts Committee

Here is a description of the composition and activities of the Planned Giving and Major Gifts Committee of the Royal Ontario Museum (ROM) Foundation:

> The Planned Giving and Major Gifts Committee is to be chaired by a member of the Board of Directors and to be composed of not less than three members. Its membership will not be limited to directors of the ROM Foundation.
>
> The Planned Giving and Major Gifts Committee will recommend to the Board of Directors policies to facilitate major gift fundraising from charitable foundations and through planned gifts. The Planned Giving and Major Gifts Committee will be involved closely in the development of recognition vehicles for major gifts.

Activities

- to receive information from the Executive Director to formulate policies and strategies in the area of planned giving and major gift fundraising for recommendation to the Board; to monitor the ROM's progress in securing major gifts including planned gifts;

- to develop fundraising targets and financial objectives for the planned giving programme and special appeals to charitable foundations;

- to develop plans for the cultivation of prospective donors;

- to participate in the evaluation of prospective donors to be reserved for solicitation of major gifts including planned gifts;

- to participate in solicitations of major gifts and planned gifts from individuals and charitable foundations for the ROM and its affiliates;

- to plan and recommend policies to the Board in regard to comprehensive campaign efforts for capital and/or endowment purposes.

Step 4. Identify Prospective Donors

The same process of identifying prospects, creating a committee, recruiting solicitors, and undertaking the personal solicitations described in Chapter 11 (Face-to-Face Solicitation) can be applied directly to soliciting planned gifts.

While your donor records and research will surely identify your best prospects, some surprises may come your way. Examples abound of individuals and couples who have led outwardly frugal lives but astonish the world by willing millions to institutions from resources that no one knew existed.

Finally, review your first two inner circles to identify individuals with the financial ability and potential willingness to purchase life insurance policies naming your organization as the beneficiary, or to participate in a pooled fund or any other form of deferred giving.

Step 5. Approach Your Prospects for a Planned Gift

Once your organization is ready to launch a planned giving effort, recruit and train your solicitors, assign prospects, and follow the same procedures outlined in Chapter 11.

While the mention in a newsletter or the enclosure of a brochure in a general mailing may lead people to call your office for more information on planned giving, face-to-face contact is usually vital to persuade donors to sign up. After thanking a caller for making an inquiry, suggest a meeting (at a place and time convenient to the prospect) so that you can explain planned giving and answer any questions.

When you meet, remember to impress upon your prospect your capability as the steward of his or her contribution. To do so, you might mention the name of your legal counsel or the bank that manages your deferred gifts. Additionally, although you want to present the different options thoroughly, it's important not to present yourself as a donor's legal or financial counsel. Suggest that the donor consult a lawyer or accountant if he or she asks such questions as, "Do you think that a contribution of X dollars is more desirable than Y dollars now for tax purposes?" or, "Do you think that I should give 100 shares of X Corporation or 150 shares of Y Company?" Better yet, suggest that you and the donor visit the advisor together. Be careful to avoid implying that you are an attorney, accountant, or financial planner unless you are certified as such. Remember that your goal is to present the opportunity and the details of how a planned gift to your organization might work. Deferred gifts of various kinds have been lost to organizations when disgruntled relatives accused the organization of "undue influence" over the now deceased donor.

Step 6. Follow Up the Gift and Continue Cultivation

Acknowledge appropriately the gifts received. In addition to sending the immediate thank-you note, consider what type of public acknowledgment donors might appreciate (if this has not already been discussed). Whereas some donors may be gratified to receive some form of public acknowledgment for their support, such as mention in a newsletter, bulletin, or annual report, others will wish to remain anonymous. Speak to other groups active in planned giving to learn how they handle public acknowledgment.

Be sure that donors receive regular updates on your programs, and treat them as specially as you do your major donors. Even though the benefits of their gifts may not be reaped immediately, their support is highly significant. Those who have designated your organization as the beneficiary of a will or some other planned gift have clearly indicated that they support your work in a substantial way, and that your ongoing success is personally important. As a result, you want to keep the door open for those donors to support you in other ways as well, unless they indicate that their support is limited to a one-time gift. The more frankly you talk to your donors, the easier it will be to assess the possibility of future gifts. Your donors will probably appreciate your candor and attention, too.

Profile:

Greenpeace Canada

Like many non-profit organizations, Greenpeace Canada had to start small when it first began seeking planned gifts in 1990. Natasha van Bentum, the director of major gifts at the time, was asked to spend just 25 percent of her time promoting bequests, the least complicated of planned gifts. The program, van Bentum says, "was the very first of its kind for an environmental group in Canada." While a few bequests had come in with no effort by Greenpeace, the organization had been almost completely dependent on direct mail. It had not actively tried to get bequests or even large cash gifts from its donors, most of whom gave in the $25 range. "No one had any experience with planned giving, so I had complete liberty in shaping the program," she recalls.

The first thing van Bentum did was to complete a rough draft of a brochure about bequests. Then she used it to conduct some simple research. She wrote letters, made telephone calls, and visited with people to share the brochure and get their reaction to Greenpeace's plan to promote bequests. She asked for feedback and conducted interviews with two groups: some 20 Greenpeace donors who were giving at a higher-than-average level, $250 or more per year, and about the same number of estate-planning lawyers who help people with their wills.

"In the early years of a program like this, visits to lawyers are just as important as visits to donors," says van Bentum. "If the donor's own lawyer does not understand charitable bequests or who we are, it can put a big damper on any effort we make with the donor." She was relieved to learn that most of the donors and lawyers she interviewed thought that bequests made sense for Greenpeace.

More important, van Bentum says, the interviews convinced her that the thought process of people who make a will is similar to that of environmental donors. People who care about the environment care about the future; they don't want to leave a mess for future generations and they are willing to do something about it, she says. The same thing is true of people who make wills: They care about what happens after they're gone and they have taken steps to put their affairs in order, so as not to leave a mess. "After I realized that," van Bentum says, "'I didn't have to do any more research. I knew that our donors would be attracted to the idea of making a bequest."

After putting the finishing touches on the brochure, which spelled out Greenpeace's accomplishments, some basic facts about the benefits of having a will, and how a will can be used to make a gift to help protect the environment, van Bentum was ready to start promoting bequests. For the first several years, she simply advertised the brochure in the organization's newsletter, which is mailed to 160,000 donors three to four times each year. The ad, which contained a photograph of animals protected by the environmental group, told donors how to get a free copy. Donors who requested the brochure could fill out a tear-off page and mail it back to Greenpeace. That response device allowed them to request more information about bequests, and to specify whether they'd already named

Greenpeace in their will or intended to do so. When donors returned the information, van Bentum followed up accordingly, calling donors to provide more information, for example, or thanking those whose plans already included a bequest to Greenpeace.

Even those modest efforts paid off, says van Bentum. Between 1990 and 1994, she says, the organization saw a 100-percent increase in the number of bequests it received. Gradually, van Bentum began to do more. Two years ago, she abandoned major gifts to work full time on bequests. She created a new brochure, a more educational pamphlet designed to enable people to write a will. "Seven out of 10 Canadians do not have a will," she says. "The number one challenge in planned giving is people not facing the issue of making a will."

Instead of just advertising the pamphlet in the newsletter, van Bentum has now mailed it to 15,000 Greenpeace donors in three groups: those who give $250 or more annually, donors who make monthly gifts to the organization, and those who give less frequently in response to direct-mail appeals. Along with the pamphlet, those donors got a low-key letter from van Bentum and were asked to fill out a short questionnaire, similar to the tear-off page in the first brochure. Those mailings have generated a response from 4 percent of the recipients; van Bentum is now busy working with that set of donors to increase bequests to Greenpeace.

To that end, she has also continued her meetings with both lawyers and donors in Vancouver, where Greenpeace is based, to make them aware of the bequest program. And she travels two or three times each year to other Canadian cities; the trips last a week to 10 days.

During the trips, van Bentum sometimes invites lawyers and donors to previously scheduled Greenpeace events, such as "Ship Visits" in which supporters are invited aboard one of the organization's two ships. There they are treated to refreshments and a presentation about how the ships further Greenpeace's efforts to monitor environmental threats like toxic dumping in ocean waters, off-shore nuclear testing, and illegal whaling.

Van Bentum's efforts have paid off handsomely. Between 1984, when Greenpeace first began keeping records on bequests, and 1992, bequest income totaled $365,000. That's an average of $45,000 per year. But from 1993 to 1998, bequests grew to an average of $525,000 annually and totaled $3,135,000.

To take the bequest program even further, van Bentum added a section on bequests to the Greenpeace Web site (www.greenpeace.org), which enables people to request the two brochures while they are on-line. The page on wills contains a humorous message: "When you come back as a whale," it says, "you'll be glad you put Greenpeace in your will." About 75,000 people have visited the page in its first two years of existence, and van Bentum gets about five or six on-line requests for the materials on wills each week.

Van Bentum says that she hopes to soon be able to seek other types of planned gifts for Greenpeace. She says she will pursue them in the following order, according to their increasing complexity: gifts of life insurance, outright gifts of appreciated stock, annuities, and then charitable remainder trusts. Despite her bequest program's steady growth and impressive returns, however, van Bentum says that there have been several challenges along the way. Perhaps the biggest, she says, is an expectation by the board of directors that a certain amount of bequest income will come in during any given year. In reality, she notes, bequest income is highly unpredictable in its first seven years or so, and can fluctuate dramatically from one year to the next.

"It is important to caution one's board when large bequests come in, so they do not become conditioned to this," says van Bentum. "I now have a situation where my board is used to seeing unusually large gifts once every 18 months. Now they're sitting back and waiting for the next one. But you can't bank on it, and you should never base the budget on it."

— Holly Hall

Planned Giving Forever

Mentioned earlier, planned giving serves donors by enabling them to extend their charitable support beyond their lifetimes; for an organization, it ensures a future source of income during its own mature years. The benefits can be substantial for both donors and nonprofits.

Tips

- Many people feel that planned giving is mysterious, or only for wealthy people, or slightly distasteful to discuss. However, everyone is going to die and most people will leave assets to someone. While some planned giving strategies for wealthy individuals are complicated and best left to professionals, everyone can understand the concept of contributing assets for charitable purposes; this is the basis of planned giving.

- Start your planned giving initiative with a bequest program. Tell people how to leave your organization money in their wills. This is simple and easy, and the results may surprise you.

- Before you begin a planned giving program, think about whether your group needs to exist in perpetuity and what kind of endowment or reserve fund you want to set up for gifts you receive. Otherwise, you may be tempted to spend gifts from a bequest on your annual needs. Because bequests are one-time gifts, this is unwise.

Summary Worksheet

for _____

(name of your organization)

Approaching Individuals for Support: Bequests, Life Insurance Premiums, and Other Forms of Planned Giving

Building on Efforts to Date

1. Have you received any bequests or other planned gifts in the past?

_____ yes _____ no

2. If Yes, from whom?

_____

_____

_____

3. What characteristics do these individuals share:

Comments:

_____

_____

_____

4. What is your sense of what they valued in your organization's work?

Comments:

_____

_____

_____

Assessing your Organization's Planned Giving Readiness Checklist

	YES	NO
1. Is your organization five years old or more?	_____	_____
2. Is your organization financially sound?	_____	_____
3. Do you expect your organization to exist and be operating thirty years from now?	_____	_____
4. Does your organization have a strong constituency that can be readily identified?	_____	_____
5. Does that constituency have property or discretionary income?	_____	_____

6. Will your board of directors support a planned giving effort?   _____ _____

7. Will your organization allot staff and professional time for a
planned giving effort?   _____ _____

8. Will your organization allot the financial resources needed for
publications, materials, travel, training, etc.?   _____ _____

9. Is your staff committed to planned giving?   _____ _____

Finding Assistance and Counsel

Name several individuals who might advise you on how to launch a planned giving campaign effectively:

a. _____

b. _____

c. _____

Rating Your Planned Giving Potential

On the basis of what you have learned, how would you rank your chances of securing bequests, life insurance premiums, and other planned gifts?

__ Very Good   __ Possible   __ Unlikely   __ Still Unknown

Additional Resources

Publications

Barrett, Richard D., and Molly E. Ware. *Planned Giving Essentials: A Step by Step Guide to Success.* Frederick, MD: Aspen Publishers (Aspen's Fund Raising Series for the 21st Century), 1997, xiii, 166 p.

> Divided into two parts. The first part introduces basic planned giving principles and practices, and the second part provides a guide to implementing a planned giving program. Includes glossary, bibliographic references, and index.

Behan, Donald F. "Planned Giving with Gift Annuities." *Nonprofit World* 14 (March–April 1996): 11–15.

> Describes what gift annuities are, what types exist, and their benefits and risks.

Billitteri, Thomas J. "All in the Family." *Chronicle of Philanthropy* 11 (15 July 1999) 33–35.

> The Internal Revenue Service has established an internal task force to investigate "charitable family limited partnerships," a tax-avoidance strategy that uses charities as partners in business ventures. It is estimated that hundreds of wealthy individuals are currently taking advantage of the "char-flip," as the strategy is known. Industry insiders estimate that at least $3 billion worth of such transactions have been completed in the past two years. The strategy, which was first promoted by a Dallas tax consulting firm in early 1997 and is now being pushed by a number of financial planning firms, allows donors to take a tax deduction for contributing a sizable portion of their family business or other assets, such as real estate, to charity while maintaining complete control over those assets.

Blum, Debra E. "Looking To Get Out of the Pool." *Chronicle of Philanthropy* 12 (24 February 2000): 31–32.

> Discusses the drop in popularity of pooled-income funds as a planned giving option, and the way that many nonprofit organizations are attempting to reorganize or close them.

Canter, MacKenzie, III. "Charitable Contributions of Real Estate." *Philanthropy Monthly* 32 (July–August 1999): 5–21.

> Discusses sources of real estate gifts; tax and non-tax risks and risk reduction strategies; and donation formats, including charitable remainder trusts. In addition, includes a discussion of the "TFR Technique." TFR is the acronym for Thornburg Foundation Realty, Inc. (previously known as American Foundation Realty, Inc.), an "all equity" real estate investment trust. The TFR Technique was developed by Garret Thornburg and John Grab, and is intended to solve many of the problems associated with real estate giving that are experienced by donors and charities. Sidebars provide illustrative examples of ways to fund charitable remainder trusts, and the benefits of the TFR Technique. Also included is a copy of a letter from the Internal Revenue Service to Thornburg Foundation Realty, Inc. providing rulings concerning transactions involving charitable trusts.

Caswell, G.M. "A Life and Death Issue." *Fund Raising Management* 26 (February 1996): 28–29.
  Discusses mortality and the role it plays in assisting donors with planned or testamentary gifts.

Chouinard, Carole. "Comparison of the Tax Treatment of Charitable Remainder Trusts in Canada and the United States." *Philanthropist/Le Philanthrope* 14 (September 1998): 3–16.
  Article compares the Canadian model to the American model in terms of tax rules and consequences, costs, and other issues.

Clough, Leonard G., David G. Clough, Ellen G. Estes, and Ednalou C. Ballard. *Practical Guide to Planned Giving*, 1998. Detroit: The Taft Group, 1997, xxvi, 930 p.
  Provides marketing and technical information to help development officers establish permanent planned giving programs. The book is divided into five main sections. The first section contains operational definitions of major forms of planned giving programs, a step-by-step guide to preparing and setting up a planned giving program, and advice on marketing the program. The second section deals with managing and evaluating the program. The third section explains federal tax aspects of planned giving, including considerations involved with donating different kinds of assets to charitable organizations. The fourth section describes the roles of the gift planning team: the financial planner, the insurance professional, the attorney, and the accountant. The fifth section provides a glossary, sample forms, resource lists, a summary of charitable gift annuity state regulations, codes of ethics, maximum gift rates, sample disclosure statements, and IRS forms and publications.

Connell, James E. "Funding Gift Annuities with Real Estate." *Planned Giving Today* (July 1997): 1, 7–9.

Copilevitz, Errol. "Potential Dilemma of Contingent Gifts." *Fund Raising Management* 26 (February 1996): 34–38.
  Advises fundraisers how to deal with donor-imposed restrictions.

Coppes, Michael L. "A Big Plan for Small-Office Planned Giving." *Currents* 25 (March 1999): 41–47.
  Fifteen steps to a successful planned giving program.

Englebrecht, Ted D., and Monica E. Selmonosky. "Contingent Bequests and Estate Tax Charitable Deductions." *Trusts & Estates* 136 (September 1997): 40, 42–47.
  Examines tax planning strategies that will ensure the tax deductibility of contingent bequests.

Fuerst, Rita A. "Dilemma of Contingent Gifts." *New Directions for Philanthropic Fundraising* 13 (Fall 1996): 73–84.
> Defines the Internal Revenue Service's qualifications of gifts, then addresses the issue of donor-imposed restrictions, and how these restrictions must be consistent with the intent to make the gift.

Giese, James O. "Tax Issues Regarding Planned Giving and Recent Legislative Developments." *New Directions for Philanthropic Fundraising* 14 (Winter 1996): 47–62.
> Offers an overview of IRS regulations concerning philanthropy and the nonprofit sector.

Grant Thornton, LLP. *Planned Giving: A Board Member's Perspective.* Washington, DC: National Center for Nonprofit Boards, 1999. 27 p.

Greene, Karen L. "Hidden Treasures: Three Varied Examples of How the Right Planned Giving Setting Can Turn Rough Prospects into True Gems." *Currents* 22 (October 1996): 40–43.
> Describes three different planned giving approaches: charitable award programs (CAPs), employee stock ownership programs (ESOPs), and deferred gift annuities.

Gregg, Keith E. *Do Well by Doing Good: The Complete Guide to Charitable Remainder Trusts.* Chicago: Bonus Books, 1996.
> Chapters cover different types and popular uses of charitable remainder trusts, and explain how to set them up and market them.

Gulbrandsen, James S., and Dan B. Roberts. "CRATS, CRUTS and NIMCRUTS: Philanthropy or Prosperity?" *Trusts & Estates* 135 (June 1996): 53–57.
> Explains that properly structured charitable plans not only provide significant benefits to charity, but also financially reward the donor. Particular focus is given to the relationship between tax issues, trust accounting rules, and investment strategies.

Hall, Holly. "Forging Ties to the Money Pros." *Chronicle of Philanthropy* 9 (7 August 1997): 1, 12, 14.
> To offset government cuts and to tap into the $10 trillion that baby boomers are expected to inherit, charities are experimenting with various means of enabling financial professionals to actively encourage their clients to consider philanthropy. Whereas some charities have already achieved impressive results using such techniques, among the many barriers to their widespread use are: the reluctance of most financial professionals to bring up the issue for fear of losing business, their lack of proficiency in the complexities of planned giving, and their discomfort in discussing value-laden matters with their clients.

Hall, Holly. "Rich Donors Cite Displeasure with Financial Advisers." *Chronicle of Philanthropy* 9 (7 August 1997): 12.

A poll conducted for the *Chronicle* has revealed that a majority of donors are dissatisfied with the help received from financial advisers or charity officers. As a consequence, only 1 to 2 percent of dissatisfied donors expect to make further planned gifts or to recommend planned giving to others. This displeasure appears to be due to an inadequate level of preparation on the part of charity officers and financial planners, most of whom failed a quiz designed to test their expertise in the planned giving field.

Hall, Holly. "Turning Baby Boomers into Big Givers." *Chronicle of Philanthropy* 8 (16 May 1996): 25–27.

Charities are experimenting with a variety of new approaches to attract planned gifts from young and middle-aged donors. Methods described include adjusting the pitch for young donors, developing appeals to unmarried couples, seeking gifts by telephone, and asking donors to return income from planned gifts.

Hartsook, Robert F. "Gifts that Go Out of the Box." *Fund Raising Management* 28 (April 1997): 16–17.

Suggests offering every gift option to a prospective donor of $100,000 or more.

Hartsook, Robert F. "Nurturing Deferred Gifts: Shaping Your Donor's Vision." *FRI Monthly Portfolio* 38 (February 1999): 1–2.

Recommends seven steps to take to acquire deferred gifts.

Heise, Suzanne. "Act Now. Give Forever." *Fund Raising Management* 30 (March 2000): 24–25, 42.

Describes Leave a Legacy, a community awareness program that encourages people to include nonprofits in their wills. Established in Connecticut, nearly 500 nonprofits in the state participated in the public awareness campaign.

Hixson, Anne. "Tapping a Rich Resource." *Fund Raising Management* 30 (November 1999): 20–23.

Profiles the Institute for Family Wealth Counseling, an organization of financial counseling professionals that provides advising services on estate planning to wealthy clients.

Jackman, Lee. "Charitable Organizations Have a Moral Obligation to Wealthy Donors Who Leave Them Their Entire Estate." *Fund Raising Management,* 30 (February 2000): 32–33.

Expresses the opinion that if a wealthy donor arranges to leave their entire estate to a nonprofit organization, then the organization is obligated to establish and maintain a strong bond with the donor and make sure that they are well cared for during the rest of their life, and ensure that the donor's wishes for the use of his or her gift are honored.

Jensen, John W. "A Check List: Audit Your Planned Giving Program." *NonProfit Times* 11 (October 1997): 46–47.

Jensen, John W. "When There's a Will: What To Do When a Bequest Comes In." *NonProfit Times* 12 (March 1998): 39, 40, 46.

Jordan, Ronald R. "Expertise on Call." *Currents* 22 (March 1996): 14, 16, 18.
   Emphasizes the importance of having a committee of allied professionals as a vital link to donors and a resource for a planned giving program.

Jordan, Ronald R., Katelyn L. Quynn, and Carolyn M. Osteen. *Planned Giving: Management, Marketing, and Law*. New York: John Wiley & Sons, 1995. xx, 372 p.
   Divided into six parts: building a development program, marketing planned giving, planned giving assets, deferred gifts, related disciplines, and planned giving in context. Accompanied by a computer disk with documents for use when creating and administering a planned giving program.

Kabaker, Thomas. "The Shape of Gifts to Come." *Advancing Philanthropy* 4 (Fall 1996): 24–27.
   Gives a brief overview of planned giving: finding prospects, structuring gifts, and advantages for donors and recipient organizations.

Kling, Paul F. "A Sea Change in Planned Giving." *Advancing Philanthropy* 6 (Fall–Winter 1998): 14–19.
   Author asserts that today's donors are more inclined to support local grassroots nonprofits than more established organizations, to seek more control over the uses of their gifts, and demand greater accountability.

Lewis, Nicole. "Gaining Donors' Trusts: Charities Step Up Their Efforts To Attract Sizable Planned Gifts." *Chronicle of Philanthropy* 12 (21 September 2000): 31–33.
   Article describes efforts by charities to increase planned gifts to their institutions. Strategies include using direct mail, offering planned giving seminars, advertising in national publications, and hiring a full-time staff member to promote planned gifts. Additional strategies include making information about planned giving available on the Internet and educating young adults about planned gifts.

Mann, Barlow T. "Are Your Donors in the Market for Planned Gifts?" *Fund Raising Management* 26 (February 1996): 30–33.
   Argues that today's economic environment provides powerful incentives for donors to plan their current and deferred gifts.

McAllister, Pamela. *The Charity's Guide to Charitable Contributions*. Seattle: Conlee-Gibbs Publishing, 1998. vii, 138 p.

> Focuses on common situations that most fundraisers encounter, and answers questions that may be asked by potential donors. Several chapters explain IRS rules; additional chapters deal with particular types of contributions and fundraising methods; one chapter is devoted to planned giving; the final chapter discusses state laws. Appendices include reprints of IRS Publication 526 (Charitable Contributions); Publication 561 (Determining the Value of Donated Property); Form 8283 (Noncash Charitable Contributions); and Form 8282 (Donee Information Return). Indexed.

McCoy, Jerry J. "Charitable Remainder Trust Regs Present Planning Opportunities." *Trusts & Estates* 138 (March 1999): 16, 18, 20, 22, 24, 26, 28.

> Geared toward estate planners, article reviews the new charitable remainder trust regulations item by item, and then examines the planning implications of the regulations.

Moerschbaecher, Lynda S. *Start at Square One: Starting and Managing the Planned Gift Program*. Chicago: Precept Press, 1998. xiv, 223 p.

Moran, William J. "Raising Planned Gifts Through a Campaign Framework: It Works But Be Careful." *Fund Raising Management* 29 (May 1998): 23–25.

National Conference on Planned Giving. *All That Jazz: Tenth Anniversary National Conference on Planned Giving Proceedings*. Indianapolis: National Committee on Planned Giving, 1997.

> Proceedings, including thirty-eight audio cassettes, of the conference that took place September 21–24, 1997.

Nicklin, Julie L. "Tact, Strategy, and Delayed Gratification Fill the Days of a Planned Giving Officer: His Delicate Job Is To Seek Gifts That His College Will Receive After the Donors Demise." *Chronicle of Higher Education* 43 (10 January 1997): A45–46.

> Describes a typical day in the life of Paul F. Kling, director of planned giving at the University of Richmond.

Peebles, Jane. *The Handbook of International Philanthropy: Policies and Procedures for Planned Giving Beyond Our Borders*. Chicago: Bonus Books, 1998. x, 125 p.

> A guide to the current IRS tax regulations on charitable giving by individuals to foreign charities, or to U.S. charities for use in other countries. Presents taxation issues for residents and nonresident aliens.

Polisher, Edward N., and Teresa M. Peeler. "A Collector's Guide to Art, Taxes and Charitable Deductions." *Trusts & Estates* 136 (September 1997): 26, 28, 30, 32-34, 36, 38.
  The federal government encourages the advancement of the arts by providing deductions from the income, estate, and gift taxes of philanthropists who donate works of art from their collections to charitable organizations. Discusses various estate planning solutions.

Prince, Russ Alan, Gary L. Rathbun, and Chris E. Steiner. *The Charitable Giving Handbook.* Cincinnati: The National Underwriter Company, 1997. ix, 310 p.
  Analyzes the charitable impulse, outlines the estate planning process, discusses what donors look for in a charitable adviser, and describes the various types of charitable gifts.

Reis, George R. "Building Bridges." *Fund Raising Management* 30 (August 1999): 19–23.
  Profiles the Planned Giving Design Center, which uses the Internet to assist charities in establishing and cultivating relationships with professional advisors in their communities, and ensuring that advisors have access to gift planning information.

Ryan, Ellen. "Shades of Gray." *Currents* 26 (February 2000): 36–40.
  Interview with Charles Collier, senior philanthropic adviser at Harvard University; Pamela Davidson, head of Davidson Gift Design and president of the National Committee on Planned Giving; and Doug White, president of the Boston-based Web site Charities Today, and author of "The Art of Planned Giving." The discussion includes planned giving issues such as: charitable intent, donor control, professional behavior, certification and incentive pay for planned giving officers, and collaboration with financial planners.

Schmeling, David G. "The 'Why' of Planned Giving." *Grassroots Fundraising Journal* 17 (December 1998): 3–5.
  Part 1 in a series on the topic of planned giving. The author begins by defining the meaning of planned giving, and the skills necessary for a planned giving fundraiser.

Schmeling, David G. "Marketing Planned Giving." *Grassroots Fundraising Journal* 18 (February 1999): 7–8.
  Part 2 in a series on the topic of planned giving. Explores the first steps in determining an organization's planned giving rationale and how to market it.

Schmeling, David G. "Budgeting for Planned Giving." *Grassroots Fundraising Journal* 18 (June 1999): 7–9.
  Part 3 in a series on the topic of planned giving. Discusses key items to consider in preparing a planned giving budget. Includes a planned giving resource list.

Schmeling, David G. *Planned Giving: For the One Person Development Office.* 2nd ed. Wheaton, IL: Deferred Giving Services, 1998. 217 looseleaf pages.
  This manual provides practical advice on establishing a donor-sensitive and market-oriented planned giving program. Schmeling begins with eight steps to take in

laying the foundation for such a program: (1) making the decision (includes a
self-assessment checklist); (2) adopting a market plan (with a discussion of the four basic
markets for a planned giving program); (3) recruiting a key board member; (4) compiling
the mailing list; (5) preparing the budget (includes a sample); (6) presenting planned giving
to the board of directors (includes a worksheet for assessing the organization's readiness
for a planned giving program); (7) integrating planned giving into the overall development
program; (8) and marketing the program. The following chapters cover quarterly and
organizational newsletters, direct mail appeals, tax-update newsletters, a
memorial/recognition program, basic follow-up procedures, a planned giving advisory
committee, financial and estate planning seminars, endowment funds, the integration of
planned giving with corporate solicitations and capital campaigns, ways to handle noncash
gifts, various gifting arrangements (describing main characteristics, target market, and
marketing strategy), policy and procedure guidelines, and substantiation. Includes sample
forms and checklists and a bibliography.

Schneiter, Paul H., ed. *Practical Guide to Planned Giving, 2000.* Farmington Hills, MI: The
Taft Group, 1999. xxiii, 997 p.
    Provides marketing and technical information to help development officers establish
    permanent planned giving programs. The book is divided into five main sections; the first
    section contains operational definitions of major forms of planned giving programs, a
    step-by-step guide to preparing and setting up a planned giving program, and how to
    market the program. The second section deals with managing and evaluating the program.
    The third section explains federal tax aspects of planned giving, including considerations
    involved with donating different kinds of assets to charitable organizations. The fourth
    section describes the roles of the gift planning team: the financial planner, insurance
    professional, the attorney, and the accountant. The fifth section provides a glossary, sample
    forms, resource lists, summary of charitable gift annuity state regulations, codes of ethics,
    maximum gift rates, sample disclosure statements, and IRS forms and publications.

Schoenhals, G. Roger, ed. *Getting Going in Planned Giving: Launch Your Program with
Powerful Ideas from the Pages of "Planned Giving Today."* Seattle: Planned Giving Today,
1997. 60 p.

Schoenhals, G. Roger, ed. *First Steps in Planned Giving: Practical Ideas from the Pages of
"Planned Giving Today."* Edmonds, WA: Planned Giving Today, 1999. 60 p.

Sciscoe, Lisa Stone, and Dan L. O'Korn. "Planned Gifts: Deferred Enjoyment."
New Directions for Philanthropic Fundraising 13 (Fall 1996): 59–72.
    Depending on the type of planned gift used, contributors of planned gifts may not receive
    immediate tax deductions, which are often deferred due to state and federal tax regulations.

Sharpe, Robert F., Sr. *Planned Giving Simplified: The Gift, the Giver, and the Gift Planner.* New York: John Wiley & Sons, 1999. xxx, 210 p.

> Divided into major sections: "The Planned Gift" describes the types of planned gift instruments available to today's donors, types of property that may be donated, deferred gifts, and other options, such as giving-for-income plans (charitable remainder unitrusts, annuity trusts, for example). "The Planned Giver" describes "typical" donors, motivations for giving, and fears of prospective planned givers. "The Gift Planner" details the types of individual gift planners as well as corporate entities that provide similar services, and describes how each operates. Concluding chapters deal with the roles of the nonprofit agency's board of trustees and the chief executive officer in building an effective planned giving program. Includes glossary and index.

Shenkman, Martin M. *The Complete Book of Trusts.* 2nd ed. New York: John Wiley & Sons, 1998. xxii, 409 p.

> Explains what a trust is, lists and describes the numerous types of trusts, explains tax consequences, and provides sample forms.

Sinclair, Matthew. "Planned Giving: Starting a Program from Scratch." *NonProfit Times* 12 (August 1998): 39, 40.

Strapp, Nancy Herrold. "The Psychology of Irrevocable Gifts." *New Directions for Philanthropic Fundraising* 14 (Winter 1996): 37–46.

> Presents an analysis of psychological factors that donors may encounter when contemplating an irrevocable charitable gift. Gives strategies gift planners can use to assist donors in coming to resolution.

Taylor, Robert R. "Transitional Development: Repositioning for Major and Planned Gifts." *New Directions for Philanthropic Fundraising* 14 (Winter 1996): 19–35.

> Discusses repositioning a nonprofit from a basic fundraising operation to a major gift enterprise through a large investment of resources, planning, patience, and hard work.

Teitell, Conrad. "Charitable Remainder Trusts—Final Regulations." *Trusts & Estates* 138 (August 1999): 36–47.

Teitell, Conrad. "IRS Keeps Things Interesting for Charitable Givers." *Trusts & Estates* 136 (February 1997): 65–66.

> Summarizes recent regulatory developments that address gifts of publicly traded stock and deductions for bequests to religious charities.

Teitell, Conrad. *Portable Planned Giving Manual.* 6th ed. Old Greenwich, CT: Taxwise Giving, 1998. xxvi, 735 p.

> Describes deductibility of gifts, valuation of gifts, substantiating charitable deductions, will and estate planning basics, charitable remainder trusts, and other planned giving options.

Thomas, Susan Decker. "Do You Hear What I Hear?: Prospects Will Indicate When They're Open to the Idea of Planned Gifts. Here's How To Recognize Their Cues and Respond Appropriately." *Currents* 14 (March 1998): 36–40.

Thompson, Todd S. "Attract Major Gifts with a CRT." *Nonprofit World* 18 (January–February 2000): 9–12.
    Discusses how charitable remainder trusts work and explains the two types of charitable remainder trusts: annuity trusts and unitrusts. An explanation of how an irrevocable life insurance trust works and the benefits of a charitable remainder trust with an irrevocable life insurance trust is also provided. In addition, describes the type of donors for which CRTs work best.

Treacy, Gerald B. Jr. "So Much Better?" *Currents* 26 (February 2000): 43–46.
    Discusses the emergence of the supporting organization as a trend in planned giving. Includes a discussion of the origins of the supporting organization as a legal entity, organizational structures for supporting organizations, and benefits to donors and campuses of supporting organizations.

Weber, Gerald A., Thomas A. Korman, Steven C. Gustafson, and John R. Silverman. "Preserving Family Assets: The Use of Planned Charitable Giving." *New Directions for Philanthropic Fundraising* 14 (Winter 1996): 89–104.
    Suggests using the family attorney as a bridge linking people's personal and philanthropic interests with a nonprofit institution's mission and services.

White, Douglas E. *The Art of Planned Giving: Understanding Donors and the Culture of Giving*. New York: John Wiley & Sons, 1998. xix, 362 p.

Internet Resources

American Philanthropy Review: Model Gift Policy Manual (www.charitychannel.com)
    Developed by the American Philanthropy Review, a company that reviews and sells books on fundraising and nonprofit management, this site provides a sample policy manual for planned giving programs. The manual outlines deferred giving options, gift acceptance procedures, and appraisal and reporting requirements. It also describes the advantages and disadvantages of different planned giving approaches, including annuities, unitrusts, pooled income funds, and charitable gift annuities. Includes a glossary.

National Committee on Planned Giving (www.ncpg.org)
    Run by the Committee, an organization for planned giving officers and others who advise donors on deferred giving, this Web site provides links to sites that provide information on planned giving.

Planned Giving Design Center (www.pgdc.net/)
   Web site created to provide professional advisors and planned giving specialists with comprehensive research and planning resources.

Planned Giving Today (Newsletter; www.pgtoday.com)
   A monthly newsletter serving the planned giving community as a practical resource for education, information, and professional linkage.

Electronic Mailing Lists

Estate planning (ESTPLAN-L) list
Send email to: mailto:listserv@netcom.comlistserv@netcom.com
Message: subscribe ESTPLAN-L

Fundraising and planned giving (FUNDLIST) list
Send email to: mailto:listserv@jhuvm.hcf.jhu.edulistserv@jhuvm.hcf.jhu.edu
Message: subscribe FUNDLIST [YOUR REAL FIRST & LAST NAME]

Fundraising and planned giving (GIFT-PL) list
Send email to: mailto:listserv@indycms.iupui.edulistserv@indycms.iupui.edu
Message: subscribe GIFT-PL [YOUR REAL FIRST & LAST NAME]

Chapter 13

Raising Money on the Internet

No sector of American society will have more influence on the future state of our social capital than the electronic mass media and especially the Internet.
— Robert Putnam

With the advent of the Internet, e-mail, e-commerce, e-philanthropy, and other electronic advances, nonprofits have at their fingertips, literally, new vehicles to further their mission. They can enhance their performance in development and fundraising; record-keeping; planning; prospect research; communications with staff, volunteer leadership, and donors; public relations and education; advocacy and constituency-building; and volunteer recruitment, to name just a few areas. While access to the Internet is still largely concentrated among those with sufficient

resources and technical training, the technology has brought countless individuals into contact with like-minded people and causes in a way that has never been seen before.

The Internet enables people to communicate more easily than ever across wide distances, and to discuss and share information on specific topics. It helps individuals and nonprofits to access more readily key information and needed intelligence, and enables them to download application forms and guidelines for proposals without using postage, telephone, or fax. A wide range of free software can be downloaded that makes it possible for an organization's computers to function as telephones and fax machines; to enable organizations' auctions, special events, planned giving, solicitation training, telethons, direct mail, planning, and other types of fundraising; and to improve operations in such areas as scheduling, payroll, financial record-keeping, database management, word processing, graphics and presentations, and planning. By downloading demonstration versions of these and other software programs, organizations can try them before buying. Those programs—as well as books, office equipment and supplies, tickets for travel, and more—can then be purchased on the Internet, usually at a significant savings.

Internet communication technologies make it possible for organizations to accept donations and perform financial transactions on the Web using secure servers that protect donors' credit or debit card numbers. In a survey conducted for America Online by Roper Starch, 29 percent of the 505 participants said they would be interested in making on-line donations to charity. Interest among young people was particularly strong—53 percent of respondents between the ages of eighteen and twenty-four said they were inclined to donate on-line, compared to only 17 percent of respondents over the age of fifty.

It is safe to conclude that there is virtually no area of a nonprofit's operations that cannot benefit from the seemingly limitless supply of information and resources the Internet makes available to any organization at any spot on the globe where people can log on. With some one billion portable Internet connections expected to be deployed around the world by 2005,[1] it is essential that nonprofits become proficient in accessing and utilizing the rapidly expanding wealth of resources available on the Internet, and learning especially how to use this tool in their development efforts.

What Are the Advantages of Using the Internet To Raise Funds?

1. A Web site can use all forms of media—text, graphics, sound, and motion—to deliver an organization's message in a far more powerful way than is possible by mail or phone.

2. In contrast to mail and phone appeals, Internet solicitations are "self-targeting"; that is, they enable prospective donors to go right to information that appeals to them, rather than wade through extensive literature or listen to a generic telephone pitch.

---

1. Thomas L. Friedman, "Social Safety News," *New York Times* (3 November 1999).

3. The Internet enables organizations to approach, in the language and format of their time, the many prospective donors under forty whose response to traditional mail and phone appeals is decreasing.

4. The Internet opens up a whole new world of volunteer recruitment possibilities.

5. The number of people using the Internet is expected to double every year for the next several years, providing organizations with a reach far exceeding that of any other medium.

What Are the Disadvantages of Using the Internet To Raise Funds?

1. There are millions of Web sites and the number is growing exponentially. To attract people to its site, an organization must have the human and financial resources to plan and design a Web site, to monitor any interactive features, and to update the site continually so that it remains interesting to those who return. The site must also load fast enough to catch people as they surf.

2. While a number of efforts at self-regulation are underway, the Web is still a relatively new phenomenon, and it is unclear how it will be controlled and regulated in the future.

3. Until libraries, town halls, and other public facilities provide easy access for groups such as the elderly and the poor, the Internet will continue to widen the gap between information haves and have-nots. People without Web access will not be reached.

4. The demographics of people who most use the Internet may not correspond to your donor profile.

5. Nonprofits must guard against the tendency to replace personal meetings with electronic interactions. While the latter are faster, easier, and less confrontational, nothing replaces face-to-face meetings as the best way to build the relationships that will secure a gift.

6. The Internet can easily capture the attention of staff members, thus diverting precious energies better spent on delivering programs and raising money.

E-Philanthropy Mini-Profiles

With near-perfect timing, the American Civil Liberty Union's "Keep Cyberspace Free" Web site went live the same week that President Clinton signed the Communications Decency Act, which provided for censorship of the Internet. As a result of an exceptional combination of good timing, an issue with special appeal for heavy Internet users, and the credibility of the ACLU on the censorship issue, more than $18,000 was raised in the site's first month, mostly via on-line credit card contributions.[2]

Kirk Gardner, Director of Major Gifts at the University of Maryland's Medical System, had to raise money for research on celiac disease, a rare digestive disorder. He contacted the editors of three e-mail newsletters on the disease, hoping to raise between $10,000 and $20,000. No one was more surprised than he was when these newsletters generated $100,000 in contributions! People had forwarded the e-mail newsletters to friends, and printed and distributed them, spreading the word far beyond anything Mr. Gardner could have imagined to "people we had no access to and didn't know existed."

In some cases, significant gifts have been negotiated on the Net. The development office at Northwestern University received an e-mail message from a couple wanting to make a significant gift to the university's capital campaign. The negotiations were carried out almost entirely by e-mail, and within three months a gift of $2 million arrived.

The director of research in the Stanford University's development office, Jerold Pearson, reports, "After the New York chapter of the Stanford Alumni Association started sending e-mail, attendance at fundraising events increased significantly."[3]

When the American Museum of Natural History in New York City created its Hall of Biodiversity, computer terminals connected to the Internet were installed in the exhibit. Through the terminals, museum-goers were able to access information on the major nonprofit organizations addressing issues of the environment and biodiversity, and then e-mail whatever appeared on the computer screen to their home or office computers. As a result, visitors not only learned about threats to the world's biodiversity but also could connect to organizations that offered ways to help.

Coupled with an Internet sell-off, a live auction—Chicago's Cows on Parade—at the Chicago Theatre netted more than $3.5 million for local charities. An on-line auction held earlier the same day netted $1.4 million. One hundred percent of the bids went to charities chosen by each cow's sponsor. "I'm in shock," said Nathan Mason, cow-ordinator for the city's department of public art programs. "We thought we were being bold early on when we estimated we would raise a quarter million. We didn't know what to expect, but this is so far beyond what we ever imagined."

The Heifer Project International's Most Important Gift Catalog in the World also enables donors to buy cows (actually, water buffalo), but in this case for the purpose of using animals to address hunger and poverty through ecologically sound, sustainable agriculture. Water buffalo "purchased" via the Heifer Project's on-line catalog provide Asian farmers with a life-changing food- and income-producing draft animal "that can slog through mud that would stall a tractor in minutes, and that can take steep mountain plots in stride. They're 'fueled' with readily renewable resources, and they yield milk, manure, and money from the sale of calves."[4]

The Net site Yahoo! Auctions gathered a group of celebrities to contribute items to be auctioned to help Kosovo refugees. Proceeds from the auction went to the American Red Cross, which needed $1 million a week to carry out its work helping Kosovo refugees.

---

2. Mal Warwick & Associates Web site: www.malwarwick.com

3. Marilyn Dickey, "E-Mailing for Dollars," *Chronicle of Philanthropy* 10 (10 September 1998): 23.

4. From the Heifer Project International Web site: www.catalog.heifer.org/buffalo.cfm

Case Study

The Red Cross

For many years, fund raising on the Internet remained an empty promise. From its inception, the Internet has seemed the perfect tool for fund raisers: a way to reach uncountable millions of donors at very little cost to the organization. But for most groups, expectations far exceeded results during the 1990s. Now, however, some organizations have finally begun to see substantial amounts of money flowing through online donations.

With the pace of change in online communications moving so rapidly, any snapshot may quickly become dated. So it may seem foolhardy to chart the course of online giving from the fund-raising success of any particular organization. Still, some groups have begun to master the art of fund raising online and their experiences may point toward a rich new resource for charities.

For example, Internet fund raising by the American Red Cross shot up dramatically in fiscal year 1999. Online contributions, which had been $172,000 in fiscal year 1998, rose to $2.5 million the following year. It would be easy to assume that the Red Cross merely benefited from a general trend in the broader environment: as more and more people have become comfortable making purchases online, it could be argued, more of them would also be willing to make contributions to charity through the Internet. But closer examination reveals a conscious effort to improve online fund-raising results at the Red Cross.

Internet fund raising started slowly at the Red Cross. Beginning in 1996, the Red Cross Website was equipped to receive donations from online visitors. But that function was essentially a passive effort, says Robert S. Guldi, director of creative services in the marketing department of the American Red Cross. When Mr. Guldi joined the Red Cross, at the beginning of 1998, he felt the Website "was a real missed opportunity" and he set out to revamp the site to become a more dynamic source of information to encourage visitors to make contributions.

At first glance, Mr. Guldi, a former theme-park designer for the Disney Corporation, might seem an unlikely choice to head creative services for an agency that deals with natural disasters and human suffering. But his past experience was actually very relevant to his efforts on the Red Cross Website, he says. Creating a dynamic charity Website "is a lot like designing a theme park ride," he says. "You begin by bringing the story to viewers impactfully. Then you suspend their outside sensations and shape their entire experience. At the end, you give them a chance to help out by donating, and the feeling of contributing is euphoric," he explains. Put another way, Internet visitors are invited to become emotionally involved, then empowered to help out. Finally, their feelings and actions are reinforced by the images and stories on the Website.

It might also be argued that the severity of disasters and crises facing the Red Cross, such as the enormous human suffering associated with the conflict in Kosovo, provoked the sharp spike in contributions. But Mr. Guldi suggests otherwise. "We had seen the same type of suffering before, but we just took a different approach in communicating what was happening."

The latest burst of donations in fiscal 1999 came in April, when the Red Cross took in about $1.2 million. Of that amount, over $115,000 was given in just one day.

One of the keys to the success for the Red Cross was the fact that there has been a huge increase in the volume of traffic coming to its Website. In 1999, the average number of hits on a normal day reached about 450,000, representing about 100,000 discrete individuals. On a big disaster day, the traffic can spike up to about 900,000. By contrast, prior to the revamping of the Website in 1998 traffic was just 8,000 hits per day. The huge increase in traffic and contributions was not related to a significant increase in staffing, however. During that time the Internet team grew by just one, to six people, says Mr. Guldi.

Rather, the increasing volume of traffic had more to do with improved design of the Red Cross Website and the development of critically important strategic partnerships with major commercial Internet sites. For example, the Red Cross established a close relationship with Excite.com, one of the most popular Internet portal sites. The Red Cross provided fresh original photographs of natural disasters and other crises—around the country and the globe—for publication on the Excite Website. From Excite, interested visitors could go directly to the Red Cross Website, where they could receive deeper information about the crisis in question and ultimately would be able to help out by making a contribution. "They quickly found out that they were not helpless. They saw us as a way they could take action," says Mr. Guldi.

From a management standpoint, the key change was recognizing that Internet fund raising is not merely a matter of streamlined fulfillment, making sure that the online donation form is accessible and functional. Instead, Internet fund raising is much more a function of communications and marketing than a simple development activity, Mr. Guldi argues. At the Red Cross, responsibility for the design of Internet fund-raising activities rests with Mr. Guldi, who serves both as director and creative director of creative services. In other words, he has administrative and creative control of the site.

Obviously, few nonprofit organizations are as large as the Red Cross. And very few charities would have a position as specialized as the creative director of creative services. But the Red Cross approach could nevertheless be instructive for smaller groups that might adopt similar strategies.

—Vince Stehle

Deciding Whether To Use the Internet To Raise Funds

After weighing the advantages and disadvantages of soliciting support on the Internet, an organization should then answer the following questions before launching an Internet fundraising initiative:

- Do staff members have enough time to devote to such an initiative? If not, can your organization recruit volunteers—or hire additional staff members—to run the operation?

- Is your organization's development infrastructure capable of handling several simultaneous revenue streams of contributions and pledges? Does it have the human and financial resources to deliver any benefits to which donors are entitled as a result of their on-line gifts?

- Is the underlying Internet fundraising strategy to expand your organization's donor base and cultivate younger prospects, who are beginning to develop their giving habits and allegiances, as opposed to raising cash quickly—a result that cannot be assured?

If you can answer these questions in the affirmative, then your organization is justified in launching an Internet-based fundraising initiative.

Organizing an Internet Fundraising Program

Step 1. Investigate Federal and State Regulations

As of the writing of this book, there is considerable confusion about what nonprofits that fundraise on the Internet should do to comply with state and federal regulations. Because organizations cannot foresee who will respond to solicitations made by e-mail or via their Web sites, the most pressing issue for U.S. nonprofits is: in which states should they register? Since a request on even a modest Web site will be viewed by people around the world, the matter of registering is not as simple as in the case of solicitations made by mail, on the phone, or in person.

As an example of the Internet's long reach, Jennifer Moore, writing in *The Chronicle of Philanthropy*, reports that, "Even small charities with seemingly local missions have sometimes received money from faraway donors . . . A Girl Scout troop in Honolulu recently raised $35,000 on the Net by selling merit badges. Many of the buyers . . . turned out to be collectors and others who lived in Japan."[5]

Since Internet technology will continue to evolve rapidly—with enterprising nonprofits taking advantage of every new development to friendraise and fundraise—state and federal regulatory laws will become increasingly complex. Organizations are, therefore, urged to consult experienced counsel with regard to their development activities on the Net.

Step 2. Create a Web Site

Creating a Web site is a wonderful way to advertise your organization, provide information, keep people up to date about your activities, recruit volunteers, and solicit contributions. The cost of creating a Web site ranges widely, and, obviously, the more interesting your site is, the more time people will spend there. However, spending a lot of money on a fancy Web site that is never updated is less effective than creating an attractive, easy-to-follow site that is updated frequently, since that will bring people back time and again.

---

5 Jennifer Moore, "A Web of Confusion," *Chronicle of Philanthropy* 12 (21 October 1999): 37–39.

Communicating by E-mail

Communicating with Staff and Board Members. E-mail is a wonderful way for staffers to communicate with each other as well as with members of the board of directors. It invites an immediate response; people generally look forward to receiving their e-mail; and reminders sent by e-mail somehow do not carry the nagging tone they might if they were communicated by fax or phone. Additionally, these messages can be easily forwarded to others, or transferred into other documents, thus saving time and avoiding mistakes.

By using e-mail, you can easily and quickly circulate memos, general information, drafts, agendas and meeting minutes, and other documents. E-mailing is not only faster than regular mail or fax transmission, but it saves time as well by facilitating early consensus on issues. Passwords ensure confidentiality, and most programs provide mechanisms for confirming receipt of these communications. Finally, if some of your board members or supporters aren't always available to make solicitations in person, e-mail offers an alternative for communicating their personal testimony and excitement.

Although Marshall McLuhan's famous proclamation, "The medium is the message," was made during the 1950s, it has never been so relevant. The physical, written word has a distinctive feel that sends a slightly different message depending on how it is transmitted. Remember, therefore, that e-mail must not become the norm, automatically replacing memos and letters delivered by regular mail or fax. Be sure to choose the means of communication—with everyone, not just board members—that best sends the intended (unspoken) message. And despite technology that allows people to speak via the Internet and see each other on-screen as they do, phone conversations and personal visits provide the human contact that so many situations demand.

Communicating with Constituencies: Cultivation and Stewardship. Nonprofits are increasingly using electronic newsletters to provide updates on their activities while simultaneously continuing to mail newsletters to those constituents who prefer hard copy. To get the e-mail addresses of your donors, simply ask on the printed requests you send them. You may then want to give the donor or member the option to receive information by e-mail: "Sign me up for your electronic newsletter." Since many Internet users pay for their connection by the minute or by the number of messages received, it's an important courtesy to make sure your constituents want to hear from you by e-mail.

You can also use e-mail to invite donors to events; to share good news such as the receipt of a grant, a major contribution, or an award; or to alert your constituents to upcoming legislation that may impact your organization's area of operations (and to provide the e-mail addresses of their elected representatives so they may contact them). Many organizations now use e-mail to thank donors for gifts and respond to their questions and concerns. Used for these purposes, e-mail enables an organization to increase its cultivation activities by providing effective, inexpensive opportunities to get in touch with donors. Encourage people to contact you by e-mail and you may find, as have many charities, that people will request information about giving and even send pledges by e-mail.

Soliciting on the Net: Where To Register?

One of the most common questions heard these days concerns whether the law as commonly understood requires that an nonprofit organization soliciting online (e.g., on a Web page) register in every state that demands registration from organizations soliciting within its jurisdiction. The short answer is yes. The laws of those states that require registration can be read to mean that solicitations carried through the Internet and presented to people in a particular state are subject to regulation by that state. Even more critically, many regulatory agencies (commonly, but not universally, the state Attorney General's office) have indicated that they will interpret the state law that way, and will enforce the registration requirements upon those soliciting online, even if the organization is located outside their jurisdiction.

However, there have been no examples of state regulators demanding registration from a nonprofit organization located outside its jurisdiction based solely upon the existence of a request for donations on a Web page. This is not because the regulators generally believe that registration requirements don't apply to this activity. The primary reason why there has not yet been any enforcement is because Internet-based solicitations are so new that it's not necessarily clear yet what all the relevant issues may be. Because regulators tend to set precedents by their actions, and are held accountable for them in court, they are initially being cautious. This will not last. Regardless of whether you believe it is fair, right or legal, it is only a matter of time before the states start enforcing registration requirements upon nonprofit organizations that solicit online.[6]

6. Eric Mercer, Online Compendium of Federal and State Regulations for U.S. Nonprofit Organizations, 1999; www.muridae.com/nporegulation/.

The Basics

Your first step is to determine the content of the site. Describe your organization, its vision and mission, and the services you offer, and provide contact information. Doing this in a clear and simple way will help capture the attention of people who are used to exploring the Web quickly, who don't want to search for basic information, and who don't want to wait while a highly designed page loads. Make sure that the graphics you use for your Web site are consistent with all your other publications, including letterhead, newsletter, and so on.

Additional Information and Material

Your Web site can also contain other elements, including the organization's newsletters, annual reports, press releases, surveys, event announcements, staff listings and contact information, job openings, and articles and white papers on subjects relating to your mission. Including links to other organizations and resources makes for a richer site, sends the message that your organization has the larger view, and helps promote your site if the organizations whose Web addresses you include will reciprocate.

Positioning Your Organization for Support

Including general news about your field of endeavor positions your organization as one with a broad view and as a key information source. This can help to generate on-line contributions.

A California nonprofit, for example, has joined the list of environmental groups using the Web to distribute information about pollution. The Silicon Valley Toxics Coalition of San Jose, California has established a Web site (www.svtc.org/svtchome) that shows where pollution has occurred in the San Jose area. The site, which took two years to build, is based on about ten databases from the U.S. Environmental Protection Agency and several state government sources.

Other environmental groups have created similar Web sites. The Environmental Defense Fund's Scorecard site (www.scorecard.org) describes pollution at a variety of locations around the country.

Volunteer Recruitment

The Web has become a powerful force for recruiting volunteers. Virtual volunteering, volunteer work that can be performed anywhere via the Internet, taps into a whole new source of volunteers by facilitating the participation of people previously constrained from volunteering on-site by time pressures, disability, or personal preference.

Soliciting Contributions

In considering the Web as a fundraising vehicle, it's important to determine if the profile of your prospective supporters matches that of regular Web users. For example, it is unlikely that top businesspeople you may have targeted spend much time surfing the Web. Such individuals usually give to, and become involved with, charities as a result of more personal contact. On the other hand, if your organization's purpose or activities have to do with education, then the Internet may be an appropriate fundraising tool, as those involved in education now form the largest Internet user group (replacing people in the computing field).

Organizations wishing to fundraise on the Net must also have a development infrastructure that enables them to deal with multiple sources of contributions and pledges. Because security on the Web is still a developing area, donors that make an on-line pledge may want to pay by sending a check or requesting a pledge card that they can fill out with a credit card number and then mail in (rather than supplying credit card information over the Web). The Pittsburgh Dance Council (www.contrib.andrew.cmu.edu/usr/cd9p/pledge.html) has streamlined this operation by including a contribution form that can be printed out, filled in, and sent to the Council with a check or credit card number.

You will need a "secure area" on your Web site to accept on-line contributions (or purchases); this requires getting a domain name, or using someone else's. People who want to buy or give on-line can go into the secure area, enter their credit card information, and indicate what

Profile of the Internet User

According to the On-line Research Group's survey in 1998 of 1,500 randomly selected Internet users, women made up 34 percent of the Internet-using population. When it comes to household income, the survey pointed primarily to middle-class users, with few very-high and very-low income users. And 43 percent of Internet users had incomes from $35,000 to $75,000 a year; 7 percent of users had household incomes from $100,000 to $150,000; and less than 1 percent had incomes above $200,000 a year. Less than 3 percent of Internet users have household incomes under $15,000 a year and 16 percent had household incomes from $15,000 to $35,000 a year.

Internet users are a younger crowd, according to the survey. The results show that while 15 percent of users fell in the 45 to 54 age range, only 3 percent were 55 or older. The largest age group of users was the 35 to 44 year olds, who made up 25 percent of the Internet crowd. At 20 percent of the Internet-using population, 18 to 24 year olds are well represented.

Very large companies and very small companies are likely to be heavy users. Companies with more than 10,000 employees made up the largest single group (19 percent of survey respondents) who said their employees are "frequent users." But companies with fewer than 50 employees make up the second-largest group, with 18 percent saying their employees are frequent Internet users. And 16 percent of companies employing from 1,001 to 5,000 employees said their employees are frequent users.[7]

7. Sebastian Rupley, "Profile of the Internet User," *PC Magazine,* 15 November 1998.

they want. Groups that both seek new donors and have products to sell will find a secure area to be worth the cost. For ideas, look at other organizations' sites and check the Additional Resources section at the end of this chapter.

When you make your appeal, be sure to enumerate the results made possible by people's contributions, and describe how those who want to help can get more information. Offering Web-related premiums is also a good idea, as Web sites are visited primarily by people who not only have access to the Web, but also enjoy surfing it. Such premiums might include screen savers (with the logo and slogan of your group, of course), mouse pads, CD-ROMs, and icons that can be placed on their own site. Surveys, electronic postcards, quizzes, and the like allow more interactivity and will keep people at your site longer.

Step 3. Create the Physical Page(s)

Impact Online (www.impactonline.org) is an excellent starting point for nonprofit organizations that seek to create a Web presence or want to use the Web to augment their resources. The site addresses a number of topics relevant to nonprofits and the Web, ranging from how to obtain free Internet access to how to use the Web to promote volunteerism at your nonprofit

E-Philanthropy Options

The key to success is to give the surfer what he came to see, then ask him for the support that makes having this resource possible....

When you sell "real estate" on your site, you place a banner ad which links your supporter to one of various e-commerce systems. There they can participate in purchasing anything from books to computer software to luggage. Your organization receives either a percentage of the sale, a commission on the traffic, or both.

The primary advantage of this method is that it requires no administration on your part and so, provides pure profit for you. It works best if your site has a lot of traffic, and your donors are comfortable with e-commerce and marketing.

The most prominent of these companies are igive.com and 4charity.com.

When you list with a donation clearinghouse, such as independentcharities.org and charityweb.com, you provide donors with the opportunity to choose your organization from the list of nonprofits the site serves.

Assume the clearinghouse advertises somewhere to drive traffic to their site so people will give. This way of receiving donations over the Web does have the advantage of needing no administration, and you need not "be present to win." You don't need a Web site to connect with potential donors.

Right now, there are two ways to take donations on your Web site. You can develop an e-commerce system yourself with your own software and customized programming. If you have the expertise and resources (up to $10,000 in set-up costs and a computer specialist on staff), this will allow you complete ownership of the system. You will be able to customize donation options and donation forms and have a seamless system to solicit donations.

For those with more limited resources, there are already established donation systems to which you can link. Those with successful track-records include givetocharity.com and donate.net.

GivetoCharity.com is designed to primarily to take donations. The system is secure, and the form allows your donors to make notes if they wish to specify a purpose for their donation. Donate.net allows you to set up your own donation options. In addition to taking donations, donate.net can sell items, tickets, reports, or e-card greetings designed specifically for your agency.

Each company charges a minimal percentage of the revenue generated, to cover the cost of programming and banking fees. If your organization cultivates your donors and makes your request on your Web site, this method provides the system for you "to walk out with the money."[8]

---

8. Eric Miller, "Surfer to Supporter: Fundraising on Your Web Site," *Philanthropy News Online* (26 October 1999).

organization. Visit the Internet Nonprofit Center's Web site (www.nonprofits.org lib/) to learn how to design and build a Web site.

Step 4. Publicize Your Web Site

After creating an attractive, stimulating site that people will want to return to, you must then do everything you can to drive traffic to your site.

1. Put your e-mail and Web site addresses on everything that leaves your office, including letterhead, business cards, correspondence, newsletters, annual reports, press releases, advertising copy, and so on.

2. Make sure your Web site address (or URL, uniform resource locator) is part of your signature on every e-mail you send.

3. E-mail your Web site address to every Web search engine you can find.[9]

4. Incorporate your Web site address into your answering machine message and announce it at speeches, trainings, meetings, etc.

5. E-mail the Webmasters at organizations similar to yours and ask them to link to your site, and offer to reciprocate.

6. Update your site frequently.

7. Announce the launching of—or important changes to—your Web site to your constituents, and send press releases to local print and electronic media and relevant professional associations.

8. Make your Web site interactive: self-scoring quizzes, bulletin boards, opportunities to sign up for your electronic newsletter, and invitations to join your organization are easy to include.

9. List your Web site on relevant Internet news groups, and on electronic bulletin boards.

---

9. To register with many search engines with one e-mail, contact: www.submit-it.com.

But Will It Bring In Cash?

It is sometimes hard to know in advance whether your Web site will be used enough to justify its cost. However, looking at the experience of others makes it clear that a Web site can attract and involve people who may not have found your group without it. A case in point is the experience of the Gay, Lesbian, & Straight Education Network (GLSEN), the largest organization of parents, educators, students, and other concerned citizens working to end homophobia in schools from grades K through 12. GLSEN's national field director, John Spear, notes that until last year, his group saw their Web site (www.glsen.org) as more of a frill than a necessity. Updated less than once a month, it was not particularly attractive and consisted mainly of text-only pages. The Webmaster was a volunteer. But a survey showed that three hundred new GLSTEN members—more than 5 percent of the entire organization—had learned about the group from its Web site. The group decided to dedicate more time and energy to the site, and today it gets about 400 visits per day and is updated five times a week. GLSEN has expanded its site to include, among many other features, an on-line bookstore and an on-line conference registration capacity.

Step 5: Train Staff

Giving your staff Internet-equipped computers is the first step, but staff members need training. Having the tools without the training is somewhat akin to receiving a grant to build a facility but not the funds to equip, staff, and operate it. In fact, surveys have shown that lack of training is for many organizations the main barrier to using the Web.

Because Internet technology is constantly developing, this training must be ongoing. Nonprofits must, therefore, take into account the cost of staff and volunteer training if they are to derive maximum benefits from Web fundraising. They should include these costs in any proposals that request funds for purchasing computer equipment or developing a presence on the Web.

While all organizations that engage in fundraising activities on the Internet may not develop new, substantial revenues, any nonprofits that are able to put up a site are likely to benefit from their presence on the Web. An initial goal for Internet fundraising initiatives would be to receive enough contributions to pay for the development and maintenance of the Web site. As security technology develops and people become more accustomed to on-line giving, those contributions will grow.

PTA's Tap Into E-Commerce As a Fund-Raiser for Schools

The workload of thousands of parent volunteers is about to change. In the last year, a number of online versions of scrip sales have emerged. Scrip is a type of gift certificate that has become a fund-raising mainstay for thousands of schools across the U.S.A. Stores sell the certificates at a discount to schools, which then sell them at face value to their supporters.

At Schoolpop (www.schoolpop.com) and Your School Shop (www.yourschoolshop.com), parents use the companies' home pages as portals to national retailers like Amazon.com, J.C. Penney, and Officemax. Each online purchase kicks back a small percentage to the school, and the merchants also pay a small percentage of each purchase to the scrip service. Escrip (www.escripinc.com) also aims to eliminate the hassle of scrip sales by turning them into electronic transactions. With Escrip, participants register their credit and debit cards, and a percentage is sent to a designated charity each time the cards are used at participating businesses.

The merchants that have signed up with Escrip include Budget Rent-a-Car, American Airlines, Payless Shoe Source, and Eddie Bauer. Escrip transfers the rebates electronically to schools, or to charities, and sends each family a detailed list of its monthly purchases, including what percentage of the sales benefited the charity.

Tips

- Don't promise anything on the front end that you can't deliver on the back end. If you have a cyberstore, don't make customers wait six weeks for their product; three days should be the most. When people contribute using a form they downloaded, process the gift and thank them within seventy-two hours.

- Don't let your site stagnate; update and work on it constantly. Simply having a home page that stays the same or has out-of-date information can be more harmful to your group than not using the Web at all.

- Use fundraising on the Web to facilitate and enhance—not replace—your repertoire of fundraising strategies.

Summary Worksheet

for _____

(name of your organization)

Raising Money on the Internet

1. Does you group have an e-mail address?

   _____ yes   _____ no

   If yes, are you able to keep up with the mail you currently receive?

2. Do you have a Web site?

   _____ yes   _____ no

   If yes, are you able to keep it up-to-date (change it or add to it at least once a month?)

3. Do you have a staff member who can devote at least five hours a week to updating the site?

   _____ yes   _____ no

4. How much money can you spend on your Web site? $ _____

   List here the firms you have gotten quotes from on helping you develop a Web site, and summarize what they have offered to do for you.

   Name:
   Quote:
   Proposal Details:

   _____
   _____
   _____

   Name:
   Quote:
   Proposal Details:

   _____
   _____
   _____

   Name:
   Quote:
   Proposal Details:

   _____
   _____
   _____

5. Where might you find money to create and maintain a good Web site?

Foundations: _____

Corporations: _____

Individuals: _____

In-kind: _____

6. If you spend the money needed to create and maintain a good Web site, is there anything that won't get done at your organization? Is the trade-off worth it?

_____

_____

_____

_____

_____

_____

_____

_____

_____

_____

Additional Resources

Publications

Abelson, Reed. "Pitfalls for Internet Shoppers with Charitable Bent." *New York Times,* 31 (March 1999). Secs. A, C.

There has been marked growth in the number of Internet sites that give a portion of proceeds to charity, but charities might not be reaping the benefits. Some sites have encountered computer problems; others have instructions that are too difficult to follow, while some might be scams. Article names several of the sites, and compares their ease of use, disclosure, causes they support, and how the site makes money. GreaterGood.com, 4charity.com, CharityWeb, Igive.com, Mycause.com, and Shop2give.com are among those described.

Abshire, Michael. "To Regulate or Not To Regulate E-Philanthropy Is the Question." *Corporate Philanthropy Report* 15 (January 2000): 11.

Discusses the possibility of the regulation of Internet fundraising, as well as the taxation of Internet business activities.

Allen, Nick. "Fundraising on the Internet: Using E-Mail and the Web To Acquire and Cultivate Donors." *Grassroots Fundraising Journal* 19 (June 2000): 3–5.

The author discusses seven ways to raise money on the Internet—and which are working best.

Allen, Nick, Mal Warwick, and Michael Stein, eds. *Fundraising on the Net: Recruiting and Renewing Donors Online.* Berkeley, CA: Strathmoor Press, 1996.

Focuses on how nonprofits can acquire new donors through the Net. Topics discussed include on-line tools, translating direct mail and telephone fundraising techniques to an electronic medium, fundraising opportunities on-line, and useful Web sites for fundraisers. Includes a glossary of Net-related terms.

Balog, Kathy. "Internet Fundraising: Should Your Organization Do It?" *Volunteer Leadership* (Spring 2000): 34–37.

Barber, Putnam. "Getting Started: Whom Do You Trust?" *Advancing Philanthropy* 8 (May-June 2000): 36–37.

Barber offers five questions that nonprofits should ask themselves before a substantial investment in Web fundraising.

Bayne, Kim M. *The Internet Marketing Plan: A Practical Handbook for Creating, Implementing and Assessing Your Online Presence.* New York: John Wiley & Sons, 1997, 400 p.

Billitteri, Thomas J. "Technology and Accountability Will Shape the Future of Philanthropy." *Chronicle of Philanthropy* 12 (13 January 2000): 10, 16, 20.

Various observers predict how new technology, including the Internet, will change the daily work of nonprofits and foundations, and their relationships with each other. Leaders will be expected to be smart about the uses of technology for fundraising and management. For charities, donor expectations will increase, the Internet will somewhat replace direct mail and telemarketing for delivery of information, and will make available to a wide public more information about the practices and finances of the nonprofit than ever before. As competition for support increases, more charities may establish for-profit ventures, continuing the commercialization of the sector. Competition will also encourage increased collaborations within the field. For foundations, technology will enhance a greater openness with grantees and contribute to their ability to communicate with each other.

Corson-Finnerty, Adam, and Laura Blanchard. *Fundraising and Friend-Raising on the Web.* Chicago: American Library Association, 1998. viii, 122 p.

Intended for library administrators, but with approaches that will succeed for any nonprofit, book offers advice on such topics as developing and measuring the impact of a Web site; creating donor recognition in cyberspace; delivering your site directly to potential donors on disk or CD-ROM; and fundraising with digital cash. Throughout, provides examples currently on the Web. Includes a CD-ROM disk.

Deulloa, John R. *The Step by Step Guide to Successfully Promoting a Web Site.* Escondida, CA: PromoteOne, 1999, 93 p.

Dickey, Marilyn, and Holly Hall. "The Pitfalls of Mining the Internet." *Chronicle of Philanthropy* (23 September 1999): 29, 32.

Discusses current issues surrounding prospect research on the Internet. Experts remark that although the Internet is making it easier and less expensive to obtain information on potential donors, many charities are not utilizing it as effectively as they could be. The increasing involvement of professional researchers in fundraising efforts and the issue of donor privacy are also discussed.

Dickey, Marilyn, comp. "Internet Sites that Click for Charity Researchers Seeking Donors." *Chronicle of Philanthropy* 11 (23 September 1999): 30–31.

Listing of Web sites useful to fundraisers.

Eckstein, Richard M., ed. *Directory of Computer and High Technology Grants.* 3rd ed. Loxahatchee, FL: Research Grant Guides, 1996. 116 p.

Provides information on more than 500 foundations and corporations that grant funds or donate equipment to nonprofit organizations seeking computers, software, and related technology. Includes four essays: "A Grant Seeker's Guide to the Internet: Revised and Revisited" by Andrew J. Grant and Suzy D. Sonenberg; "Proposal Writing Basics" by

Andrew J. Grant; "Computers and the Nonprofit Organizations" by Jon Rosen; and "Take Nothing for Granted" by Chris Petersen. Indexed by name and subject.

Ensman, Richard G., Jr. "Turn Small Shops Into Big Shops via the Internet." *Fund Raising Management* 28 (June 1997): p. 18–19.
Details myriad ways that smaller nonprofits can utilize the Internet to reach large audiences of potential donors, volunteers, and clients.

Foundation Center. *The Foundation Center's Guide to Grantseeking on the Web,* 2nd ed. New York: The Foundation Center, 2000. xv, 520 p.
A comprehensive manual including an introduction to the World Wide Web; use of Web browsers; how to locate foundation, public charity, corporate giving, and government funding information through the Web; databases, on-line journals, and interactive services of interest to grantseekers; and an in-depth tour of the features of the Foundation Center's Web site. The book also serves as a directory to hundreds of funders that have Web sites; a CD-ROM version is also available which includes live links to all those funders, for those with Web access.

Grobman, Gary M., and Gary B. Grant. *The Non-Profit Internet Handbook.* Harrisburg, PA: White Hat Communications, 1998, 216 p.
Basic work on getting connected to the Internet, why Net applications are useful, and a review of Web sites of interest to nonprofit organizations. Indexed.

Frenza, JP, and Leslie Hoffman. "Fundraising on the Internet: Three Easy Strategies for Nonprofits." *Nonprofit World* 17 (July–August 1999): 10–13.
The suggested strategies are to become a nonprofit beneficiary of one of the "shop for a cause" Web sites; establish a simple but secure Web page with a one-page form for collecting donations; and create an on-line catalog to sell products.

Fuisz, Joseph. "Internet Causes Dramatic Changes in Fund Raising World." *Fund Raising Management* 30 (October 1999): 22–24.
Discusses the impact of the Internet on fundraising, and explores the possibility of partnerships between nonprofits and on-line commercial enterprises.

Greer, Gayle. "Online Fundraising: The Time Is Now." *Fund Raising Management* 30 (August 1999): 26–29.
Encourages nonprofit organizations to utilize the Internet as a fundraising tool and a means of building relationships with donors.

Hair, Dr. Jay D. "Fund Raising on the Internet: Instant Access to a New World of Donors." *Fund Raising Management* 30 (October 1999): 16–18.
Discusses the advantages of having an on-line shopping village attached to a nonprofit organization's Web site.

Hall, Holly. "Making Sure that the Clicks Stick." *Chronicle of Philanthropy* 12 (27 January 2000): 1, 21–23.

> Many charities are reaping the rewards of their holiday on-line fundraising efforts. The article describes the approaches used by Toys for Tots, America's Second Harvest, and WNYC Public Radio. Not only have on-line techniques provided quick returns, they have reached new donors.

Hall, Holly. "States Are Split on How To Protect Donors from On-line Fraud." *Chronicle of Philanthropy* 11 (9 September 1999): 31.

> Discusses the findings of a new study of charity regulators in the U.S. which reveal that as on-line solicitations grow more popular, state officials are divided regarding the best way of protecting donors from fraud. Also discusses the growing divide between the technological "haves" and "have-nots," and the way that this affects not only individuals, but charities as well. In addition, profiles the efforts of Natasha van Bentum, director of planned giving at Greenpeace Canada in Vancouver, who has designed a new Web site to help charities use the Internet to seek gifts from elderly donors.

Hamilton, Brownie S., ed. *200 Terrific Web Sites for Nonprofit Organizations.* Virginia Beach, VA: Grantsmanship Service, Inc., 1998. xi, 57 p.

> Brief descriptions of corporate, government, foundation, and other Web sites of interest to the nonprofit community. Includes search instructions, information about listservs, and an index.

Jamieson, Doug. "Building Relationships in the Networked Age: Some Implications of the Internet for Nonprofit Organizations." *Philanthropist/Le Philanthrope* 15 (January 2000): 23–32.

> Discusses the implications of the Internet for Canadian nonprofit organizations.

Johnston, Michael. *The Fund Raiser's Guide to the Internet.* New York: John Wiley & Sons, 1998. xiv, 235 p.

> A nontechnical guide to optimizing use of the Net for nonprofit publicity and grantseeking. Includes specific recommendations for design of an effective Web presence, including how to secure on-line donations, interactivity, and copyright issues, Net security, members-only areas, and using listservs. Provides numerous real-life examples. Includes disk. Indexed.

Johnston, Michael. *The Nonprofit Guide to the Internet: How To Survive and Thrive.* 2nd ed. New York: John Wiley & Sons (Nonprofit Law, Finance and Management Series), 1999. xvii, 240 p.

> Surveys the hardware and software needed to get on-line and discusses reasons for nonprofits to utilize the Internet. Explores and gives examples of fundraising, and fundraising research, on-line. Explains how to use a Web site for marketing and public relations purposes. Includes a resource list, glossary, and index.

Lake, Howard. *Direct Connection's Guide to Fundraising on the Internet.* London: Aurelain Information Ltd., 1996. 130 p.

> British guide to fundraising on the Net. Covers such topics as how to get on the Net, Net demographics, building a fundraising Web site, and finding fundraising information on the Net. Provides a directory of Net resources for fundraisers. Includes a glossary, bibliography, and index.

Lipman, Harvy. "Big Charities Have Raised Very Little Online So Far." *Chronicle of Philanthropy* 12 (15 June 2000): 38.

> Although the American Red Cross has been successful in raising substantial amounts of money on-line, a survey by the Chronicle indicates that the charity is the exception rather than the rule. Of the 250+ nonprofits that were queried, only about one-third had raised any funds through the Internet. A list of the charities that raised more than $100,000 on-line in 1999 is given.

Moore, Jennifer, and Grant Williams. "Internet Appeals and the Law: State Charity Regulators Issue Guidelines on When Charities that Solicit Online Must Register Locally." *Chronicle of Philanthropy* 12 (7 September 2000): 21–23.

> Article describes proposed guidelines by the National Association of State Charity Officials (NASCO) on the monitoring of on-line fundraising appeals. The conditions under which nonprofits and fundraisers must file registration forms with states when asking for donations on the Internet or by e-mail are outlined.

Mudd, Mollie, ed. *The Grantseeker's Handbook of Essential Internet Sites.* 4th ed. Gaithersburg, MD: Aspen Publishers, 2000. xi, 243 p.

> Contains descriptions of more than 750 Internet sites of interest to grantseekers. Each description includes the resource's address and login or subscription instructions where applicable. Sites are arranged in the following categories: corporations, foundations and associations, government, research, and resources. Includes indexes by site name, and by major giving category for corporations and foundations.

Pulawski, Christina A. "The Effects of Technological Advances on the Ethics of Gathering Information in Support of Fundraising." *New Directions for Philanthropic Fundraising* 25 (Fall 1999): 69–79.

Reis, George R. "Fund Raising on the Web: Why Having a Dot-Org Web Site Isn't Enough." *Fund Raising Management.* 30 (January 2000): 22–24, 26–27.

> Profiles WeGo.com, a Palo Alto company whose mission is to help nonprofit organizations create or expand their Web sites, and use their Web sites to increase their effectiveness in terms of involving their members and engaging prospective donors. The company provides its services to nonprofits free of charge.

Roufa, Mike. "Can Nonprofits Really Raise Money on the Internet?" *Nonprofit World* 17 (May–June 1999): 10–12.
  Article explains what e-commerce is and how nonprofit organizations are using the Internet to raise funds.

Sellers, Don. *Getting Hits: The Definitive Guide to Promoting Your Website.* Berkeley, CA: Peachpit Press. 1997, 200 p.
  Begins with an overview of what resources you can use to build up the number of hits, or visits, to your Web site. First covers search engines and how they work, providing tips on how to get your site in the higher rankings on search engine lists and how to get listed with the top search engines, such as Yahoo!, AltaVista, and Excite. Then moves on to discuss links, showing how setting up hundreds of links can increase traffic to your site but noting that a few high-quality links can also make vast improvements in the number of hits. Sellers' lessons on "netiquette" in newsgroups and mailing lists are helpful for newcomers to these areas of the Web.

Stanek, William. *Increase Your Web Traffic In a Weekend,* rev. ed. Roseville, CA: Prima Publishers, 1998, 368 p.

Sonnereich, Wes, and Tim MacInta. *Web Developer.Com Guide to Search Engines.* New York: John Wiley & Sons, 1998, 456 p.

Tillman, Hope N., ed. *Internet Tools of the Profession: A Guide for Information Professionals.* 2nd ed. Washington, DC: Special Libraries Association, 1997, 249 p.

Zeff, Robbin Lee. *The Nonprofit Guide to the Internet.* New York: John Wiley & Sons (Nonprofit Law, Finance, and Management Series), 1996. xxii, 250 p.
  Surveys the hardware and software needed to get on-line. Includes bibliography, glossary, and directory of nonprofit-related Web sites and addresses.

Internet

This list cannot be exhaustive, but many of these sites contain excellent link libraries that will lead you to other useful sites.

Benton's Best Practices Toolkit (www.benton.org/Practice/Toolkit)
  Benton's Best Practices Toolkit provides "tools to help nonprofits make effective use of communications and information technologies." Site has a comprehensive list of links to on-line resources, including items about technology, funding, and basic communications issues.

CharityChannel (www.charitychannel.com/forums/)
  The American Philanthropy Review maintains this site on which approximately twenty discussion forums may be joined or searched. These forums, or e-mail discussion lists,

cover topics ranging across the fundraising field (capital campaigns, special events, board development, software, etc.). As an example of how the list system works, someone wrote to one of the forums on the site asking about how corporate sponsorship works. Responses came from as far away as California and Italy, from other members of the list who wished to share their perspectives. Some responses offered other Web sites and discussion groups as additional resources that could be checked.

CharityVillage (www.charityvillage.com)
A major Canadian site for the nonprofit sector, featuring an extensive list of useful links. The site is distinguished by a particularly outstanding collection of links to e-mail discussion lists, mostly American, but many Canadian as well, and with international participation. The lists are a form of discussion and exchange; it is possible to review the archives to find discussion on many topics of interest written by members, who tend to be practitioners in the field. The lists frequently include embedded links to other relevant resources.

The Chronicle of Philanthropy (www.philanthropy.com)
A key Net resource for nonprofits focusing on significant news, trends, and legal issues related to nonprofits in the areas of fundraising, governance, and Web resources.

Communications Catalyst (www.catalystcommunications.com/)
Communication Catalyst's mission is "to assist the nonprofit community in using the full resources of the 'information superhighway." There are three main activities: 1) track federal government and other information about communications grants and policy; 2) distribute the information widely; and 3) provide technical assistance to nonprofits in developing, managing, and evaluating model projects involving the information superhighway.

The Foundation Center (www.fdncenter.org)
This site, accurately called "your gateway to philanthropy on the World Wide Web," contains a wealth of information, publications, resources, and links, including those to grantmakers on the Web. It also includes *Philanthropy News Digest,* the longest running on-line news service concerning philanthropy, with a searchable archive going back to 1995. At the site you can subscribe to a number of services, including e-mail bulletins of news and job opportunities. You can also search a number of free and fee-based databases of foundation funding prospects.

Fund-Raising.com (www.fund-raising.com)
A fundraising service of the American Philanthropy Review with excellent articles and links.

Fundraising Online (www.fundraisingonline.com)
Provided by Mal Warwick & Associates, a fundraising company in Berkeley, California, this site shows nonprofits how to use e-mail and the Net in fundraising.

Give to Charity (www.givetocharity.com)
The largest on-line donation processor. Site describes its secure on-line donation service, which enables organizations to accept donations via the Internet.

Impact Online (www.impactonline.org)
An excellent starting point for nonprofit organizations seeking to establish a Web presence or hoping to use the Web to increase their resources. Addresses a number of relevant topics related to nonprofits and the Internet, ranging from how to obtain free Internet access to how to use the Internet to promote volunteerism at your nonprofit organization. The VirtualVolunteering section provides examples of how to use the Internet to mobilize volunteers for your organization.

Internet Alliance (www.internalliance.org)
Internet Alliance is a "leading association devoted to promoting and developing on-line and Internet services worldwide." The site, which provides useful standards and a guide to public policy issues related to the Internet, could help a nonprofit frame answers to ethical questions it has about marketing itself or spreading its message via the Internet.

Internet Nonprofit Center (www.nonprofits.org)
Extensive information, resources, and advice on all areas of nonprofit practice. Take some time to explore this site, in particular, the part of the extensive Nonprofit FAQ section regarding Internet use.

Internet Prospector (www.internet-prospector.org)
Provides the current and back issues of the Internet Prospector, a free monthly electronic newsletter that offers news, advice, and links to Web sites that help fundraisers "mine" the Net for information about foundations, corporations, and individuals in the United States and abroad. To receive the newsletter via e-mail, send a blank e-mail message to chlowe@uci.edu. In the subject field, type "Subscribe Net Prospector."

The Management Center (www.tmcenter.org)
Set up to support nonprofit organizations in northern California, the Management Center maintains an extensive set of very useful links of interest to nonprofit organizations regardless of their location. The site contains a nonprofit library divided into technology, advocacy, and fundraising resources; with annotated links to sites that provide technical information, services, and library resources to nonprofit organizations. Links range from the National Society of Fund Raising Executives to Independent Sector and the Nonprofit Tech library.

On-Line Directories

People and Businesses

555-1212 Searcher (www.555-1212.com)
    Find e-mail addresses, telephone numbers, area codes, etc. Includes reverse directory.

AnyWho at AT&T (www.anywho.com)
    Yellow and white pages.

FirstWorldWide.com World Yellow Pages (www.worldyellowpages.com)
    Business searches.

Infobel (www.infobel.com/)
    Many international telephone directories.

Infospace (www.infospace.com)
    Searches for people, companies, and more.

Internet Address Finder (www.iaf.net)
    Finds people and businesses.

Switchboard (www.switchboard.com)
    Finds people and businesses.

TelDir (www.teldir.com)
    Index of on-line yellow and white page international directories.

True Yellow Pages (www.trueyellow.com)
    Business listings.

Where2go (www.where2go.com)
    Business searcher.

WhoWhere at Lycos(www.whowhere.lycos.com)
    Finds people, businesses, telephones numbers, e-mail addresses, etc.

Yahoo! (www.people.yahoo.com)
    People searcher.

FAQs and Listservs CataList (www.lsoft.com/lists/listref.html)
    Catalog of LISTSERV lists at L-Soft International, Inc.

Deja.com (www.deja.com)
    Searches for Usenet articles by topic; can also search posters.

FAQs for Usenet Newsgroups at Ohio State University
(www.cis.ohio-state.edu/hypertext/faq/usenet/FAQ-List.html)
    List of Lists at Impulse

www.webcom.com/impulse/list.html
    A "one-stop information resource about e-mail discussion groups or 'lists,' as they are sometimes called."

Publicly Accessible Mailing Lists (paml.alastra.com/)
    Internet mailing list directory served by NeoSoft.

Other Resources and Lists of Resources

Argus Clearinghouse (www.clearinghouse.net)
    Contains many subjects in document categories with extensive resources. Can be searched.

December, John (www.december.com/cmc/info/index.html)
    Computer-mediated communication articles and other internet-related information.

Kovacs, Diane (www.n2h2.com/KOVACS)
    A directory of scholarly and professional e-conferences; discussion lists, newsgroups, mailing lists, interactive Web chat groups, etc.

Chapter 14

Earned and Venture Income

The best way to run a business is the way you run your life.
— Oprah Winfrey

Earned and venture income enterprises are undertaken by nonprofits to generate unrestricted income, to enhance their visibility through the sale of products and services, and to advance their mission. By approaching individuals as consumers as well as contributors, nonprofits are able to market a virtually endless array of both goods and services in support of their mission.

The Metropolitan Atlanta Council on Drugs and Alcohol in Georgia, for instance, has created a variety of fee-generating programs, including chemical abuse screening services, training for home care providers, an Internet referral system, and school programs. Families First, an

adoption agency in Georgia, is generating earned income from seminars for children of divorcing families, foster family care supervision, and teen counseling programs. The Minnesota Orchestra has begun producing series of videotapes introducing children to classical music in order to generate earned income. A nonprofit housing and development organization in New York's Times Square, the Common Ground Community, operates an ice cream store, a catering business, and a data entry company to generate income and jobs for homeless, low-income adults.

Since the 1930s, the range of revenue-generating activities and approaches that blend nonprofit and for-profit thinking has expanded enormously. An example of a pioneer in social entrepreneurship is the Delancey Street Foundation, a drug rehabilitation program in San Francisco, California. The organization has developed a number of for-profit businesses that both generate income and provide employment for its clients. The term "social entrepreneurism" is now used to describe a multitude of ventures that integrate resource generation and organizational mission. This new terminology is significant for both nonprofits and funders, for it signals a change in the way new initiatives are approached.

As you explore the many publications and internet resources on the topic, you can easily become confused. "Nonprofit enterprise," "social ventures," "venture development," "microenterprise"—these are just some of the terms you will encounter. Understanding these terms will help nonprofit managers, board members, and volunteers decide which approach may be appropriate for their organization.

Generally, *social entrepreneurs* are people who apply business practices to the work of nonprofit organizations. They bring this approach to for-profit corporations whose business practices are socially responsible; to innovative nonprofits founded to address specific causes or issues; and to nonprofit initiatives to create economic benefits for a targeted population.

In the nonprofit context, social entrepreneurship describes organizations that engage in *nonprofit enterprise* or *social purpose ventures,* the marketing of goods and services to create revenue and/or help at-risk clients reenter society through training and employment programs. Other nonprofits focus on helping low-income individuals establish small businesses; this is known as *microenterprise.*

An important underlying concept is *social return on investment* (SROI). Adapted from the business concept of return on investment, SROI provides an important index for *venture philanthropists*—individuals and institutions supporting the work of social entrepreneurs—to help measure the results of their financing. SROI assigns a dollar figure to the benefits created by new initiatives and measures such items as the amount of taxes a recovered homeless substance abuser—now gainfully employed—will pay over a lifetime; his potential consumer spending; the welfare payments and health service costs that will be saved by his recovery; and the value of any volunteer time he may devote. The concept of SROI is another example of how nonprofits are adapting strategies and concepts from the for-profit world to their own work.

Growth in Educational Offerings on Social Entrepreneurship

Colleges and universities have responded to the increasingly important role of social entrepreneurship in both the nonprofit and for-profit sectors by offering courses and programs that blend social purpose with business. At the Nonprofit Management Program at the Milano School of Management and Urban Policy at the New School University in New York, the University of Pennsylvania's Wharton School, DePaul University, the State University of Florida, Leeds University Business School, and University College Dublin, among many others, present and future community organizers, arts administrators, and NGO managers sit in classes alongside business students and executives. In her article, "Social Entrepreneurship: Profit as a Means, Not an End," Gwyer Schuyler cites the example of Robbie Pentecost, a nun who is pursuing a business degree at St. Louis University. Her business plan for a restaurant run by a Catholic charity would employ mentally ill homeless people, give them on-the-job training and also bring in revenue for the charity itself. Upon completing the MBA program, Pentecost plans to seek corporate funding to actualize her community-based plans.[1]

---

1. Gwyer Schuyler, "Social Entrepreneurship: Profit as a Means, Not an End," CELCEE DIGEST No. 98-7 (Kansas City: Kauffman Center for Entrepreneurial Leadership, 30 November 1998).

Defining Earned and Venture Income

Before discussing how nonprofits can decide if launching earned and venture income programs is right for them, let's define these concepts.

Earned Income

In contrast to unearned income—revenues received in the form of contributions or grants, etc.—earned income refers to revenues a nonprofit organization generates through program-related activities. These revenues include fees for tuition and classes, consulting fees, clinic visit fees, and any other fees generated by activities undertaken in support of an organization's mission.

The YMCA, YWCA, and YM/YWHA are classic examples of nonprofit organizations whose traditional program activities—educational, social, cultural, and athletic programs for adults and children—generate fees and admissions. Ticket sale revenues from performances given by orchestras, dance companies, and theater groups are other examples. On the international level, the cards sold by the United Nations International Children's Fund (UNICEF) are some of the most popular holiday cards in the world, and one of the main moneymakers for UNICEF's programs. In India, Child Relief and You (CRY) also raises funds from the sale of greeting cards to support projects that lift children out of poverty.

For more than sixty years, Girl Scout cookie sales have been part of American life. Through the dedication and service of everyone involved, local Girl Scout cookie sales spread the word about Girl Scouting in positive and effective ways. The purpose of Girl Scout cookie sales is twofold: first and foremost to help girls develop a wide range of skills—leadership, entrepreneurship, money management, decision-making, planning, goal-setting, teamwork, and many more. The second purpose is to generate income for Girl Scout troops/groups and local Girl Scout councils. These funds are used solely to help underwrite Girl Scout programs in the United States.

Through the cookie sales, Girl Scouting not only advances its purpose but generates a significant portion of the money it needs to fulfill that purpose. The cookie sales have shown girls, their families, their Girl Scout councils, their communities, and the nation at large that this program provides motivation and recognition and that long-term benefits resonate well beyond the activity itself. Because these benefits are directly related to the Girl Scouts' overall mission, the revenue generated by the cookie sales is considered program-related income.

Venture Income

Venture income describes income from projects that are undertaken solely to generate new revenues for an organization; they may or may not relate to the organization's mission. If the project is unrelated to the organization's mission, the revenue it generates is known as unrelated business income and is subject to unrelated business income tax, or UBIT. For example, the Museum of Modern Art (MOMA) in New York built a high-rise building for commercial and residential use that is attached to the museum. The income the building generates is categorized as unrelated business income, since renting offices and apartments is not part of MOMA's mission.

Other examples of venture income projects are the monasteries in the United States and Europe that produce and sell wine and other alcoholic beverages. The monastery of La Grande Chartreuse in the French Alps has been producing and distributing Chartreuse, an aromatic yellow liqueur, since the eighteenth century. The income generated helps support the Carthusian religious order, founded by Saint Bruno in the eleventh century. Another example is the National Museum in Phnom Penh, Cambodia, which is overrun with bats. Workers gather and sell the bat guano (used as fertilizer) to generate the funds needed for office and cleaning supplies, as well as wage supplements. Receiving no government funding, and scant funding from other sources, the sale of bat guano has helped to keep the museum open for more than thirty years.

Economic development projects that better the community by creating new jobs, building low-income housing, or revitalizing neighborhood businesses are often categorized as venture income efforts. These programs should also generate revenues, but income is secondary to the primary social objective.

Economic Development: The Fifth Avenue Committee

The Fifth Avenue Committee (FAC) is a community-based organization in New York City's Park Slope and South Brooklyn neighborhood that works with neighbors to create affordable housing, fight for the rights of tenants and for economic justice, and enable community development.

FAC develops and manages community-based affordable housing for low-income individuals and families, and helps tenants achieve resident ownership and control. The organization creates businesses to provide jobs and training opportunities, helps people with job searches, assists local merchants and new entrepreneurs, and works to spark commercial revitalization on Fifth Avenue. FAC also brings neighbors together to address important local issues and assists thousands of community residents with housing and entitlements advocacy.

FAC has created more than 500 units of affordable housing, including home-ownership housing, limited equity cooperatives, affordable rental housing for low- and moderate-income residents, housing for the homeless, and housing for people with special needs. FAC has enabled low-income residents of 14 buildings—totaling 120 units—to become resident-owners through limited equity cooperatives and the South Brooklyn Mutual Housing Association. Current development projects will create another 77 units of supportive housing for formerly homeless individuals, seniors, low-income singles, and pregnant homeless women.[2]

2. From the FAC Web site: http://198.137.240.91/Initiatives/OneAmerica/Practices/pp_19980930.6036.html

The following table and (on following pages) explanation of the spectrum of nonprofit enterprises are based on the research of James C. Crimmins and Mary Keil, authors of the important work, *Enterprise in the Nonprofit Sector.*

The preceding overview of social entrepreneurship has given us a context for looking at how—and if—a specific nonprofit should become involved in earned and venture income projects. We'll begin our consideration by looking at the potential advantages and disadvantages of such projects.

What Are the Advantages of Earned and Venture Income Initiatives?

1. Successful earned income initiatives can increase an organization's independence and sense of self-reliance by creating income streams that are not subject to the changing priorities of foundations, corporations, and governments.

| | NEAR/related to program | | | | | | Far/from program | |
| | | Convenience | | Selling the Name | | | Extensions that are | |
Program	Program Revenues	Near	Far	Giving	Royalties	Downtime	Realated	Unrelated
Services specified in the organization's charter	Revenues earned from the program delivery (earned income)	Enterprise activity related to the type of organization — Closely related	more distantly related	Marketing the name or prestige of the organization to patrons or supporters (quid pro quo giving); contributions oriented	a wider public (licensing the name)	Income derived from the down-time use of an organization's assets	Offshoot of regular program or necessities of the organization	Business venture totally unrelated to any aspect of the program
Museum: *Contemporary art exhibit*	Admission charge	Sells postcards/prints in shop	Cafeteria open to public after hours	Sells tote bag with name/logo of museum	Sells reproductions of pottery in collection	Rents out exhibit halls for parties	Sponsors tour of European museums	Sells air rights to condominium developer
University: *Undergraduate and graduate degrees*	Tuition	Bookstore; room and board (dorms and cafeterias)	Record department in bookstore	Sells football jerseys, book-covers with name of school	Takes patent on drug developed in laboratory—royalties earned; software developed, sold	Sells computer downtime; corporations use dorms and classrooms for conferences	Athletic department runs summer clinics	Leases extra land to farmers; real estate development
Rehabilitation program: *Job training and counseling to handicapped*	Fee for services (client pays and/or government reimburses)	Sells special supplies; provides family counseling	Provides taxi service for handicapped—rides for a fee	Sells T-shirts with name of organization	Sells manual explaining how to replicate its program consulting	Sells counselor downtime to corporations	Sells product produced by handicapped workers	Invests money in solar energy company
Orchestra: *Symphonic performances*	Ticket sales	Sells programs at performances	Sells drinks during intermission	Sells mugs, paperweights with orchestra name/logo	Produces records of performances; television performances	Rents out hall during downtime	Offers classes or workshops on music; offers music lessons	Runs record store

Source: Reprinted by permission of the publisher, from James C. Crimmins and Mary Keil, *Enterprise in the Nonprofit Sector* (Washington, DC: Partners for Livable Places, 1983).

2. Creating a new source of revenue diversifies and enriches an organization's funding mix, and sends the important message to current and potential funders that its fund-raising is proactive, innovative, and not reliant only on their support.

3. These initiatives can create unrestricted income—money an organization can use as it sees fit—as long as the funds are spent in ways that are consonant with the organization's legal purposes. (The organization can decide for itself whether newly generated revenues will be applied to general operating costs or to a particular program, rather than being restricted in its spending by outside funding sources.)

4. An organization's prestige and public profile can be enhanced, and its potential donor base enlarged, by its presence in the marketplace. More people, including potential contributors and consumers, will become aware of the organization, its mission, and its work. At the same time, it will be reaching out to new constituencies and spreading educational messages about its work.

5. An initiative can serve as a mechanism for recruiting volunteer leadership. Enlisting the advice and active participation of successful businesspeople, for instance, can lead to their ongoing involvement in an organization.

6. Staff will learn and develop skills that can be transferred to other agency activities, such as public relations, marketing, planning, and budgeting.

7. The creation of new revenue sources can boost the morale of staff and board.

What Are the Disadvantages of Earned and Venture Income Initiatives?

1. Risk, risk, risk. As in any small business venture, success is not assured. While there are no statistics on the failure rate of nonprofit business ventures, the overall failure rate for small businesses in the United States in their first two years of operation is staggering. For nonprofits, the risk is usually higher for venture (unrelated business) income initiatives than for earned income activities that also promote the mission of the group.

2. New income-generating ventures can be viewed—incorrectly—as immediate elixirs to replace lost income, thus diverting attention from other, more assured revenue-generating strategies.

3. Initiatives may require three to five years before becoming profitable and fully self-supporting (such enterprises are geared toward future needs and should not be expected to generate immediate profits). Regardless of how methodical an organization may have been in developing a business plan, it will probably find, as the venture proceeds, that even more time is needed before profits develop.

The Spectrum of Nonprofit Enterprise

Our survey found that nonprofit enterprise has developed across a wide spectrum, ranging, at the near end, from enterprises *closely related* to the organization's program (ticket sales, tuition, admissions) to, at the far end, business endeavors basically *unrelated* to the organization's program (real estate development, investments in industry).

Based on the data we gathered, we have "filled in" this spectrum with eight different enterprise categories under which, we believe, almost every possible nonprofit enterprise can be placed. The table outlines the categories and illustrates them with examples. It should be noted that none of the four examples represents a real institution—it is rare if not impossible to find any nonprofit that engages in all eight types of enterprise; rather, they are composites of organizations contacted during our study.

The table starts at the far left with those enterprises most closely related to the organization's program or purpose and ends on the far right with those most distantly related to the organization's program or purpose. The categories follow:

- *Program* describes what the organization actually does; that is, the services specified in the organization's charter. Examples run the gamut of nonprofits, from ballet companies to zoological societies to halfway houses for runaway teenagers.

- *Program revenues* are income earned directly from program activities themselves, such as admissions for performances, tuition for classes, fees for services.

- *Convenience* is any enterprise activity related to the purpose or character of the organization that runs it. *Near* signifies those convenience-oriented enterprises that are more *closely related* to the character of the organization: a university selling books or renting dorm rooms; a museum renting tape recorders and cassettes for exhibit tours. *Far* signifies those enterprises that are *more distantly related* to the purpose of the organization: a college bookstore selling toothpaste; a rehabilitation center providing a taxi service for handicapped clients.

- *Selling (e.g., licensing)* the name is marketing the name or prestige of the organization in order to realize a profit. *Giving* is contributions oriented and concentrates on the patrons or supporters of the organization. Opera lovers buy the company calendar and tote bag; supporters of an ecological nonprofit buy stationery and T-shirts showing the logo of the organization. *Royalties* reach a wider public and involve selling the good name or valuable assets of the nonprofit. A museum can sell reproductions of pieces in its collection; a botanical garden can license the use of its name on packets of flower seeds.

- *Downtime* represents income derived from the use of a nonprofit's assets when the organization is not using them. These can be physical assets, such as space that can be rented to other groups (concert halls, offices, conference rooms), or they can be human resources, such as skilled personnel that are "hired out" to other organizations or corporations (computer programmers, counselors).

- *Extensions that are related* to the organization take the convenience category one step further. This involves expanding an enterprise activity related to the organization beyond its immediate needs and clientele. Examples include a university opening the student laundry to the public or starting a computer software firm and a nature center expanding its hiking tours of the Alps into a travel service.

- *Extensions that are unrelated* to the function of the organization conclude the spectrum. These may evolve out of physical assets that the group can leverage into income or may be strictly business investments that have nothing to do with the organization's purpose. Examples include real estate development of unused land; investments in any type of business, ranging from oil wells to pizza parlors.

Source: Reprinted by permission of the publisher, from James C. Crimmins and Mary Keil, *Enterprise in the Nonprofit Sector* (Washington, DC: Partners for Livable Places, 1983).

4. An organization that is launching an income-generating enterprise may need to hire new staff or retrain existing staff. New employees require supervision as well as support, and this creates increased demands on management's time.

5. As its income-generating enterprise prospers, an organization may lose sight of its primary charitable mission. Its leadership should constantly bear in mind that the purpose of earned income projects is strictly to raise funds to build successful programs to realize its mission.

6. If an organization's enterprise generates unrelated business income (that is, revenues from projects unrelated to the organization's charitable purposes), financial discipline will be needed to set aside a portion of the profits to pay local, state, and federal unrelated business income tax.

7. The failure of an organization's project is likely to create adverse publicity because an earned income enterprise is such a public activity. Part of calculating the risk is assessing how much damage might be done to an organization's reputation if its venture were to fail, and what steps can be taken to lessen any potential negative fall-out.

Deciding Whether To Undertake an Income-Generating Venture

After reviewing the potential advantages and disadvantages of launching a new initiative, you're ready to examine some of the items mentioned in greater detail. Let's first make an organizational assessment, consider the products and services your organization might sell, and then consider your market. Before proceeding, however, consider this point: if you need to raise $5,000 quickly, organize a special event or ask a major donor for the money—don't start a business! The purpose of income-generating projects is to create greater long-term sources of revenues than could be developed by using other fundraising methods or approaching other constituencies.

Step 1. Assessing Your Organization's Capacities and Willingness

1. *Time.* Does your present staff have sufficient time to devote to launching a new business enterprise or will you need to hire additional personnel?

2. *Expertise.* Does your organization have ready or potential access to the business skills—planning, marketing, financial analysis, etc.—that your new venture will require? The Roberts Enterprise Development Fund (REDF) recommends that an organization have managers with "real, demonstrated business skills and experience, including: comfort with numbers and an ability to use financial calculations to help keep the venture on track; an understanding of market dynamics; the ability to manage time, people and priorities; and the ability to operate in a constantly changing environment." The REDF goes on to point out, "If you want a former social worker to run your business like a program area, fine. What you will get is a new program area for your organization. If you want a venture that is economically successful, you will need managers able to deliver."[3]

   It is possible that you may find all the business expertise you need on your board of directors, or among your constituents. The day-to-day managing of your new venture, however, is likely to require a greater investment of time than these individuals are able to make. Again, the REDF: "Every nonprofit enterprise must confront a core truth: if you want a profitable, sustainable business, you must pay for managers who are able to create market-based value—which in this case means money."[4] You may be able to launch, and even grow, your enterprise with volunteers, but you should also plan to hire skilled help as soon as possible.[5]

---

3. From Roberts Enterprise Development Fund Web site, www.redf.org, November 1999.
4. Ibid.
5. Counseling and going-into-business seminars are available, as are experienced businesspeople who belong to the Service Corps of Retired Executives (SCORE) or the Active Corps of Executives (ACE). The U.S. Small Business Administration (SBA) includes on its Web site (www.sba.gov) a start-up kit for people who want to start their own small business. See the Additional Resources list at the end of this chapter for more information.

3. *Financial resources.* Do you have access to the up-front capital needed to mount an earned income venture? In all likelihood, you will need start-up funds until such time as revenues exceed costs. You might approach individual donors, foundations, or governmental sources with whom your organization already has funding relationships. When you do approach potential funders, make sure that your materials include a professionally prepared business plan. There are many publications and software programs to help you develop your plan (refer to the Additional Resources section at the end of this chapter), but it is essential that your plan be reviewed by a person with experience in this area.

   Be aware that the main reason that business ventures fail—and most do within two years of starting up—is lack of capital. Make sure that you have carefully calculated what you are likely to need, and make sure that the money is available *before* launching your new venture.

4. *Board support.* Do your board of directors and staff support an earned/venture initiative? Undoubtedly, many of their preconceptions about how your organization conducts its affairs will be challenged. They will need, for example, to become accustomed to thinking in terms of profit and loss.

5. *Enterprising spirit.* Finally, do you and the others most closely associated with your organization have a pioneer spirit and temperament? Are you willing to live with the risks that accompany business ventures?

Step 2: Inventory the Goods and Services You Might Sell

Generally, the more program-related your "product," the more you will be able to draw from your own expertise. For example, from your past work you should already have some sense of the market for such goods or services. You may not even have to engage in much additional effort if you decide to market existing programs or services for fees.

After answering the questions posed in Step 1, answer the questions in the following checklist, adapted from *Enterprise in the Nonprofit Sector,* by James C. Crimmins and Mary Keil, to help you identify the products and services you might sell.

1. *Tangible assets.* What do you own or have the right to use? Real estate? Office, video, or other program-related equipment? Do you have any valuable items (collections, stock, materials) that could be marketed?

2. *Skills.* Make a complete list of the people and volunteers who work for your organization; include your active membership. Then identify any skills and talents they have that could be marketed to the public, to certain businesses, or to other nonprofits. More and more individuals who have worked in the voluntary sector for a number of years have developed specialized expertise that is in demand on the open market. Correspondingly, businesses are coming to appreciate some of these abilities. Many concepts that originated in the nonprofit sector have become evident

and useful in the corporate sector, particularly in the areas of human resource development and employee counseling.

3. *Programs.* Do you currently charge fees for any of your programs? Do they lend themselves to a fee scale? Can your constituency afford to pay something, or more than they are currently paying, for your program? Are there other constituencies that would pay for the programs you offer?

4. *New ideas.* Does your mission statement suggest any goods or services that might be developed into income-generating projects? Is the market already glutted with these products and services, or might there still be room for you?

5. *Traffic.* Who comes to your office and who passes by your office? What types of individuals are most likely to be near your office?

6. *Facilities.* What space do you own or lease? What are its particular advantages? Does it have a kitchen, conference facilities, parking lot, warehouse space? What other facilities are available in your community for your use?

7. *Patents, licenses, and copyrights.* Do you have a product or a program that could be licensed, patented, or published profitably for reproduction and sale?

8. *Time.* Think about when your organization's equipment, facilities, and human talent are used and when they are not. Is any of your work or usage of equipment or facilities seasonal? Are there times when equipment or people's talents are free to be used for an income-generating project?

9. *Reputation.* What does your name mean in the community, and to whom? If your name is sufficiently well known, even on a local or regional basis, you may want to approach a corporation and discuss the topic of "cause-related marketing." Refer to Chapter 16 (on corporations and businesses) for more information on how for-profit businesses "rent" a nonprofit's name for inclusion in their advertising and product labeling.

Answering the questions in this checklist provides an organization with a range of choices in choosing an income-generating project. After you have completed this exercise, select the five most promising products and services you have identified and determine which are feasible. Be as open as you can to the conclusions that emerge regarding the feasibility of your project. It's far better to conclude early on that a venture has little chance of success than to arrive at such a decision after extensive human and financial resources have been committed.

Step 3. Study Your Potential Market

What motivates individuals and businesses to purchase goods and services from nonprofit organizations? Some individuals purchase products or services from a favored nonprofit for altruistic reasons, or from a sense of obligation. Others are motivated by a desire to express their personal values by purchasing gifts from organizations that are consonant with their beliefs. This explains, in part, why many nonprofit items enjoy brisk sales around holidays such as Christmas, Hanukkah, and Kwanza. However, most people buy products and services because they need them, and are looking strictly for the best buy. Therefore, nonprofits need to identify the goods or services they can provide that match people's consumer habits. If a person can buy a quality product from a nonprofit or a local organization with whom they have a relationship, they will frequently opt to do so rather than buy the same item from a commercial source.

It's essential for organizations contemplating earned/venture income projects to do a market survey and inventory their competition. After that, products and services should be test-marketed to make sure there will be a sufficient response to warrant launching the project. These activities have been finely honed by the business community; organizations can readily enlist the services of successful marketers in the for-profit or nonprofit sectors for guidance.[6]

Step 4. Develop a Business Plan

A business plan, your blueprint for entering the field of nonprofit ventures, will ensure that you have anticipated every major consideration in advance—and have planned accordingly. As William A. Duncan wrote in *Looking at Income-Generating Businesses for Small Nonprofit Organizations,* "Preparing a full business plan is useful because it makes you think critically about what you plan to do, describes the business for potential sources of financing, and serves as a management tool once you get started. The larger the undertaking, the larger the planning task will be."

The following elements should be included in a business plan meant to guide an enterprise and also serve as a proposal to potential funders:

1. *Index and table of contents.* An important part of your presentation to potential funders, the index and table of contents should be well thought out and clearly presented. An attractively presented and well-organized business plan will increase the chance that potential funders or lenders—who may receive hundreds of proposals every week—may read it.

2. *Executive summary.* Two to four pages should be devoted to describing the project, its goals, and its potential. The summary should be strong and thorough; its impact will largely determine whether the reader chooses to continue. Additionally, the executive summary is usually the text that is extracted and sent to partners, board members, and others whose opinion bears on the funding decision.

3. *Description of the initiative and projected operation.* Be sure to position your venture in an industry-wide context by including statistics about that industry from reliable sources.

4. *Background information.* Resumes of staff members who will be involved, as well as a one-page overview of your organization, are among the most important

---

6. The book, *New Social Entrepreneurs: The Success, Challenge and Lessons of Non-Profit Enterprise Creation,* written by Jed Emerson and Fay Twersky and published by the Roberts Foundation, provides many resources to help you in this area. See the Additional Resources list at the end of this chapter for more information on this.

elements of a business plan. Projections, surveys, innovative products, and savvy marketing plans do not, by themselves, create successful ventures; people do.

5. *Marketing plan.* The plan's marketing section should describe the potential consumers for the product or service to be offered, outline the marketing strategy you have developed, and contrast that strategy to the marketing methods of your competitors.

6. *Assessment of the competition.* Inventory and assess the competition—both current and potential—that your venture will face. Consider your competitors' location, products, services, and annual sales. Also describe your organization's strengths and weaknesses, those of your proposed project, and those of the competitors you have identified. Finally, discuss how your venture may affect your competitors, as well as any steps you envision taking in reaction to their response to your initiative.

7. *Goals.* This section is the most critical part of your business plan. Discuss here the goals you expect to achieve in one, two, three, and five years, as well as your strategies for achieving these goals. Be sure to describe how you would alter your goals and strategies in response to changes in the prevailing environment.

8. *Pro forma projections of income and expenses.* These projections should cover a five-year period and include such items as the cost of equipment, financing, and operating as well as any other costs you intend to pay from the proceeds of your financing. Your projections for the first and second years of operations should be done on a monthly basis, years three and four on a quarterly basis, and year five on an annual basis.

9. *Substantiation documentation section.* This section should include items that you've referred to in the main body of the plan. Be sure to include the source of all documentation and remember that the more recent the information, the more relevant and powerful it will be.

10. *Nondisclosure agreement.* Attached to the plan, the nondisclosure agreement should be signed by anyone receiving the plan.

It is not possible to overemphasize the importance of a good business plan. Be sure to seek experienced business, legal, and financial advice as necessary, and be prepared to spend long hours developing, editing, and updating the plan.

Eight Critical Success Factors for a Business Plan[7]

1. Existence of—or the ability to create—a strong entrepreneurial team;

2. A comprehensive planning process;

3. Identification of a compelling business opportunity;

4. Understanding your unique, competitive edge;

---

7. From the Roberts Enterprise Development Fund Web site, www.redf.org, November 1999.

5. Finding a fit with your overall goals and needs;

6. The possibility to use the venture to engage in supported job training and/or employment;

7. Existence of adequate financial controls and tools for planning and monitoring the effort;

8. Access to long-term, adequate, and appropriate financing.

Legal Aspects of Earned and Venture Income Projects

United States federal and state laws permit nonprofits to engage in business enterprises within certain guidelines. Although the IRS usually expects income-generating activities to be related to an organization's charitable purposes, nonprofits may engage in an activity unrelated to its charitable purposes as long as it is not the group's primary activity and it does not account for more than approximately 25 percent of the nonprofit's total expenditures and effort. State law allows nonprofits to operate businesses as long as no distribution of income is made to members, directors, or officers. Some nonprofits that undertake totally unrelated business ventures choose to create a subsidiary for-profit corporation whose revenues revert to the parent nonprofit corporation.

In most countries, the relationship of the product or service sold to the mission of the group will determine whether the organization must pay taxes on its profit. In the United States, nonprofit organizations must pay unrelated business income tax (UBIT) on any profit from its unrelated business operations.

There is no limit on the number of related businesses a nonprofit may own and operate. However, if the principal purpose of the nonprofit is to own or operate unrelated businesses, then the organization cannot qualify for tax exemption. Generally, an organization cannot earn more than 50 percent of its revenue from an unrelated business and still be exempt from paying taxes. Sometimes an organization derives income from a facility that it uses for its mission-related purposes. In such a "dual use" arrangement, the income from the rental of the facility is not taxed.

Tax law in regard to this form of income is complex and constantly changing; every country, province, or state may have its own laws. Any organization contemplating this method of raising money must carefully investigate the prevailing laws governing such enterprises and should consult both an experienced tax lawyer and an accountant at the outset.

Profile:

Food from the Hood

South Central Los Angeles is an area well known for violent gang wars, carjackings, illicit drugs, and racism. However it is also the home of a very successful enterprise known as Food From the Hood (FFTH). Started by high school students in 1992 (shortly after the massive civil unrest that followed the Rodney King verdict), Food from the Hood has grown from a $600 surplus derived from the sale of vegetables at a farmers market to $70,000 from the sales of salad dressing. The funds provide scholarships to participating youth based on their input. FFTH annually contracts to produce 9,000 cases of salad dressing called Food from the Hood—Straight Out of the Garden. The bottles are sold in 2,000 stores in 23 states for an average of $2.59 each.

FFTH started as an organic garden grown for extra credit in a biology class at Crenshaw High School. The produce was sold at local farmer's markets, donated to those in need, and sold at reduced prices to people in the neighborhood. But after the first season's surplus, FFTH was born. Students then developed a business plan to produce a unique salad dressing. Local business leaders pitched in to help in marketing and manufacturing. The first group of students received a $15,000 grant from the Rebuild LA Fund. They sent their trial salad dressing to Sweet Adelaide, a local salad dressing company, and after several samples were sent back and forth, they figured out a winning recipe.

They then began the process of production and distribution. The work of each young person is tabulated into points. All work is valued equally; i.e., garden work and media work have equal value. Of the surplus funds generated, half goes to student scholarships and half goes back into operating costs. Based on the percentage of points earned, students are eligible for up to $15,000 annually in scholarship funding for post-secondary education. Any remaining surplus accruing after scholarships is donated to community initiatives.

The FFTH idea has spread. At the Greater Ithaca Activity Center in Ithaca, New York, kids there are now producing apple sauce called Straight Out of the Orchard using the FFTH model. In Hawaii, youth are preparing fruit mixture called Straight Out of Paradise at the Ka'u Center.[8]

---

8. Melissa Batchilder, "Youths Build Future via Philanthropy," *The Nonprofit Times* (July 1998).

Tips

- Market products and services that are most closely related to your mission; the farther afield you get, the less expertise you will have.

- Contact nonprofits similar in scope and resources to yours that are already engaged in these ventures. By learning from their experience you can avoid "re-inventing the wheel."

- As in all fundraising initiatives, leverage your time and effort by using your earned/venture income projects to cultivate individuals who could become significant assets to your organization.

Additional Resources

Publications

Abelson, Reed. "Charities Use For-Profit Units To Avoid Disclosing Finances." *New York Times* (9 February 1998).

The use of for-profit subsidiaries can effect the disclosure requirements of nonprofits and is an increasingly common practice. Unlike the nonprofit organizations with which they are associated, for-profit subsidiaries do not have to publicly disclose how much they spend on salaries, whom they employ, or to whom they award consulting contracts. Some watchdog groups express concern over these relationships.

Abelson, Reed. "Marketing Tied to Charities Draws Scrutiny from States." *New York Times* (3 May 1999): A1, A22.

Describes numerous examples of cause-related marketing efforts, such as the endorsements of pharmaceuticals, drugs, and other health products, by the American Heart Association, the American Cancer Society, and the Arthritis Foundation. Such practices are eliciting attention from regulators, who are concerned that the endorsements are misleading. Sixteen attorneys general, including those from Connecticut, New Jersey, and New York, are developing guidelines to govern these advertising campaigns. Public hearings, followed by final recommendations, are in the works.

Alpert, Gary, and Gary Pollack. *Nonprofits for Profit: The Wet Feet Insider Guide to Social Entrepreneurship*. Wet Feet Press, 1997.

Job-seeking guide for social entrepreneurs.

Backman, Elaine V., and Steven Rathgeb Smith. "Healthy Organizations, Unhealthy Communities?" *Nonprofit Management & Leadership* 10 (Summer 2000): 355–73.

Authors analyze the impact of the commercialization of nonprofit organizations in contributing to local social networks. With bibliographic references.

Berger, Harvey. "Subsidiaries and Affiliates: Check the Rules To See If You Need Them." *NonProfit Times* 13 (December 1999): 18.

Brinckerhoff, Peter C. *Financial Empowerment: More Money for More Mission.* Dillon, CO: Alpine Guild, 1996. 238 p.
> Written for the senior staff and board members of not-for-profit organizations. Based on Brinckerhoff's three core philosophies of not-for-profits: (1) a not-for-profit is a mission-based business; (2) no one gives a not-for-profit money—all money is earned; and (3) not-for-profit does not mean nonprofit. Chapters cover characteristics and outcomes of empowerment, how to estimate cash needs, working with traditional funders, how to develop a new business, financial reporting, a review of different financing options, budgeting from the bottom up, pricing for empowerment, corporate structures, roles of the CEO and the board, a sample empowerment plan, and a summary of key ideas. Includes bibliographic references and index.

Brinckerhoff, Peter C. "How To Write Your Business Plan." *Nonprofit World* 17 (March–April 1999): 10–11.

Brinckerhoff, Peter C. "Starting a Business: Too Risky for Your Organization?" *Nonprofit World* 16 (July–August 1998): 50–52.
> Provides a brief discussion about the risks an organization faces in starting a business and outlines eight steps for planning a successful business venture.

Caftel, Brad. "Business Ventures for Nonprofits: Finding the Right Legal Structure." *Grantsmanship Center Magazine* (Winter 1997): 11–14.
> Reviews the pros and cons of creating a separate for-profit subsidiary when a nonprofit starts a business venture.

Emerson, Jed. *The U.S. Nonprofit Capital Market: An Introductory Overview of Developmental Stages, Investors and Funding Instruments.* San Francisco: The Roberts Enterprise Development Fund, The Roberts Foundation, 1998.
> Presents a basic framework for understanding the work of funders and practitioners and the resources that connect the efforts of both. Helps inform the thinking of those concerned with understanding the strategic use of capital in the pursuit of charitable goals.

Emerson, Jed, and Fay Twersky. *New Social Entrepreneurs: The Success, Challenge and Lessons of Non-Profit Enterprise Creation.* San Francisco: The Roberts Foundation, 1996.
> Assesses real problems and opportunities in nonprofit enterprise development for the nonprofit, foundation, and business communities. Based on six years of experience implementing economic development projects that enable homeless individuals to become more involved members of society. Includes case studies reflecting employee, board of director, and funder perspectives and discusses nonprofit practices related to competitive advantage, capital markets, global economy, project evaluation, and more.

Fallek, Max. *Business Plan Example*. Minneapolis: American Institute of Small Business, 1997. 39 p.

A sample business plan in the format preferred by the Small Business Administration and most financial institutions. Ideal for companies and individuals funding for expansion and start-up. Includes three years of spreadsheets (including balance sheet, P & L, and cash flow), executive summary (with mission statement), finance and marketing plan, competition, production plan, company structure, etc.

Flanagan, Joan. "Generating Income from Customers and Clients." *Grantsmanship Center Magazine* 38 (Summer 1999): 25–28.

Explains how to generate earned income with sales and fees.

Froelich, Karen A. "Diversification of Revenue Strategies: Evolving Resource Dependence in Nonprofit Organizations." *Nonprofit and Voluntary Sector Quarterly* 28 (September 1999): 246–68.

Discusses and analyses the "revenue dependence" of nonprofit organizations, that is, their reliance on outside funding. Three primary sources of funding are studied here: private contributions (from individuals, corporations, and foundations), government funding, and earned income. The volatility of these income sources, the effect they may have on an organization's goals, and the strategies nonprofits may adopt to diversify their funding sources are explored, with suggestions for further research. With bibliographic references.

Glauser, Michael J. *The Business of Heart: How Social Entrepreneurs Are Changing*. Salt Lake City: Shadow Mountain, 1999. 272 p.

Henton, Douglas, John Melville, and Kimberly Walesh. *Grassroots Leaders for a New Economy: How Civic Entrepreneurs Are Building Prosperous Communities*. San Francisco: Jossey-Bass Inc., 1997.

Explains the unique leadership qualities of civic entrepreneurs (initiation, incubation, implementation and improvement, and renewal) and illustrates how these leaders can emerge from all levels of private, public, social, and civic organizations. Shows how civic entrepreneurs forge powerfully productive linkages at the intersection of business, government, education, and community, and demonstrates how they operate at the grassroots level to create collaborative advantages that make it possible for their economic communities to compete on the global stage.

I.N.E. Reports. New York: Institute for Not-for-Profit Entrepreneurship.

A free quarterly publication providing news and information about business ventures of nonprofit organizations, with emphasis on the activities of its sponsoring organization. (Order from: I.N.E. Reports, 100 Trinity Pl., Rm. 421, New York, NY 10006.)

Johnston, David Cay. "Doing Good or Doing Well: It's Starting To Get Blurry." *New York Times* (17 November 1999): H17.
> Describes commercial activities engaged in by some nonprofit organizations, and how this phenomenon may erode public confidence or create conflict-of-interest issues.

Leavins, John A., and Darshan Wadhwa. "Are Your Activities Safe from UBIT?" *Nonprofit World* 16 (September/October 1998): 49–51.
> Explains the background of the original unrelated business income tax law and the current law and its application.

Light, Paul C. *Sustaining Innovation: Creating Nonprofit and Government Organizations that Innovate Naturally.* San Francisco: Jossey-Bass, Inc., 1998.
> Shows how nonprofit and government organizations can transform the occasional act of innovation into a culture of natural innovation. Filled with success stories and practical lessons of how organizations can promote innovation, survive the inevitable mistakes, and keep their edge. Light also suggests how to fit these lessons to different management pressures facing the nonprofit sector and government.

McLaughlin, Thomas A. "Social Enterprise: Everyone Can and Should Learn from It." *NonProfit Times* 13 (February 1999): 18.
> Author defines the term "social entrepreneurialism" as a blending of business and traditional social services that attempts to use the best of both models for the benefits of clients. He goes on to discuss the five types of enterprises, which are open market services, franchise operations, sheltered services, program-based enterprises, and cooperatives. Concludes by identifying the components necessary to start an enterprise.

Mogil, Christopher, and Anne Slepian. *Welcome to Philanthropy: Resources for Individuals and Families Exploring Social Change Giving.* San Diego: National Network of Grantmakers, 1997, iv, 50 p.
> Advice for new philanthropists with an interest in "funding change, not charity."

Reder, Alan. *75 Best Business Practices for Socially Responsible Companies.* New York: G.P. Putnam's Sons, 1995.
> Many examples are included to demonstrate that the inventiveness used to create wealth can be applied to social issues as well, so that those affected by a company's decisions either benefit or at least are not harmed. Socially responsible business practice works best in a responsive culture and ought to be financially viable to be sustained. Improved employee retention and productivity, better customer goodwill, and cost savings from environmental efficiencies are common benefits of such practices. Section One deals with the employee and issues such as ownership and participatory management, job security, pay and benefits, support for working parents, and more. Section Two addresses customers and suppliers along with customer service, responsible marketing to diverse populations, and social criteria purchasing. Section Three looks at the community and society at large,

cash and in-kind philanthropy, volunteerism, community development, and more. The final section focuses on organization and accountability issues, including social auditing and governance.

Robinson, Andy. "Playing the Market: Earned Income Strategies for Grassroots Groups." *NonProfit Times* 12 (March 1998): 32–33.

Robinson, Andy. "Selling Social Change: How To Earn Money from Your Mission." *Grassroots Fundraising Journal* 17 (April 1998): 7–10.

Sanders, Michael I. *Joint Ventures Involving Tax-Exempt Organizations.* 2nd ed. New York: John Wiley & Sons (Wiley Nonprofit Law, Finance, and Management Series), 2000. xxiii, 595 p.
   A comprehensive manual on the laws, regulations, and considerations involved in direct and indirect participation of nonprofits with taxable entities. Intended for accountants, attorneys, and nonprofit executives, the book provides legal citations as well as numerous pertinent examples throughout. Reviews taxation of exempt organizations and partnerships generally, gives an overview of some types of joint ventures; lending; unrelated business income tax; debt-financed income; excess business holdings; leasing; specific issues related to healthcare institutions, housing, and universities; bonds; international ventures; and investing through limited liability companies. Indexed.

Siegel, Eric, Brian R. Ford, and Jay M. Bornstein. *The Ernst & Young Business Plan Guide.* 2nd ed. New York: John Wiley & Sons, 1993, 194 p.
   Designed to assist anyone starting a new business or expanding an existing one in creating a financial and organizational blueprint for success. Contains step-by-step instructions for devising a solid business plan.

Skloot, Edward. "Enterprise and Commerce in Nonprofit Organizations." In *Handbook of Nonprofit Organizations*, edited by Walter W. Powell. New Haven: Yale University Press, 1986.
   Background information on business ventures by nonprofit organizations including four case studies. Looks at the varieties of such activities, including program-related products and services, staff and client resources, "hard property" (sale, lease, or rental of land and buildings), and "soft property" (copyrights, patents, trademarks, art and artifacts, mailing and membership lists).

Skloot, Edward, ed. *The Nonprofit Entrepreneur: Creating Ventures to Earn Income.* New York: The Foundation Center, 1988. viii, 170 p.
   Demonstrates how nonprofits can launch successful earned income enterprises without compromising their missions. According to the Urban Institute's Nonprofit Sector Project, approximately 15 percent of nonprofits actually engage in commerce, but more than 70 percent now earn some money through fees and service charges. It is this larger cluster of

organizations for which this book is relevant. Guide shows how many nonprofit organizations have transformed themselves into entrepreneurial organizations in order to deal with sharply rising costs, diminishing government dollars, increased competition for funding, and real marketing opportunity. Includes bibliography.

Trager, Cara. "Nonprofits Selling Their Services To Replace Government Grants: Fees Support Local Development." *Crain's New York Business* 13 (11–17 August 1997): 30–31.

U.S. Internal Revenue Service. *Tax on Unrelated Business Income of Exempt Organizations* (IRS Publication No. 593). Washington, DC: U.S. Internal Revenue Service, May 1985.
    A free 18-page publication that explains unrelated income tax provisions that apply to most tax-exempt organizations. Generally, tax-exempt organizations with gross income of $1,000 or more for the year from unrelated trade or business must file and pay taxes. (Order from: Superintendent of Documents, Washington, DC 20402.)

Who Cares, Inc.
    The nation's first nonprofit business magazine for social entrepreneurs, with information on building and managing nonprofit organizations. Published six times annually, with a budget of $750,000 and national circulation of 50,000. Targets entrepreneurial nonprofit leaders, corporations and foundations, and grassroots organizations with the goal of connecting readers with a diverse network of peers. Highlights leaders on the cutting edge of social change. Twenty-five percent of the revenue comes from advertising and 75 percent from foundations and individuals. (Order: http://www.whocares.org/)

Other Resources

Ashoka: Innovators for the Public
1700 North Moore St., Suite 2000
Arlington, VA 22209
Tel: 703-527-8300
Fax: 703-527-8383
E-mail: info@ashoka.org
Web address: www.ashoka.org/
    A global nonprofit organization that finds and supports outstanding individuals with ideas for far-reaching social change. The men and women who become Ashoka Fellows share a strong entrepreneurial character as well as a passion for social causes. Ashoka's support of these social entrepreneurs yields regional and national advances in education, health, human rights, the environment, and other areas of social concern. Nominations are submitted to Ashoka Country Representatives. The Ashoka Global Fellowship now includes 825 Fellows at work in 33 countries, with more new Fellows being elected each year.

Community Wealth Ventures, Inc.
733 15th St., NW, Suite 640
Washington, DC 20005
Tel: 202-393-2925
Fax: 202-347-5868
Web address: www.communitywealth.com

A for-profit subsidiary of Share Our Strength, a nonprofit based in Washington, D.C., which generates revenue to alleviate hunger in the United States and around the world. Advises nonprofit practitioners and investors on how to strengthen their social impact by stimulating new sources of revenue. Evaluates assets of nonprofits in order to help them design revenue-generating activities, including business ventures, partnerships, and licensing agreements. Advises corporations on how to refocus community participation to reflect their values and goals by constructing mutually beneficial partnerships with nonprofits. Advises foundations on how to help their grantees achieve their revenue-generating goals.

echoing green foundation
198 Madison Ave., 8th Floor
New York, NY 10016
Tel: 212-689-1165
Fax: 212-689-9010
Web address: www.echoinggreen.org

A nonprofit foundation that applies a venture capital approach to philanthropy. The echoing green fellowship provides seed money and technical support to social entrepreneurs who want to start new public service ventures. Their network currently includes more than 300 Fellows working domestically and abroad in areas such as education, arts, health, and human and civil rights. Fellows apply through one of more than 100 participating institutions and benefit from a renewable stipend, conferences, training, and a peer network. Technical support includes strategic planning and organizational development, financial planning, staff and board development, and legal and accounting practices.

Edward Lowe Foundation: Entrepreneurial Edge
P.O. Box 8
Cassopolis, MI 49031-0008
Tel: 800-232-5693 or 616-445-4200
Fax: 616-445-4350
Web address: www.edge.lowe.org

Entrepreneurial Edge is a Web site "where entrepreneurs can find peers, share experiences, and learn how to grow their companies."

The Fund for Social Entrepreneurs (www.servenet.org/ysa/fse/)
Launched by Youth Service America to invest in visionary young leaders on their quest to start up innovative nonprofits in the national and community service field, the Fund provides professional development, training, technical assistance, networking, national visibility, and financial assistance to five to seven social entrepreneurs selected each year for a three-year period.

The Morino Institute
11600 Sunrise Valley Drive, Suite 300
Reston, VA 20191
Tel: 703-620-8971
Fax: 703-620-4102
E-mail: feedback@morino.org
Web address: www.morino.org
Dedicated to achieving systemic change—economic, educational and social—through the application of new models for continuous improvement and learning enabled by the Internet. Primary areas of focus are youth advocacy and services, entrepreneurship, social networking, and community services. Includes everything from mentoring programs to local health clinics to adult education centers.

The National Center for Social Entrepreneurs
Basset Creek Office Plaza, Suite 310
5801 Duluth St.
Minneapolis, MN 55422
Tel: 612-595-0890 or 800-696-4066
Fax: 612-595-0232
E-mail: ncse@socialentrepreneurs.org
Web address: www.socialentrepreneurs.org
A nonprofit consulting and training organization that helps nonprofits sharpen their focus, increase their impact, and become more financially self-sufficient through the adoption of entrepreneurial strategies. Using a unique array of tools and processes, the National Center works with nonprofits to assess whether they are ready for entrepreneurship and, if they are, to develop the infrastructure needed for success, to conduct portfolio analyses of their current programs, and/or to develop new social purpose business ventures.

Planware (www.planware.org)
Demo versions of business planning software can be downloaded from this Web site.

Replication and Program Strategies, Inc.
2005 Market St., Suite 900
Philadelphia, PA 19103
Tel: 215-557-4482
Fax: 215-557-4485
Web address: www.replication.org

Assists promising social programs extend their reach and widen their impact. Helps organizations develop the financial and managerial capacities needed to grow. Addresses funders and operators of expanding programs in the fields of education, human services, community development, and the like. Provides feasibility assessment, comprehensive business planning, organizational design, mid-course development, and research.

Roberts Enterprise Development Fund
Presidio Building, First Floor
P.O. Box 29266
San Francisco, CA 94129-0266
Tel: 415-561-6677
Fax: 415-561-6685
E-mail: info@redf.org
Web address: www.redf.org

Funds ten nonprofits that operate twenty-four business ventures employing very-low-income individuals throughout the San Francisco Bay area. Evolved out of a six-year effort by the Roberts Foundation to expand economic opportunity for the homeless. Provides access to business technical assistance, information management, and computer and Internet services. Available on their Web site, REDF's book *New Social Entrepreneurs: The Success, Challenge and Lessons of Nonprofit Enterprise Creation* documents their experience helping nonprofits develop for-profit enterprises. In addition to their local efforts, the Roberts Foundation is involved at the national level in the creation of nonprofit enterprises. One area of focus is the Venture Fund Initiative, which brings together foundations and social entrepreneurs in target cities throughout the country to build local venture funds.

Social Venture Network
P.O. Box 29221
San Francisco, CA 94129-0221
Tel: 415-561-6501
Fax: 415-561-6435
Web address: www.svn.org

A membership organization of successful business and social entrepreneurs dedicated to changing the way the world does business in order to create a more just, humane, and sustainable society. Provides opportunities for socially conscious entrepreneurs to exchange ideas, share problems and solutions, and collaborate on an ad hoc basis.

U.S. Small Business Administration
409 Third St., NW
Washington, DC 20416
Tel: 800-U-Ask-SBA
Web address: www.sba.gov
   This U.S. government Web site offers resources on a variety of relevant topics. The Starting Your Business area offers information about business initiatives and development, business information centers, important publications, franchise registries, the Service Corps of Retired Executives (SCORE), small business development centers, counseling help, and more. A Small Business Startup Kit can be ordered here. The Financing Your Business area provides information on loan programs, loan forms, lender programs, lending studies, loan statistics, secondary markets, etc. The SBA's Office of Entrepreneurial Development (OED) area offers the following programs: Business Initiatives, Native American Affairs, One-Stop Capital Shops, Small Business Development Centers, Veterans' Affairs, Welfare to Work Initiative, and Women's Business Ownership. A Small Business Classroom located on this site provides on-line counseling by a professional SCORE counselor, and listings of SBA training and conferences in every state in the country. The SBA's Online Business Resource Area, offered in partnership with Inc. Online and Network Solutions, provides on-line learning tools and information resources for small business owners, managers, and other students of enterprise.

PART B

APPROACHING INSTITUTIONS FOR SUPPORT

Chapter 15

Approaching Foundations for Support

In today's world, everything concerns everyone. — Vaclav Havel

Foundation giving is both the best-known and the least understood source of funding. While the word "foundation" conjures up the names of some of the world's most prominent families—Rockefeller, Ford, Laidlaw, Bronfman, and Tata, to name just a few—in fact, most foundations are smaller family foundations with names that are rarely so well known.

In the U.S., foundations are nonprofit organizations that have been established expressly to support charitable efforts, as defined by the Internal Revenue Service of the U.S. government. In most cases, their support is made through grants to nonprofit organizations. Foundations represent the philanthropic interests of their founders and the interests of their founders' appointees,

who serve as stewards of the foundation's assets. Most foundations outlive their creators, and so their wishes are likely to be interpreted, amplified, enlarged, and perhaps even changed by the trustees who stand as guardians. The founding mission of some foundations, however, still serves them well. For example, the James Irvine Foundation in California was established in 1937 as a charitable trust of James Irvine, a California agricultural pioneer, "to promote the general welfare of the people of California." It is dedicated to "enhancing the social, economic, and physical quality of life throughout California, and to enriching the state's intellectual and cultural environment." That mission statement applies as much today as when the foundation's trustees originally adopted it more than six decades ago.

Foundations may adjust their priorities to meet society's changing structure and needs. For instance, there are many foundations whose purpose is funding programs to improve the life of children. Foundations established during the early decades of the twentieth century frequently funded orphanages for children without parents, or children whose parents could not take care of them. Today, few children are without someone to care for them, and with appropriate community support, most children can remain with their family or be placed with another. Consequently, foundations that used to fund orphanages now support children's centers, parent effectiveness training programs, foster care placement, community education, and so on.

Another example of foundations addressing changing needs is found in the technology field; many proposals are funded today for the purchase of computers, or system upgrades. These items did not exist and could hardly have been imagined by the donors who, many years ago, endowed the foundations now contributing to the acquisition of this technology.

Foundations exist in most northern countries, and their numbers are growing in southern countries as well. Today there are foundations in countries as diverse as Mozambique (Mozambique Foundation for Community Development), India (India Foundation for the Arts and the National Foundation for India), Colombia (Corona Foundation), Kenya (Kenya Community Development Foundation), Nigeria (Obafemi Awolowo Foundation), and Poland (the Stefan Batory Foundation). The most visible, however, are the private foundations in the United States; this chapter focuses primarily on these.

Support from foundations can be an important part of a nonprofit's funding mix, and, as we'll discuss in the following section, can provide benefits well beyond the actual money received. Additionally, preparing a proposal for submission to a foundation affords an organization's board and managers a valuable opportunity for self-assessment. When describing its programs and their anticipated impact, listing board members and their qualifications, and reporting on finances and fundraising, an organization is brought face-to-face with its performance. If the organization has been thoughtful and diligent, the process of drafting a proposal will reflect its mastery of the nonprofit basics outlined in Section 1 of this book. Writing a proposal also can reveal gaps that need to be addressed for an organization to be effective. This chapter will explain what foundations are, how they operate, which organizations receive their grants, and how they may best be approached to secure funding.

What Are the Advantages of Raising Support from Foundations?

1. Foundations are the only institutions in the world whose mission is to give away money (except for operating foundations, which conduct programs consistent with their own purpose and IRS requirements). Foundations not only want to give away money, but are required to do so if they wish to maintain their tax-exempt status.

2. Foundations tend to give big chunks of money at one time. While $5,000 might represent a large gift from an individual or a business, it is a relatively small grant from a foundation.

3. In the United States, information on foundations is readily available to almost everyone. Foundations must disclose how much they give, to whom they give, who is on their board, and what their assets are. In addition, many foundations (particularly the larger ones) publish guidelines and annual reports that describe their interests, tell when proposals are due, and explain how best to apply. Grantseekers can find much of this information in any number of specialized directories as well as on the World Wide Web, where increasing numbers of foundations maintain home pages.

4. Foundations confer credibility. Individuals—who account for the vast majority of charitable contributions—are often persuaded to make a donation in part because they see that an organization has received foundation support. Foundation funding is like the Good Housekeeping Seal of Approval, and one foundation grant tends to lead to another as well as to gifts from individuals and corporations.

What Are the Disadvantages of Raising Support from Foundations?

1. The very accessibility of foundations makes competition for their limited funding extremely intense. At best, only one out of about 10 to 15 of all grant proposals are funded, and many only partially.

2. It can often take a foundation six months from the time a proposal is submitted to reach a decision.

3. It is extremely rare for a foundation to continue funding an organization beyond three or four years, at which time the organization may have to develop a new program in order to reapply for additional funding, or look to other sources for support.

4. Many nonprofits inadvertently develop projects solely to secure foundation funding. Their case statement becomes, "What do you fund? We can do that." They move away from their original purpose.

5. Grant money may be applied only to the program described in the proposal. Administrative expenses indirectly related to running the program (such as office rental, phone bills, and seeking more funding) must be met elsewhere, either from other funding sources or from foundation grants called "general support grants." An exception would be those indirect costs that are specified in the proposal budget, usually as a percentage of overall costs. Understandably, foundations are fairly strict about how their money is spent.

An Overview of Foundation Giving

The origins of foundations go back to countries like Turkey, where foundations have flourished for close to a thousand years. However, the roots of the modern private foundation can be traced to the Statute of Charitable Uses, enacted in 1601 by the English parliament under the reign of Queen Elizabeth. In England during the 1600s, people of means set aside assets dedicated to supporting a designated institution, such as a school, an orphanage, or a museum, or for more specific purposes, such as the assistance of elderly widows. Foundations were usually established by a benefactor and his or her family, who decided to leave a specified sum of money to be administered by a designated group of trustees for set purposes. Benjamin Franklin, Stephen Girard, and Peter Cooper established such trust funds in the early days of the United States. At the beginning of the twentieth century, Andrew Carnegie and John D. Rockefeller created the prototype of the modern foundation in the United States, as J. R. Tata did in India.

Today the term "foundation"—or "trust," "corporation," "fund," or "charity"—is used to describe a variety of charitable institutions, most of which lend support to nonprofit organizations through grants. Most foundations are endowed; in other words, their benefactors' gifts were large enough to make grantmaking possible over an extended number of years by expending accrued interest only. A *family foundation* is a trust established by one donor or family. *Community foundations* administer a number of individual charitable trust funds set up by different donors; they make most of their grants in geographically defined areas. Some corporations choose to create *corporate foundations* to administer their charitable contributions. Finally there are *public charities*, nonprofit organizations that raise funds each year from individuals and other sources, some of which distribute this money in the form of grants. Note that public charities technically aren't foundations, at least according to IRS regulations. In fact, even community foundations, which manage funds established by many donors, are technically public charities. However, because their primary activity *is* grantmaking, they have long been viewed as part of the foundation universe.

Private foundations receive distinct tax advantages that influence the extent of their benevolence. In return for these advantages, the U.S. government has set requirements for the percentage of money that foundations must distribute in grants each year; since 1986, the rate has been set as the amount equal to 5 percent of the assets of the foundation. While most foundations distribute 5 percent, some occasionally give more.

UPDATE In a survey of 450 U.S. foundations, including the 50 largest independent and 25 largest community foundations, *Giving USA* reported that non-corporate foundations expended

Public Charities and Private Foundations

The Foundation Center defines a private foundation as a nongovernmental nonprofit organization having a principal fund managed by its own trustees or directors, which maintains or aids charitable, educational, religious, or other activities serving the public good, primarily through the making of grants to other nonprofit organizations.

To understand what a private foundation is, it helps to understand what it is *not*. Every U.S. and foreign charity that qualifies under Section 501(c)(3) of the Internal Revenue Service Code as tax-exempt is a "private foundation" unless it demonstrates to the IRS that it falls into another category. Broadly speaking, organizations that are *not* private foundations are public charities as described in Section 509(a) of the Internal Revenue Service Code. Public charities generally derive their funding or support primarily from the general public, receiving grants from individuals, government, and private foundations. Although some public charities engage in grantmaking activities, most conduct direct service or other tax-exempt activities. A private foundation, on the other hand, usually derives its principal fund from a single source, such as an individual, family, or corporation, and more often than not is a grantmaker. A private foundation does not solicit funds from the public.

$19.81 billion in 1999—10.4 percent of the estimated total giving in the United States from all sources ($190.16 billion). The report points out that, "With the exception of 1994, foundation giving grew well ahead of inflation. Over each of the past four years, foundation grantmaking grew by double-digit amounts and even when adjusted for inflation."[1]

Large foundations such as Ford, W.K. Kellogg, Andrew W. Mellon, Carnegie, Hewlett, Rockefeller, and MacArthur have taken the lead in exploring new international initiatives. Together, as of 1990, these seven comprised more than 70 percent of all international grantmaking by U.S. foundations. In the last decade, U.S. grantmaking for international programs has markedly increased, although as a proportion of total grantmaking, it remained modest.[2]

---

1. Ann Kaplan, ed., *Giving USA: The Annual Report on Philanthropy for the Year 1999* (New York: American Association of Fund-Raising Counsel, 2000).
2. Loren Renz and Josefina Samson-Atienza, *International Grantmaking: A Report on U.S. Foundation Trends* (New York: The Foundation Center, 1997).

General Characteristics of Four Types of Foundations

Foundation Type	Description	Source of Funds	Decision-making Activity	Grantmaking Requirements	Reporting
Independent foundation	An independent grant making organization established to aid, social, educational, religious, or other charitable activities.	Endowment generally derived from a single source such as an individual, a family, or a group of individuals. Contributions to endowment limited as to tax deductibility.	Decisions may be made by donor or members of the donor's family; by an independent board of directors or trustees; or by a bank or trust officer acting on the donor's behalf.	Broad discretionary giving allowed but may have specific guidelines and give only in a few specific fields. About 70% limit their giving to local area.	Annual information returns (Form 990-PF) filed with IRS must be made available to public. A small percentage issue separately printed annual reports.
Company-Sponsored Foundation	Legally an independent grantmaking organization with close ties to the corporation providing funds.	Endowment and annual contributions from a profit-making corporation. May maintain small endowment and pay out most of contributions received annually in grants, or may maintain endowment to cover contributions in years when corporate profits are down.	Decisions made by board of directors often composed of corporate officials, but which may include individuals with no corporate affiliation. Decisions may also be made by local company officials.	Giving tends to be in fields related to corporate activities or in communities where corporation operates. Usually gives more grants but in smaller dollar amounts than independent foundations.	Same as above
Operating foundation	An organization that uses its resources to conduct research or provide a direct service.	Endowment usually provided from a single source, but eligible for maximum deductible contributions from public.	Decisions generally made by independent board of directors	Makes few, if any, grants. Grants generally related directly to the foundation's program.	Same as above
Community foundation	A publicly sponsored organization that makes grants for social, educational, religious, or other charitable purposes in a specific community or region.	Contributions received from many donors. Usually eligible for maximum tax deductible contributions from public.	Decisions made by board of directors representing the diversity of the community.	Grants generally limited to charitable organizations in local community.	IRS Form 990 tax returns available to public. Many publish full guidelines or annual reports.

Source: David Jacobs and Melissa Lunn, eds., *The Foundation Directory, 2000 Edition* (New York: The Foundation Center, 2000).

Foundations usually make their contributions in the form of grants of money. Grants are given out for a variety of purposes. Considering the diversity of U.S. foundations and their distinctive individual characters, it is difficult and perhaps even misleading to categorize grants, but we will attempt to differentiate the major types.

1. *General support grants* support the general work and goals of the organization, as outlined in its proposal and accompanying materials. For obvious reasons, general support grants are desirable, but many foundations are less inclined to make grants of this nature, choosing instead to award funds for specific programs or projects. Grantseekers can strengthen their case for general support by including in their proposals a self-assessment component, which signals to grantmakers that the impact of their grant can be evaluated.

2. *Program grants* underwrite a particular endeavor or project that is of value to an organization's constituency and advances its mission. For example, a school might request support to develop a new math curriculum, or a horticultural society might seek funds to train at-risk youth in urban gardening. In both instances, the program or project is specific and concrete, and its success can be measured.

   In making program grants, foundations might provide seed money—support for new, experimental, or innovative projects that need initial underwriting to get off the ground, test their wings, and establish themselves sufficiently to attract ongoing support from other sources, such as the government or the public. These projects are sometimes described as "pilot programs," or "demonstration projects," because they are designed and implemented as models for replication on a larger scale once they are evaluated. Sometimes an existing foundation supporter might consider awarding a planning grant to help an organization engage in research and development to determine how best to implement the project.

3. *Capital grants* are earmarked for "capital" purposes—for example, renovating or acquiring a building, or purchasing equipment such as computers and software, or elevators, ramps, and special doorframes that provide wheelchair access.

4. *Challenge (or matching) grants* are contingent upon an organization securing funds from other sources. If, for example, an arts organization needs $100,000 to secure a building in which to conduct its classes, a foundation may make a grant of $50,000 provided that the grantee can raise another $50,000 from other sources. The funder's intent in making a "soft" challenge is to encourage the grantee to actively seek out the required matching funds, but the funder is committed to awarding the initial sum in any event. A "hard" challenge means that the grant will become available only if—and when—matching funds have been raised.

In addition to grantmaking, some foundations make *program-related investments* (PRIs): investments of some of their assets directly in nonprofit enterprises with the intent that the funds will be returned at some point. PRIs were pioneered by the Ford Foundation, still the leading PRI provider. They are low- or no-interest loans in such fields as community development, minority business development, rural cooperatives, low-income housing, education, and the arts.

Many of the larger foundations publish annual reports listing their past grantees and specific areas of interest, as well as brochures that outline their application procedures. These are mailed out upon request at no charge, but foundations are not required to do so. However, all United States private foundations are required to file a specific annual tax return with the Internal Revenue Service (Form 990-PF).

Publicly Available Tax Returns

Since 1987, the IRS has required that public charities and private foundations make both their annual tax forms (Form 990 for public charities and Form 990-PF for private foundations) and exemption applications (Form 1023) available to any person who requests that information. All charities must make their 990 or 990-PF forms available in such a way as to make sure they are, in IRS parlance, "widely available": (1) interested parties can examine the materials at the charity's office; (2) the charity must respond to written requests for photocopies of the materials, which can then be mailed or picked up; (3) the charity can post the information on the Internet.

How Do Foundations Operate?

Foundations of sufficient size and scope employ professional staff to provide information on the foundation's interests and procedures, screen potential grantees, assist them in the application process, make recommendations for action to the governing body, and carry out other duties on its behalf. If the foundation is relatively small, these duties may be carried out by the lawyer who handles the foundation's business, or they may not be carried out at all. Applicants tend to gain a better understanding of a foundation's interests and priorities when there is a professional staff.

Grantmaking decisions are usually made by a foundation's board of trustees, or by a distribution committee whose members are designated by the board. When there is a professional staff, in most cases staff members make recommendations for action to the governing body. The board might meet as frequently as once a month or as rarely as once a year to select grant recipients and set general policy regarding the areas of interest of a foundation. These governing bodies usually make the final decisions on grant awards, but some foundations empower their staff to make a limited number of discretionary grants, which are not subject to the approval of a board of trustees or distribution committee. Discretionary grants are usually smaller than the average grants the foundation awards.

Foundations make grants ranging from $100 to more than $1,000,000 and, occasionally, many millions of dollars. Reviewing data on a foundation will reveal the dollar range of grants it makes. Sometimes foundations provide smaller amounts than the grantee has requested, in which case the grantees may then have to secure grants from other foundations, or supplement the grants with revenues from other sources. In fact, when reviewing a project that requires amounts greater than they can offer, or which they do not wish to fund entirely, foundations will generally examine the proposal for evidence of an organization's plans and ability to raise the additional funds needed to fully underwrite the project.

As part of their decision-making process, some foundations initiate personal contact with prospective grantees by mail, telephone, or visits at the organization's offices or at their own. Others may decide without having any contact at all. The presence of professional staff is one indicator that a foundation generally desires some personal contact with an organization during its decision-making process. If the foundation is seriously considering your request, you can expect to meet with one of its representatives to discuss your proposal in greater detail. A foundation staff member may also arrange a "site visit" to gauge in person the capabilities of your organization and your staff.

In many cases, a foundation may receive more qualified requests than it can fund; even the most targeted, deserving request may be rejected for reasons wholly unrelated to its value, or to the merits of the organization submitting it. And as mentioned, a foundation may not even initially provide the applicant with an explanation of the rejection; frustrated applicants can write or phone to request an explanation. The answer will help the grantee whose activity *does* fall within the foundation's concerns to determine whether their prospects for receiving support will improve in the future. This is part of all fundraising. Don't be discouraged—persevere.

Deciding Whether To Approach Foundations for Support

In making this decision, consider these questions: Are you prepared to do the work outlined in the following steps? Can you take the time to write proposals and undertake the necessary research? If not, are volunteers available who would be willing to undertake these tasks?

Be honest with yourself when you answer these questions. Success in winning grants requires careful research, thorough program planning, and conscientious approaches to funders. Typically understaffed and overworked, nonprofit managers may be tempted to skip certain stages in researching and writing a proposal. Unfortunately, there are few ways to cut corners without compromising the quality of your work, and it is wise to wait before approaching foundations if you do not have adequate time and resources.

The good news is that, over time, your skills will develop and expand. You will find that less and less time is required to write solid proposals, and that research will come more easily as your knowledge grows, as you regularly review foundation annual reports, and as you become more aware of their activities through publications and Internet resources. Finally, you will learn to resist the temptation of approaching foundations when you discover that your programs do not fall squarely within their interests, or when your minimum budget exceeds their stated maximum gift.

Securing a Foundation Grant

Step 1. Ready Your Organization
As presented in Section 1 of this book, organizations must complete certain tasks to raise funds successfully. These tasks take on added importance when you are approaching foundations for support. The prospective grantee must: (1) have a clearly articulated vision and mission; (2) be

incorporated and granted tax-exempt status by the IRS, or operate under the aegis of a 501(c)(3) organization; (3) have a functioning board of directors; (4) have a program plan; and (5) have operating budgets for the organization and for those programs for which they are seeking support. These accomplishments should, of course, precede any fundraising activity.

Step 2. Frame Your Needs as Opportunities for Prospective Foundation Supporters
Some foundations, particularly those without staffs, will consider requests for general support, but most award grants for specific projects and programs. The applicant must therefore determine which of its current or projected efforts might be most attractive to prospective foundation supporters. Think in terms of how your program will advance the work of the foundation in achieving its own stated program goals.

A successful proposal will describe in some detail how an organization's activities accomplish a specific set of objectives that are consistent with its mission. Remember that you need to present a funder with more than an idea—even a good idea. You need to present a plan of action that describes precisely how you intend to implement that idea. You also need to demonstrate why your organization and program are needed. What societal problems or opportunities are you addressing? What are the merits of your proposed solutions? Why are you particularly qualified to carry out the program for which you are requesting funds?

By thinking as concretely as possible in terms of potential outcomes, you will be better able to demonstrate to potential funders the importance of your programs. At the same time, you will be developing a valuable program plan for your organization. Use the following worksheet to list your current and projected activities that are, or could be, candidates for foundation funding.

Worksheet

Name of Organization: _____

Date: _____

 1. Current Programs and Projects
    a. _____
    b. _____
    c. _____
    d. _____
    e. _____
    f. _____
    g. _____

 2. Projected Programs and Projects
    a. _____
    b. _____
    c. _____
    d. _____
    e. _____
    f. _____

Step 3: Rank Your Programs for Possible Submission to Foundation Prospects
Next identify those programs on your list that may be of most interest to prospective foundations. Develop your own list of criteria to help you make this decision, or adopt the following list.

1. *Compatibility with mission.* Is this program consistent with your group's current stated vision and mission, or would its undertaking take your organization in a different direction?

2. *Drawn from acknowledged expertise.* Does the program flow from your organization's experience and expertise, does it require skills or personnel not currently available from within the organization?

3. *Achievability.* If you do secure the needed financial resources, will you be able to accomplish the results that you are promising within a reasonable period of time?

4. *Topicality.* Is the problem or opportunity you are addressing perceived as significant by the public, as evidenced within the last year by media coverage, legislation, speeches by civic leaders, or by some other external indices?

5. *Documentation.* Can you document the seriousness of the problem or opportunity addressed by your project?

6. *Reputation.* Are there other nonprofit organizations that have also established a reputation in this area? Are they more credible than your own or less?

7. *Rationale for foundation support.* Can you illustrate why foundations, rather than other sources of support, would be the most appropriate for this project?

Your answers to the preceding questions will help you decide whether proposals to fund your programs are ready to be submitted to foundations or require further development. If the thrust and intention of the project do not flow from your mission, a funder may question your proposal. If the foundation staffers reading your proposal are not aware of the importance of the issue you are addressing, they may not view it with the same urgency that you do, or they may view agencies other than yours as better vehicles to address it. You, the grantseeker, must consider these factors carefully in advance, and address them directly in your written and oral presentations to prospective funders.

Step 4. Research Likely Prospects
Once you have developed your program(s) and decided that foundations are the most appropriate source of financial support, develop a list of prospects whose interests most closely approximate your own. Not long ago, grantseekers would mail out blanket requests for general support to any foundation they had heard about—the shot-in-the-dark approach. This method would occasionally net a grant, but most grantseekers obtained nothing for their efforts and became discouraged in their search for foundation support.

The real problem with this broadside approach is that it makes life harder for everyone. Foundation staff must spend substantial time reading and rejecting proposals that never had any chance of success; as a result, more and more foundations are adding to their informational materials the dreaded phrase "grants to pre-selected organizations only—unsolicited applications not accepted." As Andy Robinson, one of the most successful grantseekers in the environmental movement says, "If you choose to be lazy or greedy by sending out proposals at random, you mess things up for everyone." Ellen Furnari, director of the grants program at the Ben and Jerry's Foundation, says, "60 to 70 percent of the proposals we receive don't fit our guidelines, and 50 percent miss by a wide margin. We respond to all submissions graciously, but it costs substantial staff time to reject all the proposals that should not have been sent to us in the first place. We try to limit our administrative costs to 10 percent of our budget but a lot of our time is absorbed in saying 'no'."

Grantseekers should therefore target recipients of their proposals as precisely as possible. This is not to suggest that programs should be tailored to a given foundation's interests by distorting them into something they are not; such an effort will not only prove fruitless but will in the long run reflect poorly on your organization. How, then, do you use your limited time and resources most effectively in identifying the most appropriate foundations? First and foremost, do your research.

Fortunately, the United States has an excellent resource of foundation information: the Foundation Center. The Foundation Center has libraries of resources on all aspects of fundraising, a publishing arm that produces reference works and research guides on foundations, and an excellent Web site (www.fdncenter.org) that, in addition to a wealth of other information, provides access to searchable databases of foundation and grant information. The Foundation Center's most comprehensive resource is *FC Search,* the Center's exclusive database of foundation and corporate grantmakers in a fully searchable CD-ROM format. It contains data the Center has published in its principal reference works: *The Foundation Directory*; *The Foundation Directory, Part 2*; *The Foundation Directory Supplement*; the *Guide to U.S. Foundations, Their Trustees, Officers, and Donors*; the *National Directory of Corporate Giving*; and *The Foundation Grants Index. FC Search* can be purchased from the Foundation Center, or accessed at more than two hundred locations around the country. (See Appendix C for a list of these.)

The *FC Search* CD-ROM offers grantseekers many search criteria for researching profiles of more than fifty thousand U.S. foundations, corporate givers, and community foundations and other public charities. It reduces the time needed to target prospective funders from hours, or days, to seconds. From *FC Search* users with Internet access can link directly to the Web sites of approximately fifteen hundred grantmakers. In addition, *FC Search* includes the names and foundation affiliations of more than two hundred thousand trustees, officers, and donors who make the funding decisions at these institutions. It also describes some two hundred thousand foundation grants reported in recent years.

Grantseekers and fundraisers of all kinds can visit the Foundation Center's field office libraries in New York, Washington, D.C., Cleveland, Atlanta, or San Francisco, and nearly everyone can access all their resources at its cooperating collections at more than two hundred locations throughout the country. In addition, several of their publications are available in the reference section of almost any public or university library in the United States. If you aren't located near one of these facilities, you can accomplish a tremendous amount using the Foundation Center's Web site (www.fdncenter.org).

Whether at the Foundation Center, a reference library, or the Center's Web site, grantseekers may become overwhelmed. Here is a simple way to do research and identify the foundations that may be interested in your work.

The easiest reference to start with is *The Foundation Directory*, whether using the print version, the CD-ROM version, or the searchable online version available by subscription from the Foundation Center's Web site (www.fdncenter.org). Look through the indexes and find the various descriptions that most closely match what you are trying to do. Indexes in *Foundation Directory* reference works include foundation and trustee names, fields of interest (subject areas), geographic location, types of support, types of recipient organization, and population group served.

Your goal is to narrow the list of foundations that might be interested in your work by considering all the categories within which your program might fall. The Foundation Center also publishes specialized guides and, depending on your program area, you may find that the Center has done a lot of research for you. A number of Center publications list grantmakers and the grants they have made in particular subject areas.

Narrow your list of foundations down to fifty, then write to them for a copy of their annual report and grant guidelines. Some of these reports may be available at a Foundation Center field office library or cooperating collection, or groups similar to yours may have them. Also, a growing number of foundations in the United States now have Web sites containing their latest information.

However you obtain information on a foundation, read it carefully. By noting the size of grants they make and the types of organization and programs they fund, you will be able to cut your list in half. With your list narrowed down to the best prospects, ask other organizations similar to yours if they have information on approaching these foundations. Above all else, *follow the directions* provided in the foundation's guidelines. If they ask for a letter of inquiry first, send one—do not call. If they suggest calling first, call first—don't write. If they will not accept a proposal longer than five pages, don't send six. Don't give the foundation an excuse to not read your proposal, and don't give them a reason to think your group cannot even follow simple directions. Seemingly unimportant procedural steps can, if not followed to the letter, provide a foundation with the basis for rejecting your proposal without further consideration.

The following worksheet will help you list your prospects. As you identify foundations that appear to be good prospects, place them in the appropriate section of the worksheet. On the basis of your information gathering and research, you should be able to assess those programs and projects that may be of interest to foundations, and to identify which foundations those might be.

Foundation Prospect Worksheet

Local Foundations

1. Community Foundation: _____

2. Family Foundations (staffed; annual report available)

    a. _____

    b. _____

    c. _____

    d. _____

3. Corporate Foundations

    a. _____

    b. _____

    c. _____

    d. _____

4. Unstaffed Foundations

    a. _____

    b. _____

    c. _____

    d. _____

National Foundations

5. Large National Foundations (i.e., assets over $100,000,000)

    a. _____

    b. _____

    c. _____

    d. _____

6. Smaller Foundations

    a. _____

    b. _____

    c. _____

    d. _____

Step 5. Build Your Knowledge about Foundation Prospects

1. Subscribe to foundation trade journals, such as *Foundation News & Commentary* magazine (Council on Foundations, 1828 L Street, NW, Washington, D.C. 20036; tel: 800-771-8187 or 202-466-6512; 6 issues per year, $48), and the newsletter of your local association of grantmakers, if one exists (check the Council's Web site for links to the various regional associations of grantmakers).

2. Read your major local newspaper regularly for news about foundations grants.

3. Network with other nonprofits seeking support from foundations.

4. Seek advice from receptive foundation representatives.

5. Subscribe to *The Chronicle of Philanthropy* and read their "New Grants" feature as well as their "Deadlines," which announces proposal deadlines (*The Chronicle of Philanthropy*, 1255 23rd Street, NW, Washington, D.C. 20037; tel: 800-728-2819; 24 issues per year, $67.50; available for subscription on-line).

6. Examine the files at your local Foundation Center collection regularly for new information. Read their free electronic weekly newsletter *Philanthropy News Digest* at their Web site (www.fdncenter.org) or subscribe to the free e-mail edition.

7. Visit the many Web sites that provide comprehensive information about foundations and grantseeking. (See the Additional Resources section of this chapter for addresses.)

Step 6. Make the Approach

Once you have prepared a proposal, you may be tempted to submit it without considering the following points. Don't.

1. Know thy funder. Be sure you have reviewed all the materials the foundation has published on its grantmaking policies, including brochures, annual reports, grant guidelines, etc. (see the samples that follow). Before applying, be absolutely clear on why the foundation should be interested in your project.

2. Check your organization's files to see if anyone associated with your group has been in touch with the foundation; you should be aware of any such exchanges.

3. Check if you have any personal contacts with the foundation. Do any members of your staff or board know a member of the foundation's staff, or, if the foundation is unstaffed, a member of its board of directors? A pre-existing personal contact might help pave the way for your proposal.

In approaching prospective foundation supporters, you must follow the application procedures they have outlined in their printed materials. Your goal is clear: to make the most persuasive presentation possible of your project. Ideally, you'd like the opportunity to do that in person. Your first contact will most likely be made by sending a letter in which you tell why you are approaching the foundation and outline the general thrust of your project as it relates to the foundation's stated interests. The letter should always include a sign-off such as, "We would welcome the opportunity to meet with you in person to discuss this project in greater detail, and to answer any questions that you might have."

Corporate Foundation Profile

The MONY Foundation, New York, NY

General Foundation Guidelines
Background And Philosophy

About The Company
MONY Life Insurance Company (MONY), chartered in 1842 and now known as the MONY Group, was one of the first companies in America to sell life insurance to the general public, and within its second week of operation, also the first to insure women and members of the armed forces in this country. MONY has since become a leading provider of insurance and retirement programs to individuals and companies, while continuing to demonstrate a strong commitment to social responsibility. As an insurer, investor, and employer, MONY believes that the health of and future of the Company are directly related to the health and future of the communities it serves. As a concerned corporate citizen, MONY regards its philanthropic and business endeavors as valuable investments in the development of those communities.

About The Foundation
The MONY Foundation seeks to apply available resources in specific, well-defined areas of the philanthropic community. At present, our philanthropic efforts are concentrated at MONY's Home Office in New York City, and in Syracuse, NY. In addition, the MONY Foundation partners with MONY's sales offices nation-wide.

   MONY's Foundation resources are targeted towards innovative, need responsive projects and programs within our priority areas of funding. Each site has strategic funding priorities, which seek to address the specific needs of the communities where they are located. Foundation and site contributions staff assess and refine principal areas of giving on an annual basis, emphasizing specific programs as opposed to general support grants.

Grant Application Requirements/Guidelines
The MONY Foundation accepts the "New York/New Jersey Area Common Application Form." Alternatively, the MONY Foundation will consider grant applications that include a brief cover letter (1 page), and a concise proposal (4–6 pages) providing the information specified below. Legible copies of the (most recent) documentation listed below are required for all applications.

Organization

- Name and address of organization

- Contact person, title, and telephone number

- History/background and mission of organization

- Geographic area served by organization

- Target population served by the organization

Syracuse, New York Contributions Program
"The Essential Needs of Children & Teens at Risk"

MONY's community leadership is well established, and the commitment to support the area's vital needs continues. Consequently, to address concerns impacting our youth, MONY's primary focus at its Syracuse, NY site is The Essential Needs of Children & Teens at Risk.

Our community is challenged to meet the ongoing and evolving needs of our children and our teenagers—safe, nurturing facilities providing centralized programs for children at risk and for their families; initiatives that impact stress or dysfunction resulting from difficulty of balancing job and family; structured programs that impact a child's development (self-esteem, skills building, and prevention related projects); and coordination of services that respond to the urgent needs of pregnant and other "at risk" teens.

MONY will consider grants to well-managed organizations that address the needs of children and teens at risk. Funding preferences include, but are not limited to:

- Programs which could result in systematic change—enhancing linkages, removing barriers to services, and increasing resources through volunteerism and/or collaboration;

- Pilot projects based on identification of unmet needs;

- Interventions directed at preventing or shortening a crisis situation.

To round out our concern for the quality of life in this community, limited financial, personnel, and in-kind support will be given to other volunteer-civic-health related efforts.

Grants will be made two times a year (May/June and October/November) to agencies that serve the greater Syracuse area. We prefer not to acknowledge multiple-year grant requests.

General Foundation Profile

Guidelines for the Fuller Foundation, Inc.

Mission Statement

The Fuller Foundation, Inc. is a family foundation, inspired by its forward-thinking founder, Alvan T. Fuller. Our purpose is to support non-profit agencies which improve the quality of life for people, animals and the environment. The Foundation also funds the Fuller Foundation of New Hampshire which supports horticultural and educational programs for the public at Fuller Gardens. Our geographic focus area is predominately the Boston area and the immediate seacoast area of New Hampshire. Through our grants we strive to effect change, make an impact on our community, and inspire good deeds.

General Guidelines For Focus Areas:

1. No Capital Projects will be considered unless, in the opinion of the Trustees, the Foundation gift will have a significant impact.
2. Proposals for these grants must follow all current "Application Procedures" as outlined in *The Fuller Foundation, Inc. Guidelines*.
3. Any Grant submitted that is incomplete will not be considered.
4. The Fuller Foundation does not award grants to individuals.
5. Faxed grant requests will not be accepted.

Youth at Risk

In funding *Youth at Risk* The Fuller Foundation, Inc. seeks proposals from qualified agencies that involve youth 18 and under, predominately at or below the poverty line, in programs that will:

- Help prevent youth from experiencing the detrimental effects caused by the use of alcohol, tobacco and drugs through the early education of youth and parents.

- Challenge and empower youth at risk through peer leadership, outdoor adventure education programs, and alternative educational experiences. We fund programs which help youth reach their potential and to lead productive lives. The Foundation favors programs that are year-round, or summer programs which re-enforce values and skills that are learned during the school year.

Wildlife, Endangered Species—Their Environment, and Animals Helping People

In funding Wildlife, Endangered Species—Their Environment, and Animals Helping People, The Fuller Foundation, Inc. seeks proposals from qualified agencies that will:

- Educate the public on wildlife and the adverse affects of encroachment on their habitat.

- Support shelters, animal hospitals, animal habitats, and programs that insure a healthy wildlife population.

- Protect endangered species, their environment and habitat from extinction or unnecessary human encroachment.

- Support programs which improve people's lives by interaction with animals.

The Arts

In funding the Arts, The Fuller Foundation seeks proposals from qualified agencies that carry on the life interests of Alvan T. and Viola D. Fuller in this area. The Foundation expects its grants to encourage, through the agencies, "hands-on" and participatory collaborations between established cultural institutions, artists and communities.

Specific program interests include:

- Art for viewing and listening

- Art education in school

- Art and performing arts festivals

- Art (murals & sculpture) that beautifies or inspires a community

- Programs that bring symphony, opera and theatre to the community

- Adult and/or children's museum education programs

Please note that The Fuller Foundation, Inc. also wants to support "new" and "seed" organizations who do not have a financial history. However, we shall require that these organizations have a sound business plan with an active, contributing Board of Directors. We shall require that any agency "start-up" program, or those programs with a "history," have a financial plan for sustaining their mission and building their funding base that does not continuously rely on Fuller Foundation support.

Application Procedures For The Fuller Foundation, Inc.

With your grant submission we require the following:

- A brief history of the organization's origins and its current programs

- A copy of the IRS letter of Tax Exempt Status 501(c)(3)

- A narrative which describes:
    - goals and objectives of the program/project, organization or capital campaign
    - how it will measure success both short term and long term

–the evaluation process you will use

–how the funding of this program/project will change existing conditions and benefit the constituency it serves

Please Note: The Foundation will require a commitment from the applying organization to provide an "update" on its grant on or before the anniversary date of the grant.

• A list of Board of Directors. Agencies we fund must have representatives of the community they serve on the Board of Directors (please note who meets this qualification).

• Board approved budgets:
    –Organization Operational Budget for all operations
    –Program/Project Budget for the project in question for the fiscal year, and the percentage of project budget that is being requested in this proposal

• List of grants from other Foundations or Corporations and specifying the dollar amounts committed, pending, or requested for this project

• Year-to-date Financial Statement for the current fiscal year

• Independent Audit Report (if required by law) or an Accounts Review

Recent Grants Of The Fuller Foundation, Inc.

Partial List of Organizations Funded

New Hampshire Theater Project
Sexual Assault Support Services
Women's Educational & Industrial
    Union
World Music
The Portsmouth Music Hall
Boston Public Schools Special
    Technology Resource Center
Family Services of Greater Boston
Pinewood Acres
Voices of Love & Freedom
Big Sister Assoc. of Greater Boston
Morgan Memorial - Goodwill Industries
Hampton Academy Junior High School
City Year
Thompson Island Outward Bound
    Educational Center

Rockingham Community Action
Community Education Center
Seacoast Big Brother & Big Sister
Daniel Webster Council, Inc.,
    Boy Scouts of America
Boston Freedom Summer
Bell Foundation
Cambridge YWCA
STRIVE
Hampton Pre-Court Diversion Program
Freedom from Chemical Dependence
The Center for Wildlife
New Hampshire SPCA
The Great Bear Foundation

If the foundation requests a full proposal as a result of your initial inquiry, persist in trying to arrange a meeting. Will that come to pass? Will you be able to arrange a meeting with the executive director or a program officer of the foundation? The answer will depend on the volume of requests for such meetings the foundation staff receives. But if you are fortunate enough to have the opportunity to meet a foundation representative in person, be sure to bring along one of your board officers, as well as your project or executive director to present your case. During that meeting, listen carefully to any concerns or questions the foundation representative may raise, and be sure to address them fully in your proposal or in a follow-up letter.

A proposal is akin to a passport to another country. It is the document required to get past the door of a foundation to receive a hearing. But submitting a proposal does not automatically lead to a meeting with the foundation representative, or to money in hand. For guidelines on proposal preparation, review the Proposal Design Chart and the Major Components of a Proposal, both below. Also below are the cover letter and title page of a sample proposal included in *The Foundation Center's Guide to Proposal Writing.*

In the heat of writing letters of inquiry and proposals, be sure to keep in mind one important, simple truth: foundations fund people, not paper. The ability to state your ideas clearly and succinctly is vitally important, but a wise program officer knows that words alone are insufficient; good, talented people are needed to transform ideas into successful projects. Bear this in mind as you allocate your time to the various phases of grantsmanship.

The following chart provides only one example in each proposal category. There might, in fact, be several procedures or evaluation strategies for this same objective. A complete chart, including all major items in a proposal, could be several pages long.

Proposal Design Chart

Need	Goal	Objective	Procedure	Evaluation
To provide alternative learning opportunities for students who do not benefit from the regular mathematics program.	To assist selected high school students acquire independent study skills in mathematics	Forty students selected from the tenth grade will be able to demonstrate newly acquired independent study skills by successfully completing a test on a major segment of the mathematics curriculum every two months. Success will be determined by the students achieving a score of 80 percent or more. The test will be devised by an independent consultant.	A mathematics teacher will provide one hour of orientation instruction each week, pointing out the major areas of information to be covered. Supplementary reading material will be distributed following each session. Students will also be given a set of self-tests for each curriculum component. A tutor will be available during the week to answer questions.	A mathematics teacher will administer the test every two months, grade the exams, and report the results to the project director. The director and an independent study consultant will meet with each student to discuss his or her test results and assist in designing additional independent study to remedy any deficiencies.

Source: Reprinted, by permission of the publisher, from Mary Hall, *Developing Skills in Proposal Writing* (Portland, OR: Continuing Education Publications, 1977).

The Major Components of a Proposal

Topic	Information to be provided
Title Page	Title of project, name of applicant and organization, name of agency submitted to, inclusive dates of project, total budget request, signatures of authorized personnel approving submission from the local agency.
Abstract	(or Executive Summary) Summary of the proposal with at least some reference to the major points in the statement of need, objectives, procedures, evaluation, and dissemination components. Should stress the end products. Usually 250 to 500 words.
Problem Statement (or Statement of Need)	Problem Statement: Clear and precise statement of the problem or opportunity to be addressed, and its solution. Should establish *significance, relevance, timeliness, generalizability*, and *contribution* of the project. *Innovativeness* of proposed methodology may also be substantiated. Usually includes references to previous research or earlier works. Statistical data describing the need is also cited. In research proposals, this component may have a separate section labeled "related research," which includes more lengthy discussion of previous studies.
Objectives	A very specific description of the proposed outcomes of the project stated as objectives, hypotheses, and/or questions, May also state overall goals of project. Should flow logically from the identified needs/problems.
Procedures	How the objectives will be met or the hypothesis/questions tested. In nonresearch projects, this section usually starts with a description of the overall approach and then goes into further details about the methodology, participants, organization, and timeliness. In a research project, one usually describes design, population and sample, data and instrumentation, analysis, and time schedule. This section should end with a clear identification of both the short-term and long-term end products expected.
Evaluation*	Details the means by which the local agency and the funding source will know the project has accomplished its purposes. States purpose of evaluation, type of information to be collected, details on instruments, data collection, analysis, and utilization and tells how results will be reported. Evaluation criteria should be provided for each objective.
Dissemination*	How will products and findings be shared with others? Frequently, this section will detail the reports that the foundation requires from the grantee.
Personnel	Who are the personnel that will work on the project and what will they do? What are their backgrounds and credentials? If new staff are needed, how many and of what type? How will they be selected? In a research proposal, this section may also include a description of the project's administrative organization. Individuals to serve as consultants should also be identified, their backgrounds described, and use justified.
Budget	Cost of the project. Usually divided into categories such as personnel, supplies and materials, travel, data processing, facilities or equipment, and indirect costs.

*These categories may or may not be included in research proposals; if required, they can be discussed as elements of the "procedures" component.

January 1, 1997

Andrea L. Correll
Executive Director
Good Works Foundation
Philanthropic Avenue
New York, NY   10000

Dear Ms. Correll:

I am pleased to contact you to introduce the Good Works Foundation to Mind-Builders' work with young women and their families from the Northeast Bronx and to request support for our **Family Services Center.**

   Mind-Builders Family Services Center provides intensive counseling and support services, accessible 24 hours a day, to women at risk of having their children removed from the home and placed in foster care. Family Services Center counselors and assistants work with young mothers to help them learn to overcome problems such as spousal abuse and alcohol and/or drug addiction that threaten to break up their families. The caseloads are kept small (40 girls and women a year) enabling the Family Services Center to provide an effective and cost efficient alternative to foster care services.

   Our project budget for this year is $358,281. To date, we have secured a $300,000 lead grant from the Child Welfare Administration and have received one generous commitment of $25,000 for this project from the Alternative Trust. To meet our budget, we must raise $33,281 from the private sector. Mind-Builders has approached a number of foundations to provide this support. A list of requests pending review with amounts requested is included in the appendix to our proposal.

   We request a grant of $10,000 from the Good Works Foundation to enable the Family Services Center to help girls and young women rebuild their families and their lives. Enclosed please find a proposal describing our program in detail. Please feel free to call me if you have any questions or if you would like to arrange to visit the Family Services Center.

Sincerely,

Camille Giraud Akeju
Executive Director

MIND-BUILDERS FAMILY SERVICES CENTER

Empowering Young Mothers to Maintain Strong Families

A Request for Funding Submitted to the
Good Works Foundation

by

Camille Giraud Akeju
Executive Director

Mind-Builders Family Services Center
3415 Olinville Avenue
Bronx, New York 10467-5612
(719) 652-6256

Profile:

First Place Fund for Youth: Berkeley, California

How does a brand new organization known to only a handful of people begin to get foundation funding? This is the dilemma that faced First Place Fund for Youth in Berkeley, California. Founded by Amy Lemley and Deanne Owens, First Place Fund for Youth provides loans and other kinds of support to emancipated foster youth. The issue they are addressing is one unfamiliar to almost anyone outside the foster care system. When a foster child turns 18, the state emancipates him or her. This means the state recognizes that this child is now an adult, and as such, expects this adult to become self-supporting. The foster family no longer receives any financial support for taking care of this person, and, in most cases, the former foster youth is on his or her own to find work, to find housing, to go to college.

Amy and Deanne had studied the situation of foster youth as part of a master's degree class and were appalled to learn that many foster youths go from foster care directly to the streets and become homeless youth, or worse, are arrested and go to jail.

The problems emancipated foster youth face are the same faced by the poverty-stricken. How will they get enough money together to make a deposit on a rental unit? Where do they get the money to buy nice clothes to go on an interview? Where do they turn for counseling in deciding whether to go to college or vocational school, take this job or that job, and so on? Amy and Deanne realized that much of what they had taken for granted from their biological families was not so for thousands of these young people, many of whom have more serious problems, such as substance abuse, or emotional scars left from childhood that make maintaining friendships or keeping a job difficult. Amy and Deanne believed, and intended to prove, that with financial and personal support, these young adults could become productive members of society. They simply needed a chance and a helping hand.

In response, Amy and Deanne started a micro-lending program, with a counseling component built in. First Place Fund for Youth makes loans for rent deposits, first year tuition payments, and other types of "front money" these young adults need to get started. Their counseling component provides much of the same information and support as would be present in a functional biological family.

As First Place Fund for Youth grows, Amy and Deanne plan for it to become self-supporting through gifts from young people who have been helped, from foster parents, and from those in the foster care system who see the need for what they are doing, as well as some government support. With friends, they have organized houseparties and small mailings to raise some money, but as a new group they face some of the problems that the young people they want to help also face.

They also researched a number of foundations that funded youth programs, or whose guidelines stated their interest in young people. Amy and Deanne developed and submitted excellent proposals, received a number of rejection letters, and quickly realized that a good idea and a well-written proposal weren't enough.

As part of their masters program, they had taken a course in fundraising and marketing, and they knew that the most successful fundraising method is face-to-face soliciting. They approached one of the teachers of that course for help and she suggested that they speak to several people who might be able to open some doors for them. One person was Boona Cheema, the Director of Building Opportunities for Self-Sufficiency (BOSS), a multi-million dollar 26-year-old program in Berkeley serving homeless and near homeless people. Boona agreed that BOSS would become their fiscal sponsor to give them an established institution to use in their foundation approaches, and would also provide free office space.

Because they were able to use their teacher's name in calling these people (who, in turn, let them use their names in calling others), Amy and Deanne were able to arrange meetings with some foundation staff. In these meetings, they were able to explain their vision and their plans. They are compelling and competent young women, and since some of the 'sell' of this program had to be convincing foundation staff that they were capable of running this program, personal meetings were imperative. They were then invited to submit proposals, which they did, and, as a result, received several grants; and with each grant, their legitimacy increased. As one foundation officer told them, "Once you get one grant, you will get more. Foundations look at each other to learn which are good programs to fund."

As of this writing, their largest grant was $30,000. This, along with a handful of $5,000 and $10,000 grants, money raised from family, friends, and an increasing, responsive mailing list, has enabled Amy and Deanne to pause in their fundraising and focus on program delivery. Without an excellent program, they will not continue to get funding, and without funding they will not be able to build their program.

They have realized that organizational development and fundraising is a circle, and are careful to monitor where they are on that circle on a regular basis. They have invited seven people to serve on their advisory board, and are pursuing their own nonprofit tax status. They have made their first loans, and have ongoing group and one-to-one counseling. Some of their board members are adults that were foster children and know first hand how difficult the transition can be, some are graduates of Amy and Deanne's program, and others are interested volunteers. They have been able to build a board of people who know that fundraising is part of their responsibility and this in turn, enabled them to answer the inevitable question from foundations, "How do you intend to support yourselves after our grant is spent?"

First Place Fund for Youth knows that they will probably receive grant funding for a few years, and then will need to have an individual donor program in place. By working on building their individual donor strategy and foundation and government funding fronts at the same time, they will not become overly dependent on any one source. By recognizing the role personal contacts can play in opening doors, they will not approach any foundation without an introduction or contact.

— Kim Klein, with thanks to Amy Lemley and Deanne Owens

The Yes

Let's assume that you have carefully targeted your foundation prospects, prepared your written materials conscientiously, and presented your organization skillfully in your face-to-face meeting with the foundation's representatives. Your hard work may well be rewarded with a grant! If so, be sure to express your appreciation promptly in a letter and make careful note of—and put on your calendar—any reporting requirements requested by the funder.

Then share your good fortune with any other foundations that are considering proposals from your organization. If your first funder has not fully underwritten the cost of your project, other prospective funders will be influenced by support from one of their peers. Thus, your first grant will help you to "leverage" other foundation support. Make sure to let your constituents know about your success, too.

The No

Foundations often reject proposals for reasons completely unrelated to a project's merits. They may have received more applications than they can respond to, or they may be overcommitted. If their reasons for declining to fund your proposal are not stated in their letter, write or call whoever has signed the rejection letter and politely ask for their reasons. Inquire whether there were any ways in which you could have strengthened your proposal or program design. Ask for advice and weigh any you receive carefully. If the reasons were directly related to your organization's efforts, you will want to assess whether the foundation will be receptive to a revised proposal, or whether your mission and the foundation's interests simply do not coincide at all. Be sure to review your own operations in light of their feedback.

Remember that securing foundation support is a process that may only begin with the first proposal you submit. Many nonprofits have found that ongoing research, targeted approaches, and persistence pay off. Cultivating and building relationships is just as important when fundraising from foundations as it is when soliciting individuals.

Pitfalls and Lessons

Now that it has a stake in your success and future, a foundation that has given you support will be interested in the progress you make toward the goals you've articulated in your proposal. Make sure you mail progress reports (both financial and program), press clippings, invitations to events (open houses, conferences, etc.), and newsletters; don't let the foundation hear from you only when you need funds again. Build the relationship. If a foundation is not in the position to renew its support immediately, you may find a new project in the years ahead that might again fall within its interest areas.

At the same time, beware of the danger that too much success in foundation fundraising can pose for an organization. Suppose your work was so appealing to foundations that numerous grants enabled you to hire new staff and considerably expand the scope of your organization's efforts. It does not necessarily follow that you can count on the same level of foundation funding in the years ahead.

Start to plan now for that probability and devote some of your resources to developing other sources of income so that you will be prepared. Use some of your hard-earned foundation goodwill to receive a grant that will broaden your fundraising efforts targeted at individuals, corporations, or government, for example.

Tips

- Research, research, research. Target, target, target. Be sure to research your prospects carefully, and target your requests appropriately.

- When you meet with a prospective foundation supporter, seize the opportunity to learn more about the foundation's priorities and procedures than is stated in its public materials.

Summary Worksheet

for _____

(name of your organization)

Approaching Foundations for Support

Building on Past Foundation Support

1. Have any foundations ever supported your work in the past?

    _____ yes   _____ no

    If yes, which ones?

    a. _____

    b. _____

    c. _____

    d. _____

2. What characteristics do these funders share? How do their interests correspond to each other?

    _____

    _____

    _____

    _____

3. What is your sense of what they valued in your organization's work?

    _____

    _____

    _____

    _____

4. Which ones can you approach again for future support?
    Definite Ongoing Prospects:

    _____

    _____

    _____

    _____

    Untested (further information needed):

    _____

    _____

    _____

    _____

Finding New Foundation Supporters: Research and Networking

1. Using the Foundation Center's *Foundation Directory*, *Foundation Directory Online*, *FC Search,* or other specialized guides, list the categories your work falls under:

_____   _____

_____   _____

_____   _____

_____   _____

2 List the names of some other organizations similar to yours in mission and in scope, in your own community and in other parts of the country. Which ones have been successful in securing foundation support? Place a check mark next to those that have.

a. _____

b. _____

c. _____

d. _____

3. Now, based on your own knowledge or on discussions with representatives of these groups, find out what you can about their funders. List and describe them below.

Name of foundation	Description (i.e., local, national, etc.)	Grant amount
a. _____	a. _____	a. _____
b. _____	b. _____	b. _____
c. _____	c. _____	c. _____
d. _____	d. _____	d. _____
e. _____	e. _____	e. _____
f. _____	f. _____	f. _____

For what purpose	To which organization
a. _____	a. _____
b. _____	b. _____
c. _____	c. _____
d. _____	d. _____
e. _____	e. _____
f. _____	f. _____

4. Below, list those foundation prospects that you have uncovered from your research and networking. Limit your listing to the ten most likely supporters of your organization, in other words, your ten "best bets."

a. Type of Foundation	b. Their Stated Areas of Interest that Relate to Your Work	c. Appropriate Contact: Person, Address, and Phone
Family Foundation		
Community Foundation		
Other Local Foundations		
Local Public Charities		
National Foundations		
International Foundations		

d. Any Personal Contacts	e. Your Program(s) that Correspond to Their Interests	f. Grants to Similar Organizations

Making the Match

For each prospect on the previous list, complete a worksheet like the following

Foundation name: _____

Its stated areas of interest that pertain to your work (Draw from their annual reports, reference books, newsclippings, etc.):

_____	_____
_____	_____
_____	_____
_____	_____

Write one or more short sentences demonstrating how the work of your organization reflects the interests of the foundation.

_____

_____

_____

_____

_____

_____

_____

_____

_____

Finding Assistance and Counsel

Name five or more individuals who might be able to advise you on how to most effectively approach the foundations on your best bets list (other organization directors, consultants, members of professional organizations, etc.).

a. _____

b. _____

c. _____

d. _____

e. _____

Assessing the Likelihood of Securing Foundation Support

On the basis of what you have learned, how would you rank your chances of securing support from foundations?

___ Very Good   ___ Possible   ___ Unlikely   ___ Still Unknown

Additional Resources

Publications

Briggs, Eli, and Gerard Holmes, comps. *1998 Grantmakers Directory*. 5th ed. San Diego: National Network of Grantmakers, 1998. vi, 219 p.

Reference tool and working document for members of the National Network of Grantmakers (NNG), an organization of progressive funders, as well as for their grantmaking programs and grantseekers. Fifth edition features 159 grantmaking institutions and 19 related organizations. Entries include contact information, mission, primary areas of interest, priority grants and limitations, application process, and financial data. A chart details specific issues funded for each entry. Also includes entries for affinity groups, regional associations of grantmakers, and related members. Indexed by name, grantmaking interests, target population, and geographic area.

Brisbois, Matthew W., and Pamela M. Kalte. *The Directory of Corporate and Foundation Givers, 2000*. 9th ed. Detroit: The Taft Group, 1999. 2 vols.

Descriptive profiles of approximately 8,000 philanthropic programs. Covers private foundations with assets of at least $1.8 million or $250,000 in grants paid. Also covers 1,575 corporate foundations, and 2,000 direct giving programs. Indexed by headquarters and operating locations, types of support, recipient type, products/industry, officers and directors, and grant recipients.

Cantarella, Gina-Marie, ed. *New York State Foundations: A Comprehensive Directory*. 6th ed. New York: The Foundation Center, 1999. xxxiv, 1252 p.

Lists 5,883 independent, company-sponsored, and community foundations that are currently active in New York State. Arranged alphabetically by New York counties (including the five boroughs of New York City). A separate section includes 1,260 out-of-state foundations with funding interests in New York. Each foundation entry includes address; telephone number; principal donor(s); financial data; fields of interest; types of support; limitations; publications; application information; names of officers, trustees, or directors; and a listing of selected grants, when available. Indexed by donors, officers, and trustees; geographic location; types of support; subjects; and foundation name. Introductory material includes tables showing aggregate fiscal data of New York foundations, the fifty largest New York foundations by assets and by total giving, and fiscal data of New York foundations by county. Published biannually.

Castelli, Susan. "Site Visits: The Make It or Break It Decision." *Grassroots Fundraising Journal* 16 (October 1997): 5–8.

Explains the purpose of site visits and why they are one of the most important steps in the grant application process. Provides suggestions to help nonprofit organizations and funders prepare for a site visit.

Council on Foundations. *Foundation News & Commentary*. Washington, DC: Council on
Foundations.

> A bimonthly magazine that focuses primarily on grantmakers, grantmaking activities and
> trends with some information on philanthropy in general. (Free to members; $48 per year
> for nonmembers. Order from: Council on Foundations, Inc., 1828 L Street, N.W.,
> Washington, DC 20036.)

Europa Publications. *The International Foundation Directory: 2000.* 9th ed. London: Europa
Publications, 2000. xiv 918 p.

> This edition includes information on more than 1,500 organizations in approximately 100
> countries. Arranged alphabetically by country, each entry notes the foundation's name in
> its native language followed by an English translation, year founded, and founding person
> or organization; activities, publications, and finances if available (assets and grantmaking
> expenditures in native country's currency); board of trustees; officers; address with e-mail;
> and telephone, telex, and fax numbers. Contains selected bibliography, alphabetical index,
> and index of main activities. Introduction has an overview of the evolution of foundations
> in Europe from the Middle Ages to the present.

Feczko, Margaret Mary, ed. *Foundations of the 1990s: A Directory of Newly Established
Foundations*. New York: The Foundation Center, 1998. xl, 1345 p.

> A comprehensive listing of foundations created in the United States after 1989. Organized
> by state, the book provides descriptive entries for 9,158 foundations that together held
> assets of $16.8 billion. Tables analyzing assets and total giving are presented in the
> introductory statistical material. Indexed by donors, officers, and trustees; geographic
> location and preference; international giving by country; types of support; subjects; and
> foundation name.

Garonzik, Elan, and Susan Wood, eds. *European Foundation Centre Profiles: One Hundred
and Twelve Profiles of Foundations and Corporate Funders Active in Europe or
Intercontinentally*. Brussels: European Foundation Centre, 1995.

Geever, Jane C. *The Foundation Center's Guide to Proposal Writing*, 3rd ed. New York: The
Foundation Center, 2001. xviii, 200 p.

> Guides the reader from pre-proposal planning to post-grant follow-up. Incorporates
> excerpts from actual grant proposals and interviews with foundation and corporate
> grantmakers about what they look for in a proposal. Includes chapters on researching,
> contacting, and cultivating potential funders, as well as a sample proposal and a selected
> bibliography on proposal development.

Golden, Susan L. *Secrets of Successful Grantsmanship: A Guerrilla Guide to Raising Money*.
San Francisco: Jossey-Bass Publishers, 1997. xx, 165 p.

> Provides a step-by-step method for navigating the grantmaking process. Offers strategies
> for conducting effective prospect research; making initial conversations with grantmakers;

and preparing, submitting, and following up on grant proposals. Includes bibliographic
references and index.

Government Information Services. *Winning Strategies for Developing Grant Proposals.*
Washington, DC: Government Information Services, 1999. iv, 96 p.
>   Presents general guidelines for writing proposals, and specific instructions for creating
>   proposals for private sector sources and federal agencies. Actual successful proposals are
>   given for each type.

Hale, Phale D., Jr. *Writing Grant Proposals That Win.* 2nd ed. Alexandria, VA: Capitol
Publications, 1997. 213 p.
>   Covers the major elements in any proposal: needs statement, objectives, activities,
>   personnel description, evaluation plan, and budget. Also discusses the difference between
>   applying to federal and private sector funders, writing for the reviewer, and dealing with
>   the politics of grantseeking. Appendices include list of federal and private funder Web
>   sites, resource list, sample federal application forms, and a list of contacts in state
>   governments.

Holcombe, Randall G. *Writing Off Ideas: Taxation, Foundations, and Philanthropy in
America.* New Brunswick, NJ: Transaction Publishers, 2000. x, 284 p.
>   The author posits that unlike the government and business sectors, foundations are
>   accountable to no one. He notes that in recent times, foundations have funded analysis of
>   public policy issues and ideas, rather than maintain the grantmaking modes of the earlier
>   part of the twentieth century. Chapters are devoted to the history of foundations, the impact
>   of various federal tax regulations over time, donor intent, trends in foundation giving, and
>   the role of foundations in the economy, among other issues, concentrating on "how tax
>   laws affect the ideas that are financed by nonprofit foundations." Other potential means of
>   fostering greater accountability are discussed in the conclusion. With bibliographic
>   references and an index.

Jacobs, David, ed. *The Foundation Directory: 2001 Edition.* 23rd ed. New York: The
Foundation Center, 2001. xliv, 2500+ p.
>   This annual publication provides information on the finances, governance, and giving
>   interests of the nation's largest grantmaking foundations. Contains entries for 10,000
>   private and community foundations. Arranged alphabetically by state, entries provide
>   foundation name, address, and telephone number (when supplied by the foundation);
>   foundation type; financial data (assets, total number and amount of grants paid, and high
>   and low grant amounts); fields of interest; types of support; limitations; application
>   information; names and titles of officers, principal administrators, and trustees or directors;
>   Employer Identification Number; and selected grants, when available. Appendices list
>   foundations from the previous edition which no longer qualify for inclusion, as well as
>   private operating and non-operating foundations excluded from the *Directory*. Indexed by

donors, officers, and trustees; geographic location; international giving; types of support; subject; foundations new to this edition; and foundation name.

Jacobs, David, and Melissa Lunn, eds. *Guide to U.S. Foundations, Their Trustees, Officers and Donors.* 2001 ed. New York: The Foundation Center, 2001. 2 vols.

    This annual publication provides a comprehensive listing of currently active grantmaking foundations in the United States. The Guide contains over 50,000 entries arranged alphabetically by state, and within each state in descending order by total grants paid. Entries may include foundation name, address, telephone number; application address and contact person; e-mail and Internet address; establishment date; donor; latest complete financial information; geographic limitations; publications; officers, trustees, and/or directors; and codes which indicate the other Foundation Center publications in which an entry also appears. Volume two also contains three indexes: a comprehensive name index of all the trustees, officers, and donors affiliated with the foundations; an alphabetical listing of the foundations with their state location and the codes indicating which other Foundation Center publications contain additional information; and an index and locator for community foundations.

Jankowski, Katherine E., ed. *America's New Foundations.* 13th ed. Detroit: The Taft Group, 1998. xxi, 1628 p.

    Profiles approximately 3,000 private, corporate, and community foundations created since 1988. A full profile contains the foundation's address, telephone number, establishment year, type, contact person, and employer identification number (EIN). An analysis of charitable giving follows, including principal charitable interests, typical recipients, and grant types. Gives application procedures when available; presents fiscal data; and ends with a list of up to ten recent grants made by the foundation. Indexed by headquarters, state, grant type, recipient type, officers and directors, and recipients by location.

Johnson, Pattie J., and Margaret Morth, eds. *Foundation Fundamentals: A Guide for Grantseekers.* 6th ed. New York: The Foundation Center, 1999. xv, 259 p.

    A primer designed to clarify the grantseeking process and to help grantseekers utilize information resources in locating appropriate funders. The first three chapters provide a context for understanding foundation giving, and the remaining chapters and appendices introduce the grantseeker to the resources of the Foundation Center, and outline a number of research strategies designed to help grantseekers develop a list of potential funders. Accompanied by illustrations and worksheets throughout. With bibliographic references, list of state charities registration offices, the Foundation Center's grants classification system, and glossary of type of support terms.

Jones, Francine, Michelle Kragalott, and Georgetta Toth, eds. *The Foundation 1000: In-Depth Profiles of the 1000 Largest U.S. Foundations.* 2000-2001 ed. New York: Foundation Center, 2000. xxxiv, 3070 p.

> The 2000-2001 annual edition includes information on the following: foundation name, address and Internet address if available, telephone and fax numbers, and contact person; purpose; limitations of giving program; specific programs and areas of interest; financial data consisting of fiscal year, assets, contributions received, amount of grants paid, grants made to individuals, employee matching gifts, loans to individuals; grants authorized and outstanding future payments; officers, board members, and principal staff; size of staff; sponsoring company; historical information; types of funds; policy and application guidelines; publications; subject area; recipient type; type of support for grants of $10,000 or more; population group for grants of $10,000 or more; geographic distribution for grants of $10,000 or more; and sample grants. Indexed by donors, officers, and trustees; subjects; types of support; geographic location; and international giving.

Kaplan, Ann E., ed. *Giving USA: The Annual Report on Philanthropy for the Year 1999.* 45th ed. New York: American Association of Fund Raising Counsel Trust for Philanthropy, 2000. 171 p.

> An annual statistical analysis of charitable giving contributions, distribution, donors, recipients, sources of philanthropy, and areas of philanthropic opportunity; this edition covers 1999. Sources analyzed include individuals, bequests, foundations, and corporations. Areas of philanthropic opportunity that are compared for the period of 1969-1999 are religion; education; health; human services; arts, culture, and humanities; public/society benefit; environment/wildlife; and international affairs. A separate section reviews giving worldwide. Contains numerous charts, lists, and statistical tables. Of particular note are the listings of gifts of five million dollars or more by individuals. Among the statistical tables are total giving, uses of contributions, the growth of contributions, and inflation-adjusted giving. Includes a resource guide and a table of the National Taxonomy of Exempt Entities.

Kiger, Joseph C. *Philanthropic Foundations in the Twentieth Century.* Westport, CT: Greenwood Press, 2000. viii, 222 p.

> A comprehensive treatment of the growth of foundations in modern times. Provides a narrative of the worldwide historical antecedents to the growth of modern foundations. Details the numerous investigations of the field, including the Walsh Commission in 1915, the Cox Committee in 1952, the Patman Investigation that began in 1961, and the Filer Commission, whose results were published in 1977. Discusses the expansion of the field, the characteristics of governance and personnel, supervision by governmental bodies, international activities, and the development of the third sector abroad. With bibliography and index.

Kiritz, Norton J. "Hard Data/Soft Data: How They Help You Build Strong Proposals."
Grantsmanship Center Magazine (Winter 1997): 4–5, 7, 9–10.
  Explains how to use "hard data" (statistical information) and "soft data" (anecdotal
  evidence) to give substance to a proposal.

Kosztolanyi, Istvan. *Proposal Writing.* English ed. Baltimore: Johns Hopkins University
Institute for Policy Studies, 1997. 28 p.
  Outlines the standard elements of a grantseeking proposal, and includes a handy checklist.
  Pamphlet specifically developed for nonprofit managers in Central and Eastern Europe.
  This title is also available in Bulgarian, Czech, Hungarian, Polish, Russian, Slovak, and
  Slovenian languages.

Lagemann, Ellen Condliffe, ed. *Philanthropic Foundations: New Scholarship, New
Possibilities.* Bloomington, IN: Indiana University Press, 1999. xviii, 420 p.
  Chapters contributed by various specialists. Part I: Foundations as Organizations.
  "Resolving the Dilemmas of Democratic Governance: The Historical Development of
  Trusteeship in America, 1636–1996" by Peter Dobkin Hall; "Foundations in the American
  Polity, 1900–1950" by David C. Hammack; "Private Foundations as Public Institutions:
  Regulations, Professionalization, and the Redefinition of Organized Philanthropy" by Peter
  Frumkin. Part II: Case Studies in Early-Twentieth-Century Foundation Philanthropy.
  "Constructing a New Political Economy: Philanthropy, Institution-Building, and Consumer
  Capitalism in the Early Twentieth Century" by Meg Jacobs; "Selling the Public on Public
  Health: The Commonwealth and Milbank Health Demonstrations and the Meaning of
  Community Health Education" by Elizabeth Toon; "Constructing the Normal Child: The
  Rockefeller Philanthropies and the Science of Child Development, 1918–1940" by Julia
  Grant; "Mary van Kleeck of the Russell Sage Foundation: Religion, Social Science, and
  the Ironies of Parasitic Modernity" by Guy Alchon. Part III: Foundations and Recent
  Social Movements. "The Ford Foundation and Philanthropic Activism in the 1960s" by
  Alice O'Connor; "The Ford Foundation's War on Poverty: Private Philanthropy and Race
  Relations in New York City, 1948–1968" by Gregory K. Raynor; "Grassrooting the
  System? The Development and Impact of Social Movement Philanthropy, 1953-1990" by
  J. Craig Jenkins and Abigail L. Halcli; "When Grantees Become Grantors: Accountability,
  Democracy, and Social Movement Philanthropy" by Susan A. Ostrander; "The Ford
  Foundation and Women's Studies in American Higher Education: Seeds of Change?" by
  Rosa Proietto. Part IV: Writing the History of Foundations. "Going for Broke: The
  Historian's Commitment to Philanthropy" by Barry Dean Karl; "In Search of the Ford
  Foundation" by Richard Magat; "The History of Philanthropy as Life-History: A
  Biographer's View of Mrs. Russell Sage" by Ruth Crocker; "Local Philanthropy Matters:
  Pressing Issues for Research and Practice" by William S. McKersie; and "The Future of
  Foundation History: Suggestions for Research and Practice" by Lucy Bernholz. Includes
  bibliography and index.

Lawrence, Steven. *Family Foundations: A Profile of Funders and Trends.* New York: The
Foundation Center, 2000. xiii, 55 p.

> Published in collaboration with the National Center for Family Philanthropy, the report
> provides a comprehensive measurement of the size and scope of the U.S. family
> foundation community. Through use of objective and subjective criteria, the report
> identifies the number of family foundations and their distribution by region and state, size,
> geographic focus, and decade of establishment; and includes analyses of staffing and
> public reporting by these funders. Also examines trends in giving by a sample of larger
> family foundations between 1993 and 1998 and compares these patterns with independent
> foundations overall. An appendix presents a discussion of the issues now affecting family
> foundations.

Lawrence, Steven, Carlos Camposeco, and John Kendzior. *Foundation Giving Trends:
Update on Funding Priorities.* New York: The Foundation Center (Foundations Today
series), 2000. xi, 84 p.

> The successor to "Foundation Giving," this is volume one of "Foundations Today," a
> five-part annual publication on the current state of foundations and their giving. This report
> presents a picture of how 1,000 of the top U.S. foundations distributed their grant dollars in
> 1998. Within broad major fields of education, health, human services, arts and culture,
> public/society benefit, environment and animals, science, international affairs, and social
> science, funding trends from 1980 through 1998 are given. Analyses of giving for various
> types of support and for special populations are made, and trends for independent,
> corporate and community foundations are discussed. A special analysis of family
> foundations is given. Accompanied by numerous charts and graphs.

Lawrence, Steven, Carlos Camposeco, and John Kendzior. *Foundation Yearbook: Facts and
Figures on Private and Community Foundations.* 2000 ed. New York: The Foundation Center
(Foundations Today series), 2000. xi, 98 p.

> Documents the growth in number, giving, and assets of all active U.S. foundations from
> 1975 through 1998. Provides comparisons of foundation activities by foundation size;
> breakdowns of foundation resources by geographic location and grantmaker type; and a
> brief history of foundation development since the early 1900s. Data about the largest 50
> independent, 50 corporate, 25 community, and 10 operating foundations is presented in
> charts.

League, V.C. *The Proposal Writer's Workshop: A Guide To Help You Write Winning
Proposals.* Sacramento: Curry-Co Publications, 1998. xvii, 202 p.

Lunn, Melissa, ed. *The Foundation Directory Part Two.* 2001 ed. New York: The Foundation
Center, 2001. xxxviii, 1,900+ p.

> This annual publication provides information on 10,000 mid-sized foundations. Arranged
> alphabetically by state, entries provide foundation name, address, and telephone number
> (when supplied by the foundation); foundation type; financial data (assets, total number

and amount of grants paid, and high and low grant amounts); fields of interest; types of support; limitations; application information; names and titles of officers, principal administrators, and trustees or directors; Employer Identification Number; and selected grants. Introductory material contains tables showing aggregate fiscal data by foundation type, and by region and state. Includes rankings of the 100 largest mid-sized foundations by assets and by total giving. Indexed by foundation name; geographic location; types of support; subject; and donors, officers, and trustees.

MacLean, Rebecca, and Denise McLeod, eds. *The Foundation Grants Index 2001: A Cumulative Listing of Foundation Grants Reported in 1999*. New York: The Foundation Center, 2000. 3,000 p.

This annual publication provides access to the actual grants of major foundations by subject area, geographic focus, types of support, and the types of organizations that receive the grants. Covers more than 100,000 grants of $10,000 or more awarded by almost 1,000 foundations. The grants are arranged by 28 major subject fields; within each major subject field foundations with qualifying grants are arranged alphabetically by state. Grants are indexed by recipient name, subject, type of support/geographic location, recipient categories, and name of foundation.

Miner, Lynn E., Jeremy T. Miner, and Jerry Griffith. *Proposal Planning and Writing*. 2nd ed. Phoenix, AZ: Oryx Press, 1998. vii, 174 p.

Covers the proposal development process for federal government, private foundation, and corporate funding sources. Answers twenty-five basic questions frequently asked by both inexperienced and experienced grantseekers. Presents many examples taken from successful proposals. Also gives suggestions on using computers to simplify the grant development process. Includes a bibliography and an appendix of publishers and vendors. Indexed.

Morth, Margaret, and Sarah Collins, eds. *The Foundation Center's User-Friendly Guide: A Grantseeker's Guide to Resources*. 4th ed. New York: The Foundation Center, 1996. 42 p.

Primer introduces novice grantseekers to funding resources and the fundamentals of identifying appropriate funders. Answers grantseekers' ten most commonly asked questions: how to begin the search process; how to secure tax exemption; how to find out about grants for a specific subject or field of interest; how to discover more about grantmakers in a specific city, state, or region; where to find further information on foundations; what types of organizations grantmakers fund and the types of grants available; the types of information grantmakers provide about themselves; grants for individuals; proposal development; and what information is available electronically. Includes annotated bibliographies, hints for using Foundation Center publications, and a glossary.

New, Cheryl Carter, and James Aaron Quick. *Grantseeker's Toolkit: A Comprehensive Guide to Finding Funding.* New York: John Wiley & Sons, 1998. xvii, 248 p.
  A thorough grantseeking handbook, with the stated goal of helping readers achieve competitive applications. Begins with the design of a project to solve a problem, then focuses on the research process for locating potential funders interested in the project. Covers funding research sources in federal, state, and local government, foundations, and corporations. Provides details on crafting a winning proposal, with examples. Includes numerous worksheets. Accompanying computer disk provides exercises and templates.

Orlich, Donald C. *Designing Successful Grant Proposals.* Alexandria, VA: Association for Supervision and Curriculum Development, 1996. 134 p.
  Presents the standard elements of grant writing, with checklists at the end of each section. Includes a copy of a funded proposal, and a reading list.

Orosz, Joel J. *The Insider's Guide to Grantmaking: How Foundations Find, Fund, and Manage Effective Programs.* San Francisco: Jossey-Bass Publishers, 2000. xvi, 303 p.
  Written primarily for program officers of foundations, the author provides a brief history on foundations, their structure, and their role in society. In the following chapters, he details the program officer's responsibilities from building relationships with applicants, reviewing, accepting, and declining proposals, and making site visits to writing and presenting the funding document, managing projects and leveraging their impact. The author shares real-world advice on a variety of issues confronting program officers, including how not to raise a grantseeker's expectations, what to do during a site visit, and the ethics of grantmaking. Includes bibliographic references and index.

Renz, Loren. "International Grantmaking by U.S. Foundations: Issues and Directions in the 1990s." *Nonprofit and Voluntary Sector Quarterly* 27 (December 1998): 507–521.
  Summarizes findings from *International Grantmaking: A Report on U.S. Foundation Trends*, published by the Foundation Center in 1997.

Robinson, Andy. *Grassroots Grants: An Activist's Guide to Proposal Writing.* Inverness, CA: Chardon Press, 1996. xi, 194 p.
  Foundations are a significant source of potential funding for grassroots activists and should not be ignored. Provides tep-by-step guidance on how to achieve success.

Romaniuk, Bohdan R., and LySandra C. Hill, eds. *America's New Foundations, 2000.* 14th ed. Farmington Hills, MI: The Taft Group, 1999. xxii, 1364 p.
  Profiles approximately 3,000 private, corporate, and community foundations created since 1989. A full profile contains the foundation's address, telephone number, establishment year, type, contact person, and Employer Identification Number. An analysis of charitable giving follows, including principal charitable interests, typical recipients, and grant types. Gives application procedures when available; presents fiscal data; and ends with a list of

up to ten recent grants made by the foundation. Indexed by headquarters state, grant type, recipient type, officers and directors, and recipients by location.

Romaniuk, Bohdan R., ed. *Foundation Reporter 2001.* 32nd ed. Detroit: The Taft Group, 2000. xiv, 1769 p.

Profiles more than 1,000 of the largest private foundations. Each foundation either has $10 million in assets or has made grants equaling $500,000. Entries are arranged alphabetically by foundation name and contain foundation contact, fiscal status, contributions summary, donor information, foundation philosophy, contributions analysis, typical recipients list, officers and directors (including—whenever available—place and date of birth, alma mater, current employment, and corporate and philanthropic affiliations), application and review procedures, grants analysis, and a listing of up to fifty recent grants. Indexes to entries arranged by state; location of grant recipient; grant and recipient type; donor; and name, place of birth, alma mater, corporate affiliation, club affiliation, and nonprofit affiliation of officers and directors.

Trombley, Nicole, ed. and comp. *Grantmakers Directory 2000-2001: A Resource for Social Change Funders & Grantseekers.* 6th ed. San Diego: National Network of Grantmakers, 2000. vii, 336 p.

Serves as a reference tool and working document for members of the National Network of Grantmakers (NNG), an organization of progressive funders, as well as for their grantmaking programs and grantseekers. This edition features more than 190 grantmaking institutions and related organizations. Entries include contact information, mission, primary areas of interest, priority grants and limitations, application process, and financial data. A chart details specific issues funded for each entry. Also includes entries for affinity groups, regional associations of grantmakers, and related members. Indexed by name, grantmaking interests, target population, and geographic area.

Zils, Michael, ed. *World Guide to Foundations.* 1st ed. Munich, Germany: K. G. Saur, 1998. xiv, 559 p.

Presents brief entries on 21,750 foundations in 112 countries. Work is organized alphabetically within countries. Entries contain, when available, foundation name, address, telephone and fax numbers, email address, year of establishment, chairman, manager, assets, annual income and expenses, and areas of focus. Indexed by foundation name and subject.

Internet Resources

Community Foundations by State (www.tgci.com/resources/foundations/community/)

Identifies community foundations—nonprofit, tax-exempt, publicly supported grantmaking organizations—by state. Web site is maintained by the Grantsmanship Center.

Council on Foundations (www.cof.org/)
   A nonprofit membership organization of grantmaking foundations and corporations, the
   Council on Foundations has helped foundation staff, trustees, and board members in their
   day-to-day grantmaking activities. Through one-to-one technical assistance, research,
   publications, conferences and workshops, legal services, and a wide array of other
   services, the Council addresses the important issues and challenges that face foundations
   and corporate funders. Council members include more than 1,800 grantmaking
   organizations, including community foundations, corporate foundations and giving
   programs, private operating foundations, private independent foundations, public
   foundations, and international programs.

Daily Diffs: Philanthropy and Foundations folder in Finance and Investment file
(www.dailydiffs.com/dop000rm.htm)
   "Fresh news from philanthropic, charitable, and non-profit organizations and public and
   private foundations, for donors and board members."

The Foundation Center (www.fdncenter.org)
   The Foundation Center is a nonprofit organization devoted to serving the information
   needs of grantmakers and grantseekers. The Center provides an extensive list of books,
   CD-ROMs, and searchable on-line databases, and provides libraries and training sessions
   related to the nonprofit sector. The Web site—described accurately as "your gateway to
   philanthropy on the World Wide Web"—includes searchable database applications, a
   bibliographic database of titles concerning the nonprofit world, extensive lists of links to
   foundations and other grantmakers, common grant application forms, a Reference Desk
   with an FAQ page organized by topic, a long list of annotated links for finding on-line sites
   related to nonprofits, and an on-line reference librarian who takes questions by e-mail. The
   site also offers such on-line educational materials as a "Proposal Writing Short Course."
   The site also includes *Philanthropy News Digest*, which you can receive as a free e-mail
   newsletter.

Foundation News & Commentary (www.cof.org/foundationnews/)
   The on-line version of *Foundation News & Commentary*, a bi-monthly magazine published
   by the Council on Foundations (see the Publications section, above).

Funders Online (www.fundersonline.org)
   Funders Online, an initiative of the European Foundation Centre, aims to promote the use
   of Internet technology among independent funders in Europe and to create a single point of
   reference to Europe's philanthropic community. The Funders Online Web site features the
   first Internet directory of Europe's independent funder Web sites. Through Funders Online,
   users can access the Web sites of more than three hundred foundations and corporate
   funders in Europe with a total annual expenditure of more than 3.5 billion euros.

Fundsnet Services: Nonprofit Center (www.fundsnetservices.com/nonproct.htm)
  Extensive directories in the areas of grantmaking foundations, corporate philanthropy,
  computer and technology, fundraising, international grantmaking, scholarships, and
  financial aid.

Grants and Grant Writing Resources (www.proposalwriter.com/grants.html)
  Comprehensive listings of personally selected resources on grants, grantwriting, and grants
  by topic area. Also, information and links to U.S. government grants by agency and topic
  area. Free proposal development checklist.

The Grantsmanship Center (http://www.tgci.com/)
  TGCI offers grantsmanship training and low-cost publications to nonprofit organizations
  and government agencies. TGCI conducts some 200 workshops annually in grantsmanship
  and proposal writing. More than 100 local agencies host these workshops.

North Valley Community Foundation: What Is a Community Foundation
(www.nvcf.org/aboutus_what.html)
  An introduction to community foundations.

Online Resources for Grant Seekers, Valdosta State University, Georgia
(www.valdosta.peachnet.edu/~mwatson/grants/resource)
  A list of online resources for grantseekers: resource guides, subject catalogs, magazines
  and other sources.

Polaris (www.polarisgrantscentral.net/)
  Directories, lists, hints and tips, resources, and articles for grantseekers.

Chapter 16

Corporations and Businesses

The Millenium Poll, conducted by Environics International in cooperation with The Prince of Wales Business Leaders Forum and The Conference Board, indicates that people rate social responsibility as the most important factor influencing public impressions of individual companies.

We are at a moment in history then where there is both the potential and the necessity to build a new 'social contract' among businesses, governments and civil society organizations.   —Christopher Pinney

From multinational corporations to the corner store, businesses are supporting nonprofit organizations more and more, either as an expression of social responsibility or as a business strategy to increase name recognition, productivity, and synergy—or both.

This shift is creating a significant change in thinking for both donor and recipient: for businesses, there's a heightened sense of opportunity, and for nonprofits, an increased focus on the fit between corporate goals and values and their own. Corporate support for civic endeavors is likewise becoming predicated on a balance between its own values and goals and those of recipient nonprofits. While many businesses continue their traditional support of nonprofits through gifts of cash, goods and services, and expertise, new approaches—such as strategic philanthropy, cause-related marketing, and social investing—are also taking hold. "Checkbook philanthropy won't cut it for corporations anymore," says Paul Ostergard, retired chairman and CEO of the Citigroup Foundation, and current president of the Committee to Encourage Corporate Philanthropy. "They can't just write checks to whoever walks in the door. Companies must be able to defend their giving with business value."[1] This new corporate mindset bodes well for nonprofits seeking business support.

Corporate Giving Then and Now

In North America, corporate giving took shape in the mid-nineteenth century when rapidly expanding railroads funded YMCA hostels to house their employees. During World War I, companies asked stockholders to authorize a special dividend to be given to the Red Cross for their international war relief efforts. Community Chests and, later, United Ways were organized on the same model as the Red Cross.

One of the model corporate giving programs was started in 1945–46 in Minneapolis, Minnesota by the Dayton-Hudson Corporation, which established a policy to give 5 percent of its gross profits to charity. Forty more Twin Cities corporations followed suit, and the first "5% Club" was created. Other cities have followed the Minneapolis model, with 5% Clubs, 2% Clubs, and other organized efforts to promote the concept of what was then known simply as "corporate philanthropy."

Giving USA, a publication of the American Association of Fund-Raising Counsel, reports that corporations and corporate foundations contributed an estimated $11.02 billion to U.S. nonprofits in 1999, 5.8 percent of the estimated total giving from all sources of $190.16 billion. This represents a 14.3 percent increase (11.8 percent adjusted for inflation) over 1998 corporate giving. These figures do not include support provided through marketing, public relations, and advertising services. The report points out that, "Corporate giving as a percentage of pre-tax income . . . climbed. In 1996 corporate giving represented 1.0 percent of corporate pre-tax income; by 1999, it had reached 1.3 percent."[2]

Two increasingly significant forms of corporate support are now being tracked: cause-related marketing and sponsorship. Cone, Inc., a consultancy in strategic cause-related marketing, reports that cause-related marketing "has increased by an estimated 504% since 1990, to an

---

1. Monica Langley, "Top CEO's Aim to Prod Corporate America into Giving Billions to Charity," *Wall Street Journal* (19 November 1999).
2. Ann E. Kaplan, ed., *Giving USA: The Annual Report on Philanthropy for the Year 1999* (New York: American Association of Fund-Raising Counsel, 2000).

estimated $630 million in 1999.[3] And IEG, Inc., a company that tracks and analyzes corporate sponsorship, forecast in 1998 that corporate sponsorship of sports, arts, event, and cause marketing would grow by 11.8 percent in 1999. They estimated that North American companies spent $6.8 billion in 1998, and would spend $7.6 billion in 1999.[4]

Why Do Corporations and Businesses Support Nonprofits?

As a preface to this section, let's paraphrase a point made in the chapter on face-to-face solicitation: If you know the prospect's capacity and motivation for giving, and if you remember that you are not only asking for something, you are also offering something—it is highly likely that your solicitation will be effective. In approaching corporations for support, it's equally important to know their reasons for giving so that you can tailor your solicitation in the same way you would for an individual.

Although tax advantages provide some measure of inducement, they are not the primary impetus for corporate giving. Helping communities in a manner that is consistent with overall corporate objectives is the key concept; the items on corporate giving's double agenda—altruism and self-interest—are complementary, not contrary. The work of such groups as The Conference Board, the Social Venture Network, and Businesses for Social Responsibility in the United States, Ethos in Brazil, and Philippine Business for Social Progress in Manila—as well as the strategic giving of well-known multinationals—repeatedly demonstrates the bottom line benefits of corporate philanthropy.

Here are some of the reasons corporations and businesses support nonprofit organizations:

- To fulfill their social responsibility and sense of obligation to be good "corporate citizens," and to "give back" to the employees, customers, and communities that make them successful.

- To increase visibility and enhance their reputation. These goals lie at the heart of business' cause-related and sponsorship investments.

- To increase sales and profitability. Surveys have shown that: (1) a customer faced with the choice of two products will buy the one manufactured by the company known to be charitable; and (2) that companies with a defined corporate commitment to ethical principles do better (based on annual sales/revenues) than companies that lack such a commitment.

- To accelerate growth. "Stakeholder-balanced" companies show four times the growth rate and eight times the employment growth of companies that are shareholder-only focused. "Stakeholders" are defined as all those affected by a company's behavior: its employees, suppliers, and customers as well as the citizens of the company town.[5]

---

3. Cone, Inc., *The 1999 Cone-Roper Cause-Related Trends Report: The Evolution of Cause Branding* (Boston: Cone, Inc., 1999).

4. IEG, Inc., *IEG Sponsorship Report* (Chicago: IEG Inc., 1998).

5. Ditchley Park Conference on the Future of Services Trade Liberalization, Ditchley Fork, Oxfordshire England, 26-28 April 1998.

- To achieve human resource management goals, such as employee recruitment, retention, productivity, morale, and loyalty. A survey of 150 Canadian CEOs identified positive impact on employees as "the most persuasive benefit of corporate community involvement."[6]

In an era when businesses increasingly blend community relations and strategic philanthropy, an absolute prerequisite for securing their support is knowing their reasons for giving. Whether soliciting cash donations, technical assistance, in-kind support, or some form of sponsorship, nonprofits and NGOs must apply this knowledge in creating relationships and partnerships that help both parties achieve their goals.

How Do Corporations and Businesses Extend Support?

While corporate philanthropy is most often expressed in the form of cash contributions—by placing an ad in a program book, say, or providing a grant for a specific program—these transactions represent only one dimension of corporate support. Corporations (as distinct from foundations) have vast resources to tap in assisting nonprofits; they might "loan" executives and volunteers, donate the use of their printing presses, or become involved in cause-related marketing and sponsorships. In fact, these types of support are growing at a faster pace than cash gifts, and they offer exciting new opportunities for nonprofits to enrich their funding mix.

Let's take a closer look at three forms of corporate and business support: cash donations, in-kind gifts of goods and services, and promotional arrangements.

Cash Gifts, Grants, and Contributions

Businesses provide financial support in various ways. First, they make direct grants and contributions to nonprofit organizations. In Germany, for example, the Dresden Bank partnered in rebuilding a famous church by providing donor certificates to individual givers. The church was able to raise $80 million in eight years. With backing from America Online and Time Warner's New Line Cinema, HEAVEN (Helping, Educate, Activate, Volunteer, and Empower via the Net), a national nonprofit "dedicated to using technology and new media to benefit society and bridge the digital divide," was able to create a job-training and internship program in new media for inner-city high school students.

Second, businesses provide substantial support through direct gifts and payroll deductions to the local United Way and other federated fundraising organizations, which in turn make annual allocations to various civic agencies.

Third, many businesses encourage their employees to make charitable contributions by offering to match their donations up to a certain amount. Some of these matches are extremely generous, with dollar-for-dollar being common; some go as high as three dollars for every dollar the employee gives. Generally the maximum amount corporations will match is around $1,000, but

---

6. Business Council on National Issues, reported by the Canadian Centre for Philanthropy (www.ccp.ca).

Giving Back to the Tiger

Several years ago, a shareholder stood up at a corporate meeting for Exxon, which long urged drivers to "put a tiger in their tank." The tiger had been so accommodating as a logo and sound bite, the shareholder said, that it's time to give something back to the tiger.

As a result, Exxon, with the United States Fish and Wildlife Service, began a Save the Tiger Fund in 1995 that will dispense $9 million over eight years to various tiger preservation programs, to which conservationists, ever strapped for cash, responded, "gr-r-eat!"[7]

---

7. "Improbably, the Tiger Survives," by Natalie Angier; *New York Times* (12 October 1999).

---

some match employees' contributions up to $6,000, and the contributions of management up to $12,000. Therefore, every nonprofit organization should collect information on where its donors, clients, and volunteers work and publish a list of corporations that make matching gifts so that donors can take advantage of this benefit.[8]

In-Kind Contributions

Material Support
The goods, products, and/or services that businesses market to the public are frequently donated to nonprofits. For instance, a computer company might donate computers or software, and a business that is relocating might contribute its old furniture. World Book, for example, provided more than two hundred Early World of Learning kits to Peace Corps volunteers in Saint Lucia, who distributed the supplies to disabled children. Each kit contained activity books, concept cards, story books with companion cassette tapes, and other materials to promote learning through creative play. To aid this project, UPS partnered with the Peace Corps Major Gifts Program to ship the materials to Saint Lucia.

When Nestlé Research and Development upgraded its computers, it donated ten of its old computers to the Peace Corps in Loitokitok, Kenya. The project allowed the community's residents to enhance their computer skills, which had become outdated due to lack of resources and opportunities, and to apply those skills directly in their own isolated community.

Many large corporations donate the use of their in-house printing facilities during down times, so that nonprofits can print stationery, posters, direct mail solicitations, and so on for free or at a greatly reduced cost.

---

8. A complete list of U.S. corporations that provide matching gifts, and the terms under which they do, can be obtained from the Council for the Advancement and Support of Education (CASE) in Washington, D.C., at 1-800-554-8536. CASE also publishes a leaflet on corporate matching programs called *Double Your Dollars*, which can be bought in bulk and sent out with a newsletter or mail appeal.

People Power

Businesses employ many talented, highly skilled people whose expertise in areas such as financial management, marketing, human resources, public relations, and planning relate directly to the needs of nonprofits.

For example, a small nonprofit in California was having problems with its bookkeeping. Several volunteer accountants had come and gone, and the executive director had not been able to keep on top of the group's finances and didn't know how to straighten out the problems. The group approached a local manufacturer and asked for a cash gift of $5,000 to complete an audit. As the manager learned more about their problem, he offered instead to loan the group one of the firm's accountants for three months. He guaranteed that the accountant would get them into good enough shape for an audit. The accountant set up systems, solved problems, helped the executive director understand what kind of supervision was necessary, and even participated in the hiring of a new bookkeeper. This in-kind gift was worth almost $12,000. When the group did have the audit done, the auditor commented on how professional the accounting setup was. The result was a positive audit of funds that helped the group make a successful application to the local United Way.

With many employees potentially waiting in the wings to offer their services to nonprofit organizations, the corporate world is a fertile and unlimited hunting ground for new board members and volunteers. In fact, many companies encourage their employees to become involved with nonprofits by establishing programs for corporate volunteers, loaned executives, retired executives, and senior consultants. In many U.S. cities, organizations such as Volunteer Consulting Group in New York, Business Volunteers United in Cleveland, Ohio, and National Executive Service Corps run board candidate recruitment services and provide professional management consulting, thus serving as a bridge between nonprofits and businesses. The International Executive Service Corps offers similar services around the world.

Physical Facilities

Corporations may donate the use of their conference rooms, auditoriums, and other meeting facilities to organizations for workshops, seminars, annual meetings, special events, and other public functions. On the U.S. Virgin Island of Saint Croix, for instance, the Buccaneer Hotel regularly makes its banquet facilities available free of charge to local civic groups.

Promotion and Publicity

Cause-Related Marketing

Using funds from their marketing budgets, corporations and businesses can promote a product or service by publicizing their partnership with a nonprofit; this strategy is called cause-related marketing. In this increasingly popular arrangement, a business secures a nonprofit's endorsement (through the use of its name and/or logo) for a fee or a percentage of sales, with the goal of enhancing its credibility. Cause-related marketing has been used by General Foods, Scott Paper Company, and many, many other large corporations. One well-known campaign was General Foods' marketing agreement with Mothers Against Drunk Driving to raise funds for MADD and

Influencing Consumer Choice With a Positive Image: The International Perspective

One of the specific functions in which the positive effects of superior corporate social performance can most easily be demonstrated is marketing, particularly cause-related marketing. In 1997, *The Cone-Roper Cause-Related Marketing Trends Report,* a national study of consumer attitudes and awareness toward cause-related marketing, found that 76 percent of U.S. consumers:

- believe it is acceptable for companies to engage in cause-related marketing (up from 66 percent in 1993);

- report they would be likely to switch to a brand associated with a good cause (also up from 66 percent in 1993); and

- said that when price and quality of merchandise are equal, they would be likely to switch to a retail store associated with a good cause (up from 62 percent in 1993).

As in the United States, cause-related marketing in the United Kingdom is a growing issue. It is successfully being used to develop corporate reputation, build brand image, enlist customer loyalty, and increase sales. The *London Times* has even noted a shift from straight donations to increased interest in cause-related marketing.

For small businesses, the benefits of good behavior are more immediate in terms of reputation in the local area, a finding consistent with U.S. studies. For example, one study found that 59 percent of consumers believe that business should address social problems locally, compared with 26 percent for national problems and only 9 percent for international issues.[9] And a 1997 Lucent Technologies study found that, after price and quality, being a positive presence in a particular minority or ethnic community was the most influential factor when it came to choosing a long-distance telephone service provider.[10]

Data from surveys of corporate executives on corporate image are even stronger. With all things being equal, 98 percent of South Korean executives agree that corporate image becomes the determinant in customer choice, followed by 96 percent of German, Russian, and Spanish executives, and 95 percent of U.S. executives.[11]

In reality, corporate social performance cannot substitute for superior product quality or a more competitive price. It can, however, afford a strategic advantage in a crowded and competitive marketplace, serving as a tiebreaker for competing products that are closely matched in features and price. Thus, it is not surprising that a number of companies most closely identified with a commitment to corporate social responsibility, such as Levi Strauss and Ben & Jerry's, are in the consumer products business. The Body Shop International, based in the United Kingdom, not only leveraged its social performance to its advantage in its industry, it used it to remold its market entirely.

9. Cone, Inc., *The 1997 Cone-Roper Cause-Related Marketing Trends Report* (Boston: Cone Inc., 1997)

10. Laurie Eurick, presentation to National Congress for Community Economic Development Telecommunications Conference, November 1997.

11. Stephen Garone, "Managing Reputation with Image and Brands," Report 1212-98-CH (New York: The Conference Board, 23 April, 1998): p. 6.

Profile: Cause Related Marketing

Boys & Girls Club of America

Six years after signing its first cause-related marketing contract, Boys & Girls Clubs of America, an Atlanta umbrella group for some 2,400 local clubs nationwide, has developed one of the most successful cause-related marketing programs in the country. Last year, it raised more than $3.5 million of its $16-million budget from marketing arrangements with corporations like Coca-Cola, Sears, and MasterCard.

Nonprofit groups—especially small charities that don't have a national presence or household name recognition—often think they can't do cause-related marketing, says Kurt Aschermann, Boys & Girls Clubs' senior vice-president of marketing. "But this stuff can work for a tiny group that only raises $100,000 a year. It's just as usable on a local level and it can be just as easy."

As an example, Mr. Aschermann points to the Phoenix Boys & Girls Club, which set up a five-figure marketing deal on its own, without any help from the national organization. The Phoenix club approached Circle K, a local convenience store chain, whose CEO had once been a member of the club. The club wanted to remain open on Saturdays, but had been unable to raise the necessary funds. It proposed that Circle K sponsor a year's worth of Saturdays; in exchange, the Boys & Girls Club agreed to call those days "Circle K Saturdays for Kids," and Circle K's sponsorship was publicized through the charity's press releases and advertisements placed by the company. Both parties benefited: the club got to keep its doors open on Saturdays and received some paid advertising it could not have normally afforded. The company got its name out to the public—and demonstrated to customers that it was a good "corporate citizen."

In addition to sponsorships in which companies like Circle K underwrite a program that has their name on it, Boys & Girls Clubs pursue two other kinds of cause-related marketing deals. Companies pay to use the Boys & Girls Clubs' name and logo on products through licensing and royalty agreements. Sales promotions, the other type of deal, involve a limited-time offer during which Boys & Girls Clubs gets a portion of the sales price every time a product is sold.

Aschermann says that charities need to be careful to protect their good name in marketing deals. Because charities exist to promote the public good rather than commercial interests, they should avoid any appearance of undue influence by the companies they work with, or any suggestion that they exist to sell products, he says.

Boys & Girls Clubs has a written policy that it makes clear to all its corporate marketing partners: "We do not endorse products, promote the sale of products or mandate our Clubs to endorse, purchase or sell any product," it says. "'We do not give 'official,' 'preferred,' or 'exclusive' status to any company, product or brand." Boys & Girls Clubs does take the view that associating its name with a company's may enhance the company's image and influence consumers to buy a product, but it makes no promises, says Aschermann. And, he notes, Boys & Girls Clubs works with several competing companies, thus avoiding the perception that the charity endorses a particular product or corporation.

In addition to protecting their organization's good name, nonprofit leaders need to remember that pursuing marketing deals is completely different from going after corporate grants, says Aschermann, who was Boys & Girls Clubs' chief fund raiser before taking charge of the organization's cause-related marketing initiatives. The negotiations involved in setting up a marketing deal, he says, take far longer than seeking a grant—well over a year in many cases—and charities need to approach companies differently than they do for grants.

Rather than talking about the charity's needs, how it's working to solve a social problem, or how many people the group has helped, Aschermann says that charity officials have to think, instead, about how forging a marketing affiliation with their organization will contribute to the company's image and its bottom line. They have to understand the value they bring to such business efforts.

In meetings with potential corporate marketing partners, Aschermann says he practices "proposal-less fund raising." He never brings a written proposal to initial discussions with corporate executives—even though he has possible marketing deals in mind and has already determined through research that the company could benefit from working with Boys & Girls Clubs.

Putting a proposal on the table too soon, he says, just gives a company the option of saying, "No." Instead, Boys & Girls Club staff members spend time learning about the company's objectives, and exploring whether the two organizations can work together in a mutually beneficial manner, Aschermann says. If there's a match, they write the proposal together.

But even when negotiations get to that stage after weeks and months of work, some marketing deals fall through in the end, says Aschermann. "The first big deal I thought I closed was a literacy program with a franchise that agreed to pay $20 million over a five-year period," he recalls. "We announced it to the local clubs, and then the company couldn't do it. The guy inside the company who was our champion lost his job, and the deal went south."

Aschermann says the experience taught him two lessons he has never forgotten. "First, go to the top: The CEO has to be involved. Second, never announce the deal publicly until the letter of agreement is signed." Despite dozens of successful marketing deals since then—many in the multi-million dollar range—Aschermann says that revenue from marketing will never replace the need for charitable contributions, or even come close to generating the local clubs' operating expenses, which currently total $650 million annually. "There is no company in the world that can run enough national promotions to give us the income we need," he says. "Cause-related marketing," he adds, "will never raise $650 million—or even half that amount."

The money is important, admits Aschermann, but the real benefit of marketing arrangements is the increased visibility created for Boys & Girls Clubs. The companies spend much more than they pay Boys & Girls Clubs on promoting their tie-in to the charity. Boys & Girls Clubs couldn't otherwise afford such sophisticated advertising. Without it, Aschermann says, the charity would not have been able to grow to its current level of $650 million, up from $180 million a decade ago, when there were less than half as many clubs open as there are today.

"The key to this marketing stuff," he says, "is not the revenue. It's the awareness building."

—Holly Hall

market its popular beverage Tang. General Foods also initiated cause-related marketing through Grape-Nuts, Natural Raisin Bran, children's cereals, and Maxwell House Coffee. At the other end of the spectrum are small retail outlets (e.g., restaurants and neighborhood merchants) that raise money for local causes such as Little League and volunteer fire companies.

Perhaps the first large-scale example of cause-related marketing was in 1983, when the American Express Company (AMEX) celebrated the twenty-fifth anniversary of the AMEX card throughout the United States by associating itself with the campaign to restore and preserve the Statue of Liberty and Ellis Island. In that year, AMEX made a one-penny contribution to the Statue of Liberty-Ellis Island Foundation every time its card was used in the United States, and donated a dollar for each new customer application. The promotion raised seventeen million tax-deductible dollars for the campaign. At the same time, AMEX credit card use and applications soared: card usage jumped 28 percent and applications shot up by 45 percent.

Possibly the largest corporate cause-related marketing and sponsorship endeavor involves the Olympic Games, which usually generates some $500 million from a combination of sponsorship and licensing fees for the use of the Olympic logo and name.

While it is not appropriate for all organizations and should not be considered a replacement for annual grant support, cause-related marketing can create an occasional new stream of unrestricted revenues. Nonprofits seeking a cause-related marketing partnership should make sure that the images of both organizations are compatible; negotiate and sign a contract that guarantees the nonprofit a minimum fee; and avoid actively promoting their partners' products or services. Nonprofits should also be keenly aware of their business partners' expectations, which typically include heightened visibility and credibility, access to potential customers, expertise, and the opportunity to establish a long-term relationship.

Sponsorship

In cause-related marketing, the business partner's interest is in associating the nonprofit's name with its own. In sponsorship, a business seeks to enhance its public image by placing its own name before a nonprofit's constituents or the general public. In return for visible sponsorship credit (the more generous the sponsorship, the more prominent the credit), businesses will underwrite advertisements in publications (as well as promotional flyers, brochures, banners, and invitations), and will even lend staff to assist in promotional tasks. Other forms of sponsorship include the underwriting of a dance company's season, a symphony orchestra's opening gala concert, or a high school band's uniforms. At the local level, business sponsorship is easily spotted on the backs of Little League players, on the walls of sporting fields, and in programs for fairs, bazaars, and other community fundraisers.

For more costly events and programs, NGOs and nonprofits frequently solicit multiple sponsors. An example of highly successful co-sponsorship is the New York City Marathon, organized by the New York Road Runners Club and officially sponsored in 1999 by Chase Manhattan Bank, Nike, Café de Colombia, *Runner's World,* Gatorade, Continental Airlines, Alive, and Poland Spring. Other examples include Home Box Office's support of "Comic Relief," the cable television program that raises money to meet the medical needs of homeless people; and the New Orleans Jazz and Heritage Festival, which lists Miller Brewing, Coca-Cola, House of Blues, Ray-Ban, and Sprint PCS among some twenty-five corporate sponsors.

In a slightly different form of sponsorship—sponsorship of its own event—Toys "R" Us raised $5 million for its Children's Benefit Fund at the company's annual Evening for Special Children gala. Money raised for the event was distributed to more than 200 organizations, hospitals, and foundations.

Comparing Corporate Sponsorship And Charitable Contributions

Source within the corporation	Sponsorship	Charitable contribution
	Typically from marketing, advertising, or communications budgets.	From charitable donations or philanthropy budgets.
Publicity	Highly public	Usually little fanfare
Corporate Accounting	Written off as a full business expense, like promotional printing expenses or media placement expenses.	Write-off limited to 75% of net income. (This limit was increased in 1997 from 20%, so accounting/tax considerations are less likely to influence the way a corporation designates funding of a nonprofit organization.
Corporate objectives	Generally, to raise the profile of the corporation; to sell more products/services; to increase positive awareness in markets and among stakeholders (customers, potential customers, geographic community)	To be a good corporate citizen; to enhance the corporate image with closest stakeholders (i.e. key employees, shareholders, suppliers).
What corporations want in return	Except in the case of very small sponsorships, banners and a small acknowledgement on a program are no longer sufficient. Today, corporations look for everything from employee involvement to the opportunity to mix and mingle with other top level executives at other sponsor corporations. The best relationships develop and increase in value to both sponsorship partners over a number of years.	Appropriate gratitude; confidence that the charitable dollars are used responsibly.
Where most dollars go	One of the fastest growth areas in sponsorship today is cause-related organizations. For now, however, sports (where sponsorship started) get over 50%	Education, social services, and the health sector are reported to get close to 75% of charitable donations.

Source: Judith Barker, "Sponsorship or Charitable Contribution—What's in a Name?" *Canadian FundRaiser,* 17 December, 1998.

Case Study

No Longer Bowling Alone

When Classical Action: Performing Arts Against AIDS was founded in 1993, the classical music industry enthusiastically adopted the organization as its representative in the fight against AIDS. Artists, managers, performing artists and presenters, record company executives, press representatives—every aspect of this professional world—came forward to support us in our efforts to raise funds for HIV/AIDS service organizations nationwide.

Industry support for Classical Action comes in a variety of forms, such as making individual contributions, purchasing tickets to events, and buying merchandise. Most importantly, these supporters provide their artistic or professional services at no cost to help us produce the types of events for which we have earned a stellar reputation, i.e., private house concerts and major concerts in the country's leading halls which feature well-known classical musicians, orchestras and choruses.

While this support in all its forms has proven to be the backbone of our organization, we felt it was important to provide this industry with a means to come together and demonstrate their support as a *united* front. In the past, we had produced a benefit wine tasting and a gala concert evening, both organized to appeal specifically to our friends in the performing arts industry. These events were extremely labor intensive and did not produce the income we had hoped for. So when an artist manager approached us about organizing a classical music industry bowling event, we gave the idea serious consideration.

What we discovered was that America's most popular sport was the ideal way to get this specific audience excited and involved. Classical Action's bowling event provided them with tremendous individual gratification and a fulfilling form of self-expression. At the workplace, the event afforded an opportunity to put a different stamp on themselves: They became more than members of X company's staff, they became members of X company's bowling team. This was demonstrated in a variety of ways, and believe it or not, proved to be a great motivator.

Numerous teams took the time to think up clever names for themselves and have team T-shirts designed (most impressively, each member of the Metropolitan Opera team had a handmade T-shirt with a different opera/bowling pun, e.g. "Die Fliegende Bowling Ball). A mention of a special prize for "Best Bowling Outfit" actually inspired quite a few bowlers. Most importantly, the fundraising aspect of the event was taken seriously, with a very competitive edge, and, as you'll see, a notably successful outcome.

Here, briefly, is how we went about organizing our first bowling event: After securing a good deal on one of New York City's more popular bowling alleys, our next move was to recruit bowling teams and bowlers from within the industry (a mailing list we were able to compile easily). We dubbed the event "Up Our Alley: The First Annual Classical Action Benefit Bowling Bonanza," and recruitment letters were printed on special bowling stationery with a jazzy logo and signed by representatives from four management companies, two record companies, and the New York Philharmonic Orchestra. The tone of the letter and the design conveyed three important messages about "Up Our Alley":

- Participants were going to have a great time;

- Participants would be given a unique opportunity to network with their colleagues; and

- Participants would be raising money for a worthwhile cause.

Each bowling team was asked to seek sponsorship in the form of tax-deductible contributions to Classical Action. They were informed that fabulous prizes would be awarded to those teams and individuals who raise the most money for Classical Action, and that a celebrity panel of judges would also be on hand to award prizes for such categories as "Best Form," "Best Gutter Ball," "Best Bowling Shirt," etc.

Upon receipt of a team's registration forms, we mailed or faxed detailed instructions and sponsor sheets. It was during this process of bowling team recruitment that we truly learned the benefits of e-mail and the Internet. Our Projects Manager sent weekly and then almost daily updates via e-mail and posted on our Web site about team recruitment. This fostered a sense of friendly competition and built excitement around the event. These updates continued up until the day of the event.

We also busied ourselves securing donated prizes for the winning teams and individuals. Letters were mailed to restaurants and clubs, and follow-up phone calls were made to secure donations of dinners for two. A management company gave us 14 tickets to a new Broadway show. A wine company donated wine and special gift boxes. We got tickets to the taping of Saturday Night Live and to Sony IMAX Theatres, and we even got the bowling alley to donate gift certificates.

We had been predicting the participation of 20 teams with about 150 people in attendance. With each team being asked to raise a minimum of $1,000 to participate, we'd estimated our income at $20,000. By the big day, we had 33 registered teams. Close to 300 people showed up at the bowling alley that night (many were attending merely as cheerleaders), with a line forming around the corner just to get in.

It was loud and it was crowded. People danced, bowled, and raised a ruckus. In short, it was the antithesis to the types of fundraising events to which these people were accustomed—a factor that in retrospect seems to be one of the keys to its success. And it was surprisingly successful: We netted $45,000, exceeding our net income projections by $25,000.

With just a couple of exceptions, every team managed to meet the $1,000 fundraising minimum, and many greatly exceeded it. The team from BMG Classics, the record company, decided to forgo collecting individual sponsorships and persuaded the company itself to make a $5,000 contribution. CAMI, one of the largest artist management companies, raised close to $3,400 through individual sponsorships and a matching company gifts. But company size did not seem to correlate directly with dollars raised. Stevens/Bandes, a small graphics company of five employees, ranked third as the team that raised the most money. The crowds enthusiastic response to the announcements of our fundraising total confirmed in our minds that ultimately, everyone knew why he or she was there—to recognize that the AIDS crisis is not over and that AIDS services need funding now more than ever.

—Deborah Edison

How Do Corporations and Businesses Operate Their Charitable Contributions and Community Affairs Programs?

For the smallest unit of American business—the neighborhood store—the proprietor makes all the business decisions, including which charities (if any) to support. The proprietor may belong to a local trade association or a chamber of commerce that periodically suggests nonprofit organizations worthy of support. Support can range from placing canisters near the cash register to selling calendars produced by the PTA of the nearby elementary school, to donating raffle prizes.

The next business category includes supermarkets, drugstores, banks, fast-food outlets, and the like. Here the manager of a local store or branch generally makes the decisions and can choose from a larger variety of charitable options than the corner-storeowner.

The parent company may sponsor a community-service grants program through which the branch manager can award grants (or refer local organizations to the central office for such grants); or a bank branch manager may enclose a nonprofit's literature with its monthly statements, donate the printing of ad books or raffle tickets, or offer the bank's windows or lobby for a display highlighting an organization's work. Often the only way to receive funding from the parent corporation is to be recommended by a local manager who is familiar with the nonprofit's work and reputation.

Nonprofits seeking the support of larger citywide or suburban establishments—shopping malls, department stores, utility, and transit companies, for example—should contact the public relations or community affairs offices. These departments organize the promotional events that help a store attract shoppers, and it's precisely these events that offer excellent opportunities for collaboration with nonprofit organizations. Department stores, for instance, sometimes sponsor Senior Days and bus in residents from local senior citizen centers for a day of shopping and entertainment at special discount prices; they may even include a luncheon in the store cafeteria or restaurant. A store may also donate one of its weekly display ads to promote a nonprofit's work. The marketing or publicity staffs of these businesses are usually glad to assist nonprofit organizations in planning and coordinating all the details that such activities require. The best initial contact, however, is the chief executive officer of the company or the officer most directly responsible for public relations, since his or her approval is necessary for any large-scale promotion or contribution. You should not hesitate, however, to start by contacting anyone you know in a company; once approached, that person can direct you to the appropriate department. From there, a knowledgeable employee can show you how to navigate a company's bureaucracy until you find the officer who can help. If you don't know anyone at the corporation, and are trying to identify the best person to approach, ask the personnel office.

Before approaching very large corporations, including multinationals, remember that, because of their sheer size, they may have several offices or departments that handle requests for donations. These include:

1. *Corporate contributions* (sometimes also known as *community affairs* or *community relations*). Professional staff members work in capacities not much different from their counterparts in the foundation world. A corporation's contributions

budget is usually set in the fall for the forthcoming year. Nonprofits may request information on areas of funding interest and application guidelines.

2. *Publicity or marketing.* Publicity, communications, or marketing departments are responsible for a corporation's promotional efforts, including advertising and media relations, and can allocate a portion of their substantial budgets to supporting nonprofits, either in the form of cash donations, or through cause-related marketing or sponsorship arrangements.

3. *Public affairs or governmental relations.* Some corporations maintain departments that oversee all corporate activities relating to the public. These offices stay abreast of relationships with the government on a local, state, and federal level, and focus on issues that bear on the well-being of the communities in which the corporation maintains offices, conducts its business, or sells its products or services. These departments may consist of one senior executive, or they may employ an entire professional staff.

Unless someone at a nonprofit has prior personal contact at the senior level of a company, the nonprofit's executive director or board officer usually makes the initial contact with someone in the corporation's charitable contributions office. The contributions officer is then in a position to introduce the nonprofit's representative to officials of other appropriate offices within the company for assistance.

Decisions on grants and contributions are made directly by a corporation's chief executive officer, by a committee of senior executives (a Contributions Committee, perhaps), or by one senior officer in charge of this area. The larger the grant, the greater the likelihood that the final decision will be made by a number of people. On the other hand, decisions about small requests, such as the purchase of an ad in annual program books or a table at a gala benefit, are most often made by the corporate contributions staff itself.

The size of a corporation's charitable contributions staff will largely determine whether or not an applicant can talk directly to a contributions officer or associate. Large institutions with high public profiles, such as banks, probably receive a higher volume of requests than more specialized and focused companies. The applicant, therefore, may find the latter type of company far more likely to reply to a request for personal contact.

Unless corporations have created a foundation through which to channel their charitable giving, their philanthropy is not subject to the same requirements set by the Internal Revenue Service for foundations. Corporations, for instance, are not required to report their grants in a special annual report. If they seek tax deductions for their charitable contributions, however, they must report their donations on corporate tax returns, which in the case of private companies are not available to the general public. Some corporations voluntarily publish annual reports detailing their charitable activities for the year; these are available free upon request from the charitable contributions office.

Corporations tend to be more general than most professionally staffed foundations in their grantmaking, and their interest areas are usually more broad: health, education, and welfare. As with foundations, however, it is difficult to generalize, given the scope and diversity of businesses. Some companies do have highly targeted and carefully selected priorities; fortunately, these are usually the same companies that publish annual reports.

Partly because of these broad interests, corporations often provide general support grants rather than project-specific grants. Corporate grants also differ from foundation grants in both range and size. It is not unusual for a company to make a substantial number of small grants (less than $5,000) to organizations while also making substantial grants ($50,000 to $100,000) to a select list of larger institutions.

The most significant difference between foundation giving and corporate giving lies, as described earlier, in the ability of a company to provide more than financial support. Whether or not an applicant's grant request is funded, the nonprofit should explore other types of support from that corporation. In fact, the company may welcome the opportunity to place volunteers with your organization or to publicize your work in its company newsletter or magazine.

Retrenchment in public spending to meet human needs and increased competition for foundation support characterized the fundraising landscape in the last decades of the twentieth century. These realities have brought corporate philanthropy in its many forms into the limelight as never before, and the time is ripe for nonprofits to explore the corporate resource tree actively.

Which Organizations Are Eligible for Cash and In-Kind Contributions from Businesses?

To receive a deduction from the IRS for their contributions, businesses are required to limit their financial support to organizations classified as "charitable" under Section 501(c)(3) of the IRS Code. Businesses are of course, free to support other types of nonprofit organizations as long as they do not attempt to claim tax deductions for such support. Companies can therefore support organizations with extensive lobbying or electoral activities that might exceed what the IRS allows for 501(c)(3) organizations.

A company is not restricted in deciding which organizations to designate as recipients of its many in-kind services and contributions, since these services are not deducted on a company's tax return (except for companies that do deduct for large donations of equipment, such as computers).

What Are the Advantages of Raising Support from Corporations and Businesses?

1. Once you receive support from a business, you are more likely to receive similar support in subsequent years. If you continue to meet the company's charitable goals, you've set the stage for other approaches in the future. Of course, ongoing support depends upon other factors, as well: (a) the steadiness of the company's profits, enabling it to provide funds for its giving program; (b) your organization's ability to carry out your programs successfully; (c) the quality of your ongoing

communication with your contact at the company; and (d) the perceived value of your work in relation to that of grantees of longer standing, especially if a company's charitable resources are shrinking.

2. A cash gift or grant from a company bestows credibility that will help you approach other departments of the same company for different kinds of support, such as in-kind services.

3. Indication of support for your work by one company in your community will help induce other companies to extend their own. Businesses don't regard the presence of their counterparts as competitive, and may even view their own absence as negative. The significant exception, of course, is corporate sponsorship, where the sponsoring company is seeking maximum publicity and image enhancement through its association with your program. Companies in one particular industry might, therefore, be reluctant to share the spotlight with each other, but not necessarily with businesses in other fields.

4. In-kind goods and services donated by businesses can enable smaller nonprofits to tackle larger activities than their present resources usually allow because loaned executives or other volunteers provide a tremendous boost to their people power.

What Are the Disadvantages of Raising Support from Corporations and Businesses?

1. While corporations do make grants in both large and small amounts, most awards to small, community-based organizations are for less than $5000, especially for first-time applicants. In addition, it is difficult for grantees to increase the level of business benefactors' support in subsequent years. Neighborhood businesses, usually a steady source of support for nonprofit organizations in their community, are also limited in the level of support they are able to contribute. Five hundred or a thousand dollars would be a very large gift from the traditional mom-and-pop store, and may even constitute the average grant from the local bank.

2. Since businesses frequently expect some public recognition or acknowledgment of their contributions, the recipient organization has an obligation, often unstated, to publicize the grant it has received. This sounds simple enough, but it may well not be; many social-issue and advocacy organizations may be attacking problems they believe to be fostered, or even caused, by the very same corporation offering financial support.

   Those groups may feel that their integrity will be compromised if they accept funds from the companies whose policies they are seeking to change. An environmental group, for example, may decide not to approach a particular utility company for support if the group is actively challenging that company's plans to build a nuclear reactor. On the other hand, the company may be eager to extend support to the environmental group simply to demonstrate to the public that it is, in fact, concerned with the quality of the environment, despite charges to the contrary.

3. Similarly, if a company is seeking to enhance its public profile through a grant, or sponsorship of some event or program, it might oppose the presence of other corporate supporters. Clearly, this depends on the nature of the project itself, as well as on the extent of support being provided.

4. When a company has associated its public image with your work, it wants to maximize the benefits of its support, and may ask to be involved in your promotional activities. Some organizations might welcome any offer of assistance, but others might find such involvement intrusive.

5. Businesses often look for their own peers and colleagues on the board of a nonprofit as evidence that the group is really interested in the input of business. Again, some groups might agree, while others might fear that their board nominating process might be compromised.

Deciding Whether To Approach Corporations and Businesses for Support

In order to make this decision, consider the following questions:

1. Do the local businesses and corporations you've targeted provide grants and other forms of support that could help your organization's work?

2. Are you prepared to extend public recognition to your business supporters? Do you have any philosophical or value-related conflicts that would preclude accepting support from certain types of companies?

3. Finally, in light of business' strategic giving goals, is your organization or project potentially interesting to a business in your community? Do you have a sufficiently large constituency that a business identifies as part of its market? Do you have other potentially valuable assets for your business backer? Prestige? Visible presence in the community? Wealthy connections? Or is your work of such direct value to the community in which the business operates that you can demonstrate that its support will have a direct bearing on making the community better, both for business and for its employees? In essence, what can you offer a company in return for its support?

Samsung Austin Semiconductor Corporate Giving Program Guidelines

Corporate Giving Program

The Samsung Austin Semiconductor (SAS) Corporate Giving Program is designed to contribute community support in the form of cash grants and donations to eligible non-profit organizations.

Eligibility

To be eligible, the requesting organization must be a non-profit, tax-exempt 501c(3) organization serving the communities in which our employees live. SAS gives special consideration to programs that:

- Benefit SAS employees and families

- Target under-served or minority populations

Eligible programs are in the following areas:

- Education

- Health and Human Services

- Environment

- Arts and Culture

- Other: DReAM Beyond Volunteer Program/matching fund

Exclusions

SAS does not fund:

- Individuals

- Organizations serving a limited constituency

- Political or lobbying organizations, or those supporting the candidacy of a particular individual

- Organizations dedicated to fighting specific diseases (cancer, lung, kidney, etc.)

- Traditionally parent-supported organizations (PTA, Little League, Scouts, etc.)

- Ongoing capital or endowment fundraising campaigns

- General operating expenses

- Private foundations

- Other areas at SAS discretion

Application Procedure

Applications must be submitted IN WRITING, on the SAS Request for Corporate Giving form. This form is available for download as a PDF document that can be filled out on the computer, printed and sent in. Note: When you enter your information onto the downloaded file, you can print it, but you cannot save it. If you do not have a copy of Acrobat Reader, get one free from Adobe. All requested support documentation must be attached at the time of application submittal.

Grant Distribution/Renewals

Applications are accepted on a quarterly basis, with deadlines on January 10, April 10, July 10, and October 10. Applications may only be submitted once a year. SAS may require site visits for requesting organizations. A grant award in one year does not make an organization automatically eligible the following year.

SAS will normally issue award notifications within six weeks of grant application submittal. Grant funds are generally disbursed within two weeks of award notification. Special requests for funding outside of the standard review policy will be considered on a case-by-case basis, and in a timely manner.

Other Cash Donations

SAS considers requests to sponsor select events, conferences, or community-based activities on a case-by-case basis. Donations for these types of activities must meet the SAS eligibility criteria.

Review Criteria

SAS will consider applications according to the following criteria:

1. Program addresses SAS priorities:
   Does the program: (a) improve visibility and environment for our employees/neighbors/ customers; and (b) target under-served or minority populations?

2. program will increase quality of life

3. Association with program benefits SAS:
   Does the program/request: (a) demonstrate understanding of SAS business; and (b) build SAS' citizenship image and provide good public relations exposure?

4. Requesting organization demonstrates strong organizational structure:
Does the organization: (a) have diverse income; and (b) work cooperatively with other community organizations?

The DReAM Beyond Volunteer Program

The DReAM Beyond Volunteer Program is designed to serve and support the community by providing SAS volunteer assistance for qualifying community activities.

Application Procedure

Requests for SAS volunteer assistance must be submitted IN WRITING, on the SAS Request for Volunteer Assistance form, at least three weeks prior to the event. This form is available for download as a PDF document that can be filled out on the computer, printed and sent in. Note: When you enter your information onto the downloaded file, you can print it, but you cannot save it. If you do not have a copy of Acrobat Reader, get one free from Adobe.

1. Activity addresses SAS priorities:
Does the activity: (a) improve visibility and environment for our employees/neighbors/customers; and (b) target under-served or minority populations?

2. Activity will increase quality of life:
Does the activity: (a) demonstrate significant direct benefit (immediate and meaningful contact with target group, or measurable result from efforts); and (b) reach a significant number of people?

3. Association with activity benefits SAS:
Does the request/activity: (a) request demonstrate understanding of SAS business; (b) build SAS' citizenship image and provide good public relations exposure; (c) provide employees solid training and personal growth opportunities; (d) have reasonable time frame; and (e) assure legal indemnity for SAS?

Exclusions

SAS will not provide volunteers to political or labor organizations, or to religious organizations whose volunteer activities will not directly benefit a non-profit cause regularly supported by SAS. Volunteer activities will be conducted after business hours during SAS employees' free time. Exceptions will be evaluated on a case-by-case basis, with approval of the President and Vice President/Director of Human Resources. Company supplies and equipment may be used to support volunteer activities only with prior approval from the DReAM Beyond coordinator.[12]

---

12. Samsung Austin Semiconductor Web site: www.sas.samsung.com/giving_guidelines.html

Securing Support from Corporations and Businesses

The road to business support begins in the same the way as foundation grantsmanship: with an inventory of the projects that you can offer corporations and businesses. The same criteria that you applied to your search for foundation support will serve you equally well in gauging potential business and corporate support. These include: (1) compatibility with mission, (2) acknowledged expertise, (3) achievability, (4) topicality, and (5) documentation. (See Chapter 15 for further details on these criteria.) To this list, add the following:

1. *Rationale for corporate support.* How does your project or program correspond to the interests of a particular business or corporation? Does it match its stated areas of concern? Or does it conform to a general corporate interest in the health and welfare of the community in which the business is conducted?

2. *Potential dividends to the corporate supporter.* Does the project have the potential to meet the potential corporate donor's strategic goals? Publicity? Exposure? Credibility? Enhanced public image? Increase in product sales?

3. *Strong case for your organization.* Are there other nonprofit organizations operating within the same geographic scope of a business prospect that are more established in your field? Do they have the ability to "return" more to the business on its charitable "investment" because of the size or scale of their operations? Because of their public profile? Or can you make the best case?

Your answers to these questions will help you estimate how much interest your work may hold for the businesses you plan to approach. In the process, you may also become aware of the issues to highlight in your request for support. Use the summary worksheet at the end of this chapter to gauge your chances in approaching businesses for help. Are your chances strong, moderate, poor? If you conclude that your chances are moderate or poor, should you abandon your business solicitation campaign? Do more research to locate more likely prospects? Seek advice on ways of making your programs more attractive to potential contributors?

Now develop a list of prospective businesses to approach using the following categories:

- Businesses and corporations in your immediate community

- Metropolitan area businesses

- Corporate headquarters or plant facilities in your city

- National or multinational corporations outside your community

To make sure that you haven't omitted any possibilities, review your list from the perspective of these categories:

- Businesses that your organization and its members and constituents patronize or use regularly, such as corner stores, supermarkets, banks, department stores, etc.

- Companies for which your members and constituents and their families work

• Companies that sell products to your primary constituency

• Business concerns whose activities correspond to your programs; for example, pharmaceutical companies for health-care organizations, computer companies for computer training projects, toy companies for youth programs, etc.

• Other corporations that have expressed interest in your work through their printed annual reports, grant guidelines, or news reports

Corporate prospecting affords you the opportunity to involve your board, your fundraising committee, local businesspeople, and community supporters in some creative brainstorming to develop a list of businesses for subsequent approaches. Now you are ready to make the actual approach!

Step 1
Research the interests and activities of the companies listed on your prospect list. Contact them directly, particularly if they are medium-size to large corporations, to request a copy of their grantmaking guidelines, and to establish to whom letters requesting support should be addressed. Seek out data from your local library or chamber of commerce that sheds information on the companies' customers, employees, and other constituencies they are interested in. Consult the Additional Resources section at the end of this chapter for publications and Web sites that provide extensive information.

Step 2
Check within your organization and community to see whether you have any existing contacts with the businesses on your prospect list.

Step 3
Based on the data you have collected and reviewed, decide whether your overall organization or a particular program would be of most potential interest to your prospects.

Step 4
Decide whether your organization or project lends itself to a specialized corporate or business campaign, to targeting a number of businesses and corporations, or to an appeal to just one company.

Step 5
If you decide to undertake a campaign, identify and recruit potential business leaders to serve as chairs or co-chairs of such an effort, and elicit their help in forming a campaign committee. Also, develop a timetable for the actual campaign, from the kickoff to the finale.

Step 6
Before making any actual contact with a company, ask any inside contacts you have in the company how they might facilitate your request. A letter of support? A friendly informal word? A simple mention on your part in your letter?

Step 7

Place a phone call to the individual contact whom you have previously identified at the corporation or business. If you have not yet identified this person, simply call the central switchboard of the corporation and ask for the name of the staff member in charge of charitable contributions.

Try to engage that person in conversation about your organization. Tell him or her what kind of support you are seeking from the company and why you are approaching it in particular. Request the opportunity to meet with him or her to talk more about your work. You will be told whether your project falls within the company's interests (which you should have established through your prior research), and whether you should submit a letter and/or a proposal. Some companies might ask you to put your request in writing before they will give you any indication of their interest. In either case, you have already established a personal contact.

Avoid the tendency to talk too much, and practice what you are going to say with a friend or co-worker first. Try not to tell the person things that are not important or that could be surmised easily, such as "We are a nonprofit that does good work," or "We need support and are doing our best to raise money wherever we can." Try instead, "Literacy for All works here in Ourtown with adults who have reading problems. We work with two hundred adults a year, most of whom were functionally illiterate day laborers. Ninety percent of them are able to enter the workforce after completing our course."

Be specific and focus your comments on what is important to the corporation. Even if you are talking with a sympathetic person, that person will be most interested in what will match his or her corporation's interests.

Step 8

If the company requests a letter, draft a short one (preferably no longer than two pages) to invite its support. The letter should summarize the project and establish the reasons for supporting it. In your letter, mention a mutual contact person if one exists. Close the letter with a request for a meeting to discuss your work in person. Involve your business campaign leader(s) as cosigner(s) of your letter.

Step 9

Prior to any contact, itemize the other types of support—besides a cash contribution—that the business might provide. If for some reason financial support does not appear to be immediately forthcoming, be prepared to discuss other types of assistance. In your contact with a contributions officer following receipt of your letter or phone call, be sure to determine whether there are other members of the company with whom you should be discussing in-kind support, such as the marketing or public relations staff. If so, your first contact can be helpful in arranging further introductions for you.

Step 10

If after several weeks you have not had a response to your request for a meeting, make a follow-up phone call. At this time, be prepared to explain succinctly why you have approached the company, and what its support would enable you to do. Plan to bring a board member, business campaign committee member, or community leader with you to support your request. They can speak about the importance of your work from their own perspective. Also invite your prospect to visit your organization.

Step 11

As in meetings with a foundation representative, be sure to listen to any concerns that are raised during the interview and make note of them so that you can answer them fully in your follow-up letter. Your letter should also convey your thanks for the meeting.

The Yes

Victory! The company has indicated that it finds your concerns consonant with its priorities and would like to begin working with your organization. The first order of business is to talk to the company representative about the kind of public acknowledgment they would like to receive for their support—a press release, an announcement in your newsletter, a listing in a program bulletin or annual brochure, etc.

As your work proceeds, be sure to fulfill your responsibilities as you have explained them to your corporate sponsors. If you alter the project substantially, keep your sponsors posted.

Finally, involve your corporate sponsors in your program as it progresses. Invite them to attend appropriate events and send them any press notices, particularly those that mention them. Maintain the degree of personal contact that seems natural for both parties.

The No

If your request has been rejected, contact the corporation by mail or phone to ask: "Are there ways that we could make the program stronger or more attractive to you in the future?" or "What factors entered into your decision not to provide support at this time?" Not every business will be forthcoming with this information, but some will give you some guidance for the next time you approach a company for help. You will often find that your request has been turned down simply because of the volume of requests received. In this case, you should apply again; persistence pays off with the corporate community. Take this opportunity, too, to explore in-kind services, such as volunteers, donated printing, and the like. Maintain cordial relations; you never know when you may want to return to a specific company for aid.

Not every business will respond to your requests for assistance. That does not mean that all businesses, small and large, will be equally unresponsive. These are uncharted waters for many nonprofits; the best thing to do is to get out there and explore them.

Profile: Lincoln Unified School District, Stockton, California

Like many public school districts, Lincoln Unified School District has been on the receiving end of a number of potentially devastating budget cuts. However, it has responded by creating a fundraising program, and is one of the first school districts in the United States to hire a development director. Her name is Ann Quinn, and the following event is one of her most successful efforts to involve the corporate and business community in providing funding for the schools.

In 1992, Lincoln Unified School District created an arts festival. Patterned after the age-old Italian street painting tradition enjoying a resurgence throughout Europe, it has grown to become a major fund raiser for the school district. By 1996, 200 people of all ages and from throughout San Joaquin County created 125 pictures. Entire public and private school classes, as well as children's shelters, worked on large squares, while solo artists often labored for two days to finish their individual creations.

Nearly 7,000 people attended the 1996 Festival. Admission is free to promote attendance; and the local press regularly photographs the event and chalks a square themselves. The format is simple. You close off a street (this will take permission in some places). You line out squares ranging from 4' x 6' to 12' x 12' and sell sponsorships for $75 to $1,000 to local businesses and corporations, or even family and friends. Recruit adult and student artists of all ages to create "masterpieces" in chalk over a two-day period and give them high-quality chalk to do it. Add to the festivities with live music, craft and food vendors, and a classic car show. The result is a family-oriented event that draws thousands of people to watch colorful street canvases unfold.

A local developer contributes vendor coordination and security, helping keep expenses to a minimum (only the cost of the chalk purchased wholesale); other businesses donate poster graphics and production, billboard space and media time. In 1996, the school district raised $42,000 and in 1997, $60,000. The money goes to its summer theater program, which provides a good deal of the volunteer energy needed for the event.

The secret is creatively seeking community underwriting and support, which means willingness to take the time to personally recruit such collaboration. A key to Lincoln's success is that it offers long-term recognition for participating businesses. Not only do sponsors see their names displayed on the top of their square during the two-day Festival, they are recognized for several weeks in the district's summer theater programs, on a permanent plaque and on posters if they are major donors, and in back-to-school newsletters.

Throughout the year Lincoln keeps sponsors advised of how their money is being spent for arts programs. As the years have passed, more and more businesses have bought into the Festival because of the thousands of people it attracts. The most recent year of the Festival, *VIA*, the magazine of the American Automobile Association, listed the Festival in its calendar along with a picture. The Festival is now becoming a reason to visit Stockton, which in turn makes businesses and corporations want to be part of it.

Ann Quinn, the director of development who masterminds the Festival says, "We believe this is the largest free, public art-in-action event especially for young people in the country."

Thanks to Ann Quinn and the Lincoln Unified School District in Stockton, California, for this information.

Tips

- Consider what your group has to offer a business or corporation aside from good publicity, enhanced image, and the like. Think about their work force: What do their workers need? What kind of community do they desire? What are their future needs in terms of markets, workers, research, and so on? Envision yourself in part as a partner to the business: you provide them with something they want, and they provide you with support.

- Think in broad terms about what a business could provide your organization. Remember that much corporate and business support is given in-kind rather than in cash.

Summary Worksheet

for _____

(name of your organization)

Approaching Businesses for Support

Building on Past Business and Corporate Support

1. Have any businesses and corporations ever supported your work in the past?

   _____ yes _____ no

   If yes, which ones?

   _____ _____
   _____ _____
   _____ _____
   _____ _____

2. What characteristics do these businesses share? How do their interests correspond to each other?

   Comments:

   _____
   _____
   _____
   _____

3. What is your sense of what they valued in your organization's work?

   Comments:

   _____
   _____
   _____
   _____

4. Which ones can you reapproach for future support question

   Definite Ongoing Prospects:

   _____ _____
   _____ _____
   _____ _____
   _____ _____

Untested (further information needed):

_____   _____
_____   _____
_____   _____
_____   _____

Finding New Business and Corporate Supporters:

Research and Networking

1. List those businesses that your members and constituents patronize most frequently:

_____   _____
_____   _____
_____   _____
_____   _____

2. Add to the list businesses that employ your members and constituents:

_____   _____
_____   _____
_____   _____
_____   _____

3. Are there additional businesses and corporations that are marketing their products and services to your particular constituencies?

_____   _____
_____   _____
_____   _____
_____   _____

4. See pages 438 and 439 for this part of the worksheet.

Making the Match

For each prospect in the previous list, complete the following worksheet (use your own blank paper).

Name of Business or Corporation:

Its Stated Areas of Interest that Pertain to Your Work (draw from annual reports, reference books, newsclippings, etc.):

Write one or more short sentences demonstrating how the work of your organization reflects the interests of X business.

4. List below those business prospects that you have uncovered from your research and your networking. Limit your listing to the ten most likely supporters of your organization—your ten best bets.

a. Type of Business	b. Its Stated Areas of Interest that Relate to Your Work	c. Appropriate Contact: Person, Address, Telephone Number
Neighborhood Stores		
Banks, Utility Companies, Department Stores, etc.		
Corporations with headquarters or facilities in your community		
Large National Corporations		

d. Personal Contacts	e. Your Program(s) that Correspond to Its Interests	f. Level of Potential Financial Support	f. Other Types of Possible Support

Finding Assistance and Counsel

Name five or more individuals who might be able to advise you on how to most effectively approach the businesses and corporations on your best bets list:

a. _____

b. _____

c. _____

d. _____

Addressing the Likelihood of Securing Support

On the basis of what you have learned, how would you rank your chances of securing support from businesses?

___ Very Good   ___ Possible   ___ Unlikely   ___ Still Unknown

What might you do to improve your chances?

Additional Resources

Publications

Abelson, Reed. "Marketing Tied to Charities Draws Scrutiny from States." *New York Times* (3 May 1999): A1, A22.

> Describes numerous examples of cause-related marketing efforts, such as the endorsements of pharmaceuticals, drugs, and other health products, by the American Heart Association, the American Cancer Society, and the Arthritis Foundation. Such practices are eliciting attention from regulators, who are concerned that the endorsements are misleading. Sixteen attorneys general, including those from Connecticut, New Jersey, and New York, are developing guidelines to govern these advertising campaigns. Public hearings, followed by final recommendations, are in the works.

Abshire, Michael. "Merging Traffic." *Corporate Philanthropy Report* 14 (October 1999): 1, 4–6.

> Discusses current corporate acquisitions and mergers, and their impact on corporate giving, with detailed coverage of the mergers between Bell Atlantic/NYNEX, Citicorp/Travelers, and Honeywell/Allied Signal. Provides suggestions for ways that nonprofits and merging corporate foundations can adapt to mergers and acquisitions. In addition, discusses the study that the Conference Board is conducting to assess the impact of mergers and acquisitions on corporate giving, which will be published in November of 1999.

Abshire, Michael. "Real Estate: Untapped Giving Source." *Corporate Philanthropy Report* 15 (February 2000): 1, 5.

> Discusses the promotion of an IRS-approved structure that allows and simplifies the donation of commercial real estate to nonprofit organizations by Garrett Thornburg, one of the founders of American Foundation Realty. Discusses the benefits of such donations for charities and for corporations/donors.

Adkins, Sue. *Cause Related Marketing: Who Cares Wins.* Oxford, England: Butterworth-Heinemann, 1999. xx, 307 p.

> A textbook that positions cause-related marketing within the context of management of corporate reputation, specifically drawing upon examples and research based on companies in the United Kingdom. Discusses why corporations should be involved in cause-related marketing, and provides typical models and case studies of both American and U.K. corporations. Also analyzes some marketing arrangements that went awry, such as the Sunbeam Corporation's relationship with the American Medical Association. Presents concrete steps for negotiating the partnership, and ultimate evaluation. Indexed.

Alperson, Myra. *Measuring Corporate Community Involvement: A Research Report.* New York: The Conference Board, 1996. 46 p.

Data is drawn from a 1996 Conference Board survey assessing the extent to which companies both measure and evaluate and also benchmark their contributions and community relations programs. Of the Fortune 1000 companies that received the survey, 177 responded. General findings show that 44 percent of respondents do some form of measurement or evaluation of their corporate contributions and community relations programs, while 56 percent report that they benchmark them.

Altman, Barbara W. "Transformed Corporate Community Relations: A Management Tool for Achieving Corporate Citizenship." *Business and Society Review* 102–103 (1998): 43–51.

Presents new themes in both corporate citizenship and community relations practice. Also explores new corporate citizenship models and presents common elements in corporate citizenship.

Austin, James E. "Strategic Collaboration Between Nonprofits and Businesses." *Nonprofit and Voluntary Sector Quarterly* 29 (Supplement 2000): 69–97.

The author explains and develops four components to a framework for analyzing collaborations between corporations and nonprofit organizations. Such cross-sector collaborations are considered to be more common than previously, and more important strategically to the parties involved. Also delves into the "alliance marketplace" and suggests avenues for future research. With bibliographic references.

Blum, Debra E. "Corporate Giving Rises Again." *Chronicle of Philanthropy* 12 (13 July 2000): 1, 9–16, 18.

The *Chronicle of Philanthropy's* annual survey of corporations and their giving shows a substantial increase in giving during 1999, yet the proportion of pre-tax giving remains at about one percent. Nearly 100 companies, whose combined philanthropy represents almost one third of corporate giving, responded to the survey. Twenty-nine of the companies gave internationally. A complete listing of the responses is included.

Blum, Debra E. "New Group Hopes To Increase Corporate Giving to $15 Billion a Year." *Chronicle of Philanthropy* 12 (2 December 1999): 10.

The Committee to Encourage Corporate Philanthropy has been formed by business leaders of the country's top companies, as well as the actor Paul Newman. The new nonprofit aims to spur corporate giving to reach $15 billion in the next five years. Complete list of the founders is provided.

Blum, Debra E. "New Studies Provide Insight into Why Companies Give and Who Benefits." *Chronicle of Philanthropy* 11 (15 July 1999): 16.

Three new studies conducted independently provide analysis about why companies give and who their recipients are. *Fortune* magazine commissioned a study that found that most large companies give to programs that help young people. A University of New Hampshire study found that most companies never evaluate the results of their giving programs, though they state that philanthropy is important in achieving their business goals. A survey conducted for the Dallas Foundation determined that large companies tend to give to education, while smaller businesses fund programs that benefit the homeless, poor, or hungry.

Burlingame, Dwight F., and Dennis R. Young, eds. *Corporate Philanthropy at the Crossroads*. Bloomington, IN: Indiana University Press, 1996. xv, 183 p.

Contains essays and research papers on corporate philanthropy arranged in four parts. In Chapter One, Craig Smith makes a case for connecting corporate giving directly to company strategy. The second part of the book reviews current trends and emerging paradoxes in the field. In Chapter Two, John A. Yankey examines the reason that nonprofits continue to seek corporate support even though it represents only a small proportion of the total giving to nonprofits. In Chapter Three, Alice Korngold and Elizabeth Hosler Voudouris examine in greater detail the emerging important role that corporate voluntarism plays for the modern corporation, and they offer a model to evaluate its impact. The third part focuses on the state of research on corporate philanthropy. In Chapter Four, Donna Wood and Raymond Jones provide an extensive review that frames the question of business philanthropy within the broader context of corporate social performance. In Chapter Five, Dwight Burlingame and Patricia Frishkoff provide the results of their research in Indiana and Oregon to show how firm size affects corporate philanthropy. In Chapter Six, David Lewin and J. M. Sabater report their research on how community involvement through volunteer programs affects employee morale and corporate performance. Questions of ethics and power are examined in the fourth part. In Chapter Seven, Lance Buhl offers an ethical framework for understanding corporate philanthropy. Based on his research of business executives, Jerome Himmelstein examines issues of power and corporate philanthropy in Chapter Eight. In Chapter Nine, the editors call for more research toward a new understanding of corporate philanthropy.

Clark, David, ed. *National Directory of Corporate Giving*. 6th ed. New York: The Foundation Center, 1999. 1,092 pp.

Performs a unique service for fundraisers eager to pursue corporate grants by providing reliable, fact-filled, up-to-date entries on approximately 3,000 corporate foundations and direct-giving programs. Corporate funders often make grants that reflect the interests of their parent companies—and it benefits grantseekers to discover these funding priorities before submitting proposals. Detailed portraits of 1,900+ corporate foundations and an additional 1,000+ direct-giving programs include such essential information as the names of key personnel, types of support generally awarded, giving limitations, financial data, purpose and activities statements, and application procedures.

Cone, Inc. *The 1999 Cone/Roper Cause-Related Trends Report: The Evolution of Cause Branding.* Boston: Cone, Inc., 1999. 24 p.
A five-year longitudinal analysis of cause-related marketing trends, with emphasis on the evolving effort of "cause branding." Cause branding is defined in this report as "a business strategy that integrates a social issue or cause into brand equity and organizational identity to gain significant bottom-line impacts."

Cunningham, Peggy M. "Sleeping with the Devil? Exploring Ethical Concerns Associated with Cause-Related Marketing." *New Directions for Philanthropic Fundraising* 18 (Winter 1997): 55-76.

Embley, L. Lawrence. *Doing Well While Doing Good: The Marketing Link Between Business and Nonprofit Causes.* Englewood Cliffs, NJ: Prentice-Hall, 1993. xix, 252 p.
The author promotes the idea of American business joining directly with nonprofit organizations to address the country's social needs. Numerous corporate examples are cited. Concludes with a chapter devoted to initiating a philanthropic economic business strategy.

Diane Gingold and Associates. *Fortune 500 Survey of Corporate Social Responsibility for Youth.* Washington, DC: Diane Gingold and Associates, 1999. 18 p.
Results of a survey of Fortune 500 companies and their 1998 giving (including grants, in-kind giving, cause-related marketing, and employee voluntarism) to programs that support youth in grades K–12. Nearly all of the respondents fund youth programs, and many devote most of their funding in this area.

Hill, LySandra C. *Corporate Giving Yellow Pages 2000.* 15th ed. Detroit: The Taft Group, 1999. viii, 321 p.
Provides approximately 3,500 listings of corporate contributions programs and foundations. Arranged alphabetically by the sponsoring company's name. Three indexes follow the main section: one by major products/industry, and two geographic, one by headquarters and the other by operating locations.

Hill, LySandra C., ed. *Corporate Giving Directory, 2001.* 22nd ed. Farmington Hills, MI: The Taft Group, 2000. li, 1675 p.
Provides detailed descriptive profiles of more than 1,000 of the largest corporate charitable-giving programs in the United States. Each company profiled makes annual contributions of at least $200,000, including nonmonetary donations. Indexed by headquarters state; operating and grant recipient location; type of grant; nonmonetary support; and recipient type. Also includes biographical indexes. Includes glossary.

Himmelstein, Jerome L. *Looking Good and Doing Good: Corporate Philanthropy and Corporate Power.* Bloomington, IN: Indiana University Press, 1997. xi, 185 p.

> Based on interviews with managers of the top fifty-five corporate giving programs, the Author scrutinizes how corporate philanthropy becomes politicized, how corporations respond to political controversy, and what such conflicts reveal about the nature of American corporations.

Jackson, Linda F., comp. *Matching Gift Details: Profiles of More than 7,500 Companies with Matching Gift Programs.* 44th ed. Washington, DC: Council for Advancement and Support of Education, 1999. 233 p.

> Provides information on some 7,500 U.S. corporate foundations, parent companies, and subsidiaries that match employee gifts to nonprofits, such as hospitals, educational institutions, cultural and arts groups, and various community organizations. Also provides statistics on this type of corporate giving for years 1995, 1997, and 1999. Numerous appendices list and rank company gift-matching attributes.

Jones, Francine, ed. *Corporate Foundation Profiles.* 11th ed. New York: The Foundation Center, 2000. xxviii, 660 p.

> Provides detailed profiles for 207 of the largest company-sponsored foundations. Profile information includes foundation name, address, telephone number, and name and title of contact person; limitations, program areas, and types of support; financial data concerning assets, gifts or contributions received by the foundation, expenditures including grants paid, high and low grant amounts, employee matching gifts, grants to individuals, and loans and scholarships; sponsoring company and background; grant analysis, including types of support and listing of sample grants; policies and application guidelines; and foundation publications. Indexed by donors, officers and trustees, subject interest, type of support, geographic location, and international giving.

Levy, Reynold. *Give and Take: A Candid Account of Corporate Philanthropy.* Boston: Harvard Business School Press, 1999. xxvi, 233 pp.

> Levy, former president of the AT&T Foundation as well as executive director of the 92nd Street Y (New York), offers a guidebook for both grantmakers and grantseekers. His aim is to educate in the fundamentals of corporate philanthropy, discussing general principles and precepts, conduct, and politics. Recommends strategies for development staff when approaching corporate givers (and lists the top ten sins of "corporate supplicants"). Concludes with the author's predictions of future trends. With bibliographic references and index.

Litz, Reginald A., and Alice C. Stewart. "Charity Begins at Home: Family Firms and Patterns of Community Involvement." *Nonprofit and Voluntary Sector Quarterly* 29 (March 2000): 131–48.

> In order to study the relationship between giving and corporate ownership, the authors conducted an analysis of the community involvement of 300 local hardware stores in 1995.

In brief, the data showed that family firms tended to be more involved than nonfamily firms. The survey instrument is included. With bibliographic references.

Logan, David, Delwin Roy, and Laurie Regelbrugge. *Global Corporate Citizenship: Rationale and Strategies.* Washington, DC: Hitachi Foundation, 1997. v, 185 p.
   Examines and documents international giving to social issues being practiced by numerous multinational corporations.

Marx, Jerry D. "Corporate Philanthropy: What is the Strategy." *Nonprofit and Voluntary Sector Quarterly* 28 (June 1999): 185–98.
   Has corporate philanthropy become essentially a business deal? This study, by means of a survey of 226 corporations, analyzes the extent to which strategic philanthropy is becoming the norm in corporate contributions management. Discusses the evolution of strategic philanthropy, defined in this study as "the process by which contributions are targeted to meet business objectives and recipient needs." Among other criteria and variables, the respondents ranked business goals within industry categories. With bibliographic references.

Muirhead, Sophia A. *Corporate Contributions: The View from 50 years.* New York, The Conference Board, 1999. 66 p.
   Provides a history of corporate philanthropy in the U.S. from the time when it was considered illegal to the present, dividing the growth into four developmental periods: "Prelegalization" (1870s to 1930s), "Innovation and Legalization" (1940s to 1950s), "Growth and Expansion" (mid-1950s to mid-1980s), and "Diversification and Globalization" (late 1980s to the present). Also suggests some of the challenges for the field in the coming decade. Details the history of matching gifts programs and in-kind giving. With bibliographic references.

Paprocki, Steven L., National Committee for Responsive Philanthropy. *Grants: Corporate Grantmaking for Racial and Ethnic Communities.* Wakefield, RI: Moyer Bell, 2000. 732 p.
   Profiles of 124 companies and their giving to specific racial and ethnic communities—African Americans, Asian Pacific Americans, Hispanics and Latinos, and Native Americans. For each company, gives a breakdown by community and by broad categories (arts & culture, education, health, human services and public benefit). Also provides suggestions for grantseekers regarding each company. The industries represented here include automotive, banking, beverages, brokerage and financial services, computers, consumer electronics, department stores, food and food services, gas and oil, health and pharmaceuticals, insurance, leisure wear and equipment, media and entertainment, personal care products, and publishing. Also included are giving profiles within major metropolitan regions. Numerous indexes are appended.

Pollack, Rachel H., and Christopher Toward. "Corporate Change and Corporate Giving." *Currents* 25 (June 1999): 26–31.
    How development officers should respond to corporate mergers: patience, understanding, maintaining regular contact, and staying on top of the news.

Pollack, Rachel H. "Which Way Is the Wind Blowing: Trends in Corporate and Foundation Giving and How Fund Raisers Can Stay on Top of Them." *Currents* 26 (April 2000): 43–48.
    Summarizes the key issues addressed at the "Collaborations and Partnerships" conference, held at Duke University in November 1999, which focused on current trends in corporate and foundation giving, and their impact on fundraising efforts in higher education. Includes a discussion of strategic partnerships between campuses and corporations; the decentralization of corporate giving, involving the increasing development of regional giving strategies; the use of employee-directed philanthropy, such as matching gifts and internal campaigns; the impact of corporate mergers on corporate giving; venture philanthropy; the increasing prominence of small companies, wealthy high technology entrepreneurs, family and regional foundations in philanthropy; and wealthy corporate employees as fundraising prospects. Sidebar provides an employment forecast for corporate and foundations relations officers on college and university campuses.

Pringle, Hamish, and Marjorie Thompson. *Brand Spirit: How Cause Related Marketing Builds Brands.* New York: John Wiley & Sons. 1999. Hardcover, 300 p.

Ptacek, Joseph J., and Gina Salazar. "Enlightened Self-Interest: Selling Business on the Benefits of Cause-Related Marketing." *Nonprofit World* 15 (July–August 1997): 9–13.
    Defines cause-related marketing and provides the fundamentals of its practice.

Rosa, Paul. "In-Kind Gifts: Legal, Financial & Matching Considerations." *Grassroots Fundraising Journal* 19 (February 2000): 11–12.

Sharma, Janet, Michelle Grogg, Becky Turner, and Josie McElroy. "Corporate Connections: Forging Strong Links Between Businesses and Nonprofits." *Volunteer Leadership* (Winter 1999): 9–13.
    Provides guidance on what corporations are looking for in nonprofit partnerships and what nonprofits can offer to corporations. Includes tips on how to make these partnerships a success.

Smith, Craig. "Corporate Giving at Y2K: New Rules for a New Era." *Corporate Philanthropy Report* 14 (April 1999): 1, 4–7.
    Provides an excerpt from the book "Giving by Industry: 1999–2000".

Smith, Craig, ed. *Giving by Industry: A Reference Guide to the New Corporate Philanthropy.*
1999–2000 ed. Gaithersburg, MD: Aspen Publishers, 1999. xvii, 439 p.

> Each chapter describes a different industry and explains how philanthropic support is
> shaped by the business interests specific to that industry. Shows how the system of support
> has changed through time and ponders the issues that will reshape the industry's support of
> nonprofits in the future. Short profiles of leading companies in the industry follow the
> analysis section. Indexed.

Steele, J. Valerie, Neil E. Hochman, Jeremy F. Brown, and Natacha Leonare, eds. *National
Directory of Corporate Public Affairs, 2000.* 18th ed. Washington, DC: Columbia Books,
2000.

> Profiles some 1,900 companies identified as having public affairs programs, and lists
> approximately 14,000 corporate officers engaged in public affairs. Corporate profiles
> include the addresses of the corporate headquarters and the company's Washington, D. C.,
> area office; political action committee; foundation or corporate giving program (including
> primary interests, assets, approximate total contributions, and contact person); and
> corporate publications. A separate section provides an alphabetical listing of names,
> showing the company that employs that person, his or her correct title and address, and if
> and where the individual is registered as a lobbyist.

Tillman, Audris D. *Corporate Contributions in 1997.* 32nd ed. New York: The Conference
Board (Conference Board Report, No. 1229–99-RR), 1999. 46 p.

> Summarizes the results of the Conference Board's 32nd annual survey of corporations. The
> analysis of 1997 data on the giving practices of the largest U.S. corporations contains an
> executive summary and numerous charts and tables of data. Charts include percentages of
> recipients by subject, the top 50 donors of cash and non-cash giving, and largest givers by
> industry.

Tillman, Corliss M. *Making the Corporate Connection—A Step-by-Step Guide to
Sponsorship.* PWIB Research Express Publications, 1999. 150 p.

Vacek, Lori. *Corporate Citizenship in Asia Pacific: Conference Report.* Washington, DC:
Council on Foundations, 1997. 54 p.

> Outlines the emerging practice of corporate citizenship in the Asia Pacific region. Based
> on themes that emerged from a Council on Foundations conference held in Hong Kong in
> 1995.

Weeden, Curt. *Corporate Social Investing.* San Francisco: Berrett-Koehler Publishers, Inc.,
1998.

> A breakthrough guide for businesses planning their corporate giving strategies, as well as a
> valuable fundraising tool for nonprofit organizations seeking corporate support. The
> ten-step program outlines how to transform corporate gifts into corporate social
> investments, forging creative alliances with nonprofit organizations that will bolster or

maintain profits while at the same time providing needed resources for schools, colleges, civic groups, cultural organizations, and other charities. Explains why corporations should be concerned about social investing and how such philanthropy is changing. Tells how to research and make company-appropriate investments and which ones to avoid. Provides staffing and management designs for different types of organizations. Gives suggestions for nonprofits seeking corporate investors as they face increased cutbacks in public funding.

Zukowski, Linda M. *Fistfuls of Dollars: Fact and Fantasy about Corporate Charitable Giving.* 1st ed. Redondo Beach, CA: EarthWrites Publishing, 1998. 196 p.
Covers the basics of corporate giving solicitation, as well as the elements of proposals and budgets. Also discusses how to respond to a funding decision. Indexed.

Organizations

The Business Enterprise Trust
706 Cowper Street
Palo Alto, CA 94301
Tel: 650-321-5100
Web address: www.betrust.org
Founded to celebrate the concept that responsible business behavior is more widespread than generally believed and is essential for the long-term maximization of shareholder value. Subscribes to the concept that businesses are a form of organization where various parties voluntarily come together to do what none of them could do alone. Recognizes that business leaders at all levels need to behave responsibly toward all those constituents, or stakeholders, in order to achieve optimal business performance over the long term.

Business for Social Responsibility
609 Mission Street, 2nd Floor
San Francisco, CA 94105-3506
Tel: 415-537-0888
Fax: 415-537-0889
Web address: www.bsr.org
A national association of more than 1,400 companies that are interested in implementing responsible corporate policies and practices. The Global Business Responsibility Resource Center, a project of the Business for Social Responsibility (BSR) Education Fund, provides businesses, nonprofits interested in working with the private sector, the media, and academics with information, strategic tools, and other assistance they may need to understand and implement responsible business practices. The BSR tracks emerging issues and trends, provides information on corporate leadership practices, conducts research and education workshops, develops practical business tools, and provides consulting services and technical assistance to its member companies.

The Conference Board
845 Third Avenue
New York, NY 10022-6679
Tel: 212-759-0900
Fax: 212-980-7014
Web address: http://www.conference-board.org/

> The Conference Board is a leading business membership and research organization where you can gain cross-industry knowledge and share experiences and best practices with executives from more than 3,000 companies and other organizations in 67 countries. A not-for-profit, nonadvocacy organization with a dual purpose: "To improve the business enterprise system and to enhance the contribution of business to society."

Prince of Wales Business Leaders Forum
15-16 Cornwall Terrace
Regent's Park
London NW1 4QP England
Tel: 44-0171-467-3656
Fax: 44-0171-467-3610
Web address: www.oneworld.org/pwblf

> An international not-for-profit organization founded by the Prince of Wales in 1990. Mission is to "promote socially responsible business practices which benefit business and society and to help achieve social, economic, and environmentally sustainable development."

Internet Resources

Companies Online (http://www.companiesonline.com/)
> Dun & Bradstreet list of 100,000 public and private firms.

Corporate Information (www.corporateinformation.com)
> Meta-index to Web sites for U.S. and international corporations. Provides profiles and research reports on thousands of companies around the world.

Foundation Center: Corporate Grantmakers on the Internet
(http://fdncenter.org/grantmaker/gws_corp/corp.html)
> A list of hundreds of links that take you directly to the Web sites of company-sponsored private foundations and direct corporate giving programs. For grantseekers interested in doing preliminary funding research online, provides thorough annotations that can be searched using the grantmaker search engine included in an adjacent frame.

Funders Online (http://www.fundersonline.org/)
> Funders Online, an initiative of the European Foundation Centre, aims to promote the use of Internet technology among independent funders in Europe and to create a single point of reference to Europe's philanthropic community. The Funders Online Web site features the

first Internet directory of independent funder websites. Through Funders Online, users can access the Web sites of some three hundred foundations and corporate funders in Europe with a total annual expenditure of more than 3.5 billion euros.

Guide to Understanding Financials (http://www.ibm.com/financialguide)
This IBM Web page has information on how to make sense of the financial statements in a company's annual report.

Internet Prospector: Corporate Giving (http://www.internet-prospector.org/corp-giv.html)
Site rich in information and links about corporate giving.

Internet Prospector: Locating U.S. Corporation Records Online
(http://www.internet-prospector.org/secstate.html)
A directory of state Web sites and U.S. secretaries of state, contact information, including URL's and e-mail addresses. Search official incorporation, trademark, UCC, and foundation databases, when available.

Project Involve (www.alfsv.org/involve)
A corporate community involvement project of the American Leadership Forum that is dedicated to increasing the level of corporate philanthropy in Silicon Valley. Provides building blocks for companies small and large to make a positive impact on the community by using a range of corporate resources—cash, employees, product, and in-kind gifts. Publishes a reference guide of organizations and agencies relevant for designing and implementing community-oriented programs.

STAT-USA (http://www.stat-usa.gov/)
U.S. Department of Commerce business, trade, and economic news.

Wall Street Research NET (WSRN) (http://www.wsrn.com/home/companyResearch.html)
Database of 17,000 U.S. and Canadian companies, with more than 500,000 links to additional information.

Chapter 17

Government Support

The happiness of society is the end of government.
— John Adams

Probably no debate is more important to the future of any country's neediest, most vulnerable citizens than the one concerning the role of government in delivering social services and supporting the work of nonprofits. In countries with an emerging nonprofit sector, the role of government in supporting those organizations, and encouraging them to grow and thrive, is a major part of the evolution of both the nonprofit sector and the government itself.

Support from government sources varies with the local, national, and international state of the economy; the political party in office; the popularity of a specific cause; the strength of

competing demands; and demographic considerations. Many governments have, since the worldwide Great Depression of the 1930s, played a central role in supporting nonprofit organizations. Since the Reagan and Thatcher administrations in the 1980s, however, governments around the world have reduced the level of services they provide as well as their support of nonprofits. The nonprofit sector has responded by securing more private donations, increasing fees for service, developing sources of earned income through sales of products, and so on. Unfortunately, many nonprofits have simply been forced out of existence as a result of losing government support—an unhappy fact that underlines the importance of nonprofits' diversifying their sources of support.

According to a study titled "The Nonprofit Sector and the New Federal Budget: Recent History and Future Directions," in the United States "the percentage of the gross domestic product devoted to federal spending in areas of interest to nonprofits, outside of Medicare, Medicaid, and income assistance, declined some 40 percent between FY 1980 and FY 1997, so that, by FY 1997 it was only 60 percent of what it had been in FY 1980."[1]

What Is the Relationship between Government and Nonprofits?

Government is motivated to fund nonprofit organizations because it needs their help to ensure the public good. Nonprofits comprise educational, social service, health service, research, religious, and cultural institutions, as well as the civic, social, fraternal, and advocacy groups that make up the very fabric of most societies. Nonprofits can do some things better, more quickly, or more cost effectively than government, and in many instances already have the experience it would take a public agency years to develop. Additionally, nonprofits may be less constrained by legal and bureaucratic requirements and are consequently better positioned to take risks and explore new solutions.

The relationship between government and the nonprofit sector, however, goes well beyond the fact that government is a major source of support. Historically, nonprofit organizations have tended to precede government as originators of programs and services, and to act as a testing ground for new solutions to social problems. In recent years, nonprofit groups have consolidated their interests and organized nationally so that they are now recognized as a distinct sector of the economy, referred to as the "third sector," the "social sector," "civil society," the "voluntary sector," or the "independent sector." This sector's relationships with all levels of government have assumed greater definition, fostered by increased research, publication, and education. At the same time, there are more "public–private" partnerships that cut across sectors.

Government generally plays three roles with regard to the nonprofit sector:

---

1. Alan Abramson, Lester M. Salamon, and Eugene C. Steurle, "The Nonprofit Sector and the Federal Budget: Recent History and Future Directions." Working paper, Aspen Institute Nonprofit Sector Research Fund, Washington, D.C., 1999.

1. It creates an environment that encourages—or discourages—the creation and flourishing of nonprofits, chiefly through laws governing freedom of speech, assembly, the press, etc., and the degree to which they are enforced.

2. Government can draft laws and create financial incentives to help nonprofits operate without some of the pressures for-profit business must face. Financial incentives, such as tax deductions for contributions, encourage individuals and businesses to donate time and money, and tax-exempt status enables nonprofits to operate without paying many, or all, of the taxes that for-profit businesses must pay.

3. Government can provide actual financial support to a nonprofit through a grant or a contract.

In the United States, government funding is extended either as direct or indirect support. *Direct support* is provided in two ways: *grants* and *purchase-of-service contracts*. Grants are awards to organizations for a negotiated amount of funds to carry out a project or program for a specific period of time. Purchase-of-service contracts are legal agreements between a government agency and a nonprofit that has been engaged to deliver specific services to eligible clients.

Indirect support consists of:

1. *Tax exemptions.* Nonprofits are granted federal, state, and local exemptions from corporate income tax. Some municipalities also exempt nonprofits from real estate and sales taxes.

2. *Reduced mail rates.* Nonprofits are entitled to certain privileged mailing rates.

3. *Public employee charitable solicitations.* Public agencies cooperate with local fund-raising campaigns for nonprofit organizations by providing release time to staff for solicitation purposes and by allowing payroll deductions.

4. *Support for revenue-generating programs.* Some states permit charitable organizations to raise tax-free money through bingo, casino gambling, and canvassing.

5. *Access to public forums for debate.* Legislative and commission hearings are open to nonprofits for the purpose of speaking out on issues that concern their constituencies.

Many of these advantages are available in a number of countries, but very few countries have a uniform policy code stating what their government will provide to its nonprofit organizations. This chapter focuses primarily on sources of government support for U.S.-based nonprofits. However, government plays a critical role in the life of the voluntary sector in all countries.

The Third Sector's Role in Public Debate

The right of nonprofits to criticize a standing government and to encourage debate on public policy issues is, itself, another hotly debated issue. In his book, "The International Guide to Nonprofit Law," Lester Salamon suggests the following role for government in his chapter proposing an international statement of principles:

> Government plays a significant role in the functioning of the voluntary sector. In general, governments should encourage . . . voluntary organizations while respecting their need for a significant degree of autonomy and independence. Key features of a positive government approach toward the voluntary sector include the following:

> • The right to associate must be clearly and forcefully embedded in law.

> • Voluntary organizations acting in the public interest should be eligible for preferential tax treatment.

> • Government should not discourage contributions by individuals and corporations to support the public-service activities of voluntary organizations, whether these contributions are cash or in-kind.

> • Partnership arrangements between government and voluntary sector in the delivery of needed services should be encouraged, but in ways that avoid jeopardizing the autonomy and independence of voluntary organizations.

> • Government should avoid infringing on the independence of the voluntary sector.

> • Government policy should respect and facilitate the advocacy role of nonprofit organizations.

> • Where misuse or mismanagement of voluntary organizations is charged, organizations must have recourse to the courts.[2]

2. Lester M. Salamon and Stefan Toepler, *International Guide to Nonprofit Law* (New York: John Wiley & Sons, 1997).

Overview: Securing Grants and Contracts from Federal, State, and Local Governments

Since 1980, there has been a substantial shift from the federal government as the direct source of funds to state and local government as providers of public support; this trend is popularly referred to as "devolution." The U.S. federal government's use of large block grants to the fifty states has been a means of giving individual states greater administrative responsibility for program priorities and allocations. Welfare, health care, and the regulation of food and the safety of drinking water are among the areas where state and localities have greater rule.

State and local governments also appropriate money for their own programs, which may operate independently or in complicated interrelationships with federal programs. In New York State, for example, agencies such as the Division for Youth, the Department of Social Service, the Office of Mental Retardation, the State Education Department, the Office of Mental Health, the Division of Alcohol and Alcohol Abuse, the Department of Health, the Office of the Aging, the Division of Substance Abuse Services Administration, among others, administer both federal funds coming to New York State and programs generated by the New York State legislature. Frequently, these monies are passed through the states and administered by counties, sometimes by city or village governments.

The permutations and combinations of funding programs emanating from federal, state, and local government are endlessly complex and fluid. To illustrate what could happen, a nonprofit agency may be the recipient of:

- A federal grant administered by a federal program officer

- Program funds granted and administered by a state agency, but funded by a block grant from the federal government

- A contract for services with a state agency, mandated by state legislation and funded by state tax funds

- County tax funds granted through a county agency as a match to state and federal funds

Seeking public funds requires an understanding of budgetary process and the ways information about the availability of funds is made public by federal, state, and local agencies and departments. The budget process at each level is unique in its details and timing, but there are common elements at all levels that the grant- or contract-seeker should know. In every budget process there are points at which the leadership of a nonprofit organization or coalition of nonprofit agencies can try to influence the characteristics of a program and the amount of money available to fund that program.

The beginning of any budget cycle is usually closed to outsiders. Agency staff, budget divisions, and executive staff establish agency priorities for program funding, prepare budgets, hold internal hearings, and negotiate budget proposals. To influence the process at this stage would require an outsider with significant influence at a sufficiently high level. Internal conversations, presentations, and/or research papers may be used to move a program idea into a budget proposal. Eventually, the executive budget is forwarded to Congress, or to a state or local legislative body, for action.

It is in the legislative body that the public has its best opportunity to influence the budget. The committees that deal with the budget all hold seasonal hearings at which nonprofits can express their views. In New York State, for example these important hearings take place in September, October, and November; in California they occur from February to May. Once the executive budget is passed and appropriations are made, the executive branch usually regains control of the administration of the funds. The executive branch distributes the money through contracts or grants, including block grants.

The U.S. Federal Government

Grants and contracts are allocated through a request for proposal (RFP) process. The executive staff of a government agency or department prepares an RFP that defines the type of program that will fulfill legislative intent. Project grant money from the federal government is described by federal agencies as funding that "fills gaps," or "supplements, not supplants." Federal project grant money is not meant to fund normal day-to-day operations and will not be granted for that purpose.

Catalog of Federal Domestic Assistance

The best source of information about federal funding opportunities is the *Catalog of Federal Domestic Assistance* (*CFDA*), published by the federal government. The *Catalog* describes itself as "a government-wide compendium of Federal programs, projects, services and activities that provide assistance or benefits to the American public. It contains both financial and non-financial assistance programs administered by departments and establishments of the Federal Government," and lists all funding the U.S. government provides domestically. To purchase the 2000 edition of the *CFDA*, send $87 to the Superintendent of Documents, U.S. Government Printing Office, P.O. Box 371954, Pittsburgh, PA 15250-7954; or call 202-512-1800 to charge your order. (You will also receive an update six months later.) The *CFDA* is also on-line at www.cfda.gov/. The on-line version allows users to search using key words to find programs that correspond to an organization's own mix of efforts, and is one of the best bargains around. It is important to spend time with the *CFDA* to avoid developing a proposal that has no chance of being funded. Be sure to check the section called "Deleted Programs Index" to make sure a program you have identified still exists.

Once a potential funding source has been identified, the next step is to call the program contact person and verify that your organization is eligible for funding, and ask when the RFP will be announced in the *Federal Register*.

The Federal Register

At the federal level, preliminary funding guidelines are published in the *Federal Register*. Published every day that the federal government works, the *Federal Register* includes everything from presidential proclamations and executive orders to federal agency regulations and proposed agency rules. This central resource is available at depository libraries—public or university libraries throughout the country that have been designated to receive copies of government publications for public use—or it can be purchased for $606 a year from the Superintendent of Documents, as noted above for the *CFDA*.

Funding guidelines published in the *Federal Register* are open to public comment. Professionals interested in influencing the design of programs frequently make comments in writing to the administration, sometimes visiting agencies to discuss guidelines and following up their visit with written commentary. Once an RFP has been formalized, it is reissued in the *Federal*

Register. Announcements for federal agencies seeking bids on contracts can be found in the *Commerce Business Daily*.

Commerce Business Daily

Commerce Business Daily (*CBD*) lists notices of proposed government procurement actions, contract awards, sales of government property, and other procurement information. A new edition of the *CBD* is issued every business day. Each edition contains approximately five hundred to one thousand notices and each notice appears in the *CBD* only once. The *CBD* databases on-line via GPO Access contain notices from December 2, 1996, forward. All federal procurement offices are required to announce in the *CBD* proposed procurement actions over $25,000 and contract awards over $25,000 that are likely to result in the award of any subcontracts. If you wish to review previous editions of the *CBD*, contact your local public library for assistance. Copies of the *CBD* are maintained at more than seven hundred federal depository libraries located throughout the United States. CBD*Net*, the online version of *Commerce Business Daily*, can be found at http://cbdnet.access.gpo.gov/. (A one-year subscription to the print version costs between $275 and $324. Order from the Superintendent of Documents, as noted above for the *CFDA*.)

State and Local Funding

At the state and local level, the proposal process is not so straightforward. Although most states do publish information on funding for at least some of their funding sources, there is no publication similar to the *Federal Register* or the *Commerce Business Daily* within the states or counties. There are, however, some excellent resources for nonprofit organizations seeking funding from local and state governments, including:

- *State Budget.* This document describes in detail the various programs funded by a state government and the dollar amounts allocated to them.

- *State Plans.* These documents project the programmatic plans of a state agency for a specific period of time.

- *County/City Budget.* These documents describe in detail the various programs funded by a locality.

- *Directories of state or local funding.* These can be found at a local library, or in the libraries of places like the United Way, or other organizations that receive substantial state or local funding.

In their book *The Grantseekers Toolkit*, Cheryl New and James Quick maintain, "state and local programs are frequently highly political in nature, so finding out about state and local funding availability becomes a matter of who you know and whom you have spoken with recently. Communicating regularly with other nonprofits in your field is an invaluable activity in this connection, too. In many cases, the only way to find out about state and local funding possibilities is through word of mouth."[3] Even large state agencies, such as departments of education, do not have a central publication that announces their requests for proposals. In some states, including New York and Illinois, RFPs are often published in the notice section of major newspapers in the state.

Each agency, division, or bureau that administers programs for which an RFP process is used writes and distributes its own RFPs. In New York, each of these divisions or bureaus has its own lists of potential organizations from which it seeks proposals. In other states, the lists are maintained at the department level. In Illinois, for example, the Department of Public Aid maintains central lists for all the subdivisions within that department. The grant- or contract-seeker needs to identify the individual in each bureau or division who is a potential source of funds and make sure to be included on the list of potential contract agencies that routinely receive RFPs.

It is not unusual for a legislative body to appropriate more money than the administration spends, and while a legislature may appropriate several millions of dollars for a program, the administration might actually spend only a fraction of that amount by delaying the RFP process, among other possible tactics. Naturally, program people are anxious to spend all funds that have been appropriated. Legislators who are interested in a particular program will often exert pressure on the executive body to expend allocated funds through conducting oversight hearings.

When funds have been allocated but no RFP is forthcoming, consider making a request to participate in such oversight hearings. Sometimes the state or county legislature does not grant total administrative power to the agencies but reserves some decision-making approval for itself. In these cases, support for a particular program from the legislature is vitally important.

The executive budget process is not the only channel open for nonprofit organizations; in some states, including New York and California, individual legislators are empowered to propose bills appropriating support for specific nonprofit organizations in their home districts. It is not unusual for a powerful legislator to sponsor a bill allocating money to be channeled through some state agency to a single organization in his or her home district. In these instances, the contract or grants management process is assigned to a state agency. In New York State, the time to influence this process is in January, February, and March.

Another way of obtaining public funds open to some nonprofits is by making sure an agency is licensed, certified, and approved to provide certain mandated services, such as foster care, Medicare or Medicaid, or child-abuse prevention services. Institutionalized, ongoing funding streams of this kind can offer a very secure funding source for nonprofits.

Many of the same processes and points of influence work at the local level. Local governments frequently engage in comprehensive planning, where planning committees determine priorities and agendas for local spending. Becoming involved in these processes and understanding the legislative process at the local level may be the first step in securing public funding.

Competition for funds varies at each level of government, but the most competitive market for public funds is clearly at the federal level. An inexperienced, unknown agency is, therefore, better positioned to seek federal dollars when application is made in association with a university, major research firm, or state agency. Agencies with the capacity to raise funds from private sources to match their government grants are also good partners. Seeking federal funds is a

---

3. Cheryl New and James Quick, *The Grantseekers Toolkit* (New York: John Wiley & Sons, 1998).

highly professional skill that requires large investments of time and money; small community-based organizations especially should be aware that the odds are against their receiving an adequate return on investment in the application process.

The process of seeking state funds or local funds is somewhat less competitive. Fewer organizations receive RFPs and there is some commitment to distributing funds aimed at programmatic needs according to population density, geographic location, and ethnic and racial representation.

Which Organizations Are Eligible for Government Grants and Contracts?

Governments give funds to projects conducted by businesses, unions, trade associations, and all kinds of nonprofit organizations. Governments sometimes fund individuals to produce a service on a contractual basis; however, the amount of money awarded to individuals is small—usually under $5,000.

What Are the Advantages of Securing Support from Government?

There are a variety of advantages to gaining government support:

1. *Ongoing support.* Compared with foundation and corporate giving, government funding is more likely to be renewable. The most secure funds are those provided through legislated mandates, such as services to neglected, abused, or foster care children; Medicare; and Medicaid. However, mandates and entitlements are all under scrutiny and revision, so no government funding is totally secure. Other government programs are more short-lived. Most recipients can expect a minimum of one year of support from a federal or state agency. These grants are considered "seed money" for demonstration projects. The possibility of refunding is enhanced if the program shows demonstrable results in a timely fashion and builds a positive working relationship with the funding agency. Alliances with local political figures also help promote ongoing support. Frequently, such individuals have influence on which local programs receive funding.

2. *Substantial support.* Government grants and contracts are frequently larger than those awarded by foundations or corporations. Sometimes a government grant or contract is sufficiently large to finance an entire program. Indeed, some government programs prefer that contract agencies receive no additional funds. This policy ensures programmatic control and accountability to the funding source.

3. *Credibility.* Support from one governmental agency or department, and a proven track record in managing public tax dollars, will enhance an organization's credibility with other public funding sources. Previous government support provides

evidence that a nonprofit can meet the stringent fiscal and programmatic expectations of government officials. Government funding can also help meet the expectations of other funding sources, such as foundations and corporations. Some foundations and corporations view their funds as seed support for projects that will ultimately be underwritten by government, since their resources are modest in comparison to the public sector. For example, a demonstration social services program that is clearly within the realm of governmental priorities might be initially funded by private sources, and subsequently, by a unit of government.

4. *Easier access to decision-makers and the decision-making process.* Once a nonprofit has won government support, its staff becomes known to the staff of the agency providing that support. With their help, an entire network of contacts can be built over the years to help identify other potential sources and craft proposals and programs that may gain support. Eventually a nonprofit may even become able to influence the decision-making process regarding the priorities and allocation of funds, since its experience and knowledge has become known and respected. The longer an organization is around, and the longer it serves its community, the more likely it is to be successful at building public support.

In sum, nonprofits can utilize a number of different avenues and strategies to present their cases to government officials. Applicants will usually find that there are individuals involved with every government program who can become allies and help them understand the details of their grantmaking procedures; e.g., What was the intent of the legislation authorizing their program? What would be included in a strong proposal? Who would be involved with the actual decision-making process?

Applicants can also enlist the aid of elected officials to write letters of support or even make phone calls to prospective public funders in support of a proposal. City council members, town selectmen, mayors, governors, state and county legislators, congressional representatives, state and U.S. senators, and state and local commissioners are just some of the elected officials whose stewardship can lend valuable support for a proposal. Their involvement does not necessarily guarantee forthcoming support, but their endorsement will strengthen an organization's competitive position, as government agencies are interested in maintaining the goodwill of these officials. The support of nonelected key community leaders is also important.

What Are the Disadvantages of Raising Support from Government?

1. *Time limitations.* Many government grants are time limited and cover a declining proportion of program expenses. For example, a three-year award could cover 100 percent of all expenses in year one, 75 percent in year two, and 50 percent in year three.

2. *Unanticipated or uncovered additional expenses.* A government grant or contract does not necessarily cover all expenses that might be incurred. As a result, money often must be raised from other sources.

3. *Cash Flow.* An organization may have to front initial program expenses, since government contracts are frequently awarded on a reimbursement basis. An agency lays out the money for the service, documents that the services have been provided and how much they have cost, submits this evidence to the proper agency, and waits for a check. While checks are supposed to arrive within thirty to sixty days, this is not always the case; finding the initial start-up funding until an organization is on a cycle of reimbursement sometimes makes government contracts impossible for smaller agencies.

4. *Paperwork.* The wise stewardship of public funds is a primary priority for government employees. Governments are accountable to the taxpayer. As a result, recipients of public funds are required to keep extensive records to ensure that the taxpayers' money is used wisely. Both financial and programmatic data are reported on a regular basis.

5. *Additional record-keeping.* The paperwork associated with a federal contract or grant will force an organization to expand the responsibilities and possibly the job descriptions of its management and clerical staff. Program staff will have to adapt to keeping records on services delivered in a more exhaustive manner than they may be accustomed to—entailing, perhaps, some additional training of financial and program staff. Annual audits and additional accounting assistance are also standard. Of course, all of these additional steps have built-in advantages as well, including better fiscal management control and enhanced public image. Auditors' reports also increase an agency's credibility with a public funding source and other supporters.

6. *Legal responsibility.* The use of public funds involves both moral and legal obligations. Government grants and contracts are tightly monitored, and misuse of funds can result in legal action. Government grants and contracts require compliance with regulations that are specific to the program and with other standard regulations on fiscal management and affirmative action. In the worst case the IRS could revoke an organization's tax exemption. Repayment of any misused funds might also be required.

7. *Potential negative impact on private fundraising efforts.* Potential individual donors might think, "They don't need my charitable dollars. They are receiving money from the government," or "They are already receiving my tax dollars." While most organizations that receive public support wisely continue to solicit support from other sources (or continue to need other revenues for reasons already mentioned, or for other programs), they need to make their case for such support clear to the giving public. In other words, the responsibility is on the receiving organization to be proactive and forthright in explaining to potential donors why charitable support is also needed. This is particularly true for those institutions that the public knows as

public institutions, such as land grant colleges and universities, public elementary and secondary schools, and actual departments of government that directly solicit the public for support.

8. *Potential adverse effect on the agency's internal organization.* Due to the many requirements and regulations set by public funders, an agency receiving public money has less flexibility in how it chooses to structure its delivery of services or programs. Also, public monies may result in a certain level of bureaucratization in an organization. This may be altogether desirable; however, the impulse behind such changes are externally induced—by a governmental body rather than by a mandate of your board of directors or an executive director. Such changes may affect the morale of staff and volunteers, who may have shaped the previous mode of operation. It is also harder to predict how all of these changes will impact an organization and to plan for their consequences.

Deciding Whether To Approach Government for Support

How does a new or existing nonprofit organization determine whether current or prospective programs might qualify for government support in the form of grants or contracts? The answer is not necessarily automatic or simple. You must do some research to answer this question. Begin by contacting local organizations and agencies that are active in your field of interest to develop a sense of who is doing what and to explore who is funding what; this is a perfect project for a capable volunteer or intern. The local United Way or health and welfare planning body or arts coordinating council can also be of invaluable assistance in gathering this information.

As you analyze what you've learned, ask yourself these questions: Can you address any gaps in the current service delivery system? Can you see any ways to maximize the impact of the funding sources now pouring in? Are the funds appropriately targeted to the needs of the client population?

In the search for public funds for your program, you can also check with local and government offices, elected officials, and community leaders in your field of interest to assess whether they are aware of any funds that might be available for your work. You can write or call public agencies directly and ask them for information. Request that you be put on the list of organizations that receive their program announcements.

One other possible route is to identify and contact organizations similar to yours in other parts of the country to obtain their knowledge of the subject at hand. This approach will also help you identify national foundations and corporations that are prospects for support. Librarians at your main local library can assist you in identifying these groups by suggesting standard reference materials. There may also be one or more national associations representing the interests of such organizations that can provide you with the information you seek. For example, the Center for Community Change, based in Washington, D. C., provides community-based and neighborhood organizations with information on U. S. federal programs. Additionally, there are some reference books on federal funding listed in the Additional Resources section of this chapter.

What if your work addresses an issue that is so new or pioneering that it has not yet captured the interest of government? This is often the case because nonprofits are on the cutting edge of many social issues. In deciding whether to approach government for support in these instances, consider the following questions: Does your work affect a substantial number of individuals or a specific population whose needs the government has recognized? Can you document or demonstrate the need for the programs your organization is suggesting? Will these programs, if supported, result in positive changes in regard to the problem that you have set out to address? Can you mobilize sufficient local support among: (1) those who are affected by the problem, (2) elected government representatives, and (3) recognized community leaders, such as civic and religious figures?

Be assured that this road is not an easy one. If the government has not yet acknowledged the critical nature of the issues your organization is addressing, you would probably be more successful approaching other funding sources for initial support, such as foundations or individuals. Government support might be forthcoming after the need for your program has been established. In fact, government is not usually a good candidate for initial support for the kinds of controversial and evolving issues that frequently prompt individuals or groups to establish new nonprofit organizations.

Securing Government Support

Once you have identified a prospective public funding source, you need to engage in the following tasks:

Step 1. Identify or Design a Program that Conforms to the Interests of the Funding Agency

You may find that you have an existing project or program that falls within the stated interests of a government agency or department. Those interests are usually written into the legislation that brought an agency's or department's programs into existence, as well as into the regulations the agency or department subsequently issued that governs the disbursement of grants or contracts.

If your organization, while active in the field generally, does not currently have a project that corresponds to the specific interests of a particular government source, you can design a program for your organization that does correspond to those interests. The same criteria that were presented in matching projects with foundation and corporate interests also serve in building a strong case for government support:

1. Compatibility with mission

2. Acknowledged expertise

3. Achievability

4. Topicality

5. Documentation

The ability to accomplish a specific set of objectives (criterion 3) and the capacity to demonstrate the extent of the seriousness of a problem (criterion 4) are important to government funders; they want to see a measurable return on the funds they allocate. You should document that return in the reports you submit after receiving a grant or contract by describing and, if possible, quantifying a reduction in the incidence of the problem you set out to tackle, or in an increase in the number of individuals to whom you have been able to provide mandated services.

Step 2. Enlist Local Counsel and Support for Your Work

You may have a wonderful idea, but you are unlikely to win government support unless you can first demonstrate support at the local level. Government agencies, institutes, and departments want to see evidence of popular support among the constituencies you are planning to serve as well as in the community at large. Such support indicates that they can fund you with the knowledge that your community, too, feels that your efforts will make an impact.

This kind of support can be provided by elected officials (such as city council representatives, town selectmen, mayors, state legislators, or congressional representatives); civic and community leaders (United Way officials, donors, religious leaders, or chamber of commerce officers); and board officers and/or executive directors of related organizations that are recognized leaders in your field.

These individuals can most effectively express their support by mailing a letter on their organizational letterhead that states why they believe your proposed project is worthwhile and why they believe your organization is qualified to implement it. They may know the particular official of the agency to which you are applying, or even a member of the advisory body that makes the funding decisions. Your contacts may prefer to place a phone call, or to mention their support at an upcoming meeting or gathering with the official in question. You should leave the method of contact to the discretion of the individuals you are asking, as they will know what type of contact would be most appropriate.

Step 3. Request a Pre-Application Meeting

After identifying the government department or agency most likely to provide support, contact them directly. Request any information they make available to prospective applicants, including the application form, instruction booklet, and a copy of the bill or act that authorized or established the program to which you are applying. You should then identify the public official in charge of handling all applications and request a pre-application meeting; that request is best made by a letter, followed up by a phone call.

The purpose of this meeting is to discuss what the government official's agency is really looking for in proposals or applications. In other words, are there any particular types of projects it has prioritized, or that are of special, or timely, interest? Has it already delegated certain types of programs to the low-priority heap? This information-gathering visit can help you in designing the program you will submit for consideration and also in completing the required application or proposal.

Don't hesitate to ask questions about completing the application; the government official will not expect you to be totally knowledgeable about government grantsmanship. This same official will be your ongoing contact throughout the application process and, possibly, in future years.

Strike a positive tone at your meeting and send a letter afterward thanking the person for his or her time and counsel.

Step 4. Complete and Submit the Required Application in a Timely and Thorough Fashion

Most government funding bodies have application forms or specify the format to be used for proposals; others request a proposal addressing a problem or set of tasks that they have identified. In either case, the proposal or the application provide the opportunity to describe who you are, what you hope to accomplish, and the ways in which you are particularly qualified to achieve the objectives that you have set forth.

Again, if any questions arise as you prepare your written materials, don't hesitate to contact the official with whom you have already met. Remember the importance of personal relationships, whether you are applying for a government grant or asking a friend for a donation.

Problem Statement

Typically, the application requires a well-documented statement of the problem. You can develop this statement using one of two approaches: problem analysis or needs assessment. The *problem analysis* approach identifies the causes of problems, and is usually used to define issues that will be addressed by programs designed as demonstrations of innovative new solutions. Take the *needs assessment* approach when applying for program funding to serve a population whose needs have been officially recognized. The needs assessment approach uses statistics and social indicator data to document the extent and seriousness of a recognized problem in a specific geographic location.

Program Goals and Objectives

Regardless of which approach you take in drafting the problem statement, your argument should lead logically to program goals. A program goal states in broad strokes what the program seeks to achieve and is made more specific by identifying specific objectives. Program objectives are statements of the results that can be expected from the project.

Approach and Evaluation

Your list of program objectives should be followed by a description of your approach to the problem, of your plans for achieving the objectives. This description should reflect a logical connection to both the statement of the problem and the objectives. Show how your approach to the problem will deal with the causes of the problem or will specifically address the needs laid out in the problem statement.

The approach to the problem is followed by a description of the tasks you will undertake in order to achieve your objectives. These tasks provide a blueprint for building your budget, and each task should be described in detail. The list and description of tasks is followed by a timeline that indicates the sequence in which tasks will be accomplished.

The proposal should always include an evaluation section, briefly outlining how you intend to show that the intended results were achieved and that achievement was the result of the program and not of chance.

Budget, Capability, and Future Funding

The budget section details the cost of the project. It should be justified in relationship to the tasks. Job descriptions of all staff are presented in this section along with a description of the organizational structure.

The budget section is followed by a section called the *capability of the contractor* that documents the reasons your agency is in a strong position to conduct this program. Your past history, resources, and letters of support should be included here. A final section should outline your plans for future funding.

Government grant proposals are frequently lengthier than proposals to foundations and corporations, often because of the detail required. Rich detail in clear prose, free of jargon, is appreciated. Rather than overcrowding the main text, you might want to use appendices.

The Yes

You have been awarded a grant or a contract—Congratulations! Now you can get down to business. Make sure you understand all the financial reporting requirements that accompany your award. Remember that you will be receiving public tax dollars, which carry greater fiscal responsibility than you may be accustomed to. Be sure that you and your bookkeeping staff understand all the financial forms you will be required to file on a regular basis. If you have any questions, pick up the phone and make an appointment with a fiscal officer at the agency that has awarded you the grant or contract.

You may also wish to clarify when you will receive the actual funds, since you may have to wait several months before receiving your first installment. Because of the problems produced by delays in receiving government funds, a number of foundations have established programs to provide interest-free or modest-interest loans to help the cash flow of nonprofits who are waiting to receive their approved government allocations.

The No

Don't despair. Inquire why your proposal was rejected—you are entitled to an explanation. As you can always reapply, discuss the strengths of your proposal as well as the weaknesses, and discuss the possibility of submitting an application or proposal that addresses the issues that were raised during this first review process. Persistence will be your best ally as long as any subsequent application demonstrates that you have dealt with the concerns that prompted the first rejection.

Be sure you have been added to the mailing list of the targeted agency to receive future requests for proposals and any other information that they periodically make available to prospective applicants. Thank the officials with whom you have been in touch for their time and consideration. Keep a friendly door open for the next time around.

Lessons for the Future

Federal government support has changed dramatically over recent decades. Starting with the Reagan administration and continuing to the present, there has been a concerted attempt to weaken the role of the national government in protecting and promoting the welfare of its vulnerable citizens. Although that effort may falter as intensifying social problems demonstrate their pernicious nature, national government continues to hold steady on its course toward less and less involvement with the welfare of its citizenry. To overcome these problems, a commitment needs to be made and resources allocated on a scale that only national government can provide. As Vernon Jordan said in his speech, "We Cannot Live for Ourselves Alone": "Because government has immense resources, legal powers of persuasion, and is politically accountable, it must hold a central position in marshalling our society's efforts toward political, social and economic equality."

Meanwhile, nonprofits must be prepared to operate in this current period of federal retrenchment. The federal government will be seeking to transfer more responsibilities to the states. Local governments—cities, towns, and counties—will be demanding a greater voice in state capitals, where much of the decision-making process is increasingly taking place. While some government dollars will certainly continue to flow directly to nonprofit organizations from Washington D.C., the political arena will increasingly shift to the state capitals. Fortunately, the distance to the state capital is shorter than the road to Washington, D.C. Many nonprofits will have to learn, or relearn, how the political processes of their own state governments work. State elected officials can expect more visitors on their doorsteps.

One result of the changes on the federal level is that state and local governments are experimenting with new ways to allocate resources as they weigh which programs formerly supported by federal dollars deserve their support. Some nonprofits have benefited from this transfer of fiscal resources to the local level, but others have not.

State and local governments are also experimenting with new forms of taxation and revenue generation, such as lotteries and gambling, to finance some of these programs. Lotteries have actually become the fastest-growing source of state revenues nationwide. Although results have been mixed, and a considerable portion of the money raised by these programs is being spent on their promotion and administration, lotteries have had positive effects in some cases.

Other ideas will continue to arise as both nonprofits and government seek ways to raise needed dollars. If nonprofits can organize themselves effectively, they can become a powerful force in helping direct these newfound revenues. The future will certainly provide numerous opportunities for nonprofits that are creative, resourceful, in touch with today's realities, and focused on tomorrow's possibilities.

Tips

- Find your way to your state capital—more public funding decisions will be made there in the future.

- Seek out the counsel of your elected representatives and their staff.

- Cultivate the support of important elected officials on an ongoing basis.

Profile:

Kentucky Waterways Alliance

The Kentucky Waterways Alliance (KWA) has received several Clean Water Act, Section 319(H) grants through the state of Kentucky to assist in implementing the Kentucky Nonpoint Source Pollution Prevention Program. The Kentucky Division of Water publishes a guidance document with useful information on how they rank and evaluate projects, what type of projects they fund, and specific requirements for the grant proposals. As with any grant proposal, it is important to follow the grant guidance. Kentucky's emphasis for this program is on controlling nonpoint source pollution through the implementation of best management practices by funding projects that use an appropriate combination of educational activities, technical assistance, financial assistance, training, watershed demonstration activities, and enforcement.

KWA has concentrated on funding for educational and training activities. Our most successful effort has been to secure funding for nonpoint source educational activities, which we then offer as mini-grants to our local groups. To date, we have funded a total of 23 local projects with over $85,000 in federal funds. We will soon have an additional $60,000 in mini-grant funds available for our groups.

In 1995, using grant monies for training, we sponsored a workshop on Bio-engineering for Erosion Control and Flood Management. The workshop was a great opportunity for KWA to network with other private and public groups around the state and gain credibility as well as impact policy in this critical watershed protection area. Funding for a second workshop was included and approved in a subsequent grant.

An additional benefit accruing from our nonpoint source grants is our ability to charge grant administration costs to the project. Since we spend a good deal of time administering these grants, this funding helps keep our organization in business! If all this sounds too good to be true, let me convey a few of the disadvantages of this funding. The lead time between submitting the grant proposal and actually receiving approval to spend the money and implement the project can be very long. For instance, we are still awaiting the award that is funded in the state's Fiscal Year 1997 EPA funds, written and approved over two years ago! A second disadvantage is that the entire program works on a reimbursement basis. This means that we have to spend the money and then apply to the state and wait for reimbursement. KWA has found that the time it takes for reimbursements to arrive can vary from less than one month to almost four months. This is very hard for many of our local groups and is the biggest reason why many of them do not apply. Nonpoint source grants also require a minimum 40 percent match. Finally, as with any federal/state grant program, you must agree to comply with a whole host of requirements, including the Paperwork Reduction Act. By the time you've finished complying, you may want to cite your state administrator for violating that very act!

—Judy Peterson, Executive Director of the Kentucky Waterways Alliance

Reprinted by permission from the River Network River Fundraising Alert, vol. 5, no. 2, 1998.

Summary Worksheet

for _____

(name of your organization)

Approaching Government for Support

Building on Past Government Support

1 Have any units of government ever supported your work in the past?

_____ yes   _____ no

If yes, which ones?

_____
_____
_____
_____

2. What characteristics do these funders share? How do their interests correspond to each other?

Comments:

_____
_____
_____
_____

3. What is *your* sense of what they valued in your organization's work?

Comments:

_____
_____
_____
_____

4. Which ones can you approach again for future support?

_____   _____
_____   _____
_____   _____
_____   _____

Definite Ongoing Projects:
Untested (further information needed):

_____   _____
_____   _____
_____   _____
_____   _____

Finding New Government Supporters

Research and Networking

1. List the categories of government interest that your work falls within (i.e., housing, employment, education, criminal justice, social services, etc.):

————————————————   ————————————————
————————————————   ————————————————
————————————————   ————————————————

2. List the units of the local, state, and federal governments that are responsible for these program areas (i.e., departments, agencies, bureaus, commissions, etc.):

Local

————————————————   ————————————————
————————————————   ————————————————
————————————————   ————————————————

State

————————————————   ————————————————
————————————————   ————————————————
————————————————   ————————————————

Federal

————————————————   ————————————————
————————————————   ————————————————
————————————————   ————————————————

3. List the names of other organizations similar to yours in mission and scope in your own community and in other parts of the country.

————————————————   ————————————————
————————————————   ————————————————
————————————————   ————————————————

Which ones have been successful in securing government support? Place a check mark next to those that have. Now, based on your own knowledge or on discussions with representatives of these groups, find out what you can about their funders. List them below:

Name   Unit of Government
(i.e. local, state, federal)

————————————————   ————————————————
————————————————   ————————————————
————————————————   ————————————————

4. See pages 474 and 475 for this part of the worksheet.

Making the Match

For each prospect on the previous list, complete the following worksheet (use your own blank paper).

Name of Government Program:

Its Areas of Interest that Pertain to Your Work:

Develop one or more sentences relating your work to the interests of the unit of government you are approaching. (Or write one or more short sentences demonstrating how the work of your organization reflects the interests of X unit of government.)

4. List below the government programs that you have uncovered from your research and your networking. Limit your listing to the most likely supporters of your organization (your "best bets")

a. Unit of Government	b. Its Stated Areas of Interest that Relate to Your Work	c. Appropriate Contact: Person, Address, and Phone
Local		
State		
Federal		

d. Any Personal Contacts	e. Your Program(s) that Correspond to Their Interests	f. Grants to Similar Organizations

Finding Assistance and Counsel

Name five or more individuals who might be able to advise you on how to approach most effectively the government programs on your prospect list:

a. _____

b. _____

c. _____

d. _____

e. _____

Assessing the Likelihood of Securing Government Support

On the basis of what you have learned, how would you rank your chances of securing government support?

___ Very Good   __ Possible   __ Unlikely   __ Still Unknown

Additional Resources

Publications

Alexander, Jennifer. "Adaptive Strategies of Nonprofit Human Service Organizations in an Era of Devolution and New Public Management." *Nonprofit Management & Leadership* 10 (Spring 2000): 287–303.

> Discusses the findings of a multiphase study of nonprofit human service organizations serving children and youth in Cuyahoga County, Ohio. The purpose of the study was to identify adaptation strategies for maintaining organizational viability in response to the devolution of federal social programs. The study includes an analysis of literature on best practices, and reviews the results of focus groups and a workshop devoted to the evaluation of organizational strategies. Effective adaptations that are identified include strategic expansion of client bases and services; the development of business management techniques and technological capacity building; networking as means of exchanging resources and connecting with funding opportunities; and commercialization of services. With bibliographic references.

Angelica, Emil W., and Vincent L. Hyman. *Coping with Cutbacks: The Nonprofit Guide to Success When Times Are Tight*. Saint Paul, MN: Amherst H. Wilder Foundation, 1997. xi, 114 p.

> Strategies for dealing with anticipated and actual government funding cutbacks. Suggests a six-step self-study process for an organization to determine the best possible options. Includes strategies checklist, reproducible worksheets, and a bibliography.

Billitteri, Thomas J. "For-Profit Social-Service Contracts Could Hurt the Poor, Leaders Say." *Chronicle of Philanthropy* 12 (10 February 2000): 29.

> Discusses a statement issued by 18 major social service organizations in opposition to a trend in which for-profit companies are increasingly providing social services under contracts with the government, placing them in direct competition with nonprofit organizations. The statement voices concern that such contracts could potentially hurt the poor and elderly. Signers of the statement included top executives at Big Brothers Big Sisters of America, Boy Scouts of America, Goodwill Industries International, and the Salvation Army. The effort was coordinated by Catholic Charities USA.

Boris, Elizabeth T., and C. Eugene Steuerle, eds. *Nonprofits and Government: Collaboration and Conflict*. Washington, DC: Urban Institute Press, 1999. xii, 383 p.

> Various contributors analyze the complex relationship of nonprofits to government: (1) "Nonprofit Organizations in a Democracy: Varied Roles and Responsibilities" by Elizabeth T. Boris; (2) "Complementary, Supplementary, or Adversarial? A Theoretical and Historical Examination of Nonprofit-Government Relations in the United States," by Dennis R. Young; (3) "Meeting Social Needs: Comparing the Resources of the Independent Sector and Government," by C. Eugene Steuerle and Virginia A. Hodgkinson;

(4) "The Nonprofit Sector and the Federal Budget: Recent History and Future Directions," by Alan J. Abramson, Lester M. Salamon, and C. Eugene Steuerle; (5) "Tax Treatment of Nonprofit Organizations: A Two-Edged Sword?" by Evelyn Broody and Joseph J. Cordes; (6) "Government Financing of Nonprofit Activity," by Steven Rathgeb Smith; (7) "Nonprofits and Devolution: What Do We Know?" by Carol J. De Vita; (8) "Why Not For-Profit? Conversions and Public Policy," by John H. Goddeeris and Burton A. Weisbrod; (9) "Clash of Values: The State, Religion, and the Arts," by Robert Wuthnow; (10) "Nonprofit Advocacy and Political Participation," by Elizabeth J. Reid; and (11) "Government-Nonprofit Relations in International Perspective," by Lester M. Salamon. Indexed.

Capitol Publications. *Federal Grants and Contracts Weekly*. Arlington, VA: Capitol Publications.

Weekly reports on the latest contracting opportunities and upcoming grants. Regular features include Grants Alert, RFPs Available, Grants and RFPs calendars, profiles of particular agencies, and information about contracts awarded.

Coble, Ran. "The Nonprofit Sector and State Governments: Public Policy Issues Facing Nonprofits in North Carolina and Other States." *Nonprofit Management & Leadership* 9 (Spring 1999): 293–313.

Dumouchel, J. Robert. *Government Assistance Almanac, 2000–2001*. 14th ed. Detroit: Omnigraphics, 2000. xvi, 891 p.

Outlines more than 1,400 federal domestic programs available in 2000. Each entry provides the official and popular program title; the type or types of assistance available through the program; a brief description of program objectives, purposes, and permitted uses, along with examples of funded projects; a summary of recent accomplishments; eligibility requirements; range and average amounts awarded for programs involving financial assistance; and the address and telephone number for the program. Other sections provide summary tables for program funding levels and a listing of field office contacts. Includes index.

Froelich, Karen A. "Diversification of Revenue Strategies: Evolving Resource Dependence in Nonprofit Organizations."*Nonprofit and Voluntary Sector Quarterly,* 28 (September 1999): 246–68.

Discusses and analyses the "revenue dependence" of nonprofit organizations, that is, their reliance on outside funding. Three primary sources of funding are studied here: private contributions (from individuals, corporations, and foundations), government funding, and earned income. The volatility of these income sources, the effect they may have on an organization's goals, and the strategies nonprofits may adopt to diversify their funding sources are explored, with suggestions for further research. With bibliographic references.

Green, Marc, ed. "A Guide to Federal Project Grants." *Grantsmanship Center Magazine* 37 (Winter 1999): 6–11.

> Provides a comprehensive list of all federal project grants with fiscal year 1998 expenditures.

Hodgkinson, Virginia A., Thomas H. Pollak, and Lester M. Salamon, eds. *The Impact of Federal Budget Proposals upon the Activities of Charitable Organizations and the People They Serve 1996-2002: The One Hundred Nonprofit Organizations Study.* Washington, DC: Independent Sector, 1995. vi, 334 p.

> Provides national projections of the impact of congressional budget proposals and detailed impact statements of the proposals on specific organizations. The main part of the report, the One Hundred Nonprofit Organizations Study, focuses on estimating the impact of the House of Representatives' budget resolution on 108 nonprofit organizations that provided Independent Sector with data on their recent revenues by source, program spending, and the amount of services provided by program. Appendices include the methodology for the survey, a list of participating organizations, historical data from 1992, and the survey questionnaire.

Independent Sector. *Changing Roles, Changing Relationships: The New Challenge for Business, Nonprofit Organizations, and Government.* Washington, DC: Independent Sector, 2000. iv, 24 p.

> A free discussion paper and collaborative publication of the Conference Board, Council on Foundations, Independent Sector, National Academy of Public Administration, National Alliance of Business, and the National Governors' Association. Noting that technology and our information-based economy are changing the workplace and increasing globalization, the roles and relationships of the three sectors are changing. Intersectoral collaborations are emerging as one viable option, among others.

Kramer, Ralph M. "A Third Sector in the Third Millennium?" *Voluntas* 11 (March 2000): 1–23.

> Changes in the relationship of the third sector to government in the 1970s to 1980s were profound and Kramer argues that traditional models of the sector need to be re-analyzed, especially in the area of delivery of human services. He discusses and compares four alternative paradigms. With bibliographic references.

Leadership Directories. *Federal Yellow Book.* Washington, DC: Leadership Directories. Annual, with quarterly updates.

> Directory of the executive branch of the federal government, including the White House, Executive Office of the President, and approximately 38,000 federal officials.

Reif-Lehrer, Liane. *Grant Application Writer's Handbook*. Boston: Jones and Bartlett Publishers, 1995. xx, 472 p.

Explains the process of grantseeking from both government and private funders. Chapters cover getting started; the review process; parts of the grant application; planning and writing the research plan; submitting and tracking the grant application; and summary statements, rebuttals, and revisions. Extensive appendices contain information on and examples of National Institute of Health and National Science Foundation awards, sample outline for the research plan, general checklist, sample budget justifications, sample summary statements, advice on applying for foundation grants, and strategies for successful written and oral presentations. Includes bibliographic references, a glossary, and an index.

Reiss, Alvin H. "States Establish Endowment Funds To Ensure Long-Term Arts Support." *Fund Raising Management* 29 (February 1999): 20–21, 41.

With government funding cutbacks, many state arts councils are establishing endowment funds to ensure long-term support for local arts organizations.

Saidel, Judith R., and Sharon L. Harlan. "Contracting and Patterns of Nonprofit Governance." *Nonprofit Management & Leadership* 8 (April 1998): 243–59.

Studies those nonprofit organizations that operate with government grants and contracts with a view to ascertaining the extent to which such funding affects executive leadership, board composition, and interorganizational associations. Includes bibliographic references.

Sawicky, Max B., ed. *The End of Welfare: Consequences of Federal Devolution for the Nation*. Armonk, NY: M.E. Sharpe Publishing (Economic Policy Institute series), 1999. 288 p.

Smillie, Ian. "Changing Partners: Northern Nongovernmental Organizations, Northern Governments." *Voluntas* 5 (August 1994): 155–92.

Draws on a series of studies conducted in 1993 by the Development Centre of the Organisation for Economic Cooperation and Development (OECD), covering thirteen OECD member companies and the European Commission. Examines trends and issues in the fast-changing relationship between nongovernmental organizations (NGOs) and governments. Sees a particular problem in the north, where recession and faltering public support have pushed governments into reduced aid budgets and new concepts of accountability, participation, and the role of civil society. Proposes some basic principles for remedying the problems and for treating NGOs as important elements of civil society rather than as delivery mechanisms for governments. With references.

U.S. Government Printing Office. *Catalog of Federal Domestic Assistance*. Washington, DC: U.S. Government Printing Office. Annual, with supplementary updates.

The U.S. government's most complete listing of the federal programs and activities that provide assistance or benefits to state and local governments, nonprofit organizations, etc.

Extensive descriptions of each program include eligibility requirements, application procedures, and amounts of grants. Indexed by agency program, function, popular name, applicant eligibility, and subject. (One-year subscription costs $87 for hard copy—looseleaf in three-ring binder—or $85 for CD-ROM. To order hard copy, call 202-512-1800; to order CD-ROM, call 202-708-5126. Available on-line at: www.cfda.gov/.)

U.S. Government Printing Office. *Commerce Business Daily*. Washington, DC: U. S. Government Printing Office.

Announcements about government contracts for which bids are being accepted. Also includes information on sales of surplus government property. A new edition is issued every business day, and each edition contains some five hundred to one thousand notices. (One-year subscription to print version costs between $275 and $324. To order, call 202-512-1800. CBD*Net*, at http://cbdnet.access.gpo.gov/, is the government's official free electronic version of the *CBD*.)

U.S. Government Printing Office. *Congressional Directory*. Washington, DC: U. S. Government Printing Office. Biannual, with annual supplements.

Reference source issued for each Congress, with a supplement for the second session. Biographical information on members of Congress, plus committees, staff personnel, aides, and secretaries. Less detailed information on the executive and judicial branches. Personal name index. (Paperback costs $32, hardcover costs $45. Order from: Superintendent of Documents, P.O. Box 371954, Pittsburgh, PA 15250-7954; or call 202-512-1800.)

U.S. Government Printing Office. *Federal Register*. Washington, DC: U. S. Government Printing Office.

Official news publication (issued five times a week) for the federal government; includes official announcements of granting, programs, regulations, and deadlines. (One-year subscription costs $607. Order from: Superintendent of Documents, P.O. Box 371954, Pittsburgh, PA 15250-7954; or call 202-512-1800.)

U.S. Government Printing Office. *United States Government Manual*. Washington, DC: U. S. Government Printing Office. Annual.

Official handbook of the U.S. government describes and lists the principal personnel of agencies and other bodies of all branches of government (although the executive branch is covered in the greatest depth). Arranged by department or agency but the text is concerned with programs and activities rather than administrative structure. ($46. Order from: Superintendent of Documents, P.O. Box 371954, Pittsburgh, PA 15250-7954; or call 202-512-1800.)

Internet Resources

Acquisition Reform Net (ARNet) (www.arnet.gov/NTindex.html)
Site of the Office of Federal Procurement Policy. Information on federal acquisition and procurement opportunities, best practices, a discussion forum, references, and more.

BidRadar (www.bidradar.com)
Subscribers receive new business opportunities via e-mail every weekday. Tracks federal government opportunities and will soon add state and local governments and large corporate opportunities. Subjects divided into one hundred categories, allowing you to select those that match your business objectives.

DonorData, InfoNow Grants-On-Disk (www.donordata.com)
Fundraising and fund development resources for nonprofit organizations. Offers free and full version foundation directories of private, public, community, corporate, and government grants available.

FEDIX (www.fie.com/fedix)
Free e-mail service that automatically delivers federal research and education funding opportunities within your specific areas of interest.

GovCon (www.govcon.com)
On-line community for government contractors.

NonProfit Gateway (www.nonprofit.gov)
Network of links to federal government information and services, including information about grants, regulations, taxes, and more. Linked to all cabinet departments and many federal agencies. Visitors can also search "Notices of Funding Availability" from the *Federal Register.*

Notices of Funding Availability (ocd.usda.gov/nofa.htm)
NOFAs are announcements that appear in the *Federal Register*, inviting applications for federal grant programs. This page allows you to generate a customized listing of NOFAs.

The Grant Doctors: State Grant Information (www.thegrantdoctors.com/states.htm)
Links to grant information websites of all states

TGCI's Federal Register Grants Information
(www.tgci.com/Fr/fr000419.htm#GrantAnnouncements)
Daily listing of new federal grant announcements. Summaries of each grant are also available.

TGCI's Funding through State Government (www.tgci.com/STATES/states2)

Most federal funding for services is passed on to states and counties for their use or for redistribution. Site lists links to state home pages, where you can search for agencies that relate to your work. Also contains links to other sites that contain local government grant information.

Chapter 18

Religious Institutions

It is not righteousness, that ye turn your faces towards the East or West; but it is righteousness to believe in God almighty, and the Last Day, and the angels, the Scripture, and the Prophets; to spend of your wealth for the love of God Almighty to kinsfolk, and to orphans, and the needy, and the wayfarer, and to those who ask for help . . . —Koran 2:177

The tradition of individual giving is evident in the sacred texts of all religions, and is woven into the very fabric of most people's daily lives. Tithing—an individual's obligation to contribute 10 percent of his or her annual income to charity—is a precept in all of the world's major religions.

For Buddhists and Jews, charity is equated with justice and ethical conduct. In fact, the Hebrew word *tzedakah* encompasses the meanings of both "justice" and "charity." Jews do not view giving as a generous or magnanimous act but one of justice and righteousness.

It is therefore not surprising that organized religion has been a driving force throughout history in providing assistance to the poor, the oppressed, the downtrodden, and the disadvantaged. During the last one hundred years, many of the major social movements for justice have been led by religious figures and institutions. From Mohandas (Mahatma) Gandhi to the Buddhist monks who protested the war in Vietnam to the hundreds of clergy who helped lead the civil rights movement in the United States—religious leaders have been in the forefront of justice movements all over the world.

Many such movements are closely identified with individuals, such as Mahatma Gandhi, Martin Luther King, Jr., Dietrich Bonhoeffer, Cesar Chavez, Archbishop Romero, Thich Naht Hanh, and others; but all movements represent both the charisma and brilliance of their leaders and the hard work and dedication of hundreds of thousands—in some cases millions—of followers. An exhaustive examination of the role played by religion in social movements is beyond this book's scope, but religion's extensive social impact informs much of the funding and support described in this chapter.

What Organized Religion Supports

Figures on how much money is raised by religious institutions throughout the world are not available except in a few countries. In the United States, which has the longest and most thorough documentation, faith communities and their affiliated organizations receive almost half of the country's total charitable contributions year after year. Religious groups in Canada and England also receive the lion's share of all contributions. Just how much is given to religious organizations is virtually impossible to calculate since so much is given in-kind (food, furniture, books, clothes, and so on). Furthermore, many contributions are made in cash, and donors frequently do not keep track of their gifts. But even while precise numbers are not available, simple observation tells us that if religion isn't the main beneficiary of individual giving, it is certainly among the top two or three in most countries.

The highest percentage of dollars given to religious bodies goes directly to support the charitable activities conducted by those religious bodies. According to researcher Mark Dowie, 50 percent of the revenues generated by religious institutions are designated for the delivery of social services in their respective communities. At the local, national, and international levels, religious groups channel resources to vulnerable and disenfranchised populations at home and abroad in the form of services such as food, shelter, and health care; and in the form of assistance for self-help efforts that empower local populations to better their lives.

Tzedakah:

Moses Maimonides' Levels of Giving

1. To give, but give sadly
2. To help in a way that is less than fitting, but in good humor
3. To give only after having been asked to
4. To give before being asked
5. To give in such a manner that the donor does not know the recipient's identity
6. To give in such a manner that the recipient does not know the identity of the donor
7. To give in such a way as neither the donor nor the recipient knows the identity of the other
8. To give by helping the poor by either employing them or taking them into partnership (to give so that poverty and the need for giving is ended)

How Are Religious Bodies Structured?

Religious funding sources include units of organization ranging from the local parish, church, temple, or mosque to the national denominational structure. Each unit provides varying kinds and levels of support to nonprofit efforts.

For all faiths, the common meeting ground is the local place of worship—the church, synagogue, temple, meeting house, congregation, mosque, and so on. These in turn usually belong to local, regional, national, and sometimes international structures. These structures represent their interests and missions to the public and to other members of the same faith. Regional and metropolitan bodies are usually referred to as *judicatories*; they may also be called a diocese, synod, presbytery, meeting, conference, or association. The judicatories normally belong to a national body.

Local faith communities may also belong to various metropolitan or regional ecumenical bodies, such as councils of churches or interfaith councils, through which they regularly communicate with their counterparts in other religions and act together on issues of mutual concern. Protestant denominations may also belong to national ecumenical bodies, such as the National Council of Churches.

On the regional or metropolitan level, religious bodies have created organizations such as Catholic Charities and Jewish Federations that serve as umbrella bodies for all denominationally related health, social service, and welfare agencies. For example, Jewish Federations exist first and foremost to coordinate and fund the activities of constituent agencies, which maintain a communal relationship with the Federation.

How Do Religious Sources Extend Support to Nonprofit Organizations?

Because religious leaders couple their community involvement with deeply held beliefs and values, their support is often the most reliable form of assistance a nonprofit can receive.

Religious institutions provide a wide spectrum of both financial and nonmonetary support to nonprofits, particularly those that are community based (see the table below, which outlines these types of support). Grants and contributions of money are available from some religious bodies on local, regional, national, and international levels, and houses of worship often serve as incubators for grassroots organizations by providing space for offices, meetings, rallies, and so on. Fiscal sponsorship, bookkeeping assistance, proposal writing, access to office equipment, and guidance in the early stages of development are other ways that religious institutions help groups grow and develop.

Most important, religious leaders can aid local nonprofit initiatives by serving as advocates, representatives, and brokers on behalf of their interests vis-à-vis elected officials, funders, civic leaders, and others who control local resources. The endorsement of a respected clergyperson can open doors.

Patterns of support and resources from religious institutions are extremely varied and so it is difficult to generalize about average grant size or application procedures. For example, a shelter for battered women may be given $100 from the women's group of a local church; or the chair of the women's group could recommend the shelter for a discretionary gift of $500 from the Pastor-Parish Relations Committee. These actions might bring the shelter to the attention of the Domestic Missions Committee, resulting in a $2,000 gift from their budget. On their recommendation, the shelter might apply to the local council of churches, which might then write a letter of support to a national church giving program—which in turn might grant them $10,000 a year for three years. And during Domestic Violence Awareness Month, the Council of Churches might sponsor a "Second Collection Sunday," when all its members (which would be most of the Protestant churches in town) take up a second collection during their Sunday service that can net thousands of dollars.

The structure of particular denominations varies greatly, providing myriad opportunities for the savvy fundraiser, but it also may cause some frustration. Much giving is not formalized, and so an organization must have strong contacts and be continually alert to opportunities as they arise. And since a congregation's primary functions are to provide a place for worship and to conduct its own initiatives, any philanthropic or charitable activities must be incidental or, at best, secondary to its main purposes. This holds true for most local congregations and faith communities and their regional judicatories as well as for local and national ecumenical structures and national religious bodies.

How Do Religious Structures Operate Funding Programs?

Religious funding sources can be divided into six categories:

1. Formal programs of international ecumenical groups (such as the World Council of Churches) and mission programs, and relief, humanitarian assistance, and development agencies.

2. Grantmaking bodies that are part of a specific religious denomination. In the United States, examples include the Catholic Campaign for Human Development; the Minority Group Self-Development Fund of the Commission on Religion and Race, sponsored by the United Methodist Church; and the Coalition for Human Needs of the Episcopal Church. These bodies generally operate nationally and derive their funding from local churches, which give a percentage of their overall budgets.

   Many religious grantmakers are similar to other grantmaking institutions, such as foundations and corporations. They publish guidelines, application procedures, and, sometimes, annual reports. However, in accordance with their status under the law as religious institutions, they are not subject to many of the legal requirements set for foundations. They tend to be less publicly known as grantmakers in their immediate communities.

3. Religiously motivated grantmakers that are not formally affiliated with a religious body. An example is the Jewish Fund for Justice, which gives to organizations addressing the root causes of poverty and disenfranchisement in the United States, focusing on Jewish and non-Jewish organizations that need start-up funds. Another example is the New Israel Fund, which provides grants to organizations working for peace in Israel and Palestine. Wealthy individuals of different faiths have also established family foundations that express their founders' religious beliefs.

4. On the local level, a number of socially conscious congregations around the country have established specific grantmaking mechanisms. In New York City, for instance, Trinity Church operates a local grantmaking program. And the Unitarian-Universalist Veatch Program at Shelter Rock in Long Island, New York, was established with a gift of stock from a parishioner, Caroline Veatch, enabling the church to award grants totaling several million dollars each year. The grantmaking program has its own staff and the program's board is made up of church members. These churches are unusual, however; most local faith communities do not have the resources to set up such programs.

5. Cities and other communities where significant numbers of Protestants, Catholics, or Jews reside frequently have religiously affiliated federations, such as a Jewish Federation or a Catholic Charities, that identify community needs, coordinate the programmatic response from appropriate social welfare and health agencies, and conduct annual fundraising campaigns to finance these efforts. The federations' relationship with their beneficiary agencies is communal, and involves providing technical assistance as well as funding. A beneficiary agency is expected to forego certain types of independent fundraising in exchange for the support it receives from the federated campaign.

Admittance to these federations is a very formal procedure that may be time-consuming. While member agencies are not usually sectarian in their delivery of services, they are viewed as an extension of the federations' broader responsibilities to a particular religious community. As these local federations are autonomous, the grantseeker is best advised to become acquainted with their criteria for agency membership. Additionally, some of these federations also have endowments, trust funds, or donor-advised funds that have separate allocation procedures and may, in fact, provide support to nonmember nonprofit agencies. Federations also often act in concert with other nonprofits on issues of mutual concern through co-sponsorship of conferences, coalition efforts, and other forms of advocacy.

6. Completing the list are individual members of various faith communities. Many individuals give not only through their own religious bodies but also directly to numerous nonprofit organizations. Some may even be motivated to set up family foundations or trust funds at a local community foundation or at religious federations. Faith plays a large part in whether and how much an individual gives away. Studies have shown that 90 percent of givers describe themselves as religious or spiritual.

How Do Religious Institutions Provide Nonmonetary Support?

Nonmonetary support from religious institutions may take the form of a congregation that conducts a canned food drive for the poor in its community or a national religious body that establishes domestic and overseas programs to further its faith's beliefs and mission. These groups are more likely to make available nonmonetary support rather than actual cash contributions, except to finance their own programs. For example, when the number of homeless individuals hit crisis proportions in the United States in the early 1980s, religious leaders of all persuasions helped provide food, shelter, and social services. At the same time, many churches and temples used their facilities as shelters and soup kitchens—not only for the homeless, but for the poor and unemployed as well.

Religious officials, both laity and clergy, are active in initiating programs that reflect their own values. A local council of churches, or interfaith council, will often act as a broker for local nonprofits whose activities are consonant with their own concerns. In this role, the council might aid them in obtaining financial support from other sources, or gain access to critical decision-makers within the community. There are not the same set of formal guidelines that might accompany an institution whose primary purpose is grantmaking.

Support from Religious Institutions for Nonprofit Organizations

	Individual faith communities (churches, temples, etc.)	Metropolitan or regional jurisdictions (diocese, meeting)	Metropolitan or regional Council of Churches (or other local ecumenical bodies)	Religious federated campaigns	National denominational bodies	National ecumenical bodies	National religiously affiliated social service/human welfare/peace and justice/relief and development agencies
1. Grants and contributions	some	many	few	all	some	few	few
2. Space for offices	many	few	few	some	few	few	few
3. Space for meetings	most	most	some	some	many	many	many
4. Space for social services	some	few	none	some	none	none	none
5. Advocacy support	all	all	all	all	all	all	all
6. Access to office machines	some	few	few	some	some	few	few
7. Professional counsel in fundraising and other matters	most	most	most	all	all	all	all
8. Volunteers	all	some	some	some	few	few	few

Which Nonprofits Are Most Likely To Receive Support from Religious Organizations?

A religious institution is most likely to support nonprofit organizations in which its members are involved as staff, volunteers, trustees, or constituents. Congregations also tend to support nonprofits that are active in the fields of interest that most closely correspond to their faith. Issues of interest to religious communities include social welfare and human needs; food, hunger, and nutrition; social justice; peace and disarmament; international relief, reconstruction, and development work; immigration and resettlement of refugees; human rights and antidiscrimination work; community development and empowerment; prison reform; domestic violence; child care; women's issues; and unemployment, job retraining, and worker-owned businesses. Although extensive, this list is by no means complete. Religious organizations, in fact, address the entire array of social and economic issues that relate to low-income, minority, and vulnerable populations in the Americas and throughout the world, as well as issues such as disarmament and peace that face each and every individual regardless of religious affiliation.

Within these issue areas there are some religious structures and organizations that "bind up the wounds of poverty" by supporting soup kitchens and shelters for the homeless. Others take the lead in "preventing the wounds in the first place" by supporting advocacy efforts that reduce unemployment or encourage economic investment in low-income neighborhoods, for example. Quite often the same religious organizations, or different faith communities within a particular denomination, are active in both relief and advocacy programs.

What perhaps distinguishes religious philanthropy today is its mission—and increased ability—to serve a broad variety of those in need, as well as to promote systemic social change. Most organized religions are, in fact, nonsectarian in both their service and advocacy efforts.

As indicated, a wide variety of nonprofits can successfully approach religious groups for cash contributions and grants, meeting and office space, or volunteers—especially since the interests and concerns of religious bodies also vary widely. Some organizations, however, are less likely to win support from religious sources than others. For example, religious institutions are less likely to provide financial support to arts groups, unless a particular expression of their art reflects the social concerns of that religious body. At the same time, it is common in some communities for churches and temples to provide performance space for a range of nonprofit theater, dance, music, and other arts groups.

There are no hard-and-fast rules about which nonprofits would or would not fall within the interest areas of some religious institutions. Certain issues, such as reproductive rights for women, however, clearly create conflict in some religious communities. Some religions lend support to these efforts; others oppose them.

What Are the Advantages of Raising Support from Religious Institutions?

1. *Occasional speedy assistance.* If your work is closely aligned with the interests of a religious source, you are likely to receive a small grant, useful advice, meeting space, or some other kind of assistance relatively quickly. This is particularly important for resource-poor organizations that are just getting off the ground.

2. *Credibility.* Religious support in any form is a valuable "credential" for other funders who look for evidence of community participation and support when they make grantmaking decisions.

3. *Good advice.* Clergy are often asked to serve on the boards of nonprofits because of their knowledge of the community, their expertise in working with disparate political forces, and their experience as board members. An organization can directly approach religious leaders to serve on its board or advisory group, or simply ask them for their counsel at critical junctures.

4. *Ready sources of people power.* Congregations are ready-made gatherings of individuals who share common concerns, values, and, frequently, a commitment to helping others. As a result, they are a wonderful source of people power for appropriate nonprofit groups. Congregations can provide volunteers for a board, committees, fundraising projects, canvassing, tabling, and any number of volunteer projects that a group may undertake. Very often, they will be the most reliable and hardworking volunteers. A congregation also comprises a host of potential financial contributors. It may choose to make a gift on behalf of its entire membership by conducting a special offering among all of its parishioners, by asking in its newsletter for contributions, or by hosting a special fundraising event.

What Are the Disadvantages of Raising Support from Religious Institutions?

1. *Limited financial assistance.* Most religious institutions are not able to extend substantial financial support to nonprofit organizations. Grants and contributions from those that do usually range from $100 to $5,000. There are, however, significant exceptions.

   Additionally, religious sources regard their financial support primarily as "seed money" to launch new efforts, not as ongoing financial support. Like many small foundations, they are likely to withdraw their support once a group begins to generate consistent support from large foundations, corporations, and government. However, nonprofit agencies that are sectarian in their governance, although not in their programs, may receive steady annual support from religious federations.

2. *Limited available information on sources.* Information on religious funding sources, such as annual reports or general directories, is scarce. There are few written reference tools to help guide the prospective grantseeker, who must rely instead on obtaining information through personal contacts who are more intimately involved with religious life. The Additional Resources section at the end of this chapter lists some of the major materials on organized religious giving.

3. *Need to demonstrate religious involvement.* Some religious sources may expect an organization to involve members of their faith as board members, staff, or volunteers. Given the range of skills that talented religious leaders can bring to an organization, it's worth doing so.

Deciding Whether To Approach Religious Institutions for Support

Are members of any particular faith actively involved with your organization as staff or board members, volunteers, or constituents? Does your work correspond to any of the areas of interest to the religious community enumerated earlier? Does your work provide direct benefits to a community or neighborhood where a church, temple, mosque, meeting house, or synagogue is located, or where there is a high proportion of members of a certain faith?

If your organization can answer yes to any of these questions, you should certainly consider religious groups as potential sources of support.

If your financial needs are modest, religious institutions can be a quick source of small sums for emergency needs, such as purchasing food for soup kitchens or renting buses to transport people to demonstrations on pressing social issues. If on the other hand your organization's primary need is for large sums of money—more than several thousand dollars—you would be better advised to look to other sources, unless you fit squarely within the priorities and guidelines of national or local religious grantmaking bodies.

To view religious bodies solely as financial supporters rather than also as sources of advice, people power, physical space, and advocacy help, however, is to diminish their significance to nonprofit work.

Securing Support from Religious Institutions

The best way to begin approaching religious sources for assistance is to start locally—just as you would when approaching foundations, businesses, or government agencies. First, make a list of the religious organizations—ranging from the actual faith communities to the local religious federations—that have a physical presence in your community; they are the most logical groups to contact first.

Next, identify the individual congregations to approach by applying the following criteria: prior personal contact, the congregation's reputation for community involvement, and the involvement of your organization's members in the affairs of a particular congregation or faith.

You are likely to need the assistance of a sympathetic clergy member or well-versed parishioner to serve as your guide through the maze of organizational structures that exist within each religious tradition. Now you are ready to make the actual approach.

Step 1: Identify People Who Can Help

Identify individuals in your organization with active ties to local faith communities by circulating a list of local churches, synagogues, and temples and their religious leaders.

Step 2: Inventory Your Organization's Needs

Simultaneous with Step 1, list those needs you think a religious body might be able to fill, such as financial support; volunteers; expert counsel; advocacy support; space for offices, meetings, and special events; and use of equipment, such as computers, photocopy machines, telephones, and chairs.

Step 3: Prepare Your Case for Support

Prepare a brief statement on how your organization has provided assistance, or plans to do so, to the community shared by you and the congregation. The purpose of this exercise is to aid you in thinking through why a community-minded religious institution should be interested in your work. At the same time, the resulting statement will also be useful for drafting the initial letter of inquiry.

Step 4: Make Your Appeal

Make the initial approach to the clergy members in charge of the congregations you have targeted. If a member of your group knows those religious leaders, let that individual make the first contact to request a meeting. If no one in your group knows any of your prospects personally, it is best to make the initial approach by letter requesting a meeting. The letter outlines what your plans are, drawing from your previous working statement, and requests the opportunity to meet to seek the clergy member's advice and assistance.

Step 5: Arrange a Meeting

Bring one or two other people to the meeting, preferably members of the congregation you are visiting. Speak from your heart about the issue for which you seek support. Be forthright in stating your needs. You are exploring whether there is sufficient mutuality of interest for the congregation to become involved in your work.

If some mutual interest can be established, inquire whether there are any ways in which the local congregation can help. Find out if there is a committee within the congregation that addresses social concerns, social justice, social action, or peace and justice, and if it would be appropriate for you to discuss your needs with the committee. You can also offer your organization's assistance to the congregation.

Don't suggest that money is your sole or most important need unless it really is. Also, don't ask for everything at your first meeting. Remember that you are establishing a relationship that should serve your organization over a long period of time. You will have plenty of subsequent opportunities to ask for specific assistance once a positive initial meeting has taken place.

If a particular clergy member has been responsive to your queries, you can also use the occasion to ask about others whom you should contact, and anyone in the citywide office of that particular denomination or religion whom you might approach for advice and assistance. If you are fortunate, you will have found a navigator to help steer you through the local maze of religious structures.

Step 6: Develop the Relationship

If any assistance has been offered, follow up quickly. If the clerical leader has been especially helpful and supportive, you might consider how you might more actively involve him or her in the life of your group—for example, as a board member or a formal advisor or sponsor.

Step 7: Follow Up

Your next steps are to follow the leads provided in Step 5. At the judicatory level, you will probably meet with a clergy member assigned to community issues, social concerns, social action, urban ministry, or some similar area. This new guide can tell you which denominations—on a citywide basis—have discretionary or program-related funding mechanisms. You can also seek guidance to the next level of religious organization—the national religious headquarters or policymaking body—and ask about appropriate ecumenical organizations and metropolitan religiously affiliated federations.

Step 8: Secure Giving Guidelines

If it appears that you fit within the guidelines of some of the religious grantmaking programs in your city or nationally or internationally, request from the appropriate bodies copies of their guidelines and application procedures, including deadlines for application. At this point, refer to the table above showing the types of assistance provided by the different levels of religious faiths. Also, request a list of previous grant recipients. Review these materials to make sure that your work does fall within their areas of interest.

Step 9: Carry Out the Solicitations

Make telephone contact with the groups you have targeted, and, whenever possible, follow up with a personal visit before making a formal application. Preferably, invite the person to visit your program. This pre-application interview enables you to develop a more detailed idea of the funder's priorities and may answer some of your own questions about how best to draft a proposal or application for assistance. Unlike their foundation counterparts, religious grantmakers frequently make available actual application forms. Otherwise, you should engage in the same process that you would if you were preparing a proposal for submission to a foundation. Be sure to present the support of the local congregation and judicatory when approaching the national body. Evidence of such support and involvement is sometimes crucial to receiving support from the national body. Solicit letters of support toward that end.

Religious Support Forever

The majority of nonprofit organizations that are able to secure financial support from religious bodies use that funding as an incidental source during a critical period of their development, such as their formation, or in an emergency. A small minority of nonprofits, whose activities closely match the stated interests of religious bodies, may be able to gain admittance to a religious federated fundraising campaign that will assure them of steady, ongoing support.

There is usually no time limit on the nonmonetary support that a religious institution provides to nonprofits that reflect its beliefs and interests. Due to the mutuality of concerns that can bind nonprofit endeavors and religious institutions together, many nonprofits can expect ongoing assistance of one form or another. Financial support, however, may be short-lived or sporadic, depending on the vagaries of particular religious supporters.

Tips

- Research all the religious affiliations of your staff, board, volunteers, and clients/institutions before making any approaches.

- Religious institutions provide much nonmonetary support, such as volunteers, space for events, connection to other religious institutions, and so on.

Profile: National Interfaith Committee for Worker Justice

The National Interfaith Committee for Worker Justice (NICWJ) was formed in 1996. It grew in its first four years from an idea in the director's head, and operating out of her bedroom, to a nationally significant organization with a general operating budget over $750,000 plus an additional $300,000 raised for supporting local groups around the country through a Worker Justice Fund.

Approximately 20 percent of the general operating budget, and 30 percent of the Worker Justice Fund budget comes from 44 different religious sources—primarily men and women's religious orders, national and regional denominational sources, and endowed congregations. In addition, the organization receives a fair amount of support from clergy who often contribute from congregational discretionary funds.

NICWJ has found that raising support from religious sources shares similar principles with raising funds from most other sources:

1. *Build relationships with donors.* Religious sources, like other sources, give money to people with whom they have relationships. Consequently, it is essential to get to know the key decision-makers personally. The board and the staff work to build relationships with staff or committee members at religious sources.

2. *Involve donors in the work.* The religious sources that give the most to NICWJ have people from their congregations, denominations, or orders who are actively engaged in the work. The National Interfaith Committee for Worker Justice is often asked how many Presbyterians or how many Sisters from a particular order are actually involved with groups around the country. The work must seek ways to educate and mobilize the religious community.

3. *Communicate regularly with donors.* The National Interfaith Committee sends a newsletter six times a year to everyone on its mailing list, including donors. The newsletter is a simple way to update donors and build the sense among donors that the organization is doing solid work. Every so often, the staff send donors a big pile of press clips.

4. *Do the hard work.* Religious sources, like most foundation sources, require proposals to be submitted, forms to be filled out, and reports to be sent. And all this must meet the religious sources' deadlines. Despite theologies of forgiveness and second chances, religious sources are no more merciful to groups that miss deadlines or don't send the right information than any other source. Raising money from religious sources is hard work—just like most fundraising! Some of the most complicated proposal formats the National Interfaith Committee has completed have come from religious sources.

5. *Stick to your issues.* People in the faith community are all over the place theologically and politically. The NICWJ has learned to stick solely to its issues and not discuss staff's personal views on issues that are controversial within the religious community—unless they are the ones on which the organization is working.

6. *Ask.* Religious sources have to be asked for money, just like everyone else. Otherwise, they assume you don't need their money.

7. *Ask again.* If it looks like the NICWJ work matches a religious source's priorities, NICWJ asks three years in a row before giving up. The amount of funds available for religious sources to give can vary year to year. Sometimes the decision-makers change, so you might find a more receptive committee one year over another.

8. *Keep looking for new sources.* Despite the wide variety of religious sources that support the NICWJ, there are many more out there that the organization hasn't heard about, so staff and board members are always on the lookout for leads about new sources. Unfortunately, there is no book that lists all the religious sources. The best way to find them and get to them is to talk with leaders involved with your organization who are active in the religious community.

—Kim Bobo

Summary Worksheet

for _____

(name of your organization)

Approaching Religious Institutions for Support

Building on Past Support

1. Have any religious institutions ever supported your work in the past?

_____ yes   _____ no

If yes, which ones?

_____   _____
_____   _____
_____   _____
_____   _____

2. What characteristics do these institutions share? How do their interest correspond to each other?

Comments:

_____
_____
_____
_____

3. What is your sense of what they valued in your organization's work?

Comments:

_____
_____
_____
_____

4. Which ones can you reapproach for future support?

Definite Ongoing Projects:

_____   _____
_____   _____
_____   _____
_____   _____

Untested (Further Information Needed):

_____   _____
_____   _____
_____   _____
_____   _____

Finding New Religious Supporters

1. Are there individuals within your own organization with active ties to local churches, temples, or other faith communities? If yes, who are they and what are their ties?

   _____ yes   _____ no

   _____

   _____

   _____

   _____

2. What are the particular religious congregations that have a physical presence in your community or have expressed an interest in your targeted constituency?

   _____

   _____

   _____

   _____

3. Which religious bodies have publicly expressed an interest in the issues that comprise your organization's work?

   _____

   _____

   _____

   _____

4. See pages 502 and 503 for this part of the worksheet.

Making the Match

For each prospect on the previous list, complete the following exercise (use your own blank paper).

Name of religious institution:

Its stated areas of interest that pertain to your work:

Develop one or more sentences relating your work to the interests of the religious institution that you are approaching (or write one or more short sentences demonstrating how the work of your organization reflects the interests of X religious institution).

Finding Assistance and Counsel

Name five or more individuals who might be able to advise you on how to most effectively approach the religious institutions on your best bets list.

   a. _____

   b. _____

   c. _____

   d. _____

   e. _____

4. List below the religious institutions you have uncovered from your research and your networking. Limit your listing to the ten most likely supporters of your organization—your ten best bets.

a. Type of Religious Institution	b. Their Stated Areas of Interest that Relate to Your Work	c. Appropriate Contact: Person, Address, and Phone
Individual Churches, Temples, and Other Faith Communities		
Metropolitan or Regional Jurisdictions		
Metropolitan or Regional Ecumenical Bodies		
Religious Federations		
National Religious Bodies		

d. Any Personal Contacts	e. Your Program(s) that Correspond to Their Interests	f. Grants to Similar Organizations

Assessing the Likelihood of Securing Support from Religious Institutions

On the basis of what you have learned, how would you rank your chances of securing support from religious institutions?

___ Very Good   __ Possible   __ Unlikely   __ Still Unknown

Additional Resources

Publications

Billiteri, Thomas J., and Paul Demko. "Roman Catholic Groups Start Community Foundation." *Chronicle of Philanthropy* 11 (5 November 1998).

> Lay members of a Roman Catholic group have formed the National Catholic Community Foundation. The organization is billed as the first Catholic community foundation that is national in scope. The foundation is offering several options to their donors, one of which is to disburse grants through a donor-advised fund.

Bush, Lawrence, Jeffrey Dekro, Arthur Waskow, and Letty Cottin Pogrebin. *Jews, Money and Social Responsibility: Developing a Torah of Money for Contemporary Life*. Philadelphia: Shefa Fund, 1993. x, 198 p.

> Explores how core concepts of Judaism such as charity, stewardship, and the unity of creation can be combined with principles of the social responsibility movement to envision and develop a "covenanted economy" or "Torah of money." Supplementary materials include "Women and Philanthropy," by Letty Cottin Pogrebin; "Toward an Eco-Kosher Life Path," by Arthur Waskow; a bibliography; and recommended resources. Indexed.

Cnaan, Ram A., and Robert J. Wineburg. *Social Work and the Role of the Religious Community in Social Service Provision*. Working paper, Institution for Social and Policy Studies, New Haven, CT, 1997. 65 p.

Council on Foundations. *Philanthropy and Religion in a Civil Society: Experiences at the Interface: Proceedings from the Conference on Philanthropy and Religion in a Civil Society*. Washington, DC: Council on Foundations, 1995. vi, 135 p.

Foundations and Donors Interested in Catholic Activities, Inc. *How To Run a Catholic Foundation: Increasing the Impact of Religious Giving*. Washington, DC: Foundations and Donors Interested in Catholic Activities Inc., 1998. 88 p.

> Proceedings of a conference held in January 1998 on the operations of Catholic foundations today. Topics include increasing family involvement in foundations, succession within family foundations, evaluation of church-sponsored projects, the benefits and pitfalls of funding specialization, and responsible philanthropy.

Hodgkinson, Virginia A., Murray S. Weitzman, and Arthur D. Kirsch. *From Belief to Commitment: The Community Service Activities and Finances of Religious Congregations in the U.S.* Washington, DC: Independent Sector, 1993. xiv, 143 p.

> Results of a survey undertaken to investigate the connection and contribution of religious institutions to the independent sector, and to update a larger survey from 1987. Explores the influence of these institutions on the services provided to communities, the nation, and other countries, and examines the ways religious values motivate people to give and

volunteer both to the religious institutions and to other organizations. The report also documents religious congregations as the primary voluntary service providers for neighborhoods, with nine out of ten congregations reporting their facilities were available for groups within their congregations, and six out of ten reporting their facilities were available to other groups in the community.

Lindner, Eileen W., ed. *Yearbook of American and Canadian Churches.* 68th ed. Nashville, TN: Abingdon Press, 2000. v, 408 p.

McNamara, Patrick. "Case Studies in Church Giving: A Preliminary Report from the Lilly Endowment Study of Congregational Giving." Preliminary Report, no. 4. Washington, DC: Catholic University of America, 1994. 15 p.
    Describes six congregations with exemplary giving.

Meiners, Phyllis A., and Greg A. Sanford. *Church Philanthropy for Native Americans and Other Minorities: A Guide to Multicultural Funding from Religious Sources.* Boca Raton, FL: CRC Press, 1995. xiv, 279 p.
    Organized into two sections. The first section contains church grant programs from ten denominations and several ecumenical organizations. The second section contains church loan programs offered by seven denominations and a number of ecumenical organizations. Entries provide the funder's address, telephone number, denomination, branch, order, headquarters city, year of establishment, grant range, total annual giving, grant fund governing body, grant committees, officers, special interests, geographic interests, application deadlines and procedures, sample grants, description and purpose, and restrictions. Includes subject and geographic indexes.

Meshanko, Ronald J. *National Guide to Episcopal, Lutheran, Methodist and Presbyterian Funding.* Washington, DC: Ecumenical Resource Consultants, Inc., 1993. 108 p.

Oates, Mary J. *The Catholic Philanthropic Tradition in America.* Bloomington, IN: Indiana University Press, 1995. xiii, 231 p.
    Presents the history of Catholic philanthropy in the U.S. Chronicles the church's traditional charitable activities which encompass orphanages, hospitals, schools, and social agencies. Describes the increasing tension between centralized control of giving and democratic participation. Includes bibliography and index.

Paul, Eileen, ed. *Religious Funding Resource Guide.* 16th ed. Washington, DC: ResourceWomen, 2000.
    Information on approximately thirty-eight Protestant, Roman Catholic, ecumenical, and Jewish funding organizations that accept applications from nonreligious based organizations. Lists addresses, telephone numbers, and grants; describes organizational purpose, project criteria, and application procedures. Includes a calendar of application deadlines, a discussion on seeking funds from church sources (including information on

major denominational structures), and a list of sources that fund international projects. Includes bibliography.

Ronsvalle, John L., and Sylvia Ronsvalle. *The State of Church Giving through 1992*. Champaign, IL: Empty Tomb, 1994. iv, 74 p.
    Analyzes accumulated records submitted to the *Yearbook of American and Canadian Churches* over many decades. These reports were based on congregational annual reports that are processed and analyzed in various denominational offices on an ongoing basis. Reviews data for twenty-nine denominations that include about 100,000 of the estimated 350,000 religious congregations in the U.S. Numerous tables and charts present data such as patterns in member giving from 1968 to 1992, per member giving as a percentage of income in eleven denominations from 1921 to 1992, and projected trends for giving. Appendices list denominations, denominational data tables, and income and deflators.

Scheie, David M., Jaimie Markham, Theatrice Williams, John Slettom, and Sharon Marie A. Ramirez. *Better Together: Religious Institutions as Partners in Community Based Development*. Minneapolis, MN: Rainbow Research, 1994. vii, 63 p.
    Reports on Lilly Endowment's "Religious Institutions as Partners in Community-Based Development," a project launched in 1989 to encourage a select number of partnerships in both urban and rural communities. Lilly Endowment supported twenty-eight projects; eighteen were located in urban neighborhoods, two were in suburban communities, and eight were in rural or small town settings. Ten of the twenty-eight were located in the Midwest, nine in the Northeast, four in the Southeast, and four west of the Mississippi. Chapters cover an overview of the projects and partnerships, results of the program, a critique of program design and management, and recommendations. An appendix includes a directory of grant recipients in the Lilly Endowment program.

Tobin, Gary A., Joel Streicker, and Gabriel Berger. "An Exploration of Jewish Federation Endowment Programs." Waltham, MA: Maurice and Marilyn Cohen Center for Modern Jewish Studies, 1997. ii, 43 p.

Chapter 19

Federated Fundraising Organizations

One tree receiving all the wind, breaks. A descent for the sake of a friend is
an ascent.
— Guy A. Zona
The House of the Heart is Never Full
Proverbs of Africa

In 1829, a Philadelphia publisher named Matthew Cary asked three friends to make donations to a single organization that would then distribute their gifts among the city's thirty-three charities; in doing so, Cary introduced federated fundraising to the United States. The next federated fundraising effort was initiated in Denver in 1887 by a priest, a rabbi, and two ministers. They conducted a fundraising campaign on behalf of the Charity Organization Society that raised

$21,700, of which $18,000 was distributed to ten local agencies. In 1913, the city of Cleveland established the first modern federated fund, and over the next fourteen years, more than three hundred other communities followed Cleveland's lead by establishing what was then referred to as "community chests." By 1931, these groups had raised more than $100 million, and by 1948, more than 1,000 community chests were raising and distributing funds to their member organizations.

The motive for establishing federated drives (including the United Way), however, was not entirely altruistic. Profitability was an equally compelling incentive: employers and some labor union leaders were concerned about the loss in employee productivity resulting from charitable solicitations in their workplaces. Motivated more than a little by the cost of solicitations in his factories—each drive translated into a $40,000 loss in employee labor—Henry Ford II led the auto industry in establishing the first "United Fund" citywide appeal in Detroit in the late 1940s. While it took years before federated drives became firmly established in the United States, the movement eventually took root and flourished.

Usually organized along geographic lines, federated fundraising organizations are nonprofits whose purpose is to raise and distribute funds to designated ("member") nonprofit groups, which usually reflect the values and beliefs of the federated organizations to which they belong. The hallmarks of federated campaigns are centralized allocation to recipient beneficiaries and easy access for charitable organizations to the workplace. In workplace fundraising campaigns, employees can write checks or designate a fixed sum to be deducted from their weekly paycheck for distribution to a named charitable beneficiary.

There are a number of reasons why the worksite is a particularly lucrative source of contributions:

1. Workplace fundraising taps into the largest source of funds in the United States: individuals, who in 1996 gave 80 percent of all charitable contributions (compared to 8 percent from foundations and 6 percent from corporations). In 1996, employees gave more than $2 billion to workplace fundraising campaigns.[1]

2. Contributing over time by payroll deduction enables donors to make larger contributions than they would by making a single gift. It is a generally accepted principle that people donate three times more through payroll deductions than through a one-time charitable contribution.

3. The cost of raising money in the workplace is lower than the cost of other methods of solicitation, due to the inherent efficiency of the process: one annual appeal to a large number of prospects, and simple, periodic transmission of funds to the beneficiary. Also a higher percentage of employees contribute in workplace campaigns. In the U.S. federal government, for example, 35 to 40 percent of all employees participate—and they contribute more money than they might if they made one-time gifts.

4. Organizations can tap new donors, thereby increasing revenues and visibility.

---

1. From the National Committee for Responsive Philanthropy: www.ncrp.org

5. Funds raised from workplace solicitations are usually unrestricted.

United Ways were the first federated fundraising efforts to benefit significantly from workplace payroll deduction programs, but nonprofit organizations not supported by the United Way began to organize in the early 1960s to gain access to the workplace. The U.S. government helped their efforts by allowing other national nonprofit organizations, such as international relief and health groups, to solicit federal employees in what became known as the "Combined Federal Campaign." During this campaign, the United Way and other designated charities vied for federal workplace dollars at the same time. Other large national charities soon gained access to public employees, and today most states and large municipalities allow non-United Way organizations to solicit contributions from their employees.

The Different Types of Federated Fundraising Organizations

The best-known federated fundraising organizations in the United States are United Ways, religiously affiliated federations, and alternative federated funds.

United Ways

United Ways are fundraising and allocating organizations that support a wide variety of human service agencies on the local level. United Ways may also undertake other activities to support their nonprofit member agencies and their own communities, such as providing management assistance programs, long-term planning, counsel, and information and referral services.

What is now known as the United Way of America is active in every U.S. community with a population of over 25,000. The approximately 1,400 community-based United Way organizations are autonomous, but the majority are members of the national United Way of America. Local United Ways range in size from small, predominantly volunteer bodies to large, professionally staffed enterprises in major metropolitan areas. Local United Ways are also characterized by their fundraising methods and sources of revenue. By and large, they receive the bulk of their support from company employees who have been solicited at the workplace, and from major companies through grants.

In 1997-98, United Ways received $3.4 billion in pledges and grants, and supported some 45,000 member agencies. Although the organization's growth slowed considerably in the early 90's, the United Way is clearly recovering from the downturns it experienced in the decade's middle years.

Outside the United States there are currently more than three thousand community-based fundraising organizations affiliated with United Way International. Many are known by names other than United Way, such as Matan—Your Way to Give (Israel), General Union of Voluntary Societies (Jordan), United Community Chests of Southern Africa, Asociación de Empresarios para el Desarrollo (Costa Rica), Fondo Unido (Mexico), China Charity Federation, and Central Community Chest of Japan.[2]

---

2. See the United Way International Web site (www.unitedwayinternational.org) for a complete listing and contact information.

Religiously Affiliated Federations

Religiously affiliated federations are usually established by religious institutions and/or lay leadership to raise money from individuals in houses of worship to provide financial support for organizations devoted to the social welfare and health interests of their respective faiths. Examples include local Catholic Charities and Jewish Federations (these federations are discussed in Chapter 18).

Alternative Funds

Alternative funds are public charities established to raise and distribute funds to organizations that share a distinct constituency or set of common concerns; they are often geographically based. Nineteen sixty-eight marked the arrival of alternative federated drives on the fundraising scene. In that year, Walter Bremond founded the Brotherhood Crusade of Los Angeles, the precursor of the Black United Funds that now operate throughout the United States. By the early 1980s, more than fifty more alternative federated funds had joined the ranks of the early Black United Funds. Most of them are geographically based: Tennessee's Community Shares, Earth Share of California, and Boston's Community Works are just a few examples. Some are organized nationally, such as Earth Share, the United Arts Funds, the Animal Funds of America, and the Children's Charities of America. By the late 90's, these alternative funds were raising and distributing more than $500 million each year and were growing rapidly.

These funds are "alternative" in two ways. First, they are not United Way funds and therefore represent a different system of fund collection and distribution. Second, many alternative funds support newer, nontraditional, and more change-oriented organizations. In their article, "Fund-Raising at the Workplace," Stanley Wenocur, Richard V. Cook, and Nancy L. Steketee distinguish alternative funds in the following manner: "They are called 'alternative' primarily to distinguish them from the United Way, but also because they usually represent grassroots and non-traditional organizations that seek to address the root cause of social problems rather than providing social services."[3]

United Ways have come under criticism for being unwilling to adapt their membership criteria and a number of United Ways have changed as a result. In many urban areas, for example, United Ways now fund gay and lesbian groups, AIDS organizations, shelters for battered women, and even some advocacy programs.

Examples of non-United Way funds include United Arts Funds and Community Health Charities. Some that are geared to social change are Women's Funds; Black United Funds; the Bread and Roses Community Fund in Philadelphia, which raises funds to support grassroots advocacy efforts; and the Community Solutions Fund in Minneapolis-Saint Paul, which raises funds for over forty neighborhood centers, women's groups, and other organizations. These social action

---

3. Stanley Wenocur, Richard V. Cooke, and Nancy L. Steketee, "Fund-Raising at the Workplace," *Social Policy* (Spring 1984).

funds, as they are occasionally dubbed, each raise and distribute anywhere from $25,000 to $1,000,000 a year.

Regarding the growth of both the United Way and the alternative funds, the sky is the limit. As workplaces consolidate, these organizations are developing mechanisms for raising money other than payroll deduction, although that will remain the flagship strategy.

What implications do these developments hold for today's nonprofits seeking new sources of support? Can they tap into their local federated funds for support? How can they approach workplaces in their communities directly, either as members of alternative funds or on their own? This chapter will help nonprofits answer these questions.

How Much Do Federated Funds Raise Each Year?

- In 1996, fifty-nine local United Arts Fund organizations raised a total of $83.5 million, $12.9 million of which was donated through workplace solicitations.

- Through workplace giving campaigns, International Service Agencies (ISA) raised nearly $20 million for its fifty-three humanitarian relief and development charities in 1997. ISA member programs promote sustainable development, self-sufficiency, and, in turn, dignity, pride, and hope for more than 159 million people around the world.

- In 1997–98, Women's Way, a federation of Philadelphia women's organizations, raised $1,012,989 from its workplace, individual, and corporation/foundation campaigns, and $321,222 from fundraising events and activities to support the work of its member agencies, which included Women Organized Against Rape, Elizabeth Blackwell Health Center for Women, CHOICE, Women's Law Project, and others.

- The Black United Fund (BUF) has grown from eight local BUFs, which raised $600,000 in 1975, to fifteen local BUFs, which raised more than $8,000,000 in 1996 to support programs in Black and minority communities that emphasize self-help, mutual aid, and self-determination.

As these statistics clearly show, gross revenues from federated campaigns range dramatically. Since each United Way and alternative fund is unique and independent, it is difficult to generalize about the level of financial support that federated campaigns provide to recipient groups. A United Way may fund less than 5 percent or more than 50 percent of a beneficiary organization's budget. Most alternative funds are still evolving, and so they usually provide modest support to their beneficiaries; older ones, however, give substantial support. Clearly, United Ways remain the dominant federated fundraising organizations in their communities by virtue of their history, resources, and unrestricted access to company worksites; they still distribute much larger sums than any existing alternative funds.

Basic Types of Local Alternative Funds

Black United Funds. Black United Funds (BUFs) exist in 15 locations around the country. After raising funds in the workplace, BUFs disribute grants to nonprofits assisting African Americans and other minority groups. Members include Detroit Urban League and Mothers Against System Slavery.

Asian and Hispanic Funds. Los Angeles was the birthplace of the first Asian and Latino funds. The Asian Pacific Community Fund and the United Latino Fund have raised workplace contributions since 1990. The United Latino Fund is structured along the same lines as BUFs; distributing money raised in the workplace through grants to nonprofits assisting the Hispanic community. The Asian Pacific Community Fund is a hybrid; it makes grants to nonprofit groups working in the Asian community, and also helps member agencies which donors can designate. Members include Asian Pacific American Legal Center and the Proyecto Pastoral at Dolores Mission.

Social Action Funds. Social action funds raise funds for nonprofits working on a broad range of issues, including the environment, neighborhood development, consumer needs, minority activism, women's rights, children's needs, advocacy for the elderly, and others. In 1997, there were 44 social action funds around the country working on local and statewide levels.

Women's Federations. Raising workplace money to support nonprofits that work on the issues and needs of women is the mission of eight women's federations and a number of women's foundations. All women's federations raise workplace contributions for a specific set of member organizations, while the women's foundations are tapping into the workplace as one source of revenue for their grant allocation process. Members include Women's Alliance for Job Equity and Lesbian Resource Center.

How Do Federated Funds Provide Support?

Federated funds give financial support to nonprofits in three ways:

1. They bestow *member agency status* on a nonprofit, which qualifies it for ongoing annual allocations.

2. They provide funds through various *discretionary grants*, sometimes known as venture or community development grants.

Environmental Funds. These funds solicit workplace contributions exclusively for environmental organizations. They have been the fastest growing local alternative funds for the last seven years; in 1990 there were only four local environmental funds, and in 1997, there were 19. Members include Friends of the Everglades and Animal Legal Defense Fund.

United Arts Funds. Local arts funds raise contributions from a variety of sources to support artistic and cultural institutions in communities across the nation. Of the approximately 80 arts funds in existence in 1996, 34 were involved in workplace fundraising campaigns. Members include the Allied Arts Venture Fund and Museum of Scientific Discovery.

National Voluntary Health Agencies (NVHAs). Initially participants in the Combined Federal Campaign, 22 NVHAs now seek employee contributions mainly from state government charity drives, as well as a few local government campaigns. Member agencies are the same as for Community Health Charities (CHCs). While similar to CHCs, they often exist in states where there are no CHAs.[4]

Community Health Charities (CHCs). CHCs represent health charities that participate in state and local government and corporate workplace campaigns. Member agencies include the local affiliate or chapters of national health service and research agencies, such as the American Lung Association, the Parkinson's Disease Foundation, and the National Multiple Sclerosis Society. The national organization—Community Health Charities of America—provides direction and support to 33 CHCs across the country; several of these have contractual agreements with United Ways for combined campaigns. Members include the American Diabetes Association, St. Jude's Children's Research Hospital and the Muscular Dystrophy Association.

---

4. From the National Committee for Responsive Philanthropy (www.ncrp.org).

3. They sponsor *donor option programs* (DOPs), which allow individual employees to designate as recipient a particular nonprofit, tax-exempt organization, or a federation.

Member Agency Status

Many federated funds traditionally confer the title of "member" on their beneficiaries. This suggests—in principle and in fact—a close communal relationship between the federation funder and its "grantees." In addition to enabling a nonprofit to receive ongoing funding, membership can also give an organization access to technical and management assistance resources, and publicity. However, restrictions apply to member organizations' own fundraising efforts, and federation rules usually specify how and when they may fundraise on their own behalf. All groups must decide whether these restrictions are offset by the benefits of membership; the answer to that question will vary a great deal from group to group.

A federation's board of directors, either directly or upon recommendations of a standing committee, chooses its member (recipient) agencies for the year. The application and selection process can be long, frequently entailing many site visits, extensive application forms, and numerous reviews by a variety of committees. Most federated funds also require their beneficiaries to go through some form of annual review process. However, it's rare for an agency's membership status to be terminated unless that agency has engaged in serious legal or financial misconduct, or has failed to meet ongoing requirements for membership. This is particularly true of United Ways. A federation may, however, reduce the level of support that it provides to an organization in a given year for any of a wide variety of reasons.

The composition of federation governing boards varies considerably. Most United Ways are governed by a mix of business leaders and civic, union, and member agency representatives. Their allocation committees, which make recommendations to a central board, enjoy a somewhat larger representation from the nonprofit community itself, particularly member agencies of the United Way. Allocation formulas vary from one United Way to another. In determining what each member agency receives each year, the United Ways review the entire operating budget of the recipient. The percentage of budgets underwritten by the United Way varies from agency to agency.

The governing bodies and allocation committees of alternative funds are even more varied. Since many of these funds began as coalitions of groups that did not receive United Way assistance and were seeking a slice of the charitable pie, their boards may be composed exclusively of representatives of recipient organizations. Others may have a broader representation of community and nonprofit interests. In the case of the Bread and Roses Community Fund in Philadelphia (established in 1970 as the People's Fund), each and every contributor who attends the annual convention elects members of the board of directors and community funding board for the upcoming year. Alternative federated funds also use a wide range of allocation formulas. Some funds allocate their undesignated funds equally, whereas others base their support on the size of the recipient organization's budget and the amount of time members' staff spends on a federation's fundraising campaign. All also allow their donors to designate their gifts for specific organizations.

Discretionary or Special Initiative Grants

Some United Ways and alternative federated funds set aside a pool of money each year for discretionary grants available to nonprofits on a competitive basis. Currently, a number of United Ways across the country have these programs for less-established nonprofit service organizations; guidelines for these funds vary. Since most federations raise the bulk of their funds each year from annual campaigns (usually conducted in the fall, but occasionally year-round), such grants are awarded only once a year—after their fundraising efforts have been completed. As a result, there can be a long period from grant approval to actual receipt of funding. Discretionary grants do not convey or imply membership status within the granting federation, but they can provide a nonprofit with a first step toward membership.

Donor Option Programs

In recent years, a number of United Ways have provided donors with the option of designating a nonprofit, federally tax-exempt health or human service organization as the recipient of their contribution even if it is not a United Way member. These so-called donor option plans (DOPs) provide opportunities for non-United Way agencies to benefit from charitable solicitation at the workplace. The local United Way board of directors decides whether to make this option available to contributors.

Although no two donor option programs are identical, several characteristics are fairly common to all. An employee donor wishing to participate completes a payroll authorization card and donor option form. The donor may designate any 501(c)(3) organization that meets general eligibility requirements (which sometimes include geographic and programmatic limitations). In many cases, a minimum gift may be required. An administration fee is determined and deducted from each contribution; the balance is then forwarded to the designated agency. While cash gifts are sent to the designated agency as soon as possible, all other gifts are generally paid on a monthly or quarterly basis.

Many alternative funds, as well as individual nonprofit organizations, have sought to take advantage of these DOPs, often against great odds. They have applied to the local United Way for inclusion in the list of "accredited" nonprofits that is sometimes distributed to those interested in earmarking their contribution, and have attempted to make their case directly to workers themselves.

The road to substantial workplace support for non-United Way member agencies through DOPs is a long one. A study conducted by the Neighborhoods Institute in Baltimore for the National Committee for Responsive Philanthropy reported a low percentage of workplace gifts to non-United Way charities: 6.3 percent in Philadelphia, 4.3 percent in San Francisco, and 2 percent in Sacramento. While many agencies receive donor option gifts (780 in Philadelphia and 700 in San Francisco), most get only a tiny amount of money. In Philadelphia, for example, the vast majority of groups received less than $100 each.

Case Study:

MaineShare

After several years of exploratory discussions and meetings among grassroots activists, MaineShare was incorporated in January 1989 by leaders of nine statewide nonprofit organizations. Though aware of the high-risk nature of creating a new federation for workplace giving, the incorporators were emboldened by success stories from other parts of the country. The energy and vision of two long-time Maine organizers, Larry Dansinger and the late Elly Haney, also inspired them. Indeed it was Dansinger's group, the Institute for Nonviolence Education Research & Training (INVERT), that bankrolled the majority of start-up costs over the first two years. Grants from the Haymarket People's Fund, RESIST, and the Maine Community Foundation also helped hire the first staff.

In the Fall of 1989, MaineShare's first campaign got under way, highlighted by the participation of a progressive young business, Tom's of Maine, and one of the state's most highly regarded nonprofit organizations, Pine Tree Legal Assistance Corporation. Nearly $30,000 was raised and a new message was brought to the workers of Maine: now you can "give at the office" for peace, human rights, the environment, animal welfare, and community organizing that gets to the "root causes."

Early on, however, it became very clear that Maine's local United Ways were going to make things as difficult as possible. At the City of Portland, Maine state government, the University of Maine, the Combined Federal Campaign, and countless private businesses, colleges, and even at nonprofit organizations, the United Way was there with all its power, fighting to preserve their exclusive access to employee giving drives.

But MaineShare's organizers persevered and countless public and private sector employees spoke up for charitable choice. Each year more employers invited MaineShare to participate and more Maine nonprofits were added to the list of MaineShare affiliates. By 1993, MaineShare had become a payroll giving choice for over 50,000 Maine people and its annual pledge drive exceeded $70,000. Steady growth continued through the 90's, and by the end of the decade, MaineShare had distributed over $625,000 to Maine-based organizations which previously had no way to raise money (and raise awareness) in the workplace.

MaineShare has brought an important and timely new dimension to Maine philanthropy. Beyond raising vital new dollars for social change and the environment, MaineShare has helped revitalize workplace giving by introducing new choices; attracting new donors to the process; and heightening public accountability. Employers report high levels of employee satisfaction with MaineShare and the opportunity to exercise greater latitude over payroll giving decisions. In large public sector campaigns, MaineShare has played a leading role in improving management standards and reducing costs. In 1996, MaineShare became one of the nation's first non-United Way administrators of a state employees campaign. In its four years as campaign manager of the Maine State Employees Combined Charitable Appeal (MSECCA), MaineShare reduced administrative expenses by 50% while pledge revenue increased from $253,000 in 1995 to $367,000 in 1999.

While there's much to be proud of here—many thought MaineShare would never make it this far—we still have a long way to go, particularly in terms of participation in large corporate employee campaigns. Many business leaders continue to resist offering payroll giving choices beyond United Way. This resistance is often couched in terms of concerns about administrative costs and the perceived complication of including multiple appeals, but it seems the real reasons go far deeper than that. We're up against a close-knit social network for one, but an even greater obstacle is the powerful myth about the capacity of private philanthropy to meet local needs. Over many decades, the United Way has effectively positioned itself as a community "safety net." Here in Maine, we continue to hear business and United Way leaders argue that employers should not offer MaineShare because by doing so they will undercut funding for the critical social services funded by United Way. The argument is deeply flawed.

It fails to acknowledge that United Way funding accounts for well under 10% of total United Way agency revenues. Our tax dollars (local, state, and federal) are the real force behind United Way agency funding. The United Way in Portland raised over $8 million in the fall of 1999. MaineShare raised just over $200,000 in pledges *statewide*, perhaps $75,000 of that in the Portland area. MaineShare can grow geometrically and not pose a threat to United Way agency funding.

Moreover, this thinking assumes that United Way giving will inevitably decline with the availability of other choices. This "fixed pie" model has been proven wrong many times over in campaigns around the state. With more choice overall giving rises. Sometimes United Way goes down, sometimes it goes up. A variety of variables influence how a given campaign will do in a given workplace. The amount of choice being offered is just one of them.

The paradox is that several MaineShare agencies spend considerable time advocating government funding for United Way agencies. The Maine Coalition to End Domestic Violence, Maine Coalition Against Sexual Assault, and Maine AIDS Alliance are just a few examples. In other words, MaineShare agencies are dedicated partners and allies of United Way agencies. MaineShare's campaign demonstrates how groups such as the Maine Hospice Council are not in competition with local service agencies but instead are partners with local agencies on many levels, each advancing the work of the other. MaineShare emphasizes the importance of *prevention* programs, and how groups like the Maine AIDS Alliance, Maine Coalition Against Sexual Assault, and the Natural Resources Council of Maine work to prevent the spread of HIV/AIDS; reduce sexual assault; and eliminate toxic chemicals from our environment.

As we move forward not only with the development of workplace philanthropy, but with all long-term efforts aimed at community improvement, there is an important discussion all communities need to have about the myths that cloud our understanding of the nonprofit sector and the centers of power that shape our charitable agenda.

—Matt Howe

Who Receives Support from Federated Fundraising Organizations?

A registered tax-exempt 501(c)(3) organization, or non-exempt organization with a fiscal sponsor who is a 501(c)(3) should begin by gathering application material for all the federated fundraising organizations in their community. United Ways historically favor supporting health and human service agencies whose programs fall within the following areas:

Adoption
Advocacy   Individual and family counseling
Adult education   Information and referral hotlines
Alcoholism services   Job training
Camping   Legal aid
Community health clinics   Mental health education
Consumer protection   Rape crisis relief
Crime prevention   Recreation
Day care   Rehabilitation services
Drug abuse services   Services for disabled individuals
Emergency food and shelter   Services for elderly individuals
Family counseling   Services for women
First aid   Social adjustment, development,
Food banks   functioning
Foster care   Special transportation
Health research   Suicide prevention
Home and mobile meals   voluntarism[5]

Some kinds of organizations almost certainly will not obtain United Way funding, such as those involved in arts and culture, environmental groups (unless their work has health components, such as stopping toxic dumping into a water supply), and religious organizations. Nonprofits whose work involves advocacy, community organizing, public interest law, housing and civil rights/liberties are also unlikely candidates. However, each United Way is autonomous, and there has been much change recently, so groups should find out the particular guidelines of their local federations.

Alternative funds support organizations involved in advocacy and community organizing programs around such issues as tenants' rights, disarmament, occupational health and safety, reproductive rights, and consumer rights. Other local federated funds may also be organized to support organizations that serve blacks, Hispanics, Asian-Americans, Native Americans, women, or gay men, lesbians, bisexuals, and transgender people. In most cases, recipients of alternative funds represent a cross section of the thousands of existing grassroots social-action organizations. Others were established instead to create a broader lobbying and funding base for

---

5. United Way of America, "Basic Facts About United Ways."

certain sets of social issues, such as conserving the environment or community economic development.

Nonprofits that don't qualify for support from either the United Way or existing alternative funds might choose to establish a new alternative fund in conjunction with other similar groups on the local level.

What Are the Advantages of Securing Support from Federated Funds?

1. *Reliable source of steady income.* If you are fortunate enough to become a member or beneficiary agency of a federated fund, you are generally assured of its ongoing support as long as you meet its qualifications for membership. Of course, the extent of that support varies considerably from one community to the next and from one type of federated fund to the next.

2. *Savings in your own fundraising time and budget.* One of the purposes of a federated fundraising campaign is to raise funds more efficiently than its affiliated organizations could do on their own.

3. *Workplace fundraising is the least expensive type of fundraising.* You can solicit a large number of people in a short period of time. Workplace fundraising costs fifteen cents for every dollar raised, whereas other fundraising mechanisms, such as special events or direct mail solicitation, cost much more per dollar.

4. *Heightened public profile.* The publicity that a federated campaign usually generates about its member agencies should make your organization better known to the public and to the media.

   Because federated campaigns get extensive press coverage in many locales, being a member agency almost guarantees some mention, if only in the local federation's printed material. During the campaign, individuals are often asked to make presentations at various workplaces about their organizations as part of a federation; hence, a "captive audience" will learn about your organization's specific issues or services. Of course, your public image will be intertwined with the federated fund with which you are affiliated.

   With some of the newer alternative funds that are gaining (or attempting to gain) access to the workplace, media coverage may come as a result of conflicts or disagreements with the local United Way. In a number of cities, United Way has argued that the newer funds should not be allowed into various state, city, or private sector campaigns because this would be a duplication of services. In these cases, the alternative funds have been able, through the media, to capitalize on the fact that United Way was not meeting the needs of the organizations, issues, or constituencies represented by their funds.

5. *Enhanced reputation.* Association with a federated effort can enhance your own reputation. After all, a well-organized, solid federation has extensive ties throughout the community that might reflect well on your organization.

6. *Federation membership can be a resource.* Members of the board of directors and other standing committees of your federation might serve as resources for your work. For example, if you hope to approach a local company for in-kind contributions and you are a United Way grantee, you might start with the representative of that company who sits on the United Way's board of directors. In your letter of inquiry, you can acknowledge your mutual participation in the United Way as one way to open the door.

7. *Networking.* Participation in a fundraising federation affords opportunities for networking by providing regular contact with other beneficiary organizations. You get to know their staff and trustees and broaden your base of organization-building knowledge and potentially helpful contacts.

8. *Technical assistance.* You can also benefit from some of the technical and management assistance programs that local federations operate to enhance the skills of the staff and trustees of its member organizations. For example, A Choice, a federation of community groups in Milwaukee, regularly offers workshops on such topics as grassroots fundraising, time management, grantwriting, and organizational development. The Women's Funding Alliance in Seattle has seminars on Women Managing Inherited Wealth, as well as antiracism and anti-homophobia workshops for its member organizations and other nonprofits.

Many United Ways run management assistance programs (MAPS), which conduct training sessions, consultations, and seminars, and provide technical assistance for the staff of their member agencies. They often recruit corporate executives to lend their expertise to nonprofits. Find out from your local federations whether they have such a program, and whether nonmember agencies are eligible for assistance.

What Are the Disadvantages of Securing Support from Federated Funds?

1. *Restrictions on your own fundraising.* Beneficiary organizations must usually refrain from certain fundraising activities during the federation's annual fall-to-winter campaign, or even throughout the entire year; the federation decides which activities it considers as potentially contrary to its best interests. The agreement may also limit an organization's approaches to corporations for gifts, access to individual employees at the workplace, or both. Alternative funds tend not to have comparable restrictions, except when they decide that a unified approach to a funding prospect, such as a corporation, will be strategically more effective. Again,

given the autonomy of all local federated efforts, the extent of any restrictions will vary from one community to the next and from one fund to another.

2. *Long waiting period prior for admission (or rejection).* The annual allocation and fundraising cycles of many federations often force applicants to wait a considerable period of time—a year, in some cases—before a decision is reached on their application for membership. This can also apply to acceptance into donor option programs and approval for discretionary nonmember grants. It's easy to imagine the challenges such delays might create in the operations of an applicant organization.

3. *Delay in receiving allocations.* The essence of workplace solicitation in federating fundraising is that beneficiary nonprofits receive allocations after monthly or quarterly deductions have been made from the workers' paychecks. Some organizations have had to wait inordinately long periods of time to receive funds from United Way's donor option program.

4. *Fluctuating levels of support.* Although membership status is fairly secure as long as your group is living up to its stated purpose and its programs continue to produce concrete results, your annual budget allocation (grant size) from a federation can fluctuate, especially if you are a newer, less-established member agency. Despite the fact that the level of United Way funding changes very little from one year to the next, United Ways review the entire operating budgets of their beneficiary agencies each year before determining their level of support. Because most alternative funds are still fairly young and growing, the size of their grants is determined more by the total sum of monies raised in a given year's campaign than by any internal allocation formulas. Annual employee designation patterns also affect allocations.

5. *Contribution of time and labor to actual fundraising campaigns.* Federated fundraising requires a lot of volunteer effort; member agencies are usually called on to provide volunteers for various fundraising and public speaking tasks, especially during the campaign. Minimally, they may be asked to solicit their own employees for contributions to the federated drive to which they belong. Where a local United Way encourages the management of a member agency to obtain 100 percent participation of workers in a United Way campaign, workplace charitable solicitation within that agency can fall prey to coercion and other abuses, despite the fact that the United Way discourages such practices.

6. *Subtle pressure toward conformity.* While a federation cannot formally tell a member agency what to do, it may exert subtle pressure on its members to conform to its philosophy and policies. For example, if United Way announces that it is particularly interested in funding certain types of projects in an upcoming year, member agencies know that a program addressing those concerns might be viewed more favorably than others and might ultimately affect their budget allocation. When the beneficiaries play some role in a federation's policy-making process, they are usually more comfortable with any policies that might be established in this regard.

However, when they don't have that opportunity, they can rightfully feel disenfranchised in the setting of policies.

Deciding Whether To Approach a Federated Fund for Support

Are your activities and programs service-oriented or advocacy- and organizing-oriented? Does your organization conform to the profile of other member agencies of a particular federation in your community? Does your work enjoy broad-based popular support?

The answers to these questions will help you decide whether you should approach the local United Way for support or a local alternative fund—or even trying to establish a new one with other kindred groups. Finally, you might also become involved in the donor option program (if one exists) of the local United Way, or work to gain direct access to public and private workplaces for the purposes of charitable solicitation.

Nonprofits unfamiliar with the local United Way need to decide whether they would qualify for United Way support as a member agency or as a recipient of a discretionary grant. Both determinations will depend not only on United Way's guidelines for membership and discretionary grants, but also on the nonprofit's focus. If an alternative fund does exist in the community, also check its membership or allocations guidelines to find out whether it accepts new members.

Before applying, you will also want to review carefully the fundraising restrictions that would apply if you were admitted as a member agency of a local United Way. For example, if you already enjoy substantial support from local corporations, how will United Way member agency status affect that support? Will you be restrained from approaching these companies directly again for grants? Inquire in advance how much funding you might expect to receive and measure that against the funding you might have to forego.

Securing Support from Federated Funds

A primary goal of any organization interested in support from a federation is to gain access to the lucrative workplace solicitation process. Some fundraisers see this arena as a critical source of new funds for many newer nonprofits in the decade ahead. Should this be the case, forward-looking nonprofits are advised to start staking out that field now. As mentioned, a nonprofit can work toward this goal in a variety of ways:

1. Join the local United Way as a member agency.

2. Apply to the United Way for a discretionary or a venture grant.

3. Seek participation in an existing United Way donor option program.

4. Join another federation.

5. Form a new federation with other similar organizations in your community.

Each of these strategies poses advantages and disadvantages for the uninitiated organization. You need to investigate the pros and cons of each thoroughly before you decide which is most appropriate to your needs.

Step 1. Ask Your Local United Way about Special Grant Programs

Ask your local United Way to send their most recent materials on any discretionary or special initiative grant programs for nonmember agencies, as well as membership application forms, guidelines, and a current list of past grantees and members. Make requests in writing on your organizational letterhead. Remember that very few organizations are admitted to a given United Way each year as new members. At the same time, check to see whether there are any other federated funds in your community. The National Committee for Responsive Philanthropy (NCRP) (2001 S Street, NW, Suite 620, Washington, D.C. , 20009; tel: 202-387-9177; e-mail: info@ncrp.org) or the National Alliance for Choice in Giving (P.O. Box 4572, Portland, ME 04112-4572; tel: 207-761-1110; e-mail: nacg@nacg.org) can tell you whether any exist locally, and can help you start one if there are none. Make similar inquiries with any such funds.

Step 2. Research Charitable Contributions Drives among Government Employees

Find out from your local, municipal, and/or state government whether they conduct charitable contributions drives among their employees, and whether agencies unaffiliated with a federation can participate. The personnel office of your local government will be able to provide this information, as it usually administers payroll deductions for all purposes, including charitable contributions. Also find out whether the United Way has a donor option program for nonmember agencies. If you are a national organization—or a local organization in a city with a large number of federal employees—you would be well advised to make a similar inquiry with the federal government about the Combined Federal Campaign. The National Alliance for Choice in Giving can advise groups in these matters as well. Check with your local municipal and state governments to find out whether they allow their employees to make contributions through payroll deductions to non-United Way agencies.

Step 3. Contact Other Member Organizations

Ask member organizations of local federations—both United Way and alternative funds—how they would assess the pros and cons of that support. Also find out how they obtained it. Did they find an individual within the local United Way or alternative fund who was particularly helpful to them during the application process? You might also want to obtain further materials from the National Alliance for Choice in Giving or the National Committee for Responsive Philanthropy, both of which maintain excellent publications programs. United Way of America can also provide you with some general materials (701 North Fairfax Street, Alexandria, VA 22314-2045, tel: 703-836-7100).

Step 4. Weigh the Advantages and Disadvantages for Each Strategy

You may decide to apply for a discretionary or special initiative grant from the United Way before applying for membership, or to pursue workplace solicitation directly through a donor option program. Remember that one course of action does not necessarily preclude another.

Step 5. Apply

Regardless of which action you decide to take, you will more than likely have to complete a formal application and submit a set of supporting materials. Be sure to submit required forms in a timely fashion. If you have never applied to a United Way for funding, you may want to do so for the experience as well as for the possibility that you will be funded.

Step 6. Gather Support

Solicit letters of support from community and civic leaders who can attest to the importance of your work, and don't hesitate to demonstrate your qualifications during the preapplication period. After submitting your application, forward any letters of support that come in; they will be considered at the appropriate time. This is an opportunity for you to organize your supporters toward a specific goal.

Step 7. If Accepted, Go to Work

If you have chosen to participate in a United Way donor option program or to engage directly in a workplace solicitation program of your own, your work is truly cut out for you. While workplace fundraising usually costs less than other methods and reaches more people, it is still left to the nonprofit to organize a campaign, inform the public, and mobilize teams of askers at targeted worksites. But because each United Way DOP is different, be sure to investigate the United Way's stipulations regarding your organization's publicity campaign; in some cases, publicity by an individual organization outside of United Way's presentations is prohibited.

You should also know that if you are not going to participate in a donor option plan, gaining access to workplaces in order to solicit employees is an arduous process. Because of the work involved, many of the groups that fundraise in the workplace strongly suggest that an organization join—or form—a federation before attempting to gain access. Groups in Baltimore, Pittsburgh, and Philadelphia formed fundraising coalitions to get access to donor option programs.

If you decide to go it alone, it's best to start with a limited number of workplaces. Choose ones where you have strong contacts, where your work is best known and/or relevant, and where the management is amenable to your presence. This approach is more effective initially than a massive-scale campaign, unless your work has received a lot of recent positive publicity.

Step 8. Participate in Federation Fundraising Activities

If you decide to apply to a local federated fund for support and membership and your application is approved, you will undoubtedly be asked to become active in the fund. You might participate in its governance, in some of its fundraising activities, or both, depending on the nature of the specific fund.

Tips

- Be very clear about your obligation to assist the federation that you join in its fundraising efforts, and make sure that you have the resources available for that effort; full-hearted participation is crucial to membership.

- Take advantage of the increased opportunities you will have as a member of a federation to network with your nonprofit colleagues and to learn about new funding sources and fundraising approaches.

- Educate yourself and your staff about the ongoing requirements for federation membership and monitor your work continually to make sure that you comply with them.

Summary Worksheet

for _____

(name of your organization)

Approaching Federated Fundraising Organizations

Identifying Federated Fundraising Organizations in Your Community

1. List the federated fundraising organizations (i.e., United Way, alternative funds, etc.) that operate in your community.

   _____   _____

   _____   _____

   _____   _____

   _____   _____

2. Enumerate the ways that each of those listed provide financial support to nonprofit organizations.

Name of Feder- ated Fundraising Organization	Membership Organization (yes/no)	Operating Grants Available (yes/no)	Discretionary Grants Available (yes/no)	Donor Option Programs Available
a. _____				
b. _____				
c. _____				
d. _____				

1. Are any of the federated fundraising organizations in your community supporting organizations similar to yours? If yes, what are they?

   _____

   _____

   _____

   _____

2. On the basis of its printed guidelines, does your organization reflect the interest areas or priorities of your community's federated fundraising organizations? Which ones?

   _____

   _____

   _____

   _____

3. Does your local United Way have a donor option program? If yes, is your organization eligible to participate?

_____ yes   _____ no

4. See pages 530 and 531 for this part of the worksheet.

Making the Match

For each prospect on the previous list, complete the following worksheet (use your own blank paper):

Name of Federated Fundraising Organization:

Its Stated Areas of Interest that Pertain to Your Work (draw from its annual report):

Write one or more short sentences demonstrating how the work of your organization reflects the interests of the federated fundraising organization.

Finding Assistance and Counsel

Name those individuals who might be able to advise you on how to most effectively approach the federated fundraising organization(s) on your list:

a. _____

b. _____

c. _____

d. _____

a. _____

Assessing the Likelihood of Securing Support from Federated Fundraising Organizations

On the basis of what you have learned, how would you rank your chances of securing support from federated fundraising organizations?

___ Very Good   ___ Possible   ___ Unlikely   ___ Still Unknown

4. List below the federated fundraising organizations that might provide support for your work. Limit your listing to the most likely supporters of your organization.

a. Name of Federated Fund-raising Organization	b. Its Stated Areas of Interest that Relate to Your Work	c. Appropriate Contact Person and Telephone Number

d. Personal Contacts	e. Your Program(s) that Correspond to Their Interests	f. Level of Potential Financial Support

Additional Resources

Publications

Billitteri, Thomas J. "United Ways Seek a New Identity." *Chronicle of Philanthropy* 12 (9 March 2000): 1, 21, 23–26.

> Discusses the current trend in which many United Ways across the country are shifting from focusing only on the collection and distribution of charitable contributions to becoming organizations that actively collaborate with nonprofits and community activists to combat social problems. Sidebars provide charts of statistical data regarding how the percentage of earmarked gifts to United Way has grown from 1990-1998; how United Way giving has fared against inflation from 1968-1998; and a comparison of United Ways' 1993 and 1998 campaigns, noting the increase of large gifts.

Bothwell, Robert O., and Beth M. Daley. "Charting a New Future in Work-Place Fundraising." *Fund Raising Management* 24 (October 1993): 34–35.

> Suggests the United Way of America should "abandon pretensions to being the preeminent community problem-solver" for a more flexible, responsive, and diverse future in work-place fundraising.

Carson, Emmett D. "The National Black United Fund: From Movement for Social Change to Social Change Organization." *New Directions for Philanthropic Fundraising* (Fall 1993): 53–71.

> Presents the history of the National Black United Fund, a federation of fifteen independent organizations, which raised over $7 million in 1990 and opened up workplaces for fundraising by black organizations and other groups. With references.

Carter, Woody. "Creating Something Solid To Stand On." *Advancing Philanthropy* 8 (July–August 2000): 30–31.

> Discusses the growth of the Bay Area Black United Fund, one of 20 black United Funds in the country. The fund is transforming itself from traditional workplace giving to being a community foundation to benefit African-American causes.

DaSilva, Raquel, and Maureen Curran, eds. *The 1998–1999 CARES Directory: A Guide to Social and Health Services in the Greater New York Area*. New York: United Way of New York City and Dorland Directories, 1998. xxxv, 1710 p.

> Formerly titled *The Source Book*. Contains detailed information on nearly 2,200 health and social service agencies and some 9,500 programs in the greater New York area. Indexed by program, keyword/target group, and personnel name.

Delany, Dan, and Robert O. Bothwell. *Charity in the Workplace, 1997.* Washington, DC: National Committee for Responsive Philanthropy, 1998.
> Sections cover the slow growth in United Way giving, the rise in alternative fund giving, basic types of alternative funds, profiles of regional and national alternative funds, and corporations that have open charity drives. Includes numerous tables and charts.

Dickey, Marilyn, and Jennifer Moore. "United Way Sees End to Dry Spell: Giving Rises Four Percent to Five Percent Nationwide as New Strategies Pay Off." *Chronicle of Philanthropy* (12 March 1998): 27–31.
> Based on preliminary results, many United Ways across the country are celebrating a rise in giving.

Georgeson, Lance. "Building an Employee Giving Program in the Smaller Nonprofit." *Fund Raising Management* 28 (May 1997): 30–32.

Greene, Stephen G. "High-Tech Giving at Work." *Chronicle of Philanthropy* 12 (24 August 2000): 1, 17–21.
> Describes how federations, such as United Ways, plan to incorporate recent technological advances into their fundraising efforts and the reasons why they believe this is necessary. A sidebar details how the United Way of the Bay Area is positioning itself as an authority on which nonprofit groups are the most effective in accomplishing their program goals. Statistical report on p. 20–21 lists donations by 362 of the largest United Ways for 1999-2000.

Millar, Bruce. "Beneficiaries of a Scandal: United Way of America Controversy Has Opened Company Doors for Other Federations of Charities." *Chronicle of Philanthropy* 5 (20 April 1993): 25–26.

Marx, Jerry D. "Corporate Philanthropy and United Way: Challenges for the Year 2000." *Nonprofit Management & Leadership* 8 (Fall 1997): 19–30.
> Reports the results of a national survey of corporate philanthropy programs, focusing on the influence of strategic philanthropy on corporate contributions to the United Way.

National Committee for Responsive Philanthropy. "Federal Employees Want Choice in CFC." *Responsive Philanthropy* (Fall 1996): 9–10.
> Recently convened focus groups revealed a continued interest in donor choice as a critical element of the Combined Federal Campaign (CFC).

National Committee for Responsive Philanthropy. *Workplace Fundraising: A Primer.* Washington, DC: National Committee for Responsive Philanthropy, 1997. 36 p.

Patten, Monica. "Community Foundations and United Way: Getting from Competition to Collaboration." *Philanthropist/Le Philanthrope* 13 (February 1996): 21–26.
    Describes the different roles and strengths of community foundations and United Way.

Reiss, Alvin H. "Workplace Giving a Growing Source of Arts Support." *Fund Raising Management* 29 (December 1998): 24-25.
    Discusses the use of United Arts Funds as a source of support for arts organizations. United Arts Funds, which is patterned on the United Way, brings together arts groups from communities and conducts a combined annual fund drive on behalf of its member arts organizations.

Sinclair, Matthew. "AFL-CIO Offering Choice in Giving." *NonProfit Times* 14 (February 2000): 1, 8, 10, 12.
    Discusses the AFL-CIO's creation of the Union Community Fund (UCF), which will be creating and launching workplace giving campaigns in several pilot cities. According to Jim Sessions, UCF's incoming executive director, the new nonprofit will be a way for the union to encourage giving and volunteering among members and support agencies. Discusses the United Way of America's concerns about the impact that UCF's development will have on its long-standing partnership with labor.

Sinclair, Matthew. "Moving United Way Ahead Will Take Big Coordinated Effort." *NonProfit Times* 13 (July 1999): 1, 6, 8.
    There are almost 1,400 independent United Ways in the United States, and moving them ahead in a coordinated fundraising program can be a challenge.

Stehle, Vince. "Diversifying Jewish Philanthropy: As Donors Seek More Control Over Use of Their Gifts, Federations Fear a Loss of Collective Decision Making." *Chronicle of Philanthropy* (15 May 1997): 1, 27–29.

United Way of America. *United Way of America, Annual Report*. Alexandria, VA: United Way of America. Annual.
    Report of the yearly activities of the national organization.

United Way of America Fact Sheets. Alexandria, VA: United Way of America.
    Series (free upon request) explains various aspects of United Way's history and activities. Titles include "Basic Facts About United Ways," "United Way and Services for New Agencies, Minorities and Women," and "Information and Referral Services," among others.

Organizations

The following organizations are resources for learning about federated funds. For a thorough listing of alternative federated funds, please refer to the Web links mentioned in the description of the National Committee for Responsive Philanthropy.

American Red Cross
Attn: Public Inquiry Office
431 18th Street, NW
Washington, D.C. 20006
Tel: 202-639-3520
E-mail: info@usa.redcross.org
Web address: www.redcross.org

>   The American Red Cross supports disaster relief and emergency preparedness efforts throughout the country. Interested donors can contribute directly to the national organization or use the online search engine to find local Red Cross agencies.

Combined Federal Campaign
Office of CFC Operations
1900 E Street, NW, Room 5450
Washington, D.C. 20415
Tel: 202-606-2564
Web address: www.opm.gov/cfc

>   The U.S. Office of Personnel Management oversees this yearly fundraising campaign, which allows federal employees and military personnel to make charitable contributions through a payroll deduction plan. Organizations interested in becoming affiliated with the CFC can download an application form from their Web site.

Independent Charities of America (ICA)
21 Tamal Vista Boulevard, Suite 209
Corte Madera, CA 94925
Tel: 800-477-0733
Web address: www.independentcharities.org

>   ICA is a nonprofit organization that "pre-screens high-quality national and international charities and presents them to potential givers in fund drives at work and on the web." Potential donors can search through ICA's database of organizations on-line.

National Alliance for Choice in Giving
P.O. Box 4572
Portland, ME 04112
Tel: 207-761-1110
Fax: 207-761-1115
E-mail nacg@nacg.org
Web address: www.nacg.org

> The National Alliance for Choice in Giving (NACG) is an association of 52 local and statewide federations committed to increasing awareness of and support for nonprofit organizations in your community. The federation members of NACG work for social and economic justice, women's rights, and environmental protection and preservation. NACG members partner with public and private businesses to develop programs that increase employee awareness of the community in which they live, while increasing involvement and support. One of the primary activities is the annual workplace charity drive.

National Committee for Responsible Philanthropy
2001 S Street, NW
Washington, DC 20009
Tel: 202-387-9177
Fax: 202-332-5084
E-mail: info@ncrp.org
Web address: www.ncrp.org

> The mission of the National Committee for Responsive Philanthropy (NCRP) is to make philanthropy more responsive to people with the least wealth and opportunity, more relevant to critical public needs, and more open and accountable to all, in order to create a more just and democratic society. NCRP has issued an excellent list of alternative funds. Please refer to *The Green Directory: Alternative Funds & Federations Around the World*, found on NCRP's Web site at http://www.ncrp.org/afap/greendirectory.htm. The directory is downloadable from http://www.ncrp.org/afap/afap.htm.

United Way of America
701 North Fairfax Street
Alexandria, VA 22314-2045
Tel: 703-836-7100
Web address: www.unitedway.org

> Local United Way agencies throughout the United States and Canada raise funds through payroll deduction campaigns and other means and reallocate charitable dollars for social services and community development programs in local communities. UWA also provides guidance to member agencies on funding priorities and fundraising strategies.

Chapter 20

Associations of Individuals

> *A modern democratic state cannot consist merely of civil service, political parties, and private enterprises. It must offer citizens a colorful array of ways to become involved, both privately and publicly, and must develop very different types of civic coexistence, solidarity, and participation.*
> —Vaclav Havel

The Art of the Impossible

An association is a group of individuals who come together voluntarily to work toward a common objective based on a shared belief, value, or experience. They may organize for social

purposes, professional enrichment, philanthropic concerns, or any number of reasons. Individuals often join associations to tackle through concerted effort a problem that they could not solve alone. Associations can range in size from the smallest neighborhood-based block club to a global service club such as Rotary International.

Most individuals belong to one kind of association or another because banding together with others for a common purpose is a familiar and important aspect of our lives. You may belong to a block club, a parents' group, a book club, a food co-op, or a civic association; your neighbor may belong to Alcoholics Anonymous, a service organization such as the Lions or the Soroptomists, or a sports team—the array is virtually endless.

Associations would appear to be an inherent part of life in the United States. Alexis de Tocqueville, one of the most renowned travelers to this country, commented on this phenomenon in his work, *Democracy in America*:

> Americans of all ages, all conditions, and all dispositions constantly form associations. They have not only commercial and manufacturing companies, in which all take part, but associations of a thousand other kinds, religious, moral, serious, futile, general or restricted, enormous or diminutive. The Americans make associations to give entertainment, to found seminaries, to build inns, to construct churches, to diffuse books, to send missionaries to the antipodes; in this manner they found hospitals, prisons and schools. If it is proposed to inculcate some truth or to foster some feeling by the encouragement of a great example, they form a society. Wherever at the head of some new undertaking you see the government in France, or a man of rank in England, in the United States you will be sure to find an association.[1]

Although more than 150 years have passed since Tocqueville made this observation, what he described is even more evident today in the United States and around the world. Countless individuals come together to share and develop their common interests in hobbies, social service, spiritual growth, community, neighborhood beautification, and so on. As noted in *America's Voluntary Spirit, A Book of Readings*, "There are certain common elements, however, in the whole range of associational life. Members are expected to be 'active.' They belong to committees, take part in campaigns, try to get publicity for their activities in the local press, lay a good deal of stress on fundraising (especially in the case of women's groups), and engage in a kind of gift exchange by a reciprocity of contributions," that the chapter's author compares to "the potlatches of some of the American Indian tribes."[2]

Self-help is clearly a basic element of many voluntary associations. Individuals who have experienced loss, discrimination, or illness often form associations to help others who find themselves in similar situations as well as themselves. That concern may extend to people in one's immediate community, one's own country, and even to the entire world.

Some associations trace their origins to philanthropic concerns. For example, the first Junior League in America was founded in New York City in 1901 by Mary Harriman, who, with a

1. Alexis de Tocqueville, *Democracy in America*, trans. Henry Reeve, rev. Francis Bouer (1835, 1840; reprint, 2 vols. New York: Alfred A. Knopf, Inc., 1945).

2. Brian O'Connell. *America's Voluntary Spirit, A Book of Readings* (New York: The Foundation Center, 1983).

group of eighty-five young women, worked to promote volunteer service in the settlement houses of the city. Early Junior Leagues rapidly expanded their activities to include the founding of well-baby clinics, conducting classes in home nursing, establishing orphanages, and organizing garment factories to employ needy women. Today, more than 193,000 women are active in 295 Junior Leagues across the nation.

In Zambia, a group of women has formed an association called Kwasha Mukwena to care for the rapidly growing number of orphans created by the AIDS pandemic. The women of Kwasha Mukwena bake bread, sew and batik fabrics, and weave doormats to feed and pay school fees for hundreds of orphans.

In the United States, the Southwest Florida chapter of the Video Software Dealers Association received $5,000 from its national headquarters to pass along to its favorite charity. The donations from the Fast Forward to End Hunger Fund promoted by actors Jeff Bridges and Jeff Goldblum were given to the Harry Chapin Good Bank.[3] And members of two Lee County, Florida Rotary Clubs helped raise more than $75,450 to assist destitute people in Haiti through a concert and silent auction. Funds went to help build seventy-five structurally sound houses and to provide thousands of meals for the island's children.[4]

A number of associations have evolved in the United States to represent the concerns of professions and trades. Their functions include keeping members informed of industry trends, acting as an advocate for member causes, playing an integral role in determining industry standards, performing research and development, maintaining relations with government, and lobbying for favorable legislation.

The existence of the wide variety of associations is only now being documented. John Kretzmann and John McKnight, co-directors of the Asset-Based Community Development Institute at the Institute for Policy Research at Northwestern University, researched the number and type of voluntary associations in a poor neighborhood on Chicago's South Side. They found 319 different associations in this community of 36,000 residents, 99 percent of whom were African-American and 82 percent living below the poverty line. They found a large number of church-related groups, such as a Singles Ministry, Bible Study groups, several choirs, chapters of the Elks Club and the Masons, twenty-six block clubs, fifteen neighborhood-improvement organizations, six merchant associations, and a plethora of cultural, parental concern, and school support groups. Many of these associations were not formally incorporated, but all raised money to help people and other organizations in their particular area of interest.[5]

How Do Associations Extend Support to Nonprofits?

Unfortunately, statistics are not readily available on the total contributions made by associations to other nonprofits each year, or how much money associations help raise for individual

---

3. Mary Ann Husly, *The News-Press,* 12/27/99

4. Ibid.

5. John P. Kretzmann, John L. McKnight, and Nicol Turner, "Voluntary Associations in Low-Income Neighborhoods: An Unexplored Community Resource," working paper, Institute for Policy Research, Northwestern University, Evanston, IL, 1996.

nonprofits. The range of charitable distributions made by associations is quite diverse. A local chapter of a national service organization might make a contribution of a hundred dollars in response to a speaker at its monthly meeting; or it could make a much more substantial contribution through its sponsorship of an annual charity ball. A local association might donate $500 to an organization and then sponsor a special event that raises $10,000.

A survey released by the American Society of Association Executives in 1998 found that nearly half of the 8,662 associations it represents raise money, donate supplies, or perform pro bono services for charities. This number is particularly striking when you consider that the Society represents only U.S. associations with paid staff. Extrapolating from their survey would be impossible, but it is clear that millions of dollars are raised or given by hundreds of thousands of groups all over the world. Furthermore, associations probably provide even more volunteers than dollars.

Some groups, such as the 140,000-member National Federation of Business and Professional Women's Clubs, Inc. (BPW/USA), include grantmaking as an integral part of their program agenda. As BPW's founders stated in 1919, their purpose is to serve, in this regard, the career advancement needs of business and professional women. The Federation established the Business and Professional Women's Foundation in 1956 to provide services and support to all working women. The Foundation is both an operating and a grantmaking body; its efforts include research, information and referral, and a diverse program of educational financial aid.

How Do Associations Operate?

A local association can be an informally structured grassroots group or a formally organized chapter of a national association. For the most part, associations are membership organizations in which members vote on most important decisions directly or through elected representatives. At their monthly meetings local civic associations might poll members on an important issue, such as support for or opposition to a redevelopment project slated for their neighborhood. Local chapters of large national associations, such as the League of Women Voters, or the American Association of Retired Persons (AARP), would be more likely to vote on issues such as universal health care at state and national conventions. Local chapters would thus ordinarily make decisions on major policy within the confines set by the voting membership from across the country.

The decision to support other nonprofit organizations with funds or volunteers usually rests with the local chapter of an association. Some chapters may also belong to a city- or statewide body of their association, which, on occasion, may make contributions. However, the majority of requests for support from nonprofits are usually first received by the local chapter.

Some associations see their role as supporting the charitable work of other existing organizations, whereas others become directly involved in projects by providing volunteer workers; some associations are willing to do both. Many associations exist exclusively to carry out projects relating to their own stated interests; these interests may not correspond to those of other nonprofits, and such associations would, therefore, not be candidates for a funding proposal.

Larger associations may have paid staff at both the local and national levels, although local chapters usually do not have staff unless they cover a major metropolitan area. An association may have officers, such as president or chair or co-chairs, vice president, treasurer, and secretary, who direct the work of the association between the regularly scheduled meetings of its members.

Associations usually derive their income from members' annual dues. If there is a national body, each member's dues are usually shared by the local chapters and the national body. For example, dues of 75¢ per member raise more than $100,000 each year for the National Federation of Business and Professional Women to support its work. They also organize special events, such as house tours and benefit concerts, to raise additional funds for their philanthropic purposes.

Membership in associations is generally open to anyone with an interest in joining, although some associations do set requirements for membership, such as references from existing members, professional experience, and the like.

Associations can also provide benefits that are consistent with their purposes. As an example from the past, with the emergence of cities in Europe in the Middle Ages, medieval guilds were founded to provide assistance to craftsmen and their families. Some of their services included a type of insurance to provide for the needs of widows and children of prematurely deceased guild members. Such programs enabled their members to practice their craft more effectively.

Which Nonprofits Are Most Likely To Receive Support from Associations?

Hundreds of thousands of associations exist, counting national organizations, their local chapters, and independent local and regional groups as well as thousands of grassroots associations, such as block clubs, cooperatives, tenants' groups, community organizations, and village-based groups. There are far more associations than foundations, and it is therefore even harder to make generalizations about their areas of interest. The nonprofit fundraiser's task is made even more complicated because sympathetic associations that wish to support an organization's work may choose to provide volunteers, rather than donate funds.

Nevertheless, the myriad of associations on both the local and national levels makes it likely that some will extend support in one form or another. As in most fundraising efforts, the two best ways to involve an association in supporting your group are: (1) find a sympathetic member of the association to take your cause to the rest of the group, and (2) find an association with a natural affinity to your cause. When you can do both, you are likely to find a large and steady source of funds and volunteers!

Here are some examples researched and reported by Marilyn Dickey in *The Chronicle of Philanthropy*:

- When real estate agent Renee Kaplan, a member of the Greater Tulsa Association of Realtors, survived breast cancer, she approached her association colleagues to ask if they would help raise seed money for a local chapter of Y-ME

National Breast Cancer Organization she was starting in Tulsa. The association agreed, and sponsored silent auctions and golf tournaments that raised $12,500—half of the charity's budget for its first year of operations.

- Rawhide Boys Ranch, in New London, Wisconsin, helps youngsters who have been in trouble with the law. They enlisted the aid of the Wisconsin Automobile and Truck Dealers Association in a fundraising effort to encourage people to donate used cars for Rawhide to sell and keep the profits. With the help of the association, Rawhide was able to go from selling 50 donated cars a year to 7,000 cars in 1998, netting the ranch more than $1 million and doubling the number of children it serves. The association also donated $300,000 to enable Rawhide to build a new facility.[6]

What Are the Advantages of Raising Support from Associations?

1. *Quick source of small amounts of money.* Suppose you need to raise several hundred dollars, or even a thousand, as soon as possible. Where can you turn? Local associations might respond to your request by inviting you to address its members at a monthly meeting and paying you a speaker's honorarium, or passing the hat among those in attendance. Some groups may even have a contributions fund specifically established for philanthropic purposes. While the financial capacity of associations varies considerably, an organization can raise hundreds of dollars by appealing to a number of them for support in a relatively short time.

2. *Source of volunteers.* Because associations usually attract civic-minded people who are interested in the well-being of their communities, they can be a good source of volunteers. Furthermore, association members are often organization-minded in the sense that they understand how groups function best, based on their own experiences as workers and board members in an association. This background makes them good prospects for serving on a board of directors or a standing committee of a nonprofit that is seeking new volunteer leaders. Association members may possess some of the skills that you currently lack on your board, and can also be recruited to work as skilled volunteers in some of your programs.

3. *Source of useful civic contacts.* Have you ever been unsuccessful in getting an appointment, only to discover that the door swings wide open when you bring an associate who has a personal relationship with somebody on the other side? Most nonprofits are always in need of new contacts within government agencies, corporations, and larger nonprofit institutions. Individuals from these groups frequently

---

6. Marilyn Dickey, "Raising Money by Association," *Chronicle of Philanthropy* 10 (16 July 1998): 37-38.

belong to local service associations. By approaching an association for assistance, or even becoming personally involved yourself, you broaden your own network of people to turn to in times of need.

4. *Partner in advocacy efforts.* If you are building popular support for a bill pending before the state legislature that affects your constituency, or are working to galvanize popular opinion around a broad public issue, associations are excellent channels for reaching out to other circles within your own community. Also, because many associations are familiar with electoral and legislative processes, and know how they can be used to advance issues, they can be useful allies. The skills of such groups as the League of Women Voters and the American Association of University Women are well known. In any coalition-building efforts, therefore, be sure to include some associations on your list.

5. *Evidence of community support.* Indeed, there is no better way to demonstrate community support for your organization and its issues than by highlighting the associations that your organization works with. That support can be useful when approaching government or corporations for support. The official backing of associations helps show the depth of popular support that your organization enjoys among the public.

What Are the Disadvantages of Raising Support from Associations?

1. *Limited financial support.* Most associations are not sources of substantial financial support for nonprofit organizations. There are some major exceptions, but the vast majority of associations extend financial assistance in hundreds of dollars rather than thousands. For some programs and emergency needs, however, even a few hundred dollars can make a significant difference.

2. *The time involved.* You can't secure help from most associations simply by dropping a letter in the mail; social, civic, fraternal, ethnic, and professional groups transact their affairs through personal contact. To elicit their assistance, you must first meet with one of their officers and then address a meeting of the membership. You may prefer such direct personal contact yourself, but such meetings do take time from an already crowded schedule. Moreover, you may have to wait, since many groups meet only once a month and schedule their speakers several months in advance.

3. *Potential for disappointment.* Have you ever been a luncheon speaker for a group in which your comments stirred no more interest than the rubbery chicken your listeners dined on? And yet they invited you to speak!

Associations are occasionally eager to find new speakers for monthly get-togethers, but the chair of a group's program committee may have run out of new ideas and turned to you out of desperation. If this is the case, you may discover that your audience has no interest in, or even sympathy for, your views; responses may range from indifference to hostility. Your time has been wasted and you have been left with an unpleasant memory or a challenge to your mettle—or both. The lesson here is to choose your audiences carefully.

At the same time, there will often be at least one person who is not indifferent and whose interest you might develop if approached after the meeting. As you speak, keep a sharp lookout for such people; their smiles or body language may communicate interest.

4. *Reduction or termination of support.* Associations can decide to reduce or terminate their support of your organization and move onto another cause. This is particularly likely if your contact was, say, the president of a local trade association who was replaced by a new person with new interests. Consequently, an event that your organization and the association may have developed over several years might have a new beneficiary. Or, the association may decide that the work it is doing for your group is taking too much time and end the project altogether.

Deciding Whether To Approach Associations for Support

How well do you know the associations in your community? Is there a match of interests? Are there potential allies who might support your work if you were to approach them? Some alliances are logical and self-evident. For example, the Academy of Facial Plastic and Reconstructive Surgeons has worked with the National Coalition Against Domestic Violence to provide plastic surgery for women who have been disfigured by domestic violence. Says Rita Smith, executive director of the coalition, "Plastic surgery is considered cosmetic to the rest of the world, but it's a real gift to women who want to have scars removed."

The basis for other alliances can be less obvious. For example, the Foundation for the Peoples of the South Pacific, a Washington-based development agency organized to foster self-help efforts among South Pacific peoples, eventually found a receptive audience in the Veterans of Foreign Wars (VFW), since many VFW members served in the armed forces in the South Pacific during World War II. During their overseas experiences, many soldiers developed an appreciation for South Pacific culture, and so were inclined to respond favorably to the Foundation's appeals for funds fifty years later.

Your potential association supporters may be evident or not; the challenge for every non-profit organization is to identify the most likely candidates. If your work involves coalition-building and advocacy, your time will be well spent in developing relationships with associations in your community. If you ever have an occasional need for small sums of money or for volunteers, these alliances will serve you well.

Securing Support from Associations

Step 1. Identify Potentially Supportive Associations in Your Community

Your first step is to inventory the associations in your community that you feel might support your work. You are developing a prospect list, just as you would with foundations. Look for logical allies as well as less apparent ones. The Yellow Pages of your local phone book list local associations under Associations or under Service Organizations. Review the results of your circles exercise from Chapter 7. What kinds of organizations might some of your prime constituents belong to? Which professional bodies? Religiously oriented groups? Civic associations? Women's organizations? Sororities or fraternities? Merchants or trade associations? By thinking through who your individual supporters are and what their professional and personal interests are, you'll begin to develop a sense of which associations will support your work.

Your elected officials are in a good position to know which associations in their districts might be responsive to your issue. After all, their staff spends much of its time doing such constituent work as responding to inquiries, requests, and positions put forth by a wide array of local groups. You could benefit in your prospecting by speaking to staff members in the district offices of your city, state, and federally elected officials. There are also several excellent reference works on nationally oriented associations to guide the uninitiated; see the Additional Resources section at the end of this chapter.

After brainstorming with your staff, board, or organizing committee, speaking to staff members of friendly elected officials, and checking some of the available reference materials, you should be able to develop a fairly solid prospect list of five to fifteen local associations to explore.

Step 2. Make the Approach

Associations are generally less formal in conducting their affairs than other institutions. You can approach them initially by placing a phone call to a member of an association whom you already know, or to an officer.

Introduce yourself and explain that you are seeking the opportunity to address the members of the association to elicit support for your organization's work. Suggest that you would be most willing to meet to discuss your work with officers of the association so that they will be able to judge whether their members would be interested in learning more about the problems that your organization tackles. Plan to bring one or two others to the initial exploratory meeting, as well as some organizational literature, such as pamphlets, brochures, and newsletters.

Step 3. Hold the Meeting

Your goal is to get the members of an association involved by educating them about the extent of the problem, the work your organization does to create solutions, and the ways in which individuals and associations can help. By virtue of your work, you are an authoritative source of information on certain issues. You will need to articulate why any civic-minded group would have an interest in those problems and their resolution. You are building a case on the basis of mutually understood concerns. Be clear about the types of assistance that would benefit your organization.

If your listeners have been receptive to your story, you can then seek out a wider audience with the association's membership. Inquire how you can best proceed to let others within the local association learn about your work. Are there regular meetings that you can address? If the association is a chapter of a statewide or a national body, are there conferences or conventions that other chapters also attend? With luck, you will have won over the officers at your first presentation to the degree that they will be willing to help you approach the membership for assistance.

Step 4. Address the Association's Membership

You've secured an opportunity to make your case to the membership of an association at its regular meeting. Congratulations! How can you make the most effective presentation?

Nothing makes a speech more effective than visual aids. Do you have any slide shows, charts, Powerpoint presentations, or photographs you can use to illustrate and enhance your comments? If you happen to be an excellent artist, you might even illustrate your comments on a blackboard or flip-chart paper as you proceed. You could also recruit the services of a graphic artist to prepare some visuals to accompany your remarks. If you plan to make a number of presentations in the course of a year, such an investment will serve you many times over.

In your prepared comments, tell your audience how, as members of the association and as individuals, they can assist your work. In essence, a presentation has three components:

1. A vivid description of a problem or an opportunity and how it bears on the lives of your constituents—as well as your listeners

2. An illustration of how your organization is tackling the situation that you described

3. A statement of how your audience can help you reduce the incidence or consequences of that particular problem (e.g., by providing you with funds or volunteers, adding its voice to a lobbying effort you might be engaged in, etc.)

Leave enough time at the end of your speech so that listeners can ask questions, and thank them for the opportunity to address their group. If your audience has been receptive to your remarks, offer to return the following year to give an update on your progress.

Step. 5. Follow-Up

An association may thank you for your speech by awarding you a speaker's honorarium. If you have the permission of the association, you can solicit memberships and contributions. Because associations vary in their rules about the degree to which you can solicit—or if you can solicit funds at all—be sure to ask your host ahead of time, and, if appropriate, bring appropriate literature to distribute.

Profiles

- The National Association of Homebuilders (U.S.A.) has made Habitat for Humanity one of its favorite charities. It encourages employees to donate their time to build houses for Habitat and provides funding on a regular basis. Further, NAHB has introduced Habitat to a number of valuable contacts by donating booth space for Habitat at its annual trade show, which attracts 70,000 members and nonmembers. One particularly successful introduction was to Dow Chemical, which now annually donates all of the rigid foam insulation used in Habitat houses in all of North America, valued at $350,000. In addition, Dow Chemical makes a $250,000 cash donation each year.

- The Video Software Dealers Association in Encino, California, raised $2 million in 1998 for Fast Forward to End Hunger, a local charity, by putting 5,000 collection canisters in its member video-rental stores to solicit gifts from customers.

- The American Pulpwood Association raises money for the Children's Miracle Network, which supports children's hospitals in the United States and Canada, through a program called Log-a-Load. Association members make donations of $200 to $500—the value of a truckload of logs—and through events such as auctions and fishing tournaments. Log-a-Load has raised $8.1 million for children's hospitals since 1988.[7]

7. Marilyn Dickey, Raising Money by Association," *Chronicle of Philanthropy* 10 (16 July 1998): 37–38.

Thank your host in a follow-up letter that acknowledges any support you receive (at the meeting or afterwards) and states how the contributions will be put to use. The association's potential further involvement in your work will be enhanced if you demonstrate to what specific end you have put their monies. You might earmark the contribution for a particular program that evoked interest during the course of your presentation. Generally, this course of action is wiser in the long run than designating the contributions for general use.

If you have not been offered any financial stipend for your presentation, you can request a contribution in your follow-up letter. If the experience has proven fruitful, you can inquire about other chapters or associations that your hosts might suggest you approach. If the association has an active local philanthropic program or belongs to a national body that does, you can also inquire how you might qualify for further support.

Be sure to add your official host and the association itself to your mailing list so they will receive newsletters, ongoing membership appeals, and invitations to any special events or open houses you might sponsor in the future. As is the case with religious leaders, you are initiating a relationship that you hope will serve your organization for a long time to come.

Summary

Reaching out to associations deepens your support base in your own community and may provide you with concrete assistance. You have enlarged your reservoir of potential allies to turn to when the occasion calls for a show of support. Addressing their membership meetings also provides you with the opportunity to sharpen your public speaking skills as well as those of your board and staff members. While the financial rewards might be limited, the returns in enhanced people power and strong political clout are incalculable.

Tips

- Be creative and thorough when identifying the associations whose interests may correspond to those of your group. Every community the world over has formal and informal associations of people who come together out of shared interest or values.

- Know to what groups your staff, volunteers, and board members belong.

Summary Worksheet

for _____

Approaching Associations for Support

Building on Past Association Support

1. Have any associations ever supported your work in the past?

_____ yes   _____ no

If yes, which ones? How?

_____

_____

_____

_____

_____

_____

2. What characteristics do these associations share? How do their interests correspond to each other?

Comments:

_____

_____

_____

_____

3. What is your sense of what they valued in your organization's work?

Comments:

_____

_____

_____

_____

4. Which ones can you re-approach for future support?

Definite Ongoing Projects

_____   _____

_____   _____

_____   _____

_____   _____

Untested (further information needed)

_____   _____
_____   _____
_____   _____
_____   _____

Finding New Association Supporters: Research and Networking

1. Using reference materials at your local library, such as the ones listed in the Additional Resources at the end of this chapter, list some associations that might support your work.

_____
_____
_____
_____

2. What are some of the reasons why such associations would be attracted to your work?

_____
_____
_____
_____

3.   See pages 552 and 553 for this part of the worksheet.

Making the Match

For each prospect on the previous list, complete the following worksheet (use your own blank paper):

Name of Association:

Its Stated Areas of Interest that Pertain to Your Work (draw from printed literature, informal conversations, news clippings, etc.):
Write one or more short sentences demonstrating how the work of your organization reflects the interests of the association.

Finding Assistance and Counsel

Name five or more individuals who might be able to advise you on how to most effectively approach the associations on your best-bets list:

a. _____
b. _____
c. _____
d. _____
e. _____

Addressing the Likelihood of Securing Support from Associations

On the basis of what you have learned, how would you rank your chances of securing support from associations?

___ Very Good ___ Possible ___ Unlikely ___ Still Unknown

3. List below the association prospects you have uncovered from your research and your networking. Limit your listing to the most likely supporters of your organization.

a. Type of Association	b. Their Stated Areas of Interest that Relate to Your Work	c. Appropriate Contact: Person, Address, and Phone
Neighborhood or Community-Based		
Citywide		
National		

d. Personal Contacts	e. Your Program(s) that Correspond to Their Interests	f. Type and Amount of Support Available

Additional Resources

Publications

Alliance for International Educational and Cultural Exchange. *International Exchange Locator: A Resource Directory for Educational and Cultural Exchange.* 5th ed. Washington, DC: Alliance for International Educational and Cultural Exchange, 1998. x, 249 p.

> Arranged in six sections: organizations involved in international exchanges, industry-specific exchanges, research/support organizations, foreign affairs agencies and exchange programs, other federal government exchanges, and key Congressional committees and members of congress. Includes index.

Angus, Susan G., ed. Invest Yourself: *The Catalogue of Volunteer Opportunities. A Guide to Action.* New York: Commission on Voluntary Service and Action, Inc., 1993. xxxiv, 302 p.

> Guide to voluntary service opportunities throughout North America and worldwide. Organization profiles include address, telephone number, general information about the agency, and skills needed. Indexed by agency name, work camps, opportunities for volunteers under eighteen years old, program location, skills and interests needed, international/intercultural opportunities, and full- and part-time opportunities.

Barrett, Jacqueline K., ed. *Encyclopedia of Women's Associations Worldwide.* Detroit: Gale Group, 1993. lxvi, 471 p.

> A guide to more than 3,400 organizations around the world concerning women and women's issues. Lists organizations by geographic region, and then by country within those regions. Entries include information describing the activities/objectives of the organization, information on any publications they may produce, as well as standard directory information. Indexed by name and by activities.

Boyd, Alex, ed. *Guide to Multicultural Resources 1997/1998.* 6th ed. Fort Atkinson, WI: Highsmith Press, 1997. x, 580 p.

> Profiles more than three thousand African-American, Asian-American, Hispanic-American, and Native American associations, institutions, organizations, and other entities, as well as local, state, and federal government agencies with a multicultural mission. Indexed by organization name, executives, subjects, geographic location, and agency publications and videos.

Brennan, Shawn, ed. *Women's Information Directory.* Detroit: Gale Group, 1992. xviii, 795 p.

> Provides more than 10,800 listings of organizations, agencies, institutions, programs, publications, services, and other resources with direct relevance to women or women's issues. Listings are arranged in twenty-six separate chapters according to resource type. All entries contain contact information, and many also contain descriptive information. Includes name and subject index.

Downs, Buck J., ed. *National Trade and Professional Associations of the United States.* 35th ed. Washington, DC: Columbia Books, 2000. 959 p.

Lists 7,600 trade associations, professional societies, labor unions, and similar national groups. Indexed by subject, geography, budget size, executives, and acronyms.

Downs, Buck J., ed. *State and Regional Associations of the United States.* 12th ed. Washington, DC: Columbia Books, 2000. 719 p.

Organized alphabetically by the name of the association. Entries are indexed by subject, budget size, executives names, and acronyms. A final index lists names of firms that provide management services to associations on a contract basis.

Eldridge, Grant J., ed. *National Directory of Nonprofit Organizations.* 12th ed. Farmington Hills, MI: The Taft Group, 2000. 3 vols.

Provides brief informational profiles for more than 264,000 tax-exempt organizations. Each entry contains name, address, reported annual income, IRS 501(c) contribution deduction eligibility and filing status, and activity code (activity groups table and activity look-up table in the front of each volume list activity codes based on major subject groups as described by the IRS). Volume one (parts one and two) contains entries for those organizations with annual revenues estimated at $100,000 or more; volume two contains entries for organizations with annual revenues estimated between $25,000 and $99,999. Includes IRS Filing Status table. Indexed by organizational activity and geographic location.

Estell, Kenneth, ed. *African Americans Information Directory.* 4th ed. Detroit: Gale Group, 1998. xiii, 560 p.

Provides information on more than 5,200 nonprofit organizations, government agencies, publications and programs for and about African-Americans. Entries are arranged under such topics as: national, regional, state, and local organizations; library collections, museums and cultural institutions; colleges and universities with Black Studies programs; federal, state and local government agencies; federal domestic assistance programs; the top 100 black businesses; and publications, publishers, broadcast media, and Internet resources serving the Black community. Master name and keyword index.

Leadership Directories. *Associations Yellow Book: Who's Who at the Leading U.S. Trade and Professional Associations.* New York: Leadership Directories, Inc., 1996. xvi, 1028 p.

Profiles 1,179 of the leading U.S. trade and professional associations. Included in the profiles are names of officers and staff; Washington representatives and political action committee contacts; and board members. Focuses on associations that are vocational in nature, that operate on a national level, and that have annual operating budgets of at least one million dollars. Organized alphabetically by association name; the book also includes numerous indexes.

Montney, Charles B., ed. *Hispanic Americans Information Directory.* 3rd ed. Detroit: Gale Group, 1994. xv, 515 p.

Provides information on approximately 5,400 organizations, agencies, publications, and programs for and about Hispanic-Americans. Entries are organized into seventeen chapters, including national, regional, state, and local associations; library collections, museums, and cultural organizations; research centers; awards, honors, and prizes; colleges and universities with Hispanic Studies programs; state, local, and federal government agencies; federal domestic assistance programs; the top 500 Hispanic businesses in the United States; and publications, publishers, videos, and television and radio stations serving the Hispanic community. All entries include an address, with telephone numbers and contact names provided whenever possible. Many chapters contain descriptive annotations. Master name and keyword index.

Moran, Amanda M., ed. *CyberHound's Guide to Associations and Nonprofit Organizations on the Internet.* Detroit: Gale Group, 1996. xxxii, 694 p.

Provides entries for 2,500 Web sites of associations and other nonprofit organizations. Entries contain the uniform resource locator (URL); site description; updating frequency; site establishment date; geographic area and time span covered; language; target audience; contact information; and ratings of site content, design, and technical merit. Includes bibliography, glossary of Internet terms, and indexes of organization name, contact person, and subject.

Oakes, Elizabeth H., ed. *Minority Organizations: A National Directory.* 5th ed. Chicago: Ferguson Publishing Company, 1997. 636 p.

A reference volume to African-American, Hispanic-American, Asian-American or Pacific Islander-American, and Native American organizations. This edition cites nearly 6,000 organizations, providing names, address, telephone, fax, e-mail, and Web site information; description of membership; types of activities and programs; and publications. Indexed by state and activity category.

Russell, John J., ed. *National Trade and Professional Associations of the United States.* 32nd ed. Washington, DC: Columbia Books, 1997. 694 p.

Schorr, Alan Edward, ed. *Hispanic Resource Directory.* 3rd ed. Juneau, AK: Denali Press, 1996. 493 p.

Sheets, Tara, ed. *Encyclopedia of Associations: International Organizations.* 35th ed. Detroit: Gale Group, 1999. 2 vols.

Guide to some 20,800 international nonprofit membership organizations, including multi-national and bi-national groups and national organizations based outside the United States. Part One includes descriptive listings, arranged under fifteen general subject categories and includes location, size, objectives, and information on publications, conventions/meetings, annual budget, commercial exhibits, language and affiliations. Part

Two contains a comprehensive alphabetical name and keyword index, geographic, and executive indexes.

Sheets, Tara E., ed. *Encyclopedia of Associations: National Organizations of the U.S.* 36th ed. Detroit: Gale Research, 2000. 2 vols.
  Provides detailed information on nearly 23,000 American nonprofit organizations of national scope. Categories for organizations include trade, business, and commercial organizations; social welfare, health and medical, and public affairs organizations; legal, governmental, public administration, and military organizations; educational and cultural organizations; religious organizations; chambers of commerce and trade and tourism organizations; and labor unions, associations, and federations. Part three is an alphabetical index to organization names and keywords, including citations to selected organizations in six additional reference works.

Walls, David. *The Activist's Almanac: The Concerned Citizen's Guide to the Leading Advocacy Organizations in America.* New York: Simon & Schuster, 1993. 431 p.
  Profiles organizations that are national in scope or impact, have a membership structure that is open to the general public, are classified as nonprofit organizations, have an orientation toward changing public policy rather than providing services, and influence public policy or promote ideas with significant potential for policy impact across the political spectrum. Entries provide basic contact information plus date founded, number of members, budget, staff size, tax status, related political action committees, purpose, detailed background and history, priorities, membership profile, structure, resources, publications and services. Extensive bibliographical notes and index.

Chapter 21

Labor Unions

by Ellen Cassedy

What does labor want? It wants the earth and the fullness thereof . . . We want more schoolhouses and less jails; more books and less arsenals; more learning and less vice; more constant work and less crime; more leisure and less greed; more justice and less revenge.

—Samuel Gompers

The time is ripe for nonprofit organizations to approach unions. Many unions are actively seeking ties with organizations in their communities, and developing ties with unions can strengthen

a nonprofit in many ways. Unions can be a valuable source of advice, skilled volunteers, political contacts, resources such as meeting rooms and printing facilities—and, on occasion, money.

An organization approaching a union for support can expect to be asked to reciprocate—to support the union in return. A nonprofit organization can offer important support for union goals both at work and in the broader community, resulting in a long-lasting relationship with many benefits for both sides.

While many of the ideas in this chapter can be applied internationally, our discussion focuses exclusively on labor and nonprofits in the United States. After religious organizations, unions are the largest social institution in the United States. Through unions, working men and women and their families seek to make their voices heard, both on the job and in their communities. More than sixteen million Americans belong to unions today, and some forty million live in union households. Union members include women and men of all ages, races, and ethnic groups. They work in hospitals and nursing homes, at auto assembly plants and on trains, buses, and planes. They are security guards, teachers, musicians, electricians, postal workers, janitors, doctors, and more.

The largest group of union members are government workers, followed by workers in manufacturing, services, transportation, and retail. Union members live in every state. In Michigan, close to one in four workers is a union member, whereas in South Carolina, only four percent of workers carry a union card.

Men and women join unions to gain a voice in workplace decisions, better wages and benefits, job security, and safety and fairness on the job. Union members earn higher pay than non-union workers—32 percent more—and are more likely to have health insurance and a pension.

In addition to bargaining over pay, benefits, and working conditions for their own members, unions have a long and proud tradition of supporting social justice for all. Today, the AFL-CIO, the nationwide labor federation, states that its overall mission is "to improve the lives of working families and to bring economic justice to the workplace and social justice to the nation."

The tradition of workers helping workers stretches back in history. Before unions existed, workers would pass the hat to help feed the family of an injured employee. Neighbors pitched in to rebuild a home destroyed by fire or storm. Early unions organized relief funds and death benefits. Over the years, unions in America have played a major role in shaping living conditions for all members of society. Unions have won better wages, benefits, dignity, and justice on the job—not just for their own members, but for millions of Americans who don't belong to unions.

Many of the public policies we take for granted today—the ban on child labor, the eight-hour work day, Social Security, pension protections, the minimum wage, workplace health and safety rules—were won primarily by America's unions. Unions have been in the forefront of efforts for housing, education, health care, civil rights, consumer rights, and the struggle to close the wage gap between men and women. That's the history behind the popular bumper sticker: "The labor movement: the folks who brought you the weekend."

In addition to advocating social change, unions contribute to their communities in other ways. Across the country, thousands of union volunteers participate in community service efforts: raising funds for charities, collecting food, building wheelchair ramps, donating blood, and providing services for the elderly, the unemployed, children, and the disabled.

Unions Today

In the mid-1950s, the percentage of union members in the workforce as a whole reached its peak; at that time, 35 percent of all workers were union members. Over the past twenty years, however, changes in the economy and aggressive antiunion efforts by employers led to a decline in union membership as a percentage of all workers. By the 1990s, union membership hovered at about 14 percent of the workforce—the lowest level since 1935. Union members saw the results in diminished power at the bargaining table. Productivity soared and salaries for business executives increased exponentially—yet wages for working people stagnated. More and more families found themselves working longer hours just to stay even. Workers' political power suffered, too. Policies to benefit working families met with rough sailing in Congress, state legislatures, and city councils alike.

In 1995, unions across the United States launched an effort to reverse the decline. Under the slogan "A New Voice for American Workers," John J. Sweeney was elected president of the AFL-CIO. Sweeney announced a vigorous effort to recruit new members and to mobilize union members in grassroots efforts for social and economic change. Today, following Sweeney's lead, many unions are devoting more resources than ever before to reaching potential new members and developing allies in their communities. They're looking for nonprofit organizations with which they can pursue a common agenda.

Unions are joining together with health-care advocates to expand health coverage and improve the quality of care. They're working with community organizations to pass "living wage laws" to move families up from poverty. They're working with senior citizens on Medicare and Social Security issues. They're working for education reform—to reduce class size, repair school buildings, and hire more teachers. They're working with civil rights allies for racial equality and with women's organizations for pay equity, child care, and after-school programs. Unions have stepped up their activities in the political arena. In each election cycle, unions field tens of thousands of volunteers who register voters, educate voters about issues and candidates, and get people to the polls on election day. In the 1998 elections, one voter in four came from a union household.

Today's unions need ties with nonprofit organizations. In fact, for today's unions, forming lasting partnerships with allies in the community is a matter of tremendous urgency. To meet the needs of their members, many unions must increase their bargaining power by expanding their ranks. Yet organizing new members tends to be difficult. Workers who seek to join unions often face intense hostility from employers who view them as disloyal troublemakers. Each year, more than ten thousand workers are illegally fired for exercising their "right to organize."

Mobilizing community support may be the only way that unions can create a climate that allows workers to choose to join a union and bargain effectively. Likewise, unions and community organizations may find they must join together if they are to become strong enough to achieve their goals—whether in the field of community services, economic development, or legislative victories.

Understanding the Structure of America's Unions

Approaching unions for support requires understanding two parallel structures and some related bodies. The first is the structure of individual unions, such as the Steelworkers Union, the Communication Workers of America, and the American Federation of State, County, and Municipal Employees (AFSCME). These are known as *international unions* because they have members in Canada. International unions number more than one hundred in the United States today. Most are headquartered in Washington, D.C.

Unions are grounded in collective action. Before an individual can join a union, a majority of workers at a particular workplace, workplace unit, or group of worksites must choose to join up together. A union local can consist of workers from a single workplace, a single employer with a number of worksites (such as a city government), or a large number of employers.

The union locals you'll encounter in your community will vary greatly. Some are small, numbering only a few hundred workers; others have thousands of members. Some are stable, active, and growing; others stagnant, shrinking, or struggling. Some may have thousands of members, a large paid staff, printing facilities, and a building of their own; others may have few members, no paid staff, and no resources to share. Some are eager to develop ties with partners in their communities; others are not.

Union locals elect officers and an executive board. Most have committees—for example, a committee on community service or political action. Locals have a system of union representatives called *stewards* or *delegates,* at each worksite. These are often the core of union activists. Some locals have full- or part-time staff, either elected or appointed. The most important leader tends to be the president or business agent.

In some internationals, locals join together in larger bodies known as *joint councils, joint boards, state councils,* or *regional structures.* These may have paid or unpaid leaders. Some internationals and regional bodies direct their locals to participate in various issue campaigns or to reach out to their communities in various ways. Different locals will follow these directives to varying degrees.

Based on their wages, union members pay dues to the local they belong to—frequently a few hundred dollars a year per member. The local sends on a fraction of these dues to the higher bodies of the union, but most dues money remains at the local level, where it goes into bargaining, organizing, education, and other union activities. Most locals have only very limited funds, if any, to donate to nonprofits or other organizations.

Parallel to the structure of individual unions is the national federation of America's unions, the AFL-CIO (American Federation of Labor-Congress of Industrial Organizations). Nearly one hundred internationals belong to the AFL-CIO, which sets policy for labor and carries out nationwide efforts in the fields of organizing, education, and politics. (A few international unions, such as the National Education Association, the American Nurses Association, and the National Association of Social Workers, don't belong to the AFL-CIO.) The AFL-CIO operates at the city or county level through *central labor councils,* or *central labor bodies,* and at the state level through *state federations,* or "state feds."

The central labor council is a voluntary coalition of union locals in a particular community. Locals join in order to work together on community, legislative, and political efforts. The state federation is a coalition of unions on a statewide level. It is the primary legislative arm of unions in a particular state. The largest and most active locals tend to set the direction of the central labor council and the state federation.

The AFL-CIO carries out a number of nationwide efforts that may have an impact on U.S. communities.

Labor and the United Way

For more than half a century, the AFL-CIO and United Way of America have worked together to provide community services. In more than two hundred communities across the country, AFL-CIO Community Services Liaisons are funded by the United Way to link unions with community agencies. The AFL-CIO holds twenty statewide community services conferences each year and trains some six thousand union members annually as counselors who provide information and referrals, linking those in need to community agencies.

Union Cities

A more recent effort, the AFL-CIO's Union Cities project operates on the metropolitan level to link unions with one another and with community organizations in order to strengthen the voice of working families. Central labor councils in some cities carry out the Union Cities program by strengthening community alliances and generating community support for union organizing campaigns and economic development policies that benefit workers and their families. A related project, Street Heat, mobilizes union and community members to support organizing drives and other union efforts.

AFL-CIO Constituency Groups

Several groups represent constituencies within the AFL-CIO. These operate on the community level and can be a good source of local activists interested in the mission of a particular nonprofit organization. See the Additional Resources section at the end of this chapter for the addresses and phone numbers of their Washington, D.C., headquarters.

- The A. Philip Randolph Institute, named after the veteran fighter for African-Americans in the labor movement, seeks to build support for unions in African-American communities. It has 150 chapters in 36 states.

- The Asian Pacific American Labor Alliance (APALA) seeks to build ties between unions and the Asian Pacific American community.

- The Coalition of Labor Union Women brings together union women to advance the rights of women at the workplace and through political and legislative action.

- The Labor Council for Latin American Advancement encourages Hispanic workers and their families to vote, runs citizenship classes and forums on immigrant workers' rights, and supports legislation to benefit all workers.

- Pride at Work is the national organization of lesbian, gay, bisexual, and transgender union members. It has fifteen regional chapters, which fight discrimination based on sexual orientation, educate the labor movement about the concerns of lesbian and gay union members, educate the lesbian and gay community about unions, and assist with union organizing efforts.

- Not an official arm of the AFL-CIO, the National Council of Senior Citizens mobilizes retired union members to protect Social Security, expand Medicare, and support other social and economic causes. It has more than five hundred thousand members and two thousand affiliated clubs and councils. NCSC members are experienced activists who may have time and expertise to devote to a nonprofit organization.

- Also not an official arm of the AFL-CIO, Jobs with Justice brings together union locals, community groups, and religious organizations in more than thirty cities. Through local coalitions, community leaders develop lasting ties and work together to improve health care coverage, support union organizing campaigns, and fight for fairness at the workplace.

America's unions are diverse from top to bottom. Some locals, and some internationals, are large, well-funded, and powerful. Others are small, with few resources. In some states and communities, unions are active and highly visible; in others, the union presence is hard to notice. But don't jump to conclusions. The relative size, power, and presence of unions in your area will not necessarily tell you how fruitful it will be to approach them for support. One large, stable local may be enthusiastic about sharing its resources; another may not feel compelled to build alliances. One small local may be too strapped to help you; another may be desperate for allies. The only way to find out is to ask.

How Do Unions Provide Monetary and Nonmonetary Support to Nonprofits?

While some unions receive government grants or funding from other sources, the great majority of union money comes from local members' dues. Likewise, the bulk of union giving takes place on the local level. In addition, the AFL-CIO gives away about a million dollars each year. International unions also give away small amounts of funds. Several unions run small foundations at the national level; these tend to fund union projects or scholarships for children of union members.

Direct monetary support flowing from local unions to nonprofit organizations is generally small—in the range of one hundred or a few hundred dollars annually per group. Traditionally, requests for union grants come to the president or the executive board through union officers or members. A union officer who sits on the board of the local diabetes foundation, for example, may ask the local to buy a table at the annual fundraising dinner. Or a rank-and-file member of the local may make such a request.

Increasingly, the AFL-CIO is urging unions to provide monetary and nonmonetary support on a strategic basis—to allocate resources in a way that directly supports the broad interests of the union. Nonprofit organizations seeking funding will be wise to make a strong case for why their project advances the union's agenda. Union decisions about granting monetary or nonmonetary support to nonprofit organizations can be made in several venues. Some unions make such decisions by formal vote of the executive board; others leave the decisions to the discretion of the president or staff.

Likewise, central labor councils also have executive boards, officers, and, sometimes, staff. They, too, can decide such matters either formally or informally. International unions concern themselves with supporting national efforts. Generally, they would consider a proposal for support of a nonprofit organization only if the project were of national or regional scope, and only upon the recommendation of local and regional union leaders.

Most union support for nonprofit organizations is nonmonetary. Unions can help nonprofits in many ways:

- Unions can provide meeting space or an auditorium, free printing, or a phone bank for a phonathon. They can publicize a nonprofit event, service, or program through the union newsletter or workplace bulletin boards.

- Union members in the building trades will sometimes be happy to paint your office, build new shelves, or even put on a new roof.

- Unions can supply volunteers—some of them with organizational expertise such as coordinating a rally or designing a leaflet. Some unions have databases of activists listed by neighborhood or precinct.

- Unions can supply speakers for press events.

- Unions can send a representative to sit on your board or advisory committee. Such a representative can be a skilled organizational veteran with much to contribute.

- Unions can help build your reputation in the community by lending their endorsement to your event or fundraiser.

- Unions can be an excellent source of information about your community—about other groups with aims similar to yours, about how the government or the school system works, about other unions to approach.

• Finally, in an advocacy campaign, unions can supply invaluable clout and expertise. They can help you plan your pressure campaign, advise you on how to deal with public officials, exert their own pressure on an official, co-sign a letter to the newspaper. They can circulate petitions or send people to your rally or lobby day. Allying with a union could spell the difference between success and failure for your campaign to expand health coverage, improve public transit, or reduce class size in local schools.

Community Services Liaisons

In hundreds of communities across the country, community services liaisons are funded by United Way of America to serve on the staff of the AFL-CIO's central labor councils. The job of these liaisons is to link unions with their communities, and they can be an excellent entree for nonprofits seeking support from unions. Here are some of the ways community services liaisons help nonprofits:

• Community services liaisons develop networks of active union volunteers.

• They help build community coalitions.

• They plan events on public policy issues, such as community summits on Social Security reform.

• They assist union families with drug and alcohol problems, child care, services for the elderly, food, housing, legal aid, medical care, and other personal and family problems.

• They have a comprehensive knowledge of social service agencies in the community.

• They seek to place union members on the boards of health and human service organizations.

• They know the local union scene and the community as a whole. They know which unions have ties with which community groups, which unions can turn out members for community projects, and which unions have meeting halls, printing facilities, and other resources.

As an outgrowth of the AFL-CIO's ties with United Way, at the end of the 1990s the labor federation was considering launching a national labor charity. The new charity would raise funds during United Way drives through the donor option program, which allows employees to contribute to charities that are not members of United Way itself. Funds would go to union/community partnerships at the local level. A union that saw a need for child care for swing shift workers at a local factory, for example, could present a funding proposal in partnership with a local child-care agency.

Which Nonprofits Are Most Likely To Receive Union Support?

Unions are most likely to support nonprofit organizations that advance their interests. These interests are varied:

- Unions want to serve their members' needs on the job.

- Unions want to grow.

- Unions want to elect pro-worker candidates and pass legislation that helps working families.

- Unions want to create goodwill in their community—to build a positive reputation, thereby boosting community support for organizing, bargaining, and legislative and political efforts.

- Unions want to help meet the broader needs of union families, from the need for a safe and stable community to good schools, day care, elder care, and other social services. Nonprofit organizations that serve the needs of individual union members and their families will be of interest to unions as official bodies.

With the election of AFL-CIO President John J. Sweeney, unions' approach to their communities is undergoing a change. Though individual unions and locals vary, many of today's unions lean more toward alliances with activist organizations than they did in the past. As one AFL-CIO staffer put it, "Less charity, more advocacy." More unions than in the past are seeking to work with community groups in strategic ways—ways that build the power of the union and further its social justice agenda—rather than simply on an ad hoc basis.

Even "charity" work, however, can be strategically important for a union. Community service programs that help people pay their utility bills or feed their children can bring union volunteers into contact with low-wage workers—providing an opening to encourage these workers to join the union. Sponsoring citizenship classes for immigrant workers or building low-income housing can help unions establish trust in racial and ethnic communities that they need to reach. Unions may well be interested in nonprofits—either advocacy or service-oriented—that provide them with these kinds of opportunities.

Across the country, central labor councils are discussing how to break down the isolation of unions and strengthen ties within their communities. "Every community has many groups that are potential allies," an AFL-CIO publication advises central labor council leaders. "Make a list of local religious, women's, civil rights, neighborhood, advocacy, ward and precinct and senior citizen organizations . . . Look for connections." In cities where unions are indeed looking for connections, nonprofit organizations that can advance union interests may be welcomed with open arms.

Some relationships between unions and nonprofits feature a "tit-for-tat" exchange of in-kind services. A church mission in Alabama, for example, provided food baskets for striking workers. In return, members of the painters' union renovated a room at the mission. And when the mission wanted to set up a sewing room for low-income mothers, union leaders used their connections with the union at a nearby sewing machine manufacturing plant to obtain a donation of free sewing machines from the plant. In other cases, the reciprocal relationship develops beyond an exchange of services into a strategic partnership.

In Milwaukee, Wisconsin, in 1996, unions and community groups formed a coalition to ensure that in the building of the new convention center, construction jobs would pay a living wage and members of minority groups would be hired. In Massachusetts, women's groups and community organizations joined with building trades unions to oppose legislation that would have eliminated prevailing wage standards for construction workers. African-American store workers in Greensboro, North Carolina worked with community leaders in a successful effort to organize a union and bring their wages up to par with white store workers in other cities. They held town hall meetings, circulated petitions, and marched in thousand-person demonstrations. The coalition won higher wages for the workers—which added millions of dollars to the local economy.

Here are some ways that nonprofits may be asked—or may offer—to support unions:

1. Send a representative to participate in the union's legislative phonathon - either a formal representative or an individual attending informally.

2. Invite workers who are seeking to organize a union to make a presentation at your group's general meeting.

3. Print an article about the union's activities in your newsletter.

4. Pass a resolution officially endorsing the union's campaign.

5. Urge public officials to support a union organizing drive. Send a letter to an employer who is seeking to obstruct union organizing. Join a delegation visiting a public official or employer.

6. Help plan an event such as a rally or community summit.

7. Join a demonstration or picket line. Bring a sign identifying your organization.

8. Speak at a rally.

9. Participate in a committee or workers' rights board that holds employers accountable to fair rules when workers are seeking to organize a union.

10. Support a political candidate. Publicize a candidate's views. Help get out the vote.

Nonprofit organizations that can support unions in some of these ways are most likely to be able to build the ties with unions that result in long-lasting support. But other factors matter, too. "Who's most likely to get support from unions?" one veteran community organizer asks. "The organization with the best program—the best marketing plan—the best ties—the best strategy for getting the support."

What Are the Advantages of Seeking Union Support?

1. *Occasional speedy assistance.* Unions can help out with a place to meet, a quick print job, a call to a recalcitrant official. But such assistance probably won't be offered until after a connection has been established.

2. *Good advice.* Some union members and leaders have a wealth of knowledge about recruiting volunteers; running meetings, phone banks, and picnics; building community support; and winning victories.

3. *People power.* Some union leaders and members wear many hats in their communities. They're involved in a variety of community efforts and are generous with their time and energy.

4. *Political power.* Union leaders can sometimes call on their history with elected officials to get results for your organization. Union involvement in your advocacy campaign can add valuable clout.

5. *Long-term support for a common agenda.* Unions and nonprofits that share common goals can grow and progress together over many years.

What are the Disadvantages of Seeking Union Support?

1. *Limited money.* Local unions and central labor councils are unlikely to give a direct grant of more than a few hundred dollars to a nonprofit organization. Regional and national union structures give support to only a small number of nonprofits—generally those with which they have an extensive working relationship.

2. *Limited information available.* Unions aren't in the business of giving away money or making in-kind donations. They don't publish directories or annual reports. The union structure is complex. Given the various names by which unions are known—Local 15, Teamsters Local 15, International Brotherhood of Teamsters 15—even finding a union in the telephone book can be difficult. Exploring the union landscape in your community can be an arduous endeavor.

3. *Barrier to corporate support.* In some cases, antiunion employers will be reluctant to support an organization that receives aid from unions.

4. *Special sensitivities.* Some union officials may take offense if you build your new building with nonunion labor, hire a nonunion printer to produce your flyers or business cards, use a nonunion telephone company, or drive a foreign car. These obstacles can be difficult to overcome.

5. *Internal politics.* As with any institution, maintaining a relationship with a union over the long term can be a challenge. Some unions are characterized by lively internal disputes and power struggles that are hard to keep up with. Union officers with

whom you've succeeded in developing a trusting relationship can be voted out of office. Other unions may be led, year in and year out, by veteran officials who aren't interested in meeting new people.

Securing Support from Unions

Step 1. Identify Potential Union Supporters and Organization Contacts

Begin by thinking through what you know about unions in your community.

Which unions are visible in your area? Which are known for community involvement? Have you had contact with any union leaders? Which unions would be interested in your particular issues? (Construction unions might be interested in your housing program, teachers in your education program, and so on.) Identify individuals in your organization or your network who have active ties with unions. You might circulate a list of local unions among your active members. If you run a social service agency, find out if any of your clients are union members. To find out more, you might start by:

- Calling the state federation (nearly always located in the state capital and listed under "[Name of State] AFL-CIO" in your state capital). Ask whether your community has a central labor council and which local unions you should be in touch with.

- Calling the community services coordinator in the AFL-CIO Department of Field Mobilization at the AFL-CIO in Washington, D.C. Ask for names of union activists in your community who could help you.

- Calling the central labor council in your community. Ask for the community services liaison, if there is one. In a small town, the central labor council may not have a full-time staff. Don't be put off if your call is not returned promptly—just call again.

- Consulting the Yellow Pages under "Labor Organizations" or "Unions."

Of course, finding a union activist or leader who can be your guide can make a big difference. If you don't know such a person yet, keep your eyes open for one as you go along.

Step 2. Determine Your Needs

At the same time, list the needs you have that a union or unions might be able to fill. Think in terms of small actions as well as long-term partnerships.

Step 3. Determine How Your Organization Can Help a Union

Think through how your organization helps the union and its members, or how you plan to do so. Ask yourself: Why is my organization of interest to the union? What has my organization or anyone close to my organization done to help the union? How do union members benefit from my organization? How would involvement with my organization help the union reach out to new members? How would involvement with my organization help the union build goodwill within the community? How could my organization help the union advance its organizing, bargaining, legislative, or political agenda?

Step 4. Choose One or More "Target" Unions

These could be unions whose leaders you happen to know, or unions you've decided might have a special interest in your program. Find out what you can about them. Who leads the union? Who belongs to the union? What size is the union? What kind of workers belong—what jobs do they do; which employers do they work for; what neighborhoods do they live in; what is their income level, sex, race? Is the union growing or declining? Is it active in community affairs? Has it been in the news recently? What are its priorities? But don't get hung up trying to gather all of this information before you make the initial contact. Do the best you can while moving ahead.

Step 5. Ask for a Meeting

Your initial approach may be to the community services liaison, the head of the central labor council, or the leader of an individual union. Ask your members to set up a meeting with the union they belong to. You can use a phone call, a letter, or a brief visit to the union office to request the meeting.

Step 6. Decide Who Should Come to the Meeting

An articulate leader of your organization, or a member of your group who has a personal tie to the union—preferably someone who is a member of the union—should attend. If that's not possible, invite any member of your group who can speak convincingly about why the union's members would benefit from your organization. Possibly a friend or ally may know the person you're meeting. Your target union leader will want to hear from someone he or she feels comfortable with. At every level of the union structure, if an "insider" can help carry the ball for you, so much the better.

Step 7. Hold the Meeting

At the meeting, describe the effort for which you need support and why it's important to you. State your needs clearly. Ask whether the union would be interested in working with you. If the union is interested, explore how you could work together. Have in mind some limited and specific actions the union could take to meet your needs. But also keep in mind that your goal is to build a trusting relationship for the long haul. Be flexible. Good early questions include:

"Is there one activist in the union who could become active in our organization?" This first volunteer could be the key to developing a long-term relationship."How can we get the word out within the union? Are there committees we could speak with? Which other unions and union leaders should we reach out to? Can you help?

What about money? Given the very limited funds that unions have to offer, if money is your only need, you probably shouldn't be at the meeting in the first place. If possible, wait until a later meeting to ask for funding. But don't hesitate to ask for specific in-kind resources, such as a room for an upcoming meeting.

To have a friend, you must be a friend. Make clear that you are seeking a mutual relationship. Ask what you can do to help the union.

Step 8. Follow Up Right Away

If the union has offered to help you, or if you have offered to help the union, set the wheels in motion. If a union leader has been particularly helpful, consider asking him or her to join your board or advisory board. Once on board, he or she could not only provide valuable advice but serve as your voice within the union community as a whole.

Follow up any leads that come out of the meeting, whether individual activists, a union committee, a higher body of the union, or other union or community leaders.

Finally, write a letter of thanks, and make sure to give public recognition when a union helps your organization.

Step 9. Plan for an Ongoing Relationship

Keep the union informed of your progress. Invite union activists to attend your events or visit your program. Take the time to get to know what the union is doing and participate where you can. Be persistent. Some unions are more willing to work with community groups than others. Some have more experience than others. Many union leaders take a while to warm up to the idea of working with other organizations. Don't take a rejection personally.

Solidarity Forever

Seeking support from unions can lead to long-lasting and mutually beneficial relationships. While few nonprofits should expect to raise significant amounts of money from unions, those organizations that share a common agenda with unions can expect a sustained and productive partnership. In the union movement, they call it solidarity.

Profile:

UHCAN Ohio and the Cleveland AFL-CIO

In Cleveland, Ohio, the Universal Health Care Action Network (UHCAN Ohio) and the Cleveland AFL-CIO work closely together on a variety of projects. The mutually beneficial relationship is typical of the close ties developing today between nonprofits (especially advocacy organizations) and unions.

In deciding which community groups to work with, the Cleveland AFL-CIO looks for "a common agenda and true respect for working people," says Executive Secretary John Ryan. "We ask, 'How does this organization's program make the community better for working people?'" Ryan met UHCAN Ohio's associate director, Athena Godet-Calogerass, through Jobs with Justice, a coalition of unions, religious organizations, and community groups. After hearing about UHCAN Ohio's campaign to expand health coverage for low-income families, Ryan agreed to call a meeting of UHCAN Ohio and unions representing low-income workers.

Following this meeting, unions representing service workers, hotel workers, and clothing workers signed on as active UHCAN Ohio supporters. Union activists and staff received training from UHCAN Ohio in how to register children of union members for free health care. Using talking points prepared by UHCAN Ohio, union leaders spoke about the campaign on TV talk shows. Union members testified at legislative hearings.

Together with other supporters, UHCAN Ohio and the Cleveland AFL-CIO achieved their goal. They increased the number of children eligible for free health care under the Child Health Insurance Program (CHIP). The next goal is to expand the program to cover the children's parents as well.

UHCAN Ohio and Cleveland unions have cooperated closely on other projects, too. When concession workers at the Cleveland baseball stadium sought to join a union, they ran into fierce opposition from their employer. In response, the AFL-CIO assembled a delegation of religious and community leaders to meet with the management of the Cleveland Indians, who in turn urged the concession employer to stop fighting the union drive.

Together, Cleveland unions and community groups, including UHCAN Ohio, conducted a "living wage" campaign to guarantee decent wages in the Cleveland area. UHCAN Ohio focused on the need for decent health benefits. UHCAN Ohio leaders speak at union rallies, such as a demonstration organized by the clothing workers union to put pressure on a local sweatshop. UHCAN Ohio also supported nurses who were seeking to organize a union at the public hospital by signing on to a letter urging hospital management not to obstruct the union drive.

Direct monetary support is not a big part of the relationship between the Cleveland AFL-CIO and UHCAN Ohio. Of the approximately $15,000 that the Cleveland AFL-CIO gives away each year, only about $200 goes to UHCAN Ohio. Individual unions that work closely with UHCAN Ohio have made donations of up to $1,000. In recognition of their support, these unions are listed as "organizational members" of UHCAN Ohio. The AFL-CIO donates in-kind services such as printing, and it helps groups like UHCAN to apply for grants from other sources.

Why does the partnership work? "It's natural," says Godet-Calogerass. "There's a justice orientation. We each serve one another's interest." But more than a shared agenda brings the two organizations together. "The personal relationships count, too," Godet-Calogerass says. "At first, people at meetings just glanced my way. Now everybody knows me. It's real."

Tips

- Apply the same kind of thinking about how a nonprofit can help meet unions' needs to other sources of funding; make sure you consider what prospective union supporters might want as carefully as what you want for your organization.

- A union official may have contacts in a variety of companies; be alert, therefore, to ways in which union contacts can lead you to other potential sources of funding.

- Before meeting with union officials, prepare yourself by doing some background reading on labor, generally, and the union you're approaching and its issues, specifically.

Acknowledgments

Thanks go to: Chris Marston, Karen Nussbaum, and Janet Shenk of the AFL-CIO; Anne Hill and John Ryan of the Cleveland AFL-CIO; Athena Godet-Calogerass of UHCAN Ohio; Kim Bobo of the National Interfaith Committee for Worker Justice; Jackie Kendall and Steve Max of the Midwest Academy; Jeff Blum of the Committee for the Future.

Summary Worksheet

for _____

(name of your organization)

Approaching Labor for Support

Building on Past Labor Support

1. Have any labor unions ever supported your work in the past?

   _____ yes   _____ no

   If yes, which ones?

   _____

   _____

   _____

   _____

   _____

2. What characteristics do these labor unions share? How do their interests correspond to each other?

   Comments:

   _____

   _____

   _____

   _____

   _____

3. What is *your* sense of what they valued in your organization's work?

   Comments:

   _____

   _____

   _____

   _____

4. Which ones can you reapproach for future support?

   Definite Ongoing Prospects:

   _____

   _____

   _____

   _____

   _____

Untested (further information needed):

_____

_____

_____

_____

_____

Finding New Labor Support: Research and Networking

1. List those labor unions to which your members and constituents belong:

_____

_____

_____

_____

_____

_____

2. See pages 578 and 579 for this part of the worksheet.

Making the Match

For each prospect in the previous list, complete the following worksheet (use your own blank paper).
Name of Labor Union:

Its Stated Areas of Interest that Pertain to Your Work (draw from annual reports, reference books, newsclippings, etc.):

Write one or more short sentences demonstrating how the work of your organization reflects the interests of X labor union.

Finding Assistance and Counsel

Name five or more individuals who might be able to advise you on how to most effectively approach the labor unions on your "Best Bets" list:

_____

_____

_____

_____

_____

Addressing the Likelihood of Securing Support

On the basis of what you have learned, how would you rank your chances of securing support from labor unions?

___ Very Good   ___ Possible   ___ Unlikely   ___ Still Unknown

2. List below those unions that you have uncovered from your research and networking. Limit your listing to the ten most likely supporters of your organization—your ten "Best Bets."

a. Labor Union	b. Its Stated Areas of Interest that Relate to Your Work	c. Appropriate Contact Person, Telephone Number
District-Level		
City-Level		
State-Level		
National		

d. Personal Contacts	e. Your Program(s) that Correspond to Their Interests	f. Other Types of Support Available

Additional Resources

Publications

Billitteri, Thomas J. "Organizing Better Links to Labor." *Chronicle of Philanthropy* 11 (25 March 1999): 1, 9–10, 12.

> In the past, private foundations and labor unions were suspicious of each other's motives; that has now changed and the two sectors are focusing their concerns on improving economic conditions for low-wage service employees.

Bobo, Kim, Jackie Kendall, and Steve Max. *Organize! Organizing for Social Change: A Manual for Activists in the 1990s.* Cabin John, MD: Seven Locks Press, 1991.

> See especially Chapter 18 on unions.

Downs, Buck J., ed. *National Trade and Professional Associations of the United States.* 35th ed. Washington, DC: Columbia Books, 2000. 959 p.

> Lists 7,600 trade associations, professional societies, labor unions, and similar national groups. Indexed by subject, geography, budget size, executives, and acronyms.

Magat, Richard. "Organized Labor and Philanthropic Foundations: Partners or Strangers?" *Nonprofit and Voluntary Sector Quarterly* 23 (Winter 1994): 35–70.

> Examines the relationship between foundations and labor unions, which has involved both approach and avoidance. With references.

Magat, Richard. "Unions and Foundations: The Twain Meet ... Sometimes." *Foundation News & Commentary* 35 (November–December 1994): 24–28.

> Traces the relationships of labor unions and private foundations, past and present. Cites specific programs in the past, and analyzes survey results of labor-related grants made since the mid-1980s.

Magat, Richard. *Unlikely Partners: Philanthropic Foundations and the Labor Movement.* Ithaca, NY: Cornell University Press, 1998. x, 242 p.

> Provides an in-depth history of the relation of foundations and public charities to the labor union movement in the twentieth century. The first great foundations were born during times of turbulent labor activism, and the first foundation to address these issues was the Russell Sage Foundation. Much of the book examines union–foundation connections in various fields, including health and safety, public policy, economic development, education, farmworkers, women and blacks. Discusses some of the challenges created by changes in the modern workplace. With bibliographic references and index.

Rotolo, Thomas. "Trends in Voluntary Association Participation." *Nonprofit and Voluntary Sector Quarterly* 28 (June 1999): 199–212.

> Through data on voluntary association memberships between 1974 and 1994, information is provided about Americans' involvement in organizations such as fraternal and veterans groups, political clubs, youth groups, hobby or garden clubs, school fraternities or sororities, professional societies, labor unions, church-affiliated groups and other entities. Trend analysis is given, and author concludes with recommendations for future research. With bibliographic references.

Sinclair, Matthew. "AFL-CIO Offering Choice in Giving." *NonProfit Times* 14 (February 2000): 1, 8, 10, 12.

> Discusses the AFL-CIO's creation of the Union Community Fund (UCF), which will be creating and launching workplace giving campaigns in several pilot cities. According to Jim Sessions, UCF's incoming executive director, the new nonprofit will be a way for the union to encourage giving and volunteering among members and support agencies. Discusses the United Way of America's concerns about the impact that UCF's development will have on its long-standing partnership with labor.

Organizational Resources

AFL-CIO
Community Services Coordinator
Department of Field Mobilization
815 Sixteenth Street, NW
Washington, DC 20006
Tel: 202-637-5000
Fax: 202-637-5058
E-mail: feedback@aflcio.org
Web address: www.aflcio.org

A. Philip Randolph Institute (APRI)
1444 I Street, NW
Suite 300
Washington, DC 20005
Tel: 202-289-2774
Fax: 202-289-5289
E-mail: info@aprihq.org
Web address: www.aprihq.org

Asian Pacific American Labor Alliance (APALA)
1101 Fourteenth Street, NW
Suite 310
Washington, DC 20005
Tel: 202-842-1263
Fax: 202-842-1462
E-mail: APALA@erols.com
Web address: www.apalanet.org/index.htm

Coalition of Labor Union Women (CLUW)
1126 Sixteenth Street, NW
Suite 104
Washington, DC 20036
Tel: 202-466-4610
Fax: 202-776-0537
E-mail: CLUW@Pressroom.com
Web address: www.cluw.org

Jobs with Justice
501 Third Street, NW
Washington, DC 20001
Tel: 202-434-1106
Fax: 202-434-1477
E-mail: jobswjustice@jwj.org
Web address: www.jwj.org

Labor Council for Latin American Advancement (LCLAA)
815 Sixteenth Street, NW
Suite 310
Washington, DC 20006
Tel: 202-347-4223
Fax: 202-347-5095
E-mail: Natlclaa@aol.com
Web address: www.lclaa.org

National Council of Senior Citizens
8403 Colesville Road
Suite 1200
Silver Spring, MD 20910-3314
Tel: 301-578-8800
Fax: 301-578-8999
Web address: www.ncscinc.org

Pride at Work
815 Sixteenth Street, NW
Suite 4020
Washington, DC 20006
Tel: 202-429-1023
E-mail: llualii@aflcio.org
Web address: www.igc.org/prideatwork/

Internet Resources

Catherwood Library
NYS School of Industrial and Labor Relations
Cornell University
Tel: 607-255-2184
Web address: www.ilr.cornell.edu/library/reference/Guides/LUI_Manual/union_dirs.htm
    List of union directories accessible via the Internet; includes URLs and brief descriptions.

LaborNet's Directory of Union Organizations and Resources on the Internet
(www.igc.org/igc/ln/resources/unions.html)
    Includes four separate lists: Directory of Unions, Directory of Union-Friendly
    Organizations, Directory of Institutes and Libraries, and Directory of Labor Media.

LabourStart: Global Labour Directory of Directories (www.labourstart.org/gldod.shtml)
    Where trade unionists start their day on the net.

Section 3

DEVELOPING YOUR OVERALL FUNDRAISING PLAN

Chapter 22

Choosing Your Funding Mix and the Strategies To Secure It

As a cousin of mine once said about money, money is always there but the pockets change; it is not in the same pockets after a change, and that is all there is to say about money.   —Gertrude Stein

Section 1 outlined the tasks that any nonprofit must complete before it can launch a successful fundraising campaign. An organization must complete such vital tasks as program planning and budgeting not only to operate but also to show stakeholders that its house is in order. Prospective supporters may give short-term support on blind faith, but they need to see evidence of an organization's proficiency in both programs and operations to feel lasting confidence.

Section 1 prepared you to venture into the world of resources and financing. As you go forth, you will immediately encounter a variety of potential funding sources. The key questions to answer at this point are: Which of the many sources and strategies described in Section 2 are most appropriate for your organization? Should you put your energies into pursuing government grants and contracts, for example? Obtaining a grant from the local community foundation? Or both? How can you best proceed to develop an individual membership base? Which approaches to individuals will net the greatest return—face-to-face solicitation, direct mail, special events, a combination of these, or some other strategy? Does your organization need new donors? Should your current donors be asked to give more? Should you try to identify donors or funders beyond your immediate constituency? And what resources do you need for applying the strategy you pick?

As we have stressed throughout this book, you are looking not for one source of revenue but rather for the most likely *mix* of sources to ensure maximum long-term organizational viability.

Envision your funding as a multi-legged stool. Each leg represents a different major source of revenue; if one is significantly reduced, or even eliminated, your organization may suffer somewhat but will still be able to function on the income provided by the other sources. The stool will continue to stand. An organization totally dependent on government grants and contracts, for example, is extremely vulnerable. Another group that receives support from foundations, a fundraising federation, and a pool of individuals in addition to government is clearly stronger and more secure.

Section 2 provided an introduction to the world of money available to nonprofits. It showed how to secure support most effectively from any of the sources enumerated, and how to decide which are most appropriate to your situation. You still need to answer the following questions: Which mix will build the strongest multi-legged financial base for your organization? What should be the proportions of each source? How can you best develop a fundraising strategy that will succeed? What is the best way to plan your fundraising work?

Section 3 will help you answer these questions. It provides you with a blueprint for planning and implementing your efforts to secure financial support. The ten phases of this process are summarized below and then discussed in detail.

Phase 1. Taking Stock of Your Strengths and Assets. Because fundraising is, in the finest sense, a collaboration among different parties moved to act on the same set of concerns, you must consider what can *you* bring to the tables of prospective donors and funders. What are your competencies? Phase 1 enables the leaders of both new and mature efforts to inventory their assets and strengths.

Phase 2. Choosing Funding Partners. As Section 2 showed, there are numerous potential stakeholders from which to choose. The task before you is to select the ones most likely to become your committed partners. During Phase 2, you will review your answers to the questionnaires at the ends of Chapters 8 through 21 and create a list of the best prospects and strategies.

Phase 3. Setting Fundraising Goals. How can you present your financial needs to prospective supporters most effectively? How much should you ask them for? Phase 3 builds on the budgeting and program planning work discussed in Chapters 4 and 5 to help you set fundraising goals, which are an important element in eliciting positive responses from prospective supporters.

Phase 4. Developing a Strategy To Secure Support from Individuals. As we have discussed and documented, individuals are the largest source of philanthropic funding. They are also the most consistent supporters of nonprofit organizations; their dollars are both reliable and renewable. Chapters 8 through 14 presented some popular methods for generating support from individuals. Phase 4 shows you how to identify the individuals most likely to provide support, and how to secure it.

Phase 5. Developing a Strategy To Secure Support from Institutions. The world of institutional support is vast and often intimidating. Institutions represent the corporate interests of their boards of directors, members, and constituents. These interests produce distinct cultures, each with its own rules and regulations. Chapters 15 through 21 showed how these various prospective stakeholders operate and how you can match your own efforts to their priorities. Phase 5 outlines a procedure for identifying the institutions most likely to support your work and explains how to successfully elicit their support.

Phase 6. Making The Case. A script can often aid you in asking others for support; the writing exercises presented in Phase 6 will help you organize your information. This work will be easier if you have spent considerable time developing your vision and mission statements (Chapter 1) and identifying what you can offer to funding partners (Phase 1, Taking Stock of Your Strengths and Assets). By completing Phases 4 and 5, you will also have identified the audiences for your fully developed materials.

Phase 7. Preparing the Final Fundraising Plan and Calendar. The research and preparation stages of your fundraising are now drawing to a close. You will have chosen your most likely sources of support and developed the materials you need to approach them. In Phase 7, you create a blueprint for action by organizing and scheduling the work that lies ahead.

Phase 8. Making the Approach. The style of your presentation will influence the outcome of your appeal. Although your program may be worthy and your prospects well chosen, your fundraising efforts may nonetheless falter if you take the wrong approach. Phase 6, Making the Case, will have provided solicitors with the necessary background for representing your organization's work. Chapters 8 through 21 offer detailed suggestions for approaching particular individual and institutional supporters. Phase 8 guides you through the asking process.

Phase 9. Building the Relationship with Your Supporters. Securing funding from both individual and institutional sources can be the first stage of a long-lived collegial and professional relationship. You can choose to nurture that incipient relationship, or, unwisely, to ignore it. Phase 9 discusses how to sustain and strengthen your supporters' interest and involvement in your work.

Phase 10. Monitoring and Evaluating Your Fundraising Efforts: Laying the Groundwork for Next Year. Your efforts to secure funds will benefit immensely from ongoing monitoring and evaluation. After all, your own experiences provide the best data about what does and does not work. Phase 10 offers guidance on how to monitor and evaluate your fundraising activities so that you can achieve—and maintain—the most success.

The planning process outlined in these ten phases is both cyclical and ongoing. Different events and outcomes (for example, a rejection letter or unforeseen revenues) may cause you to return to an earlier phase.

Phase 1: Taking Stock of Your Strengths and Assets

By taking stock of your organizational assets and strengths, you put yourself in the best position to build a strong case for support to prospective funders or donors.

Why should taking such an inventory be so important? Simply because we are often so busy doing the work of our organization that we fail to pay sufficient attention to what makes us unique. Yet it is those very attributes that frequently lead to new support from the individuals and institutions that were previously unfamiliar with our work.

Where do you look for your assets and strengths? Every existing organization has a history and a reputation. Its past probably reveals successes, accomplishments, and a few false starts as well. An organization's history is a treasure trove of assets that may readily be converted into credentials—and credentials are important. It is not enough simply to state the issues and problems your group is addressing and describe its plan of action. Such statements may elicit some initial support, but they are too abstract to attract significant, ongoing support. You will need to describe in precise terms how your organization is qualified both to address this problem and to make genuine headway toward solving it.

Don't despair, however, if your organization is new. The experience and expertise of all the people involved with your effort testify to your group's ability to create beneficial change. Your core group members have earned a reputation on their own, by working for other organizations, or both. It is important, therefore, to begin by reviewing their professional and personal resumes for the qualifications that will establish credibility. In this way, you are pinpointing your organization's capabilities and giving current, new, and prospective funders good reason to believe in you.

The following worksheet is designed to help you collect evidence—past or present—that illustrates your organization's competency as it relates to the issues and programs that define the purpose of your work. Don't hesitate to add your own questions to this list, of course.

Worksheet

Taking Stock of Your Strengths and Assets

Program History

a. _____ _____ (year)
b. _____ _____ (year)
c. _____ _____ (year)
d. _____ _____ (year)

1. What projects or programs has your organization successfully implemented?

a. _____ Results: _____
_____ _____
_____ _____

b. _____ Results: _____
_____ _____
_____ _____

c. _____ Results: _____
_____ _____
_____ _____

d. _____ Results: _____
_____ _____
_____ _____

2. Explain why these efforts succeeded. What changes did they effect?

3. What skills and abilities enabled you to succeed in these efforts—personal or organizational or both?

_____
_____
_____
_____
_____
_____

4. In what ways can you document the success of your past work?
   a. Statistics:

_____
_____
_____

   b. Letters of appreciation:

_____
_____
_____
_____

c. Assessments by outside bodies (i. e. funders, government agencies, professional associations, etc.; awards and honors bestowed on your organization or people in it):

_____

_____

_____

_____

d. Media Coverage (i.e., articles in local and national newspapers and magazines, television and radio coverage, etc.):

_____

_____

_____

_____

e. Miscellaneous:

_____

_____

_____

_____

Board and Staff History

1. What are the qualifications of your past and current board members and staff?

2. What commendations have they received in recognition of their talents and contributions?

Board   Staff

_____   _____

_____   _____

_____   _____

3. How would you describe their most unique talents?

Board   Staff

_____   _____

_____   _____

_____   _____

4. What percentage of your board members make financial contributions to your organization? _____ %

Board   Staff

_____   _____

_____   _____

_____   _____

Organizational History

1. How long has your organization been in existence?
   ___ brand new ___ years old

2. What distinguishes your past work from that of similar organizations? List the specific ways in which your work differs from theirs, and why you are unique.

   _____
   _____
   _____
   _____
   _____

3. What recognition has your organization as a whole received since its inception? (e.g., invitations to speak at conferences, workshops, public rallies, legislative hearings; certificates of commendation; quotations in scholarly or popular journals and magazines; letters of appreciation, etc.):

   _____
   _____
   _____
   _____
   _____

Funding History

1. What kinds of institutions have supported your work? Who are they?
   a. Foundations:

   _____
   _____
   _____
   _____
   _____

   b. Corporations or businesses:

   _____
   _____
   _____
   _____
   _____

   c. Religious sources:

   _____
   _____
   _____
   _____
   _____

   d. Associations of individuals:

   _____
   _____
   _____
   _____
   _____

   e. Labor Unions:

   _____
   _____
   _____
   _____
   _____

   f. Federations:

   _____
   _____
   _____
   _____
   _____

   g. Government:

   _____
   _____
   _____
   _____
   _____

   h. Other:

   _____
   _____
   _____
   _____
   _____

2. How many individuals pay dues, make contributions, or do both to support your work? _____
   What percentage renew their support each year? _____

3. How diversified is your financial base? For example, how many different sources extend support to you? _____
   What percentage of your total income does each comprise? _____ _____ _____

4. What reports do you file annually with government agencies to satisfy their reporting requirements for nonprofit organizations?

   _____
   _____
   _____

All nonprofits should maintain up-to-date "credibility files," and gather this type of information on a steady basis. Staff and board members should do the same for their own use, as well as for the organization. Such files will make it easier when you need to assemble data for fundraising proposals and also for promotional materials such as brochures, annual reports, and press releases.

Phase 2. Choosing Funding Partners

Fundraising is a collaboration between a nonprofit organization and a group of financial backers. Just as a bank underwrites a business, so do individuals, foundations, government agencies, corporations, and the other sources presented in Section 2 underwrite the operations of a nonprofit. A bank looks for a strict financial return on its investment; *your* financial partners want to see that they've helped make the concrete changes suggested by your group's vision and mission statements, objectives, and program plans. Selecting these financial partners can be an exhausting pursuit unless you are methodical.

The following worksheet consolidates the results of the worksheets at the end of each chapter in Section 2. In cases where you can be more specific in listing your prospects, go ahead and do so. If you know, for example, that your local community foundation is a solid prospect but that other foundations are not, place that particular foundation in the "very good" column. Be as specific as your information permits.

Worksheet

Selecting Prospective Funding Partners for Your Nonprofit Endeavor

Sources	Assessing Chances of Support			
	Very Good	Possible	Unlikely	Still Unknown

1. Individuals via:

   a. Face-to-face solicitation

   b. Telephone

   c. Direct mail

   d. Internet (e.g. Web site, electronic newsletter)

   e. Special events

   f. Planned giving

   g. Earned or venture income projects

   h. Other:

2. Foundations

   a. Family foundations

   b. Community foundations

   c. Other local foundations

   d. Local public charities

   e. National foundations

3. Business and Corporations

   a. Neighborhood stores

   b. Banks, utility companies, department stores, etc.

   c. Corporations with headquarters or facilities in your community

   d. Large national corporations

   e. Multinational companies

4. Government (grants and contracts)

   a. Local government units:

Sources	Assessing Chances of Support			
	Very Good	Possible	Unlikely	Still Unknown
b. State government units:				
c. Federal government units:				
5. Religious Institutions				
a. Individual churches, temples, and other faith communities				
b. Metropolitan and regional religious bodies				
c. Metropolitan and regional ecumenical bodies				
d. Religious federated organizations				
e. National religious bodies				
f. International structures				
6 Federated Fundraising Organizations				
a. United Way				
b. Other community chests				
c. Alternative funds				
7. Associations of Individuals				
a. Neighborhood or community-based associations				
b. Citywide associations				
c. National associations				
8. Labor Unions				
a. Local unions				
b. Citywide unions				
c. National unions				

Completing the preceding worksheet will help you identify your strongest potential supporters, those who are capable of and, possibly, willing to support your work at some level.

Historically, many nonprofit leaders have engaged in "stop-and-go" fundraising in which one particular type of funding—such as foundation or government—is obtained and used exclusively until it is exhausted. At that point, the search for a replacement source begins. A better strategy is to identify your entire array of partners *before* you charge off in pursuit of just one on your prospect list.

The following procedure will help you visualize your specific range of supporters by transposing your responses onto the archery target below. Place your *best* prospects in the bull's-eye, your remaining *possible* sources in the second circle of the target, and your *unlikely* possibilities in the outer circle. Finally, place the funding sources whose ability and willingness to support your work has yet to be ascertained outside the target on your list of *unknowns*.

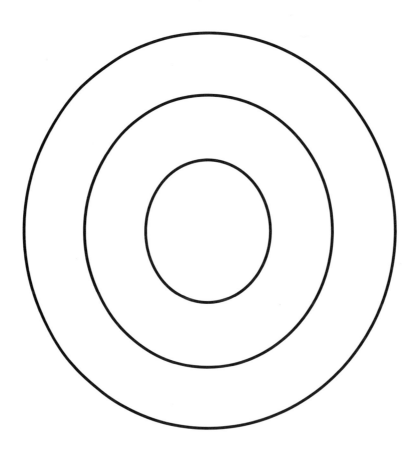

As you complete your information-gathering, remember that research and networking will enable you to move sources from your unknown list into the target. Don't limit your choices at this stage by the actual amount of funds that a source may be able to provide. Your objective is to define the mix of funding sources by identifying the sources that are, in principle, your most likely partners.

You have ranked your prospective funders through the exercises outlined in this phase. In lieu of stop-and-go fundraising, you can now take a comprehensive look at your best-bets list (those in the bull's-eye). You will then need to answer some questions about these prospects.

- What level of potential support can they provide?

- Do you have access to individuals in a decision-making capacity?

- Which sources appear to have the potential for significant long-term support?

- How much time and up-front expenditure of human and financial capital is needed to tap these particular sources?

Your answers to these questions will make your forthcoming fundraising activity more targeted and potentially more successful. Use the earlier worksheet titled "Selecting Prospective Funding Partners for Your Nonprofit Endeavors" to gather your responses. As you analyze the information, certain patterns will emerge. For example, neighborhood and grassroots groups will probably find that individual residents of their own communities are their easiest targets. Arts organizations will find that their initial universe is broader, since they have programs that likely extend beyond one single community. Citywide advocacy and public interest nonprofits may find more institutional prospects at the top of their list. Be sure to trust your own experience and knowledge, for each and every nonprofit organization is trailblazing its own path when its leadership sets out in search of support.

Keeping in mind that your future is best secured by tapping into a mix of sources, turn your attention to matching your prospects with your specific fundraising needs.

Phase 3. Setting Fundraising Goals

Your organization's budgeting and program planning work (see Chapters 4 and 5) helps you calculate the goals that will guide your fundraising activities. Clearly stated financial goals enable you to tell individual prospects how their contributions would fit into your overall needs, and show foundations and corporations how you would spend the funds requested in your grant applications.

Setting fundraising goals is also important for two others reasons. First, it motivates individuals to give. Just as program objectives encourage people to work harder, fundraising goals can inspire your constituents to give—and to keep giving—until you can finance your programs or special project(s) for a year. Additionally, comparing your goals to the amount that has actually been raised helps you to make better program decisions. If you achieve your fundraising goals, you can undertake the programs you've planned. If you raise less, you may have to modify—or eliminate—one or more. If, on the other hand, you exceed your goals, you can expand your programs or use the money for other purposes.

Budgeting and fundraising go hand in hand. Without a comprehensive sense of how much money an organization plans to expend, it cannot possibly project realistic fundraising goals. At the same time, unless an organization raises all the money it considers necessary to support its year's activities, the budget has to be reduced accordingly.

Your organization can set fundraising goals in three ways:

1. Establish the total you need to raise *in a given year* to carry out the programs you have planned, as well as the administrative costs.

2. Calculate the total sum of monies you need to implement *a particular project*, such as constructing a new building or purchasing a computer.

3. Ascribe a dollar expense amount to a service or program—that is, a *unit of service*—that your organization performs.

You can draw on one or all of these methods to assist you in your fundraising. Let's examine each of these methods to determine how they can best serve your organization.

Setting Annual Fundraising Goals

Completing the budgeting process outlined in Chapter 5 enables you to determine the total organizational expenditures for personnel and non-personnel items for the upcoming year. The total of that organizational budget (see the sample worksheet titled "Organizational Expense Budget" on page XXX) is what's needed to underwrite your projected activities. Once this figure is established, you can launch a community-wide drive to raise it, or you can design a strategy to raise that total from a mix of funding sources.

For example, an after-school care center projects its payroll, rent, utilities, and other ancillary expenses at $150,000 for the coming year. Since it receives close to $100,000 in day-care fees (earned income), the organization may decide to set a fundraising (unearned income) goal of $50,000 for the year.

Chart A: Setting Your Annual Organizational Fundraising Goal

Total Anticipated Expenses for the Year	$ _____
Minus	
Anticipated Income from Program Fees	$ _____
Equals	
Annual Fundraising Campaign Total	$ _____

Setting Program Fundraising Goals

In the same way that you have budgeted all the expenditures in your organization's entire operating costs, you can assess the expenses inherent in any particular project or program (see the sample worksheet titled "Program Expense Budget" on page XXX). If, for example, a group wishes to create a public information and referral program on consumer issues, it can cost out the equipment (computer and accompanying software) as well as the salaries of the personnel needed to implement the program.

Chart B: Setting Your Program Fundraising Goal

Total Projected Expenses for X Project $ _____

Minus

Donated, or In-kind Services $ _____

Equals

Program Fundraising Goal $ _____

Setting Unit-of-Service Fundraising Goals

Review your programs to determine whether you provide any services that can be valued in a way that might appeal to prospective donors. Likely candidates include direct service programs and capital expenditures, such as purchase of buildings, vehicles, and computers. Less attractive are programs that improve an organization's administrative capacities, such as upgrading filing systems, renovating offices, increasing salaries, or purchasing a new photocopy machine.

For example, a counselor at a domestic violence center may report assisting ten individuals every week to regain a sense of well-being and dignity after a sexual assault. Since there are five counselors who work full-time and see an average of ten victims each week, the center can report that it assists 2,600 individuals each year (5 counselors x 10 clients x 52 weeks = 2,600 cases). By dividing the organization's entire annual budget by the number of client interventions, you can ascertain the cost of assistance to one individual. If the organization's annual operating budget is $200,000, the cost to assist one individual—the unit-of-service cost—is approximately $77 ($200,000/2,600 clients = $ 76.92).

This valuation is based on the assumption that crisis counseling is the center's only program activity. If, however, there are other programs—such as training hospital emergency room personnel to work effectively with rape victims, or training police officials to counsel women immediately on the scene—the formula for determining the unit-of-service cost changes.

In such instances you would determine the total direct costs of the counseling program and add a percentage of the indirect administrative expenses that correspond to the ratio of that program to the entire programmatic budget of the center. If the counseling program costs $50,000 and the training program costs $25,000, the percentage of administrative costs attached to the counseling program would be twice the costs attached to the training program. If the administrative costs total $25,000, then two-thirds of that cost can be associated with the counseling program ($16,666.67) and one-third with the training program ($8,333.33).

Using Your Fundraising Goals

Depending on the audience and the occasion, a nonprofit may use any or all of the three different fundraising goals. For example, if you want to establish a goal for a special event, you might choose a program goal. If you want to determine a goal for your entire year's fundraising efforts to include in your campaign literature, you would choose the annual fundraising goal. If you want to set a goal for a direct mail appeal, you could easily select a unit-of-service fundraising goal. During the course of a year's fundraising activities, you will no doubt use all three goals. Let's examine how the hypothetical domestic violence center uses these goals in its development efforts.

The center's annual budget is $200,000, of which $100,000 is received from foundations and city and county agencies. One September, the center announces its annual campaign to raise the remaining $100,000 from the community in order to provide desperately needed services during the upcoming year. As one of its first outreach efforts, the center sends out a direct mail appeal to its past supporters, asking for contributions of $38.50 ($100,000 divided by the number of people using the service). The appeal says, "Your gift of $38.50 allows us to provide immediate and appropriate counseling and advocacy for one victim of domestic violence."

The center may designate those who respond as "angels," "supporters," "patrons," "benefactors," or "sponsors." (The exact membership category need not, by the way, come from this conventional list. You are free to use terms that may convey more of the personal flavor of your work or values.)

As part of its annual fund campaign, the center segmented its mailing and targeted donors who at some point had given more than $100. To encourage these donors to increase their level of giving, the center decided to use a variation of the unit-of-service approach. The solicitation letter in the direct mail pack might read as follows:

Dear [name of donor],

We are conducting our annual campaign effort to provide services to the thousands who are abused domestically in our city each year. Here is the impact you can make with your contribution:

- If you make a gift of $150, we will be able to help five individuals this year.

- A monthly pledge of $38.50 ($462 for the year) enables us to assist one person each month—a total of twelve during the year!

- If you can make an outright gift of $1,000, this year we will be able to help twenty-five people who turn to us out of desperation and fear for sensitive help and support.

In its approaches to foundations and corporations, the center makes greater use of its program-related fundraising goals as part of its proposals. For example, it may decide to approach the local community foundation for a grant of $17,000 to set up a pilot counseling program directly in the emergency room of the major municipal hospital. It may also decide to approach a local corporation for a grant of $12,000 to underwrite the costs of a subway and bus poster campaign announcing the center's hot-line number and some of the services it provides.

In each of these examples, the staff, fundraising volunteers, and board members have approached targeted funders with requests tailored to their respective abilities to give. Your audience of supporters is not homogeneous. It includes both individuals and institutions, all with varying abilities and inclinations to support your work. You are responsible for setting their sights on the amount to give. Putting it bluntly, people usually give when they are asked, and if they can, they give what they are asked for. No matter which approach you take—annual goals, program goals, or unit-of-service goals—you are defining for your potential supporters the levels of assistance that you need and the total amount required for maintaining your operations for a given year.

Challenge and Matching Grants

Another variation of "customized" fundraising involves the challenge, or matching, gift or grant. It is not unusual for a foundation, corporation, government agency, or even an individual to make a gift contingent on another funder or funders matching that gift, either on a one-to-one or two-to-one basis. For example, an initial funder agrees to contribute $5,000 on the condition that other sources match it one-to-one ($5,000) or two-to-one ($10,000). If the organization is able to satisfy the funder's condition, it will receive a total of either $10,000 or $15,000 from the initial gift of $5,000. The donors who respond to these challenges are gratified that their dollars are producing additional dollars of support, and the initial donor receives that same sense of gratification.

Foundations and corporations that are concerned about an organization's ability to raise all the funds needed to implement a program may make a challenge, or matching, grant. In this way, they protect their resources until the potential recipient organization has raised the match stipulated by the grant.

Phase 4: Developing a Strategy To Secure Support from Individuals

Individuals should provide the core support for practically any kind of nonprofit endeavor. Such support is important for a number of reasons. Individuals are, beyond a doubt, the most reliable, consistent source of income for nonprofit organizations throughout the world. Their investment in your work will rarely waiver as long as you fulfill your mission adequately and acknowledge the individual supporters for their aid. Individuals form very personal relationships with the charitable organizations they support. As long as you encourage, recognize, and nurture that relationship, you can count on retaining most of your individual donors year in and out. They serve as your life insurance policy for the future, for they will be around even if institutional supporters withdraw their support.

Nevertheless, some organizations scoff at the idea of reaching out to individuals for support, believing that the public is apathetic to their issues or that their immediate constituency is too poor or hard-pressed to provide any significant help. Other groups simply don't know how to petition the public effectively for financial support and find themselves bewildered by the variety of techniques available for securing contributions from individuals.

But the nonprofits that overcome these obstacles will be rewarded in the long run with a growing base of individual supporters who outlast practically every other form of support and who may be even more responsive than institutional sources to pleas for certain types of programs that otherwise would languish. The most modest start at soliciting gifts from individuals may soon prove worthwhile and, ultimately, create a substantial level of support.

Encourage Donors To Become Members

Membership is the most common method that groups use to encourage individual support. Membership sometimes carries certain rights within an organization, such as voting for officers and board members, but in most cases membership simply gives a donor a sense of belonging to an organization.

People who make donations without becoming members do not seem to feel that their gifts establish a mutually understood commitment, nor do they have any real incentive to repeat their gifts in the future—unless they are solicited again. However, people who join an organization tend to recognize that they have made a commitment.

Organizations that encourage individuals to become members benefit in other ways. A membership is generally perceived by both donor and institution as something to be renewed. This allows donors to project their annual membership as a regular part of their yearly budget while allowing the institution to project a specific amount of income from membership support (taking into account some attrition, of course).

Donors can be encouraged to become members at a level commensurate with their interest and means. A pattern of graduated perquisites ("perks") can give donors an incentive to increase their giving, and so be upgraded from one category of membership to another.

Some groups strive to make their membership invitations more attractive by offering concrete benefits to individuals who join. Even small groups can offer such perks as T-shirts, buttons, discounted admissions to special events and educational programs, and invitations to members' parties. Actually, your imagination and knowledge of your own constituency can help you design a membership package of benefits to suit almost any organization.

Don't lose sight of the fact, however, that while tangible membership benefits serve as an incentive to give, and to give more, they rarely provide the primary stimulus. Individuals become members and make contributions for a variety of other, usually intangible, reasons (see Chapter 7). You can best decide if you need to sweeten your membership program with distinct benefits, for you know your constituents best.

If they feel a strong sense of kinship with your organization, your constituents will inevitably respond well to requests for funds, whether received through the mail or at their doorstep. When your donors are already quite loyal, you may not need to sweeten your membership offer to elicit the desired response. You can, however, still consider motivating your supporters to increase their level of support by offering specific benefits tied to different giving levels. For example, you can offer a silkscreen poster signed by the artist to all contributors who give, say, $250 or more. If your organization's claim on the conscience and wallets of your public is less strong, then benefits can serve as a greater incentive to prompt individuals to respond to your requests.

If you're considering offering tangible benefits, be sure to reread Chapter 5 on budgeting, and to stay within the guidelines given by the Federal Accounting Standards Board (FASB). If your perquisite has market value—that is, it could be sold outside your organization—then you must deduct the market value of the product from the donation, and only the remaining portion may be claimed as a deduction by the member. T-shirts, mugs, and tote bags bearing your organization's logo are not items that generally could be sold in a regular store, but art could be. These regulations are not entirely cut-and-dried; but they must be kept in mind.

Identify Likely Supporters

The first step in tapping individuals for membership is to identify the particular constituencies most likely to be committed to your work—your board, volunteers, and even your staff members. This may seem offensive to some of these individuals, who already give generously of their time and feel that this sufficiently demonstrates their commitment. And in part, that's true. Still, there is nothing like a commitment of money to signal to others the importance donors ascribe to their organization. Since many of your board members, staff, and volunteers will, at some point, ask others to give to your organization, they will be able to say to a prospective member, "I joined because I felt that what we are doing is critically important. Won't you join, too?"

Now that you are ready to go beyond your own organization for support, your task becomes one of identifying and targeting which individuals are most likely to develop an interest in, and extend support to, your work. Undoubtedly, you will be able to develop some sense of how to identify these individuals and to decide what constituencies they might belong to. Brainstorm with other members of your organizing committee, board of directors, or fundraising committee. The circles exercise in Chapter 7 will help.

If your organization already receives support from individuals through a variety of ways, start out by analyzing those supporters. List them by their common denominators, such as occupation: Are they teachers, social workers, lawyers, parents, activists, doctors, or computer programmers? Demographics: What is their age? Gender? Political affiliation? What distinguishes them? You are not trying to stereotype your supporters, only to differentiate them so that you know how you can reach them most effectively.

If you decided to undertake a direct mail campaign, you'll need to select lists of names to mail to. The more you know about your current members, the more readily you will be able to identify other kindred souls. For example, which magazines do most of your members subscribe to, and which newspapers do they read? This information will help you target your public relations efforts.

You may be surprised at who is giving you money and who is not. On the one hand, you may realize that a certain segment of the population you had thought would contribute has provided only minimal support; you should reach out to them. The opposite may also be true. For example, a shelter for battered women used to routinely delete men's names from direct mail lists they used until they examined their donor base and learned that 20 percent of their supporters were men. And the Gay Men's Health Crisis in New York City was very surprised to discover how many of their individual donors were lesbians. As an exercise, make your own list of the five most frequent types of contributors to your organization.

1. _____
2. _____
3. _____
4. _____
5. _____

Think through what you know about these constituencies. Would they prefer to go to a movie, a ballet party, or an educational seminar? Do they enjoy opportunities to socialize with their peers? Would they prefer a picnic or a testimonial dinner? Do any other groups of concerned individuals come to mind that you currently do not have among your present membership? If so, name them:

1. _____
2. _____
3. _____

Determine Ways To Approach Individuals for Support

The sharper your sense of your current and prospective donors, the easier it will be to select the most productive way of approaching them—which brings us to the second step: brainstorming a variety of ways to ask individuals for support.

Let's examine the Redding Youth Violence Project as a hypothetical example to illustrate the process. At its monthly meeting, the core group came up with the following list of potential individual supporters:

1. Core group members (including their families and friends)

2. Local civic clubs and PTAs in their neighborhood

3. Local business people

4. Local clergy

5. Local federations

6. Local unions

The Project's task was to list the possible ways each of these groups of prospective supporters could give money, or how to best ask them for support on a regular basis. Let's see what they came up with:

Constituencies
All constituents can be asked to:

- Make personal contributions

- Become members through the annual fund

- Purchase raffle tickets, buttons, bumper stickers, etc.

- Attend and sell tickets to fundraising events

- Identify and approach local business, government, foundation, federation, association, religious, and labor contacts to explore fundraising possibilities

1. Core group members

- Pass the hat at regular meetings

- Pay monthly membership dues

- "Sponsor" the cost of one client

2. Local civic clubs and neighborhood PTAs

- Using their official letterhead, publicize and ask for contributions

- Make contributions and/or pledges in response to presentations at their monthly meetings

- Purchase newsletter subscriptions

- Purchase ads in newsletter

- Provide information about the Project through various channels

3. Local business

- Make contributions in response to personal solicitations

- Place canisters near cash registers

- Donate items for raffles and special events

- Purchase ads in newsletter

- Provide in-kind goods and services

- Allow workplace solicitations

- Employ the Project's clients/youths at risk

- Develop modest cause-related marketing program
- Provide information about the Project through various channels
- Include Project's fundraising materials with monthly statements/invoices

4. Local clergy

- Appeal for funds through their own newsletters
- Help Project solicit funds from national religious organization
- Host a special event
- Hold a special collection

5. Local federations
   - Apply for membership status in local United Way or other local federated fundraising organization to be eligible for workplace contributions

6. Local unions
   - Develop and publicize training programs for the Project's clients/youths at risk to raise visibility and enhance the image of both organizations

Let's take another hypothetical example to illustrate once more how an organization can identify its key individual supporters. Members of the core group of Art in Schools (AIS) asked themselves the following question: Which individuals are the most likely supporters of our work to help ensure that music, drama, and fine arts programs are included in schools' curricula?

As a result of their brainstorming, AIS found that they had many constituencies, owing to the community's deep concern about the quality of education. These included:

1. Core group members, especially artists. (including their families and friends)

2. Other politically aware or socially concerned artists

3. Socially concerned members of the arts-oriented public in their community

4. Art, music, and drama teachers

5. Parents, particularly those parents who had themselves enjoyed art as part of their education

6. Liberal arts professors, particularly those who teach undergraduates, who were dismayed at the lack of cultural awareness of many of the incoming freshmen

7. Teachers union members and officials

8. Members of dinner theaters, art clubs, book groups, and the like

Clearly, AIS has many potential constituencies to turn to for support. Let's list the possible ways each of these groups of prospective supporters can give support, or how to best ask them for support on a regular basis:

Constituencies

All constituents can be asked to:

- Make personal contributions

- Become members through the annual fund

- Purchase raffle tickets, buttons, bumper stickers, etc.

1. Core group members

   - Attend and sell tickets to fundraising events

   - Identify and approach local business, government, federation, association, religious, and labor contacts to explore fundraising possibilities

   - Ask friends and other artists to donate works of art (or other related or appropriate items) for an annual auction

   - Arrange for exhibitions of student artwork

2. Other politically aware or socially concerned artists

   - Donate works of art for sale or auction

   - Design special art postcards as a source of earned income

   - Attend and sell tickets to fundraising events

   - Solicit their dealers and galleries

   - Make personal contributions, and become AIS members through annual fund

3. Socially concerned members of the arts-oriented public

   - Buy tickets to special events and purchase postcards

   - Host exhibitions of donated art in their homes to sell to other friends

4. Arts, music, and drama teachers

   - Organize house parties

   - Provide names of parents who might be concerned

   - Provide access to other teachers not in the arts who might give money

   - Attend events

   - Help promote the political message of AIS to students, school administrators, and other teachers

5. Parents

   - Provide access to PTA meetings and mailing lists

- Post notices in newsletters

- Host houseparties

- Attend events

6. Liberal arts professors

- Write articles for journals

- Provide interviews to the media

- Provide names of professors and alumni who might be sympathetic

7. Teachers members union and officials
   - Provide mailing lists for a direct mail solicitation

8. Members of dinner theaters, arts clubs, book groups, etc.

- Provide names for direct mail appeals

- Announce events at their performances

As these hypothetical cases illustrate, there are many ways individuals can support a particular nonprofit undertaking. Both of these groups, just like your own, can expand their lists by sharing them with others. In many cases, you will observe that the strongest members of your group will be people who cross several lines. For example, university professors who were also members of amateur theater groups, who had children in the public school system, and who were active in the PTA or their own union, are most likely to become committed AIS members and donors.

Furthermore, anyone who was identified as someone who could come to an event could also be approached by mail or phone. People who would donate art can be approached to donate cash, and people who buy art at auctions should be asked to become members of the group. If you do a thorough job in analyzing your constituency, you will soon be overwhelmed by possibilities and realize that you can raise funds successfully as long as you plan your work and work your plan.

Which approaches did your core group identify?

Constituencies

1._____

_____

_____

_____

_____

2._____

_____

_____

_____

_____

3._____

_____

_____

_____

_____

4._____

_____

_____

_____

_____

5._____

_____

_____

_____

_____

Approaches

1._____

_____

_____

_____

_____

2._____

_____

_____

_____

_____

3. _____

_____

_____

_____

_____

4._____

_____

_____

_____

_____

5._____

_____

_____

_____

_____

Choose Your Approaches

The third step is to choose from your lists those approaches or methods your core group wants to pursue. Ask your planning committee, which is responsible for your fundraising efforts, to suggest which approaches you should use—perhaps three or so to start with. Let's put this task before our two hypothetical organizations.

The Redding Youth Violence Project decided to focus on a membership dues program; passing the hat at monthly meetings; two special events; and two "free" holiday open houses (in December and July). These four approaches afforded the Project a way of asking their constituents regularly for support. The benefits and open houses also provided them with opportunities to strengthen personal relationships with their supporters. In addition, they decided to list in their monthly newsletter the names of their members as they joined or renewed their memberships.

The core group of Art in Schools decided to focus on a campaign to sell specially designed art postcards to the memberships of other sympathetic organizations through direct mail; asking famous socially concerned artists known to them to donate works of art for an annual auction; and conducting a phonathon to ask teachers and professors to join. Note that these approaches include a mix of face-to-face solicitation (Chapter 11), direct mail (Chapter 9), special events (Chapter 8), telephone solicitation (Chapter 10), and earned income (Chapter 14).

AIS chose this particular mix of approaches to individuals for several reasons. As artists, they realized that they had access to something of value to others—their work and the works of other artists. They also knew that their targeted constituencies were regularly solicited by other more established organizations. As a result, they decided to raise money by selling art postcards in lieu of simple solicitation for support. They were also capitalizing on the knowledge and skills of their core group. Some of their members had personal relationships with famous artists, and one member had experience in designing and marketing postcards for sale.

After discussing their plans with more resource people outside their immediate circles, including the local art auction house and several gallery owners, they were able to make reasonable estimates of projected income from these activities. They decided to drop the tour of artists' studios, for others did not find the concept very appealing. They discovered that their friends were not members of any existing human rights organizations, so they decided to institute a membership program. Since their friends included both struggling and successful artists, they developed a two-tiered membership program to enable both groups to give according to their means.

Estimate Your Proceeds

The final step before the actual fundraising gets under way is to make some conservative estimates on how much each of the chosen efforts can net in a year. Art in Schools came up with the following summary:

Strategies for Reaching Individuals:

a. 250 dues-paying members @ $20/year	=	$5,000
b. 100 dues-paying patrons @ $50/year	=	$5,000
c. 500 packets of 10 postcards each sold @ $5/packet	=	$2,500
d.1 annual art auction of donated works	=	$15,000
TOTAL RAISED FROM INDIVIDUALS	=	$27,500

AIS decided to list all the artists who joined as members and patrons, or who contributed their own work, in a full-page ad in the local arts newspaper each year to thank them publicly for their support.

Our Redding Youth Violence Project has to ask itself the following questions: How much can we ask each person to donate at a monthly meeting? How many people will be able to contribute that amount at each meeting? How much can we expect people to pay in membership dues? How many members can we sign up in a year? What kinds of special events should we plan? How much can we expect to net from each one? And so on....

By answering such specific questions, the Project could make a reasonable estimate of how much it might raise from individuals in a given year. They came up with this summary:

a. 1,000 dues-paying members @ $10/year	=	$10,000
b. 12 monthly collections x 20 people x $2 each	=	$480
c. Two special events (tag sale and bazaar @ $2,000 ea.)	=	$4,000
TOTAL RAISED FROM INDIVIDUALS	=	$14,480

Acknowledge Your Supporters

Finally, you want to make sure that you recognize your supporters both privately and publicly for their contributions. Private acknowledgment should always begin with a personalized thank-you note. Further private recognition can take the form of mailing newsletters, "insiders' memos," annual reports, and other publications to donors to keep them posted about the work that they have made possible. Let them know regularly that your flourishing, ongoing work would be impossible without their help.

Public acknowledgment can be as simple as listing your new members (if they aren't too numerous) in a newsletter on an ongoing basis. If you offer different categories of membership, you can list supporters by the categories they have chosen. You've seen these lists of benefactors in the playbills of nonprofit theater groups and on the walls of buildings of nonprofit facilities. Just as a university recognizes major donors by naming buildings or other facilities after them, smaller nonprofits can express their appreciation to supporters through some form of public listing.

To make sure that you are aware of the methods available to secure memberships and contributions from individuals, re-read Chapters 8–14, which outline the strategies employed by most organizations: special events, direct mail, telephone solicitiation, face-to-face solicitation, planned giving, raising money through the Internet, and earned and venture income endeavors. Refer to them for a fuller explanation of the pros and cons of each of these methods. Just as our two hypothetical organizations chose a mix of these approaches, you can now do the same.

In choosing your approaches to individuals, remember to look for ways in which to ask them for money regularly and to provide them with opportunities for personal involvement in your work.

Which approaches are your final choices? Make your own conservative estimates of what these strategies to secure individual support will net.

Strategies to Garner Support from Individuals:

a. _____   = $ _____

b. _____   = $ _____

c. _____   = $ _____

d. _____   = $ _____

e. _____   = $ _____

ESTIMATED TOTAL RAISED FROM INDIVIDUALS   = $ _____

To build up your individual support base, keep the following guidelines in mind:

1. *Always talk up membership.* Wherever your members go, they should always seek out new members for your organization. It's the first way for others to become involved in your work. Don't neglect any personal opportunity to ask someone to become a member—nothing succeeds as much as a personal approach.

2. *Be on the lookout for prospective new constituencies.* Be alert to other like-minded groups with whom you may be in touch. Are there other organizations that you belong to, or magazines or periodicals that you subscribe to? Their membership or subscription lists could prove to be good prospects for your own effort. In the words of the direct mail consultant, "keep on prospecting."

3. *Make it clear that membership lasts one year only, and remember that it's your responsibility to solicit renewals.* You might be well advised to consider labeling your membership dues by year; for example, "We are writing you to ask you to renew your membership for 20__." This helps reinforce the annual renewal process in the minds of donors, and helps all parties keep track of their dues. Send out renewal notices about eleven months after you receive a membership check, and don't hesitate to send out a second or even a third reminder notice to encourage renewals. In the time that's passed since you mailed the first renewal notice, news and needs may have developed that you could include in subsequent reminders to provide added motivation for membership renewal.

4. *Try to "upgrade" your givers each year.* Don't miss this opportunity to ask your members to increase the size of their gift and class of membership. The increase you suggest may be as modest as 10 percent or much more if you know the member has the means. Publicize your classes of membership each year so you can ask each and every member to consider renewing at the next highest category. You can also sweeten the request by giving each category of membership its own distinct benefits and, perhaps, adding a new or different perk in each category every year. You have only to notice how frequently advertisements for products include the word "new" to realize the appeal of this concept.

   There is no law that says you cannot ask loyal supporters to increase their level of support each year; yet you would be surprised to learn how few organizations actually do. Remember that your members have no way of knowing that you need more money unless you tell them. If you do not regularly ask them to increase the size of their gifts, you are sending the message that you do not need more money. Donors may interpret this to mean the organization is not growing, or is not doing anything, and is, therefore, a bad investment. Almost every nonprofit needs more money every year, and your group should be no exception.

5. *Thank contributors promptly and graciously.* There is nothing so important for retaining donors as personalized notes acknowledging receipt of their donation. Your efforts will be repaid ten times over if you send a personalized thank-you note within seventy-two hours of receiving the gift. Such a note can be short and simple:

   Dear Ms. Jones,

   Thank you so much for your generous gift of $35 to the work of Tenants United for Fair Housing. Your donation makes you a member or TUFH, and you join 300 other concerned neighbors and friends. You will receive our [monthly, quarterly, annual] newsletter, and are warmly invited to join us and other friends of TUFH at our annual general meeting on [date]. I look forward to seeing you there, and to staying in touch. Thanks again!

   Sincerely,

   Gina Volunteer.

The spirit of a gift is somehow violated if it is not acknowledged promptly and graciously. Test this idea on yourself: If you sent in a membership check, what would you ordinarily expect in return? Take special care, too, that you don't rely excessively upon the word processor. Nothing can take the place of a personal hand-written note, whether added as a postscript to a form letter or as the entire letter itself. The more personally you treat your donors, the more likely they are to be generous in return.

6. *Gather data on your supporters, especially your large donors.* Don't view your individual donors solely as sources of funds; rather, get to know them as individuals with varying and particular interests. Appreciate those interests and take them into account when you select special events or membership benefits. Try to find out what especially interests them in your organization.

7. *You can treat different kinds of members differently, and you should.* Obviously, the contribution from a $100 supporter is more valuable than that of a $25 donor, and that of a $500 sustainer is more important to your work than that of the $100 supporter. Generally, the larger the amount of a donor's gift, the more personal contact there should be. If you can visit only X number of donors, it logically follows that you should visit those who have given the most money or have the potential to do so. However, there are many exceptions to this rule, which is another reason for you to gather information on your donors.

Suppose, for example, that Donor A gives $100 and Donor B gives $250. Donor B would seem to be a higher priority for a visit and more personal contact thereafter. Say, however, that your research shows that Donor A is close a friend of Volunteer C, and that if C asked A instead of a staff or board member, A would give $1,000. This makes Donor A a higher priority than Donor B.

However, B's gift of $250 gift represents a big sacrifice, as B is a person with a low income. Nevertheless, if your research indicates that Donor B is willing to ask a number of his friends for money, and can probably raise $3,000, Donors A and B become equal priorities. The real priority is, therefore, training enough solicitors to ask for money so that at any given time, several people in your organization can make these visits. In this way, the organization is not reliant on one person prioritizing donors.

8. *Keep accurate, up-to-date records.* In order to nurture your members' interests, you need to know what they are. Develop individual files on your large donors, just as you would on a foundation, and maintain your records so that is easy to review the giving history of all your members. Computerization of membership records is desirable for this reason alone.

9. *Don't contact your members only when you need money.* Let your members hear from you throughout the year. That is why a membership newsletter, or some other form of regular communication, is valuable.

Since membership contributions do not preclude people from making additional gifts to an organization, you can solicit support from members more than once a year. If you can make a good case for needing financial help, you should certainly not hesitate to make an appeal to your membership. There is no magic rule about how many times a year you can ask the same people to give, but most groups find that they net a decent return without alienating donors when they ask three to four times a year. Some groups are able to ask up to twelve times, but most find that they lose money if they ask more than twelve times or less than three. Your membership may forget about you if you solicit less than three times a year.

The bottom line is, you can mail out as many appeals as will net consistent positive responses and cover more than their printing and mailing costs. Again, use your own judgment: How many solicitations would you be willing to receive? If each appeal had merit on its own, you would probably feel differently than if each appeal sounded exactly like the one preceding it. Beware of crying wolf more than once! You can go to your membership once for funds to meet a crisis or emergency, but success the second time around is unlikely.

Phase 5: Developing a Strategy To Secure Support from Institutions

Some nonprofit organizations have supported their work through individual contributions alone. Undoubtedly, these are organizations that constantly reach out to new donors and have a very strong renewal program in place, as well as a consistent major donor effort. Other groups have used their revenues from individuals to underwrite the general operating expenses of their group while reaching out to institutional sources for support of particular programs and projects. Either of these routes can achieve desirable results for nonprofits.

To reiterate, individual support remains the most reliable, renewable, and consistent source of funding, and in the best of worlds, institutional support would only be incidental to your financial base. However, some would argue that government should be the main funder of nonprofit activity, since both the public and the nonprofit sector share responsibility for the public good; in many countries, this is the case. As we have previously pointed out, many governments around the world do not assume their rightful responsibility, and leave nonprofits to figure out other ways to raise money.

Most nonprofit groups are not totally supported by a single category of funders—individuals, foundations, or government—but, rather, by a mix of sources. It is their job to identify, cultivate and pursue aggressively the mix of individual and institutional prospects deemed most likely to extend support.

Your next set of tasks, then, is to research and identify your universe of prospective institutional supporters and select your best bets. You will then be ready to approach them for funding.

As Chapters 15 to 21 illustrate, the world of institutional funding is truly a vast one that includes:

- Government: town, county, village, city, state, region, and federal

- Foundations: family, private, company-sponsored, community, local and national, grantmaking public charities

- Businesses and Corporations: neighborhood stores, chain stores, bank branches, utility companies, department stores, specialty shops, restaurants, small companies, local and national corporations

- Religious Institutions: churches, temples, synagogues, and other faith communities; local and regional religious decision-making bodies; local and national ecumenical structures; national religious bodies

- Labor Unions: individual unions, central labor councils, state federations

- Federated Fundraising Organizations: United Way, Community Chest, Catholic Charities, United Jewish Appeal, and the hundreds of other workplace giving campaigns

- Associations of Individuals: service clubs such as Rotarians, Lions, Soroptomists, Junior League, Hadassah, American Association of University Women; professional, business, and trade associations, such as the local Bar Association and Chamber of Commerce

These chapters outline in detail how each of these institutional sources extends support to nonprofits; how much they make available in grants and in-kind (noncash) contributions; the advantages and disadvantages of raising support from them; what motivates them to provide philanthropic assistance; and how to approach them for assistance. At the end of each of these chapters is a worksheet to help you decide whether you should explore this particular type of support for your own organization. Your sources of funds should comprise a mix of these institutional sources to further strengthen the legs of your funding base.

We now turn back to the task before us: identifying those particular institutional sources that are the most likely to extend support. *Remember that you are looking to identify a manageable number of prospects that can be pursued with some fair measure of success.* It is best to narrow down your list of prospects as much as possible so that you will be free to give adequate personal attention to each of them. Successful institutional fundraising requires careful personal approaches to your prospects. Therefore, the fewer prospects you target, the more likely you will be able to devote the appropriate time and attention to making the best approach and subsequent follow-up. Your first prospect list will be broader and more inclusive than your final one. Now your research, networking, and other information-gathering pursuits begin.

Research Your Prospects

Research involves reviewing the printed materials and informed gossip that are publicly available on foundations, businesses, government, religious sources, fundraising federations, labor unions, and associations of individuals. There are standard reference materials available at your local library or the local regional collection of the Foundation Center (see Appendix X to locate your nearest collection). The Internet should be explored thoroughly. Specific reference sources have been listed in the Additional Resources section at the end of some of the previous chapters. In addition, some institutional sources—a number of foundations, corporations, most government agencies, most federated campaigns, and some religious sources—make available free upon request application guidelines, lists of past grantees, and annual reports. You are looking for:

1. Funders similar to those that already support you or have supported you in the past

2. Funders with an interest in your work based on your locale

3. Funders with an interest in your work based on the subject of your program

4. Funders able to provide the level of financial support you are seeking

First, explore funders similar to those that already support you. If you receive grants from national foundations because of your groundbreaking work in an area of national import, research other national foundations to learn if there are others that share an interest in this area. In the same way, if you have elicited positive responses from a certain type of corporation in the past, you will want to explore other corporations in the same industry for support. Success in securing a grant from a foundation or corporation does not automatically lead to success with their counterparts. It does, however, suggest a possibility worth exploring. Most funding sources are influenced in their decision-making by the evidence of their colleagues' involvement, for that translates into credibility.

Second, you are now ready to explore other sectors of support apart from the ones you are currently tapping. In exploring these new sources, start at the most local level. For instance, approach your local parish before going to the metropolitan religious body or to its national headquarters. For one thing, you are more likely to have some personal contacts at this level of organization already; for another, you face less competition from other similar organizations. Competition for funding tends to increase as you reach out to sources with a wider geographic scope. The closer to your locale your sources are, the greater investment they have in the political success of your effort.

There are, however, exceptions to this theory. Some national sources, including religious bodies, government, corporations, and foundations, might well be attracted to your work for a variety of factors, such as: a high correlation to their particular interests; unique characteristics of your efforts; the potential for your work to serve as a model or demonstration project for other communities; or the vanguard nature of your work.

An example is provided by the early years of the women's movement in the United States, when a number of progressive-minded national foundations made grants to local women's organizations before their local foundation counterparts did. In these cases, national foundations set an example for local foundations to follow. A similar scenario took place in the mid-1980s regarding funding for disarmament projects, and the 90's saw the same pattern for funding HIV/AIDS organizations.

Additionally, it would not be unusual for a national foundation to fund a local organization perceived by its local funding community as being too controversial owing to its area of interest or its form of advocacy. For these reasons, some organizations should engage in subject-related research as well as geographic-based research into prospective funding sources.

Network

Another method for gaining information is networking, a concept that has fortunately gained popular support. Networking is no more than cooperation among individuals and organizations with similar needs (and goals) to aid each other. Each and every nonprofit has counterpart organizations locally and around the country whose experiences can save them valuable time so that they don't have to reinvent the wheel. Those counterparts might work in a similar field, involve a similar constituency, or operate in the same geographic locale.

The first step in networking is to brainstorm a list of your most likely counterpart organizations. Think in terms of issues, geography, and constituency. Find out what they have learned from their own fundraising efforts. Other groups can share with you valuable information that may not necessarily be printed in any materials, such as: Which funders are the most likely to give pre-application meetings? What is of most interest to staff in a funding proposal? How much work is involved in making an appropriate application?

You can also network with development (fundraising) professionals at nearby large nonprofit institutions, such as hospitals, colleges and universities, museums, and the like to elicit their suggestions. Finally, conferences, seminars, and meetings provide splendid opportunities to network, not only with other nonprofits but with funders as well. Network until you feel that you have a comprehensive understanding of your prospects.

Fill in the following worksheet ("Summarizing the Information Gathered on Your Institutional Prospects") with the results of your research and networking. It will thus provide you with a handy list of the universe of your funding prospects. To make your prospect list even more helpful, add information on potential grant size and existing contacts or door openers.

Don't hesitate to eliminate any prospects from your list because of the small size of their grants, the absence of personal contacts, or because your work is not a funding priority, to cite just a few examples.

You would best spend your time by making thorough approaches to a small number of select funders than by trying to cover the entire waterfront. You will not be able to pursue all the prospective sources of support that you have discovered with the same degree of vigor. Reduce your list to a manageable number, and look for reasons to eliminate prospects rather keep them. In other words, choose the prospects that really are your best bets. You might aim for a final prospect list of no more than ten institutional sources as candidates for support.

Estimate Your Proceeds

In the same way that you projected total support from individuals, you should now make some conservative estimates of how much you might raise by approaching your institutional prospects. Conservative estimates are made on the basis of what you can assuredly expect rather than what you hope to receive. If you have received support from institutions in the past year, gauge which of them are really likely to renew their grants, contracts, or contributions in the upcoming year, and project a realistic financial estimate of their support.

Now turn to all your best bets lists. Ascribe an average grant size to each of them. Garner this information either through your research or your networking. Review the list: Are there sources whose support you are confident of receiving? Who are they? What level of support can you assuredly predict, if any? Where you are not confident or are unsure, err on the conservative side; don't count any "questionables" in your final projections. That way, you will be pleasantly surprised if you exceed your goal rather than disappointed if you fall below.

Another approach is to select the three prospects on your best bets list that most closely match your specific programs and purposes. Use the average grant size they award to organizations similar to your own as the basis for projecting your total revenue from institutions. You will, of course, have to decide how many of those prospects might award funding, if any. Again, it is better to err on the safe side unless you have strong indications of these prospects' inclination to fund your organization.

If this is your first foray into approaching institutions for support, you will probably find it difficult to estimate your chances for success. Don't panic; most nonprofits just starting out are in the same position. If you are still in the dark after all your information-gathering, you can simply decide not to project any support from institutions. That does not mean, of course, that you won't pursue your best bets—only that you will not count on their support without strong evidence.

Unfounded fundraising projections can be very dangerous. If the goals are not realized, programs may have to be eliminated, fundraising volunteers may become discouraged, and your credibility is likely to suffer. It is far better to build slowly and surely than to be faced with a shortage of funds due to projections that were based more on hope than on fact.

To build up your institutional support base, keep the following guidelines in mind:

1. *Do your homework.* The days of successful "shotgun" grantsmanship are over, if they ever really existed at all. Mailing out a large number of proposals to a group of institutional sources simply because you have their names and addresses, is the least effective way to achieve your fundraising goals. Your only success is likely to be in alienating funders—who speak to each other regularly, by the way; they will identify your organization as one that sends proposals that don't fit their guidelines and doesn't do its homework

2. *Target your approach.* In today's competitive climate especially, it's important to spend your limited time and resources researching prospective supporters to determine which may be appropriate and sympathetic to your work. Immerse yourself in their literature—annual reports, newsletters, and guidelines for applicants—and gather additional information by networking with people familiar with their work. Arming yourself with the fruits of careful preparation and thought will put you in the best position to select a group of funders.

   To further target your approach, in your letter of inquiry, or in the cover letter accompanying your proposal, make sure you articulate your reasons for approaching that *particular* institution for support.

Worksheet

Summarizing the Information Gathered on Your Institutional Prospects

Present or Past Institutional Funders	Prospects Similar to Present or Past Ones	Prospects Interested on the Basis of Locale

Prospects Interested on the Basis of Program Activity	Level of Potential Financial Support Available	Your Degree of Access to Decision-makers (Existing Contacts)

Your research and information-gathering will force you to abandon some prospects, since your activities will fall outside their interest areas. That's fine. Remember that you are honing down your prospect list to your ten best bets.

3. *Establish personal contact as early as possible in the application process.* This can be quite difficult, as foundations and corporations are increasingly deluged with requests for support in the wake of federal cutbacks, and their staffs have less time to respond to the volume of worthy inquiries they regularly receive. Yet, people still respond most readily to personal appeals. Paper does not sell programs; people do. Suggest a meeting in your letter of inquiry or in the cover letter accompanying your proposal and use that meeting to provide the human dimension that complements your plans on paper.

   If your letter doesn't result in a meeting, don't give up. You may still have an opportunity to meet later on. Think about upcoming events such as open houses, conferences, forums, or seminars, to which you can personally invite targeted funders. Consider carefully which activities would interest them. In other words, focus on *their* interests and on developing a long-term relationship, just as you would in building a relationship with a prospective individual donor. (More suggestions on nurturing such a relationship are included in Phase 9.)

4. *Keep your eyes on the long-term relationship.* Disappointment is only natural when you receive a rejection letter from a prospective institutional supporter. Its decision not to back your efforts, whose value you believe in strongly, strikes deep. But remember that its rejection may have had nothing to do with the quality of your work. The institution may have received a volume of deserving requests for funding that far surpassed its resources; or it may have distributed its grants in a different geographic area.

   Once you have determined that you were not rejected because your work fell outside the scope of your prospect's interests, make sure to keep the door open by keeping them posted on your ongoing work. The opportunity to reapply may arise in the future.

5. *Show that you have strong leadership.* Organizational leadership is integral to success in grantsmanship. Although grants are made to organizations, funders know that individuals are the key to organizational success, and they will seek evidence of the strength and quality of your organization's leadership from the very beginning of your relationship. Accordingly, you can best give evidence of the capabilities of your leadership by stating your case clearly and completely in your initial letter of inquiry. Don't hesitate to refer to one of your past successes if it is pertinent. Later on, when you submit your full proposal, include concise resumes of the staff members who will be directly involved in the work outlined in the proposal.

   It is important, too, that the acknowledged leaders of your organization be present at the first meeting with a prospective institutional supporter. In most cases, this means the executive director and the board chair or president. Depending on the agenda of the meeting, you might include one or two other individuals, such as program staff, other board members, constituents, or key community supporters, provided that they can make a concrete contribution to the meeting that no one else can. Choose the attendees carefully to ensure that you are presenting the strongest and most well rounded case for support.

6. *Prepare for the meeting.* An essential step in beginning the application process is to list the questions you think a particular prospect is likely to ask. Take the time to ask the hard questions and to play devil's advocate; the tougher you are now, the stronger your final proposal will be.

Once you have completed your list, answer all the questions one by one in writing. Then incorporate your responses into your initial letter and proposal. Do not wait until you are face-to-face with prospective supporters to address their concerns. Seize the opportunity in advance and answer them head-on in your first communication. They will realize quickly that you are thoroughly familiar with the problem you propose to address, and that your thoughtful and well-planned strategy merits a closer look.

7. *Know your niche.* Many nonprofits operate in a field of endeavor in which other organizations also work. Each group has its own particular strengths and makes a unique contribution. More often than not, institutional supporters are aware of the matrix of groups on an issue of mutual concern. They will be the first to ask such questions as: How is your work different from that of other existing organizations? It is your responsibility as the grantseeker to articulate the unique resources that distinguish your organization from the others. Your uniqueness, whether it is in your philosophy, your constituency, or your approach to a problem, will be a major factor in winning institutional backing.

Grantseekers often try to be all things to all people. This obfuscates your own strengths and blurs your mission. The materials you send to institutional funders should clearly state your approach and how it sets you apart from other groups active in the same field.

8. *Be prepared to discuss your organization's non-monetary needs.* Make a list of the other types of support that your prospect might provide and keep it handy. Since competition for non-cash assistance is less fierce, you may be able to leave a meeting with an important piece of information, or the promise of an in-kind contribution. You will have also established the basis for an ongoing relationship and, hopefully, financial support in the future. Remember that it is better to walk away with something than with nothing at all.

If you have done your homework well, your prospects will be in a position to aid you in a number of ways, such as introducing you to other funders, sending your staff to seminars, allowing your group to use the funders' space for meetings, and so on. Corporate funders can sometimes donate products, office furnishings, or printing, or provide consulting. Money may be your top priority, but don't fail to consider other forms of support. After all, an institution's financial resources may be limited or fully committed when you make your request.

9. *Be alert for opportunities to provide something of value to funders.* While some corporate backers may be quick to point out ways grantees can be of assistance to them, other funders may be less forthcoming. You can strengthen your relationships with funders by anticipating occasions on which you can help them. That assistance might take the form of information on a subject of interest or public recognition of their support. In the growing climate of partnership between the nonprofit sector and the private and public sectors, more opportunities for collaboration are emerging whereby nonprofits can contribute to funders' initiatives.

10. *Prepare your written materials conscientiously.* Personal communication is always important, but your written communications form the permanent record of your relationship with a funder. They are also often the first contact that a source has with your organization.

    The proposal is the most important piece of documentation. Funders may summarize it or circulate it in its entirety to a board of trustees or to others who have a say in their decision-making process. The proposal must speak for your work until—and if—you can.

    Preparing the proposal provides you with a chance to organize all of the data relevant to your work and to build a strong case for support. Be sure to include your strongest arguments in the proposal or the accompanying cover letter and to incorporate any information that reinforces your organization's credentials and its ability to succeed. You might do this by referring to past successes, including a letter of support from a recognized authority in your field, or by mentioning recognition your organization has received in the press.

11. *Explore possible personal contacts before making a cold approach.* This guideline is probably the most controversial of any on this list. Many funders' staff members decry the process whereby the executive director of a nonprofit makes an initial overture to a member of the funder's board of directors, who in turn makes a recommendation to the staff member. After all, it is the staffer's job to screen and recommend to the board potential projects for support, not the other way around. Make these contacts carefully, since you will be circumventing established procedure and possibly risking the loss of a staff member's support. And if written guidelines tell you not to go around the staff, then don't. Some foundations have noted the following in their guidelines, "Approaching trustees will not help and may hurt your chances for receiving funding."

    On the other hand, grantsmanship is a competitive process, and the personal factor certainly does affect the outcome of an appeal. The lesson here is to tread lightly, but do tread nonetheless (again, unless the guidelines specifically tell you not to). If any of your institutional prospects are totally new to you, compose a list of the contact people and others involved in the decision-making process. Circulate the list among your own active constituents (staff, board, key volunteers, etc.) to find out whether any of them know anybody on your list personally. When a connection is made, ask your own contact if he or she knows an appropriate way to approach that funder. Trust intuition and experience: let him or her decide whether placing an inquiry with the friend would be wise.

Your contact can also pose a question, such as "X organization, on whose board of directors I serve, is considering making an approach to your foundation for support. Could I take a moment of your time to tell you why I think our work is worthy of your support?" If the response is encouraging, ask for a suggestion about how to present your work effectively to the institution.

People always debate whether who you know or what you know is more important, and they often conclude that who you know is the key. But in fact, the real key is *what* you know when you approach *who* you know; if that person thinks you should have known something before coming to him or her that you *didn't* know, your chance for funding could be hurt.

Phase 6: Making the Case

What role does writing play in nonprofit fundraising? Regardless of which funding sources you target, you will invariably need written materials: brochures, proposals, direct mail appeals, newsletters, annual reports, and letters of inquiry, for example. And even though face-to-face solicitations raise more money than letters, the written materials you send to a prospect before the solicitation—as well as those you may leave afterward—are very important. And there's always the possibility that you won't be able to meet with institutional funding sources, so your written materials must speak for you.

One way to avoid the perennial writer's anxiety and to save time as well is to do exactly what most veteran professional fundraisers and development officers at hospitals, museums, universities, and other large nonprofit institutions do: write one document in advance of a fundraising campaign that will satisfy your needs before they arise. That document has the rather lofty-sounding title of *case statement*.

A case statement is simply a written document that states the most important facts about an organization. It can range in length from a wallet-size card to twenty pages or more. The most common case statement for the small to medium-size nonprofit probably ranges between five and ten pages. Preparing such a statement provides you with the opportunity to amass data that will best illustrate the competence of your staff and the effectiveness of your work. Your objective is to present sufficient information to your potential investors to elicit a positive response. In many ways, the case statement is not unlike the general support proposal that you might prepare for submission to a foundation; both provide the reader with answers to the following questions in an organized fashion:

1. Why does your organization exist? What are the problems in society that you plan to address? Describe the magnitude of those problems in a concrete way. Your objective is to assure the reader that your work is a response to proven and defensible needs.

2. How do you plan to alleviate these problems? What can you realistically hope to accomplish? Your objective here is to state succinctly your organizational purpose or mission and your specific program objectives.

3. Why is your staff and board qualified to tackle these problems with any expectation of success? Your objective here is to present the skills, qualifications, and experiences of your staff, board, and volunteers, whose combined efforts will have impact on the stated problem.

4. How much in revenues is needed to enable you to advance your efforts? Your objective here is to illustrate the costs of your efforts through budgeting.

5. How do you anticipate raising all the revenues you will need? Your objective here is to describe all your fundraising and income-generating plans to show that you can, with some degree of certainty, raise all the funds you need.

Your work in Section 1 of this book should provide you with much of the information you need to answer these questions thoroughly. Furthermore, the data from your completed exercises in Phases 1 and 3 (Taking Stock of Your Strengths and Assets, and Setting Fundraising Goals) will also be useful, as will the materials in your credibility file. In preparing a case statement, remember to present the most compelling, rational arguments you have to convince potential supporters of the worthiness of your organization.

Once you have finished writing your case statement, you'll need to present it in a clear and tasteful manner. A crisp, clean-looking document on quality paper will do the job. Be aware that graphics can enhance the visual appearance and appeal of your written materials, and pay attention to design, not only of your case statement, but also of direct mail appeals, newsletters, proposals, and brochures. Your materials do not have to be fancy, but they should be attractive enough to enhance the text and send a message to readers that your organization does things tastefully and appropriately.

Writing a clear and concise case statement or general support proposal (or whatever you choose to name this working document) will serve you in a number of important ways. It will give you a way to engage others early on in the fundraising process. You can circulate your draft for comments and suggestions to people whose help you need when the fundraising actually begins. In doing so, you foster their investment in your efforts and improve the chances that they will devote time and energy to your fundraising when you need them later on.

You now have a document from which you will be able to draw sentences, paragraphs, pages, and even sections for all the written materials you are required to prepare as your fundraising efforts continue. You will have saved yourself precious time, since you won't have to compose every new proposal or direct mail appeal from scratch. You may even choose to use your case statement as your primary fundraising document with large individual donors and foundations. In addition, you'll have a versatile set of materials to put in the hands of others associated with your group for a variety of purposes. The materials will be useful, for example, to those who make speeches, conduct workshops, or write articles for publication. The materials will also lend invaluable support to your face-to-face solicitors by serving as their briefing papers.

Your case statement can also be used as a tool for recruiting new board members. Since you have put your best foot forward in the body of this statement, it should serve you well in correspondence and in meetings with prospective board candidates.

Finally, you might circulate a draft to some significant donors whom you plan to approach as part of your campaign. In soliciting their feedback and suggestions, you are recognizing their importance to your organization and engaging their intellects before asking them to dip into their wallets. Inevitably, they will be more motivated to give later, when formally approached.

For all of these reasons, preparing written materials well in advance will strengthen your fundraising efforts. Spare yourself anxiety and frustration; start writing now. You will reap the rewards many times over later on!

Writer's Block—A Nonprofit's Monkey Wrench

If you are like many people in nonprofit pursuits—and most others—you will do your utmost to postpone writing tasks until time has run out. Deadline pressures, simple procrastination, and lack of confidence in writing skills can have serious adverse effects on the best of projects.

Reluctance to write is altogether common. J.R.R. Tolkien, one of the world's most prolific writers, speaks for many people when he says, "I play cards, or draw marvelously intricate patterns on backs of old newspapers while I am solving the crossword. Then I feel ashamed and try to get back to work, but the phone rings, or [my wife] Edith calls me to tea, and so I put it off for a later day."

If you share Tolkien's reluctance, you are not alone. If, however, you are among those chosen few who warm to every writing task with the greatest ease, cherish your gift. The rest of us must find someone to help us in our writing endeavors or learn to overcome our writing blocks. Obviously, taking the latter road will serve you best in the long run.

If You Need Help

Fortunately, a number of resources do exist to help frustrated writers develop confidence in their abilities. You will find a bookshelf of how-to titles at your local library or major bookstore. Recommended are:

- *The Elements of Style*, by William Strunk and E. B. White (New York: Macmillan, 1979)

- *Writing Without Teachers*, by Peter Elbow (London: Oxford University Press, 1975)

- *Writing Down the Bones: Freeing the Writer Within,* by Natalie Goldberg (Boston: Shambala Publications, 1996)

Phase 7: Preparing the Fundraising Plan and Calendar

You've established your fundraising goal for the year (Phase 3), targeted your potential individual and institutional backers and set conservative estimates on their potential level of support (Phases 4 and 5), and prepared the documents necessary to develop a variety of fundraising materials (Phase 6). This information provides you with the framework for your own particular fundraising strategy. Summarize your results on the following worksheet:

Worksheet

Summary of Fundraising Strategy

Fill in the results from your exercises in Phases 4 and 5:

Individual Supporters:

a. _____ Memberships @ $ ___/each   = $ _____

b. _____ Special events @ ___/each   = $ _____

c. _____ Large contributions @ ___/each   = $ _____

d. _____ Other forms of individual support:

_____   = $ _____

_____   = $ _____

_____   = $ _____

_____   = $ _____

                                    Subtotal   = $ _____

Institutional Supporters:

a. Foundations   = $ _____

b. Corporations and businesses   = $ _____

c. Government   = $ _____

d. Religious institutions   = $ _____

e. Federated fundraising organizations   = $ _____

f. Associations of individuals   = $ _____

g. Unions   = $ _____

                                    Subtotal   = $ _____

                                    TOTAL   = $ _____

You now have a realistic sense of the funding you may anticipate in the forthcoming year. Does this match the fundraising goals you set in Phase 3? If so, you're in good shape. If not, you need to reduce your operating budget or reasonably increase your fundraising projections. Don't initiate programs against revenues that aren't reasonably assured unless the program can be implemented in phases, and it is possible to wait between phases to raise money for the next phase.

The next step in implementing your strategy is to make a chart on some poster paper on a wall, or secure a large yearly calendar, with columns for each of the coming twelve months. At the top of each column, write the dollar amount that you need for monthly operating expenses (cash flow sheet). You are now ready to schedule your efforts (see the "Fundraising Calendar" worksheet).

1. Mark on the calendar your "proven traditions" for securing individual support, such as past membership appeals, special events, raffles, etc., and projected income from each for the coming year.

2. Fill in the amounts of grants and contributions from past institutional supporters that you can safely anticipate receiving again.

3. Add to the calendar the tasks you will need to complete in order for this support to be forthcoming. For example, under direct mail to membership, place all the tasks that are involved in a direct mail membership effort, such as: preparing copy for the letter; printing letter and enclosures; arranging artwork; arranging for mailing; recording receipts; and sending out thank-you notes. For past renewable institutional sources, place on your calendar not only writing proposals and cover letters but also sending final reports and occasional updates. You should now have on your calendar all the tasks you will need to complete in order to solicit funds from your past supporters.

4. Turn to your new prospects and schedule the tasks needed to solicit their support. You are choosing here from all the various approaches outlined in Section 2 (face-to-face, direct mail, special events, etc.). In scheduling, pay particular attention to two major considerations: (1) the months when you will need the funds to meet your operating expenses; and (2) the times of the year most appropriate for the activities you are planning. Try to be as detailed as possible in listing all the tasks involved in any particular fundraising activity.

5. Schedule your approaches to new prospective institutional supporters. When will your staff, board, and volunteers be free for additional fundraising? Use the calendar and your sense of other organizational priorities to pinpoint the time of year when you can most effectively mount this effort.

6. Place on the calendar all the tasks that accompany these approaches to new sources, such as:

   a. identifying prospects through research and networking

    b. developing program and/or general organizational proposals, including budgets and sample cover letters

    c. identifying personal contacts as prospects

    d. making the initial approach, either by telephone or by letter of inquiry, depending on the targeted sources and the nature of the personal relationship

    e. submitting a formal proposal or application, with back-up supporting materials

    f. scheduling follow-up appointments and visits with appropriate parties, at either your office or theirs

    g. submitting any requested additional materials.

7. You can take your planning process one step further by assigning individuals to all the tasks listed. This will aid the organization in defining responsibilities for the individuals involved, as well as ensuring that the timeline and tasks set are realistic. You are anticipating the people power inherent in each step of the way and assigning these responsibilities as the plan unfolds.

8. Next, place conservative income projections for each source on the calendar and the date when you might expect to receive the funds. You should continually keep track of the totals of gross receipts versus gross expenses each month to determine whether you will have sufficient revenues. Don't forget to carry over any unspent revenues from one month to the next. Thus, your calendar will help you project cash flow as well.

9. In listing tasks, don't overlook evaluation of each of your fundraising efforts as part of your list. You can place all your necessary fundraising activities and tasks on the calendar. Also, note that there is a line for monthly income totals, so you can keep track of your incoming revenues on a regular basis.

    Use this calendar as an ongoing tool in your work. Review it at least once a month with all the people who are intimately involved with your organization's fundraising work. Make whatever changes and modifications are warranted. This is the blueprint of your fundraising strategy for the upcoming year.

Phase 8: Making the Approach

Who Should Ask for Financial Support on Behalf of Your Organization?

The executive director and the officers of the board of directors are an organization's prime solicitors and the best choices for approaching a major prospective supporter. Yet each and every person associated with a nonprofit can ask others for support, including board members, staff members, volunteers, constituents, former constituents (i.e., alumni), family members, supporters, friends, civic leaders, public officials, contacts, and peers. The decision depends on each particular situation.

Worksheet

Fundraising Calendar

List on this calendar under the appropriate month all the tasks and activities inherent in your fundraising plan, and the individuals responsible for their implementation.

Jan	Feb	Mar	Apr	May	Jun	Jul	Aug	Sept	Oct	Nov	Dec
Monthly projection											
$	$	$	$	$	$	$	$	$	$	$	$

Individual fundraising

Institutional fundraising

Profile:

Arkansas Coalition for Choice

Although fundraising can seem like a daunting task, the Arkansas Coalition for Choice (ACC), a statewide coalition of women's, business, religious, and civil liberties groups, believes that once you set the fundraising wheels in motion, "things start happening." Carol Nokes, President of the ACC, explains, "If you know what you need to do and how much you need to do it, all you need to do is ask. The most successful way to raise money is to call on people directly. It's hard for someone to say no."

ACC's overall fundraising strategy has met with great success. Whether fundraising by phonebanking, by mail, or in person, ACC asks potential donors to help fund specific activities (i.e., "We need 20 people to give $ ___ to do ___"). This enables donors to take ownership of an event and become more invested in the organization.

ACC also puts a unique twist on some traditional fundraising devices. For example, when phonebanking, ACC typically recruits volunteers to make the calls. People who want to participate but don't feel comfortable asking for money over the phone, drive around to pick up the donations. This door-to-door collection eliminates the usual delay, cost, and coordination involved in collecting funds and provides a perfect opportunity to thank the donor personally.

Other creative fundraising ideas have also paid off. ACC raised several thousand dollars when it paid to sponsor the dress rehearsal of a local repertory theater in exchange for the right to sell tickets to the performance. During the event, ACC hosted a cocktail hour to introduce its officers and mingle with supporters. The event, held during two consecutive years, has drawn many people who were not already affiliated with the organization.

The Coalition's most recent fundraising achievement was the receipt of a Ms. Foundation grant. Ms. has challenged the Coalition to match half of it, which it will do through a highly targeted phonebank. Because ACC is always looking ahead, the job of fundraising is never over, but ACC knows what it takes to make it happen.[1]

---

1. The ProChoice Resource Center, Inc. *Strategies for Action: A Grassroots Organizing Manual* (Port Chester, NY: The ProChoice Resource Center, 1997).

Remember that you needn't feel alone in your fundraising work; there are many others to call on for assistance. You might even mobilize everyone on your list for a fundraising effort. And there are instances when the automatic constituencies within an organization can be called on to raise money; the Girl Scouts are unquestionably the best example. Moreover, certain activities—selling raffle or benefit tickets, or recruiting sponsors for walkathons—can be done by anybody and everybody involved with—or simply attracted to, your work.

Drawing from a list of potential solicitors, the leadership of a nonprofit must determine the most appropriate person or persons to make a particular request. Experience shows that people

Who Should Speak on Your Behalf?

I recall vividly a meeting with David Ramage in Philadelphia in the mid-1970s. At that time, I was co-director of the Philadelphia Clearinghouse for Community Funding Resources, a nonprofit technical assistance organization serving the Delaware Valley, and David was the president of the New World Foundation. He was visiting us with Karl Mathiasen, a member of his board, to assess our work, since we had applied for a grant from his foundation. Representing the Clearinghouse were the two co-directors, Linda Richardson and myself, and two of our board members, Bill Taylor, a finance secretary with the American Friends Service Committee, and Myesha Jackson, co-director of the Tenant Action Group. Bill represented what we referred to as "resource people," those who made their skills available to community-based organizations by serving on our board. Myesha represented a group that had received technical assistance from the Clearinghouse staff. At the close of the meeting, David told us why he had felt that it had been particularly good. He said, "Not only have you demonstrated the importance of your work by Myesha's comments, but you have attested to the quality of your work through Bill's remarks." David had shared with us a valuable insight. And yes we did receive a grant from them as well. The most ironic element of this story is that David Ramage gave significance to something that we were apt to take for granted: organizations found our work valuable, and experts felt that we were providing quality assistance. We had been so busy doing our job that we forgot to take a few steps back to assess it from an outsider's perspective.

—Michael Seltzer

respond most generously when asked by someone they know or respect. Thus, peer-to-peer solicitation is usually very effective: alumni to fellow alumni; students to other students; parents to parents; businesspeople to their counterparts; youth to youth. As a general rule, ask board members to ask their peers for support, staff to ask other staff, volunteers to ask other volunteers, major donors to ask other major donors, and so on. When approaching a particular constituency for the first time, you would do well to ask your top prospects to make a contribution and also to join you in asking others for support. In this way, you will be recruiting those who are best suited to ask their peers for assistance.

Unfortunately, some fundraisers most fear asking their own friends and contacts for money—even though they are likely to be the best prospects. They know the value of a particular organization's work, since they will have heard first-hand accounts from their fundraiser friends. You would be overlooking a prime constituency by giving in to such fears. You are likely to discover that your friend appreciates being asked and is pleased to join the life of your organization as a contributor and member.

To reiterate, your prime task is to identify who should make a particular fundraising request on behalf of your organization and then to brief that individual or those individuals adequately in preparation for the meeting with your candidate. As the executive director or member of the board, you may be a member of the team of two or three who might participate in the visit.

What Should You Ask Support For?

Again, you are matching up your prospective donor's interests with those activities of your organization that the donor would be most interested in supporting. Some people will be willing to give you money simply on the basis of your stated purpose, or to attend a special event you are sponsoring just to have a good time. More often than not, however, they will be more moved to be charitable when they hear or read about the specifics of your work.

Your task, then, is to anticipate which of your projected programs and efforts will have the greatest appeal to your prospects. Phase 3 provided some examples of the ways an organization can present its different needs. In other instances, your research, networking, and other information-gathering activities will provide you with some clues to your prospects' interests.

You may be tempted to present a foundation prospect with a number of choices. This strategy can be useful under certain circumstances, but you would be advised instead to gauge what aspect of your work would most interest a particular prospect and to present only that aspect. This demonstrates not only that you have done your homework but that you are reserving the right to set your own program priorities.

How Much Should You Ask For?

Your various prospective supporters can afford to make contributions of varying amounts to support your work. It is your responsibility to give them that opportunity. Some groups choose to suggest an amount in a direct mail solicitation or a proposal.

Certain fundraising approaches, such as direct mail and special events, do lend themselves to a range of gift sizes. A special event, whether a banquet or dinner, is a perfect occasion to offer your contributors a range of options. People can decide to be sponsors, patrons, or benefactors, to mention just some of the traditional terms. You can ascribe a different dollar amount to distinguish each level of support. That range should reflect the amounts of money you believe your supporters are capable of giving. This approach is also helpful when you lack basic information about your prospective donors' giving habits.

In deciding how much you can ask prospective contributors to give, your information-gathering and networking can once more be valuable aids. If you are approaching past donors, the simplest method would be to determine the amount you request based on their highest previous gift to your organization. You can ask them either to repeat their past gift or to consider making a larger gift. There are always a number of arguments you can use to provide a rationale to your contributors for increasing their giving, such as increased costs, inflation, greater demand for services, or new threats and challenges to your constituencies. More often than not, you will have a sound rationale for such a request.

What if you are writing a donor who has never given before to your organization? How can you gauge in advance what amount to request? You can turn to other organizations for advice. While some groups may be reluctant to share data on their donors, others will quickly see that it is to their advantage. After all, you may be able to do the same for them. Development officers at large nonprofits such as hospitals, universities, and museums rely also on a variety of standard reference materials to garner vital facts about prospective major donors. These include *Who's Who in America*, *The Social Register*, *Standard and Poor's Register of Corporations*, and *Directors and Executives*.

All of these books are standard reference materials, so you are certainly not invading anyone's privacy by using them. Building a profile of your prospects will bring you closer to gaining a sense of how much financial support they are capable of providing to your organization. You also will be surprised about the information that is available to you from your local newspapers, which regularly report on philanthropic individuals in your community. Since it is usually desirable for nonprofits to provide some form of public recognition of their strongest supporters, you are also apt to find valuable tidbits about them in an organization's newsletters, annual reports, special event programs, or other publications.

Remember that your financial needs are real. They reflect the costs of programs that you and others value highly. You can assert these needs clearly to your current and prospective supporters so that they are invited to respond according to their own abilities. By asking them to make contributions, you are extending an invitation to them.

A note about approaching institutional sources: foundations, corporations, governmental agencies, and religious institutions, as previously indicated, often make information available about their average grant size in their annual reports, guidelines for applicants, requests for proposals, and other literature they publish on their grantmaking programs. It is preferable to approach these sources with requests for targeted amounts that are gauged on the institution's stated financial capabilities. You will, of course, state the entire budget of the project for which you are requesting support, but you want to be clear about what part of that budget you are asking them to underwrite. If you still have doubts about the desirable level of support to request, you can ask the counsel of a sympathetic contact at the institution you are approaching.

To summarize, when approaching either a prospective individual or institutional donor, you should:

1. Decide in advance the specific amount to request.

2. Target that amount to the capacity of the prospect you are approaching.

3. Offer a range of gift options for large mass appeals.

All of the approaches discussed have merit depending on the specific situation. You have to decide which ones you want to use.

When and Where Can a Request for Financial Support Best Be Made ?

Institutions usually make decisions about when and where to request support easy for the grantseeker, since they have established procedures that may be printed in their guidelines. Your goal is always to seek as personal a contact as possible with a member of the staff who is engaged in the grant review process. This suggests a visit, to either their office or yours. First, mail an initial letter of inquiry and request a meeting. Since many sources (such as foundations and

House Parties

If you decide to throw a house party at a member's home for his or her neighbors, should you charge an admission in advance or at the door, make an appeal once people have congregated, or use the event only to set the stage for a later one-on-one solicitation? How do you make this decision?

The safest response is to charge a fixed amount for a ticket, in advance or at the door, or both. You should set your benefit price on the basis of the ability of your audience to pay, the "going rate" for such events in your community, and the entertainment value of your program. You can determine the going rate by checking what other nonprofits charge for similar events. On the basis of these three factors, you can then proceed to set the optimal ticket price.

If you are reaching out to constituents who can afford to make contributions of different amounts, some larger than the ticket price, give them the opportunity to do so. In such an instance, you can use the house party to introduce your work to these prospects and either make a pitch at the party or approach them later. If you do a pitch at the party, someone (usually not directly associated as staff with the organization) addresses the gathering at an appropriate moment. He or she makes a testimonial to the value of the work of the organization and asks for contributions. The emcee might start by asking for contributions at a designated high level. Once he or she gets as many pledges as are forthcoming for such sized gifts, the emcee drops to a request for a lower amount, and so on. The atmosphere resembles that of an art auction. Alternatively, the host or emcee might simply ask that everyone take a few moments and write out a check for the most they can afford. Ask everyone to be silent while people write out their checks, and have a couple of friends be prepared to take out their checkbook as soon as the pitch is complete.

corporations) are deluged with requests for support, some may request a full proposal prior to meeting. Again, their printed guidelines will usually state such procedures.

If you do your homework well and know that your targeted supporters are strong prospects, you might choose other ways to introduce yourself to them before making a request for funds. You can extend an invitation to activities, programs, or special events that you are planning. You can offer to mail them some materials on your work due to *their* stated interest in your field of endeavor. All these ideas will distinguish your approach from those of the legions of grantseekers who are always knocking on the doors of foundations and corporations. If your assumptions about a particular institution's priorities are correct, polite persistence will eventually pay off.

Your choices about when and where to approach individuals for support are more varied. Again, your goal is the same: you want to establish face-to-face contact as soon as possible. You can do that by canvassing door-to-door in your community, by inviting people to a wine and

---

Profile:

Defeating a Health Initiative

In 1994, the people of the state of California put an initiative on the ballot that called for single payer health care, the kind of health coverage found in a number of other countries around the world, but not in the United States. The health insurance industry and for-profit medical chains and hospitals were the formidable opponents of this grassroots effort, which was called Proposition 186. Money had to be raised quickly, but fundraising and organizing had to go hand-in-hand to try to get enough votes to pass this initiative. New York-based consultant Dave Fleischer suggested a house-party method which he had used in other political campaigns. The goal was to have a thousand house parties in six months raising $1,000 each, for a total of $1,000,000. The campaign created a house-party packet, which had a timeline, a generic invitation that you could take to any copy place and have duplicated, sample signs, sample information forms, return envelopes, and buttons and bumper stickers. Hosts were given a party packet that allowed anyone, even someone who had never had a party at their house, to walk step-by-step through this process and complete a successful party. The goal of $1,000 could be met by getting twenty-five people to give $40, ten people to give $100, or fifty people to give $20, or some combination. A second goal of each house party was also to get two people to agree to host their own house party. By the third month, there were minimally thirty house parties every weekend day all over the state, and five or six every evening. While not all of them raised their quota of $1,000, many went above it, some as high as $10,000. At the end of the campaign, 1,300 house parties had raised $1.4 million and reached thousands of voters. Although Prop. 186 was defeated, the house party strategy was very successful.

---

cheese party, by staffing a booth at an annual street festival in your town or city, or making an appointment to visit a prospective donor in his or her home, to mention just a few options.

Phase 9: Building the Relationship with Your Supporters

On rare occasions, supporters find that they are rewarded for their contributions with ingratitude. With gift in hand, the nonprofit's leaders simply rush off on their mission and ignore their benefactors.

This is foolhardy. When a contribution is made, it signals the possibility of a long-term relationship taking root between donor and the recipient. Remember that it always takes more time and effort to find a new donor than to keep an existing donor committed to your organization. The lesson is to value your supporters for the lifeline that they provide to your work.

How can you sustain and strengthen your supporters' interest and involvement in your work? If you really perceive your supporters as partners in your undertaking, you will have to treat

Case Study

Capital Campaign: A Small Town Tackles a Big Project

On September 28, 1990, just two weeks after Roann, Indiana's annual Covered Bridge Festival, someone set the historic bridge afire. Although firemen from eight departments responded, flames shot high into the evening sky, and the bridge was left a charred, smoking hulk.

A landmark built in 1877, Roann Covered Bridge is on the National Register of Historic Places.

Over the years, this small rural community had lost its school, its merchants, and its major enterprises to larger towns. Losing the bridge was a big blow. "It was," said Ann Mullenix, "almost like losing a member of your family."

When stunned citizens gathered the next morning, their meeting amounted to a wake. But about ten days later, they met again to consider what could be done.

The Town Takes Heart

The meeting began on a doubtful, downbeat note, voices negative, faces gloomy. Repairs that might take years and cost a million dollars seemed impossible for a rural village of 500.

That's where Amos Schwartz came in.

A contractor from Geneva, Indiana, Schwartz chided the people of Roann for faint heart. In his slight Swiss accent, he said not only should the bridge be saved, but the job could be done for $250,000 to $300,000. Says Henry Becker, "Schwartz was just the man we needed. A sense of purpose seized us." Everybody in town began to believe the bridge could be reconstructed.

And everyone cared. That's where the town's strength lay.

Townsfolk formed the Roann Covered Bridge Association and began to consider how to proceed. If they were going to do anything, there was no time to waste. The Historic Landmarks Foundation of Indiana had a grant available, but only about four days were left in which to apply. To qualify, they first had to raise $10,000 in matching funds.

Volunteers went door-to-door, and within those four days $8,000 funneled in. "It was a good cause. We didn't have to explain or sell," one solicitor noted. A couple of $1,000 donations put them over the top and the grant was theirs.

That was a big boost toward the Covered Bridge Association's next effort—an auction held the day after Thanksgiving. As word went around, auction items came in by the truckload—things that might ordinarily have gone into a spate of garage sales. When the last "Sold!" sounded, $17,700 had been raised. Best of all, no cash outlay had been necessary. Everything from several exercycles to the services of the auctioneer and his crew had been donated.

Small Events Add Up

Bridge repair estimates had now been finalized at $320,000. They could not hope to raise that much in one swoop. Meeting each Thursday to brainstorm, they came up with a potpourri of fundraisers. No idea was too small to be considered.

In conjunction with the November auction, a craft and bake sale had gone well. They held another bake sale. Canisters placed in stores of surrounding towns brought in more than $3,000 for the fund. Softball games cleared $500.

Indiana is well known for basketball fervor. What is not so well known is that after graduation, Hoosier players form community, factory, and church teams and continue playing for fun. The fundraising group decided to use them, setting up a tournament to which teams from nearby towns of Warsaw, Huntington, and Peru were invited. Henry Becker, treasurer for the bridge fund, was able to bank another $2,100 from the basketball tourney. They "played pretty good ball, too," said Becker.

Aluminum collection stations, set up at convenient spots on nearby highways, brought in nearly $3,500, thanks to the generosity of the local aluminum company, which gave a 20-cent premium for cans collected.

The group's biggest single money-maker, however, was a 300-page cookbook, put together by Louttia Krow. All recipes were donated. As first and second printings of 1,500 quickly sold out, 3,000 more copies were ordered and they, too, are nearly gone. The cookbook cleared $24,000.

Wabash County originally had five covered bridges. Local artist Gladys Schuman had sketched all five. Her sketches, donated by her son, Philip Fawley, were reproduced in miniature to make unique note paper. Sales of these added to the cause.

Many other small projects sprang up. A donation of $2 lit a colored bulb on the community Christmas tree, each light in honor of friend or family. The tree came to growing life, and credits listed in the weekly *Bridge Bulletin* sparked interest

The *Bridge Bulletin* was another project that grew from the association's Thursday night brainstorming sessions. Published weekly by association member Ann Mullenix, the *Bulletin* kept interest high and information current. Copies were left on post-office counters, distributed through stores and businesses, and placed beside the salt, pepper, and ketchup on each table in Roann's sole restaurant. Not only did the *Bulletin* increase turnout for fundraising activities, but weekly updates of funds raised won over early disbelievers.

Some fundraisers sprang up as private projects. Jim Huffman bought Rubbermaid bird feeders in the shape of a covered bridge. Painting these barn-red, Huffman attached a miniature "Roann Covered Bridge" sign and a price tag of $25. In all, 80 were sold, 75 of them donated (25 by the Rubbermaid Company).

Jim's brother Chuck crafted bridge belt buckles, clocks with a wood-burned bridge design, and sweatshirts printed with the Roann Bridge. All proceeds went into the fund.

Several people had had the presence of mind to photograph the bridge in flames, and one of these dramatic photos went onto a brochure. When businesses enclosed these with client or vendor correspondence, some sizeable donations drifted in—$75, $100. Eventually, corporate donations totaled $5,200, even without an organized industrial drive. The Bridge Association felt businesses already got asked too often.

County school teachers, who saw the covered bridge fire as an opportunity to enliven history lessons, also pitched in. One roomful of children at O. J. Neighbors School, Wabash, Indiana, raffled toys donated by Toys-R-Us, adding $80 to the bridge fund. Responding to letters from teachers of Metro North Elementary School, school children from elementary schools all over Indiana sent small amounts. Their contributions totaled $2,740.

The Roann Covered Bridge Association's Thursday sessions were open to all and any ideas. However, realizing that a small fundraising base hasn't room for long odds, they turned down things like a book of coupons usable in local stores that would return only $1 for every $29 worth of sales. Uh-uh. As their fund grew, the bridge association could proudly say that for every dollar collected, approximately 96 cents stayed in the fund,

The effort was run on a business-like basis, with month-to-month reports of contributions, expenses, and banking printed for committee meetings. Cannily invested in interest-bearing accounts, the fund also grew of itself. As contributions were deposited, interest income mounted to $3,500, and will continue to grow until all the money is spent for construction costs.

Minimal Expenses

The biggest fundraising plus for this group may have been in keeping advertising and other expenses to a minimum. Merchants sponsored ads for basketball games, auctions, suppers, and other projects. Printing costs of the *Bridge Bulletin* were underwritten by anonymous donors. Volunteers contributed many hours and few turned in requests for reimbursement of expenses. Little or no financial layout was required for a spring street festival, with games, dunk tank, etc., staffed by volunteers. Farmers donated hot dogs for the sausage and pancake breakfast and the hog roast supper, and the festival cleared $4,200.

Suppers put on by volunteers were also a smash success. This was partly because everyone in town reachable by telephone received a personal invitation. Callers divided up the phone book—"You take the A's and D's, I'll take the Cs and D's"—and telephoned every household, For the chili supper, more supplies had to be rushed in—twice. Fresher chili was never served.

Government Agencies Take Notice

In the midst of these efforts, Wabash County commissioners, taking notice of the unique value of a covered bridge, voted $35,000 for its repair. That, and a grant of $19,000 from the Indiana Department of Commerce, put Roann Bridge Association's fundraising over the top.

At the beginning of their undertaking, the group had no idea that such a large grant was available. When they learned about it, they didn't much care for the idea of hiring professionals to process an application. However, as amateurs in the ways of governments they may not have secured this grant without help. Certainly, they would not have received it so quickly.

The firm from Fort Wayne that was hired to handle the application will also administer the grant. "They charge a lot," said a committee member, "$2,800 to apply, $9,500 to administer the grant. We didn't really like that, but it seemed necessary to have someone who knew the ropes."

Recommended by a representative from the Department of Commerce, the firm secured the grant from the department in three months. By now, Roann Covered Bridge Association had raised $65,000, and this favorable percentage of local money seemed to impress the grant committee.

Thus, only six short, busy months after their bridge burned, the village of Roann raised the final dollar needed for its repair—$320,000. Roann celebrated.

Grace Notes

Their fundraising effort has ended on a grace note. In fact, more than one. At the 1991 annual bridge festival, Roann Covered Bridge Association sponsored wagon rides and a tour of the old river mill—closed to tour groups for several years—as a small return for the town's outpouring of goodwill and funds. Amos Schwartz, the contractor, plans to video-tape reconstruction of the bridge, which began December 1, 1991, and donate tapes to schools to public service. Spliced into tapes of the bridge burning, this video will become a vivid reminder of the lasting damage carelessness and vandalism can inflict.

The aluminum recycling effort begun to raise bridge funds will continue as an anti-littering conservation project.

Meanwhile, fundraising has not quite ended after all. Counting on the momentum they've created, the members of Roann Covered Bridge Association will try to raise an additional $32,000 to install a sprinkler system in the repaired bridge.

Thanks to a potpourri of fundraising ideas and many willing volunteers, a continuing place on the map has been ensured for this gutsy Indiana village and its unique bridge.

—Shirley Wilcox, North Manchester, Indiana, from the *Grassroots Fundraising Journal.*

them as such. Some nonprofits actually bestow on their members voting privileges in the governance of their organizations. Their members elect the board of directors of the nonprofit corporation. Short of this, nonprofit leaders can do many things to heighten the sense of affiliation between their constituents and their organizations. The following chart illustrates the variety of ways in which individuals can choose to become more active in the affairs of a nonprofit.

Chart:

The History of John Doe's Participation in the Work of the Bumblebee Day-Care Center

- John has brought his daughter to the day-care center for the last two years; the center noted on his registration form that he is a human resources senior manager at a local company, and designed a cultivation strategy.

- After receiving the center's newsletter and attending several open houses, John is asked by the center's development staff if he would be willing to review the center's personnel practice handbook and policies.

- He agrees, reviews the material, makes recommendations, and checks implementation. He receives a letter of thanks and is also thanked in the center's next newsletter.

- The center's development staff asks if he would be willing to contact other parents to identify skills and experience they might be willing to share with the center. John accepts because his experience with the center—both as a parent and a volunteer—has been consistently positive. He suggests that he form a small committee to undertake the project.

- The development staff helps John organize the committee and its work. It is during this time that the center sends out its annual fund appeal. John receives a solicitation letter with a handwritten note from the center's board chairman thanking him for all his work. The children in his daughter's group have made a thank-you poster, which is also enclosed. How can John resist making a generous contribution?

- He continues to receive newsletters and other publications from the center, and receives recognition for his work and support in a profile article in the newsletter.

- John is then asked to become a member of a standing committee of the board; he accepts and makes another, larger, contribution.

- As a result of his committee work, he accepts a nomination to the board of directors and makes the largest donation he can afford to the day-care's capital campaign.

- He steps down from the board after serving two terms, joins the advisory committee, and is honored at the center's annual dinner for his years of service.

The benefits the center derives from John Doe's contributions are self-evident, but what may be less apparent are those John Doe has personally derived. They may include public recognition, social opportunities, leadership experience, respect from his neighbors and peers, and skill enhancement, to mention a few. In any case, it is safe to assume that both parties have reaped benefits from the association.

Correspondingly, relationships with institutional supporters need not begin and end with the receipt of a grant. There are ways to increase the participation of institutional representatives in the work and life of your organization. The following chart illustrates some of these ways.

Chart

The History of Joan Swan, Program Officer of the Miracle Foundation, and the Echo Park Job Training Project

- Joan receives an invitation to a reception honoring the first graduating class of the Echo Park Job Training Project (EPJTP), and decides to attend when a colleague at another foundation calls to extend a second invitation.

- Aware that Joan will be attending, EPJTP's executive director sends a short note saying how pleased she is that Joan will attend, and includes some basic material on the organization. At the ceremony, Joan is welcome by the executive director, and they sit with the board president and several graduates at the post-ceremony luncheon.

- Later that week, Joan receives a letter thanking her for attending. The letter also mentions a project that falls squarely within the Miracle Foundation's guidelines and asks for a meeting. After the meeting, Joan asks EPJTP to submit a proposal for the project they discussed.

- She receives the proposal and requests additional information. At the same time, she receives letters from several colleagues and community leaders that speak about EPJTP's importance to the community, the expertise of its staff, and the commitment of its board.

- Miracle Foundation approves a grant! Joan calls the executive director with the good news and sends out a grant agreement and a check.

- She receives a thank-you letter, a signed copy of the grant agreement, and a request for a meeting for advice on other prospective funders. The following week, she reads about the Miracle Foundation's grant in the local newspaper.

- She requests and receives a six-month narrative and financial report on the progress of the project, and asks EPJTP staff to meet with a brand-new job training project in another part of town to provide technical advice.

- She accepts an invitation for a site visit.

- She recommends the executive director of EPJTP as a speaker at a local funder's program on "Decreasing Chronic Unemployment."

- She receives a final end-of-the-year report on the accomplishments of the project, including a glossy photograph of the program participants.

The history of Joan Swan and the Echo Park Job Training Project illustrates a key ingredient in a successful partnership between an organization and an institutional supporter: continuity. In this particular example, several things are presumed. The grantee is conducting a program that corresponds to the funder's interests and that is accomplishing its stated objectives. The grantee can choose to decline any request made by the funder that it deems inappropriate or that it cannot fulfill due to pressures of time or other reasons. But in the majority of cases, the grantee will be willing and able to satisfy requests.

These two examples are meant to be neither prescriptive nor exhaustive. They only suggest that the nonprofit organization and its supporters each have something to offer the other. It is the responsibility of the nonprofit to make the first overture and to nurture the relationship. Not every supporter will be interested in ongoing collaborations, but those who are will respond to your initiatives. The reward for both parties will be found in the fruits of an ongoing partnership.

Phase 10: Monitoring and Evaluating Your Fundraising Efforts: Laying the Groundwork for Next Year

As in most aspects of fundraising, common sense is the rule in monitoring and evaluating your efforts. Whether a special event succeeds or fails, find out why. Ask all those involved to participate in an evaluation. Are the mistakes or miscalculations correctable? Did the event require more staff, member, and volunteer time than was warranted by the money it generated? What should be done differently the next time around in order to enhance the event's success? Sometimes burnout or disappointment after a frustrating event are so rampant within an organization that questions such as these never get addressed.

Feedback is vital to other efforts, too. For example, find out why a targeted corporation has sent a form rejection letter in response to your letter of inquiry. Call or write the corporation's charitable contributions officer and ask what might make your organization more attractive to the company for possible future consideration. Gather feedback wherever you can. Such information helps in redefining and refocusing the organization's fundraising strategy.

Most people have a tendency to walk away quickly from both successes and disappointments without reviewing them critically. As part of your planning process, schedule evaluation meetings after every special event and campaign. Ask people who were involved questions such as: What can we learn from this experience for the future? What would we do the same way again? What would we do differently?

Check with others for their perceptions. You can even survey your members if you are assessing fundraising programs aimed at them. Finally, be sure to schedule dates for your evaluation meetings as part of your planning process for next year's fundraising efforts. Build on your previous experiences.

Final Thoughts on Securing Your Organization's Future

As described in this book, effective fundraising produces two equally important, simultaneous results: (1) you secure funds to support your organization in its immediate work; (2) you lay the financial groundwork for your future endeavors as well, thereby freeing yourself and your organization from reinventing a new fundraising wheel each year.

Through building a strong organization (Section 1), choosing appropriate funding partners (Section 2), and crafting a well-thought-out strategy and plan to secure their support (Section 3), you will be positioned to serve your constituents and supporters well. All will derive satisfaction from the knowledge that your nonprofit organization is on the right course.

Now you are prepared to go out and start your fundraising for the year!

Additional Resources

Publications

American Association of Fund Raising Counsel. *Fund Raising Review*. Bimonthly. New York: American Association of Fund Raising Counsel.

    Summary of significant articles, speeches, and trends in fundraising.

Brody, Leslie. *Effective Fund Raising: Tools and Techniques for Success.* Acton, MA: Copley Publishing Group, 1994. x, 157 p.

    Basic primer for executive directors, board members, and volunteers wishing to raise funds to maintain needed services or develop new programs. Covers mobilization, annual appeals, phonathons, corporate approaches, soliciting foundations, special events, and consultants. Includes an appendix of master forms for reproduction, and an acrostic.

Bryce, Herrington. *Financial & Strategic Management for Nonprofit Organizations: Comprehensive Guide to Legal, Financial, Management, Fundraising, and Other Key Areas.* 3rd ed. San Francisco: Jossey-Bass, 1999. Hardcover, 608 pp.

    This invaluable guide for nonprofit managers provides encyclopedic coverage of the key legal, accounting, and financial issues facing their organizations. It lays out the fundamentals of nonprofit laws, strategic planning, fundraising, risk management and compensation, and budgeting. Now extensively revised and updated, the third edition offers expanded coverage of the rules for attaining and maintaining nonprofit status; growing the organization through strategic alliances; handling gifts of stocks; finding tax-favored medical and retirement plans; reorganizing through mergers, divestitures, conversions, and much more. It is the only book to offer such a wide-ranging coverage of key topics in a single volume.

Burlingame, Dwight F., ed. *Critical Issues in Fund Raising.* New York: John Wiley & Sons (NSFRE/Wiley Fund Development series), 1997. xxii, 266 p.

    Researchers and practitioners address the major issues in the current state of fundraising, including demographics and donor motivation, strategies, marketing, ethics, regulation and law, cost-effectiveness and financial management. Also provides perspective on fundraising in Western Europe. Indexed.

Carlson, Mim, and Cheryl Clarke. *Team-Based Fundraising Step-by-Step: A Total Organization Model.* San Francisco: Jossey-Bass, 1999. Hardcover 208 p.

    This new team-based approach to fundraising brings the entire organization together to raise the money nonprofits need to survive. Two nonprofit experts have developed a model that gets every member of the group—from the board of directors down to the volunteers – involved. This book shows how this approach can work at every step of the process, laying out specific tasks for each team member, and providing sample forms. Includes examples from organizations that have successfully used the model to increase their own fundraising effectiveness.

Ciconte, Barbara Kushner, and Jeanne Gerda Jacob. *Fund Raising Basics: A Complete Guide.* Frederick, MD: Aspen Publishers (Aspen's Fund Raising Series for the 21st Century), 1997. xvii, 315 p.
> Addresses all aspects of the development field. Chapters cover the roles of board, staff, and volunteers in fundraising; setting up and managing a development office; using technology; and developing and evaluting a fundraising plan.

Dove, Kent E. *Conducting a Successful Capital Campaign.* 2nd ed. San Francisco: Jossey-Bass 1999. Hardcover 608 pp.
> A comprehensive, systematic guide – packed with practical tools and advice – for planning and managing a successful campaign. Expanded resource section offers samples of key elements of a capital campaign, including a complete volunteer kit, sample budget report, program brochures, newsletters, a strategic plan, and market survey questionnaires, among other tools.

Edles, L. Peter. *Fundraising: Hands-On Tactics for Nonprofit Groups.* New York: McGraw-Hill, 1993. xiii, 288 p.
> Step-by-step guide to organizing, developing, and conducting membership and constituent fundraising drives. Includes sections on soliciting major and intermediate gifts, and on running a small-gifts drive.

Ferree, G. Donald, Jr., John W. Barry, and Bruno V. Manno. *The National Survey on Philanthropy & Civic Renewal 1997-1998: Americans on Giving, Volunteering, and Strengthening Community Institutions.* Washington, DC: National Commission on Philanthropy and Civic Renewal. 96 pp.
> Presents the findings of the "National Survey on Philanthropy and Civic Renewal" conducted by researchers at the University of Connecticut, who interviewed more than one thousand people by telephone. Additional surveys were conducted with representatives from racial/ethnic and other minority groups, and with wealthy persons. The survey questions are reprinted in Appendix 1.

Flanagan, Joan. *The Grass Roots Fundraising Book: How to Raise Money in Your Community.* Chicago: Swallow Press, 1982. 344 pp.
> One of the most important guides to a wide range of grassroots and community fundraising activities. Provides step-by-step details on how to set up a fundraising program, how to choose the right strategy for a given group, and how to raise money and build an organization at the same time. Extensive references to other resource materials.

Flanagan, Joan. *The Successful Volunteer Organization: Getting Started and Getting Results in Nonprofit, Charitable, Grass Roots, and Community Groups.* Chicago: Contemporary Books, 1981. 376 pp.

> How-to manual for volunteer organizations. Discusses getting started, getting results, getting organized, and getting advice. Principles for strengthening organizations include how to conduct productive meetings, do fundraising and publicity, and build a stronger membership and board of directors. Includes an annotated bibliography.

Firstenberg, Paul B. *The Twenty-First Century Nonprofit: Remaking the Organization in the Post-Government Era.* New York: Foundation Center, 1996. xxii, 247 p.

> Provides a road map for organizations seeking to enhance their performance both in program design and execution and in achieving financial health. Encourages managers to adopt the strategies developed by the for-profit sector in recent years; expand their revenue base by diversifying grant sources and exploiting the possibilities of for-profit enterprises; develop human resources by learning how to attract and retain talented people; and explore the nature of leadership. Provides profiles of three nonprofit CEOs: McGeorge Bundy, William G. Bowen, and Joan Ganz Cooney. Includes bibliographic references and index.

Golden, Susan L. *Secrets of Successful Grantmanship: A Guerilla Guide to Raising Money.* Jossey-Bass, 1997, 192 pp.

Graham, Christine P. *Blueprint for a Capital Campaign: An Introduction for Board Members, Volunteers and Staff.* Shaftsbury, VT: CPG Enterprises, 1997. 21 p.

> A concise guide on how to plan and implement a capital campaign, together with a recommended reading list.

Grassroots Fundraising Journal.

> A bimonthly journal published by Chardon Press. Each issue features a how-to article on a specific fundraising method or some related issue. Includes ideas submitted by readers. Ideal publication for community-based organizations.

Greenfield, James M. *Fund Raising Cost Effectiveness: A Self Assessment Workbook.* New York: John Wiley & Sons (NSFRE/Wiley Fund Development Series), 1996. xxxviii, 333 p.

Greenfield, James M. *Fund-Raising Fundamentals: A Guide to Annual Giving for Professionals and Volunteers.* New York: John Wiley & Sons (Nonprofit Law, Finance, and Management Series), 1994. xix, 407 p.

Greenfield, James M., ed. *The Nonprofit Handbook: Fund Raising.* 2nd ed. New York: John Wiley & Sons (NSFRE/Wiley Fund Development Series), 1997. xxv, 716 p.

> Provides information on the entire scope of fundraising, including the how-to of actual solicitation activities. Divided into six parts: Managing Fund Development, Fund-Raising

Readiness, Annual Giving Program, Major Giving Programs, Select Audiences and Environments, and Support Ingredients. Includes index.

Harrison, Bill J. Fundraising: *The Good, the Bad, and the Ugly, and How To Tell the Difference*. 3rd ed. Madison, WI: Society for Nonprofit Organizations, 1997. 300 p.
Covers multiple topics in workbook format: types of fundraising, special events, volunteers, individual solicitation, donor clubs, telemarketing and direct mail, corporate solicitation, capital campaigns, and planned giving. The "bad" are solicitation companies that skirt the law, and the "ugly" are charity scams. Provides tips on protecting against these frauds.

Hartsook, Robert F. "77 Reasons Why People Give." *Fundraising Management* 29 (December 1998): 18–19.

Henley, Michael J., and Diane L. Hodiak. *Fund Raising & Marketing in the One-Person Shop: Achieving Success with Limited Resources*. 2nd ed. Minneapolis: Development Resource Center, 1997. viii, 189 p.

Joyaux, Simone P. *Strategic Fund Development: Building Profitable Relationships that Last*. Frederick, MD: Aspen Publishers (Aspen's Fund Raising Series for the 21st Century), 1997. xiii, 213 p.
Argues that four relationships are critical for a nonprofit organization's survival. The first relationship is within the organization and involves creating a healthy infrastructure. The second is with the community, which evolves through strategic planning. The third is with the organization's constituents so they will be ready to give. The fourth is with the organization's volunteers to enable them to take action on behalf of the organization. Includes bibliographic references and index.

Kelly, Kathleen S. *Effective Fund-Raising Management*. Mahwah, NJ: Lawrence Erlbaum Associates, 1998. xvi, 663 p.
Comprehensive work organized into three main sections: practice, principles, and process of fundraising. Chapters cover fundraising as a profession, including types of jobs in the field; organizational context of fundraising, both historically and presently; legal and ethical issues; fundraising theories; and specific types of fundraising (annual giving, major gifts, planned giving, capital campaigns, and soliciting individuals, corporations, and foundations). Each chapter provides a suggested reading list. Indexed.

Kihlstedt, Andrea, and Catherine Schwartz. *Capital Campaigns: Strategies that Work*. Frederick, MD: Aspen Publishers (Aspen's Fund Raising Series for the 21st Century), 1997. xv, 232 p.
Written for small- to mid-sized nonprofit organizations that are considering a capital campaign. Covers the entire process from planning the campaign through using consultants

to finishing, evaluating, and reporting on the campaign. Includes bibliographic references, a glossary, and an index.

Klein, Kim, ed. *Como Recaudar Fondos en Su Comunidad* (*How To Raise Money in Your Community*). Trans. Norma del Rio. Berkeley, CA: Chardon Press, 1998. 39 p.
Compilation of articles about special events and direct mail fundraising strategies as they relate to individual solicitation. In Spanish.

Lansdowne, David. *Relentlessly Practical Guide To Raising Serious Money*. Medfield, MA: Emerson & Church, 1997. 264 p.

Lant, Jeffrey L. *Development Today: A Fund Raising Guide for Nonprofit Organizations*. 5th ed., rev. Cambridge, MA: JLA Publications, 1993. iv, 298 p.
Guide for those who find fundraising a frustrating process, providing practical information and techniques for overcoming fundraising fears. The author guides the reluctant fundraiser through a series of basic steps such as the planning process; the documents required; the key people involved and how to work with them; the function of the coordinating committee; corporate, federal, and foundation fundraising; the capital campaign; special events; and direct mail. Includes a fundraising planning and implementation time-line, and samples of such items as a cover letter, precis, proposal, several letters, pledge cards, and newsletter. Includes bibliography.

Mills-Groninger, Tim. "Gearing Up the Small Shop." *Advancing Philanthropy* 6 (Summer 1998): 10–13.
Argues that the one- to three-person fundraising office must make smart use of technology, and offers practical advice for getting started.

Mixer, Joseph R. *Principles of Professional Fundraising: Useful Foundations for Successful Practice*. San Francisco: Jossey-Bass Publishers (Jossey-Bass Nonprofit Sector Series), 1993. xx, 277 p.
Applies concepts and theories from psychology, organizational behavior, and management to provide a framework that enhances the effectiveness of professional fundraising. Offers models for soliciting donations by discerning the attitudes, influences, and values of potential donors. Includes illustrative planning charts, criteria for selecting fundraising methods, and key elements in the organization of fundraising activities. Indexed.

Muir, Roy, and Jerry A. May, eds. *Developing an Effective Major Gift Program: From Managing Staff to Soliciting Gifts*. Washington, DC: Council for Advancement and Support of Education, 1993. iv, 134 p.
Designed for fundraisers in education, but with a wealth of information applicable to all fundraising. Individually authored chapters discuss management of a major gift campaign, developing staff, setting guidelines, prospect research, prospect management, using

volunteers, narrowing the field, special events, solicitation, and stewardship of major donors. Extensive annotated bibliography of donor research resources.

Murray, Dennis J. *Guaranteed Fund-Raising System: A Systems Approach to Developing Fund-Raising Plans.* 2nd ed. Poughkeepsie, NY: American Institute of Management, 1994. xi, 297 p.

National Society of Fund Raising Executives. *NSFRE Journal.* Twice a year. Washington, DC: National Society of Fund Raising Executives.
   How-to articles and reports of successful fundraising activities for professional fundraisers. (Order from: National Society of Fund Raising Executives, 1101 King Street, Suite 700 Alexandria, VA 22314 (703) 684-0410).

Noriega, Maria Elena, and Milton Murray. *Apoyo Financiero: Como Lograrlo.* Mexico D.F., C.P.: Editorial Diana S.A., 1995. 182 p.
   Outlines the preparation, implementation, and evaluation of a fundraising campaign. In Spanish.

Oster, Sharon M. Strategic *Management for Nonprofit Organizations: Theory and Cases.* New York: Oxford University Press, 1995. ix, 350 p.
   Applies the concepts of strategic management developed originally in the for-profit sector to the management of nonprofits. Describes the preparation of a strategic plan that is consistent with the resources available, analyzes the operational tasks in executing the plan, and outlines the ways in which nonprofits need to change in order to remain competitive. Topics include the role and mission of the nonprofit, fundraising, accounting, evaluation, volunteers, and the board of directors. Provides in-depth case studies of nine nonprofit organizations from diverse areas of the nonprofit sector. Includes numerous charts and graphs, bibliographic references, and index.

Poderis, Tony. *It's a Great Day to Fund-Raise: A Veteran Campaigner Reveals the Development Tips and Techniques that Will Work for You.* Willoughby Hills, OH: FundAmerica Press, 1996. ix, 116 p.
   A concise guide that covers most aspects of fundraising. Contains chapters on planning; prospecting for donors; evaluating prospects; annual, endowment, capital, and underwriting campaigns; developing, preparing, and managing a campaign; and developing the fundraising team. Includes index.

Scanlan, Eugene A. *Corporate and Foundation Fund Raising: A Complete Guide from the Inside.* Frederick, MD: Aspen Publishers (Aspen's Fund Raising Series for the 21st Century), 1997. xv, 276 p.
   Presents an overview of the various types of corporate foundations and giving programs as well as private and community foundations, followed by appropriate techniques of approaching them effectively.

Setterberg, Fred, and Katy Schulman. *Beyond Profit: The Complete Guide to Managing the Nonprofit Organization.* New York: Harper and Row. 1985. 271 pp.

> Strategies for managing all aspects of nonprofit organizations including long-range planning, publicity, and fundraising. The section on fundraising discusses why and how to ask for money, where the money is, and how to get it.

Society for Nonprofit Organizations. *Nonprofit World Report.* Madison, WI: The Society for Nonprofit Organizations.

> Bimonthly publication with articles about all issues of interest to those in the nonprofit field including information about pending legislation and successful fundraising approaches and practices.

Sturtevant, William T. *The Artful Journey: Cultivating and Soliciting the Major Gift.* Chicago: Bonus Books, 1997. viii, 219.

> The manual explores the principles and tenets of fundraising philosophy, focusing mainly on major gifts. Marketing concepts, determinants of success, gift solicitation, and active listening techniques are among the topics covered.

Warwick, Mal, Stephen Hitchcock, Joan Flanagan, and Robert H. Frank. *The Hands-On Guide to Fundraising Strategy and Evaluation.* Looseleaf. Frederick, MD: Aspen Publishers, 1995. 1 v.

> Accessible fundraising manual arranged in five parts:. "How Fundraising Really Works," which offers advice on assessing a fundraising program; "Ingredients of Successful Fundraising," which details the costs associated with various fundraising methods; "The Fundraiser's Toolbox," which covers a range of procedures from choosing the right computer system to tips for hiring a consultant; "Talking Sense about Fundraising," which discusses a new way to explain fundraising to the board, staff, and donors; and "Resources for the Serious Fundraiser," which gives guidelines and standards of fundraising associations. Provides numerous charts, forms, and questionnaires to facilitate the fundraising process. Includes bibliographic references and index.

Weinstein, Stanley. *The Complete Guide to Fund-Raising Management.* New York: John Wiley & Sons, 1999. xii, 307 p.

> A comprehensive treatment of fundraising principles and practices, including information about creating case statements, record-keeping, prospect research, cultivating donors, major gifts, grants, direct mail, telemarketing, special events, planned giving, and capital campaigns. Covers management and human resources issues, planning, budgeting, ethics, and evaluation of a fundraising program. Includes disk. Indexed.

Internet

About.com Guide to Nonprofit Charitable Organizations (www.about.com)

> A miniWeb site within the comprehensive About.com site (formerly the Mining Company) that serves as a useful guide to resources and information about nonprofit organizations,

foundations, jobs, educational opportunities, and the latest developments in the field. Visitors can search feature archives as well as the entire About.com site, participate in chats, and receive newsletters via e-mail.

ActionAid (www.actionaid/home.html)
ActionAid helps poor people in developing countries to address and overcome the causes and effects of poverty by planning and implementing long-term development programs.

The Alliance of European Voluntary Service Organizations (www.workcamps.com/alliance)
The Alliance of European Voluntary Service Organisations, founded in 1982, is an "International Non-Governmental Youth Organisation that represents national organisations which promote intercultural education, understanding, and peace through voluntary services."

CharityChannel (www.charitychannel.com/forums)
The American Philanthropy Review maintains this site on which approximately twenty discussion forums may be joined or searched. These forums, or e-mail discussion lists, cover topics ranging across the fundraising field (capital campaigns, special events, board development, software, etc.). As an example of how the list system works, someone wrote to one of the forums on the site asking how corporate sponsorship works, and responses came from other members (from as far away as California and Italy) of the list who wished to share their perspectives. Some responses offered other Web sites and discussion groups as additional resources.

CharityVillage (www.charityvillage.com)
CharityVillage is a major Canadian site for the nonprofit sector, featuring an extensive list of useful links. The site is distinguished by a particularly outstanding collection of links to e-mail discussion lists – mostly American, but many Canadian as well, and with international participation. The lists are a form of discussion and exchange; it's possible to review the archives to find discussion on many topics of interest written by members who tend to be practitioners in the field. Lists frequently include embedded links to other relevant resources, such as papers that have been written and presented on the subject at hand.

The Chronicle of Philanthropy (www.philanthropy.com)
A key Internet resource for nonprofits. Focuses on significant news, trends, and legal issues related to nonprofits in the areas of fundraising, governance, and Web resources.

The Cutting Edge Bookstore (www.thecuttingedge.com)
This site provides a handy list of titles available in the areas of fundraising and marketing, with a selection of titles focused on the web.

The Foundation Center (www.fdncenter.org)
One of the richest sources of information about foundations and fundraising.

Grants Web (web.fie.com/cws/sra/resource)
Links to a wide range of grants-related Internet sites and resources. Includes funding opportunities and grants databases.

GuideStar (www.guidestar.com)
GuideStar offers a searchable database of nonprofit organizations, philanthropic news, and a resource exchange. Nonprofits can post (for free) classifieds, news, and other information.

Idealist – Action Without Borders, Inc. (www.idealist.org)
An enormously helpful site, the Idealist pages provide links to a full range of sites that serve nonprofit organizations. The site provides a clearinghouse of links to organizations and services, ranging from volunteer opportunities and jobsearch links, to accessing services.

IGC's Activism/Internet Resource Center (www.igc.org)
A comprehensive directory of links to nonprofit resources on the Internet. The "activist toolkit" includes links to a number of e-zines, Web-based publications, and helpful legislative directories.

Independent Sector (www.indepsec.org)
Committed to promoting philanthropy, volunteering, and citizen action, this coalition group brings together nonprofit organizations, foundations, and corporate giving programs. The site gives an overview of IS programs and includes a section on the basics of lobbying by charitable organizations. A media section includes facts and figures on the size and scope of the nonprofit sector and a statistical overview of the IS survey on giving and volunteering. "Giving Voice to Your Heart" is a starter kit to help guide visitors in their public relations efforts. The IS publications catalog can be searched electronically for material of interest.

Internet Nonprofit Center (www.nonprofits.org)
An exceptionally useful site that provides solid technical information on an extensive range of topics directly relevant to nonprofits, and maintains extensive links to other sites. Includes an excellent FAQ (frequently asked questions) section with authoritative responses to questions and helpful links and references for further information. A recommended starting point for almost any inquiry of interest to nonprofits. The FAQs tend to be written by practitioners and academicians, with subject-specific expertise provided by lawyers, accountants, etc.

Internet Prospector (www.internet-prospector.org)
   This nonprofit service to the prospect research community is produced by volunteers nationwide who "mine" the Net for prospect research nuggets for nonprofit fundraisers. Includes an online newsletter and archives of past issues, a directory of U.S. secretary of state incorporation records, search engine prospecting and test results, and tips for foundation searches.

Library of Congress (www.lcweb.loc.gov)
   The entire Library of Congress catalog searchable on-line, as well as information on programs and services.

The Management Center (www.tmcenter.org)
   Set up to support nonprofit organizations in northern California, the Management Center maintains an extensive set of very useful links of interest to nonprofit organizations regardless of their location. The site contains a nonprofit library divided into technology, advocacy, and fundraising resources, with annotated links to sites that provide technical information, services, and library resources to nonprofit organizations. Links range from the National Society of Fund Raising Executives to Independent Sector and the Nonprofit Tech library.

National Center for Charitable Statistics – A Project of the Center on Nonprofits and Philanthropy at the Urban Institute (www.nccs.urban.org)
   Visitors to this site can download microdata on nonprofit organizations, view or download database documentation and data dictionaries, and download blank IRS forms from which most of the data is collected.

National Committee for Responsive Philanthropy (www.ncrp.org)
   The mission of the National Committee for Responsive Philanthropy (NCRP) is to make philanthropy more responsive to people with the least wealth and opportunity, more relevant to critical public needs, and more open and accountable to all, in order to create a more just and democratic society.

Nonprofit Outreach Network, Inc. (www.norn.org)
   Organizational site dedicated to helping other nonprofit organizations utilize the power of the Internet and World Wide Web to disseminate information.

Nonprofit Prophets (www.bluewebn.com/wired/prophets/prophets.teaching.guide.html)
   A comprehensive index of annotated links to resources for investigating problems/research organized by topic. Categories include the environment/ecology; global conflict/politics; family issues; homelessness, hunger, and poverty; disasters; and major on-line news sources.

Nonprofit Sector Research Fund (www.nonprofitresearch.org/)
A program of the Aspen Institute in Washington, D.C., the Nonprofit Sector Research Fund makes grants for researching and disseminating information about nonprofit activities, impacts, and values, and promotes the use of that information to enhance nonprofit practices and inform public policy. The Fund also seeks to bolster nonprofit research by increasing the legitimacy and visibility of nonprofit scholarship, thereby attracting more investors and researchers to the field. The organization's site includes application guidelines, special initiatives, publication content and summaries, research abstracts, a list of grant recipients, and links to nonprofit resources.

Philanthropy News Digest (www.fdncenter.org/pnd/current/)
Weekly abstracts concerning philanthropic news presented by the Foundation Center. Includes a job corner, an RFP bulletin, a nonprofit spotlight, and a searchable archive dating back to 1995.

Resources for Nonprofit Organizations
(www.library.wisc.edu/libraries/Memorial/grants/nonprof.htm)
This Web page, presented by the Grants Information Center at the University of Wisconsin at Madison, "includes funding resources for organizations and sponsored individuals, as well as information on varied aspects of philanthropy and fund raising." Includes links to other Internet resources.

SERVEnet (www.servenet.org)
SERVEnet, an on-line program of Youth Service America, is designed to encourage more citizens to become actively engaged in their communities by volunteering; to provide volunteer-based nonprofit organizations the best resources available to them in a quick and easy manner; and to match the skills, experience, and enthusiasm of dedicated volunteers with nonprofit organizations who need their participation. The site includes a zip code search feature for national volunteer opportunities.

U.S. Census Bureau (www.census.gov)
The Census Bureau's sprawling site is the source of social, demographic, and economic information about the United States on the Web. Offerings include all Census Bureau publications (in PDF format) released since January 1996; statistical profiles for states, congressional districts, and counties; current economic indicators; state and county maps, and more.

A Compilation of State Laws Regulating Charitable Organizations

GIVING USA™ Update

Issue 1, 2000

a newsletter published by the
AAFRC Trust for Philanthropy

Annual Survey of State Laws Regulating Charitable Solicitations
As of January 1, 2000

State Regulatory Agency	Registration or Licensing Requirements for Charitable Organizations	Reporting Dates and Requirements for Charitable Organizations	State Accepts Uniform Registration Form[4]	Solicitation Disclosure Requirements for Charitable Organizations	Organizations Using Paid Solicitors Note Additional Disclosure Requirements if Paid Solicitor Used[1]	Organizations Using Fund-Raising Counsel Note Registration/ Licensing/Bonding Requirements for Counsel[2]	Organizations Using Paid Solicitors Note State Imposes Additional Requirements for Solicitors[3]
Alabama Attorney General Consumer Affairs Division 11 S. Union Street Montgomery, AL 36130 334-242-7334	Annual registration, $25 fee.	Registration expires 3 months after fiscal year end. Annual financial report due at that time.	✓	None	✓	$100 fee and $10,000 bond.	✓
Alaska Fair Business Practices Section Dept. of Law 1031 W. 4th Avenue Suite 200 Anchorage, AK 99501 907-269-5100	Annual registration, no fee.	Registration expires on September 1 of each year.		None	✓	None	✓
Arizona Secretary of State 1700 West Washington, 7th Floor Phoenix, AZ 85007-2808 602-542-6670	Annual registration, no fee.	Registration renewal due on January 31. File Form 990 or financial report with renewal on January 31.		None	✓	None	✓
Arkansas Office of the Attorney General Consumer Protection Division 200 Tower Building 323 Center Street Little Rock, AR 72201 501-682-2341	Annual registration.	Annual registration. Financial report due 4¹/₂ months after fiscal year end if fiscal year ends December 31. If fiscal year end is other than December 31, reports due May 15 or, upon request, within 6 months of fiscal year end. Financial report may be Form 990. If gross revenue exceeds $500,000, an independent CPA audit is required.	✓	None	✓	Registration, $100. No bond.	✓
California Registry of Charitable Trusts P.O. Box 903447 Sacramento, CA 94203-4470 916-445-2021	Initial registration for organizations located doing business, or raising funds in state. Foreign charitable organizations must obtain certificate of authority and franchise tax exemption. $25 fee. Over 200 cities and counties have solicitation ordinances which may require registration. Contact Registry of Charitable Trusts for more information.	Financial report, consisting of Form 990, 990 EZ, or 990 PF, due 4¹/₂ months after fiscal year end. Form RRF-1 due January 15 of each year. $25 fee for organizations with assets or revenue exceeding $100,000 during preceding fiscal year.	✓	None	✓	Registration, $200 fee.	✓
Colorado Secretary of State 1560 Broadway, 2nd Floor Denver, CO 80202 303-894-2200	Organizations employing professional solicitors must file Solicitation Notice prior to each campaign. $62.50 fee.	Campaign financial report required within 90 days of close of campaign. $12.50 fee.		None	✓	None	✓
Connecticut c/o Department of Consumer Protection Attorney General Public Charities Unit 55 Elm Street Hartford, CT 06106 860-808-5030 860-808-5030	Initial registration, $20 fee.	Annual financial report due within 5 months of fiscal year end, $25 fee. Independent CPA audit required if gross revenue less government grants and fees exceeds $100,000. Late filing fee, $25.	✓	None	✓	No registration or bond for counsel not having custody of funds. Counsel must file with Department of Consumer Protection a copy of contracts with charitable oranizations.	✓

State Regulatory Agency	Registration or Licensing Requirements for Charitable Organizations	Reporting Dates and Requirements for Charitable Organizations	State Accepts Uniform Registration Form[4]	Solicitation Disclosure Requirements for Charitable Organizations	Organizations Using Paid Solicitors Note Additional Disclosure Requirements if Paid Solicitor Used[1]	Organizations Using Fund-Raising Counsel Note Registration/Licensing/Bonding Requirements for Counsel[2]	Organizations Using Paid Solicitors Note State Imposes Additional Requirements for Solicitors[3]
Delaware Department of State Division of Corporations John G. Townsend Building P.O. Box 898 Dover, DE 19903 302-739-3073	None	None		None	✓	None	
District of Columbia Dept. of Consumer & Regulatory Affairs Business Services Division 614 H Street, NW P.O. Box 93160 Washington, DC 20090 202-727-7086	Annual licensing is $80 per year.	Financial report due within 30 days after end of licensing period and 30 days after a demand by the mayor.	✓	None	✓	None	
Florida Dept. of Agriculture & Consumer Services Attn: Solicitation Section P.O. Box 6700 Tallahassee, FL 32314-6700 850-410-3705	Annual registration; fees range from $10 to $400, based on annual gross receipts.	Financial report or Form 990 to accompany registration annually or by 4 1/2 months after fiscal year end. Late fee, $25 per month.		The statement below is required on all written solicitations. "A copy of the official registration and financial information may be obtained from the Division of Consumer Services by calling toll-free, within the state 1-800-HELP-FLA. Registration does not imply endorsement."	✓	Registration, $300 fee. No bond.	✓
Georgia Secretary of State Business Services and Regulation 2 Martin Luther King Jr. Drive, SE Suite 802-West Tower Atlanta, GA 30334 404-656-4911	Annual registration, $25 fee.	Annual report due on organization's renewal date, $10 fee. Certified financial statement required if proceeds are $500,000 or more; independent CPA review required for proceeds of $100,000-$500,000; file Form 990 if proceeds are under $100,000.	✓	Organization must disclose to donor names of solicitor and organization. If telephone solicitation, the location of the caller and that full description of charitable program and financial statement are available upon request.	✓	None	✓
Hawaii Dept. of Commerce & Consumer Affairs Business Registration Division 1010 Richards Street P.O. Box 40 Honolulu, HI 96810 808-586-2727	None	None		None		Registration, $60 fee and $5,000 bond.	✓
Idaho Attorney General Business Regulation Division Statehouse Room 210 Boise, ID 83720 208-334-2400	None	None		None		None	
Illinois Attorney General Charitable Compliance Section 100 W. Randolph, 12th Floor Chicago, IL 60601-3175 312-814-2595	Initial registration. $15 fee.	Annual financial report due within 6 months of fiscal year end. $15 Fee. CPA opinion must accompany report if revenues exceed $150,000 or if professional solicitor is engaged and contributions exceed $25,000. If registration expires, $100 late penalty fee.	✓	None		Registration every two years. No fee.	✓
Indiana Attorney General Consumer Protection Division Indiana Government Center South 402 W. Washington Street, 5th Floor Indianapolis, IN 46204-2770 317-232-6201	Organizations must register annually with the Department of Revenue, Not-for-Profit Division, 100 N. Senate Avenue, Room 201, Indianapolis, IN 46204-2253.	Form File IT-35AR 4 1/2 months after fiscal end.		None	✓	Initial registration, $1,000 fee. Notice filing due prior to campaigns. Renewal registration fee $50.	✓

This chart is for information purposes only. Readers are advised to contact appropriate state regulatory agencies for legal compliance procedures.
© All rights reserved. Obtain written permission from the publisher to reproduce or excerpt.

State Regulatory Agency	Registration or Licensing Requirements for Charitable Organizations	Reporting Dates and Requirements for Charitable Organizations	State Accepts Uniform Registration Form[4]	Solicitation Disclosure Requirements for Charitable Organizations	Organizations Using Paid Solicitors Note Additional Disclosure Requirements if Paid Solicitor Used[1]	Organizations Using Fund-Raising Counsel Note Registration/ Licensing/Bonding Requirements for Counsel[2]	Organizations Using Paid Solicitors Note State Imposes Additional Requirements for Solicitors[3]
Iowa Attorney General Consumer Protection Division 1300 E. Walnut Hoover State Office Building, 2nd Floor Des Moines, IA 50319 515-281-5926	None	None		Charity's financial information must be provided upon request.		None	✓
Kansas Kansas Secretary of State Ron Thornburgh First Floor, Memorial Hall 120 SW 10th Avenue Topeka, KS 66612-1594 785-296-4564	Annual registration, $20 fee.	Financial report due within 6 months of fiscal year end.	✓	Name, address and telephone number of charity and state registration number, that annual financial report is filed with secretary of state.	✓	Registration and $5,000 bond.	✓
Kentucky Attorney General Division of Consumer Protection 1024 Capitol Center Drive Frankfort, KY 40601-8204 502-696-5389	Initial registration. No fee.	Form 990 due 4 1/2 months after fiscal year end.	✓	None	✓	Registration, $50 fee. No bond.	✓
Louisiana Department of Justice Public Protection Division Consumer Protection Section P.O. Box 94095 Baton Rouge, LA 70804-9095 504-342-7900	Registration prior to campaigns for organizations using professional solicitors. $25 fee.	Renew registration annually. $25 fee. File Form 990 and updated information, if any.	✓	This state has substantial disclosure requirements for police and firefighter groups. Consult statute for details.	✓	None	✓
Maine Charitable Solicitations Department of Professional & Financial Regulation 35 State House Station Augusta, ME 04333-0035 207-624-8624	Initial registration, $50 fee. State will issue renewal notice.	Financial report must be filed with commissioner by November 30, at the same time as the registration renewal. $100 renewal filing fee. If more than $30,000 raised, must file audited financial statement, additional $50 filing fee, for a total of $150.	✓	None	✓	Registration, $200 fee with one-time $50 application fee and $10,000 bond.	✓
Maryland Secretary of State Charities Division State House Annapolis, MD 21401 410-974-5534	Annual registration. $50 to $200 fee, depending on annual gross proceeds. No fee if proceeds are less than $25,000 and no professional solicitor is used.	Form 990 due within 6 months of end of most recently completed fiscal year. If proceeds are in excess of $200,000, audit is required by independent CPA; accountant's review if gross income from contributions is $100,000-$200,000.	✓	Written solicitations must state that documents and information filed under the Maryland charitable organizations laws can be obtained from the secretary of state for the cost of postage and copies.		Registration, $200 fee. No bond.	✓
Massachusetts Attorney General Division of Public Charities One Ashburton Place Boston, MA 02108 617-727-2200	Annual registration, $35 to $250 fee, depending on annual gross proceeds.	Organizations receiving $250,000 or more must file an audited financial statement. Organizations receiving less than $250,000 must file a financial statement with accountant's review. File Forms PC and 990 4 1/2 months after fiscal year end.	✓	None	✓	Registration, $200 fee. No bond.	✓
Michigan Attorney General Charitable Trust Section P.O. Box 30214 Lansing, MI 48909 517-373-1152	Annual licensing, no fee.	Licensing renewal, with financial report due within 6 months of fiscal year end. CPA audit or review required where public support is at least $100,000. CPA audit required if public support is $250,000 or more. Audit and review requirements not supported by Michigan statute.	✓	Attorney General encourages display/disclosure of charity's registration number on all solicitations. Not supported by Michigan statute.		Licensing and $10,000 bond.	✓
Minnesota Attorney General Charities Division NCL Tower, #1200 445 Minnesota Street St. Paul, MN 55101-2131 612-296-6172	Annual registration, $25 fee.	Renew registration within 6 months of fiscal year end. Annual report, financial statement, and copy of Form 990. Audit required if public contributions exceed $350,000. Late filing fee, $50.	✓	None	✓	Registration, $200 fee. No bond.	✓

This chart is for information purposes only. Readers are advised to contact appropriate state regulatory agencies for legal compliance procedures.

State Regulatory Agency	Registration or Licensing Requirements for Charitable Organizations	Reporting Dates and Requirements for Charitable Organizations	State Accepts Uniform Registration Form[4]	Solicitation Disclosure Requirements for Charitable Organizations	Organizations Using Paid Solicitors Note Additional Disclosure Requirements if Paid Solicitor Used[1]	Organizations Using Fund-Raising Counsel Note Registration/ Licensing/Bonding Requirements for Counsel[2]	Organizations Using Paid Solicitors Note State Imposes Additional Requirements for Solicitors[3]
Mississippi Secretary of State Charities Division P.O. Box 136 Jackson, MS 39205-0136 601-359-1371	Annual registration, $50 fee.	Financial report due annually with registration. File audited financial statement if proceeds exceed $100,000 or if professional fund raiser was used.	✓	Written solicitations require the following statement verbatim: "The official registration and financial information of the organization may be obtained from the Mississippi Secretary of State's office by calling 1-888-236-6167. Registration by the Secretary of State does not imply endorsement by the Secretary of State."	✓	Registration, $250. No bond.	✓
Missouri Attorney General Public Protection Unit P.O. Box 899 Jefferson City, MO 65102 573-751-1197	Annual registration, $15 fee. Note: 501(c)(3) organizations are exempt from registration. A copy of the organization's IRS tax exemption determination letter may be filed with the state to obtain exemption.	Annual report due within 2$\frac{1}{2}$ months of fiscal year end.	✓	None	✓	None	✓
Montana Office of the Attorney General P.O. Box 20146 Helena, MT 59620-1401 406-444-2026	None	None		None		None	
Nebraska Secretary of State 2300 State Capitol Lincoln, NE 68509 402-471-2554	None	None		None	✓	None	
Nevada Secretary of State Capitol Complex Carson City, NV 89710 702-687-5203	No fund-raising registration. Foreign non-profit corporations having assets or an office in Nevada must qualify before doing business in Nevada.	Corporate annual report due by July 1.		None	✓	None	
New Hampshire Attorney General Register of Charitable Trusts 33 Capitol Street Concord, NH 03301-6397 603-271-3591	One-time registration, $25 fee.	Annual report and Form 990 due within 4$\frac{1}{2}$ months of fiscal year end. Annual reporting fee, $50.	✓	None	✓	Registration, $75 fee and $10,000 bond.	✓
New Jersey Division of Consumer Affairs Charities Registration Section 124 Halsey Street, 7th Floor P.O. Box 45028 Newark, NJ 07101 973-504-6259	Annual registration. Fee scale: $60 to $250, depending on annual gross receipts.	Annual financial report due within 6 months of fiscal year end. Late fee $25, if registration submitted more than 30 days after due date.	✓	Printed solicitations, written confirmation, receipts or written reminders issued by a charitable organization, independent paid fund raiser or solicitor must contain the statement below, which must be conspicuously printed. "Information filed with the attorney general concerning this charitable solicitation may be obtained from the attorney general of the state of New Jersey by calling 201-504-6215. Registration with the attorney general does not imply endorsement."	✓	Registration, $250 fee. No bond.	✓
New Mexico Office of the Attorney General Charitable Organization Registry P.O. Drawer 1508 Santa Fe, NM 87504-1508 505-827-6000	Annual registration. No fee.	Form 990 or financial report due within 4$\frac{1}{2}$ months of fiscal year end.	✓	None	✓	None	

This chart is for information purposes only. Readers are advised to contact appropriate state regulatory agencies for legal compliance procedures.
© All rights reserved. Obtain written permission from the publisher to reproduce or excerpt.

State Regulatory Agency	Registration or Licensing Requirements for Charitable Organizations	Reporting Dates and Requirements for Charitable Organizations	State Accepts Uniform Registration Form[4]	Solicitation Disclosure Requirements for Charitable Organizations	Organizations Using Paid Solicitors Note Additional Disclosure Requirements if Paid Solicitor Used[1]	Organizations Using Fund-Raising Counsel Note Registration/ Licensing/Bonding Requirements for Counsel[2]	Organizations Using Paid Solicitors Note State Imposes Additional Requirements for Solicitors[3]
New York For Fund-Raising Counsel and Professional Fund Raisers (Paid Solicitors): State of New York Office of the Attorney General Charities Bureau The Capitol Albany, NY 12224 518-486-9797 *For Charitable Organizations:* Department of Law Charities Bureau Registration Section 120 Broadway, 3rd Floor New York, Ny 10271 212-416-8430	Initial registration, $25 fee.	Annual financial report due 4¹/₂ months after fiscal year end. Fees range from $10 to $25. Where receipts are in excess of $150,000 for preceding year, report must be accompanied by opinion signed by independent CPA. Accountant's "review report" required where receipts are between $75,000 and $150,000. Unaudited financial report required where receipts are below $75,000. Any organization compensating a person for fund raising, including staff person, must submit financial statement, regardless of revenue levels. In all cases, copies of the filed Form 990 must be submitted.	✓	Solicitations must include the statement below. The disclosure statement must be placed conspicuously in the material with print no smaller than 10-point bold-face type or, alternatively, no smaller than the size of print used for the most number of words in the statement. "A copy of the latest annual report may be obtained from the organization or from the Charities Bureau, Department of Law, 120 Broadway, New York, NY 10271."	✓	Registration, $800 fee. No bond.	✓
North Carolina Department of Secretary of State 2 Salisbury Street, Suite 5014 Raleigh, NC 27601 or P.O. Box 29622 Raleigh, NC 27626-0622 919-807-2214	Annual registration, $50 to $200 fee, based on receipts. Parent organizations filing on behalf of chapters or affiliates $100 to $400 fee, based on number of chapters.	Annual renewal due 4¹/₂ months after fiscal year end. File Form 990; audited financial statement optional. Late fee, $25 per month.		Charitable organizations or sponsors are required to register and must conspicuously display the following statement on every solicitation, written confirmation, receipt or reminder: "Financial information about this organization and a copy of its license are available from the State Solicitation Licensing Branch at 919-733-4510. The license is not an endorsement by the state." The statement should be printed in 9-point type and made conspicuous by use of one or more of the following: underlining, a border, or bold type.	✓	Licensing, $200 fee. No bond.	✓
North Dakota Secretary of State Licensing Division 600 E. Boulevard Avenue Bismarck, ND 58505 701-328-3665	Annual registration. Initial fee, $25.	Financial report due September 1 each year. $10 fee.	✓	None		Registration, $100 fee.	✓
Ohio Attorney General Charitable Foundation Section 101 E. Town Street 4th Floor Columbus, OH 43215-5148 614-466-3180	Annual registration for out-of-state charities and Ohio organizations not already registered under the state's Trust Act. $50 to $200 fee, depending upon amount of contributions received in state.	Financial report due within 4¹/₂ months of fiscal year end.	✓	Name and address of charity. If not a 501(c) (3) organization, charitable purpose of appeal.	✓	None	✓
Oklahoma Secretary of State 2300 N. Lincoln Boulevard, Room 101 Oklahoma City, OK 73105-4897 405-521-3911	Annual registration, $15 fee.	Financial report due with renewal registration. Due date is anniversary date of original registration.	✓	None		None	✓
Oregon Department of Justice 1515 S.W. 5th Avenue, Suite 410 Portland, OR 97201 503-229-5548	Initial registration. No fee.	Annual report due within 4¹/₂ months of fiscal year end. Fees: $10 to $200. (Multiply national gross by 0.0118 to obtain Oregon receipts to determine fee.) Late fee, $20.	✓	None	✓	Registration for counsel who advise on direct mail, or who have access to contributions, or have authority to pay expenses. $250 fee.	✓
Pennsylvania Dept. of State Bureau of Charitable Organizations 124 Pine Street, 3rd Floor P.O. Box 8723 Harrisburg, PA 17105 717-783-1720	Annual registration. Fee, $15-$250.	File within 4¹/₂ months of fiscal year end. Annual financial statement and Form 990. Reviewed statement for organizations with revenues $25,000-$100,000; audited statement for organizations receiving $100,000 and more. Late fee, $25 per month.	✓	Solicitation disclosure statement: "The official registration and financial information of [legal name of charity as registered with the Department of State] may be obtained from the Pennsylvania Department of State by calling toll free, within Pennsylvania, 800-732-0999. Registration does not imply endorsement."	✓	Registration for counsel who advise on direct mail, or who have access to contributions, or have authority to pay expenses. $250 fee.	✓

This chart is for information purposes only. Readers are advised to contact appropriate state regulatory agencies for legal compliance procedures.

State Regulatory Agency	Registration or Licensing Requirements for Charitable Organizations	Reporting Dates and Requirements for Charitable Organizations	State Accepts Uniform Registration Form[4]	Solicitation Disclosure Requirements for Charitable Organizations	Organizations Using Paid Solicitors Note Additional Disclosure Requirements if Paid Solicitor Used[1]	Organizations Using Fund-Raising Counsel Note Registration/Licensing/Bonding Requirements for Counsel[2]	Organizations Using Paid Solicitors Note State Imposes Additional Requirements for Solicitors[3]
Rhode Island Dept. of Business Regulations Charitable Organization Section 233 Richmond Street Suite 232 Providence, RI 02903-4232 401-222-3048	Annual registration, $75 fee.	Financial report audited by independent CPA due annually. Where proceeds are less than $100,000, no audit required.	✓	None		Registration, $200 fee and $10,000 bond.	✓
South Carolina Office of the Secretary of State P.O. Box 11350 Columbia, SC 29211 803-734-1790	Annual registration, $50 fee.	Financial report due within 4 1/2 months of fiscal year end.	✓	None	✓	Registration, $50 fee.	✓
South Dakota Attorney General State Capitol 500 E. Capitol Pierre, SD 57501-5070 605-773-4400	None	None		None		None	✓
Tennessee Secretary of State Division of Charitable Solicitations James K. Polk Bldg., Suite 1700 Nashville, TN 37243-0308 615-741-2555	Annual registration, $50 initial fee; thereafter fees range from $100 to $300, depending upon annual gross receipts.	Annual registration and financial report due within 6 months of fiscal year end. Organizations with revenues between $25,000 and $100,000 must submit Form 990. Organizations with revenues above $100,000 must submit audited financial statement.(No audit required if proceeds do not exceed $10,000.) New registrants in their first year of operation must file quarterly financial reports.	✓	None	✓	Registration, $250 fee and $25,000 bond.	✓
Texas Secretary of State Statutory Documents Section P.O. Box 12887 Austin, TX 78711-2887 512-475-0775	Annual registration for public safety organizations and veterans' groups. Fees: $150-$250. Bonding required of veterans' groups. Foreign charitable organizations are required to obtain a Certificate of Authority if they have a physical location in Texas.	Renew annually.		This state has substantial disclosure requirements for public safety and veterans organizations. Consult statute for details.		None	✓
Utah Dept. of Commerce Division of Consumer Protection 160 East 300 South P.O. Box 146704 Salt Lake City, UT 84114-8704 801-530-6601	Annual registration, $100 fee.	Renew annually. Groups required to register must file quarterly financial reports the first year of registration. Late fee, $25 per month.		None	✓	Registration, $150 fee and $25,000 bond.	✓
Vermont Attorney General 109 State Street Montpelier, VT 05609 802-828-3171	None	None		None		None	✓
Virginia Department of Agriculture and Consumer Services Office of Consumer Affairs P.O. Box 1163 Richmond, VA 23218 804-786-1343	Annual registration. $30 to $325 fee based on previous year's gross receipts. Initial registration may require $100 surcharge.	Annual registration within 4 1/2 months of fiscal year end. Certified treasurer's report for proceeds under $25,000; certified audit or accompanying Form 990 if proceeds over $25,000. Late filing fee, $100.	✓	All written solicitations must disclose that financial statements are available from the Office of Consumer Affairs.	✓	Registration, $100 fee. No bond.	✓
Washington Office of Secretary of State Charities Division 505 E. Union P.O. Box 40234 Olympia, WA 98504-0234 360-753-7120	Annual registration, $20 initial registration fee: $10 annually thereafter.	Annual registration and financial report due within 4 1/2 months of fiscal year end.	✓	Written solicitations must disclose name of organization, purpose of solicitation, whether organization is registered; secretary of state's toll-free number (1-800-332-4483). Commercial fund raisers must disclose name, name of firm, name and city of the charitable organization.	✓	None	✓

This chart is for information purposes only. Readers are advised to contact appropriate state regulatory agencies for legal compliance procedures.

STATE REGULATORY AGENCY	REGISTRATION OR LICENSING REQUIREMENTS FOR CHARITABLE ORGANIZATIONS	REPORTING DATES AND REQUIREMENTS FOR CHARITABLE ORGANIZATIONS	STATE ACCEPTS UNIFORM REGISTRATION FORM[4]	SOLICITATION DISCLOSURE REQUIREMENTS FOR CHARITABLE ORGANIZATIONS	ORGANIZATIONS USING PAID SOLICITORS NOTE ADDITIONAL DISCLOSURE REQUIREMENTS IF PAID SOLICITOR USED[1]	ORGANIZATIONS USING FUND-RAISING COUNSEL NOTE REGISTRATION/ LICENSING/BONDING REQUIREMENTS FOR COUNSEL[2]	ORGANIZATIONS USING PAID SOLICITORS NOTE STATE IMPOSES ADDITIONAL REQUIREMENTS FOR SOLICITORS[3]
West Virginia Secretary of State Building 1, 1900 Kanawha Blvd. East Charleston, WV 25305-0770 304-558-8000	Annual registration, $15 to $50 fee, depending on annual gross receipts.	Annual registration with audited financial report and Form 990. No audit required if proceeds are less than $50,000.		Every printed solicitation should include the following statement. "West Virginia residents may obtain a summary of the registration and financial documents from the Secretary of State, State Capitol, Charleston, WV 25305. Registration does not imply endorsement."	✓	Registration, $50 fee and $10,000 bond.	✓
Wisconsin Dept. of Regulation & Licensing 1400 E. Washington Avenue Room 285 P.O. Box 8935 Madison, WI 53708 608-267-7132	Initial registration, $15 fee.	Registration renewed July 31st. $15 fee. Annual financial report due within 6 months of fiscal year end. Independent CPA audit required where proceeds exceed $50,000 or paid fund raiser is used.	✓	None	✓	None	✓
Wyoming Secretary of State Capitol Bldg. 200 W. 24th Cheyenne, WY 82002 307-777-7378 or Office of the Attorney General 123 Capitol Building Cheyenne, WY 82002 307-777-7841	None	None		None		None	

Glossary and notes

Registration and Licensing: Most states require charities and fund-raising professionals to register with a regulatory agency before fund raising. In 1988, licensing provisions in North Carolina were declared unconstitutional by the Supreme Court in *Riley v National Federation of the Blind of North Carolina*. Many states changed their statutes accordingly.

Reporting Dates: Dates when financial or annual reports of charities must be filed with a regulatory agency.

Commercial Co-Ventures: A number of states regulate the relationship and resulting activities between charitable organizations and for-profit sales companies that enter into agreements to use the name and goodwill of a charity in conjunction with the sale of goods or services. These commercial co-venture relationships require certain contractual provisions as well as registration in limited circumstances. Consult the various state statutes for details about the regulation of this activity.

[1]Solicitation Disclosure Requirements: Disclosures are statements that must be made to the prospective contributor in an appeal for funds. Many states have both oral and written disclosure requirements for charitable organizations that use and pay for the fund-raising services of an outside firm. This is especially true when using door-to-door solicitors or a telemarketing firm. These disclosures vary from jurisdiction to jurisdiction, and organizations should consult individual state statutes or requirements or legal counsel to ensure the organization is in compliance. States have to word required statements carefully so that they do not violate Supreme Court rulings regarding unconstitutional abridgments of the right to free speech.

[2]Fund-Raising Counsel: Fund-raising counsel, as defined in the Model Charitable Solicitation Act, provide advice and counsel to charitable organizations in the development of their fund-raising appeals but do not actually solicit or retain custody of contributions. Because fund-raising counsel do not directly contact potential contributors or handle funds, many states do not require them to file a bond or, in some cases, registering. This *Update* outlines the general registration,

fee, and bond requirements for fund-raising counsel. However, these laws are continually changing, and organizations should consult the particular state statute or requirements or legal counsel to determine the current requirements.

[3]Paid Solicitors: Professional fund raisersófirms or individuals paid by a charitable organization to actually solicit and/or collect contributions on the organizationís behalfómust register and post bond in many states. Organizations should consult individual state statutes or requirements or legal counsel for specific requirements.

[4]Uniform Registration Form: This form was developed to aid charitable organizations with multiple state filings. The form was developed through the cooperation of the American Association of Fund-Raising Counsel (AAFRC), the National Society of Fund Raising Executives (NSFRE), and the National Association of State Charity Officials (NASCO). The states indicated on the chart accept the Uniform Registration Form. All of these states continue to require annual filing of financial information or some other type of annual report. It is anticipated that additional states will begin to accept the Uniform Registration Form this year. The following Internet web site provides a current list of the states that accept the form and a copy of the form that can be downloaded: *http://www.nonprofits.org/library/gov/urs*. The following states also require the filing of supplemental forms and/or information in addition to the Uniform Registration Form: Arkansas, California, Georgia, Illinois, Michigan, Mississippi, Missouri, New Hampshire, North Dakota, Rhode Island, Tennessee. Massachusetts accepts the Uniform Registration Form for initial registrations only.

Important Note: This information is designed to provide an introduction to the registration requirements of charitable organizations and the fund-raising counsel they hire. This material is to inform organizations prior to engaging in fund-raising and related activities. It is not intended as a substitute for specific legal advice. Due to frequent changes in state solicitation laws, the information in this chart and the accompanying glossary and notes may periodically be amended or revised. Organizations should consult legal counsel for specific legal advice.

APPENDIX B

Links to Resource Organizations

The list below is not exhaustive. These links and others may be found in the Additional Resources sections of individual chapters. These selected Web sites include a wealth of valuable resources, and they will link you to many more.

Alliance for Nonprofit Management
www.allianceonline.org

American Association of Fund-Raising Counsel (AAFRC)
www.aafrc.org

American Management Association (AMA)
www.amanet.org

American Society of Association Executives (ASAE)
www.asaenet.org

ASAE's Gateway to Associations
www.asaenet.org/Gateway/GatewayHP.html

Association for Healthcare Philanthropy
www.go-ahp.org

Association for Research on Nonprofit Organizations and Voluntary Action
www.arnova.org

Association for Volunteer Administration (AVA)
www.avaintl.org

Association of Professional Researchers for Advancement
www.aprahome.org

The Aspen Institute Nonprofit Sector Research Fund
www.nonprofitresearch.org

Center for Community Change
www.communitychange.org

Charities Today
www.charitiestoday.com

Charity First
www.charityfirst.com

CharityTalk
www.CharityChannel.com

Catalog of Federal Domestic Assistance
www.cfda.gov

Conference Board
www.conference-board.org

Contact Center Network Directory
www.contact.org

Council for Aid to Education (CAE)
www.cae.org

**Council for the Advancement and
　　Support of Education**
www.case.org/CURRIndex/main.html

Council on Foundations
www.cof.org

Contact Center Network
www.contact.org

The Chronicle of Philanthropy
www.philanthropy.com

The Chronicle of Higher Education
www.chronicle.com

David Lamb's Prospect Research Page
www.lambresearch.com

The Drucker Foundation
www.drucker.org

Federal Information Exchange, Inc.
www.sciencewise.com/fedix

Federal Register
www.access.gpo.gov/su_docs/aces/
　　aces140.html

**Forum of Regional Associations of
　　Grantmakers**
www.rag.org

The Foundation Center
www.fdncenter.org

Funding Exchange
www.fex.org

Fundsnet Online Services
www.fundsnetservices.com

Grantsmanship Center
www.tgci.com

GuideStar
www.guidestar.org

HandsNet on the Web
www.handsnet.org

IGC's Activism/Internet Resource Center
www.igc.org

Independent Sector
www.indepsec.org

InnoNet's Toolbox
www.inetwork.org

Internal Revenue Service
www.irs.ustreas.gov/prod

Internet Nonprofit Center
www.nonprofits.org

Internet Prospector
www.internet-prospector.org

**Internet Resources for Non-Profit
　　Organizations**
www.sils.umich.edu

**Management Assistance Program for
　　Nonprofits**
www.mapnp.org

**Michigan State University Grants and
　　Related Resources**
www.lib.msu.edu/harris23/grants/grants.htm

National Assembly of National Voluntary Health and Social Welfare Organizations, Inc.
www.nassembly.org

National Assembly of State Arts Agencies
www.nasaa-arts.org

The National Center for Charitable Statistics
nccs.urban.org

National Center for Nonprofit Boards
www.ncnb.org

National Committee for Responsive Philanthropy
www.ncrp.org

National Council of Nonprofit Associations
www.ncna.org

National Society of Fund-Raising Executives
www.nsfre.org

NonProfit Gateway
www.nonprofit.gov

Nonprofit Genie
www.genie.org

Nonprofit Online News
www.gilbert.org/news

Nonprofit Outreach Network, Inc.
www.norn.org

Nonprofit Prophets
www.kn.pacbell.com/wired/prophets/index.html

Nonprofit Resources Catalog
www.clark.net

Nonprofit Times
www.nptimes.com

OMB Watch
www.ombwatch.org

Philanthropic Advisory Service Council of the Better Business Bureaus Inc.
www.bbb.org/about/pas.asp

Philanthropy Journal Online
www.pj.org

Philanthropy New Digest
www.fdncenter.org/pnd/current/index.html

The Philanthropy News Network
pnnonline.org

Philanthopy Roundtable
www.philanthropyroundtable.org

PhilanthropySearch.com
www.philanthropysearch.com

Resources for Nonprofit Organizations
www.library.wisc.edu/libraries/Memorial/grants/nonprof.htm

Support Center for Nonprofit Management
www.supportcenter.org/sf

United Way of America
www.unitedway.org

Voluntech.org
www.voluntech.org

International Resources

Asia-Pacific Philanthropy Consortium Information Center
iews.yonsei.ac.kr/appcic

Canadian Association of Gift Planners
www.cagptoronto.org

Canadian Centre for Philanthropy
www.ccp.ca

Charity Aid Foundation
www.charitynet.org

Charity Village
www.charityvillage.com

CIVICUS: World Alliance for Citizen Participation
www.civicus.org

Civnet
civnet.org

Funders Online
www.fundersonline.org

German Charities Institute (Deutsches Spendeninstitut Krefeld: DSK)
www.dsk.de

International Center for Nonprofit Law
www.icnl.org

International Nonprofit Support Organizations
www.idealist.org/support.html

Internet Prospector
www.internet-prospector.org/inter.html

NGOnet
www.ngonet.org

One World Online
www.oneworld.org

Pact
www.pactworld.org

PRAXIS
www.ssw.upenn.edu/~restes/praxis.html

Union of International Associations
www.uia.org

United Nations NGO Link
www.un.org/MoreInfo/ngolink/dpingo.htm

Appendix C

The Foundation Center's Cooperating Collections

FOUNDATION CENTER COOPERATING COLLECTIONS   FREE FUNDING INFORMATION CENTERS

The Foundation Center is an independent national service organization established by foundations to provide an authoritative source of information on foundation and corporate giving. The New York, Washington D.C., Atlanta, Cleveland, and San Francisco reference collections operated by the Foundation Center offer a wide variety of services and comprehensive resources on foundations and grants. Cooperating Collections are libraries, community foundations, and other nonprofit agencies that make accessible a collection of Foundation Center publications, as well as a variety of supplementary materials and education programs in areas useful to grantseekers. The collection includes:

FC SEARCH: THE FOUNDATION CENTER'S DATABASE ON CD-ROM	FOUNDATIONS TODAY SERIES	GUIDE TO U.S. FOUNDATIONS, THEIR TRUSTEES, OFFICERS, AND DONORS
THE FOUNDATION DIRECTORY 1 AND 2, AND SUPPLEMENT	FOUNDATION GRANTS TO INDIVIDUALS	NATIONAL DIRECTORY OF CORPORATE GIVING
FOUNDATION FUNDAMENTALS	THE FOUNDATION CENTER'S GUIDE TO GRANTSEEKING ON THE WEB	NATIONAL GUIDE TO FUNDING IN.... (SERIES)
THE FOUNDATION 1000	THE FOUNDATION CENTER'S GUIDE TO PROPOSAL WRITING	

All five Foundation Center libraries and most Cooperating Collections have FC: Search: The Foundation Center's Database on CD-ROM available for public use and provide Internet access. Increasingly, those seeking information on fundraising and nonprofit management are referring to our Web site (http://www.fdncenter.org) and others for a wealth of data and advice on grantseeking, including links to foundation IRS information returns (990-PFs). Because the Cooperating Collections vary in their hours, it is recommended that you call the collection in advance of a visit. To check on new locations or current holdings, call toll-free 1-800-424-9836, or visit our site at http://fdncenter.org/collections/index.html.

REFERENCE COLLECTIONS OPERATED BY THE FOUNDATION CENTER

THE FOUNDATION CENTER 2nd Floor 79 Fifth Ave. New York, NY 10003 (212) 620-4230	THE FOUNDATION CENTER 312 Sutter St., Suite 606 San Francisco, CA 94108 (415) 397-0902	THE FOUNDATION CENTER 1627 K St., NW Washington, DC 20036 (202) 331-1400	THE FOUNDATION CENTER Kent H. Smith Library 1422 Euclid, Suite 1356 Cleveland, OH 44115 (216) 861-1933	THE FOUNDATION CENTER Suite 150, Grand Lobby Hurt Bldg., 50 Hurt Plaza Atlanta, GA 30303 (404) 880-0094

ALABAMA

BIRMINGHAM PUBLIC LIBRARY
Government Documents
2100 Park Place
Birmingham 35203
(205) 226-3620

HUNTSVILLE PUBLIC LIBRARY
915 Monroe St.
Huntsville 35801
(256) 532-5940

UNIVERSITY OF SOUTH ALABAMA
Library Bldg.
Mobile 36688
(334) 460-7025

AUBURN UNIVERSITY AT
MONTGOMERY LIBRARY
7300 University Dr.
Montgomery 36124-4023
(334) 244-3200

ALASKA

UNIVERSITY OF ALASKA AT
ANCHORAGE
Library
3211 Providence Dr.
Anchorage 95508
(907) 786-1848

JUNEAU PUBLIC LIBRARY
292 Marine Way
Juneau 99801
(907) 586-5267

ARIZONA

FLAGSTAFF CITY-COCONINO COUNTY
PUBLIC LIBRARY
300 W. Aspen Ave.
Flagstaff 86001
(520) 779-7670

PHOENIX PUBLIC LIBRARY
Information Services Department
1221 N. Central Ave.
Phoenix 85004
(602) 262-4636

TUCSON PIMA LIBRARY
101 N. Stone Ave.
Tucson 87501
(520) 791-4393

ARKANSAS

WESTARK COMMUNITY COLLEGE—
BOREHAM LIBRARY
5210 Grand Ave.
Ft. Smith 72913
(501) 788-7200

CENTRAL ARKANSAS LIBRARY SYSTEM
100 Rock St.
Little Rock 72201
(501) 918-3000

PINE BLUFF-JEFFERSON COUNTY
LIBRARY SYSTEM
200 E. 8th
Pine Bluff 71601
(870) 534-2159

CALIFORNIA

HUMBOLDT AREA FOUNDATION
Rooney Resource Center
373 Indianola
Bayside 95524
(707) 442-2993

VENTURA COUNTY COMMUNITY
FOUNDATION
Resource Center for Nonprofit Organizations
1317 Del Norte Rd., Suite 150
Camarillo 93010-8504
(805) 988-0196

FRESNO REGIONAL FOUNDATION
Nonprofit Advancement Center
3425 N. First St., Suite 101
Fresno 93726
(559) 226-0216

CENTER FOR NONPROFIT
MANAGEMENT IN SOUTHERN
CALIFORNIA
Nonprofit Resource Library
606 South Olive St. #2450
Los Angeles 90014
(213) 623-7080

PHILANTHROPY RESOURCE CENTER
Flintridge Center
1040 Lincoln Ave, Suite 100
Pasadena 91103
(626) 449-0839

GRANT & RESOURCE CENTER OF
NORTHERN CALIFORNIA
Bldg. C, Suite A
2280 Benton Dr.
Redding 96003
(530) 244-1219

LOS ANGELES PUBLIC LIBRARY
West Valley Regional Branch Library
19036 Van Owen St.
Reseda 91335
(818) 345-4393

RICHMOND PUBLIC LIBRARY
325 Civic Center Plaza
Richmond 94804
(510) 620-6555

RIVERSIDE PUBLIC LIBRARY
3581 Mission Inn Ave.
Riverside 92501
(909) 782-5201

NONPROFIT RESOURCE CENTER
Sacramento Public Library
328 I St., 2nd Floor
Sacramento 95814
(916) 264-2772

SAN DIEGO FOUNDATION
Funding Information Center
1420 Kettner Blvd., Suite 500
San Diego 92101
(619) 235-2300

NONPROFIT DEVELOPMENT LIBRARY
1922 The Alameda, Suite 212
San Jose 95126
(408) 248-9505

PENINSULA COMMUNITY
FOUNDATION
Peninsula Nonprofit Center
1700 S. El Camino Real, #R201
San Mateo 94402-3049
(650) 358-9392

LOS ANGELES PUBLIC LIBRARY
San Pedro Regional Branch
931 S. Gaffey St.
San Pedro 90731
(310) 548-7779

VOLUNTEER CENTER OF GREATER
ORANGE COUNTY
Nonprofit Resource Center
1901 E. 4th St., Suite 100
Santa Ana 92705
(714) 953-5757

SANTA BARBARA PUBLIC LIBRARY
40 E. Anapamu St.
Santa Barbara 93101-1019
(805) 962-7653

SANTA MONICA PUBLIC LIBRARY
1343 6th St.
Santa Monica 90401-1603
(310) 458-8600

SONOMA COUNTY LIBRARY
3rd & E Sts.
Santa Rosa 95404
(707) 545-0831

SEASIDE BRANCH LIBRARY
550 Harcourt Ave.
Seaside 93955
(831) 899-8131

SONORA AREA FOUNDATION
20100 Cedar Rd., N.
Sonora 95370
(209) 533-2596

COLORADO

PENROSE LIBRARY
20 N. Cascade Ave.
Colorado Springs 80903
(719) 531-6333

DENVER PUBLIC LIBRARY
General Reference
10 W. 14th Ave. Pkwy.
Denver 80204
(303) 640-6200

CONNECTICUT

DANBURY PUBLIC LIBRARY
170 Main St.
Danbury 06810
(203) 797-4527

GREENWICH LIBRARY
101 W. Putnam Ave.
Greenwich 06830
(203) 622-7900

HARTFORD PUBLIC LIBRARY
500 Main St.
Hartford 06103
(860) 543-8656

NEW HAVEN FREE PUBLIC LIBRARY
Reference Dept.
133 Elm St.
New Haven 06510-2057
(203) 946-7091

DELAWARE

UNIVERSITY OF DELAWARE
Hugh Morris Library
Newark 19717-5267
(302) 831-2432

FLORIDA

VOLUSIA COUNTY LIBRARY CENTER
City Island
105 E. Magnolia Ave.
Daytona Beach 32114-4484
(904) 257-6036

NOVA SOUTHEASTERN UNIVERSITY
Einstein Library
3301 College Ave.
Fort Lauderdale 33314
(954) 262-4601

INDIAN RIVER COMMUNITY COLLEGE
Learning Resources Center
3209 Virginia Ave.
Fort Pierce 34981-5596
(561) 462-4757

JACKSONVILLE PUBLIC LIBRARIES
Grants Resource Center
122 N. Ocean St.
Jacksonville 32202
(904) 630-2665

MIAMI–DADE PUBLIC LIBRARY
Humanities/Social Science
101 W. Flagler St.
Miami 33130
(305) 375-5575

ORANGE COUNTY LIBRARY SYSTEM
Social Sciences Department
101 E. Central Blvd.
Orlando 32801
(407) 425-4694

SELBY PUBLIC LIBRARY
Reference
1331 1st St.
Sarasota 34236
(941) 316-1181

TAMPA–HILLSBOROUGH COUNTY
PUBLIC LIBRARY
900 N. Ashley Dr.
Tampa 33602
(813) 273-3652

COMMUNITY FOUNDATION OF PALM
BEACH & MARTIN COUNTIES
324 Datura St., Suite 340
West Palm Beach 33401
(561) 659-6800

GEORGIA

ATLANTA–FULTON PUBLIC LIBRARY
Foundation Collection–Ivan Allen
Department
1 Margaret Mitchell Square
Atlanta 30303-1089
(404) 730-1909

UNITED WAY OF CENTRAL GEORGIA
Community Resource Center
277 Martin Luther King Jr. Blvd.,
Suite 301
Macon 31201
(912) 738-3949

SAVANNAH STATE UNIVERSITY
Asa Gordon Library
Thompkins Rd.
Savannah 31404
(912) 356-2185

THOMAS COUNTY PUBLIC LIBRARY
201 N. Madison St.
Thomasville 31792
(912) 225-5252

HAWAII

UNIVERSITY OF HAWAII
Hamilton Library
2550 The Mall
Honolulu 96822
(808) 956-7214

HAWAII COMMUNITY FOUNDATION
FUNDING RESOURCE LIBRARY
900 Fort St., Suite 1300
Honolulu 96813
(808) 537-6333

IDAHO

BOISE PUBLIC LIBRARY
Funding Information Center
715 S. Capitol Blvd.
Boise 83702
(208) 384-4024

CALDWELL PUBLIC LIBRARY
1010 Dearborn St.
Caldwell 83605
(208) 459-3242

ILLINOIS

DONORS FORUM OF CHICAGO
208 S. LaSalle, Suite 735
Chicago 60604
(312) 578-0175

EVANSTON PUBLIC LIBRARY
1703 Orrington Ave.
Evanston 60201
(847) 866-0300

ROCK ISLAND PUBLIC LIBRARY
401 19th St.
Rock Island 61201-8143
(309) 732-7323

UNIVERSITY OF ILLINOIS
AT SPRINGFIELD, LIB 23
Brookens Library
Springfield 62794-9243
(217) 206-6633

INDIANA

EVANSVILLE–VANDERBURGH
PUBLIC LIBRARY
22 SE 5th St.
Evansville 47708
(812) 428-8200

ALLEN COUNTY PUBLIC LIBRARY
900 Webster St.
Ft. Wayne 46802
(219) 421-1200

INDIANAPOLIS–MARION COUNTY
PUBLIC LIBRARY
Social Sciences
40 E. St. Clair
Indianapolis 46206
(317) 269-1733

VIGO COUNTY PUBLIC LIBRARY
1 Library Square
Terre Haute 47807
(812) 232-1113

IOWA

CEDAR RAPIDS PUBLIC LIBRARY
500 1st St., SE
Cedar Rapids 52401
(319) 398-5123

SOUTHWESTERN COMMUNITY
COLLEGE
Learning Resource Center
1501 W. Townline Rd.
Creston 50801
(515) 782-7081

PUBLIC LIBRARY OF DES MOINES
100 Locust
Des Moines 50309-1791
(515) 283-4152

SIOUX CITY PUBLIC LIBRARY
Siouxland Funding Research Center
529 Pierce St.
Sioux City 51101-1203
(712) 255-2933

KANSAS

DODGE CITY PUBLIC LIBRARY
1001 2nd Ave.
Dodge City 67801
(316) 225-0248

TOPEKA AND SHAWNEE COUNTY
PUBLIC LIBRARY
1515 SW 10th Ave.
Topeka 66604-1345
(785) 233-2040

WICHITA PUBLIC LIBRARY
223 S. Main St.
Wichita 67202
(316) 261-8500

KENTUCKY

WESTERN KENTUCKY UNIVERSITY
Helm-Cravens Library
Bowling Green 42101-3576
(270) 745-6163

LEXINGTON PUBLIC LIBRARY
140 E. Main St.
Lexington 40507-1376
(859) 231-5520

LOUISVILLE FREE PUBLIC LIBRARY
301 York St.
Louisville 40203
(502) 574-1617

LOUISIANA

EAST BATON ROUGE PARISH LIBRARY
Centroplex Branch Grants Collection
120 St. Louis
Baton Rouge 70802
(225) 389-4967

BEAUREGARD PARISH LIBRARY
205 S. Washington Ave.
De Ridder 70634
(318) 463-6217

OUACHITA PARISH PUBLIC LIBRARY
1800 Stubbs Ave.
Monroe 71201
(318) 327-1490

NEW ORLEANS PUBLIC LIBRARY
Business & Science Division
219 Loyola Ave.
New Orleans 70112
(504) 596-2580

SHREVE MEMORIAL LIBRARY
424 Texas St.
Shreveport 71120-1523
(318) 226-5894

MAINE

UNIVERSITY OF SOUTHERN
MAINE LIBRARY
Maine Philanthropy Center
314 Forrest Ave.
Portland 04104-9301
(207) 780-5029

MARYLAND

ENOCH PRATT FREE LIBRARY
Social Science & History
400 Cathedral St.
Baltimore 21201
(410) 396-5430

MASSACHUSETTS

ASSOCIATED GRANT MAKERS
55 Court St.
Room 520
Boston 02108
(617) 426-2606

BOSTON PUBLIC LIBRARY
Soc. Sci. Reference
700 Boylston St.
Boston 02116
(617) 536-5400

WESTERN MASSACHUSETTS FUNDING
RESOURCE CENTER
65 Elliot St.
Springfield 01101-1730
(413) 452-0697

WORCESTER PUBLIC LIBRARY
Grants Resource Center
160 Fremont St.
Worcester 01603
(508) 799-1655

MICHIGAN

ALPENA COUNTY LIBRARY
211 N. 1st St.
Alpena 49707
(517) 356-6188

UNIVERSITY OF
MICHIGAN–ANN ARBOR
Graduate Library
Reference & Research Services
Department
Ann Arbor 48109-1205
(734) 763-1539

WILLARD PUBLIC LIBRARY
Nonprofit & Funding Resource
Collections
7 W. Van Buren St.
Battle Creek 49017
(616) 968-8166

HENRY FORD CENTENNIAL LIBRARY
Adult Services
16301 Michigan Ave.
Dearborn 48124
(313) 943-2330

WAYNE STATE UNIVERSITY
Purdy/Kresge Library
265 Cass Ave.
Detroit 48202
(313) 577-6424

MICHIGAN STATE UNIVERSITY
LIBRARIES
Main Library
Funding Center
100 Library
East Lansing 48824-1048
(517) 353-8818

FARMINGTON COMMUNITY LIBRARY
32737 W. 12 Mile Rd.
Farmington Hills 48334
(248) 553-0300

UNIVERSITY OF MICHIGAN—FLINT
Frances Willson Thompson Library
Flint 48502-1950
(810) 762-3413

GRAND RAPIDS PUBLIC LIBRARY
60 Library Plaza NE
Grand Rapids 49503-3093
(616) 456-3600

MICHIGAN TECHNOLOGICAL
UNIVERSITY
Van Pelt Library
1400 Townsend Dr.
Houghton 49931
(906) 487-2507

NORTHWESTERN MICHIGAN COLLEGE
Mark & Helen Osterlin Library
1701 E. Front St.
Traverse City 49684
(616) 922-1060

MINNESOTA

DULUTH PUBLIC LIBRARY
520 W. Superior St.
Duluth 55802
(218) 723-3802

SOUTHWEST STATE UNIVERSITY
University Library
N. Hwy. 23
Marshall 56253
(507) 537-6108

MINNEAPOLIS PUBLIC LIBRARY
Sociology Department
300 Nicollet Mall
Minneapolis 55401
(612) 630-6300

ROCHESTER PUBLIC LIBRARY
101 2nd St. SE
Rochester 55904-3777
(507) 285-8002

ST. PAUL PUBLIC LIBRARY
90 W. 4th St.
St. Paul 55102
(651) 266-7000

MISSISSIPPI

JACKSON/HINDS LIBRARY SYSTEM
300 N. State St.
Jackson 39201
(601) 968-5803

MISSOURI

CLEARINGHOUSE FOR
MIDCONTINENT FOUNDATIONS
University of Missouri—Kansas City
Center for Business Innovation
4747 Troost
Kansas City 64110-0680
(816) 235-1176

KANSAS CITY PUBLIC LIBRARY
311 E. 12th St.
Kansas City 64106
(816) 701-3541

METROPOLITAN ASSOCIATION FOR
PHILANTHROPY, INC.
211 N. Broadway, Suite 1200
St. Louis 63102
(314) 621-6220

SPRINGFIELD-GREENE
COUNTY LIBRARY
The Library Center
4653 S. Campbell
Springfield 65810
(417) 874-8110

MONTANA

MONTANA STATE UNIVERSITY—
BILLINGS
Library—Special Collections
1500 N. 30th St.
Billings 59101-0298
(406) 657-2320

BOZEMAN PUBLIC LIBRARY
220 E. Lamme
Bozeman 59715
(406) 582-2402

MONTANA STATE LIBRARY
Library Services
1515 E. 6th Ave.
Helena 59620-1800
(406) 444-3004

UNIVERSITY OF MONTANA
Mansfield Library
32 Campus Dr. #9936
Missoula 59812-9936
(406) 243-6800

NEBRASKA

UNIVERSITY OF NEBRASKA—
LINCOLN
Love Library
14th & R Sts.
Lincoln 68588-2848
(402) 472-2848

OMAHA PUBLIC LIBRARY
W. Dale Clark Library
Social Sciences Dept.
215 S. 15th St.
Omaha 68102
(402) 444-4826

NEVADA

CLARK COUNTY LIBRARY
1401 E. Flamingo
Las Vegas 89119
(702) 733-3642

WASHOE COUNTY LIBRARY
301 S. Center St.
Reno 89501
(775) 785-4190

NEW HAMPSHIRE

CONCORD PUBLIC LIBRARY
45 Green St.
Concord 03301
(603) 225-8670

PLYMOUTH STATE COLLEGE
Herbert H. Lamson Library
Plymouth 03264
(603) 535-2258

NEW JERSEY

CUMBERLAND COUNTY LIBRARY
800 E. Commerce St.
Bridgeton 08302
(856) 453-2210

NEWARK ENTERPRISE COMMUNITY
RESOURCE DEVELOPMENT CENTER
303-309 Washington St.
Newark 07102
(973) 624-8300

COUNTY COLLEGE OF MORRIS
Learning Resource Center
214 Center Grove Rd.
Randolph 07869
(973) 328-5296

NEW JERSEY STATE LIBRARY
185 W. State St.
Trenton 08625-0520
(609) 292-6220

NEW MEXICO

ALBUQUERQUE COMMUNITY
FOUNDATION
3301 Menaul NE, Suite 30
Albuquerque 87176-6960
(505) 883-6240

NEW MEXICO STATE LIBRARY
Information Services
1209 Camino Carlos Rey
Santa Fe 87505-9860
(505) 476-9702

NEW YORK

NEW YORK STATE LIBRARY
Humanities Reference
Cultural Education Center, 6th Fl.
Empire State Plaza
Albany 12230
(518) 474-5355

SUFFOLK COOPERATIVE
LIBRARY SYSTEM
627 N. Sunrise Service Rd.
Bellport 11713
(516) 286-1600

THE NONPROFIT CONNECTION, INC.
One Hanson Place, Room 2504
Brooklyn 11243
(718) 230-3200

BROOKLYN PUBLIC LIBRARY
Social Sciences/Philosophy Division
Grand Army Plaza
Brooklyn 11238
(718) 230-2122

BUFFALO & ERIE COUNTY
PUBLIC LIBRARY
Business, Science & Technology Dept.
1 Lafayette Square
Buffalo 14203-1887
(716) 858-7097

HUNTINGTON PUBLIC LIBRARY
338 Main St.
Huntington 11743
(631) 427-5165

QUEENS BOROUGH PUBLIC LIBRARY
Social Sciences Division
89-11 Merrick Blvd.
Jamaica 11432
(718) 990-0700

LEVITTOWN PUBLIC LIBRARY
1 Bluegrass Ln.
Levittown 11756
(516) 731-5728

ADRIANCE MEMORIAL LIBRARY
Special Services Department
93 Market St.
Poughkeepsie 12601
(914) 485-3445

ROCHESTER PUBLIC LIBRARY
Social Sciences
115 South Ave.
Rochester 14604
(716) 428-8120

ONONDAGA COUNTY PUBLIC LIBRARY
447 S. Salina St.
Syracuse 13202-2494
(315) 435-1900

UTICA PUBLIC LIBRARY
303 Genesee St.
Utica 13501
(315) 735-2279

WHITE PLAINS PUBLIC LIBRARY
100 Martine Ave.
White Plains 10601
(914) 422-1480

YONKERS PUBLIC LIBRARY
Reference Department, Getty
Square Branch
7 Main St.
Yonkers 10701
(914) 476-1255

NORTH CAROLINA

PACK MEMORIAL LIBRARY
Community Foundation of Western North
Carolina
67 Haywood St.
Asheville 28802
(704) 254-4960

THE DUKE ENDOWMENT
100 N. Tryon St., Suite 3500
Charlotte 28202-4012
(704) 376-0291

DURHAM COUNTY PUBLIC LIBRARY
300 N. Roxboro
Durham 27702
(919) 560-0100

STATE LIBRARY OF NORTH CAROLINA
Information Services Branch
109 E. Jones St.
Raleigh 27699-4641
(919) 733-3683

FORSYTH COUNTY PUBLIC LIBRARY
660 W. 5th St.
Winston-Salem 27101
(336) 727-2680

NORTH DAKOTA

BISMARCK PUBLIC LIBRARY
515 N. 5th St.
Bismarck 58501-4081
(701) 222-6410

FARGO PUBLIC LIBRARY
102 N. 3rd St.
Fargo 58102
(701) 241-1491

OHIO

STARK COUNTY DISTRICT LIBRARY
715 Market Ave. N.
Canton 44702
(330) 452-0665

PUBLIC LIBRARY OF CINCINNATI &
HAMILTON COUNTY
Grants Resource Center
800 Vine St.—Library Square
Cincinnati 45202-2071
(513) 369-6000

COLUMBUS METROPOLITAN LIBRARY
Business and Technology
96 S. Grant Ave.
Columbus 43215
(614) 645-2590

DAYTON & MONTGOMERY COUNTY
PUBLIC LIBRARY
Grants Information Center
215 E. Third St.
Dayton 45402
(937) 227-9500

MANSFIELD/RICHLAND COUNTY
PUBLIC LIBRARY
42 W. 3rd St.
Mansfield 44902
(419) 521-3100

TOLEDO–LUCAS COUNTY
PUBLIC LIBRARY
325 Michigan St.
Toledo 43624-1614
(419) 259-5209

PUBLIC LIBRARY OF YOUNGSTOWN &
MAHONING COUNTY
305 Wick Ave.
Youngstown 44503
(330) 744-8636

MUSKINGUM COUNTY LIBRARY
220 N. 5th St.
Zanesville 43701
(740) 453-0391

OKLAHOMA

OKLAHOMA CITY UNIVERSITY
Dulaney Browne Library
2501 N. Blackwelder
Oklahoma City 73106
(405) 521-5822

TULSA CITY–COUNTY LIBRARY
400 Civic Center
Tulsa 74103
(918) 596-7940

OREGON

OREGON INSTITUTE OF TECHNOLOGY
Library
3201 Campus Dr.
Klamath Falls 97601-8801
(541) 885-1770

PACIFIC NON-PROFIT NETWORK
Education Resource Center
1600 N. Riverside #1094
Medford 97501
(541) 779-6044

MULTNOMAH COUNTY LIBRARY
801 SW 10th Ave.
Portland 97205
(503) 248-5123

OREGON STATE LIBRARY
State Library Bldg.
250 N.Winter St. NE
Salem 97301-3950
(503) 378-4277

PENNSYLVANIA

NORTHAMPTON COMMUNITY
COLLEGE
Learning Resources Center
3835 Green Pond Rd.
Bethlehem 18017
(610) 861-5360

ERIE COUNTY LIBRARY SYSTEM
160 E. Front St.
Erie 16507
(814) 451-6927

DAUPHIN COUNTY LIBRARY SYSTEM
Central Library
101 Walnut St.
Harrisburg 17101
(717) 234-4976

LANCASTER COUNTY PUBLIC LIBRARY
125 N. Duke St.
Lancaster 17602
(717) 394-2651

FREE LIBRARY OF PHILADELPHIA
Regional Foundation Center
1901 Vine St.
Philadelphia 19103-1189
(215) 686-5423

CARNEGIE LIBRARY OF PITTSBURGH
Foundation Collection
4400 Forbes Ave.
Pittsburgh 15213-4080
(412) 622-1917

POCONO NORTHEAST
DEVELOPMENT FUND
James Pettinger Memorial Library
1151 Oak St.
Pittston 18640-3795
(570) 655-5581

READING PUBLIC LIBRARY
100 S. 5th St.
Reading 19602
(610) 655-6355

MARTIN LIBRARY
159 E. Market St.
York 17401
(717) 846-5300

RHODE ISLAND

PROVIDENCE PUBLIC
LIBRARY
225 Washington St.
Providence 02906
(401) 455-8088

SOUTH CAROLINA

ANDERSON COUNTY LIBRARY
300 N. McDuffie
Anderson 29622
(864) 260-4500

CHARLESTON COUNTY LIBRARY
68 Calhoun St.
Charleston 29401
(843) 805-6930

SOUTH CAROLINA STATE LIBRARY
1500 Senate St.
Columbia 29211-1469
(803) 734-8666

COMMUNITY FOUNDATION OF
GREATER GREENVILLE
27 Cleveland St., Suite 101
Greenville 29601
(864) 233-5925

SOUTH DAKOTA

SINTE GLESKA UNIVERSITY LIBRARY
Rosebud Sioux Reservation
Mission 57555-0107
(605) 856-2355

SOUTH DAKOTA STATE LIBRARY
800 Governors Dr.
Pierre 57501-2294
(605) 773-3131
(800) 592-1841 (SD residents)

DAKOTA STATE UNIVERSITY
Nonprofit Grants Assistance
132 S. Dakota Ave.
Sioux Falls 57104
(605) 367-5380

SIOUXLAND LIBRARIES
201 N. Main Ave.
Sioux Falls 57104
(605) 367-8720

TENNESSEE

UNITED WAY OF GREATER
CHATTANOOGA
Center for Nonprofits
406 Frazier Ave.
Chattanooga 37405
(423) 265-0514

KNOX COUNTY PUBLIC LIBRARY
500 W. Church Ave.
Knoxville 37902
(865) 215-8751

MEMPHIS & SHELBY COUNTY
PUBLIC LIBRARY
1850 Peabody Ave.
Memphis 38104
(901) 725-8877

NASHVILLE PUBLIC LIBRARY
Business Information Division
225 Polk Ave.
Nashville 37203
(615) 862-5842

TEXAS

NONPROFIT RESOURCE CENTER
Funding Information Library
500 N. Chestnut, Suite 1511
Abilene 79604
(915) 677-8166

AMARILLO AREA FOUNDATION
Grants Center
801 S. Filmore, Suite 700
Amarillo 79101
(806) 376-4521

HOGG FOUNDATION
Regional Foundation Library
3001 Lake Austin Blvd., Suite 400
Austin 78703
(512) 471-5041

BEAUMONT PUBLIC LIBRARY
801 Pearl St.
Beaumont 77704-3827
(409) 838-6606

CORPUS CHRISTI PUBLIC LIBRARY
Funding Information Center
805 Comanche St.
Reference Dept.
Corpus Christi 78401
(361) 880-7000

DALLAS PUBLIC LIBRARY
Urban Information
1515 Young St.
Dallas 75201
(214) 670-1487

SOUTHWEST BORDER NONPROFIT
RESOURCE CENTER
1201 W. University Dr.
Edinburgh 78539
(956) 384-5920

CENTER FOR VOLUNTEERISM &
NONPROFIT MANAGEMENT
1918 Texas Ave.
El Paso 79901
(915) 532-5377

FUNDING INFORMATION CENTER
OF FORT WORTH
329 S. Henderson
Ft. Worth 76104
(817) 334-0228

HOUSTON PUBLIC LIBRARY
Bibliographic Information Center
500 McKinney
Houston 77002
(713) 236-1313

NONPROFIT MANAGEMENT AND
VOLUNTEER CENTER
Laredo Public Library
1120 E. Calton Rd.
Laredo 78041
(956) 795-2400

LONGVIEW PUBLIC LIBRARY
222 W. Cotton St.
Longview 75601
(903) 237-1352

LUBBOCK AREA FOUNDATION, INC.
1655 Main St., Suite 209
Lubbock 79401
(806) 762-8061

NONPROFIT RESOURCE CENTER
OF TEXAS
111 Soledad, Suite 200
San Antonio 78212-8270
(210) 227-4333

WACO-MCLENNAN COUNTY LIBRARY
1717 Austin Ave.
Waco 76701
(254) 750-5941

NORTH TEXAS CENTER FOR
NONPROFIT MANAGEMENT
1105 Holliday
Wichita Falls 76301
(940) 322-4961

UTAH

SALT LAKE CITY PUBLIC LIBRARY
209 E. 500 S.
Salt Lake City 84111
(801) 524-8200

VERMONT

VERMONT DEPT. OF LIBRARIES
Reference & Law Info. Services
109 State St.
Montpelier 05609
(802) 828-3261

VIRGINIA

WASHINGTON COUNTY
PUBLIC LIBRARY
205 Oak Hill St.
Abingdon 24210
(540) 676-6222

HAMPTON PUBLIC LIBRARY
4207 Victoria Blvd.
Hampton 23669
(757) 727-1312

RICHMOND PUBLIC LIBRARY
Business, Science & Technology
101 E. Franklin St.
Richmond 23219
(804) 646-7223

ROANOKE CITY PUBLIC
LIBRARY SYSTEM
Main Library
706 S. Jefferson
Roanoke 24016
(540) 853-2471

WASHINGTON

MID-COLUMBIA LIBRARY
1620 South Union St.
Kennewick 99338
(509) 783-7878

SEATTLE PUBLIC LIBRARY
Fundraising Resource Center
1000 4th Ave.
Seattle 98104
(206) 386-4620

SPOKANE PUBLIC LIBRARY
Funding Information Center
901 W. Main Ave.
Spokane 99201
(509) 444-5300

GREATER WENATCHEE COMMUNITY
FOUNDATION AT THE WENATCHEE
PUBLIC LIBRARY
310 Douglas St.
Wenatchee 98807
(509) 662-5021

WEST VIRGINIA

KANAWHA COUNTY PUBLIC LIBRARY
123 Capitol St.
Charleston 25301
(304) 343-4646

WISCONSIN

UNIVERSITY OF WISCONSIN–MADISON
Memorial Library, Grants Information
Center
728 State St.
Madison 53706
(608) 262-3242

MARQUETTE UNIVERSITY
MEMORIAL LIBRARY
Funding Information Center
1415 W. Wisconsin Ave.
Milwaukee 53201-3141
(414) 288-1515

UNIVERSITY OF WISCONSIN—
STEVENS POINT
Library—Foundation Collection
900 Reserve St.
Stevens Point 54481-3897
(715) 346-2540

WYOMING

CASPER COLLEGE
Goodstein Foundation Library
125 College Dr.
Casper 82601
(307) 268-2269

LARAMIE COUNTY COMMUNITY
COLLEGE
Instructional Resource Center
1400 E. College Dr.
Cheyenne 82007-3299
(307) 778-1206

CAMPBELL COUNTY PUBLIC LIBRARY
2101 4-J Rd.
Gillette 82718
(307) 687-0115

TETON COUNTY LIBRARY
125 Virginian Ln.
Jackson 83001
(307) 733-2164

ROCK SPRINGS LIBRARY
Grantwriting Collection
400 C St.
Rock Springs 82901
(307) 352-6667

PUERTO RICO

UNIVERSIDAD DEL SAGRADO
CORAZON
M.M.T. Guevara Library
Santurce 00914
(787) 728-1515

Participants in the Foundation Center's Cooperating Collections network are libraries or nonprofit information centers that provide fundraising information and other funding-related technical assistance in their communities. Cooperating Collections agree to provide free public access to a basic collection of Foundation Center publications during a regular schedule of hours, offering free funding research guidance to all visitors. Many also provide a variety of services for local nonprofit organizations, using staff or volunteers to prepare special materials, organize workshops, or conduct orientations.

The Foundation Center welcomes inquiries from libraries or information centers in the U.S. interested in providing this type of public information service, particularly for communities with special need for this information. If you are interested in establishing a funding information library for the use of nonprofit organizations in your area or in learning more about the program, please contact a coordinator of Cooperating Collections: Erika Wittlieb, The Foundation Center, 79 Fifth Avenue, New York, NY 10003 (e-mail: eaw@fdncenter.org) or Janet Camarena, The Foundation Center, 312 Sutter Street, Suite 606, San Francisco, CA 94108 (e-mail: jfc@fdncenter.org).

INDEX